Optimal Event-Triggered Control Using Adaptive Dynamic Programming

Sarangapani Jagannathan, Vignesh Narayanan, and Avimanyu Sahoo

CRC Press
Taylor & Francis Group
Boca Raton London New York

CRC Press is an imprint of the
Taylor & Francis Group, an **informa** business

System Modeling and Control with Resource-Oriented Petri Nets
MengChu Zhou, Naiqi Wu

Deterministic Learning Theory for Identification, Recognition, and Control
Cong Wang, David J. Hill

Optimal and Robust Scheduling for Networked Control Systems
Stefano Longo, Tingli Su, Guido Herrmann, Phil Barber

Electric and Plug-in Hybrid Vehicle Networks
Optimization and Control
Emanuele Crisostomi, Robert Shorten, Sonja Stüdli, Fabian Wirth

Adaptive and Fault-Tolerant Control of Underactuated Nonlinear Systems
Jiangshuai Huang, Yong-Duan Song

Discrete-Time Recurrent Neural Control
Analysis and Application
Edgar N. Sánchez

Control of Nonlinear Systems via PI, PD and PID
Stability and Performance
Yong-Duan Song

Multi-Agent Systems
Platoon Control and Non-Fragile Quantized Consensus
Xiang-Gui Guo, Jian-Liang Wang, Fang Liao, Rodney Swee Huat Teo

Classical Feedback Control with Nonlinear Multi-Loop Systems
With MATLAB® and Simulink®, Third Edition
Boris J. Lurie, Paul Enright

Motion Control of Functionally Related Systems
Tarik Uzunović, Asif Sabanović

Intelligent Fault Diagnosis and Accommodation Control
Sunan Huang, Kok Kiong Tan, Poi Voon Er, Tong Heng Lee

Nonlinear Pinning Control of Complex Dynamical Networks
Edgar N. Sanchez, Carlos J. Vega, Oscar J. Suarez, Guanrong Chen

Adaptive Control of Dynamic Systems with Uncertainty and Quantization
Jing Zhou, Lantao Xing, Changyun Wen

Robust Formation Control for Multiple Unmanned Aerial Vehicles
Hao Liu, Deyuan Liu, Yan Wan, Frank L. Lewis, Kimon P. Valavanis

Variable Gain Control and Its Applications in Energy Conversion
Chenghui Zhang, Le Chang, Cheng Fu

For more information about this series, please visit: https://www.crcpress.com/Automation-and-Control-Engineering/book-series/CRCAUTCONENG

Dedication

The first author would like to dedicate the book to his mother Janaki and spouse Sandhya

The second author would like to dedicate the book to KA Kamakshi, R Jayalakshmi, VEV Ramani, KA Gopal, T Vijayalakshmi Krishnan, K Jagadisan, and R Narayanan

The third author would like to dedicate the book to his mother Kumudini, spouse Praveena, and daughter Anaaya

First edition published 2024
by CRC Press
2385 NW Executive Center Drive, Suite 320, Boca Raton FL 33431

and by CRC Press
4 Park Square, Milton Park, Abingdon, Oxon, OX14 4RN

CRC Press is an imprint of Taylor & Francis Group, LLC

ISBN: 978-1-032-46865-5 (hbk)
ISBN: 978-1-032-79150-0 (pbk)
ISBN: 978-1-003-49075-3 (ebk)

DOI: 10.1201/9781003490753

Publisher's note: This book has been prepared from camera-ready copy provided by the authors.

Access the Instructor and Student Resources/Support Material:
www.routledge.com/9781032468655

Author Bios

Dr. Sarangapani Jagannathan is a Curator's Distinguished Professor and Rutledge-Emerson Endowed Chair of Electrical and Computer Engineering at the Missouri University of Science and Technology (former University of Missouri-Rolla). He has a joint Professor appointment in the Department of Computer Science. He served as a Director for the NSF Industry/University Cooperative Research Center on Intelligent Maintenance Systems for 13 years. His research interests include learning, adaptation and control, secure human-cyber-physical systems, prognostics, and autonomous systems/robotics. Prior to his Missouri S&T appointment, he served as a faculty at University of Texas at San Antonio and as a staff engineer at Caterpillar, Peoria.

He has coauthored over 500 refereed IEEE Transaction/journal and conference articles, written 18 book chapters, authored/co-edited 6 books, received 21 US patents and one patent defense publication. He delivered over 30 plenary and keynote talks in various international conferences and supervised to graduation 33 doctoral and 31 M.S thesis students. He was a co-editor for the IET book series on control from 2010 until 2013 and served on many editorial boards including IEEE Systems, Man and Cybernetics, and has been on organizing committees of several IEEE Conferences. He is currently an associate editor for IEEE Transactions on Neural Networks and Learning Systems and others.

He received many awards including the 2020 Best Associate Editor Award, 2018 IEEE CSS Transition to Practice Award, 2007 Boeing Pride Achievement Award, 2001 Caterpillar Research Excellence Award, 2021 University of Missouri Presidential Award for sustained career excellence, 2001 University of Texas Presidential Award for early career excellence, and 2000 NSF Career Award. He also received several faculty excellence and teaching excellence and commendation awards. As part of his NSF I/UCRC, he transitioned many technologies and software products to industrial entities saving millions of dollars. He is a Fellow of the IEEE, National Academy of Inventors, and Institute of Measurement and Control, UK, Institution of Engineering and Technology (IET), UK and Asia-Pacific Artificial Intelligence Association.

Dr. Vignesh Narayanan is an Assistant Professor in the AI institute and the Department of Computer Science and Engineering at University of South Carolina (USC), Columbia. He is also affiliated with the Carolina Autism and Neurodevelopment research center at USC. His research interests include dynamical systems and networks, artificial intelligence, data science, learning theory, and computational neuroscience.

He received his B.Tech. Electrical and electronics engineering and M. Tech. Electrical engineering degrees from SASTRA University, Thanjavur, and the National Institute of Technology, Kurukshetra, India, respectively, in 2012 and 2014, and his Ph.D. degree from Missouri University of Science and Technology, Rolla, MO in 2017. He was a post-doctoral research associate at Washington University in St. Louis, before joining the AI institute of USC.

Avimanyu Sahoo received his Ph.D. in Electrical Engineering from Missouri University of Science and Technology, Rolla, MO, USA, in 2015 and a Master of Technology (MTech) from the Indian Institute of Technology (BHU), Varanasi, India, in 2011. He is currently an Assistant Professor in the Electrical and Computer Engineering Department at the University of Alabama in Huntsville (UAH), AL. Before joining UAH, Dr. Sahoo was an Associate Professor in the Division of Engineering Technology at Oklahoma State University, Stillwater, OK.

Dr. Sahoo's research interests include learning-based control and its applications in lithium-ion battery pack modeling, diagnostics, prognostics, cyber-physical systems (CPS), and electric machinery health monitoring. Currently, his research focuses on developing intelligent battery management systems (BMS) for lithium-ion battery packs used onboard electric vehicles, computation, and communication-efficient distributed intelligent control schemes for cyber-physical systems using approximate dynamic programming, reinforcement learning, and distributed adaptive state estimation. He has published over 45 journal and conference articles, including IEEE Transactions on Neural Networks and Learning Systems, Cybernetics, and Industrial Electronics. He is also an Associate Editor in IEEE Transactions on Neural Networks and Learning Systems and Frontiers in Control Engineering: Nonlinear Control.

Contents

Preface

Modern feedback control systems have resulted in major successes in the fields of mechanical and aerospace engineering, automotive, space, defense, and industrial systems. A feedback controller proactively alters the system behavior to meet a desired level of performance by optimizing a performance index. Modern control techniques, whether linear or nonlinear, were developed using state space or frequency domain techniques. These techniques were responsible for effective flight control systems, engine and emission controllers, space shuttle controllers, and for industrial systems.

In the past decade, significant advances in theoretical and applied research have occurred in computation, communication, and control to address performance in cyber-physical systems wherein cyber and physical system components interact through a communication network. Wireless communication is preferred over wired communication as it allows mobility though maintaining control performance for such systems is a challenge. Recently, a communication network is combined with the modern control system to form a networked control system (NCS) and this novel cyber-physical system (CPS) concept is considered a 3rd generation control system. In NCS, a communication packet carries the reference input, plant output, and control input which are exchanged by using a communication network among control system components such as sensors, controllers, and actuators.

Compared with traditional control systems, an NCS reduces system wiring with ease of system diagnosis and maintenance while increasing the system agility and is therefore considered as part of Industry 4.0. Because of these advantages, the NCS/CPS concepts have been considered in manufacturing and power industries despite the increasing complexity of the system. The complexity of such man-made systems has placed severe constraints on existing feedback design techniques. More stringent performance requirements in the face of system uncertainties and unknown environments such as a communication network within the control loop have challenged the limits of modern control. Operating a complex system with network imperfections such as random delays, packet losses, and quantization errors within the feedback loop and functioning in different operating regimes requires that the controller be intelligent with adaptive and learning capabilities in the presence of unknown disturbances, unmodeled dynamics, and unstructured uncertainties. A novel framework, referred to as performance-based sampling and control, or event-triggered control, has been proposed and the control design has to be developed to address these challenges.

Recently, neural network-based optimal adaptive controllers that function forward-in-time manner, to perform regulation and trajectory tracking, have been developed using reinforcement learning and adaptive dynamic programming both in continuous and discrete time. Controllers designed in discrete time have the important advantage that they can be directly implemented in digital form on modern-day embedded hardware. Unfortunately, the discrete-time design is far more complex than the continuous-time design when Lyapunov stability analysis is used since the first difference in the Lyapunov function is quadratic in the states not linear as in the case of continuous-time. This coupled with uncertainty in system dynamics along with event-triggered sampling and control for uncertain linear and nonlinear systems require an advanced optimal adaptive controller design.

This book presents the neural networks and Q-learning-based event-triggered control design to address regulation and tracking for linear and nonlinear dynamical systems. Several powerful modern control techniques are used in the book for the design of such controllers. Thorough development, rigorous analysis, and simulation examples are presented in each case. Proof sketch are provided for stability.

The first chapter introduces an introduction to event-triggered and traditional, fixed, and adaptive model-based event-triggered control methods designed after providing background on stability. Chapter 2 discusses the background of adaptive dynamic programming (ADP), optimal control of dynamic systems using value and policy iterations, and fundamental aspects of ADP for continuous and discrete-time systems including Q-learning and actor-critic neural network-based frameworks.

Chapter 3 lays the foundation of the traditional Q-learning-based optimal adaptive event-triggered control scheme design for uncertain linear discrete-time dynamic systems using infinite time horizon with state and output feedback. The case of NCS is also attempted with the Q-learning-based event-triggered design. In Chapter 4, we introduce adaptive event-triggered state feedback design for uncertain nonlinear continuous-time systems without and with a communication network within the control loop by using the function approximation property of neural networks with event sampling. Minimum intersample time and Zeno behavior are also presented.

Chapter 5 confronts the additional complexity introduced by optimizing both the event trigger sampling instants and uncertain dynamical systems by treating sample selection and control input as a co-optimization problem. Both linear and nonlinear dynamical systems are considered. Chapter 6 presents the optimal control of linear interconnected systems with hybrid parameter updates. In Chapter 7, we discuss optimal event-triggered control design for nonlinear interconnected systems using output feedback and non-zero-sum games. Chapter 8 covers the event-triggered design of nonlinear interconnected systems with exploration through NN identifier. Chapter 9 treats the applications of event-triggered control of robot manipulators, unmanned aerial vehicles, and cyber-physical systems. Since Lyapunov analysis is done within the event triggered instants, the control schemes covered in the book from chapter 3 and beyond do not require Input to State (ISS) assumption. The MATLAB code for the examples included in the book can be downloaded.

This book has been written for senior undergraduate and graduate students in a college curriculum, for practicing engineers in industry, and for university researchers. Detailed derivations, stability analysis, and computer simulations show how to design optimal event-triggered controllers as well as how to build them.

Acknowledgments and grateful thanks are due to our former doctoral students who have forced us to take our work seriously and be part of it.

This research work is supported by the National Science Foundation under grant ECCS#1406533 and CMMI#1547042 and Missouri University of Science and Technology.

Jagannathan Sarangapani
Rolla, Missouri

Vignesh Narayanan
Columbia, South Carolina

Avimanyu Sahoo
Huntsville, Alabama

List of Figures

List of Tables

1 Background and Introduction to Event-Triggered Control

CONTENTS

This chapter provides a concise overview of dynamical systems, including ordinary differential and difference equations representing continuous-time and discrete-time systems, respectively. Additionally, it introduces hybrid systems that combine characteristics of both differential and difference equations. It then delves into fundamental stability principles, utilizing Lyapunov-based methodologies, essential for analyzing these systems. Furthermore, it explores feedback control systems, emphasizing the practical implementation of control policies using embedded processors as sampled-data controllers employing periodic sampling of system states or outputs. Finally, aperiodic sampling-based control frameworks, also referred to as the *event-triggered control*, is introduced later in the chapter, where we shall review some of the basic event-based sampling and controller execution techniques that are aimed at optimizing system performance while minimizing computational overhead. The final section introduces conventional event-triggered control strategies documented in the existing literature with the necessary mathematical prerequisites provided for completeness.

1.1 INTRODUCTION

During the early 1960s, the field of control systems underwent a profound transformation with the advent of state space methods. This paradigm shift marked a departure from the conventional approaches grounded in Laplace transforms and transfer functions. Instead, it ushered in a new era centered around vector spaces, as well as the study of differential and difference equations. This pivotal period also cast a bright spotlight on the concept of stability, particularly within the framework of Lyapunov theory (Kalman, 1963; Kalman and Bertram, 1960; Brockett, 2014). Furthermore, it witnessed significant advancements in optimization theory, most notably Pontryagin's maximum principle (Bittner, 1963), along with the emergence of innovative adaptive control techniques, including model-reference adaptive control, gain-scheduling, etc. (Annaswamy and Fradkov, 2021). In parallel, developments in reinforcement learning theory for solving sequential decision making problems along with the emergence of artificial neural networks as universal function approximators spurred the development of data-driven control methodologies (Sutton and Barto, 1998; Narendra and Parthasarathy, 1990; Lewis et al., 1998). These methodologies proved exceptionally well-suited for managing complex dynamical systems that often defy concise modeling using traditional first-principle techniques.

Fast forward to the present day, and we find ourselves in an era characterized by substantial progress in computing power, communication technologies, and control systems. These advancements have paved the way for cyber-physical systems (CPS), which integrates cyber and physical system components, and are increasingly used in safety- or infrastructure-critical applications. These developments have enhanced the design and deployment of sophisticated systems in domains such as manufacturing, energy, and transportation, wherein complex networks of interconnected physical systems enabled by cyber infrastructures are commonplace. These systems are often described as 'smart' because they possess the capability to self-monitor, communicate, and autonomously govern their operations. Given the intricacy of tasks performed by these CPS, efficient control components are often needed to ensure efficiency and robustness. This has contributed to the advancements in resource-efficient control design techniques and data-driven optimal control methods. These methodologies play a crucial role in minimizing communication overhead, computational costs, and ensuring a predetermined level of performance. For instance, *event-triggered control* techniques and *adaptive or approximate dynamic programming*-based controllers are valuable tools developed to address the demands of CPS.

In the following chapters, we will systematically delve into these tools and dissect their design principles. In this chapter, we shall lay the foundation by providing a brief review of fundamental building blocks necessary for constructing efficient controllers capable of managing large and complex dynamical systems. We shall start by reviewing various system descriptions, followed by essential mathematical preliminaries. Subsequently, we shall review stability concepts and conclude with an overview of event-triggered control techniques. Several excellent expositions on dynamical systems and control are available, for instance, in Kwakernaak and Sivan (1972); Luenberger (1979); Chen (1984); Dorf and Bishop (2000); Ogata (2011); Åström and Murray (2021). For more information on mathematical preliminaries, see Royden and Fitzpatrick (1968), and on event-triggered control, see Lemmon (2010).

1.1.1 CONTINUOUS-TIME SYSTEMS

Engineered and naturally occurring systems, encompassing physical, chemical, and biological domains, often exhibit dynamic behavior. These systems possess internal memory, respond to external perturbations or stimuli, and evolve over time based on governing first-principles and external influences. The formalization of the concept of a system was initiated in the early 1900s, and in this context, a system is regarded as a distinct entity from its environment, defined by its interactions through input and output signals.

In the realm of feedback control, dynamical systems assume a pivotal role. These systems, be they drones, robots, or temperature regulation setups, possess a *state* evolving over time, governed by differential or difference equations. The essence of feedback emerges when we measure the current system state or a derived *output* and employ this information to shape the system's behavior in line with our objectives. Through judicious manipulation of these governing principles via feedback mechanisms, we seek to exert control over the system, achieving desired outcomes such as guiding a drone along a predefined trajectory or maintaining a specific room temperature. Some of these systems exhibit continuous state evolution, characterized by differential equations, and are thus classified as *continuous-time dynamical systems* or continuous systems.

A continuous-time dynamical system is typically defined by a differential equation of the form

$$\frac{dx(t)}{dt} = \dot{x}(t) = f(x(t),t), \quad x(t_0) = x_0, \tag{1.1}$$

where $x(t) \in \mathbb{R}^n$ is the state of the system at time t, t_0 is the initial time, and x_0 is the initial state of the system at t_0. The vector function $f : \mathbb{R}^n \times \mathbb{R} \to \mathbb{R}^n$ specifies the rate of change of the system's state. This function is often referred to as the dynamics of the system in (1.1) or the drift vector field. For a system to be well-defined, f is typically required to be Lipschitz continuous, which guarantees the existence and uniqueness of solution to (1.1) (Khalil, 2002).

In a more formal way, we can define a dynamical system as a tuple $\{T, X, \Phi\}$, where $T \subseteq \mathbb{R}$ is the time set. This set could represent continuous time (for instance, $T = \mathbb{R}$ or $T = [0, \infty)$) or discrete time (such as $T = \mathbb{Z}$ or $T = \mathbb{N}$). The set X is a nonempty set known as the state space. This set contains all possible states that the system can occupy. Usually, $X \subseteq \mathbb{R}^n$ for some positive integer n, but X can be any set in general. The function $\Phi : T \times T \times X \to X$ is a function describing the evolution of the system over time. For a given time $t \in T$ and a state $x \in X$, $\Phi(t, t_0, x)$ returns the state of the system at time t if the system started in the state x at time t_0. Without loss of generality, we may set $t_0 = 0$ and represent $\Phi(t, t_0, x)$ as $\Phi(t, x)$ with the initial time argument suppressed.

The function Φ must satisfy the following two conditions for all $t, s \in T$ and $x \in X$

1. $\Phi(0, x) = x$,
2. If $t + s \in T$, then $\Phi(t + s, x) = \Phi(s, \Phi(t, x))$.

The first condition indicates that if no time has passed, the state of the system remains unchanged. The second condition, known as the semigroup property (Layek et al., 2015), represents the idea that to find the state of the system at time $t + s$, one may first track the system evolution from state x for time t units so that state becomes $\Phi(t, x)$, and then let it evolve from this state for an additional time s units. These two properties are fundamental axioms of dynamical systems and ensure a degree of consistency and predictability in the system's time evolution. We can verify that the system represented in (1.1) satisfies the above two conditions (Layek et al., 2015).

Controlled dynamical systems are defined by a set of n coupled first-order ordinary differential equations, which can be compactly represented as

$$\dot{x}(t) = f(t, x(t), u(t)) \tag{1.2}$$

where $x(t) = (x_1(t), \ldots, x_n(t))^T$ is the state vector, $u(t) = (u_1(t), \ldots, u_m(t))^T$ is the input vector or control, $f : \mathbb{R} \times \mathbb{R}^n \times \mathbb{R}^m \to \mathbb{R}^n$ is a vector function with n components, i.e., $f = (f_1, \ldots, f_n)^T$, and $\dot{x}(t) = (\dot{x}_1(t), \ldots, \dot{x}_n(t))^T$ denotes the derivative of $x(t)$ with respect to time. Each function f_i for $i = 1, \ldots, n$, gives the rate of change of the corresponding state variable x_i as a function of time t, the current state x, and the current input u.

The equation in (1.2) is also referred to as the state equation. The output equation can be expressed as

$$y(t) = h(t, x(t), u(t)) \tag{1.3}$$

where $y(t) \in \mathbb{R}^p$ is the p-dimensional output vector and the function $h : \mathbb{R} \times \mathbb{R}^n \times \mathbb{R}^m \to \mathbb{R}^p$ is a vector-valued function. The equations (1.2) and (1.3) are known as the state-space model or state model. Specifically, the state equation is a non-autonomous (the evolution explicitly depends on time) and non-affine form. An autonomous system takes the form

$$\dot{x}(t) = f(x(t)), \quad x(t_0) = x_0, \tag{1.4}$$

where the function $f(\cdot)$ does not explicitly depend on time t.

A control system in an affine form is a dynamical system expressed as

$$\dot{x}(t) = f(x(t)) + \sum_{i=1}^{m} g_i(x(t))u_i(t), \quad x(t_0) = x_0, \tag{1.5}$$

where $x(t) \in \mathbb{R}^n$, $u(t) = (u_1(t), \ldots, u_m(t))^T \in \mathbb{R}^m$ is the input (or control) vector, $f : \mathbb{R}^n \to \mathbb{R}^n$ is the drift vector field representing the system's internal dynamics in the absence of control, $g_i : \mathbb{R}^n \to \mathbb{R}^n$ for $i = 1, \ldots, m$ are control vector fields or control coefficients modeling the influence of the control inputs on the system dynamics. Each of these functions, i.e., $f, g_1, \ldots, g_m$, can either be a linear or a nonlinear function of the system state. Each control input $u_i(t)$ influences the state dynamics through the corresponding control vector field $g_i(x)$, and these influences are added together to give the total rate of change of the system's state. The term "affine" here refers to the fact that the dependence of the system dynamics on the control inputs $u_i(t)$ is *affine* (linear with a constant offset due to the internal drift). We can write the state equation in (1.5) in a compact form as

$$\dot{x}(t) = f(x(t)) + g(x(t))u(t), \quad x(t_0) = x_0, \tag{1.6}$$

where the control coefficient $g : \mathbb{R}^n \to \mathbb{R}^{n\times m}$ is a matrix-valued function and the control input $u(t) \in \mathbb{R}^m$ for all time t.

In the state feedback control framework, the goal is to design a control input for the system that renders the closed-loop system stable. This control input is designed as a continuous function of time, taking the form

$$u(t) = \mu(x(t)), \tag{1.7}$$

where $\mu : \mathbb{R}^n \to \mathbb{R}^m$ is the *control policy or control law* that is dependent on the system state obtained as feedback. Then the controlled system or the closed-loop system can be represented as

$$\dot{x}(t) = f(x(t), \mu(x(t))), \quad x(t_0) = x_0. \tag{1.8}$$

There are several approaches available to design the state feedback nonlinear controllers to synthesize control laws when the system dynamics (i.e., the drift and control vector fields) are known. Examples range from PID controllers to feedback linearization, backstepping, sliding mode controllers, and so on, and can be found in several nonlinear control system texts such as Khalil (2002); Lewis et al. (2012b); Åström and Murray (2021).

As a special case of the nonlinear time-invariant affine system (1.6), we have the linear time-invariant (LTI) system expressed as

$$\dot{x}(t) = Ax(t) + Bu(t), \quad x(t_0) = x_0, \tag{1.9}$$

$$y(t) = Cx(t) + Du(t), \tag{1.10}$$

where $A \in \mathbb{R}^{n\times n}$ and $B \in \mathbb{R}^{n\times m}$ are the internal dynamics and control coefficient matrices, respectively. The matrices $C \in \mathbb{R}^{p\times n}$ and $D \in \mathbb{R}^{p\times m}$ are the output matrices. Here the drift vector field $f(x(t))$ is a linear function of the state $Ax(t)$ and the control vector field $g(x(t))$ is a constant matrix B. The state feedback control input in the case of a linear system can be expressed as

$$u(t) = Kx(t), \tag{1.11}$$

where $K \in \mathbb{R}^{m\times n}$ is the control gain and can be designed using techniques such as pole placement (Chen, 1984) or linear quadratic regulation (LQR) approaches (Lewis et al., 2012b; Kwakernaak and Sivan, 1972).

1.1.2 DISCRETE-TIME SYSTEMS

A discrete dynamical system is typically defined by a difference equation capturing the evolution of the system state and the output equation, taking the form

$$\begin{aligned} x_{k+1} &= f(k, x_k, u_k), \quad x_0 \text{ is the initial state}, \\ y_k &= h(x_k, u_k), \end{aligned} \tag{1.12}$$

where $x_k \in \mathbb{R}^n$ is the state, $u_k \in \mathbb{R}^m$ is the control input, y_k is the output of the system at the discrete time steps $k \in \mathbb{Z}$. The function $f : \mathbb{Z} \times \mathbb{R}^n \times \mathbb{R}^m \to \mathbb{R}^n$ specifies how the state of the system changes from one-time step to the next and the function $h : \mathbb{R}^n \times \mathbb{R}^m \to \mathbb{R}^p$ maps the states and control to the output. Without loss of generality, we shall consider the initial time to be zero and the initial state is defined as x_0. Similar to the continuous case, a minimum that f be Lipschitz continuous can ensure the existence and uniqueness of solutions to the difference equation (1.12). Note that the time index in a discrete-time system is an integer k instead of a real number t in a continuous-time system.

In the state feedback control framework, the goal is to design a sequence of control inputs

$$u_k = \mu(x_k), \tag{1.13}$$

which renders the closed-loop system

$$x_{k+1} = f(x_k, \mu(x_k)), \tag{1.14}$$

stable. Similar to the continuous-time case, a linear time-invariant (LTI) discrete-time system can be represented by a linear difference equation as

$$x_{k+1} = Ax_k + Bu_k, \tag{1.15}$$

$$y_k = Cx_k + Du_k, \tag{1.16}$$

where $A \in \mathbb{R}^n$, $B \in \mathbb{R}^{n \times m}$, $C \in \mathbb{R}^{p \times n}$ and $D \in \mathbb{R}^{p \times m}$ are all constant matrices. The discrete-time state feedback control input can be defined as

$$u_k = Kx_k \tag{1.17}$$

where K is the control gain matrix.

The discrete-time dynamics of a system as expressed in the equation (1.12) may be derived in two ways. They might originate directly from analyzing the dynamical system or process under consideration, where the system state evolves naturally in discrete time-steps. For example, the time evolution of a counter, population of bacterial cells (broadly, population models), epidemic models, etc. Alternatively, they could represent discretized or sampled versions of continuous-time dynamical system. In contemporary settings, controllers are predominantly implemented in a digital form due to the widespread use of embedded hardware. This necessitates a discrete-time representation of the controller, which could be established through design based on the discrete-time system dynamics.

1.1.3 SAMPLED-DATA CONTROL SYSTEMS

In many practical applications, the system or the plant operates in continuous time but the controller operates in discrete time. This is often the case when the controller is implemented digitally using embedded processors. The controller samples the output of the plant at discrete time intervals, and these samples are used to compute control inputs. The system dynamics are described by a combination of differential equations (for the plant) and difference equations (for the controller).

To understand the implementation, we start by considering a nonlinear continuous-time system in nonaffine form, represented as

$$\dot{x}(t) = f(x(t), u(t)), \quad x(t_0) = x_0, \tag{1.18}$$

where $x : \mathbb{R} \to \mathbb{R}^n$ is the state with $x(t_0) = x_0 \in \mathbb{R}^n$ being the initial condition and $u : \mathbb{R} \to \mathbb{R}^m$ is the control input. In order to implement the controller u, we resort to an embedded processor that inherently operates in a digital domain. This entails utilizing a sampled version of the state for computing the control input.

To formalize this, we can define the sequence of sampling instants as $\{t_k\}_{k=0}^{\infty}$ such that $t_{k+1} > t_k$ for $k = 1, 2, \ldots$. The kth sampling instant is denoted by $t_k \in \mathbb{R}$. The sampler output yields a sequence of sampled states, $\{\hat{x}_k\}$, where $\hat{x}_k = x(t_k)$. A state-feedback controller $K : \mathbb{R}^n \to \mathbb{R}^m$ then maps this sampled state onto a control vector $\hat{u}_k \in \mathbb{R}^m$. The sequence $\{\hat{u}_k\}_{k=0}^{\infty}$ of these controls is transformed into a continuous-time signal via a zero-order hold without delay. This renders the control signal, $u : \mathbb{R} \to \mathbb{R}^m$, employed by the plant as a piecewise constant function.

Although both the discrete-time systems and the sampled-data control systems have components of discreteness, they represent different concepts. In the discrete-time systems, all variables change at certain discrete moments in time. The system's state is updated at these discrete instants based on a discrete-time state-transition function. The changes in the system are only registered at these specific instants and the changes at any other time are ignored or assumed non-existent. On the other hand, in the sampled-data control systems, the control input to a continuous-time plant or system is updated only at discrete time instants, with the control input held constant (or varying according to some specified rule) between these instants. The system's dynamics are continuous in time, but the controller only "observes" and "acts" on the system at discrete instants. This is a form of hybrid system, as it has both continuous and discrete elements. Sampled-data control systems are common in practice due to the prevalence of digital control implementations.

1.1.4 IMPUSIVE HYBRID DYNAMICAL SYSTEMS

An impulsive hybrid dynamical system exhibits a mix of continuous and discrete (impulsive) behaviors. A general impulsive hybrid system can be represented as

$$\begin{aligned} \dot{x}(t) &= f(x(t), u(t)), \quad x(0) = x_0, \quad (t, x(t)) \notin \mathbb{D}, \\ x(t^+) &= F(x(t)), \quad (t, x(t)) \in \mathbb{D}, \end{aligned} \tag{1.19}$$

where $x(t) \in \mathbb{C} \subseteq \mathbb{R}^n$ represents the state of the system at time t with initial state $x(t_0) = x_0$, $\mathbb{C}$ is an open set containing the origin, and $u(t) \in \mathbb{R}^m$ represents the control input. The first equation describes the *flow dynamics*, where $f : \mathbb{C} \to \mathbb{R}^n$ is continuous and the second equation describes the systems' *jump dynamics* with a continuous function $F : \mathbb{D} \to \mathbb{R}^n$. The set $\mathbb{D} \subset [0, \infty) \times \mathscr{X}$, referred to as *jump set* or *resetting set*, represents the set of times and the associated states when impulsive changes occur. Here $x(t^+) = F(x(t)) = \lim_{\varepsilon \to 0} x(t + \varepsilon)$ and $\mathscr{X} \subset \mathbb{C}$ denotes the set of resetting time instants.

In some cases, $\mathbb{C}$ and $\mathbb{D}$ can intersect, meaning the system may either flow or jump. The specific behavior, in this case, depends on the exact form of the hybrid system model. These sets can be characterized based on the physical properties of the system. For instance, in a bouncing ball system, the flow set consists of times during which ball is in the air or at rest on the ground, while the jump set consists of times when the ball is impacting the ground. For more information on the hybrid dynamical systems see Bainov and Simeonov (1993); Goebel et al. (2009).

The impulsive hybrid dynamical systems and sampled data systems have distinct characteristics and uses. They differ primarily in the nature of their discrete and continuous dynamics and their typical application domains. An impulsive hybrid dynamical system exhibits behavior that is a mix of continuous dynamics and instantaneous, discrete changes (impulses). The impulsive actions can occur at fixed times (as in clock-driven systems), at variable times determined by the state of the system (as in event-driven systems), or in a manner that is a combination of the two. The defining characteristic of impulsive hybrid systems is that they can change their state instantly in response to certain events, as determined by the jump set and map. These systems are used to model various real-world phenomena, such as bouncing balls, circuit switchings, or biological systems with sudden events. On the other hand, in a sampled data system, the control input is updated only at discrete time instants resulting from a sampling process. The system evolves continuously between these updates, typically driven by a held (constant) input. This type of system is common in digital control implementations, where the controller reads sensor data (sampling), computes control actions, and updates the control inputs only at discrete times. The controller may use a zero-order hold or some other method to maintain the control input between updates. As we shall see later in the chapter, event-triggered control systems can be seen as both sampled data systems with aperiodic sampling intervals as well as impulsive dynamical system.

1.2 MATHEMATICAL PRELIMINARIES

In this section, some of the mathematical tools required for the analysis and design of optimal event-triggered control systems are reviewed. We restrict our focus to the most important tools and techniques that are applied throughout the rest of the book. To gain a broader perspective and a more comprehensive understanding of these topics, refer to Rudin (1953), Royden and Fitzpatrick (1968), and Strang (2022).

1.2.1 VECTOR NORMS

The norm of a vector in an n-dimensional real space is a non-negative value that, in some sense, measures the length (or size) of the vector. Consider $\mathbb{R}^n$, the set of all n-dimensional vectors $x = (x_1, x_2, \cdots, x_n)^T$, where $x_1, \cdots, x_{n-1}$, and x_n are real numbers.

Definition 1.1. *The norm $\|\cdot\|$ of vectors in $\mathbb{R}^n$ is a real-valued function with the following properties:*

1. $\|x\| \geq 0$ *for all* $x \in \mathbb{R}^n$, *with* $\|x\| = 0$ *if and only if* $x = 0$
2. $\|x+y\| \leq \|x\| + \|y\|$, *for all* $x, y \in \mathbb{R}^n$ *(triangle inequality)*
3. $\|\alpha x\| = |\alpha|\|x\|$, *for all* $\alpha \in \mathbb{R}$ *and* $x \in \mathbb{R}^n$

The concept of a norm can be extended to measure the distance between two vectors. Let x and y be two vectors in $\mathbb{R}^n$. The distance between these two vectors can be defined as $\|x-y\|$. There are several commonly used metrics that satisfy the Definition 1.1. For instance, a class of p-norm, where $p \geq 1$, can be defined as

$$\|x\|_p = (|x_1|^p + |x_2|^p + \cdots + |x_n|^p)^{1/p}, \quad \forall x \in \mathbb{R}^n.$$

For $p = 1, 2, \infty$, the corresponding norms $\|x\|_1$, $\|x\|_2$, and $\|x\|_\infty$ are defined as shown in Table 1.1.

Listed below are some frequently employed inequalities involving various vector norms (p-norms) in $\mathbb{R}^n$, which we will frequently refer to in this book.

1. **Triangle Inequality:** For any vectors x and y, and any $p \geq 1$,

$$\|x+y\|_p \leq \|x\|_p + \|y\|_p.$$

2. **Reverse Triangle Inequality:** For vectors x, y and any $p \geq 1$,

$$|\|x\|_p - \|y\|_p| \leq \|x-y\|_p.$$

Table 1.1
Commonly used p-norms on $\mathbb{R}^n$

p-norm on $\mathbb{R}^n$	Expression
$\|\|x\|\|_1$	$\|x_1\|+\|x_2\|+\cdots+\|x_n\|$
$\|\|x\|\|_2$ (Euclidean norm)	$(\|x_1\|^2+\|x_2\|^2+\cdots+\|x_n\|^2)^{1/2}=(x^Tx)^{1/2}$
$\|\|x\|\|_\infty$ (infinity norm)	$\max_i \|x_i\|$

3. **Holder's Inequality:** For any vectors $x=(x_1,x_2,...,x_n)^T$ and $y=(y_1,y_2,...,y_n)^T$, and any p, $q \geq 1$ such that $\frac{1}{p}+\frac{1}{q}=1$,
$$|x_1y_1+x_2y_2+...+x_ny_n| = |x^Ty| \leq ||x||_p||y||_q.$$
4. **Cauchy-Schwarz Inequality:** This is a special case of Holder's inequality when $p=q=2$. For any vectors x and y,
$$|x_1y_1+x_2y_2+...+x_ny_n| = |x^Ty| \leq ||x||_2||y||_2.$$

All p-norms are equivalent in the sense that if $||\cdot||_\alpha$ and $||\cdot||_\beta$ are two different p-norms, then there exists positive constants c_1 and c_2 such that
$$c_1||x||_\alpha \leq ||x||_\beta \leq c_2||x||_\alpha$$
for all $x \in \mathbb{R}^n$. For the norms $||x||_1$, $||x||_2$, and $||x||_\infty$, these inequalities take the forms of
$$||x||_2 \leq ||x||_1 \leq \sqrt{n}||x||_2 \quad \text{and} \quad ||x||_\infty \leq ||x||_2 \leq \sqrt{n}||x||_\infty.$$

1.2.2 MATRIX NORMS

For $x \in \mathbb{R}^n$, an $m \times n$ matrix A of real elements defines a linear mapping $y = Ax$ from $\mathbb{R}^n$ to $\mathbb{R}^m$. The norm of a matrix is a non-negative value that can represent the "size", "length", or "magnitude" of the matrix.

Definition 1.2. *A function $||\cdot||: M \to \mathbb{R}$, where M is a set of matrices in $\mathbb{R}^{m\times n}$, is called a matrix norm if it satisfies the following properties for all matrices $A, B \in M$ and all scalars λ*

1. $||A|| \geq 0$ *(non-negativity)*
2. $||A|| = 0 \Leftrightarrow A = 0$ *(definiteness)*
3. $||\lambda A|| = |\lambda|\cdot||A||$ *(homogeneity or absolute scalability)*
4. $||A+B|| \leq ||A||+||B||$ *(subadditivity or triangle inequality)*

These four properties are the defining characteristics of a matrix norm. Different norms might weigh the elements of the matrix differently, but they all have to satisfy these properties. There are three more commonly used matrix norms.

1. **Frobenius Norm:** This is the direct analogue to the Euclidean norm for vectors. For an $m \times n$ matrix $A = [a_{ij}]$, the Frobenius norm is defined as
$$||A||_F = \sqrt{\sum_{i=1}^{m}\sum_{j=1}^{n}|a_{ij}|^2}.$$

2. **Induced matrix or Operator Norm:** This is induced by the vector p-norm. For any matrix $A \in \mathbb{R}^{m \times n}$ and $x \in \mathbb{R}^n$, the p-norm (or operator norm) is defined as

$$\|A\|_p = \sup_{x \neq 0} \frac{\|Ax\|_p}{\|x\|_p},$$

where "sup" denotes the supremum. In other words, it is the maximum ratio of the norm of the output vector $Ax \in \mathbb{R}^m$ to the norm of the input vector x, over all non-zero input vectors. For $p = 1, 2$, and ∞, the corresponding induced norms are given as follows:
   a. **1-Norm (or Maximum Absolute Column Sum Norm):** This is the maximum absolute column sum of the matrix. If $A = [a_{ij}]$ is a matrix, then the 1-norm of A is defined as

$$\|A\|_1 = \max_j \sum_i |a_{ij}|.$$

   b. **Induced 2-Norm (or Spectral Norm):** The 2-norm (Euclidean norm) of a matrix is the square root of the largest eigenvalue of the matrix product A^T and A, given as

$$\|A\|_2 = [\lambda_{max}(A^T A)]^{\frac{1}{2}}.$$

   It is also equal to the largest singular value of the matrix.
   c. **Infinity Norm (or Maximum Absolute Row Sum Norm):** This is the maximum absolute row sum of the matrix. If $A = [a_{ij}]$ is a matrix, then the infinity norm of A is defined as

$$\|A\|_\infty = \max_i \sum_j |a_{ij}|.$$

There are several matrix inequalities we will use in this book and are listed below.

1. **Triangle Inequality:** The triangle inequality applies to any matrix norm (by definition). For any matrices A and B

$$\|A + B\| \leq \|A\| + \|B\|.$$

2. **Inverse of a Matrix:** If A is invertible, then the norm of the inverse matrix satisfies

$$\|A^{-1}\| \geq \frac{1}{\|A\|}.$$

3. **Submultiplicativity:** For any two matrices A and B

$$\|AB\| \leq \|A\| \|B\|.$$

4. **Spectral Radius:** The spectral radius $\rho(A)$ of a matrix A (the maximum absolute value of its eigenvalues) is always less than or equal to any matrix norm

$$\rho(A) \leq \|A\|.$$

5. **Consistency of Norms:** All matrix norms are equivalent in the sense that for any two norms $\|\cdot\|_\alpha$ and $\|\cdot\|_\beta$, there exist positive constants c_1 and c_2 such that

$$c_1 \|A\|_\alpha \leq \|A\|_\beta \leq c_2 \|A\|_\alpha$$

for all matrices A.
6. **Cauchy-Schwarz Inequality:** For matrices A, B with compatible dimensions

$$|\langle A, B \rangle| \leq \|A\|_F \|B\|_F,$$

where $\langle A, B \rangle$ represents the Frobenius inner product of A and B, defined as the trace of the matrix product B^T and A, and $\|\cdot\|_F$ is the Frobenius norm.

7. **Norm of a Transpose:** The norm of a matrix and its transpose are equal

$$\|A^T\| = \|A\|.$$

These equalities and inequalities provide useful ways to estimate the magnitude of matrices, compare different matrices, and analyze the stability and convergence of numerical algorithms involving matrices. The interpretation of the matrix norms depends on the type of norm being used. For example, the Frobenius norm can be interpreted as a measure of "magnitude" or "size" of the matrix. The induced p-norm (or operator norm) measures the maximum amount by which the matrix can "stretch" a vector when the vector norm is measured using the corresponding vector p-norm.

Example 1.1. *Let* $x = \begin{bmatrix} 1 & -10 & 2 & 0 \end{bmatrix}$. *Compute the vector p-norms for* $p = 1, 2,$ *and* ∞.

The vector norms can be found as

$$\|x\|_\infty = |-10| = 10$$

$$\|x\|_1 = 13$$

$$\|x\|_2 = \sqrt{105}$$

Example 1.2. *Given a matrix* $A = \begin{bmatrix} 4 & -4 & 2 \\ -1 & 2 & 3 \\ -2 & 1 & 0 \end{bmatrix}$. *Compute the matrix p-norms for* $p = 1, \infty$, *and the Frobenius norm.*

Solution: The norms can be calculated as follows: The 1-norm of a matrix is the maximum of the absolute column sum, which is computed as

$$\|A\|_1 = \max\{4+1+2, 4+2+1, 2+3+0\} = \max\{7,7,5\} = 7$$

The ∞-norm of a matrix is the maximum of the absolute row sum, which is computed as

$$\|A\|_\infty = \max\{4+4+2, 1+2+3, 2+1+0\} = \max\{10,6,3\} = 10$$

The Frobenius norm of a matrix is the square root of the sum of squares of all the elements of the matrix and it is computed as

$$\|A\|_F = \sqrt{4^2 + (-4)^2 + 2^2 + (-1)^2 + 2^2 + 3^3 + (-2)^2 + 1^2 + 0^2} = \sqrt{55}$$

1.2.3 QUADRATIC FORMS AND DEFINITENESS.

Given a real symmetric matrix $A \in \mathbb{R}^{n \times n}$ (i.e., $A^T = A$) and a vector $x \in \mathbb{R}^n$, the quadratic form is defined as

$$f(x) = x^T A x,$$

where x^T denotes the transpose of x, and the result of this expression is a scalar. For example, given a 2×2 matrix $A = \begin{bmatrix} a & b \\ b & d \end{bmatrix}$ and a two dimensional vector $x = \begin{bmatrix} x_1 \\ x_2 \end{bmatrix}$, the quadratic form can be written as

$$f(x) = \begin{bmatrix} x_1 & x_2 \end{bmatrix} \begin{bmatrix} a & b \\ b & d \end{bmatrix} \begin{bmatrix} x_1 \\ x_2 \end{bmatrix} = ax_1^2 + 2bx_1x_2 + dx_2^2.$$

Definition 1.3. *A symmetric matrix $A \in \mathbb{R}^{n\times n}$ is said to be*

1. ***Positive definite:*** *if $f(x) > 0$ for all $x \in \mathbb{R}^n$ with $x \neq 0$.*
2. ***Negative definite:*** *if $f(x) < 0$ for all $x \in \mathbb{R}^n$ with $x \neq 0$.*
3. ***Positive semi-definite:*** *if $f(x) \geq 0$ for all $x \in \mathbb{R}^n$.*
4. ***Negative semi-definite:*** *if $f(x) \leq 0$ for all $x \in \mathbb{R}^n$.*
5. ***Indefinite:*** *if it is neither positive semi-definite nor negative semi-definite.*

In the above definition, we assumed A is symmetric. However, the notion of the definiteness is not restricted to symmetric matrices. Any square matrix can be decomposed into a sum of a symmetric and a skew symmetric matrices, i.e., for any $A \in \mathbb{R}^{n\times n}$, we have $A = \frac{1}{2}(A - A^T) + \frac{1}{2}(A + A^T)$, where the second term yields a symmetric matrix and the first term yields a skew-symmetric matrix. It can be shown that for a nonzero vector $x \in \mathbb{R}^n$ and a nonzero matrix $A \in \mathbb{R}^{n\times n}$ the quadratic form $x^T Ax = 0$ if and only if A is a skew-symmetric matrix. Determining the positive definiteness of a matrix from the above definition is cumbersome. Alternatively, we can use the following definition to evaluate the positive definiteness of a symmetric matrix.

Definition 1.4. *Let $A \in \mathbb{R}^{n\times n}$ be a symmetric matrix. The matrix A is positive definite if and only if any of the following conditions hold*

1. *$\lambda_i(A) > 0$, $i = 1,2,\ldots,n$, where $\lambda_i(\cdot)$ is the ith eigenvalue of A. Note that the eigenvalues of A are real since the matrix is symmetric.*
2. *Every principal minor of A is positive.*
3. *There exists a nonsingular matrix A_1 such that $A = A_1 A_1^T$.*
4. *$x^T Ax \geq \alpha \|x\|^2$ for some $\alpha > 0$ and $\forall x \in \mathbb{R}^n$.*

These properties are crucial in many fields, including optimization, as they help determine the nature of a function. For example, if the Hessian of a function evaluated at a critical point, which is a symmetric matrix, is positive definite, it means that the critical point is a local minimum.

A symmetric matric $A \in \mathbb{R}^{n\times n}$ can be decomposd as

$$A = V^T \Lambda V$$

where V is an orthogonal matrix (i.e., $V^T V = I$) composed of n-orthogonal eignvectors of A, and Λ is a digonal matrix with eigenvalues of A as the diagonal elements.

Example 1.3. *Let $x = \begin{bmatrix} x_1 \\ x_2 \end{bmatrix} \in \mathbb{R}^2$ and $V(x) = x_1^2 + x_2^2 \in \mathbb{R}$. Show that $V(x)$ is positive definite (PD).*

Solution One can check that

$$V(x) = x_1^2 + x_2^2 = 0$$

when $x_1 = 0$ and $x_2 = 0$ and $x_1^2 + x_2^2 > 0$ for all $x_1 \neq 0$ or $x_2 \neq 0$. Alternatively, we can rewrite $V(x)$ in a quadratic form as $V(x) = x^T \begin{bmatrix} 1 & 0 \\ 0 & 1 \end{bmatrix} x$. Since the matrix $\begin{bmatrix} 1 & 0 \\ 0 & 1 \end{bmatrix} x$ has positive eigenvalues, the function $V(x)$ is PD.

Example 1.4. *Let $x = \begin{bmatrix} x_1 \\ x_2 \end{bmatrix} \in \mathbb{R}^2$ and $V(x) = x_1^2$.*

For $x = \begin{bmatrix} 0 \\ x_2 \end{bmatrix}$ with $x_2 \neq 0$, we have $V(x) = x_1^2 = 0$. Therefore, the function $V(x)$ is not positive definite. It is positive semidefinite.

1.2.4 PROPERTIES OF FUNCTIONS AND THEIR NORMS

Before discussing the properties of the functions, we will review the definitions of the various sets we will use throughout the book.

An *open ball* B centered at $x \in \mathbb{R}^n$ with a radius of $r \in \mathbb{R}_{>0}$ is the collection of points $y \in \mathbb{R}^n$ such that $\|y-x\| < r$. Alternatively, we can express this as

$$B(x,r) := \{y \in \mathbb{R}^n \mid \|y-x\| < r\}.$$

A *closed ball* $\bar{B}$ centered at $x \in \mathbb{R}^n$ with a radius of $r \in \mathbb{R}_{>0}$ is the collection of points $y \in \mathbb{R}^n$ such that $\|y-x\| \leq r$, and is expressed as

$$\bar{B}(x,r) := \{y \in \mathbb{R}^n \mid \|y-x\| \leq r\}.$$

A *sphere* S centered at $x \in \mathbb{R}^n$ with a radius of $r \in \mathbb{R}_{>0}$ is the collection of points $y \in \mathbb{R}^n$ such that $\|y-x\| = r$. This set is given by

$$S(x,r) := \{y \in \mathbb{R}^n \mid \|y-x\| = r\}.$$

To generalize the above definitions, we can use the distance function $d(x,y)$ defined in a metric space instead of the $\|\cdot\|$ in the definition of these sets.

The *ε-neighborhood* of a point $x \in \mathbb{R}^n$ is the open ball of radius ε centered at x, i.e., $B(x,\varepsilon)$.

A set $D \subseteq \mathbb{R}^n$ is called open iff

$$\forall x \in D, \exists \varepsilon > 0 \text{ such that } B(x,\varepsilon) \subseteq D.$$

A set $D \subset \mathbb{R}^n$ is called *closed* iff its complement D^c is open.

A set $D \in \mathbb{R}^n$ is *bounded* if there is $r > 0$ such that $\|x\| \leq r$ for all $x \in D$.

A set $D \in \mathbb{R}^n$ is *compact* if it is closed and bounded.

Some of the important properties of functions are introduced next.

Definition 1.5. *(Continuity) A function $f : D \to \mathbb{R}^m$ is called continuous at $x \in D \subseteq \mathbb{R}^n$ iff*

$$\forall \varepsilon > 0, \exists \delta > 0 \text{ such that } \|x-y\| < \delta \implies \|f(x) - f(y)\| < \varepsilon. \tag{1.20}$$

A function f is continuous on a set D iff it is continuous at x for all $x \in D$.

Definition 1.6. *(Uniform continuity) A function is uniformly continuous on D, if given $\varepsilon > 0$ there is a $\delta > 0$ (dependent only on ε) such that for all x, $y \in D$, we have $\|x-y\| < \delta \implies \|f(x) - f(y)\| < \varepsilon$.*

Note that uniform continuity is defined on a set and continuity is defined at a point. For uniform continuity, the same constant δ works for all pair of points in D. If f is uniformly continuous on a set D, then it is continuous on D. If the set D is compact (closed and bounded), then continuity and uniform continuity are equivalent.

Example 1.5. *There are many examples of functions that are both continuous and uniformly continuous. A very common one is the linear function $f(x) = mx + b$, where m and b are constants.*

This function is defined for all real numbers. The function $f(x) = mx + b$ is continuous everywhere in its domain ($\mathbb{R}$). This is because for any $\varepsilon > 0$, we can always choose $\delta = \frac{\varepsilon}{|m|}$ (assuming $m \neq 0$, if $m = 0$, then $f(x) = b$ which is constant and hence continuous). Then, if $|x-c| < \delta$, we have

$$|f(x) - f(c)| = |mx + b - mc - b| = |m||x-c| < |m|\delta = \varepsilon.$$

So, the function $f(x) = mx + b$ is continuous at every point in its domain. The function $f(x) = mx + b$ is also uniformly continuous. This is because the δ that we chose above works for all pair of points in the domain of the function.

Example 1.6. *Consider the function $f(x) = x^2$ on the set of real numbers.*

This function is continuous at every point in its domain, which includes all real numbers. This can be confirmed using the $\varepsilon - \delta$ definition of continuity. Given any point $c \in \mathbb{R}$ and any $\varepsilon > 0$, choose a $\delta = \frac{\varepsilon}{|x+c|+1}$ such that if $|x-c| < \delta$, then $|f(x) - f(c)| = |x^2 - c^2| = |(x+c)(x-c)| \leq |x+c||x-c|$. Substituting the choice of δ, we have $|f(x) - f(c)| \leq |x+c||x-c| < |x+c|\delta = \frac{|x+c|}{|x+c|+1}\varepsilon < \varepsilon$. So, $f(x) = x^2$ is continuous. However, $f(x) = x^2$ is not uniformly continuous on the set of all real numbers. This is because the function becomes increasingly steep as x increases or decreases, so there is no single δ that works for all x. To see this more explicitly, consider two points $x = n$ and $x = n + 1/n$, where n is any positive integer. The difference in the function values at these points is

$$f(n+1/n) - f(n) = (n+1/n)^2 - n^2 = 2 + 1/n^2.$$

So even though the difference $|x-n| = 1/n$ can be made arbitrarily small by choosing a large enough n, the difference $|f(x) - f(n)| = 2 + 1/n^2$ can never be made less than 2. Thus, there is no δ such that $|f(x) - f(n)| < \varepsilon$ whenever $|x-n| < \delta$ for all x and n, as would be required for uniform continuity. So $f(x) = x^2$ is continuous but not uniformly continuous on the set of all real numbers.

Example 1.7. *Consider another common example of a function $f(x) = \sin(x^2)$ on the interval $[0,\infty)$ that is continuous but not uniformly continuous.*

This function is continuous on the interval $[0,\infty)$. This is because the sine function is continuous for all real numbers and the composition of continuous functions is also continuous. However, $f(x) = \sin(x^2)$ is not uniformly continuous on $[0,\infty)$. To check this, consider two sequences of points, $x_n = \sqrt{2\pi n}$ and $y_n = \sqrt{2\pi n + \frac{\pi}{2}}$, where $n \geq 0$. The distance between x_n and y_n is $|x_n - y_n| = \sqrt{2\pi n + \frac{\pi}{2}} - \sqrt{2\pi n}$, which tends to 0 as n approaches infinity. However, the distance between the function values at these points, $|f(x_n) - f(y_n)| = |\sin((2\pi n)^2) - \sin((2\pi n + \frac{\pi}{2})^2)| = |0-1| = 1$, which does not tend to 0 as n approaches infinity. Therefore, there is no $\delta > 0$ such that $|x-y| < \delta$ implies $|f(x) - f(y)| < \varepsilon$ for all x, y in $[0,\infty)$ and all $\varepsilon > 0$. This shows that the function is not uniformly continuous on the interval $[0,\infty)$.

Definition 1.7. *(Absolutely Continuous) A function $\psi : [a,b] \to \mathbb{R}^n$ is absolutely continuous if, for all $\varepsilon > 0$, there exists $\delta > 0$ such that, for each finite collection $\{(a_1,b_2),\ldots,(a_n,b_n)\}$ of disjoint open intervals contained in $[a,b]$ with $\sum_{i=1}^{n}(b_i - a_i) < \delta$, it follows that*

$$\sum_{i=1}^{n} |\psi(b_i) - \psi(a_i)| < \varepsilon.$$

Definition 1.8. *(Lipschitz Continuity) A function $f : I \times D \to \mathbb{R}^n$, where $I = [a,b]$, is called Lipschitz continuous over D, uniformly in I, if $\exists\, L > 0$ such that*

$$\forall x,y \in D \text{ and } \forall t \in I, \|f(t,x) - f(t,y)\| \leq L\|x-y\|.$$

Definition 1.9. *(Locally Lipschitz Continuity) A function $f : I \times D \to \mathbb{R}^n$, where $I = [a,b]$, is called locally Lipschitz continuous in x over D, uniformly in t, if $\exists\, L > 0$ and $\delta > 0$ such that*

$$\forall z,y \in B(x,\delta) \text{ and } \forall t \in I, \|f(t,z) - f(t,y)\| \leq L\|z-y\|$$

Definition 1.10. *(Global Lipschitz Continuity) A function $f : I \times D \to \mathbb{R}^n$, where $I = [a,b]$, is called globally Lipschitz continuous in x over D, uniformly in t, if it is Lipschiz continuous in x over D uniformly in t and $D = \mathbb{R}^n$.*

Definition 1.11. *(Piecewise Continuity) A function $f : I \times D \to \mathbb{R}^n$ is piecewise continuous in t for all $x \in D \subset \mathbb{R}^n$ if for every fixed $x \in D \subset \mathbb{R}^n$ and every bounded interval $J \subset I$ the function $t \mapsto f(t,x)$ is continuous on J at all but a finite number of points, and at every point of discontinuity t^d, the left and right-sided limits, i.e., $\lim_{h \downarrow t^d} f(t^d + h, x)$ and $\lim_{h \uparrow t^d} f(t^d - h, x)$, exists and are finite.*

Function Norms Given a function $f(t) : [0,\infty) \to \mathbb{R}^n$, its $\mathscr{L}_p$ (function) norm is given in terms of the vector norm $\|f(t)\|_p$ at each value of t by

$$\|f(\cdot)\|_p = \left(\int_0^{\infty} \|f(t)\|_p^p dt \right)^{\frac{1}{p}},$$

and for $p = \infty$, i.e., $\mathscr{L}_\infty$ norm, is given by

$$\|f(\cdot)\|_\infty = \sup_{t \geq 0} \|f(t)\|_\infty.$$

If the $\mathscr{L}_p$ norm exists, we say $f(t) \in \mathscr{L}_p$. Note that a function is in $\mathscr{L}_\infty$ if and only if it is bounded.

If we have a function defined over the positive intergers including zero, i.e., $Z_+ = \{0,1,2,\ldots\}$ and $f(k) : Z_+ \to \mathbb{R}^n$, then the ℓ_p (function) norm is given in terms of the vector $\|f(k)\|_p$ at each value of k by

$$\|f(\cdot)\|_p = \left(\sum_{k=0}^{\infty} \|f(k)\|_p^p \right)^{\frac{1}{p}},$$

and if $p = \infty$, i.e., ℓ_∞ norm, given by

$$\|f(.)\|_\infty = \sup_k \|f(k)\|_\infty.$$

If the ℓ_p norm is finite, we say $f(k) \in \ell_p$. Note that a function is in ℓ_∞ if and only if it is bounded.

1.3 STABILITY

In this section, we will review various stability concepts used in the book for developing event-triggered, adaptive, and neural network control for linear and nonlinear systems. In particular, we focus on stability concepts based on Lypunov stability theory, such as local and global Lyapunov stability, local and global asymptotic stability, input-to-state stability, uniformly ultimately bounded stability, and $\mathscr{L}_2$ stability. More details on these stability concepts can be found in Khalil (2002).

1.3.1 EQUILIBRIUM POINT

A point x^* is called an equilibrium point of

$$\dot{x}(t) = f(x(t)) \tag{1.21}$$

implies that if $x(\tau) = x^*$ for some τ then $x(t) = x^*$ for all $t \geq \tau$, i.e., $\dot{x}(t) = 0$. In other words, if the state of a system starts at x^*, it will remain at x^*. For an autonomous system (1.21), the equilibrium points are the real roots of the equation

$$f(x) = 0.$$

Example 1.8. *Find the equilibrium points of the linear time-invariant system*

$$\dot{x}(t) = Ax(t). \tag{1.22}$$

Solution: 1. It has a single equilibrium point (the origin, 0) if A is nonsingular;
2. if A is singular, it has infinitely many equilibrium points, which are contained in the null space of the matrix.

A linear system can not have multiple isolated equilibrium points.

Example 1.9. *For the system*

$$\ddot{x}(t) + \dot{x}(t) = 0, \tag{1.23}$$

find the equilibrium points.

Solution: In state space representation with $x_1(t) = x(t)$ and $x_2(t) = \dot{x}(t)$

$$\dot{x}(t) = \begin{bmatrix} 0 & 1 \\ 0 & -1 \end{bmatrix} x(t).$$

Alternatively, we can write each state equation as

$$\begin{aligned} \dot{x}_1(t) &= x_2(t), \\ \dot{x}_2(t) &= -x_2(t). \end{aligned}$$

Therefore, it can be concluded that $x_2 = 0$ for any x_1 is an equilibrium point. The equilibrium points are not isolated.

Example 1.10. *Consider the dynamics of a pendulum given by a nonlinear autonomous equation*

$$MR^2\ddot{\theta}(t) + b\dot{\theta}(t) + MgR\sin\theta(t) = 0,$$

where R is the pendulum length, M its mass, b the friction coefficient at the hinge, and g is the gravity constant. Compute the equilibrium points.

Solution: A state space representation for this system is given by

$$\begin{aligned} \dot{x}_1(t) &= x_2(t) \\ \dot{x}_2(t) &= -\frac{b}{MR^2}x_2(t) - \frac{g}{R}\sin x_1(t). \end{aligned}$$

Therefore, the equilibrium points can be obtained as

$$x_2 = 0 \text{ and } \sin x_1 = 0,$$

i.e., the points $(n\pi, 0)$ with $n = 0, \pm 1, \pm 2, \cdots$.

1.3.2 STABILITY DEFINITIONS

In this section, several definitions characterizing the stability of equilibrium points of a system are introduced.

Definition 1.12. *Let the origin be an equilibrium point of the system $\dot{x}(t) = f(x(t))$, where $f(x)$ is locally Lipschitz over the domain $D \subset \mathbb{R}^n$ that contains the origin. Then equilibrium point $x^* = 0$ is locally stable if, for each $\varepsilon > 0$, there exists a $\delta > 0$, such that if $\|x_0\| < \delta$, then $\|x(t)\| < \varepsilon$ for all $t \geq 0$. Unstable, if the equilibrium point is not stable. Locally asymptotically stable if it is stable and $\exists \delta > 0$ such that $\|x_0\| < \delta$ implies that $x(t)$ exists for all $t \geq 0$ and $\lim_{t\to\infty} \|x(t)\| = 0$.*

Definition 1.13. *(Globally Asymptotically Stable) An equilibrium point of the dynamical system $\dot{x}(t) = f(x(t))$ is globally asymptotically stable if it is asymptotically stable and its domain of attraction is $\mathbb{R}^n$.*

Definition 1.14. *(Exponential Stability) The equilibrium point $x = 0$ is said to be exponentially stable if there exist three strictly positive numbers c, α, and λ such that for $\|x_0\| < c$*

$$\|x(t)\| \leq \alpha \|x_0\| e^{-\lambda t}$$

for all $t \in \mathbb{R}_{\geq 0}$. It is said to be globally exponentially stable if the above inequality holds for $x_0 \in \mathbb{R}^n$.

1.3.3 LYAPUNOV THEOREMS FOR STABILITY

1.3.3.1 Lyapunov Stability Theory for Continuous-Time Systems

We shall begin with some definitions.

Definition 1.15. *(Positive and Negative Definite) A function $V : D \to \mathbb{R}$ is positive definite if*

$$V(0) = 0 \text{ and } V(x) > 0 \quad \text{in} \quad D \setminus \{0\}.$$

The function is negative definite if $-V(x)$ is positive definite.

Definition 1.16. *(Positive and Negative Semidefinite) A function $V : D \to \mathbb{R}$ is positive (negative) semidefinite if*

$$V(0) = 0 \text{ and } V(x) \geq 0 \quad (V(x) \leq 0) \quad \text{in} \quad D \setminus \{0\}.$$

Definition 1.17. *(Radially Unbounded) A function $V : \mathbb{R}^n \to \mathbb{R}$ is radially unbounded if it satisfies the following condition:*

$$V(x) \to \infty \quad \text{as} \quad \|x\| \to \infty.$$

Definition 1.18. *(Invariant Set) A set $M \subset \mathbb{R}^n$ is invariant with respect to $\dot{x}(t) = f(x(t))$ with $x_0 \in M$ implies that the solution $x(t) = \phi(t, x_0) \in M$ for every $t \in \mathbb{R}$.*

Definition 1.19. *(Positively Invariant Set) A set $M \subset \mathbb{R}^n$ is forward (or positively) invariant with respect to $\dot{x}(t) = f(x(t))$ of $x_0 \in M$ implies that the solution $x(t) = \phi(t, x_0) \in M$ for every positive interval of existence of ϕ.*

Now we are ready to review the Lyapunov theorems to assess the stability of an equilibrium point directly without solving for the system dynamics. A detailed proof of the theorems can be found in (Khalil, 2002).

Theorem 1.1. *Let $x = 0$ be an equilibrium point for the system $\dot{x}(t) = f(x(t))$, where f is locally Lipschitz continuous, and $D \subset \mathbb{R}^n$ contains the origin. Let $V : D \to \mathbb{R}$ be a continuously differentiable function and positive definite, Then, the following statements are true:*

1. *If $\dot{V}(x(t)) = \frac{\partial V(x)^T}{\partial x} f(x) \leq 0, \forall x \in D$, then equilibirum point $x = 0$ is stable.*
2. *If $V \in C^1(D)$ and $\dot{V}(x(t)) = \frac{\partial V(x)^T}{\partial x} f(x) < 0, \forall x \in D$, then equilibrium point $x = 0$ is asymptotically stable, where C^1 is the set of continuous functions with continuous first derivatives.*

Theorem 1.2. *Let $x = 0$ be an equilibrium point for the system $\dot{x}(t) = f(x(t))$, where f is locally Lipschitz continuous. Let $V : \mathbb{R}^n \to \mathbb{R}$ be a continuously differentiable function and radially unbounded. If $\dot{V}(x(t)) = \frac{\partial V(x)^T}{\partial x} f(x) < 0, \forall x \in \mathbb{R}^n \setminus \{0\}$. Then, the equilibrium point $x = 0$ is globally asymptotically stable (GAS).*

Theorem 1.3. *(Lyapunov's Indirect Theorem) Let $x = 0$ be an equilibrium point of the nonlinear system $\dot{x}(t) = f(x(t))$, where $f : D \to \mathbb{R}^n$ is continuously differentiable, $f(0) = 0$ and D is a neighborhood of the origin ($0 \in D$). Let*

$$A = \frac{\partial f}{\partial x}(x)\bigg|_{x=0}$$

is Hurwitz, i.e., every eigenvalue of A has strictly negative real part. Then, the origin is locally asymptotically (exponentially) stable.

Example 1.11. *For the system given below*

$$\begin{aligned}\dot{x}_1(t) &= -x_1^3(t) + x_2(t)\\ \dot{x}_2(t) &= -x_1(t) - x_2(t),\end{aligned} \tag{1.24}$$

find if the eqilliborum point $x = 0$ is stable or unstable. Comment on the type of stability.

Solution: Choose a Lyapunov function candidate

$$V(x) = \frac{1}{2}(x_1^2 + x_2^2).$$

Note that the function $V(x)$ is positive definite. The first derivative can be computed as

$$\begin{aligned}\dot{V}(x) &= x_1\dot{x}_1 + x_2\dot{x}_2 = x_1\left(-x_1^3 + x_2\right) + x_2\left(-x_1 - x_2\right)\\ &= -x_1^4 + x_1x_2 - x_2x_1 - x_2^2 = -x_1^4 - x_2^2 = \alpha(x).\end{aligned}$$

One needs to check for the following conditions to determine the stability of the equilibrium point $x = 0$. If

$\alpha(x) = -x_1^4 - x_2^2 \leq 0$ (PSD) $\Rightarrow x = 0$ is stable.
$\alpha(x) = -x_1^4 - {x_2}^2 < 0$ (PD) $\Rightarrow x = 0$ is AS.
$\alpha(x) = -x_1^4 - {x_2}^2 < 0$ (PD) and $V(x) \to \infty$ as $\|x\| \to \infty$ (radially unbounded) $\Rightarrow x = 0$ is GAS.

To check the radial unboundedness of $V(x)$, we have

$$V(x) = \frac{1}{2}(x_1^2 + x_2^2) \to \infty \text{ as } \|x\| \to \infty.$$

From the above, $V(x)$ is radially unbounded, and $\dot{V}(x)$ is PD. Therefore, the equilibrium point $x = 0$ is globally asymptotically stable (GAS).

A nonautonomous system is represented in the form

$$\dot{x} = f(t,x).$$

The vector field is time-varying. In the time-invariant case, we saw the solution of $\dot{x} = f(x)$ starting from any time t_0 only depends on $t - t_0$. Without loss of generality, we assumed $t_0 = 0$. In nonautonomous cases, when the vector field depends on time, then the solution depends on t_0 in addition to $t - t_0$. Therefore, the concept of stability will also have some dependence on t_0.

Definition 1.20. *(Khalil (2002)) An equilibrium point $x = 0$ of $\dot{x}(t) = f(t,x)$ is said to be*

1. ***locally stable*** *if and only if $\forall \varepsilon > 0$ and $\forall t_0 \in \mathbb{R}_{\geq 0}$, $\exists \delta(t_0, \varepsilon) > 0$ such that $\forall t > t_0$, $\|x_0\| < \delta \implies$ the solution $\|\phi(t,t_0,x_0)\| < \varepsilon$;*

2. ***locally uniformly stable*** *if and only if* $\forall \varepsilon > 0$, $\exists \delta(\varepsilon) > 0$ *(*δ *is independent of* t_0*) such that* $\forall t_0 \in \mathbb{R}_{\geq 0}$ *and* $\forall t > t_0$, $\|x_0\| < \delta \implies \|\phi(t,t_0,x_0)\| < \varepsilon$;
3. ***uniformly globally stable*** *if and only if it is uniformly stable and* δ *can be selected such that* $\lim_{\varepsilon \to \infty} \delta(\varepsilon) = \infty$;
4. ***locally asymptotically stable (AS)*** *if and only if it is stable and for all* $t_0 \in \mathbb{R}_{\geq 0}$, $\exists c = c(t_0) > 0$ *a constant such that* $\forall \varepsilon > 0$, $\exists T(c,\varepsilon,t_0) \geq 0$ *such that* $\|x_0\| < c \implies \|\phi(t,t_0,x_0)\| < \varepsilon$ *for* $t \geq t_0 + T$;
5. ***locally uniformly asymptotically stable (UAS)*** *if and only if it is* ***uniformly stable*** *and* $\exists c > 0$, c *is independent of* t_0, *such that* $\forall \varepsilon > 0$, $\exists T(c,\varepsilon) \geq 0$, T *is independent of* t_0, *such that* $\forall t_0 \in \mathbb{R}_{\geq 0}$, $\|x_0\| < c \implies \|\phi(t,t_0,x_0)\| < \varepsilon$ *for* $t \geq t_0 + T$;
6. ***globally asymptotically stable (GAS)*** *if and only if it is asymptotically stable for all* $t_0 \in \mathbb{R}_{\geq 0}$ $c > 0$, $\varepsilon > 0$, $\exists T(c,\varepsilon,t_0) \geq 0$ *such that* $\|x_0\| < c \implies \|\phi(t,t_0,x_0)\| < \varepsilon$ *for* $t \geq t_0 + T$.
7. ***uniformly globally asymptotically atable (UGAS)*** *if and only if it is* ***uniformly globally stable*** *and for all* $c > 0$ *and* $\varepsilon > 0$, $\exists T(c,\varepsilon) \geq 0$, T *independent of* t_0, *such that* $\|x_0\| < c \implies \|\phi(t,t_0,x_0)\| < \varepsilon$ *for* $t \geq t_0 + T$.

Definition 1.21. *(Class* $\mathcal{K}$ *and* $\mathcal{K}_\infty$ *Functions) A function* $\alpha : [0,a) \to \mathbb{R}$ *is said to belong to*

1. *class* $\mathcal{K}$ $(\alpha \in \mathcal{K}([0,a),\mathbb{R}))$ *if and only if it is strictly increasing and* $\alpha(0) = 0$, *and*
2. *class* $\mathcal{K}_\infty$ *if and only if* $\alpha \in \mathcal{K}([0,a),\mathbb{R})$, *with* $a = \infty$, *and* $\alpha(r) \to \infty$ *as* $r \to \infty$.

Definition 1.22. *(Class* $\mathcal{KL}$ *Functions) A function* $\beta : [0,a) \times \mathbb{R}_{\geq 0} \to \mathbb{R}$ *is said to be class* $\mathcal{KL}$ $(\beta \in \mathcal{KL}([0,a) \times \mathbb{R}_{\geq 0},\mathbb{R}))$ *if and only if for every fixed* s, $\beta(r,s) \in \mathcal{K}([0,a),\mathbb{R})$ *and for every fixed* r, $\beta(r,s)$ *is nonincreasing with* $\lim_{s \to \infty} \beta(r,s) = 0$.

Definition 1.23. *(Khalil (2002)) A system* $\dot{x}(t) = f(t,x,u)$ *is said to be input-to-state stable if there exist a class* $\mathcal{KL}$ *function* β *and a class* $\mathcal{K}$ *function* γ *such that for any initial state* x_0 *and any bounded input* $u(t)$, *the solution* $x(t)$ *exists for all* $t \geq t_0$ *and satisfies*

$$\|x(t)\| \leq \beta(\|x(t_0)\|, t - t_0) + \gamma\left(\sup_{t_0 \leq \tau \leq t} \|u(\tau)\| \right).$$

We shall now look at some of the definitions concerning the stability of nonautonomous systems.

Theorem 1.4. *Let the origin* $x = 0$ *be an equilibrium point of the system* $\dot{x}(t) = f(t,x)$ *and* $D \subset \mathbb{R}^n$ *be a domain (open and connected set) containing* $x = 0$. *Suppose* $f(t,x)$ *is piecewise continuous in* t *and locally Lipschitz in* x *for all* $t \geq 0$ *and* $x(t) \in D$. *Let* $V(t,x)$ *be a continuously differentiable function such that*

$$W_1(x) \leq V(t,x) \leq W_2(x)$$

$$\frac{\partial V}{\partial t} + \frac{\partial V}{\partial x} f(t,x) \leq 0$$

for all $t \geq 0$ *and* $x \in D$, *where* $W_1(x)$ *and* $W_2(x)$ *are continuous positive definite functions on* D. *Then, the origin is uniformly stable.*

Theorem 1.5. *Let the hypothesis of Theorem 1.4 be satisfied*

1. *If a stronger inequality*

$$\frac{\partial V}{\partial t} + \frac{\partial V}{\partial x} f(t,x) \leq -W_3(x)$$

for all $t \geq 0$ *and* $x \in D$, *where* $W_3(x)$ *is continuous positive definite function on* D. *Then, the origin is uniformly asymptotically stable (UAS).*

Theorem 1.6. *(Khalil, 2002) (Input-to-State Stability) Let $V : [0,\infty)\times\mathbb{R}^n \to \mathbb{R}$ be continuosly differentiable function such that*

$$\alpha_1(\|x\|) \le V(t,x) \le \alpha_2(\|x\|)$$

$$\frac{\partial V}{\partial t} + \frac{\partial V}{\partial x} f(t,x) \le -W_3(x), \quad \forall \|x\| \ge \rho(\|u\|) \ge 0$$

for all $(t,x,u) \in [0,\infty)\times\mathbb{R}^n\times\mathbb{R}^m$, where α_1 and α_2 are class $\mathcal{K}_\infty$ functions, ρ is a class $\mathcal{K}$ function and $W_3(x)$ is a continuous positive definite function on $\mathbb{R}^n$. Then the system $\dot{x}(t) = f(t,x,u)$ is input-to-state stable (ISS) with $\gamma = \alpha_1^{-1}\circ\alpha_2\circ\rho$.

Example 1.12. *(Khalil, 2002) The system*

$$\dot{x}(t) = -x^3(t) + u(t)$$

has a globally asymptotically stable origin when $u = 0$. Show that it is ISS.

Solution: Select a Lyapunov function candidate $V = \frac{1}{2}x^2$, the derivative of V along the trajectory of the system is given by

$$\begin{aligned}\dot{V}(t) &= -x^4 + xu = -(1-\theta)x^4 - \theta x^4 + xu \\ &\le -(1-\theta)x^4, \forall |x| \ge \left(\frac{|u|}{\theta}\right)^{\frac{1}{3}},\end{aligned}$$

where $0 < \theta < 1$. Thus, the system is ISS.

Definition 1.24. *(Boundedness) Let f be piecewise continuous in t and locally Lipschitz in x for all $t \ge 0$ and $x(t) \in D$ for some domain $D \subset \mathbb{R}^n$ that contains the origin, then the solution of the system $\dot{x}(t) = f(t,x)$ with $x(t_0) = x_0$ are*

1. ***uniformly bounded*** *if there exists $c > 0$, independent of t_0, and for every $a \in (0,c)$, there is $\beta > 0$, dependent on a but independent of t_0, such that*

$$\|x(t_0)\| \le a \implies \|x(t)\| \le \beta, \forall t \ge t_0$$

2. ***globally uniformly bounded*** *if the above condition holds for arbitrarily large a.*
3. ***uniformly ultimately bounded*** *with ultimate bound b if there exists a positive constant c, independent of t_0, and for every $a \in (0,c)$, there is $T \ge 0$, dependent on a and b, but independent of t_0, such that*

$$\|x(t_0)\| \le a \implies \|x(t)\| \le b, \forall t \ge t_0 + T$$

4. ***globally uniformly ultimately bounded*** *if the above inequality holds for arbitrarily large a.*

Theorem 1.7. *(Boundedness and Ultimate Boundedness) Let $D \subset \mathbb{R}^n$ be a domain that contains the origin and $V : [0,\infty)\times D \to \mathbb{R}$ be continuously differentiable function such that*

$$\alpha_1(\|x\|) \le V(t,x) \le \alpha_2(\|x\|)$$

for all $t \ge 0$ and $\forall x \in D$, where α_1 and α_2 are class $\mathcal{K}$ functions and $W_3(x)$ is a continuous positive definite function. Take $r \ge 0$ such that $B_r \subset D$ and suppose that

$$\mu < \alpha_2^{-1}(\alpha_1(r)).$$

Then there exists a class $\mathcal{KL}$ function β for every initial state $x(t_0)$, satisfying $\|x(t_0)\| \le \alpha_2^{-1}(\alpha_1(r))$, there is $T \ge 0$, such that the solution of $\dot{x}(t) = f(t,x)$ satisfies

$$\|x(t)\| \le \beta(\|x(t_0)\|,\ t-t_0), \quad \forall t_0 \le t \le t_0 + T$$

$$\|x(t)\| \le \alpha_1^{-1}(\alpha_2(\mu)), \quad \forall t \ge t_0 + T.$$

Moreover, if $D = \mathbb{R}^n$ and α_1 belongs to class $\mathcal{K}_\infty$, then the above inequalities hold for any initial state $x(t_0)$, with no restriction on how large μ is.

1.3.3.2 Lyapunov Stability Theory for Discrete-time Systems

Consider a nonlinear autonomous discrete-time system given by

$$x_{k+1} = f(x_k) \tag{1.25}$$

where $f: D \to D$ is a nonlinear function with $D \subseteq \mathbb{R}^n$. Analogous to the equilibrium point defined for a continuous time system, a *fixed-point* x^* for the discrete-time system is one where $x_{k+1} = x_k = x^*$. In other words, for a given $\kappa \in \mathbb{Z}$ if $x_\kappa = x^*$, then $x_{\kappa+1} = f(x_\kappa) = f(x^*) = x^*$.

The following theorem guarantees the stability of the system in (1.25).

Theorem 1.8. *Let $x = 0$ be a fixed point of the time-invariant autonomous discrete-time system in (1.25), where $f: D \to D$ is locally Lipschitz with $f(0) = 0$ and $D \subseteq \mathbb{R}^n$ contains the origin. Let $V: D \to \mathbb{R}$ satisfies*

$$V(0) = 0 \text{ and } V(x(k)) > 0, \forall x(k) \in D \setminus \{0\},$$

then

1. *if $\Delta V(x_k) \leq 0, \forall x_k \in D$ implies $x = 0$ is stable,*
2. *if $x = 0$ is stable and $\Delta V(x_k) < 0, \forall x \in D \setminus \{0\}$ implies $x = 0$ is locally asymptotically stable.*
3. *if $x = 0$ is stable and $\Delta V(x_k) < 0, \forall x \in D \setminus \{0\}$, $D = \mathbb{R}^n$ and $V(x_k)$ is radially unbounded $V(x_k) \to \infty$ as $\|x_k\| \to \infty$ implies $x = 0$ is globally asymptotically stable.*

Here $\Delta V(x_k)$ is the first difference operator, i.e., $\Delta V(x_k) = V(x_{k+1}) - V(x_k)$.

Definition 1.25. *A function $V: D \to \mathbb{R}$ satisfying the condition of positive definiteness, i.e.,*

$$V(0) = 0 \text{ and } V(x) > 0, \forall x \in D \setminus 0$$

and

$$\Delta V(x_k) \leq 0, \forall x \in D$$

is called a Lyapunov function for the system (1.25).

Definition 1.26. *(Jiang and Wang, 2001) The control system*

$$x_{k+1} = f(x_k, u_k) \tag{1.26}$$

is input-to-state stable (ISS) if there exists a $\mathcal{KL}$-function $\beta: \mathbb{R}_{\geq 0} \times \mathbb{R}_{\geq 0} \to \mathbb{R}_{\geq 0}$ and a $\mathcal{K}$-function γ such that, for each $u \in \ell_\infty^m$ and each $\xi \in \mathbb{R}^n$, it holds that

$$|x(k, \xi, u)| \leq \beta(|\xi|, k) + \gamma(\|u\|) \tag{1.27}$$

for each $k \in \mathbb{Z}_+$.

Definition 1.27. *(Jiang and Wang, 2001) A continuous function $V: \mathbb{R}^n \to \mathbb{R}_{\geq 0}$ is called an ISS-Lyapunov function for the system* (1.26) *if the following holds:*

1. *There exists a $\mathcal{K}_\infty$- functions α_1, α_2 such that*

$$\alpha_1(|\xi|) \leq V(\xi) \leq \alpha_2(|\xi|), \quad \forall \xi \in \mathbb{R}^n. \tag{1.28}$$

2. *There exists a $\mathcal{K}_\infty$-function α_3 and a $\mathcal{K}$-function σ, such that*

$$V(f(\xi, \mu)) - V(\xi) \leq -\alpha_3(|\xi|) + \sigma(|\mu|), \quad \forall \xi \in \mathbb{R}^n, \forall \mu \in \mathbb{R}^m. \tag{1.29}$$

Theorem 1.9. *Consider system* (1.26). *The following are equivalent:*

1. *It is ISS.*
2. *It admits a smooth ISS-Lyapunov function.*

Theorem 1.10. *The fixed point $x = 0$ of the linear time-invariant discrete-time system*

$$x_{k+1} = Ax_k \tag{1.30}$$

where $A \in \mathbb{R}^{n\times n}$ is

1. *stable iff all the eigenvalues of A defined as $\lambda_1, \dots, \lambda_n$ satisfy $|\lambda_i| \leq 1$ for $i = 1, \dots, n$, and the algebraic and geometric multiplicity of the eigenvalues with absolute value 1 coincide,*
2. *globally asymptotically stable iff all the eigenvalue of A are such that $|\lambda_i| < 1$.*

Remark 1.1. *A matrix A with all the eigenvalues with an absolute value less than 1 is called a Schur Matrix.*

Lyapunov function for linear systems. Consider a Lyapunov function candidate $V : \mathbb{R}^n \to \mathbb{R}$ given by

$$V(x_k) = x_k^T P x_k,$$

where $P \in \mathbb{R}^{n\times n}$ is a symmetric positive definite matrix. The first difference

$$\Delta V(x_k) = V(x_{k+1}) - V(x_k).$$

Along the system dynamics (1.30), the first difference

$$\begin{aligned}\Delta V(x_k) &= x_{k+1}^T P x_{k+1} - x_k^T P x_k \\ &= x_k^T A^T P A x_k - x_k^T P x_k \\ &= x_k^T (A^T P A - P) x_k = -x_k^T Q x_k\end{aligned}$$

For the Lyapunov function candidate

$$V(x_k) = x_k^T P x_k,$$

where $P \in \mathbb{R}^{n\times n}$ is a symmetric positive definite matrix, the first difference

$$\Delta V(x_k) = -x_k^T Q x_k$$

1. If $Q \geq 0$ (PSD), the fixed point $x = 0$ is stable.
2. If $Q > 0$ (PD), the fixed point $x = 0$ is asymptotically stable.

Theorem 1.11. *A matrix A is Shur iff for any $Q = Q^T > 0$ there exists a unique matrix $P = P^T > 0$ that satisfies*

$$A^T P A - P = -Q.$$

The proof for the theorem can be found in Ogata (2011).

1.3.3.3 Lyapunov Stability Theory for Impulsive Hybrid Systems

Recall the dynamics of an impulsive hybrid system defined in (1.19). A function $x : I_{x0} \to \mathbb{C}$ is a solution to the impulsive dynamical system (1.19) on the interval I_{x0} with initial condition $x(0) = x_0$, if $x(\cdot)$ is left-continuous and $x(t)$ satisfies (1.19) for all $t \in I_{x0}$. In addition, we use the notation $\phi(t, \tau, x_0)$ to denote the solution $x(t)$ of (1.19) at time $t \geq \tau$ with initial condition $x(\tau) = x_0$. Finally, a point $x_e \in \mathbb{C}$ is an equilibrium point of (1.19) if and only if $\phi(t, \tau, x_e) = x_e$ for all $\tau \geq 0$ and $t \geq \tau$. Note that $x_e \in \mathbb{C}$ is an equilibrium point of (1.19) if and only if $f(x_e) = 0$ and $F(x_e) = x_e$.

Definition 1.28. *(Haddad et al., 2006) The nonlinear impulsive dynamical system* (1.19) *is locally bounded if there exists a* $\gamma > 0$ *such that, for every* $\delta \in (0, \gamma)$*, there exists* $\varepsilon = \varepsilon(\delta) > 0$ *such that* $\|x(0)\| < \delta$ *implies* $\|x(t)\| < \varepsilon,\ t \geq 0$*.*

Definition 1.29. *(Haddad et al., 2006) The nonlinear state-dependent impulsive dynamical system* (1.19) *is UB with bound* ε *if there exists* $\gamma > 0$ *such that, for every* $\delta \in (0, \gamma)$*, there exists* $T = T(\delta, \varepsilon) > 0$ *such that* $\|\xi(0)\| < \delta$ *implies* $\|\xi(t)\| < \varepsilon$*, for* $t \geq T$*, and globally UB with bound* ε *if, for every* $\delta \in (0, \infty)$*, there exists,* $T = T(\delta, \varepsilon) > 0$*, such that* $\|x(0)\| < \delta$ *implies* $\|x(t)\| < \varepsilon,\ t \geq T$*.*

The following theorem will be used to prove the ultimate boundedness of impulsive dynamical systems in some of the later chapters in this book.

Theorem 1.12. *(Haddad et al., 2006) Consider the impulsive dynamical system* (1.19)*. Assume that the jumps occur at distinct time instants and there exists a continuously differentiable function* $V : \mathbb{C} \to \mathbb{R}$ *and class* $\mathscr{K}$ *functions* $\alpha(.)$ *and* $\beta(.)$ *such that*

$$\alpha(\|x\|) \leq V(x) \leq \beta(\|x\|), x \in \mathbb{C}, \tag{1.31}$$

$$\frac{\partial V(x)}{\partial x} f(x, u) < 0,\ x \in \mathbb{C},\ x \notin \mathscr{Z},\ \|x\| \geq \chi, \tag{1.32}$$

$$V(F(x)) - V(x) \leq 0,\ x \in \mathbb{C},\ x \in \mathscr{Z},\ \|x\| \geq \chi, \tag{1.33}$$

where $\chi > 0$ *is such that* $B_{\alpha^{-1}(\beta(\chi))}(0) = \{\xi \in \mathbb{R}^n : \|x\| < \alpha^{-1}(\beta(\chi))\} \subset \mathbb{C}$ *with* $\eta > \beta(\chi)$*. Further, assume* $\theta \triangleq \sup_{\xi \in \bar{B}_\chi(0) \cap \mathscr{Z}} V(F(x))$ *exists. Then the nonlinear state-dependent impulsive dynamical system* (1.19) *is UB with bound* $\Xi \triangleq \alpha^{-1}(\eta)$*, where* $\eta \triangleq \max\{\beta(\chi), \theta\}$*. The sets* $B_{\alpha^{-1}(\beta(\chi))}(0)$ *and* $\bar{B}_\chi(0)$ *denotes an open ball centered at* 0 *with radius* $\alpha^{-1}(\beta(\chi))$ *and a closed ball centered at* 0 *with radius* χ*.*

So far, we have explored essential mathematical tools and theorems relevant to the design and analysis of closed-loop control systems within the event-triggered control framework. We shall now explore event-triggered control and review traditional event-triggered control techniques.

1.4 EVENT-TRIGGERED CONTROL SYSTEMS

The advent of embedded processors spurred research on the digital implementation of controllers, leading to the development of foundational theories of sampled data and discrete-time control systems. In the sampled-data systems approach, a discrete-time controller controls a continuous-time plant, whereas in a discrete-time control system, the system and controllers operate in discrete-time (Kuo, 2012; Ogata, 2011). In both schemes, a periodic, fixed sampling time is determined *a priori* and used to sample the feedback signals and execute the controller. This fixed sampling time is generally governed by the well-known Nyquist sampling criterion. However, this periodic sampling scheme leads to ineffective resource utilization (Astrom and Bernhardsson, 2002; Tabuada, 2007; Dong et al., 2017) and increases the computational burden on the controller. The problem aggravates in the case of systems with shared digital communication networks in the feedback loop, referred to as networked control systems (NCS) (Shousong and Qixin, 2003; Walsh et al., 2002; Liou and Ray, 1991), due to limited bandwidth. In this case, periodic sampling and transmission exacerbates the problem of network congestion, leading to longer network-induced delays.

Furthermore, the periodic sampling and transmission of feedback data and control execution can be redundant when there is no significant change in the system performance, and when the system is operating within a desired operating envelope. As an alternative, various sampling schemes were proposed to alleviate the burden of needless computational load and network congestion (Ellis, 1959; Dorf et al., 1962; Phillips and Tomizuka, 1995; Hristu-Varsakelis and Kumar, 2002; Rabi and Baras, 2007). In recent times, performance-based sampling schemes have been developed to reduce the computational cost and are formally referred to as "event-triggered control" (Arzen, 1999; Tabuada, 2007; Mazo and Tabuada, 2011; Heemels et al., 2008; Lunze and Lehmann, 2010; Tallapragada and Chopra, 2013; Heemels et al., 2012; Tallapragada and Chopra, 2012; Cogill, 2009; Wang and Lemmon, 2008; Donkers and Heemels, 2012; Heemels and Donkers, 2013; Garcia and Antsaklis, 2012; Eqtami et al., 2010; Stocker and Lunze, 2011; Mazo Jr. and Cao, 2011; Mazo and Tabuada, 2011). In this sampling scheme, the determination to transmit and execute control updates takes place when a significant alteration in the system state or output errors is identified. These alterations have the potential to jeopardize stability or diminish the desired performance. Therefore, the control is updated using the latest state or output information. To facilitate this sampling and transmission processes, an additional hardware device, referred to as the *event-triggering mechanism*, has been developed. This mechanism evaluates event-triggering conditions to orchestrate the timing of sampling instants or the *events*. Since the objective of this sampling is to facilitate controller execution and not signal reconstruction, this is equally applicable for both continuous (Wang and Lemmon, 2008; Tabuada, 2007; Mazo and Tabuada, 2011; Heemels et al., 2008; Lunze and Lehmann, 2010; Tallapragada and Chopra, 2013; Heemels et al., 2012; Cogill, 2009; Donkers and Heemels, 2012) and discrete-time systems (Heemels and Donkers, 2013; Eqtami et al., 2010) to either regulate the system (Wang and Lemmon, 2008; Mazo and Tabuada, 2011; Heemels et al., 2008) or enable the system state to track a desired trajectory (Tallapragada and Chopra, 2013).

In the case of a continuous-time system, the sensor measures the system state or output vectors continuously, and the triggering mechanism determines the sampling instants by evaluating the event-triggering condition (Wang and Lemmon, 2008; Mazo and Tabuada, 2011; Heemels et al., 2008; Cogill, 2009; Lunze and Lehmann, 2010). The event-triggering condition is usually defined using a state or output error function, referred to as the *event-triggering error*, and a suitably designed state-dependent threshold (Tabuada, 2007). The feedback signals are transmitted and the control is executed when the event-triggering error breaches the threshold. Typically, stability techniques (e.g., Lyapunov analysis, small-gain theorem, etc.) are used to design the event-triggering condition. In between events, various techniques are used to preserve some form of continuity in the feedback signal and the control signal. We shall see some of these methods later in this chapter. Similarly, in the discrete-time case (Heemels and Donkers, 2013; Eqtami et al., 2010), the sensor measures the system state or output, and the triggering mechanism evaluates the event-triggering condition periodically, and a decision is made whether to transmit or not. In both continuous and discrete-time cases, the event-triggering instants turn out to be aperiodic and, hence, reduces computational load and bandwidth usage. These inherent advantages of event-triggered control are proven to be more beneficial in large-scale systems such as decentralized systems (Mazo Jr. and Cao, 2011; Mazo and Tabuada, 2011; Tabuada, 2007), distributed, multi-agent systems (Mazo Jr. and Dimarogonas, 2010), and cyber-physical systems (Mazo Jr. and Dimarogonas, 2010).

A related approach called *self-triggered control* (Wang and Lemmon, 2009b; Mazo Jr. and Dimarogonas, 2010; Sahoo et al., 2018; Gommans et al., 2014) is also developed for systems where the extra hardware for realizing the trigger mechanism can be obviated. This software-based scheme, a special case of the event-triggered control, predicts the sampling instants by using the previously sampled data and the system's dynamics, i.e., using the complete model of the system. Hence, a continuous evaluation of the event-triggering condition is not necessary. For more information, see (Wang and Lemmon, 2009b; Mazo Jr. and Dimarogonas, 2010; Sahoo et al., 2018; Gommans et al., 2014) .

1.4.1 BACKGROUND AND HISTORY

The study of aperiodic sampling for sampled-data control dates back to the late fifties and early sixties (Ellis, 1959; Dorf et al., 1962; Phillips and Tomizuka, 1995; Hristu-Varsakelis and Kumar, 2002; Rabi and Baras, 2007) and was first studied in (Ellis, 1959) for quantized systems to share the communication channel without increasing its bandwidth. Moreover, a state-based adaptive sampling method for sampled data servo-mechanisms was proposed by Dorf et al. (1962), where the absolute value of the first derivative of the error signal controls the adaptive sampling rate. Later, this aperiodic state-dependent sampling was studied under various names, such as multi-rate sampling (Phillips and Tomizuka, 1995), interrupt-driven triggering (Hristu-Varsakelis and Kumar, 2002), and level-triggered sampling (Rabi and Baras, 2007). In the last two decades, this scheme has been studied under the name of event-triggered sampling (Tabuada, 2007). Various theoretical (Astrom and Bernhardsson, 2002; Tabuada, 2007) and experimental (Arzen, 1999; Heemels et al., 2008) results emphasizing its inherent advantages in computation and communication-saving have been reported in the literature. In the last few years, theoretical results started to appear in the literature for both deterministic (Tabuada, 2007; Mazo and Tabuada, 2011; Heemels et al., 2008; Lunze and Lehmann, 2010; Tallapragada and Chopra, 2013; Heemels et al., 2012; Tallapragada and Chopra, 2014; Cogill, 2009; Wang and Lemmon, 2008; Donkers and Heemels, 2012; Heemels and Donkers, 2013; Garcia and Antsaklis, 2012) and stochastic (Henningsson et al., 2008; Astrom and Bernhardsson, 2002; Sahoo and Jagannathan, 2016) event-triggered control. Thereafter, various controller design strategies incorporating event-triggered feedback were introduced.

Emulation-based approach (Tabuada, 2007; Tallapragada and Chopra, 2012) is one of the design strategies used for the event-triggered system design. In the emulation-based design, the continuous controller is presumed to be stabilizing and an event-triggering condition is developed to aperiodically update the controller to maintain stability and a certain level of performance. In the earlier works (Tabuada, 2007; Mazo and Tabuada, 2011), the system was assumed to be ISS (Khalil, 2002) with respect to the measurement error, and event-triggering conditions were designed to reduce computation and guarantee asymptotic stability. This assumption primarily serves to preclude system instability in the inter-event time, ensuring that the states do not grow unbounded with a finite escape time. A non-zero positive lower bound on the inter-event times was also guaranteed to avoid *accumulation* of events leading to Zeno behavior. The event-triggered control approach was also extended to accommodate other design considerations, such as output feedback design (Tallapragada and Chopra, 2012; Donkers and Heemels, 2010), decentralized designs (Si et al., 2004; Lehmann and Lunze, 2011), and trajectory tracking control (Hu and Yue, 2012).

The event-triggered control approach was also studied in the context of discrete-time systems (Heemels and Donkers, 2013; Garcia and Antsaklis, 2012; Eqtami et al., 2010), where the sensor senses the system state periodically in a time-triggered approach and the transmission of the feedback signals and controller executions are carried out at the event-triggering instants. In the discrete-time event-triggered control, the minimum inter-event time is the periodic sampling interval of the discrete-time system (Lehmann and Lunze, 2011). Similar to the event-triggered control in a discrete-time domain, a periodic event-triggered control approach for continuous-time systems was presented by Donkers and Heemels (2010), where the sensor sampled periodically and the events were determined as in the case of discrete-time case (Eqtami et al., 2010). The triggering condition was evaluated periodically with a fixed sampling interval, and the transmission decision was made at the violation of a trigger condition. This design framework enforces a positive lower bound on the minimum inter-event times. The stability analysis was carried out using three different modeling techniques for hybrid systems: impulsive systems (Haddad et al., 2006), piecewise linear systems, and perturbed linear systems. In all the above design approaches, the system state or output and the control input are held between two consecutive events by a zero-order hold (ZOH) for implementation.

In the second event-triggered control design strategy (Lunze and Lehmann, 2010; Garcia and

Antsaklis, 2013), a model of the system is used to reconstruct the system state vector and, subsequently, used for designing the control input. As the control input is based on the model states, no feedback transmission is required unless there is a significant change in the system performance due to external disturbance or internal parameter variation. In the area of model-based event-triggered control design, Lunze and Lehmann (2010) used an input generator as a model to predict the system state and compute the control. Further, Garcia and Antsaklis (2013) considered the nominal dynamics of the system with uncertainty, usually of smaller magnitude and bounded, to form a model. The asymptotic stability was guaranteed by designing the event-triggering condition. A discrete-time model-based approach was also presented by Heemels and Donkers (2013) for systems subjected to disturbance. Two modeling approaches (perturbed linear and piecewise linear system) were used to analyze the stability and sufficient conditions for global exponential stability were derived in terms of linear matrix inequalities (LMI). It is observed that the model-based approach reduces the number of events or transmissions more effectively when compared to the ZOH-based approach but with a higher computational load due to the induction of the model.

The event-triggered control scheme was also extended to NCS with inherent network constraints (Wang and Lemmon, 2011b; Hu and Yue, 2012; Wang and Lemmon, 2009a) such as constant or time-varying delays, packet losses, and quantization errors (Sarangapani and Xu, 2018). In these design approaches, the event-triggering condition was tailored (Wang and Lemmon, 2011b, 2009a) to handle the maximum allowable delays, packet losses (Wang and Lemmon, 2009a), and quantization error for both state and control input (Hu and Yue, 2012) so as to ensure stability. Furthermore, information-theoretic perspective of event-triggered control techniques was explored in a series of efforts (Tallapragada and Cortés, 2015; Khojasteh et al., 2019). Event-triggered control was also applied in the context of optimal control, both for deterministic and stochastic systems (Cogill, 2009; Molin and Hirche, 2013; Rabi et al., 2008; Imer and Basar, 2006). Molin and Hirche (2013) extended the optimal control designs to the event-triggered control framework and characterized the certainty equivalence principle-based controller as optimal in a linear quadratic Gaussian (LQG) framework. The optimal control input and the optimal event-triggering instants were designed using the separation principle. The optimal solution of the event-based control (Molin and Hirche, 2013) used the system dynamics to solve the Riccati equation backward-in-time. Later, the optimal event-triggered control for stochastic continuous-time NCS was formulated as an optimal stopping problem (Rabi et al., 2008), and an analytical solution was obtained. The optimal control in a constrained networked environment was also studied by researchers (Imer and Basar, 2006). Learning and adaptation with sparse, aperiodic feedback data are challenging tasks due to the need for stabilization under system uncertainty, dependence on adaptation rules tied to aperiodicity, and the impact of channel losses. Consequently, two primary challenges have emerged, leading to efforts that prioritize stability without emphasizing the convergence of parameter errors (Karafyllis and Krstic, 2018; Karafyllis et al., 2019). Alternatively, there are efforts that opt to sacrifice feedback sparsity to facilitate both learning and system stabilization (Sahoo, 2015). In the later chapters, we will explore data-driven optimal control strategies that enable learning and stabilization at the expense of frequent triggering. Additionally, we will observe that a better trade-off between learning and stabilization can be achieved with game-theoretic techniques.

We will begin with the review of data-driven optimal control design strategies in Chapter 2. In general, these strategies build-upon classical dynamic programming and reinforcement learning-based approaches to obtain optimal solutions forward-in-time. These techniques, often referred to as the adaptive dynamic programming (Watkins, 1989; Si et al., 2004), approximate dynamic programming (ADP) (Werbos, 1991a), and neuro-dynamic programming (NDP) (Bertsekas, 2012), use online approximator-based parameterization and value and/or policy iterations (Wang et al., 2011; Werbos, 1991a) to solve the Bellman or Hamilton-Jacobi-Bellman (HJB) equation to obtain the optimal control. However, these approaches are computationally intensive due to iterative learning and function approximation. Event-sampled ADP and Q-learning schemes have also been proposed in the literature to implement these computationally intensive learning-based near-optimal control approaches with limited resources (Sahoo, 2015; Vamvoudakis et al., 2017b; Narayanan and Jagannathan, 2016b). We shall learn about these data-driven approaches in Chapters 3 to 8. In the following, we shall review some of the basic event-triggered control strategies and their implementation in continous- and discrete- time systems. For more information on the event-triggered control techniques, see Lemmon (2010).

1.4.2 EVENT-TRIGGERED CONTROL OF CONTINUOUS-TIME SYSTEMS

In this chapter, we shall discuss the traditional ZOH-based, model-based, and adaptive event-triggered control schemes both in continuous- and discrete-time domains. The event-triggered optimal control approaches using ADP are discussed in Chapters 3 to 8, along with applications in Chapter 9.

1.4.2.1 ZOH-based Event-Triggered Control

In this section, the ZOH-based event-triggered control, first introduced by Tabuada (2007), is discussed. Consider a nonlinear system in the nonaffine form

$$\dot{x}(t) = f(x(t), u(t)), \quad x(0) = x_0, \tag{1.34}$$

where $x(t) \in \mathbb{R}^n$ and $u(t) \in \mathbb{R}^m$ are the state and control input vectors. The internal dynamics is the vector function $f : \mathbb{R}^n \times \mathbb{R}^m \to \mathbb{R}^n$. Let the feedback-based control input

$$u(t) = \mu(x) \tag{1.35}$$

guarantees ISS of the controlled system with respect to the event-triggering error $e(t)$ defined as

$$e(t) = \hat{x}(t) - x(t), \quad t_k \le t < t_{k+1}, \tag{1.36}$$

where $\{t_k\}_{k=0}^{\infty}$ is the sequence of the sampling instants, referred to as *events*. At times t_k, $k = 0, 1, \cdots$, the system states are sampled and sent to the controller. The sampled states $\{\hat{x}_k\}_{k=0}^{\infty}$ form a sequence in which $\hat{x}_k = x(t_k)$ held by a ZOH to compute control input. In certain following chapters in the book, we employ $x_e(t)$ to denote the sampled states, while $\hat{x}(t)$ is reserved for denoting states estimated through observers or identifiers. The output of the ZOH is a piecewise continuous signal defined as

$$\hat{x}(t) = x(t_k), \quad t_k \le t < t_{k+1}. \tag{1.37}$$

The event-based control input is computed as

$$u_e(t) = \mu(\hat{x}). \tag{1.38}$$

Then the event-triggered closed-loop system can be represented as

$$\dot{x}(t) = f(x(t), \mu(x(t) + e(t))). \tag{1.39}$$

Since the control input u renders the system ISS, there exists a Lyapunov function $V : \mathbb{R}^n \to \mathbb{R}$ (by converse Lyapunov theorem (Khalil, 2002)). Alternatively, there exists class $\mathcal{K}$ functions $\underline{\alpha}, \bar{\alpha}, \gamma$, and β such that

$$\underline{\alpha}(\|x\|) \le V(x) \le \bar{\alpha}(\|x\|), \tag{1.40}$$

$$\frac{\partial V}{\partial x} f(x, \mu(x+e)) \le -\gamma(\|x\|) + \beta(\|e\|). \tag{1.41}$$

Table 1.2
ZOH-based Event-Triggered Control

System dynamics	$\dot{x}(t) = f(x(t), u(t)),\ x(0) = x_0$
Control input	$u(t) = \mu(x)$
Event-triggering error	$e(t) = \hat{x}(t) - x(t),\ t_k \le t < t_{k+1}$
Feedback at the controller	$\hat{x}(t) = x(t_k),\ t_k \le t < t_{k+1}$
Control input at the actuator	$u_e(t) = \mu(\hat{x}(t))$
Event-triggering conditions	$\beta(\|e(t)\|) \le \sigma\gamma(\|x(t)\|)$

The first inequality in (1.40) states that V is positive definite, and the second inequality in (1.41) ensures the directional derivative is dissipative. Further, we have the directional derivative of the Lyapunov function V upper bounded as

$$\dot{V}(t) \le -\gamma(\|x(t)\|) + \beta(\|e(t)\|). \tag{1.42}$$

If we restrict the evolution of the event-triggering error $e(t)$ so that for some $\sigma \in (0,1)$

$$\beta(\|e(t)\|) \le \sigma\gamma(\|x(t)\|), \tag{1.43}$$

for all $t \ge 0$, the first derivative of the Lyapunov function is upper bounded by

$$\dot{V} \le -(1-\sigma)\gamma(\|x(t)\|). \tag{1.44}$$

By Lyapunov direct theorem, the event-triggered system is asymptotically stable.

Remark 1.2. *The event-triggering condition is the restriction on the function β in* (1.43). *The events are triggered upon the violation of this condition. Note that the term $\sigma\gamma(\|x(t)\|)$ in* (1.43) *is referred to as threshold and is a function of system state. Therefore, it is referred to as a state-dependent threshold condition (Tabuada, 2007).*

The evolution of the event-triggering error is important to get a better insight into the behavior of the closed-loop event-triggered control. The event-triggering error is reset to zero at the beginning of the interval $[t_k, t_{k+1})$, i.e., $e(t_k) = 0$ for all $k = 0, 1, \cdots, \infty$. The system is fed with a piecewise constant control input as in (1.38). Therefore, the event-triggering error increases when β (the function of the norm of $e(t)$) satisfies the inequality $\beta(\|e_k(t)\|) \le \sigma\gamma(\|x(t)\|)$, the system state is sampled, and the state at the controller $\hat{x}$ is updated as $\hat{x} = x(t_k)$, when this inequality is violated, forcing the error $e(t)$ to zero again. To implement this event-triggered control scheme, a triggering mechanism is employed to evaluate the inequality (1.43) continuously. Upon detecting a violation of the inequality, the sampler in the mechanism triggers an event.

A Special Case of Linear System

Consider the special case of a linear system represented by

$$\dot{x}(t) = Ax(t) + Bu(t), \tag{1.45}$$

where $x(t) \in \mathbb{R}^n$ and $u(t) \in \mathbb{R}^m$ are the state and control input vector. The matrics $A \in \mathbb{R}^{n\times n}$ and $B \in \mathbb{R}^{n\times m}$ are the system matrices. The pair (A,B) is assumed to be controllable. Therefore, there exists a control gain matrix $K \in \mathbb{R}^{m\times n}$, such that the control input

$$u(t) = Kx(t) \tag{1.46}$$

renders the closed-loop system asymptotically stable. We can write the closed-loop dynamics of the system with event-based control $u(t) = K\hat{x}(t)$ as

$$\begin{aligned} \dot{x}(t) &= Ax(t) + Bu(t) = Ax(t) + BK(x(t) + e(t)), \\ &= Ax(t) + BKx(t) + BKe(t). \end{aligned} \tag{1.47}$$

In the case of a linear system, since the control gain matrix K renders the closed-loop system asymptotically stable, it also ensures that the system is ISS with respect to the measurement error. Therefore, by the ISS Lyapunov theorem for the linear system, there exists a Lyapunov function $V : \mathbb{R}^n \to \mathbb{R}_{\geq 0}$ satisfying

$$\underline{a}\|x\|^2 \leq V(x) \leq \bar{a}\|x\|^2, \tag{1.48}$$

$$\frac{\partial V}{\partial x}(Ax + BKx + BKe) \leq -a\|x\|^2 + b\|e\|\|x\|, \tag{1.49}$$

where $V(x)$ can be selected as a quadratic functions $V(x) = x^T Px$. Then we have $\underline{a} = \lambda_{min}(P)$ and $\bar{a} = \lambda_{max}(P)$, where $\lambda_{min}(P)$ and $\lambda_{max}(P)$ are the minimum and maximum eigenvalues of the matrix P and the variable $a = \lambda_{min}(Q)$, where the positive definite matrix Q satisfies the Lyapunov equation

$$(A + BK)^T P + P(A + BK) = -Q. \tag{1.50}$$

The variable b in (1.49) is given as $b = K^T B^T P + PBK$. From inequality (1.49), we have

$$\dot{V}(x) \leq -a\|x\|^2 + b\|e\|\|x\|.$$

Selecting an event-triggering condition to restrict the evolution of the event-triggering error

$$\|e(t)\| \leq \sigma\|x\|, \tag{1.51}$$

where $0 < \sigma < 1$, we have

$$\dot{V}(x) \leq -a\|x\|^2 + \sigma b\|x\|^2 = -(a - \sigma b)\|x\|^2.$$

Consequently, by ensuring that $a > \sigma b$, the closed-loop event-triggered linear system can be made asymptotically stable.

1.4.2.2 Zeno-free Behavior of Event-triggered System

One of the challenges in event-triggered control of continuous-times systems is to ensure that the events are not accumulated. In other words, it is important to avoid triggering an 'infinite' number of events in a finite interval. Triggering very large (in the limit, infinite) number of events in finite time is referred to as *Zeno behavior*. To avoid this Zeno behavior, a nonzero positive lower bound on the inter-event times, i.e., $\delta t_k = t_{k+1} - t_k$, should be guaranteed.

A common approach to derive a lower bound on the inter-event time is to examine the evolution of the event-triggering error $e(t)$. Assume that the closed-loop system is Lipschitz with respect to the state x and the event-triggering error e, i.e., there exists a positive constant L such that for all x and e in $\mathbb{R}^n$,

$$\|f(x, \mu(x + e))\| \leq L\|x\| + L\|e\|. \tag{1.52}$$

For the kth event, the event-triggerining error e violates the event-triggering condition (1.43) at time t_{k+1}, then

$$\beta\left(\|e(t)\|\right) > \sigma\gamma(\|x(t)\|). \tag{1.53}$$

Assume there exists a positive constant P such that

$$P\|e(t)\| \geq \gamma^{-1}\left(\frac{1}{\sigma}\beta_1\left(\|e(t)\|\right)\right) \geq \|x(t)\|. \tag{1.54}$$

From this relation, the ratio of the event-triggering error with respect to the system state must be greater than a positive constant $1/P$. In other words, an event occurs when

$$\frac{1}{P} \leq \frac{\|e(t)\|}{\|x(t)\|}. \tag{1.55}$$

This is a more conservative condition than the original event-triggering condition in (1.43). Since the goal is to show the existence of the nonzero positive δt_k, we shall examine this condition and derive the bounds on inter-event time. Then it should also be a bound for the event-triggering condition in (1.43). In addition, this also provides a tractable approach to solve for t_k.

During an inter-event time $t_k \leq t < t_{k+1}$ for $k = 0, 1, \cdots, \infty$, the evolution of the ratio of the trajectories for $\|e(t)\| / \|x(t)\|$ satisfies

$$\frac{d}{dt}\frac{\|e(t)\|}{\|x(t)\|} \leq \left(1 + \frac{\|e(t)\|}{\|x(t)\|}\right)\frac{L\|x(t)\| + L\|e(t)\|}{\|x(t)\|} = L\left(1 + \frac{\|e(t)\|}{\|x(t)\|}\right)^2. \tag{1.56}$$

By Comparison principle (Khalil, 2002), the solution to the differential inequality, for any $\delta t \in (0, t_{k+1} - t_k)$, satisfies

$$\frac{\|e(t)\|}{\|x(t)\|} \leq \frac{\delta t L}{1 - \delta t L} \tag{1.57}$$

for all $k = 0, 1, \cdots, \infty$. Furthermore, using (1.55), at the next trigger instant $t = t_{k+1}$, we have

$$\frac{1}{P} \leq \frac{\|e(t_{k+1})\|}{\|x(t_{k+1})\|} \leq \frac{\delta t_k L}{1 - \delta t_k L}. \tag{1.58}$$

From the above relation, the inter-event times δt_k is lower bounded as

$$t_{k+1} - t_k = \delta t_k \geq \frac{1}{L + LP} \tag{1.59}$$

Remark 1.3. *The inter-event times δt_k for $k = 0, 1, \cdots, \infty$ is greater than a nonzero positive value. Alternatively, its lower bound is non-zero, positive constant. Therefore, the Zeno-free behavior is guaranteed. Note that the lower bound approaches to zero when the Lipschitz constant L approaches infinity. This would happen only when the function f is not Lipschitz.*

1.4.2.3 Model-based Event-triggered Control

The ZOH event-triggered control scheme can save network resources when compared with the periodic sampling and control scheme. An alternative to this approach is to use a model of the system and implement this model along with the controller to estimate the system state and update control inputs between any two events using the model states. In other words, instead of using the state and control transmitted during an event and holding this value at the controller and at the actuator, in the model-based event-triggered control scheme introduced by Garcia and Antsaklis (2013), the estimated states obtained from the model are used to continuously update the control input.

Consider the model of a linear time-invariant system (1.45) given by

$$\dot{\hat{x}}(t) = \hat{A}\hat{x}(t) + \hat{B}u(t), \tag{1.60}$$

where $u(t) = K\hat{x}(t) \in \mathbb{R}^m$ represents the control input, which is a function of the estimated system state $\hat{x}(t) \in \mathbb{R}^n$ and K is the constant feedback control gain matrix obtained by using $(\hat{A}, \hat{B})$. In this case, if the control inputs are computed using the model states, the lack of actual state information from the sensors to the controllers will lead to an error. Unlike the measurement error in the ZOH-based event-triggered controller, in the model-based controllers, the error is due to the discrepency between the system state and the model state and is called as the *state estimation error*, which is defined as

$$e(t) = x(t) - \hat{x}(t).$$

The model uncertainties will cause this error to grow. Hence, in this control scheme, the events are designed to keep this estimation error $e(t)$ under a predefined threshold. During an event, the controller resets the estimated state $\hat{x}$ equal to the received system state x (i.e., $\hat{x}(t) = x(t)$ at $t = t_k$) and estimation error $e(t)$ to zero, i.e., $e(t) = 0$ at $t = t_k$.

It is important to note that the model uncertainties of fixed model-based event-triggered control system (i.e., $\Delta_A = \|A - \hat{A}\|, \Delta_B = \|B - \hat{B}\|$) need to be small for maintaining the stability, and for fully exploiting the model for reducing potentially redundant events. Consider the fixed model in (1.60) with the control input

$$u(t) = \begin{cases} Kx(t), & t = t_k \\ K\hat{x}(t), & t_k \le t < t_{k+1}. \end{cases} \tag{1.61}$$

By using $u(t)$ and (1.60), the fixed model-based event-triggered closed-loop system dynamics can be represented as

$$\dot{x}(t) = (\hat{A} + \hat{B}K)x(t) + (\widetilde{A} + \widetilde{B}K)x(t) - BKe(t), \tag{1.62}$$

where $\widetilde{A} = A - \hat{A}, \widetilde{B} = B - \hat{B}$ represent model uncertainties between actual system dynamics (A, B) and constant model matrices $(\hat{A}, \hat{B})$ with the state estimation error

$$e(t) = \begin{cases} 0 & t = t_k \\ x(t) - \hat{x}(t) & t_k \le t < t_{k+1} \end{cases}. \tag{1.63}$$

Both state estimation error $e(t)$ and system uncertainties $(\widetilde{A}, \widetilde{B})$ will affect system stability.

Theorem 1.13. *(Garcia and Antsaklis, 2013) Given a linear event-triggered continuous-time system* (1.45) *and a model with constant matrices* (1.60)*, the closed-loop system with feedback selected as* (1.61) *is asymptotically stable when the following relation defined as the event-triggering condition*

$$\|e(t)\| \le \frac{\sigma(\lambda_{min}(Q) - \Delta)}{\bar{b}} \|x(t)\| \tag{1.64}$$

is violated, where $0 < \sigma < 1$, $\bar{b} = 2\|P\hat{B}K\| + 2\eta\|PK\|$ *with* $\|\tilde{B}\| \le \eta$, $\|(\tilde{A} + \tilde{B}K)^T P + P(\tilde{A} + \tilde{B}K)\| \le \Delta < \lambda_{min}(Q)$ *with* Q, P, *and* K *are positive definite matrices, and constant feedback control gain matrix respectively. Here the feedback gain matrix* K *is obtained by using*

$$(\hat{A} + \hat{B}K)^T P + P(\hat{A} + \hat{B}K) = -Q. \tag{1.65}$$

Table 1.3
Model-based Event-Triggered Control

System dynamics	$\dot{x}(t) = Ax(t) + Bu(t),\, x(0) = x_0$
System model	$\dot{\hat{x}}(t) = \hat{A}\hat{x}(t) + \hat{B}u(t),\, \hat{x}(0) = \hat{x}_0$
Control input	$u(t) = \begin{cases} Kx(t) & t = t_k \\ K\hat{x}(t) & t_k \leq t < t_{k+1} \end{cases}$
Event-triggering error	$e(t) = x(t) - \hat{x}(t),\, t_k \leq t < t_{k+1}$
Event-triggering conditions	$\\|e(t)\\| \leq \frac{\sigma(\lambda_{min}(Q)-\Delta)}{\bar{b}} \\|x(t)\\|$

1.4.2.4 Event-based Trajectory Tracking

Consider a nonlinear system

$$\dot{x}(t) = f(x(t), u(t)), \quad x(0) = x_0, \tag{1.66}$$

where $x(t) \in \mathbb{R}^n$ and $u(t) \in \mathbb{R}^m$. The control objective is to track a feasible reference trajectory $x_d(t) \in \mathbb{R}^n$ generated by a reference system represented by

$$\dot{x}_d(t) = f_d(x_d(t), v(t)), \quad x_d(0) = x_{d0}, \tag{1.67}$$

where $x_d(t) \in \mathbb{R}^n$ is the reference state with $x_d(0) = 0$, $v(t)$ is the external input to the reference system, and $f_d(x_d, v) \in \mathbb{R}^n$ is the internal dynamics. Following standard characteristics of the systems in (1.66) and (1.67) are assumed.

Assumption 1.1. *System* (1.66) *is stabilizable and the system states are available for measurement. The feasible reference trajectory $x_d(t) \in \Omega_{x_d}$, where Ω_{x_d} is a compact set, is bounded such that $\|x_d(t)\| \leq b_{x_d}$, where $b_{x_d} > 0$ is a constant.*

Define the error between the system state and the reference state as the *tracking error*, $e_r(t) \triangleq x(t) - x_d(t)$. A control signal that enables the system to track the reference trajectory depends on the tracking error and can be represented in the form

$$u(t) = \gamma(\xi(t)), \tag{1.68}$$

where $\xi = [e_r \ x_d \ v]^T$. Then the tracking error system, utilizing (1.66) and (1.67), can be defined by

$$\dot{e}_r(t) = \dot{x}(t) - \dot{x}_d(t) = f(e_r + x_d, \gamma(\xi)) - f_d(x_d, v). \tag{1.69}$$

In the event-triggered control framework, the controller (1.68) is executed at time instants t_k for $k = 0, 1, \cdots$, and can be expressed as

$$u(t) = \gamma(\xi(t_k)), \quad t_k \leq t < t_{k+1}. \tag{1.70}$$

Using this control signal, the tracking error dynamics can be rewritten as

$$\dot{e}_r(t) = f(e_r + x_d, \gamma(\xi(t_k))) - f_d(x_d, v), \quad t_k \leq t < t_{k+1}. \tag{1.71}$$

We can also define the measurement errors due to event-based sampling as

$$e_\xi(t) = \begin{bmatrix} e_{e_r}(t) \\ e_{x_d}(t) \\ e_v(t) \end{bmatrix} = \begin{bmatrix} e_r(t_k) - e_r(t) \\ x_d(t_k) - x_d(t) \\ v(t_k) - v(t) \end{bmatrix}, \quad t_k \le t < t_{k+1}. \tag{1.72}$$

Using the measurement errors, the tracking error dynamics can be expressed as

$$\dot{e}_r(t) = f(e_r + x_d, \gamma(\xi + e_\xi)) - f_d(x_d, v). \tag{1.73}$$

Adding and subtracting $f(e_r + x_d, \gamma(\xi))$, we have

$$\dot{e}_r(t) = f(e_r + x_d, \gamma(\xi)) - f_d(x_d, v) + f(e_r + x_d, \gamma(\xi + e_\xi)) - f(e_r + x_d, \gamma(\xi)). \tag{1.74}$$

Note that the reference trajectory generated by (1.67) should be a *feasible trajectory* for the system (1.66) to track. To characterize feasible reference trajectories, authors Tallapragada and Chopra (2013) introduced a family of compact sets and assumed that f, f_d, and γ are Lipschitz continuous on compact sets. Using this assumption, yields the following inequality

$$f(e_r + x_d, \gamma(\xi + e_\xi)) - f(e_r + x_d, \gamma(\xi)) \le L\|e_\xi\|, \tag{1.75}$$

where L is a (local) constant that is dependent on the compact set. It can then be shown that if the continuously implemented control policy $\gamma(\xi)$ admits a Lyapunov function V satisfying

$$\alpha_1(\|e_r\|) \le V(e_r) \le \alpha_2(\|e_r\|), \tag{1.76}$$

$$\frac{\partial V}{\partial e_r}[f(e_r + x_d, \gamma(\xi)) - f_d(x_d, v)] \le -\alpha_3(\|e_r\|), \tag{1.77}$$

where $\alpha_1(\cdot)$, $\alpha_2(\cdot)$, and $\alpha_3(\cdot)$ are class $\mathcal{K}_\infty$ functions, then the closed-loop tracking controller renders the tracking error uniformly ultimately bounded provided the events are triggered when the inequality condition $L\|e_\xi\| < \sigma \frac{\alpha_3(\|e_r\|)}{\beta(\|e_r\|)}$ with $\sigma \in (0,1)$ and $\beta(\|e_r\|) \ge \max_w \|\frac{\partial V(w)}{\partial w}\|$ is violated. It should be noted that with the tracking error dynamics defined as in (1.74), the tracking control problem associated with the system (1.66) can be viewed as a regulation problem for the tracking error system. However, unlike the regulation problem, where a continously implemented asymptotically stabilizing control input implemented aperiodically in a ZOH-based event-triggered control scheme retains asymptotically stability, the regulation problem associated with the tracking error system does not retain asymptotic convergence of the tracking error to zero. Rather, the tracking error signals are only guaranteed to be uniformly ultimately bounded with the event-triggered tracking control implementation. For more information on event-triggered tracking controllers, see Tallapragada and Chopra (2013).

1.4.3 EVENT-TRIGGERED CONTROL OF DISCRETE-TIME SYSTEMS

We shall now review the event-triggered control strategies for discrete-time systems.

1.4.3.1 ZOH-based Event-Triggered Control Design

Consider a nonlinear system

$$x_{k+1} = f(x_k, u_k), \tag{1.78}$$

where $x_k \in \mathbb{R}^n$ and $u_k \in \mathbb{R}^m$ are the state and control input vectors. The internal dynamics is the vector function $f : \mathbb{R}^n \times \mathbb{R}^m \to \mathbb{R}^n$. Let the feedback-based control input

$$u_k = \mu(x) \tag{1.79}$$

guarantees ISS of the controlled system with respect to the event-triggering error e_k defined as

$$e_k = \hat{x}_k - x_k, \quad k_l \leq k < k_{l+1}, \tag{1.80}$$

where $\{k_l\}_{l=0}^{\infty}$ is the sequence of the sampling instants, referred to as *events* and $\hat{x}_k$ is the previously defined sampled state as defined next. At times k_l, $l = 0, 1, \cdots$, the system states are sampled and sent to the controller. The sampled states $\{\hat{x}_l\}_{l=0}^{\infty}$ form a sequence in which $\hat{x}_l = x(k_l)$ is used to compute the control input that is held at the actuator until a new event. The output of the ZOH is a piecewise continuous signal defined as

$$\hat{x}_k = x_{k_l}, \quad k_l \leq k < k_{l+1}. \tag{1.81}$$

The event-based control input is computed as

$$u_k = \mu(\hat{x}). \tag{1.82}$$

Then the event-triggered closed-loop system can be represented as

$$x_{k+1} = f(x_k, \mu(x_k + e_k)). \tag{1.83}$$

Since the control policy μ renders the system ISS, there exists an ISS-Lyapunov function $V : \mathbb{R}^n \to \mathbb{R}_{\geq 0}$. Additionally, there exists class $\mathscr{K}$-functions $\underline{\alpha}, \bar{\alpha}, \gamma$, and β such that

$$\underline{\alpha}(\|x_k\|) \leq V(x_k) \leq \bar{\alpha}(\|x_k\|), \quad \forall x_k \in \mathbb{R}^n, \tag{1.84}$$

$$V(f(x_k, e)) - V(x_k) \leq -\gamma(\|x_k\|) + \beta(\|e_k\|), \quad \forall x_k \in \mathbb{R}^n, \forall e_k \in \mathbb{R}^n. \tag{1.85}$$

From these results, we have the first-difference of the Lyapunov function V upper bounded as

$$\Delta V_k \leq -\gamma(\|x_k\|) + \beta\left(\|e_k\|\right). \tag{1.86}$$

If we restrict the evolution of the event-triggering error e_k so that for some $\sigma \in (0, 1)$

$$\beta\left(\|e_k\|\right) \leq \sigma\gamma(\|x_k\|), \tag{1.87}$$

for all $k \geq 0$, the first difference of the Lyapunov function is upper bounded by

$$\Delta V_k \leq -(1 - \sigma)\gamma(\|x_k\|). \tag{1.88}$$

By Lyapunov direct theorem, the event-triggered control system is asymptotically stable.

A Special Case of Linear System

This section introduces a traditional ZOH event-triggered control scheme and an event-triggering condition for discrete-time linear systems. Different from the periodic sampling scheme, the ZOH event-triggered controller might not receive the system state at every sampling time instant. Hence the controller will hold the latest received system state vector for control input design until a new state vector is received due to an event. Now, consider the linear discrete-time

$$x_{k+1} = Ax_k + Bu_k \tag{1.89}$$

where $x_k \in \mathbb{R}^n, u_k \in \mathbb{R}^m$ are the system states and control inputs respectively, and $A \in \mathbb{R}^{n \times n}, \quad B \in \mathbb{R}^{n \times m}$ denote the system matrices. Let the event-triggered control input be given by

$$u_k = K\hat{x}_k, \tag{1.90}$$

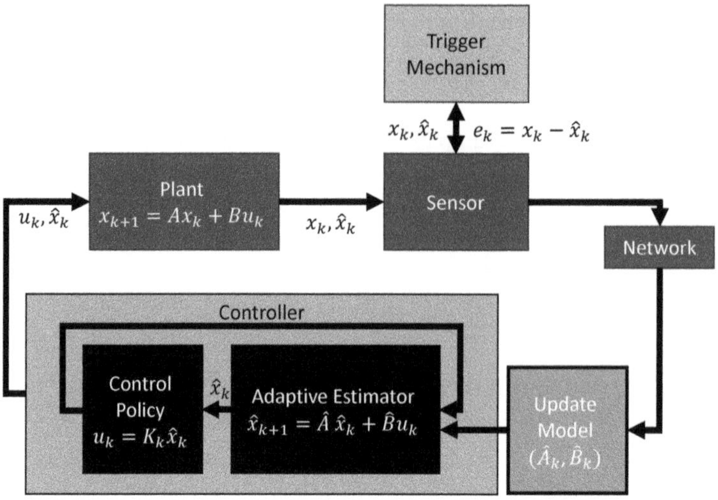

Figure 1.1 Adaptive model-based event-triggered control system.

where $\hat{x}_k$ is the latest state measurement at the time k_l and K is a stabilizing control gain matrix for the system given by (1.89) with known system matrices (A, B). The latest state measurement is not updated for any k such that $k_l \leq k < k_{l+1}$ and it is updated at the occurence of the next event at k_{l+1}. Due to this, the control input will introduce a measurement error $e_k = \hat{x}_k - x_k$ into the closed-loop system. After substituting control input u_k from (1.90), the closed-loop system dynamics can be expressed as

$$x_{k+1} = (A + BK)x_k + BKe_k. \tag{1.91}$$

As the inter-event time is elongated, the effect of the state measurement error e_k in (1.91) might accumulate and affect the stability of the system. Therefore, a threshold (Eqtami et al., 2010) is derived for e_k to ensure stability. Note, however, that the delay between the sensor, controller, and actuator is assumed to be negligible.

Theorem 1.14. *For the linear discrete-time event-triggered control system* (1.89)*, let an event be triggered when the event-triggering condition*

$$\|e_k\|^2 \leq \Gamma \|x_k\|^2 \tag{1.92}$$

is violated, where $\Gamma = \sigma \frac{\|Q\|}{\|BK\|^2 \|P\|}, 0 < \sigma < 1$, *and* Q, P, K *are positive definite matrices with the feedback control gain matrix selected as the solution of*

$$2(A + BK)^T P(A + BK) - P = -Q. \tag{1.93}$$

Then the closed-loop system is asymptotically stable.

Proof. Consider a Lyapunov function candidate as $V = x_k^T P x_k$. Using system representation (1.91) and Cauchy-Schwartz inequality, the first difference of the Lyapunov function candidate can be derived as

$$\Delta V \leq -\|Q\| \, \|x_k\|^2 + 2\|BK\|^2 \|P\| \, \|e_k\|^2 \leq -(1-\sigma)\|Q\| \, \|x_k\|^2 \tag{1.94}$$

after applying the event-trigger condition (1.92). Then ΔV is negative definite while V is positive definite when the state of the system is nonzero. Therefore, the event-triggered closed-loop control system is globally asymptotically stable. In other words, as $k \to \infty$, $x_k \to 0$. □

Table 1.4
ZOH-based Event-Triggered Control of Linear Discrete-time System

System dynamics	$x_{k+1} = Ax_k + Bu_k$
Control input	$u_k = \begin{cases} Kx_k & k = k_l \\ K\hat{x}_k & k_l \leq k < k_{l+1} \end{cases}$
Event-triggering error	$e_k = \hat{x}_k - x_k,\ k_l \leq k < k_{l+1}$
Event-triggering conditions	$\|e_k\|^2 \leq \Gamma \|x_k\|^2,\ \Gamma = \sigma \frac{\|Q\|}{\|BK\|^2\|P\|},$
	$0 < \sigma < 1$ and $2(A+BK)^T P(A+BK) - P = -Q$

1.4.3.2 Fixed Model-based Event-triggered Control Design

Although ZOH event-triggered control can save the network resource compared with periodic time-triggered control, its efficiency is low since the measured state and control inputs are not updated between any two events. As an alternative, the model-based event-triggered control scheme maybe used to provide state estimates between events to update the control input. This section presents a (fixed) model-based event-triggered control scheme and the corresponding event-trigger condition design procedure for linear time-invariant discrete-time systems. We shall assume that the communication delay (within the closed-loop) is negligible, the system's initial conditions are known, the uncertainities in the system dynamics are bounded above, and the bounds are known.

Consider the linear discrete-time system as in (1.89). Let a model for this system be defined as

$$\hat{x}_{k+1} = \hat{A}_k \hat{x}_k + \hat{B}_k u_k, \quad \hat{x}_0 = x_0, \tag{1.95}$$

with $u_k = K_k \hat{x}_k \in \mathbb{R}^m$ denoting the control input vector based on estimated states, $K_k \in \mathbb{R}^{m \times n}$ is the time-dependent feedback control gain matrix which is derived based on estimated system matrices, i.e., $\hat{A}_k \in \mathbb{R}^{n \times n}, \hat{B}_k \in \mathbb{R}^{n \times m}$.

We shall assume that the model is fixed, i.e., $\hat{A}_k, \hat{B}_k$, and K_k are fixed for all k. The event-triggered control input is designed as

$$u_k = \begin{cases} Kx_k, & k = k_l \\ K\hat{x}_k, & k_l \leq k < k_{l+1}. \end{cases} \tag{1.96}$$

where $K_k = K$ is a feedback control gain matrix selected using fixed model parameters $(\hat{A}_k = \hat{A}, \hat{B}_k = \hat{B})$. The model-based event-triggered closed-loop system can be represented as

$$x_{k+1} = (\hat{A} + \hat{B}K)x_k + (\widetilde{A} + \widetilde{B}K)x_k + BKe_k \tag{1.97}$$

where $\widetilde{A} = A - \hat{A}, \widetilde{B} = B - \hat{B}$ represent model uncertainties between actual system dynamics (A, B) and constant model matrices $(\hat{A}, \hat{B})$ with the state estimation error

$$e_k = \hat{x}_k - x_k. \tag{1.98}$$

The state estimation error e_k is reset to zero whenever an event occurs, setting the estimated state equal to the actual state of the system. One of the key assumptions to designing the event-triggering condition to ensure system stability is that the constants A_m and B_m that satisfy $\|\widetilde{A}\| < A_m$ and $\|\widetilde{B}\| < B_m$ are known.

Theorem 1.15. *Consider a linear discrete-time system as in* (1.89) *with event-triggered control input* (1.96)*, where $\hat{x}_k$ is the model states updated via* (1.95)*. Assume that the constants A_m and B_m satisfying $\|\widetilde{A}\| < A_m$ and $\|\widetilde{B}\| < B_m$ are known. Let an event be triggered when the inequality condition*

$$\|e_k\|^2 \le \Gamma \|x_k\|^2 \tag{1.99}$$

is violated, where $\Gamma = \sigma \frac{\|Q\| - 4\Delta_m^2 \|P\|}{4\|BK\|^2\|P\|}$ with $0 < \sigma < 1$, $A_m + B_m\|K\| = \Delta_m$, Q, P are positive definite matrices, and K is constant feedback control gain matrix. Here the feedback gain matrix is obtained by using

$$2(\hat{A}+\hat{B}K)^T P(\hat{A}+\hat{B}K) - P = -Q. \tag{1.100}$$

Then the closed loop system is asymptotically stable if Q and P satisfy $\Delta_m^2\|P\| < \frac{\|Q\|}{4}$.

Proof. Consider the Lypaunov function candidate as $V_k = x_k^T P x_k$. Using system representation (1.97) and Cauchy-Schwartz inequality, the first difference of Lyapunov function candidate can be expressed as

$$\begin{aligned}
\Delta V_k &= x_{k+1}^T P x_{k+1} - x_k^T P x_k \\
&= \left[(\hat{A}+\hat{B}K)x_k + (\tilde{A}+\widetilde{B}K)x_k + BKe_k\right]^T P \left[(\hat{A}+\hat{B}K)x_k + (\tilde{A}+\widetilde{B}K)x_k + BKe_k\right] - x_k^T P x_k \\
&\le x_k^T \left[2(\hat{A}+\hat{B}K)^T P(\hat{A}+\hat{B}K) - P\right] x_k + 2\left[(\widetilde{A}+\widetilde{B}K)x_k + BKe_k\right]^T P \left[(\widetilde{A}+\widetilde{B}K)x_k + BKe_k\right] \\
&\le -x_k^T Q x_k + 4x_k^T(\tilde{A}+\widetilde{B}K)^T P(\tilde{A}+\widetilde{B}K)x_k + 4e_k^T K^T B^T PBKe_k \\
&\le -\|Q\|\,\|x_k\|^2 + 4\|\widetilde{A}+\widetilde{B}K\|^2\|P\|\|x_k\|^2 + 4\|BK\|^2\|P\|\|e_k\|^2.
\end{aligned}$$

Define Δ_m such that $\|\widetilde{A}+\widetilde{B}K\| \le \|\widetilde{A}\| + \|\widetilde{B}K\| \le A_m + B_m\|K\| = \Delta_m$. Then we have

$$\Delta V_k \le -\|Q\|\,\|x_k\|^2 + 4\Delta_m^2\|P\|\,\|x_k\|^2 + 4\|BK\|^2\|P\|\,\|e_k\|^2. \tag{1.101}$$

Applying event-triggering condition (1.99) into (1.101) , we get

$$\Delta V_k \le -(1-\sigma)\left(\|Q\| - 4\Delta_m^2\|P\|\right)\|x_k\|^2. \tag{1.102}$$

With $0 < \sigma < 1$, assuming $\Delta_m^2\|P\| < \frac{\|Q\|}{4}$ and Q a positive definite matrix, ΔV_k is negative definite. Hence, using (1.97), the model-based event-triggered closed-loop system is globally asymptotically stable. □

Remark 1.4. *Compared with the ZOH event-triggered scheme, the fixed model-based approach can reduce network traffic since the model can estimate the system state vector between two events, and the control input is updated accordingly. However, the control gain matrix K is fixed. The model uncertainties $(\widetilde{A}, \widetilde{B})$ need to be small satisfying $\|\widetilde{A}+\widetilde{B}K\|^2\|P\| < \frac{\|Q\|}{4}$ in order to maintain stability. In other words, large model uncertainties can affect performance and stability.*

1.4.3.3 Adaptive Model-based Event-triggered Control Design

In the adaptive model-based event-triggered control scheme, the model parameters are constantly adjusted once per event when the controller receives the system state vector from the sensor. At the update times, the state vector of the model is also updated with the measurements obtained from the system; the update times are generally non-periodic and are triggered by the size of the state estimation error. Consequently, the model update is also not periodic in contrast with traditional adaptive control literature (Luders and Narendra, 1973). We shall employ estimation (Luders and

Table 1.5
Fixed Model-based Event-Triggered Control of Discrete-time System

System dynamics	$x_{k+1} = Ax_k + Bu_k$
System model	$\hat{x}_{k+1} = \hat{A}\hat{x}_k + \hat{B}u_k, \quad \hat{x}_0 = x_0$
Control input	$u_k = \begin{cases} Kx_k & k = k_l \\ K\hat{x}_k & k_l \le k < k_{l+1} \end{cases}$
Event-triggering error	$e_k = \hat{x}_k - x_k, \quad k_l \le k < k_{l+1}$
Event-triggering conditions	$\|e_k\|^2 \le \Gamma \|x_k\|^2, \Gamma = \sigma \frac{\|Q\| - 4\Delta_m^2 \|P\|}{4\|BK\|^2 \|P\|}, \Delta_m = A_m + B_m\|K\|$
	$0 < \sigma < 1$ and $2(\hat{A} + \hat{B}K)^T P(\hat{A} + \hat{B}K) - P = -Q$

Narendra, 1973) and adaptation (Werbos, 1983) techniques to derive an event-triggered control scheme with unknown system dynamics. First, system states are estimated by using an adaptive state estimator or adaptive model. By using the current model parameters, the feedback gain matrix is generated during an event. In the inter-event times, the model will generate the state estimates for updating the control input, but the control gain matrix is fixed between the events. Then an adaptive model-based event-triggered control scheme is derived based on the estimated state vector, which can maintain stability even with unknown system dynamics.

Adaptive State Estimator Design

Based on event-triggered control schemes (Anta and Tabuada, 2010; Eqtami et al., 2010; Tabuada, 2007; Sontag, 2008; Dimarogonas and Johanson, 2009a,b; Rabi et al., 2008; Pekir and Shiryaev, 2006; Garcia and Antsaklis, 2011)), the parameters of the adaptive state estimator will be updated only when an event is triggered and sensed system states are received at the controller. Recalling (1.89) and (1.95), event-triggered control system can be represented as

$$x_{k+1} = Ax_k + Bu_k = \theta^T z_k \tag{1.103}$$

and the adaptive state estimator as

$$\hat{x}_{k+1} = \hat{A}_k x_k + \hat{B}_k u_k = \hat{\theta}_k^T z_k, \tag{1.104}$$

where $\theta = \begin{bmatrix} A & B \end{bmatrix}^T$ and $\hat{\theta}_k = \begin{bmatrix} \hat{A}_k & \hat{B}_k \end{bmatrix}^T$ represent the target and estimated system matrices, respectively, and $z_k = \begin{bmatrix} x_k^T & u_k^T \end{bmatrix}^T$ denotes the augmented state and control vector. The state estimation error dynamics e_{k+1} can be derived as

$$e_{k+1} = x_{k+1} - \hat{x}_{k+1} = \theta^T z_k - \hat{\theta}_k^T z_k = \tilde{\theta}_k^T z_k, \tag{1.105}$$

with $\tilde{\theta}_k = \theta - \hat{\theta}_k = \begin{bmatrix} \tilde{A}_k & \tilde{B}_k \end{bmatrix}^T$ is the parameter estimation error. Now define the update law for the unknown parameters $\hat{\theta}_k$ as

$$\hat{\theta}_{k+1} = \hat{\theta}_k + \alpha_e \gamma_{k+1} z_k e_{k+1}^T, \tag{1.106}$$

where α_e is the tuning parameter satisfying $0 < \alpha_e < 1$ and γ_{k+1} is an indicator for the event trigger condition, i.e.,

$$\gamma_{k+1} = \begin{cases} 1 & \text{event is initiated} \\ 0 & \text{event is not initiated.} \end{cases} \tag{1.107}$$

Meanwhile, adaptive parameter estimation error dynamics $\widetilde{\theta}_k$ can be expressed as

$$\tilde{\theta}_{k+1} = \tilde{\theta}_k - \alpha_e \gamma_{k+1} z_k e_{k+1}^T. \tag{1.108}$$

Compared with traditional adaptive estimator schemes (Luders and Narendra, 1973), where the updates are done periodically, event-based nonperiodic tuning law (1.106) used here updates the parameters aperiodically. As a result, convergence of the parameters is coupled with the frequency of events. Let the proposed adaptive estimator be defined as (1.104) and the adaptive estimator parameter update law be given by (1.106). Then using Taylor's theorem (Goodwin and Sin, 2014) or by using Lyapunov theory (Xu, 2012), sufficient conditions for designing the positive constant tuning parameter α_e can be derived such that the parameter estimation errors $\widetilde{\theta}_k$ (1.108) converge to zero asymptotically as time $k \to \infty$.

Event-triggered Controller Design

Consider the linear discrete-time system and adaptive estimator represented by (1.103) and (1.104), respectively, with adaptive model-based event-triggered control input $u_k = K_k \hat{x}_k$, where K_k is a time-varying feedback gain matrix. The closed-loop system can be represented after applying the control input as

$$x_{k+1} = Ax_k + Bu_k = (A + BK_k)x_k - BK_k e_k, \tag{1.109}$$

where the feedback gain matrix is based on adaptive estimator parameter at time k (i.e., $\hat{\theta}_k = \begin{bmatrix} \hat{A}_k & \hat{B}_k \end{bmatrix}^T$) and estimated state error vector. It is important to note that the control gain matrix K_k can be time-dependent until the model parameters attain their target values (i.e., when $\hat{\theta}_k \to \theta, \hat{A}_k \to A, \hat{B}_k \to B$, then $K_k \to K$). In an adaptive model-based event-triggered scheme, the designed control input $u_k = K_k \hat{x}_k$, which is based on adaptive the model $(\hat{A}_k, \hat{B}_k)$, can render the state estimator $\hat{x}_{k+1} = (\hat{A}_k + \hat{B}_k K_k)\hat{x}_k$ asymptotically stable. Any such K_k can also render the closed-loop adaptive model-based event-triggered system ISS (Eqtami et al., 2010; Garcia and Antsaklis, 2011) with respect to the estimation error e_k.

Remark 1.5. *Given symmetric positive definite matrices P and Q, the feedback gain matrix $u_k = K_k \hat{x}_k$ can be selected such that the following holds*

$$2\left(\hat{A}_k + \hat{B}_k K_k\right)^T P \left(\hat{A}_k + \hat{B}_k K_k\right) - P = -Q. \tag{1.110}$$

In the model-based event-triggered linear discrete-time system, the adaptive state estimator and feedback gain matrix should be updated when

$$\|e_k\|^2 \leq \Gamma \|x_k\|^2, \tag{1.111}$$

is satisfied, where

$$\Gamma = \sigma \frac{\|Q\|}{4\|P\| \, \|BK_k\|^2} \tag{1.112}$$

with Q, P are obtained as symmetric positive definite solutions of (1.110) and $0 < \sigma < 1$.

Remark 1.6. *It is important to note the difference between adaptive model $(\hat{A}_k, \hat{B}_k)$ and actual system matrixes (A, B) or parameter estimation errors will converge to zero with the adaptive model-based scheme when compared to a fixed model scheme. Therefore, an adaptive model-based event-triggered control scheme can reduce more network traffic than a fixed model-based scheme when the uncertainties are compensated via adaptation.*

Table 1.6
Adaptive Model-based Event-Triggered Control of Linear System

System dynamics	$x_{k+1} = Ax_k + Bu_k$
System model	$\hat{x}_{k+1} = \hat{A}_k\hat{x}_k + \hat{B}_k u_k, \quad \hat{x}_0 = x_0$
Control input	$u_k = \begin{cases} K_k x_k & k = k_l \\ K_k \hat{x}_k & k_l \le k < k_{l+1} \end{cases}$
Event-triggering error	$e_k = x_k - \hat{x}_k, \quad k_l \le k < k_{l+1}$
Event-triggering conditions	$\lVert e_k \rVert^2 \le \Gamma \lVert x_k \rVert^2, \Gamma = \sigma \frac{\lVert Q \rVert}{4\lVert BK_k \rVert^2 \lVert P \rVert},$
	$0 < \sigma < 1, \quad 2(\hat{A}_k + \hat{B}_k K_k)^T P(\hat{A}_k + \hat{B}_k K_k) - P = -Q$
Model parameterization	$\hat{\theta}_k = \begin{bmatrix} \hat{A}_k & \hat{B}_k \end{bmatrix}^T$
Model parameter adaptation rule	$\hat{\theta}_{k+1} = \hat{\theta}_k + \alpha_e \gamma_{k+1} z_k e_{k+1}^T$

Remark 1.7. *From event triggering condition (1.111),* $\lVert e_k \rVert^2 \le \Gamma \lVert x_k \rVert^2$*. Thus, when* $\lVert x_k \rVert \to 0$, $\lVert e_k \rVert^2 \to 0$ *and* $e_k \to 0$.

Example 1.13. *Consider the linear discrete-time system*

$$x_{k+1} = \begin{bmatrix} 1.0559 & -0.0397 \\ 0.0298 & 0.9318 \end{bmatrix} x_k + \begin{bmatrix} 0.1008 \\ 0.0981 \end{bmatrix} u_k$$

with initial system states given by $x_0 = \begin{bmatrix} -0.2 & 0.5 \end{bmatrix}^T$ *and the event-triggering condition parameter* $\sigma = 0.8$.

First, the performance of the ZOH event-triggered control scheme is evaluated. As shown in Figure 1.2, the measurement error will be reset to zero when the norm of measurement error exceeds the threshold, and the sensor will transmit sensed system state to the controller since the event is triggered. In Figure 1.2, compared with periodic control, ZOH event-triggered control significantly reduces network traffic due to the increased time intervals between consecutive events. Figure 1.2 also shows that the measurement error and its threshold (1.92) will converge to zero.

Next, the fixed model-based event-triggered control scheme is considered. This scheme, as described by Garcia and Antsaklis (2011), uses the model

$$\hat{A} = \begin{bmatrix} 1.0503 & -0.0358 \\ 0.0268 & 0.9385 \end{bmatrix}, \hat{B} = \begin{bmatrix} 0.1009 \\ 0.0886 \end{bmatrix},$$

where the uncertainties are given by $\Delta_A = 0.01$ and $\Delta_B = 0.01$. As shown in Figure 1.3, fixed model-based event-triggered control can reduce more network traffic than ZOH event-triggered scheme

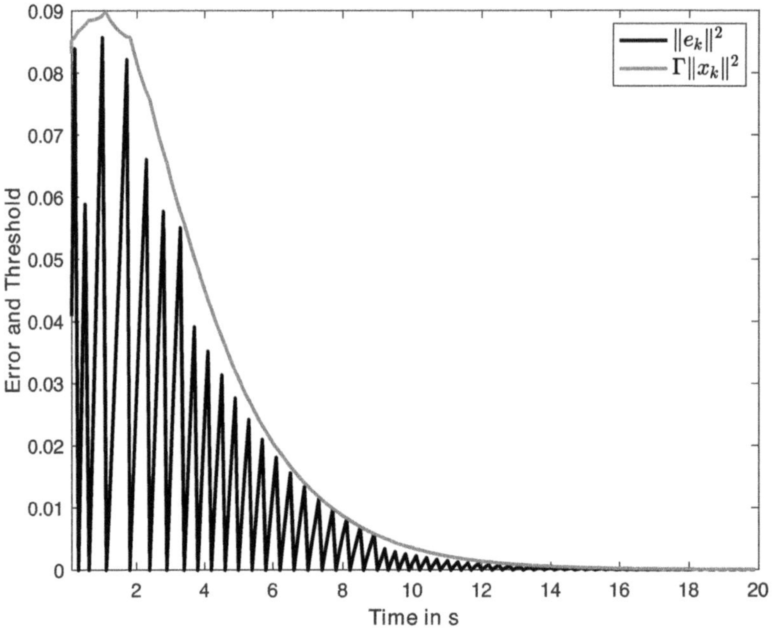

Figure 1.2 Performance of ZOH-based event-triggering mechanism.

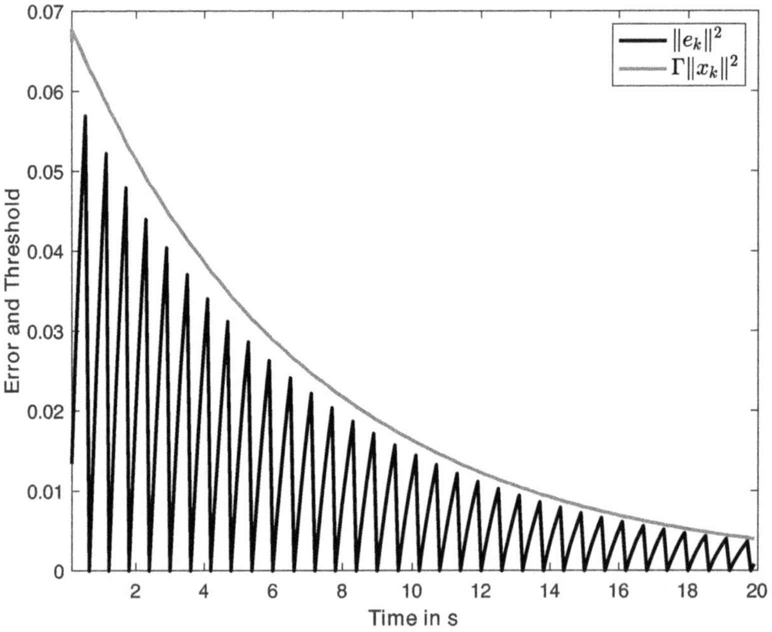

Figure 1.3 Performance of the fixed model-based event-triggering mechanism.

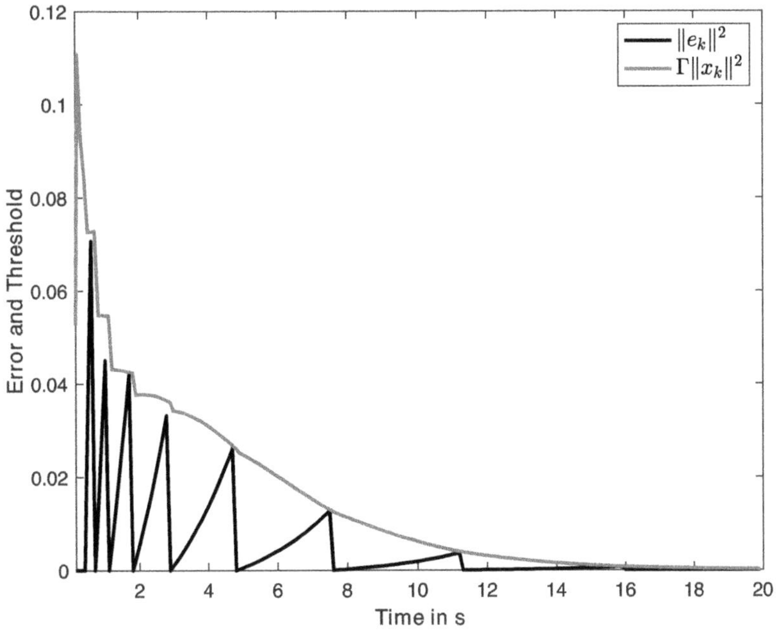

Figure 1.4 Performance of the adaptive model-based event-triggering mechanism.

shown in Figure 1.2 due to elongated update interval. Since the model can estimate system states, events were triggered less frequently than the ZOH-based event-triggered control scheme. However, the drawback of a fixed model-based event-triggered scheme is that uncertainties (i.e., Δ_A, Δ_B) need to be small and more computations are required. If the uncertainties are increased to $\Delta_A = 0.3324$ and $\Delta_B = 0.6295$, then the fixed model-based event-triggered control cannot even maintain the system stability since the constant control gain matrix K is developed from inaccurate model parameters $(\hat{A}, \hat{B})$. If model$(\hat{A}, \hat{B})$ is far away from the actual system parameters (A, B), control gain matrix K might not be stabilizing.

In the adaptive model-based event-triggered control scheme, the model estimates A_0, B_0 were initialized randomly and tuned subsequently. The model parameters were tuned online to attain their target values (A, B) over time. The adaptive tuning parameter was selected as $\alpha_e = 0.01$. Figure 1.4 shows the performance of event-triggering mechanism. At the beginning, the estimation error is large and events are triggered more frequently since the model needs to be tuned. After a short period, the events are triggered less frequently, which reduced the network traffic much more than both the ZOH- and the fixed model- based event-triggered control schemes. In the end, to demonstrate the benefit of all the event-triggered control schemes (i.e., ZOH, fixed model-based with small uncertainties, and adaptive model-based) from the network side, the network performance of all the three schemes are compared in Figure 1.5. Assume that every system states need 20 bits for transmission. From this figure, it can be seen that the network traffic of all event-triggered control schemes decreased significantly compared with periodic time-based sampling. However, the advantage of the adaptive model-based event-triggered control scheme is that it reduces network traffic and relaxes the requirement of system dynamics or the assumption that the uncertainties are small with the fixed-model-based scheme.

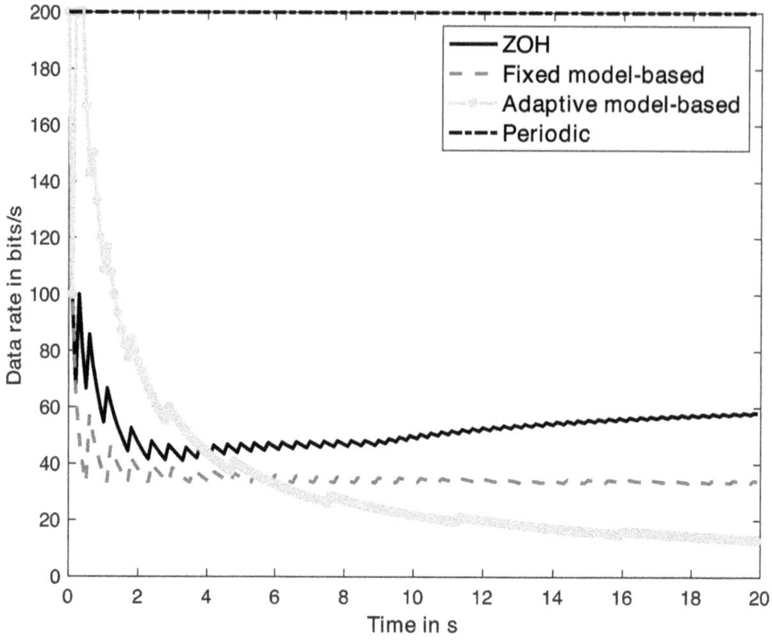

Figure 1.5 Comparison of network traffic for the event-triggered schemes.

1.5 CLOSING REMARKS

This chapter briefly introduced event-triggered control with necessary concepts of dynamical control systems operating in continuous, discrete, sampled-data, and hybrid time domains. Mathematical preliminaries are also introduced, which will be used throughout the book. In the second part of the chapter, the traditional event-triggered control designs both in continuous- and discrete- time frameworks, are also introduced. The three main architectures are introduced, i.e., ZOH-based, fixed-model-based, and adaptive model-based designs. It is observed that fixed model-based event-triggered control can save more computational resources when compared to their ZOH-based counterparts. In addition, the adaptive model-based event-triggered control can save more computation when compared with the other two approaches without complete knowledge of the system dynamics.

1.6 PROBLEMS

1.6.1 Show that the following inequalities hold for any $x \in \mathbb{R}^n$:

$$||x||_2 \leq ||x||_1 \leq \sqrt{n}||x||_2 \quad \text{and} \quad ||x||_\infty \leq ||x||_2 \leq \sqrt{n}||x||_\infty,$$

where n is a scalar.

1.6.2 Check if the following inequalities are true. For two real matrices A and B of dimension $m \times n$ and $n \times l$, the following inequities hold

a. $\frac{1}{\sqrt{n}}||A||_\infty \leq ||A||_2 \leq \sqrt{m}||A||_\infty$

b. $\frac{1}{\sqrt{m}}||A||_1 \leq ||A||_2 \leq \sqrt{n}||A||_1$

c. $||A||_2 \leq \sqrt{||A||_1 ||A||_\infty}$

d. $||AB||_p \leq ||A||_p ||B||_p$

1.6.3 Explain the nature of the equilibrium point(s) of the following autonomous nonlinear systems.

a. $\dot{x}(t) = x^2(t)$

b. $\dot{x}(t) = \sin(x(t))$
c. $\dot{x}(t) = \sin(\frac{1}{x(t)})$

1.6.4 (Khalil, 2002) Consider a function

$$V(x) = \frac{x_1^2}{1+x_1^2} + x_2^2,$$

where $x = (x_1 \ x_2)^T \in \mathbb{R}^2$. Is this function radially unbounded?

1.6.5 Show that for a linear time-invariant dynamical system state $x(t) \in \mathbb{R}^n$ and control $u(t) \in \mathbb{R}^m$, if the control input renders the closed-loop system asymptotically stable, then the system is ISS with respect to the measurement error.

1.6.6 (Lewis et al., 2012b) The longitudinal dynamics of an F-16 aircraft in straight and level flight at 502 ft/sec are given by

$$\dot{x} = Ax + Bu = \begin{bmatrix} -2.0244\times10^{-2} & 7.8761 & -3.2169\times10^{1} & -6.502\times10^{-1} \\ -2.5373\times10^{-4} & -1.0189 & 0 & 9.0484\times10^{-1} \\ 0 & 0 & 0 & 1 \\ 7.9472\times10^{-11} & -2.498 & 0 & -1.3861 \end{bmatrix} x \tag{1.113}$$

$$+ \begin{bmatrix} -1\times10^{-2} \\ -2.09\times10^{-3} \\ 0 \\ -1.99\times10^{-1} \end{bmatrix} u \tag{1.114}$$

The state is $x = \begin{bmatrix} v_T & \alpha & \theta & q \end{bmatrix}^T$, with v_T the forward velocity, α the angle of attack, θ the pitch angle, and q the pitch rate. The control input $u(t)$ is the elevator deflection δ_e.

(a) Plot the response of the open-loop system to initial conditions of $x_0 = \begin{bmatrix} 0 & 0.1 & 0 & 1 \end{bmatrix}^T$ (note that the angular units are in radians).

1.6.7 The dynamics of the Lorenz attractor system are given by

$$\begin{aligned} \dot{x}_1 &= -\sigma(x_1 - x_2) \\ \dot{x}_2 &= rx_1 - x_2 - x_1x_3 \\ \dot{x}_3 &= -bx_3 + x_1x_2. \end{aligned}$$

This system exhibits chaotic behavior. Simulate the trajectories using MATLAB with $\sigma = 10, r = 28, b = 8/3$. Use initial conditions of $x_1 = 0.1, x_2 = 0.1, x_3 = 0.1$, and a time window of 200sec. Plot the states versus time, and also the phase-plane plot in (x_1, x_2, x_3)-space.

1.6.8 The dynamical interaction of two populations, one predatory on the other (e.g. foxes and rabbits) is described by (Luenberger, 1979)

$$\begin{aligned} \dot{x}_1 &= ax_1 - bx_1x_2 \\ \dot{x}_2 &= -cx_2 + dx_1x_2 \end{aligned}$$

with a, b, c, d positive constants. The number of prey at time t is described by $x_1(t)$ and of predators by $x_2(t)$. This model exhibits oscillatory behavior corresponding to alternating periods where the prey is scarce then plentiful. In the first equation, the first term reveals that $x_1(t)$ will increase if x_2 is zero; the second term shows the effect of encounters between predator and prey, indicating that a positive x_2 causes $x_1(t)$ to decrease. In the second equation, the first term reveals that $x_2(t)$ will decrease if x_1 is zero; the second term shows that a positive x_1 causes $x_2(t)$ to increase.

Simulate this system in MATLAB using different values of the constants (begin on the first run with all values equal to 1). Plot $x_1(t), x_2(t)$ versus t, and also the phase-plane plot x_1 versus x_2. Be sure to use a sufficiently long simulation run time to observe all effects. Start with nonzero initial conditions.

1.6.9 The effects of overcrowding of prey in the presence of scarce food resources can be included to the model described in the previous problem by adding a term so that the model becomes

$$\dot{x}_1 = ax_1 - bx_1x_2 - ex_1^2$$
$$\dot{x}_2 = -cx_2 + dx_1x_2$$

with $e > 0$. Simulate this system in MATLAB and compare its behavior to the model in the previous problem.

1.6.10 The development of an epidemic can be described by (Luenberger, 1979)

$$\dot{x}_1 = -\beta x_1x_2$$
$$\dot{x}_2 = \beta x_1x_2 - \gamma x_2$$
$$\dot{x}_3 = \gamma x_2$$

with x_1 the number of susceptible individuals, x_2 the number of infected individuals, and x_3 the number of individuals who are either immune or removed by isolation or death. The infection rate constant is $\beta > 0$, and the removal rate constant is $\gamma > 0$. Simulate this system in MATLAB using different values of the constants. Plot $x_1(t), x_2(t), x_3(t)$ versus t, and also phase-plane plots x_i versus x_j. Plot the 3-D plot in x_1, x_2, x_3-space. Be sure to use a sufficiently long simulation run time to observe all effects. Start with nonzero initial conditions.

1.6.11 Many congenital diseases can be explained as the result of both genes at a single location being the same recessive gene (Luenberger, 1979). Under some assumptions, the frequency of the recessive gene at generation k is given by the recursion

$$x(k+1) = \frac{x(k)}{1+x(k)}.$$

Simulate in MATLAB using $x(0) = 80$. Observe that $x(k)$ converges to zero, but very slowly. This explains why deadly genetic diseases can remain active for hundreds of generations. Simulate the system starting for a small negative value of $x(0)$ and observe that it tends away from zero.

1.6.12 Simulate the system

$$x_1(k+1) = \frac{x_2(k)}{1+x_2(k)^2}$$
$$x_2(k+1) = \frac{x_1(k)}{1+x_2(k)^2}$$

using MATLAB. Plot $x_1(k), x_2(k)$ versus k and the phase-plane plot.

1.6.13 The system

$$\dot{x}_1 = x_2$$
$$\dot{x}_2 = x_3$$
$$\dot{x}_3 = -2x_1x_3 + \sin x_2 + 5u$$

is in Brunovsky form. If $x_1(t)$ is required to track a desired trajectory $y_d(t)$ the feedback linearization design is very easy. However, in this example it is desired for $y(t) \equiv x_2(t)$ to track $y_d(t)$. Perform the design and study the zero dynamics. Simulate the closed-loop system using MATLAB with initial conditions of $x_1(0) = 1, x_2(0) = 1, x_3(0) = 1$.

1.6.14 For the system

$$\dot{x}_1 = x_1x_2 + x_3$$
$$\dot{x}_2 = -2x_2 + x_1$$
$$\dot{x}_3 = \sin x_1 + cx_1x_2$$

Find the equilibrium points.

1.6.15 Using Lyapunov techniques examine stability for the following systems. Plot time histories to substantiate your conclusions.
   (a) $\dot{x}_1 = x_1 x_2^2 - x_1$ and $\dot{x}_2 = -x_1^2 x_2 - x_2$
   (b) $\dot{x}_1 = x_2 \sin x_1 - x_1$ and $\dot{x}_2 = -x_1 \sin x_1 - x_2$.
   (c) $\dot{x}_1 = x_2 + x_1\left(x_1^2 - 2\right)$ and $\dot{x}_2 = -x_1$.

1.6.16 Using Lyapunov techniques design controllers to stabilize the following systems. Plot time histories, both open-loop and closed-loop.
   (a) $\dot{x}_1 = x_1 x_2$ and $\dot{x}_2 = x_1^2 - \sin x_1 + u$
   (b) $\dot{x}_1 = x_1 + \left(1 + x_2^2\right) u$ and $\dot{x}_2 = x_2 \sin x_1$.
   (c) $\dot{x}_1 = x_1\left(x_1^2 - 2\right)$ and $\dot{x}_2 = \cos(x_1) + (2 + \sin(x_1))\, u$.

1.6.17 (Bounded Stability) Using Lyapunov Extensions. Use the UUB extension to show that the Van der Pol oscillator

$$\ddot{y} + \alpha\left(y^2 - \gamma\right)\dot{y} + y = u$$

is UUB. Find the radius of the region of boundedness. Simulate the system in MATLAB and plot phase-plane trajectories to verify the result.

1.6.18 Consider the system

$$\begin{aligned}\dot{x_1} &= x_1 x_2^2 - x_1\left(x_1^2 + x_2^2 - 3\right)\\ \dot{x_2} &= -x_1^2 x_2 - x_2\left(x_1^2 + x_2^2 - 3\right).\end{aligned}$$

Show that the system is UUB. Select the Lyapunov function

$$L = \left(x_1^2 + x_2^2 - 3\right)^2$$

to demonstrate that this system has two equilibria: a stable limit cycle and an unstable equilibrium point at the origin. Simulate the system using MATLAB and make phase-plane plots for several initial conditions to convince yourself that, in this example, the limit cycle is the cause of the UUB nature of the stability.

1.6.19 The system

$$\dot{x} = Ax + Bu + d$$

has a disturbance $d(t)$ that is unknown but bounded so that $\|d\| < d_M$, with the bound d_M known. Show that by selecting the control input as $u(t) = -Kx(t)$ it is possible to improve the UUB stability properties of the system by making the bound on $\|x\|$ smaller. In fact, if feedback is allowed, the initial system matrix A need not be stable as long as (A, B) is stabilizable.

2 Adaptive Dynamic Programming and Optimal Control

CONTENTS

This chapter delves deep into the foundational concepts of neural network (NN)-based approximation and its application in optimal control. The core focus here is the integration of these fundamentals into the broader framework of event-based optimal control, a topic to be thoroughly explored in the subsequent chapters. We shall begin with the notion of function approximation, a significant feature of artificial NNs. Alongside this, the principles of dynamic programming and its adaptive variant, referred to as adaptive/approximate dynamic programming (ADP), shall be examined in both discrete and continuous time domains. Neural networks, particularly those with multiple layers, are universally acknowledged for their capacity to approximate nonlinear functions. This inherent property, when applied to learning dynamical systems, facilitates the computation of control policy (a process known as indirect adaptive control of nonlinear systems) or enables the direct approximation of control policies. We shall briefly review the journey of neural network evolution, taking a deep dive into their mathematical structures, universal approximation property, and training mechanisms. Following the discourse on neural networks, we shall focus on optimal control theory. This field of mathematical optimization strives to synthesize a control policy that optimizes a specified objective function and helps steer dynamical systems over time. We shall see that the "curse of dimensionality," a notorious issue that precludes dynamic programming from being employed in large state space, has led to the advent of ADP. We shall see that, as a unifying approach, ADP allows for the design of optimal control solutions without comprehensive knowledge of system dynamics by combining adaptive control, dynamic programming, and reinforcement learning techniques.

2.1 NEURAL NETWORK (NN) CONTROL: INTRODUCTION

In this section, we will provide a concise overview of artificial neural networks (NN), emphasizing aspects most pertinent to their applications in closed-loop control of dynamical systems. The material related to NN presented in this chapter are based on earlier texts by Lewis et al. (1998) and Jagannathan (2006). Specifically, the discussion will encompass various NN topologies, key properties, and essential training techniques, all contributing to their versatility in controlling complex systems. Control architectures will also be elaborated, elucidating how NN can be integrated into existing control paradigms. Among the many applications, particular attention will be given to the function approximation capability of NN. This property enables the creation of adaptive/learning-based controllers that can model intricate, nonlinear system behaviors, making it a vital tool for effective control. The section will equip the reader with the foundational understanding required to explore and exploit NN's potential in modern control systems by focusing on these elements.

In the landscape of NN, a multitude of surveys and texts have shaped the field, including those by Lippmann (1987), Simpson (1992), Narendra and Parthasarathy (1990), and Hush and Horne (1993). Some of the contributions are also found in the works of Haykin (1994), Kosko (1992), Kung (1993), Levine (1991), Peretto (1992), Goodfellow et al. (2016) among others too extensive to list here. However, a comprehensive mastery of NN's pattern recognition and classification applications is not indispensable for the understanding of feedback control. The focus here is narrowed to select network topologies, fine-tuning methods, and essential properties, underscoring the importance of the NN function approximation characteristic, as illuminated by Lewis et al. (1999). These elements serve as the core topics of this chapter, offering a tailored introduction to NN. For those seeking a more in-depth exploration of the background on NN, additional insights can be sought from Lewis et al. (1999); Haykin (1994); Goodfellow et al. (2016), and related sources.

In the realm of digital control, the use of NN presents a sharp contrast between closed-loop and open-loop applications, with the latter predominantly focused on digital signal processing (DSP). Within DSP, tasks like pattern recognition, classification, and the approximation of static functions (possibly involving time delays) are common. Over the years, a robust methodology has been developed in DSP to choose suitable network topologies and weight configurations, ensuring reliable performance, and the nuances of weight-training algorithms are now well understood (LeCun et al., 2002). On the other hand, the approach to employing NN in closed-loop control for dynamic systems has been more exploratory and less standardized. Techniques adapted from open-loop systems, such as backpropagation for weight adjustments, are often applied in a somewhat unsophisticated but optimistic fashion. The challenges here are multifaceted, involving the need to dynamically evolve NN within a feedback loop, ensuring both system stabilization and convergence of weights. Literature on this subject typically contains limited analysis, supported mainly by simulation examples, and practical demonstrations on hardware remain notably scarce.

Over the years, the study of NN in closed-loop control applications has matured, with an increasing number of researchers offering rigorous mathematical analyses (Narendra and Parthasarathy, 1990; Lewis et al., 1998; Jagannathan, 2006). The foundation for this sophisticated exploration was laid by Narendra and Parthasarathy (1990), Werbos (1991b), and several follow-up efforts in the early 1990s. Lewis and associates subsequently expanded upon this ground-breaking research during the early to mid-1990s (Lewis et al., 1998). A significant discovery emanating from this body of work is that conventional open-loop weight-tuning algorithms, such as backpropagation or Hebbian tuning, need to be restructured to ensure stability and tracking in feedback control systems (Lewis et al., 1999). This realization has deepened our understanding of NN and spurred further investigations into their potential applications within the field of closed-loop control.

2.1.1 HISTORY OF NEURAL NETWORK

The roots of neural networks can be traced back to 1943 when McCulloch and Pitts proposed the first mathematical model of a biological neuron, establishing a basic concept for artificial neural networks (McCulloch and Pitts, 1943). This early work laid the groundwork for Rosenblatt's introduction of the perceptron in 1958, a model that enabled simple binary pattern recognition (Rosenblatt, 1958). Interest in neural networks grew in the 1960s, but was stymied by Minsky and Papert's "Perceptrons" in 1969. This book highlighted the limitations of single-layer perceptrons, casting doubts on the potential of neural networks (Minsky and Papert, 1969). During the 1970s, Werbos introduced the backpropagation algorithm for training multi-layer networks but remained largely unnoticed until the next decade (Werbos, 1974).

The 1980s marked a resurgence in neural network research. Rumelhart, Hinton, and Williams popularized the backpropagation algorithm, leading to new possibilities in training complex, multi-layered networks (Rumelhart et al., 1986). LeCun and his team further extended this by applying backpropagation to convolutional neural networks (CNNs), initiating a new era in handwriting recognition (LeCun et al., 1989). The 1990s saw the exploration of neural networks in closed-loop control systems. Narendra and Parthasarathy began to investigate the application of neural networks to dynamical systems (Narendra and Parthasarathy, 1990). Lewis and his team delved into neural network control of nonlinear systems, setting a precedent for further exploration in this field (Lewis et al., 1999).

The 2000s heralded the age of deep learning, with Hinton and Salakhutdinov's introduction of deep belief networks in 2006 (Hinton and Salakhutdinov, 2006). The watershed moment came in 2012 when Krizhevsky, Sutskever, and Hinton demonstrated the efficacy of deep CNNs in the ImageNet competition (Krizhevsky et al., 2012). This inspired further innovations, including sequence-to-sequence learning with recurrent neural networks in 2014 (Sutskever et al., 2014) and the development of residual networks (ResNets) in 2015 (He et al., 2016a). Numerous other neural network architectures, such as Long Short-Term Memory (LSTMs) networks, autoencoders, Generative Adversarial Networks (GANs), transformers, graph neural networks, reservoir networks, graph convolutional networks, and more advanced generative networks like diffusion models, have been introduced. The history of neural networks is rich and marked by periods of intense innovation, skepticism, and resurgence. From the foundational ideas of McCulloch and Pitts to the present era of deep learning and diffusion models, neural networks have evolved into a powerful and versatile tool, finding applications in diverse domains.

2.1.2 NEURAL NETWORK ARCHITECTURES

Artificial neural networks (ANNs) draw inspiration from biological information processing systems, specifically the nervous system and its fundamental unit, the neuron. Within these networks, signals are transmitted as potential differences between the interior and exterior of cells. In a neuronal cell, where dendrites carry signals from other neurons into the soma (cell body), potentially multiplying each incoming signal by a transfer weighting coefficient. The soma integrates these signals, accumulating them at the axon hillock. When the combined signal surpasses a specific cell threshold, it triggers an action potential that travels through the axon. Nonlinearities within the cell cause the composite action potential to be a nonlinear function of the incoming signal combination. The axon forms connections, or synapses, with the dendrites of subsequent neurons. Synapses operate by releasing neurotransmitter chemicals across intercellular gaps, and they can either be excitatory, promoting the firing of the next neuron, or inhibitory, hindering the firing of the next neuron.

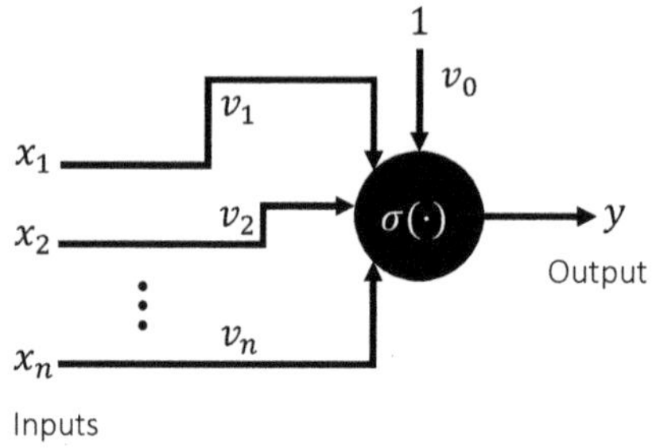

Figure 2.1 Computational model of a single neuron inspired by the anatomy of a biological neuron.

2.1.2.1 Mathematical Model of a Neuron

A mathematical model of the neuron is depicted in Figure 2.1, which shows the dendrite weights v_j, the firing threshold v_0 (also called the "bias"), and the nonlinear function $\sigma(\cdot)$. The cell inputs are the n signals at the time instant k, i.e., $x_1(k), x_2(k), x_3(k), \dots, x_n(k)$ and the output is the scalar $y(k)$, which can be expressed as the summation of weighted input signals including the bias as

$$y(k) = \sigma\left(\sum_{j=1}^{n} v_j x_j(k) + v_0\right). \tag{2.1}$$

Positive weights v_j correspond to excitatory synapses and negative weights to inhibitory synapses. This network was called the *perceptron* by Rosenblatt in 1959 (Haykin, 1994).

In continuous time the output can be expressed as a function of time $y(t)$ and written as

$$y(t) = \sigma\left(\sum_{j=1}^{n} v_j x_j(t) + v_0\right). \tag{2.2}$$

The nonlinear function is known as the *activation function*. The activation functions are selected specific to the applications though some common choices include sigmoid, radial basis, tangent hyperbolic tangent, and rectified linear functions. The activation function introduces nonlinearities to the neuron and often used to generate outputs between $[0,1]$, giving a probabilistic interpretation to the NN. Sigmoid functions are a general class of monotonically nondecreasing functions taking on bounded values between $-\infty$ and $+\infty$. As the threshold or bias v_0 changes, the activation functions shift left or right. For many NN training algorithms (including backpropagation), the derivative of $\sigma(\cdot)$ is needed to make the activation function selected differentiable.

The expression for the neuron output $y(k)$ at the time instant k (or $y(t)$ in the case of continuous-time) can be streamlined by defining the column vector of NN weights $\bar{v}(k) \in \mathbb{R}^n$ as

$$\bar{x}(k) = \begin{bmatrix} x_1 & x_2 & \cdots & x_n \end{bmatrix}^{\mathrm{T}}, \quad \bar{v}(t) = \begin{bmatrix} v_1 & v_2 & \cdots & v_n \end{bmatrix}^{\mathrm{T}} \tag{2.3}$$

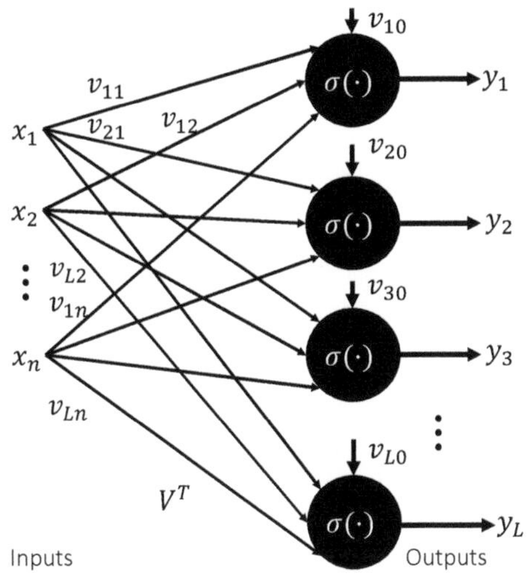

Figure 2.2 One-layer neural network.

Then, it is possible to write in matrix notation

$$y = \sigma\left(\bar{v}^{\mathrm{T}}\bar{x}\right) + v_0 \tag{2.4}$$

Note that while defining the NN output equation y in (2.4), the arguments k for discrete time and t for continuous time are omitted. Defining the augmented input column vector $x \in \mathbb{R}^{n+1}$ as

$$\begin{aligned} x &= \begin{bmatrix} 1 & \bar{x}^{\mathrm{T}} \end{bmatrix}^{\mathrm{T}} = \begin{bmatrix} 1 & x_1 & x_2 & \cdots & x_n \end{bmatrix} \\ v &= \begin{bmatrix} v_0 & \bar{v}^{\mathrm{T}} \end{bmatrix}^{\mathrm{T}} = \begin{bmatrix} v_0 & v_1 & v_2 & \cdots & v_n \end{bmatrix}^{\mathrm{T}} \end{aligned} \tag{2.5}$$

one may write

$$y = \sigma\left(v^{\mathrm{T}}x\right). \tag{2.6}$$

Though the input vector $\bar{x} \in \mathbb{R}^n$ and the weight vector $\bar{v} \in \mathbb{R}^n$ have been augmented by 1 and v_0, respectively, to include the threshold, we may at times loosely say that x and v are elements of $\mathbb{R}^n$. The neuron output expression vector y is referred to as the cell recall mechanism. They describe how the output is reconstructed from the input signals and the values of the cell parameters.

2.1.2.2 Single-layer Neural Network with Vector Output

Figure 2.2 shows an NN consisting of L cells, all fed by the same input signals x_j, $j = 1,\ldots,n$, and producing one output y per neuron. We call this a one-layer NN. The recall equation for this network is given by

$$y_l = \sigma\left(\sum_{j=1}^{n} v_{lj}x_j + v_{l0}\right) \quad l = 1,2,\ldots,L. \tag{2.7}$$

It is convenient to write the weights and the thresholds in matrix and vector forms, respectively. By defining the matrix of weights and the vector of thresholds as

$$\bar{V}^{\mathrm{T}} \equiv \begin{bmatrix} v_{11} & v_{12} & \cdots & v_{1n} \\ v_{21} & v_{22} & \cdots & v_{2n} \\ \vdots & \vdots & & \vdots \\ v_{L1} & v_{L2} & \cdots & v_{Ln} \end{bmatrix} \quad b_v = \begin{bmatrix} v_{10} \\ v_{20} \\ \vdots \\ v_{L0} \end{bmatrix}. \tag{2.8}$$

One may write the output vector $y = \begin{bmatrix} y_0 & y_1 & y_2 & \cdots & y_L \end{bmatrix}^{\mathrm{T}}$ as

$$y = \bar{\sigma}\left(\bar{V}^{\mathrm{T}}\bar{x} + b_v\right). \tag{2.9}$$

The vector activation function is defined for a vector $w \equiv [w_1 w_2 \cdots w_L]^{\mathrm{T}}$ as

$$\bar{\sigma}(w) \equiv [\bar{\sigma}(w_1)\bar{\sigma}(w_2)\cdots\bar{\sigma}(w_L)]^{\mathrm{T}}. \tag{2.10}$$

A further refinement may be achieved by inserting the threshold vector as the first column of the augmented matrix of weights as

$$V^{\mathrm{T}} \equiv \begin{bmatrix} v_{10} & v_{11} & \cdots & v_{1n} \\ v_{20} & v_{21} & \cdots & v_{2n} \\ \vdots & \vdots & & \vdots \\ v_{L0} & v_{L1} & \cdots & v_{Ln} \end{bmatrix}. \tag{2.11}$$

Then, the NN outputs may be expressed in terms of the augmented input vector x as

$$y = \bar{\sigma}\left(V^{\mathrm{T}}x\right). \tag{2.12}$$

2.1.2.3 Multi-layer Perceptron (MLP)

A two-layer ANN consists of two neuron layers (or computational layers), where the first layer containing L neurons, known as the *hidden layer*, feeds into a second layer made up of m neurons, known as the *output layer* (see Figure 2.3). This architecture is part of a category known as multilayer perceptrons, distinguished by their enhanced computational abilities compared to the one-layer NN. The one-layer NN is capable of performing basic digital operations like AND, OR, and COMPLEMENT but fell out of favor in the research community after it was proven incapable of handling the EXCLUSIVE OR (X-OR) operation, a fundamental logic operation in digital logic design (Minsky and Papert, 1969). This limitation led to a temporary halt in NN research. Later, it was found that the two-layer NN could effectively implement the X-OR operation, rejuvenating interest in NNs during the early 1980s (Rumelhart et al., 1986). Notably, solutions to the X-OR problem utilizing sigmoid activation functions were proposed by several scholars such as Hush and Horne (1993). The diagnosis of the X-OR problem and the proposed solution approach highlighted the concept of *separability*, a crucial characteristic that influences a model's ability to categorize inputs into distinct clusters or groups.

The output of the two-layer NN is given by the recall equation

$$y_i = \sigma\left(\sum_{l=1}^{L} w_{il}\sigma\left(\sum_{j=1}^{n} v_{lj}x_j + v_{l0}\right) + w_{i0}\right) \quad i = 1, 2, \ldots, m. \tag{2.13}$$

Defining the hidden-layer outputs z_l allows one to write

$$\begin{aligned} z_l &= \sigma\left(\sum_{j=1}^{n} v_{lj}x_j + v_{l0}\right) \quad l = 1, 2, \ldots, L, \\ y_i &= \sigma\left(\sum_{l=1}^{L} w_{il}z_l + w_{i0}\right) \quad i = 1, 2, \ldots, m. \end{aligned} \tag{2.14}$$

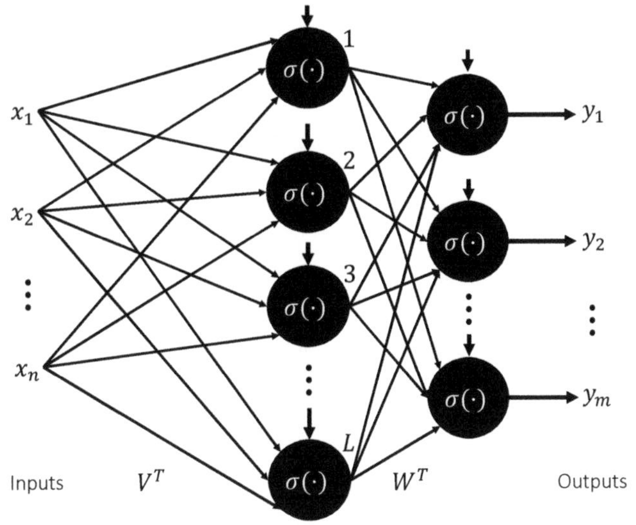

Figure 2.3 Two-layer neural network.

Defining first-layer weight matrices $\bar{V}$ and V as in the previous subsection, and second-layer weight matrices as

$$\bar{W}^{\mathrm{T}} \equiv \begin{bmatrix} w_{11} & w_{12} & \cdots & w_{1L} \\ w_{21} & w_{22} & \cdots & w_{2L} \\ \vdots & \vdots & & \vdots \\ w_{m1} & w_{m2} & \cdots & w_{mL} \end{bmatrix} \quad b_w = \begin{bmatrix} w_{10} \\ w_{20} \\ \vdots \\ w_{m0} \end{bmatrix},$$
$$W^{\mathrm{T}} \equiv \begin{bmatrix} w_{10} & w_{11} & w_{12} & \cdots & w_{1L} \\ w_{20} & w_{21} & w_{22} & \cdots & w_{2L} \\ & \vdots & \vdots & & \vdots \\ w_{m0} & w_{m1} & w_{m2} & \cdots & w_{mL} \end{bmatrix}, \tag{2.15}$$

one may write the NN output as,

$$y = \bar{\sigma}\left(\bar{W}^{\mathrm{T}}\bar{\sigma}\left(\bar{V}^{\mathrm{T}}\bar{x} + b_v\right) + b_w\right), \tag{2.16}$$

or, in streamlined form as

$$y = \sigma\left(W^{\mathrm{T}}\sigma\left(V^{\mathrm{T}}x\right)\right). \tag{2.17}$$

In these equations, the notation $\bar{\sigma}$ means the vector is defined in accordance with (2.10). In (2.17), it is necessary to use the augmented vector.

$$\sigma(w) = \begin{bmatrix}1 & \bar{\sigma}(w)^T\end{bmatrix}^T = \begin{bmatrix}1 & \sigma(w_1) & \cdots & \sigma(w_L)\end{bmatrix}^T \tag{2.18}$$

where a "1" is placed as the first entry to allow the incorporation of the thresholds w_{i0} as the first column of W^{T}. In terms of the hidden-layer output vector $z \in \mathbb{R}^L$ one may write

$$\begin{aligned} \bar{z} &= \sigma\left(V^{\mathrm{T}}x\right) \\ y &= \sigma\left(W^{\mathrm{T}}z\right), \end{aligned} \tag{2.19}$$

where $z \equiv \begin{bmatrix}1 & \bar{z}^{\mathrm{T}}\end{bmatrix}^{\mathrm{T}}$.

In the remainder of this book, we shall not show the overbar on vectors. The reader can determine by the context whether the leading "1" is required. We shall generally be concerned in later chapters with two-layer NN with linear activation functions in the output layer so that

$$y = W^{\mathrm{T}} \sigma\left(V^{\mathrm{T}} x\right). \tag{2.20}$$

2.1.2.4 Linear-in-the Parameter NN

If the first-layer weights and the thresholds V in (2.20) are predetermined by some apriori method, then only the second-layer weights and thresholds W are considered to define the NN, so that the NN has only one layer of weights. One may then define the fixed function $\phi(x) = \sigma\left(V^{\mathrm{T}} x\right)$ so that such a one-layer NN has the recall equation

$$y = W^{\mathrm{T}} \phi(x), \tag{2.21}$$

where $x \in \mathbb{R}^n$ (recall that technically x is augmented by " 1 "), $y \in \mathbb{R}^m, \phi(\cdot) : \mathbb{R} \rightarrow \mathbb{R}^L$, and L is the number of hidden-layer neurons. This NN is linear in the NN parameters W. It is easier to train such NN as they often lead to linear regression. This one-layer having only output-layer weights W should be contrasted with the one-layer NN discussed in (2.12), which consists of only input-layer weights V.

More generality is gained if $\sigma(\cdot)$ is not diagonal, for example, as defined in (2.10), but $\phi(\cdot)$ is allowed to be a general function from $\mathbb{R}^n$ to $\mathbb{R}^L$. This is called a functional link neural net (FLNN) (Sadegh, 1993). We often use $\sigma(\cdot)$ in place of $\phi(\cdot)$, with the understanding that, for linear-in-the-parameter (LIP) nets, this activation function vector is not diagonal but is a general function from $\mathbb{R}^n$ to $\mathbb{R}^L$. Some special FLNNs are now discussed. It is important to mention that in a class of neural networks, called the random vector functional link (RVFL) networks (Lewis et al., 1998), the input-to-hidden-layer weights will be selected randomly and held fixed, whereas the hidden-to-output-layer weights will be tuned. This will minimize the computational complexity associated with using NN in feedback control applications while ensuring that one can use NN in control.

Gaussian or Radial Basis Function Networks. The selection of a suitable set of activation functions is considerably simplified in various sorts of structured nonlinear networks, including radial basis functions (RBFs) and cerebellar model articulation controllers (CMAC). We shall see here that the key to the design of such structured nonlinear networks lies in a more general set of NN thresholds than allowed in the standard equation (2.13), and in the Gaussian or RBF (Sanner and Slotine, 1991), given when x is a scalar

$$\sigma(x) = \mathrm{e}^{-(x-\mu)^2/2p}, \tag{2.22}$$

where μ is the mean and p the variance. RBF NN can be written as (2.21), but have an advantage over the usual sigmoid NN in that the n-dimensional Gaussian function is well understood from probability theory, Kalman filtering, and elsewhere, making the n-dimensional RBF easier to conceptualize.

The j-th activation function can be written as

$$\sigma_j(x) = \mathrm{e}^{-1/2\left[\left(x-\mu_j\right)^{\mathrm{T}} P_j^{-1}\left(x-\mu_j\right)\right]} \tag{2.23}$$

with $x, \mu_j \in \mathbb{R}^n$. Define the vector of activation functions as $\sigma_j(x) \equiv P_j = \operatorname{diag}\left\{p_{jk}\right\}$, then (1.24) becomes separable and may be decomposed into components as

$$\sigma_j(x) = \mathrm{e}^{-1/2 \Sigma_{k=1}^{n} -\left(x_k-\mu_{jk}\right)^2/P_{jk}} = \prod_{k=1}^{n} \mathrm{e}^{-1/2\left[\left(x_k-\mu_{jk}\right)^2 P_{jk}\right]}, \tag{2.24}$$

where x_j, μ_{jk} are the k-th components of x, μ_j. Thus, the n-dimensional activation functions are the product of n scalar functions. Note that this equation is of the form of the activation functions in (2.13), but with more general thresholds, as a threshold is required for each different component of x at each hidden-layer neuron j; that is, the threshold at each hidden-layer neuron in Figure 2.3 is a vector. The variances p_{jk} are typically identically selected and the offsets μ_{jk} are usually selected with different values while designing the RBF NN and they are all left fixed; only the output-layer weights W^{T} are generally updated during training. Therefore, the RBF NN is a special sort of FLNN (1.22), where $\phi(x) = \sigma(x)$.

2.1.2.5 Dynamic NN

The NNs that have been discussed so far contain no time-delay elements or integrators. Such NNs are called *static* or *non-dynamic* networks as they do not have any memory. Further, the networks that we have seen so far have connections that are unidirectional, i.e., they have signals going from input to output via hidden layers and do not have connections that create a feedback path or loop for signals to flow backwards toward the input. There are many different dynamic NN, or recurrent NN, where some signals in the NN are either integrated or delayed and fed back into the network.

Hopfield Network. One well-known instance of dynamic NN is the Hopfield net, as depicted in Figure 2.4. This specific two-layer NN design has a feedback loop, where the output, represented by y_i, is looped back into the hidden layer's neurons (Haykin, 1994). Its first-layer weights v_{ii} are characterized as the identity elemants, while the second-layer weight matrix composed of w_{ij} assumes a square form. The activation function employed in the output layer is linear. The hidden layer of the Hopfield net is notable for its enhanced functionalities, including memory capabilities. These neurons, capable of internal signal processing, are often referred to as neuronal processing elements (NPEs) (Simpson, 1992).

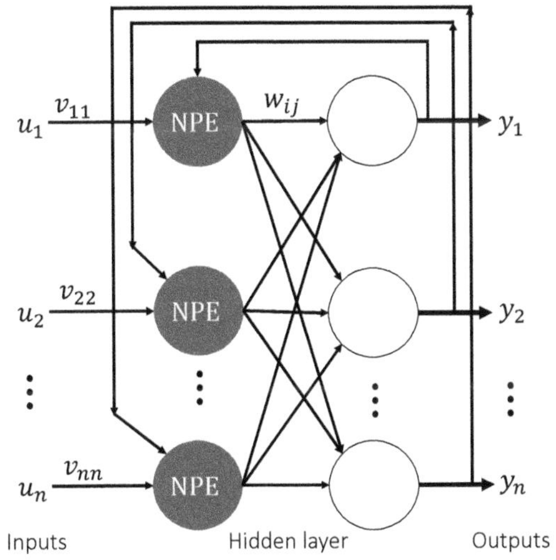

Figure 2.4 Hopfield neural network.

In the continuous-time case, the internal dynamics of each hidden-layer NPE contains an integrator $1/s$ and a time constant τ_i in addition to the usual nonlinear activation function $\sigma(\cdot)$. The internal state of the NPE is described by the signal $x_i(t)$. The ordinary differential equation describing the continuous-time Hopfield net is given as

$$\tau_i \dot{x}_i(t) = -x_i(t) + \sum_{j=1}^{n} w_{ij}\sigma_j(x_j(t)) + u_i(t) \tag{2.25}$$

with the output equation

$$y_i = \sum_{j=1}^{n} w_{ij}\sigma_j(x_j(t)). \tag{2.26}$$

This is a dynamical system of special form that contains the weights w_{ij} as adjustable parameters and positive time constants τ_i. The activation function has a subscript to allow, for instance, for scaling terms g_j as in $\sigma_j(x_j) \equiv \sigma(g_j x_j)$, which can significantly improve the performance of the Hopfield net. In the traditional Hopfield net the threshold offsets u_i are constant bias terms. It can be seen that (2.25) has the form of a state equation in control system theory, where the internal state is labeled as $x(t)$. It is for this reason that we have named the offsets as u_i. The biases play the role of the control input term, which is labeled as $u(t)$. In traditional Hopfield NN, the term "input pattern" refers to the initial state components $x_i(0)$. In the discrete-time case, the internal dynamics of each hidden-layer NPE contains a time delay instead of an integrator. The NN is now described by the difference equation

$$x_i(k+1) = p_i x_i(k) + \sum_{j=1}^{n} w_{ij}\sigma_j(x_j(k)) + u_i(k) \tag{2.27}$$

with $|p_i| < 1$. This is a discrete-time dynamical system with time index k.

Defining the NN weight matrix W^{T}, vectors $x \equiv [x_1\ x_2\ x_3\ \cdots\ x_n]^{\mathrm{T}}$ and $u \equiv \begin{bmatrix} u_1 & u_2 & u_3 \cdots u_n \end{bmatrix}^{\mathrm{T}}$, and the matrices $\Gamma \equiv \mathrm{diag}\left\{\frac{1}{\tau_1}\frac{1}{\tau_2}\cdots\frac{1}{\tau_n}\right\}^{\mathrm{T}}$, one may write the continuous-time Hopfield network dynamics as

$$\dot{x}(t) = -\Gamma x(t) + \Gamma W^{\mathrm{T}}\sigma(x(t)) + \Gamma u(t). \tag{2.28}$$

Generalized Recurrent NN. A generalized dynamical system is shown in Figure 2.5. In this figure, $H(z) = C(zI - A)^{-1}B$ represents the transfer function of linear dynamical system or plant given by

$$\begin{aligned} x(k+1) &= Ax(k) + Bu(k) \\ y(k) &= Cx(k) \end{aligned} \tag{2.29}$$

with internal state $x(k) \in \mathbb{R}^n$, control input $u(k)$, and output $y(k)$. An additional feedback of the output via a two-layer net described by (2.16) and (2.17) can be augmented to (2.29). This dynamic NN is described by the equation

$$x(k+1) = Ax(k) + B\left[\sigma\left(W^{\mathrm{T}}\sigma\left(V^{\mathrm{T}}(Cx(k) + u_1(k))\right)\right)\right] + Bu_2(k), \tag{2.30}$$

where $u_2(k) = u(k)$ and $u_1(k)$ models an input fed to the network in its feedback path. From examination of (2.27) it is plain to see that the Hopfield net is a special case of this equation, which is also true of many other dynamical NN in the literature. A analogous version for the continuous-time case can also be defined as

$$\dot{x}(t) = Ax(t) + B[\sigma(W^T\sigma(V^T(Cx(t) + u_1(t)))] + Bu_2(t). \tag{2.31}$$

In these two cases, the properties of the matrix A are different, and often, chosen to stabilize the respective dynamical systems.

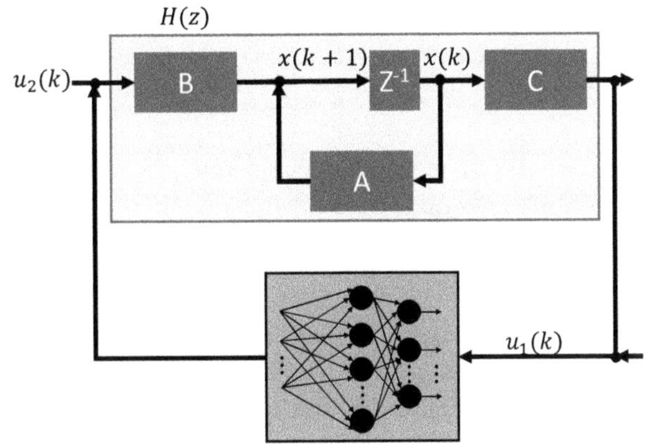

Figure 2.5 Generalized discrete-time dynamical NN.

2.1.3 FUNCTION APPROXIMATION PROPERTY OF NN

The potential of NN in closed-loop control applications is rooted in their universal function approximation capability. This fundamental attribute pertains specifically to NNs with at least two layers. Various researchers, such as Cybenko (1989), Hornik et al. (1989), and Park and Sandberg (1991), have extensively analyzed the approximation functionalities of NNs.

The universal approximation theorem posits that a two-layer NN can approximate any smooth function $f(x)$ to any desired degree of accuracy within a compact set, given the appropriate weights. This principle has been proven to be true for different types of activation functions, including sigmoid and hardlimit. More formally, let $f(x) : \mathbb{R}^n \to \mathbb{R}^m$ be a smooth function, and given a compact set $S \in \mathbb{R}^n$ along with a positive number ε_N, there exists a two-layer NN such that it approximates the function such

$$f(x) = W^{\mathrm{T}}\sigma\left(V^{\mathrm{T}}x\right) + \varepsilon(x) \tag{2.32}$$

with $\|\varepsilon(x)\| = \varepsilon_N$ for all $x \in S$, for some sufficiently large number (L) of hidden layer neurons. The value ε (generally a function of x) is called the NN *function approximation error* or the *reconstruction error*, and it decreases as the hidden layer size L increases. We say that, on the compact set S, as S becomes larger, the required L generally increases correspondingly. Approximation results have also been shown for smooth functions with a finite number of discontinuities. Even though the results says that there exists an NN that approximates $f(x)$, it should be noted that it does not show how to determine the required weights. It is in fact not an easy task to determine the weights so that an NN does indeed approximate a given function $f(x)$ closely enough. In the next section we shall show how to accomplish this using backpropagation tuning.

2.1.3.1 Functional Link Neural Networks (FLNNs)

In Section 2.1.2.4, a special class of one-layer of NN known as Functional-Link NN (FLNN) written as

$$y = W^{\mathrm{T}}\phi(x) \tag{2.33}$$

with NN output weights W (including the thresholds) and a general function $\phi(\cdot)$ from $\mathbb{R}^n$ to $\mathbb{R}^L$ was discussed. FLNN maintain the ability to approximate functions as long as their activation functions, denoted by $\phi(\cdot)$, adhere to two essential requirements within a compact, simply connected set S of $\mathbb{R}^n$ (Sadegh, 1993):

1. A constant function on set S can be described by equation (2.33) for a finite number L of hidden-layer functions.
2. The functional range of equation (2.33) is dense within the continuous function space from S to $\mathbb{R}^m$ for a countable L.

In other words, if $\phi(\cdot)$ forms a basis set, then a smooth function $f(x) : \mathbb{R}^n \to \mathbb{R}^m$ can be approximated within a compact set S of $\mathbb{R}^n$, represented as

$$f(x) = W^T \phi(x) + \varepsilon(x) \tag{2.34}$$

with some optimal weights and thresholds W and a specific number of hidden-layer neurons L. Indeed, for any chosen positive number ε_N, a feedforward NN can be constructed to ensure $\|\varepsilon(x)\| < \varepsilon_N$ for all x in S. Barron (1993) established an essential restriction on all LIP approximators, highlighting that the error ε possesses a fundamental lower limit, constrained by expressions on the magnitude of $1/L^{2/n}$. Consequently, the effectiveness of enlarging the number of NN inputs, denoted by n, to boost the precision of the approximation becomes diminished as L increases. This limitation, interestingly, is not applicable to multilayer nonlinear-in-the-parameters networks, where the constraints of lower bounds do not impose the same restrictions.

2.1.3.2 Multilayer NN

Presently, there exists a variety of NN architectures that are adept at approximating unknown nonlinear functions. Cybenko (1989) demonstrated that a M dimensional continuous function $f(x) \in C(S)$, lying within a compact subset S of $\mathbb{R}^N$, can be closely represented by an n-layer feedforward NN. This can be visualized in Figure 2.6, where the approximation is given by the expression

$$y = f(x) = W_n^{\mathrm{T}} \phi\left[W_{n-1}^{\mathrm{T}} \phi(\cdots \phi(x)] + \varepsilon(x)\right., \tag{2.35}$$

where $\varepsilon(x)$ represents the approximation error, $y = (y_1, y_2, \ldots, y_M)^T$, and ϕ denotes the activation function used within the layers of the network, $W_n, W_{n-1}, \ldots, W_2, W_1$ are target weights of the hidden-to-output- and input-to-hidden-layers, respectively, and x is the input vector. The target weights are the weights that are needed to faithfully represent the function $f(x)$ within a desired accuracy in the domain of approximation. The actual NN output (i.e., untrained NN output) is defined as

$$\hat{f}(x) = \hat{W}_n^{\mathrm{T}} \hat{\phi}_n, \tag{2.36}$$

where $\hat{W}_n$ is the actual output-layer weight matrix. For simplicity, $\phi\left(\hat{W}_{n-1}^{\mathrm{T}} \phi_{n-1}(\cdot)\right)$ is denoted as $\hat{\phi}_n$. For an NN architecture with fixed number of layers and fixed number of neurons, if there exists constant ideal weights $W_n, W_{n-1}, \ldots, W_2, W_1$ such that $\varepsilon(x) = 0$ for all $x \in S$, then $f(x)$ is said to be in the functional range of the NN.

2.1.3.3 Random Vector Functional-Link Networks

The challenge of choosing activation functions in LIP NNs to serve as a basis can be tackled, as specified earlier, by randomizing the selection of the matrix V as outlined in equation (2.21). Igelnik and Pao (1995) demonstrated that for RVFL nets, the resultant function $\phi(x) = \sigma\left(V^{\mathrm{T}} x\right)$ indeed functions as a *stochastic basis*. Consequently, the RVFL network is endowed with the universal approximation property, showcasing its ability to mimic any given continuous function over a particular domain. Within this methodology, the function $\sigma(\cdot)$ may be represented by conventional sigmoid functions. Specifically, the technique involves the random selection of activation function scaling parameters v_{lj} and shift parameters v_{l0} within the expression $\sigma\left(\sum_j v_{lj} x_j + v_{l0}\right)$. As a result,

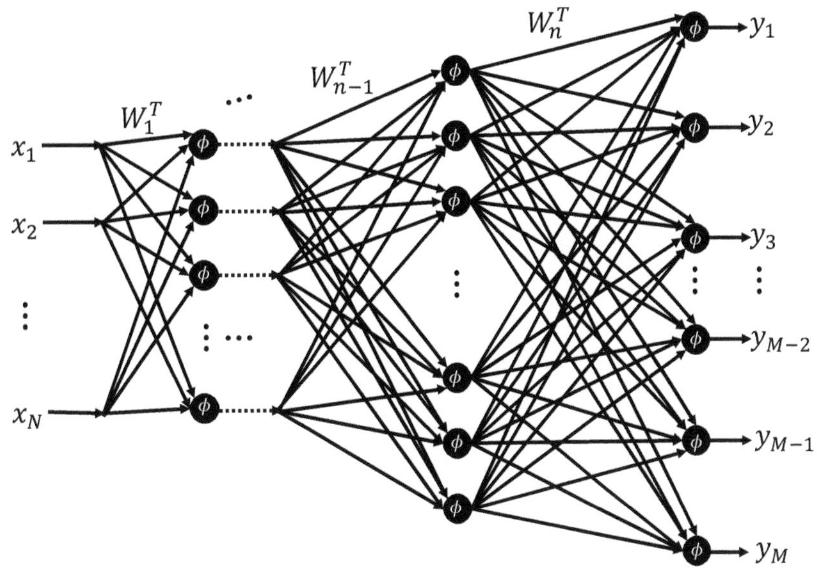

Figure 2.6 A multilayer neural network.

a family of L distinct activation functions emerges, each characterized by unique scaling and shifting parameters. This property was elucidated by Kim (1996), who provided insights into the underlying mechanics of such activation functions.

2.1.3.4 Event-based Approximation Properties of NNs

When the NNs are employed in a feedback control system, they are often used in the controllers to learn the system dynamics, "value function" (introduced later in this chapter), and/or the control inputs. These functions are typically state-dependent functions and their domain is specified by the state space of the dynamical system. Hence, the data required to learn these functions are dependent on the sampling and feedback availabililty, especially in the context of online learning and control. With intermittent event-based transmission of the system state vector x, introduced in Chapter 1, the universal NN approximation property can be extended to achieve a desired level of accuracy by properly designing a trigger condition. The trigger condition will generate required number of events for the availability of system state vector for approximation. The theorem introduced next extends the approximation property of NN for event-based sampling.

Theorem 2.1. *(Sahoo, 2015) Let $f(x) : S \to \mathbb{R}^n$, be smooth and uniformly continuous function in a compact set for all $x \in S \subset \mathbb{R}^n$. Then, there exists a single layer NN with sufficient number of neurons such that the function $f(x)$ can be approximated with constant weights and event-driven activation function, such that*

$$f(x) = W^T \varphi(\hat{x}) + \varepsilon_e(\hat{x}, e_s), \tag{2.37}$$

where $W \in \mathbb{R}^{l \times n}$ is the target NN weight matrix with l being the number of hidden-layer neurons, $\varphi(\hat{x})$ is the bounded event-driven activation function, and $\varepsilon_e(\hat{x}, e_s)$ is the event-driven NN reconstruction error with $\hat{x}$ representing the last event-based sampled state held at the ZOH.

Remark 2.1. *The event-based reconstruction error $\varepsilon_e(\hat{x}, e_s)$ is a function of the traditional reconstruction error $\varepsilon(\cdot)$ and event-trigger error e_s due to aperiodic feedback. A event-based reconstruction error $\varepsilon_e(\hat{x}, e_s)$ can be made small by increasing the frequency of event-based samples in* *addition to increasing the hidden layer neurons. This requires a suitable event-trigger condition for obtaining both approximation accuracy and a reduction in computation. A small event-based reconstruction error means a higher number of events, which results in more computations and transmissions. Hence, a trade-off exists between reconstruction error and transmission when NN are used in an event-based control scheme as function approximators.*

2.1.4 NEURAL NETWORK TRAINING METHODS

In this section, we shall review the gradient-based weight tuning methods for NN. The gradient descent algorithm is a one of the widely-used optimization technique to solve nonlinear optimization problems. In the context of machine learning, it is often used to tune parameters of a model using data in a supervised, unsupervised, or reinforcement learning paradigm. It operates by iteratively adjusting the model's parameters to minimize a given loss or cost or objective function. The process begins with an initial guess for the model's parameters and then proceeds to calculate the gradient of the loss function with respect to the model parameters, which points in the direction of the steepest increase in the loss. The algorithm updates the parameters in the opposite direction of the gradient, with the learning rate controlling the step size. This process repeats until a termination criterion is met, such as a predefined number of iterations or a desired level of loss. Geometrically, gradient descent can be envisioned as traversing a multi-dimensional loss surface, where each dimension represents a model parameter, in search of the lowest point on the loss surface, which corresponds to the optimal parameters for minimizing the loss. As the algorithm iteratively descends along the loss surface, the steps become smaller, eventually converging to the minimum as the gradient approaches zero. Gradient-based algorithm in the context of neural network training leads to the *backpropogation* algorithm that uses chain rule for computing the required gradients.

This part of the section is a brief summary of the material from Lewis et al. (1998). Several variations to gradient-based optimization algorithms are available. These include variations in the choice of learning rate, batch size (i.e., the number of data samples used during each step of the algorithm), and the stopping criterion. For more information, see Boyd and Vandenberghe (2004); Lewis et al. (1998); LeCun et al. (2002).

2.1.4.1 Gradient Descent Tuning in Continuous Time

In continuous time, the gradient descent algorithm for a single-layer neural network can be expressed as

$$\dot{V}(t) = -\eta \frac{\partial E(t)}{\partial V(t)}, \tag{2.38}$$

where $E(t)$ denotes the defined cost function at time t and $\eta > 0$ is the *learning rate* or *step-size*. Given an input-output pair (X,Y) targeted by the NN, the output error can be formulated as

$$e(t) = Y - y(t) = Y - \sigma\left(V^T(t)X\right). \tag{2.39}$$

Using this error, a cost function can be formulated, for example, as the least-squares output-error cost given by

$$E(t) = \frac{1}{2}e^T(t)e(t) = \frac{1}{2}\operatorname{tr}\left\{e(t)e^T(t)\right\}. \tag{2.40}$$

The trace of a square matrix $\operatorname{tr}\{\cdot\}$ is defined as the sum of the diagonal elements. Disregarding the derivative of $\sigma(\cdot)$ (or equivalently, assuming linear activation functions), the continuous-time perceptron training rule emerges as

$$\dot{V}(t) = \eta X e^T(t). \tag{2.41}$$

Continuous time batch updating techniques are recommended in scenarios involving multiple input/output patterns.

2.1.4.2 Gradient Descent Tuning in Discrete Time

Given the input-output pair (X,Y) that the NN should associate, define the NN output error vector as

$$e(k) = Y - y(k) = Y - \sigma\left(V^{\mathrm{T}}(k)X\right) \tag{2.42}$$

and the least-squares output-error cost as

$$E(k) = \frac{1}{2}e^{\mathrm{T}}(k)e(k) - \frac{1}{2}\operatorname{tr}\left\{e(k)e^{\mathrm{T}}(k)\right\} \tag{2.43}$$

In terms of matrices, the gradient descent algorithm is

$$V(k+1) = V(k) - \eta\frac{\partial E(k)}{\partial V(k)}. \tag{2.44}$$

Writing the cost function explicitly, we have

$$E(k) = \frac{1}{2}\operatorname{tr}\left\{\left(Y - \sigma\left(V^{\mathrm{T}}(k)X\right)\right)\left(Y - \sigma\left(V^{\mathrm{T}}(k)X\right)\right)^{\mathrm{T}}\right\}, \tag{2.45}$$

where $e(k)$ is the NN output error associated with input vector X using the weights $V(k)$ determined at iteration k. Assuming linear activation functions $\sigma(\cdot)$, one has

$$E(k) = \frac{1}{2}\operatorname{tr}\left\{\left(Y - V^{\mathrm{T}}(k)X\right)\left(Y - V^{\mathrm{T}}(k)X\right)^{\mathrm{T}}\right\}. \tag{2.46}$$

Then the gradient can be computed as

$$\frac{\partial E(k)}{\partial V(k)} = -Xe^{\mathrm{T}}(k), \tag{2.47}$$

So that the gradient descent tuning algorithm is written as

$$V(k+1) = V(k) + \eta Xe^{\mathrm{T}}(k), \tag{2.48}$$

which updates both the weights and the thresholds.

2.1.4.3 Backpropagation Training

Backpropagation training refers to a fundamental algorithm for training ANNs. It is used to optimize the parameters of the NN, such as weights and biases, to minimize a cost function. It is a gradient-based optimization algorithm and uses chain rule to compute the gradient of the cost or loss function with respect to weights in the hidden layers. The algorithm works in a two-phase process. In the forward pass, the input data is fed through the network to make predictions. In the backward pass, the gradient of the loss function with respect to the network's parameters are computed using the chain rule, beginning from the output layer and moving backward through the hidden layers. This gradient represents the direction and magnitude of parameter adjustments needed to reduce the prediction error. The parameters are updated using gradient descent method. This process is iteratively repeated for numerous training examples until the network's performance converges to a satisfactory level.

Backpropagation essentially distributes the error signals backward through the network, enabling it to learn and adapt its internal representations to make more accurate predictions.

Consider a two-layer NN as in (2.13). The forward recursion becomes

$$\begin{aligned} z &= \sigma\left(V^{\mathrm{T}} X\right) \\ y &= \sigma\left(W^{\mathrm{T}} z\right) \end{aligned} \tag{2.49}$$

and the backward recursion is

$$\begin{aligned} e &= Y - y \\ \delta^2 &= \operatorname{diag}\{y\}(1-\operatorname{diag}\{y\})e \\ \delta^1 &= \operatorname{diag}\{z\}(1-\operatorname{diag}\{z\})W\delta^2 \end{aligned} \tag{2.50}$$

Then the computation of the updates for the NN weights and thresholds for the two-layer NN can be obtained as

$$W = W + \eta z(\delta_i^2)^T, \tag{2.51}$$

$$V = V + \eta X(\delta_l^1)^T. \tag{2.52}$$

As with the gradient-descent algorithm, the NN weights and thresholds are typically initialized to small random (positive and negative) values. The backpropogation training is only guaranteed to find a local minimum, provided the step size or the learning rate parameter η is chosen appropriately. The backpropogation algorithm in continuous time can be derived similar to the discrete time algorithm presented in this section. For example, if we index the recursive relation as $W_{k+1} = W_k + \eta_k z(\delta_i^2)^T$, we may view this recursive equation as a first-order Euler approximation of the update rule represented in continuous time, i.e., the first-order approximation of the differential equation $\dot{W}(t) = \eta z(\delta_i^2)^T$. For details, see Lewis et al. (1998).

Up to this point, we have explored fundamental concepts related to ANNs and their training processes. Moving forward, we will delve into optimal control techniques, encompassing dynamic programming and reinforcement learning methods. The subsequent content in this chapter draws upon Lewis et al. (2012a,b); Bertsekas (2012) for its foundation.

2.2 OPTIMAL CONTROL AND DYNAMIC PROGRAMMING

Optimal control theory is a branch of mathematical optimization that deals with finding a control for a dynamical system over a period of time such that an objective function is optimized. It has numerous applications in science, engineering, economics, and more. The development of optimal control theory dates back to the 17th century. One of the first problems that led to the concept of optimal control was the brachistochrone problem posed by Johann Bernoulli in 1696 (Struik, 1986). In this problem, one must find the shape of the curve down which a bead sliding from rest and accelerated by gravity will slip (without friction) from one point to another in the least time. In the 18th century, optimal control took a significant step forward with the development of the calculus of variations by mathematicians like Euler and Lagrange (Kline, 1990). The calculus of variations (Liberzon, 2011; Boltyanskii et al., 1961; Weinstock, 1974) is a field of mathematical analysis that uses variations to find maxima and minima of functionals.

The modern development of optimal control theory started in the 1950s with the work of Lev Pontryagin (Pontryagin et al., 1962), Richard Bellman (Bellman, 1966), and Rudolf Kalman (Kalman, 1960a). Russian mathematician Lev Pontryagin and his students developed the maximum principle (referred to as *Pontryagin's maximum principle*) (Pontryagin et al., 1962), which is considered one of the cornerstones of optimal control theory. On the other hand, Richard Bellman introduced the *principle of optimality* and *dynamic programming* (Bellman, 1966), a method for

Table 2.1
Backpropogation Algorithm

Forward Recursion to Compute NN Output	$z_\ell = \sigma\left(\sum_{j=0}^{n} v_{\ell j} X_j\right); \quad \ell = 1,2,\ldots,L$
	$y_i = \sigma\left(\sum_{\ell=0}^{L} w_{i\ell} z_\ell\right); i = 1,2,\ldots,m$
with $x_0 = z_0 = 1$ and Y_i is the desired output at the output neuron i	
Backward Recursion for Backpropagated Errors	$e_i = Y_i - y_i; i = 1,2,\ldots,m$
	$\delta_i^2 = y_i(1-y_i)e_i; \quad i = 1,2,\ldots,m$
	$\delta_\ell^1 = z_\ell(1-z_\ell)\sum_{i=1}^{m} w_{i\ell}\delta_i^2; \quad \ell = 1,2,\ldots,L$
Computation of the NN Weight and Threshold Updates	$w_{i\ell} = w_{i\ell} + \eta z_\ell \delta_i^2; i = 1,2,\ldots,m; \quad \ell = 0,1,\ldots,L$
	$v_{\ell j} = v_{\ell j} + \eta X_j \delta_\ell^1; \quad \ell = 1,2,\ldots,L; j = 0,1,\ldots,n$

solving complex problems by breaking them down into simpler subproblems. This approach forms the basis for many algorithms in optimal control and search, including those used to control discrete event systems. In the early 1960s, Rudolf Kalman introduced the Kalman filter, which is an optimal recursive Bayesian filter for estimating the internal state of a linear dynamic system from a series of noisy measurements (Kalman, 1960b). In the latter half of the 20th century, optimal control theory was further developed and refined and saw an increasing range of applications from economics (optimal growth theory, optimal saving, etc.) (Lucas and Stokey, 1983; Ramsey, 1928), engineering (optimal control of industrial processes, etc.) (Kirk, 2004; Lewis et al., 2012b; Liberzon, 2011; Kumar and Varaiya, 1986) to computer science (optimal routing, resource allocation, etc.) (Bertsekas, 2012). Optimal control theory continues to be an area of active research with recent developments, including in stochastic control, robust control, and applications to complex systems. Despite its theoretical complexity, it is a fundamental tool for engineers, economists, and computer scientists alike.

A significant amount of research on optimal control using dynamic programming and approximate dynamic programming has been conducted in the discrete-time domain. Therefore, in this section, we shall start with the discrete-time case and then review the continuous-time case. For detailed treatments, see Bertsekas (2012); Lewis et al. (2012b,a).

2.2.1 DISCRETE-TIME OPTIMAL CONTROL

To formalize the concept of dynamic programming from a dynamical system perspective, let us consider a discrete-time dynamical system described by the equation

$$x_{k+1} = f(x_k, u_k), \tag{2.53}$$

where k is the discrete time step, $x_k \in \mathbb{R}^n$ is the state at time k, $u_k \in \mathbb{R}^m$ is the control input at time k, and $f : \mathbb{R}^n \times \mathbb{R}^m \to \mathbb{R}^n$ is a function describing the dynamics of the system. A special class of nonlinear dynamics can be expressed in the affine state space difference equation form, given by

$$x_{k+1} = f(x_k) + g(x_k)u_k. \tag{2.54}$$

The goal of the optimal control problem is to find a sequence of control inputs $u_0, u_1, \dots, u_{N-1}$ that minimizes the cost functional

$$J(x_0) = \Phi(x_N) + \sum_{k=0}^{N-1} r(x_k, u_k), \tag{2.55}$$

subject to the dynamics of the system (2.54), where $\Phi : \mathbb{R}^n \to \mathbb{R}$ is the terminal cost function, $r : \mathbb{R}^n \times \mathbb{R}^m \to \mathbb{R}$ is the stage cost function, and N is the horizon length (since N is finite, it is referred to as a *finite-horizon optimal control problem*). As a special case, by letting $N \to \infty$, the performance index can be rewritten as

$$J(x_0) = \sum_{k=0}^{\infty} r(x_k, u_k), \tag{2.56}$$

which leads to *infinite horizon optimal control problem*. The function $r(x_k, u_k)$ (in both finite and infinite horizon cases), often referred to as the *utility function*, serves as a metric to evaluate the one-step expense of control. It can be tailored to reflect various optimization objectives, such as minimizing fuel consumption, reducing energy usage, mitigating risk, and so forth. For example, one common representation of this function is the quadratic energy form given by

$$r(x_k, u_k) = x_k^T Q x_k + u_k^T R u_k. \tag{2.57}$$

In some cases, it might be expressed more generally as

$$r(x_k, u_k) = Q(x_k) + u_k^T R u_k. \tag{2.58}$$

It is necessary to ensure that $Q(x_k)$ and R are positive definite to ascertain that the cost function remains properly defined. The system is presumed to be stabilizable within a specified set $\Omega \in \mathbb{R}^n$. In other words, there exists a control policy

$$u_k = \mu(x_k), \tag{2.59}$$

ensuring that the closed-loop system defined by

$$x_{k+1} = f(x_k) + g(x_k)\mu(x_k) \tag{2.60}$$

exhibits asymptotic stability within Ω.

Remark 2.2. *A control strategy is referred to as admissible if it accomplishes stabilization and results in a determinate cost* $J(x_k)$.

We refer to the cost or value of any admissible strategy $u_k = \mu(x_k)$ as $V(x_k)$. Strategies yielding lower values are considered superior. It is worth highlighting that the value of any given admissible strategy can be ascertained by examining the infinite sum denoted as (2.56). Optimal control theory revolves around the determination of a control policy $\mu(x_k)$ that yields the minimum possible cost, leading to

$$V^*(x_k) = \min_{\mu(\cdot)} \left(\sum_{i=k}^{\infty} r(x_i, \mu(x_i)) \right), \tag{2.61}$$

referred to as the optimal cost or optimal value. The associated control policy that achieves this minimal cost is represented by:

$$u_k^* = \mu^*(x_k) = \arg\min_{\mu(\cdot)} \left(\sum_{i=k}^{\infty} r(x_i, \mu(x_i)) \right). \tag{2.62}$$

where $u_k^* = \mu^*(x_k)$ is the optimal control policy. In other words, the goal is to identify a function that maps states to control actions such that the sum of one-step costs is minimized across the system's evolution.

A planner with a short-sighted or myopic perspective would focus solely on reducing the immediate one-step cost or utility. Yet, the actual challenge extends beyond minimizing this immediate cost to include the minimization of the cumulative sum of all the one-step costs, commonly referred to as the *cost-to-go*. Addressing this challenge precisely for general nonlinear systems can often be very difficult, and in some cases, unattainable. To alleviate the complexities of this optimization problem, diverse methods and approaches have been devised. In the following sections, we will discuss two approaches: 1) dynamic programming and 2) adaptive/approximate dynamic programming.

2.2.2 DYNAMIC PROGRAMMING

Mathematician Richard Bellman developed the concept of dynamic programming in the 1950s (Bellman, 1966). He described the principle of optimality as follows: *An optimal policy has the property that whatever the initial state and initial decision are, the remaining decisions must constitute an optimal policy with regard to the state resulting from the first decision.* In simpler terms, the principle says that if a particular route is optimal, then every sub-route must also be optimal. For example, if the fastest route from city A to city C is via city B, then the fastest route from city B to city C must be a part of the fastest route from city A to city C. In the context of an optimal control problem with the cost-to-go defined as in (2.54), if $u^* = \{u_0^*, u_1^*, \ldots, u_{N-1}^*\}$ is an optimal control sequence for this problem with the associated states at each k given by $\{x_0, x_1^*, \ldots, x_{N-1}^*, x_N^*\}$, then for every k and for every x_k^*, the remaining part of the sequence $u^* = \{u_k^*, u_{k+1}^*, \ldots, u_{N-1}^*\}$ must be an optimal control sequence for the problem starting from state x_k^* at time k.

Additionally, the Bellman's principle of optimality naturally leads to a recursive formulation of the value or the cost-to-go function. If $V^*(x)$ is the optimal value function which gives us the minimum cost-to-go from state x, and u is the control input, then

$$V^*(x_k) = \min_{u_k} \{r(x_k, u_k) + V^*(x_{k+1})\}, \tag{2.63}$$

where $r(x_k, u_k)$ is the cost at time k, and x_{k+1} is the state at the next time step, which results from applying control u_k at state x_k. This equation says that the optimal cost-to-go from a state x_k under an optimal policy is the optimal one-step-cost at this state plus the cost-to-go from the next state under the optimal policy.

This principle leads to the definition of the value function $V(x_k)$ recursively, giving rise to the optimization problem for each time k. The value function can be computed recursively, *backward-in-time*, using dynamic programming with the relation

$$V(x_k) = \min_{u_k} \{r(x_k, u_k) + V(x_{k+1})\} \tag{2.64}$$

In particular, if we have the solution to the subproblems, often referred to as the *tail subproblems*, i.e., the optimal policy from x_{k+1}, x_{k+2}, ..., x_∞, then the optimal policy from x_k to x_∞ can be computed using (2.63). The dynamic programming algorithm uses the solutions to the tail subproblems, that is, the value functions $V(x_{k+N})$, to compute the solution of the subproblem from x_{k+N-1}. This solution is then used step by step, working backward in time, to address the current problem, which is to determine the value function $V(x_k)$ from x_k. Given the value functions, the optimal control sequence can be computed by choosing the control input at each time step that minimizes the right-hand side of the dynamic programming equation

$$u_k^* = \arg\min_{u_k} \{r(x_k, u_k) + V(x_{k+1})\}. \tag{2.65}$$

Example 2.1. *(Lewis et al., 2012b) Consider a linear discrete-time plant given by*

$$x_{k+1} = x_k + u_k. \tag{2.66}$$

The finite horizon performance index is defined as

$$J_0 = x_N^2 + \sum_{k=0}^{N-1} u_k^2, \tag{2.67}$$

where the final time index is $N = 2$. The feasible/admissible control inputs are

$$u_k \in \{-1, -0.5, 0, 0.5, 1\}, \tag{2.68}$$

and the feasible states are given by

$$x_k \in \{0, 0.5, 1.0, 1.5\}. \tag{2.69}$$

Find an admissible control sequence u_0^* and u_1^*, that minimizes J_0 while resulting in an admissible state trajectory x_0^*, x_1^*, and x_2^*.

Solution: We will use the principle of optimality in (2.63) to solve this problem. We will consider only the admissible control inputs in (2.68) that result in admissible states x_{k+1} in (2.69).

If $x_0 = 0$, the admissible u_0 are $u_0 = 0, 0.5$, and 1. To see this, for $x_0 = 1$ let us evaluate x_1 for each of these control inputs as follows

$$\begin{aligned} x_1 &= 0 + 0 = 0, \\ x_1 &= 0 + 0.5 = 0.5, \\ x_1 &= 0 + 1 = 1. \end{aligned}$$

Note that $u_0 = -1$ and $u_0 = -0.5$ are not admissible control since they results in states $x_1 = -1$ and $x_1 = -0.5$, respectively, which are not admissible.

If $x_0 = 0.5$, the admissible u_0 are $-0.5, 0$, and 0.5. To see this, for $x_0 = 0.5$ let's evaluate x_1 as follows

$$\begin{aligned} x_1 &= 0.5 - 0.5 = 0 \\ x_1 &= 0.5 + 0 = 0.5 \\ x_1 &= 0.5 + 0.5 = 1 \end{aligned}$$

The control input $u_0 = -1$ is not an admissible control input since it results in the state $x_1 = -0.5$ that is not feasible.

For $x_0 = 1$, the admissible u_0 are $-1, -0.5, 0$, and 0.5. For $x_0 = 1$, the feasible next state x_1 are computed for each feasible control input as follows

$$\begin{aligned} x_1 &= x_0 + u_0 = 1 - 1 = 0 \\ x_1 &= 1 - 0.5 = 0.5 \\ x_1 &= 1 + 0 = 1 \\ x_1 &= 1 + 0.5 = 1.5 \end{aligned}$$

The control input $u_0 = 1$ is not admissible.

Similarly, if $x_0 = 1.5$, the admissible u_0 are $-1, -0.5, 0$, and 0.5, and the possible next states x_1 are

$$\begin{aligned} x_1 &= x_0 + u_0 = 1.5 - 1 = 0.5 \\ x_1 &= 1.5 - 0.5 = 1 \\ x_1 &= 1.5 + 0 = 1.5 \end{aligned}$$

The control inputs $u_0 = 0.5, 1$ are not admissible.

Using the Bellman equation, an admissible cost can be expressed as

$$J_k = \frac{1}{2}u_k^2 + J_{k+1}^*. \tag{2.70}$$

Then, the optimal cost by the Bellman principle of optimality is given by

$$J_k^* = \min_{u_k}(J_k). \tag{2.71}$$

To compute the optimal policy u_k^* and J_k^* for each x_k using (2.71), we need to solve it backward from $k = N$.

Step 1: Given $N = 2$, the final cost

$$J_N^* = x_N^2 = x_2^2 \tag{2.72}$$

must be calculated for each admissible state with the value x_N. For the final states $x_2 = 0, 0.5, 1.0$, and 1.5, the terminal costs respectively are $J_2^*(x_2 = 0) = 0, J_2^*(x_2 = 0.5) = 0.25, J_2^*(x_2 = 1.0) = 1$, and $J_2^*(x_2 = 1.5) = 2.25$.

Step 2: One step backward, i.e., $k = 1$, for each possible state x_1 and for each admissible cost u_1, we will use (2.70) to compute the incurred cost as follows

$$J_1(x_1 = 1.5, u_1 = -1) = \frac{1}{2}u_1^2 + J_2^*(x_2 = x_1 + u_1) = \frac{1}{2}(-1)^2 + J_2^*(x_2 = 0.5) = 0.5 + 0.25 = 0.75$$

$$J_1(x_1 = 1.5, u_1 = -0.5) = \frac{1}{2}(-0.5)^2 + J_2^*(x_2 = 1) = 0.125 + 1 = 1.125$$

$$J_1(x_1 = 1.5, u_1 = 0) = \frac{1}{2}(0)^2 + J_2^*(x_2 = 1.5) = 0 + 2.25 = 2.25$$

From the above J_1, the value of u^* with $x_1 = 1.5$ is $u^* = -1$ and $J_1^* = 0.75$. Now for $x_1 = 1.0$ and admissible control policies $u_1 = 0.5, 0, -0.5, -1$, we can compute the J_1 similarly. The smallest value of $J_1 = 0.375$, which occurs for $u_1 = -0.5$. Hence, if $x_1 = 1.0$, then $u^* = -0.5$ and $J_1^* = 0.375$. Computing in a similar fashion, if $x_1 = 0.5$, then $u^* = -0.5$ and $J_1^* = 0.125$ and if $x_1 = 0$, then $u^* = 0$ and $J_1^* = 0$.

Step 3: Decrement $k = 0$. For $x_0 = 1.5$ and admissible control $u_0 = 0, -0.5, -1$, the associated cost $J_0 = \frac{1}{2}u_0^2 + J_1^*$, where J_1^* is the optimal cost calculated in the Step 2 for $x_1 = 1.5 + u_0$. Then, we have for

$$x_0 = 1.5, \quad J_0^* = 0.5 \text{ and } u_0^* = -0.5$$
$$x_0 = 1.0, \quad J_0^* = 0.25 \text{ and } u_0^* = -0.5$$
$$x_0 = 0.5, \quad J_0^* = 0.125 \text{ and } u_0^* = 0 \text{ or } -0.5$$
$$x_0 = 0.0, \quad J_0^* = 0 \text{ and } u_0^* = 0$$

Note that the optimal control for the state $x_0 = 0.5$ is not unique.

From the above computation, the optimal control sequence that minimizes the cost J and results in admissible states can be easily found. For example, if $x_0 = 1$, then the optimal control sequence will be $u_0^* = -0.5$ and $u_1^* - 0.5$, which will result in an optimal state trajectory of $x_0^* = 1.0, x_1^* = 0.5$, and $x_2^* = 0$. The optimal cost will be $J_0^* = 0.25$.

The principle laid down by Bellman establishes a backward-in-time procedure that is essential for solving the optimal control problem, as the optimal policy at time $k+1$ must be known to determine the optimal policy at time k as per equation (2.64). This algorithm, by its very nature, functions as an offline planning method. A prominent example of such a method within feedback control design is employing the *Riccati equation* in solving the *Linear Quadratic Regulator* (LQR) problem. This process demands an offline resolution of the Riccati equation, assuming the dynamics of the system are known.

2.2.3 LIMITATIONS OF DYNAMIC PROGRAMMING

Dynamic programming is a powerful methodology for solving a variety of optimization problems, particularly in the realm of control theory and operations research. However, it also comes with several limitations:

1. **The Curse of Dimensionality:** The computational and memory requirements of dynamic programming grow exponentially with the dimensionality of the state space and action space (or the set of admissible control inputs). This is known as Bellman's "*curse of dimensionality*". For a system with n state variables, discretizing each variable into m points would require m^n points in the state space. Thus, the number of computations and memory required scales exponentially, making dynamic programming computationally intractable for high-dimensional problems.

2. **Discretization:** Dynamic programming typically requires discretizing the state and/or control spaces. This can introduce approximation errors. Additionally, choosing the right discretization can be problem-specific and challenging.

3. **Full Knowledge Requirement:** Dynamic programming assumes that the model of the system (the transition function f and the cost function L) are known perfectly. In many real-world problems, this assumption is not valid. The model might be unknown, partially known, or it might change over time.

There are ways to address or mitigate these limitations:

1. **Model-free methods:** If the model of the system is not known perfectly, one can use model-free methods, which do not require a system model. Examples of such methods include reinforcement learning techniques like Q-learning and SARSA.

2. **Approximation Methods:** These methods try to reduce the impact of the curse of dimensionality by approximating the value function or the policy with simpler functions. Some common approximation methods include linear function approximation, neural networks, and other machine learning techniques. These methods are often referred to as adaptive/approximate dynamic programming.

2.3 ADAPTIVE DYNAMIC PROGRAMMING FOR DISCRETE-TIME SYSTEMS

Dynamic programming provides a backward-in-time optimal solution procedure, making it suitable for offline planning but unsuitable for online learning. Derived from the Bellman equation (2.63), several iterative methods have been developed for learning the solution to the optimal control equation without the need to solve the so-called *Hamilton-Jacobi-Bellman* (HJB) equation. These methods include *Policy Iteration* and *Value Iteration*. In this section we shall see how these methods can be transformed into online real-time reinforcement learning techniques. We shall see that these methods can efficiently tackle the optimal control problem using data collected along system trajectories. Key references in this domain include works by Sutton and Barto (1998), Bertsekas (2012), Werbos (1974, 1989, 1991a, 1992), and others (see Lewis et al. (2012a)).

ADP or neurodynamic programming (NDP) is an extension of dynamic programming (DP), addressing DP's limitations by employing approximation structures and real-time learning. It originated in the 1960s with the concept of reinforcement learning, a notion proposed by Minsky (Minsky and Papert, 1969) in the field of artificial intelligence. The integration of DP and reinforcement learning into neurocontrol during the late 1980s laid the groundwork for ADP, culminating in the development of deep reinforcement learning in the 2010s. ADP's unique capability to handle systems with uncertainties or unknown dynamics makes it a significant advancement in optimal control, leveraging function approximators like NN (Sutton and Barto, 1998).

Reinforcement Learning (RL), a machine learning paradigm where an agent learns through interactions with its environment, serves as the foundational learning mechanism in ADP (Sutton and Barto, 1998). In the context of ADP, the RL agent learns optimal control policies by approximating an optimal value function, adapting to feedback, and maximizing cumulative rewards. This powerful amalgamation of DP, RL, and function approximation makes ADP a versatile and promising methodology with extensive applications in robotics, power systems, traffic control, and more (Bertsekas, 2012; Werbos, 1992).

2.3.1 VALUE AND POLICY ITERATION-BASED ONLINE SOLUTION

Unlike traditional DP methods that require offline design and knowledge of the system dynamics $f(x)$, $g(x)$, RL allows for online learning in real-time, making them particularly useful when the exact system dynamics are not known. By leveraging the fundamental concept that the Bellman optimality equation act as fixed point equation, we can develop methods that operate forward-in-time. This direction facilitates the solution of the optimal control problem via learning, without utilizing or needing the system models.

To see this, let us start with a given admissible control policy $u_k = \mu(x_k)$ that results in a value $V(x_k)$. Guided, by equation (2.64), we can derive a new policy from this value by employing the following operation:

$$\mu'(x_k) = \arg\min_{\mu(\cdot)} \left(r(x_k, \mu(x_k)) + V(x_{k+1})\right). \tag{2.73}$$

Bertsekas (2012) demonstrated that the new policy $\mu'(x_k)$ represents an enhancement as it has a value $V'(x_k)$ that is either less than or equal to the original value $V(x_k)$. This phenomenon is referred to as the one-step improvement property of rollout algorithms, meaning that (2.73) is an improved policy. Repeating this iterative procedure can systematically improve the control strategy and move it closer to an optimal solution. This leads to an iterative method known as *Policy Iteration* for determining the optimal control policy. This concept has been extensively discussed in works such as Sutton and Barto (1998), and Bertsekas (2012).

2.3.1.1 Policy iteration

The policy iteration algorithm is an iterative procedure that involves two key steps: policy evaluation and policy improvement. The algorithm is presented below.

1. **Initialization:** Start with an arbitrary control policy $\mu_0(x_k)$.

2. **Policy Evaluation**: For the current policy $\mu_j(x_k)$, j denotes the iteration number, compute the value function $V_j(x_k)$ by using the Bellman equation, which is also a consistency condition that satisfies

$$V_j(x_k) = r(x(t), \mu_j(x_k)) + V_j(x_{k+1}). \tag{2.74}$$

3. **Policy Improvement:** Compute an improved policy $\mu_{j+1}(x_k)$ by solving the following minimization problem

$$\mu_{j+1}(x_k) = \arg\min_{\mu(\cdot)} \{r(x_k, \mu(x_k)) + V_{j+1}(x_{k+1})\}. \tag{2.75}$$

If the system dynamics is in affine form as in (2.54) and utility function $r(x_k, u_k)$ is in quadratic form as in (2.57), the policy improvent can be computed in one-shot as

$$\mu_{j+1}(x_k) = -\frac{1}{2} R^{-1} g^T(x_k) \frac{\partial V_{j+1}(x_{k+1})}{\partial x_{k+1}}. \tag{2.76}$$

4. **Check for Convergence:** If the policy $\mu_{j+1}(x_k)$ is the same as the policy $\mu_j(x_k)$ (or close enough), then stop the iterative process. The current policy and value function are optimal in the sense that they cannot be improved further to yield a better cost. Otherwise, go back to step 2 (Policy Evaluation) with the updated policy.

Remark 2.3. *The policy iteration method requires an initial admissible policy ($\mu_0(x_k)$). The convergence of this algorithm to the optimal value and control policy—equivalently, to the solution of* *equations* (2.63) *and* (2.65) *has been established under certain conditions. This finding has been corroborated by several researchers, as detailed in Bertsekas (2015).*

This algorithm provides an effective way to solve the optimal control problem. However, it is worth mentioning that it can be computationally expensive since it requires solving the system of Bellman equations in the policy evaluation step for each policy.

2.3.1.2 Value Iteration

The value iteration algorithm is an iterative method that computes the value function and the optimal control policy by solving the Bellman equation.

1. **Initialization:** Begin by choosing any control policy $\mu_0(x_k)$. This policy can be chosen arbitrarily and does not need to be a stabilizing policy.
2. **Value Update Step:** Update the value by employing the following equation

$$V_{j+1}(x_k) = r(x_k, \mu_j(x_k)) + V_j(x_{k+1}). \tag{2.77}$$

3. **Policy Improvement Step:** Identify an enhanced policy utilizing

$$\mu_{j+1}(x_k) = \underset{\mu(\cdot)}{\arg\min}\left(r(x_k, \mu(x_k)) + V_{j+1}(x_{k+1})\right). \tag{2.78}$$

An interesting aspect to observe is that, unlike the policy iteration, the old value is applied on the right-hand side of the equation in (2.74). It has been theoretically demonstrated that the value iteration converges under certain conditions. One essential difference between value iteration and policy iteration is that value iteration does not necessitate an initial stabilizing policy. Value iteration's foundation rests on the idea that the Bellman optimality equation in (2.63) also represents a fixed point equation. The alternating steps of value updating and policy improvement serve as the iterative method for the contraction map associated with the equation (2.63).

A critical distinction between the two iterative algorithms lies in the complexity of their respective solutions. Policy iteration mandates the resolution of the equation in (2.74) at every stage, a nonlinear Lyapunov equation, posing challenges for general nonlinear systems. Conversely, value iteration relies on solving equation (2.77), a mere recursion, making it more computationally accessible. Lastly, it is worth noting that the fixed-point equation can be the underlying principle for online RL algorithms, given appropriate structuring. These algorithms have the ability to learn through observation of data gathered along the system's trajectories.

2.3.2 TEMPORAL DIFFERENCE AND VALUE FUNCTION APPROXIMATION

To realize RL-based algorithms for solving optimal control problems, one must deal with two key ideas: temporal difference (TD) error and value function approximation (VFA).

2.3.2.1 Temporal Difference (TD) error

We have seen that given an infinite horizon cost function (2.56), we can rewrite the value function as

$$V(x_k) = r(x_k, u_k) + \sum_{i=k+1}^{\infty} r(x_i, u_i), \tag{2.79}$$

where $r(x_k, u_k)$ is the cost to go at time instant k and the second term involving the summation in (2.79) is the cost from $k+1$ to infinity. We have also seen that this can be rewritten as a difference equation given by

$$V(x_k) = r(x_k, \mu(x_k) + V(x_{k+1}), \quad V(0) = 0, \tag{2.80}$$

where $u_k = \mu(x_k)$ is the current control policy. The Bellman equation (2.80) is a version of the Lyapunov equation. From (2.80), the discrete-time Hamiltonian can be expressed as

$$H(x_k, \mu(x_k), \Delta V_k) = r(x_k, \mu(x_k) + \Delta V_k, \tag{2.81}$$

where $\Delta V_k = V(x_{k+1}) - V(x_k)$.

Remark 2.4. *The Hamiltonian function, commonly encountered in the context of Pontryagin's maximum principle, captures the cost function along with the constraint expression, which is often introduced by the system dynamics, using a Lagrangian multiplier or costate. In* (2.81)*, the Hamiltonion captures the one-step-cost, $r(x_k, \mu(x_k))$, and the constraint, which is given by the first difference of the value function $\Delta V_k = V(x_{k+1}) - V(x_k)$. We shall see that in the continuous-time, this translates to $\frac{\partial V(x(t))}{\partial t} = \frac{\partial V^T(x(t))}{\partial x(t)} \frac{dx(t)}{dt}$, where $\frac{\partial V^T(x(t))}{\partial x(t)}$ forms the Lagrange multiplier.*

As discussed in the previous section, the Bellman equation provides a backward-in-time solution approach. To solve the problem online, forward-in-time, one can define an error equation using the Hamiltonian function (2.81) given by

$$e_k = r(x_k, \mu(x_k)) + V(x_{k+1}) - V(x_k). \tag{2.82}$$

The error e_k is referred to as the temporal difference (TD) error. The TD error becomes zero when the Bellman equation is satisfied, which implies that the Hamiltonian becomes zero or the consistency condition is satisfied. Algorithmically, this also implies that, given a fixed control policy $u = \mu(x)$, one could seek to solve the equation $e_k = 0$ for each time step k. This results in the determination of a value function $V(\cdot)$, which represents the solution to the TD equation satisfying

$$0 = r(x_k, \mu(x_k)) + V(x_{k+1}) - V(x_k). \tag{2.83}$$

Solving (2.83) leads to the best estimate of the value related to the current policy application equivalently to the evaluation of the infinite sum in the cost function (2.56). The TD error is thus interpretable as a measure of discrepancy between anticipated and actual system performance following a chosen action. It acts as a metric to assess the prediction error in estimating the system's future states under the influence of the current policy. This error can be used to guide how the policy is updated to better align with the optimal trajectory. However, this needs to be accomplished without detailed knowledge of system dynamics, relying solely on the data gathered along the system trajectories. This task presents a significant challenge, particularly for general nonlinear systems, where the complexity of the system dynamics makes the TD equation notoriously difficult to solve. Note that in the policy iteration, the TD error is completely reduced to zero in the policy evaluation step while in the value iteration, the TD error is reduced (but not eliminated) in each step before the policy is updated.

2.3.2.2 Value Function Approximation

A practical approach to solving the TD equation involves approximating the value function $V(\cdot)$ through a parametric approximator. This method is often synonymously called approximate dynamic programming (ADP) (Werbos, 1974, 1989, 1991a, 1992) and neurodynamic programming (NDP) (Bertsekas, 2012). An NN-based function approximator, introduced in Section 2.1.3, is utilized to approximate the value function $V(x_k)$ in ADP/NDP algorithms.

Recalling the universal approximation property of NNs, the value function in a compact set can be written as

$$V(x_k) = W^T \phi(x_k) + \varepsilon(x_k), \tag{2.84}$$

where $W \in \mathbb{R}^l$ is the unknown target NN weights, $\phi(x_k) \in \mathbb{R}^l$ is the activation function which forms a basis for approximation, and $\varepsilon(x_k) \in \mathbb{R}$ is the approximation error with l denoting the number of neurons in the output layer. Note that we can use a NN with three or more layers for the approximation, and it is a design choice.

The estimated value function can be represented as

$$\hat{V}(x_k) = \hat{W}^T \phi(x_k), \tag{2.85}$$

where $\hat{W}$ is the estimated weights, tuned during the learning process. Substituting the value function estimates from (2.85), the TD error (2.82) becomes

$$e_k = r(x_k, \mu(x_k)) + \hat{W}^T \phi(x_{k+1}) - \hat{W}^T \phi(x_k). \tag{2.86}$$

The equation $e_k = 0$ represents a fixed point equation, acting as a consistency equation that holds true at every time instance k for the value $V(\cdot)$, which corresponds to the prevailing policy $u = \mu(x)$. Consequently, iterative methods can be employed to solve the TD equation, by updating the weights ($\hat{W}$) using optimization algorithms including the backpropogation to minimize the error e_k.

2.3.3 ONLINE POLICY AND VALUE ITERATION WITH APPROXIMATED VALUE FUNCTION

By utilizing the TD error and the value function approximation, we shall see that the policy and value iteration algorithms can be formulated so as to obtain the optimal policies online and forward-in-time.

2.3.3.1 Online Policy Iteration

1. **Initialize.** Choose any admissible control policy $\mu_0(x_k)$.
2. **Policy Evaluation Step.** Calculate the least-squares solution $\hat{W}_{j+1}$ with the following equation

$$\hat{W}_{j+1}^T (\phi(x_k) - \phi(x_{k+1})) = r(x_k, \mu_j(x_k)). \tag{2.87}$$

3. **Policy Improvement Step.** Ascertain an improved policy using the equation

$$\mu_{j+1}(x_k) = \underset{\mu(.)}{\arg\min} \left(r(x_k, \mu(x_k)) + \hat{W}_{j+1}^T \phi(x_{k+1}) \right). \tag{2.88}$$

If the utility has the special quadratic form and the dynamics are given by an affine expression, then the policy improvement step looks like

$$\mu_{j+1}(x_k) = -\frac{1}{2} R^{-1} g^T(x_k) \nabla \phi^T(x_{k+1}) \hat{W}_{j+1}, \tag{2.89}$$

where $\nabla \phi(x) = \frac{\partial \phi(x)}{\partial x} \in \mathbb{R}^{l \times n}$ is the Jacobian of the activation function vector.

Remark 2.5. *The estimated weights for the value function $\hat{W}_{j+1}$ can be computed using least squares (LS) (Ljung, 1999; Söderström and Stoica, 1989; Goodwin and Sin, 2014), recursive LS (Ljung, 1999; Söderström and Stoica, 1989; Goodwin and Sin, 2014), or gradient-based algorithms (Aström and Wittenmark, 1995). For recursive least squares (RLS) and gradient-based algorithms, the regression vector must satisfy the persistency of excitation (PE) condition (Narendra and Annaswamy, 2012) to ensure convergence.*

After the weights for the value function are estimated, the control policy is updated according to equations (2.88) or (2.89). Subsequently, the procedure (policy evaluation and improvement) is repeated again for the next step, $j+1$. This entire process continues until convergence to the optimal control solution, which is the approximate solution to equations (2.63) and (2.65). This results in an online RL algorithm capable of solving the optimal control problem while gathering data along the system trajectories. In a similar fashion, an online RL algorithm can also be derived based on value iteration.

2.3.3.2 On-Line Value Iteration Algorithm

1. **Initialize.** Select any control policy $\mu_0(x_k)$, not necessarily admissible or stabilizing.
2. **Value Update Step.** Determine the least-squares solution $\hat{W}_{j+1}$ to

$$\hat{W}_{j+1}^T \phi(x_k) = r(x_k, \mu_j(x_k)) + \hat{W}_j^T \phi(x_{k+1}). \tag{2.90}$$

3. **Policy Improvement Step.** Determine an improved policy using

$$\mu_{j+1}(x_k) = -\frac{\gamma}{2} R^{-1} g^T(x_k) \nabla\phi^T(x_{k+1}) \hat{W}_{j+1}. \tag{2.91}$$

Note that the old weight parameters are on the right-hand side of (2.90). Thus, the regression vector is now $\phi(x_k)$, which must be persistently exciting for convergence of RLS.

Additionally, Werbos (1974, 1989, 1991a, 1992) introduced four foundational methods of ADP. He defined a version of RL that learns the scalar value function $V_h(x_k)$ via heuristic dynamic programming (HDP). The extension of HDP, known as action-dependent HDP (AD-HDP), was presented as Q-learning for discrete-state Markov decision processes (MDP) by Watkins (Watkins, 1989). AD-HDP learns the Q-function, which is also a scalar function, and enables RL without using the model of the system dynamics. Dual heuristic programming (DHP) involves the online learning of the costate function $\lambda_k = \frac{\partial V(x_k)}{\partial x_k}$, which is an '$n$'-vector gradient and carries more information than the scalar value. The final method, action-dependent DHP (AD-DHP), is founded on learning the gradients of the Q-function.

2.3.4 ACTOR-CRITIC ARCHITECTURE

In the previous section, we reviewed how a value function can be approximated using an NN. This NN is often referred to as the *critic network*, in the online policy iteration and value iteration. However, the implementation of the equation (2.88) for a nonlinear system can be challenging, as the control is implicitly integrated, given that x_{k+1} is reliant on $\mu(\cdot)$ and is used as an argument for a nonlinear activation function. These issues are addressed by incorporating a second NN dedicated to the control policy, commonly referred to as the *actor network* (Werbos, 1974, 1989, 1991a, 1992; Barto et al., 1983). Consequently, the actor-network has a parametric approximator structure given by

$$u_k = \mu(x_k) = \hat{V}^T \sigma(x_k), \tag{2.92}$$

where $\sigma(x) : \mathbb{R}^n \to \mathbb{R}^M$ represents a vector of M activation functions and $\hat{V} \in \mathbb{R}^{M \times m}$ is a matrix of weights or unidentified parameters.

Once the critic NN parameters converge to W_{j+1} in the policy iteration or value iteration steps, it becomes necessary to execute the policy update steps denoted by equations (2.88) and (2.91). A gradient descent method (Lewis et al., 2012b) can be employed to update the actor weights $\hat{V}$, as given below

$$\hat{V}_{j+1}^{i+1} = \hat{V}_{j+1}^i - \beta\sigma(x_k)\left(2R\left(\hat{V}_{j+1}^i\right)^T \sigma(x_k) + g(x_k)^T \nabla\phi^T(x_{k+1}) W_{j+1}\right)^T. \tag{2.93}$$

Here, $\beta > 0$ serves as a tuning parameter, and the tuning index i increases along with the time index k.

2.3.5 Q-LEARNING

In the realm of HDP or value function learning, knowledge of system dynamics is required, as shown by equations (2.89) and (2.91). At a minimum, the knowledge of the input coupling function $g(\cdot)$

(the matrix B in the case of the linear system) is necessary. This need arises from the minimization operation shown in equation (2.88)

$$\mu_{j+1}(x_k) = \arg\min_{\mu(\cdot)} \left[r(x_k, \mu(x_k)) + W_{j+1}^T \phi(x_{k+1}) \right]. \tag{2.94}$$

Given the cost-to-go $r(x_k, u_k) = Q(x_k) + u^T R u_k$, to compute 'argmin' in (2.94), differentiate with respect to the control to yield

$$\begin{aligned} 0 =& \frac{\partial}{\partial u_k}[Q(x_k) + u_k^T R u_k] + \frac{\partial}{\partial u_k} W_{j+1}^T \phi(x_{k+1}) \\ =& 2Ru_k + \left(\frac{\partial \phi(x_{k+1})}{\partial u_k} \right)^T W_{j+1} \\ =& 2Ru_k + \left(\frac{\partial x_{k+1}}{\partial u_k} \right)^T \nabla \phi(x_{k+1})^T W_{j+1}. \end{aligned} \tag{2.95}$$

However, when evaluating $\frac{\partial x_{k+1}}{\partial u_k} = g(x_k)$, the system input matrix $g(\cdot)$ is required. Even when a secondary actor NN is used, the function $g(\cdot)$ is needed to adjust the actor NN weights, as per (2.93).

To avoid the need for knowledge of the system dynamics, an alternative method for taking partial derivatives with respect to the control input must be conceived, without going through the system. Werbos employed the concept of backpropagation through time using AD-HDP to achieve this. Watkins (1989) introduced similar concepts for discrete-space MDPs, termed as Q-learning. Given the Bellman equation (2.80), the value of any given admissible policy $\mu(\cdot)$ can be computed. The optimal control is determined using equations (2.65). Thus, the *Q-function* or the quality function associated with policy $u = \mu(x)$ is defined as

$$Q(x_k, u_k) = r(x_k, u_k) + V(x_{k+1}). \tag{2.96}$$

The optimal Q-function is then given by

$$Q^*(x_k, u_k) = r(x_k, u_k) + V^*(x_{k+1}). \tag{2.97}$$

Utilizing Q^*, the Bellman optimality equation can be expressed in a simplified form

$$V^*(x_k) = \min_u Q^*(x_k, u), \tag{2.98}$$

and the optimal control policy can be written as

$$\mu^*(x_k) = \arg\min_u Q^*(x_k, u). \tag{2.99}$$

The minimum value can be found by solving

$$\frac{\partial}{\partial u} Q^*(x_k, u_k) = 0. \tag{2.100}$$

Unlike (2.95), (2.100) does not require any derivatives involving system dynamics. Assuming the Q-function is known for all (x_k, u_k), there is no need to compute $\frac{\partial x_{k+1}}{\partial u_k}$. Value function learning (or HDP) necessitates learning and storing the optimal value for all possible states x_k. On the other hand, Q-learning requires storing the optimal Q-function for all possible values of (x_k, u_k), i.e., for all possible control actions taken in each possible state, demanding more information storage. The following discussion will address how to manage this using Q-function approximation for applying online RL techniques.

Applying online RL techniques to learn the Q-function requires
1. A fixed point equation in terms of the Q function to use the TD learning, and
2. An appropriate parametric approximator structure for the Q-function approximation (QFA).

To establish a fixed point equation for the Q-function, note that $Q(x_k, \mu(x_k)) = V(x_k)$. This allows the construction of a Bellman equation for Q-function as

$$Q(x_k, u_k) = r(x_k, u_k) + Q(x_{k+1}, \mu(x_{k+1})), \tag{2.101}$$

or equivalently,

$$Q(x_k, \mu(x_k)) = r(x_k, \mu(x_k)) + Q(x_{k+1}, \mu(x_{k+1})). \tag{2.102}$$

The optimal Q-value, denoted by Q^*, satisfies

$$Q^*(x_k, u_k) = r(x_k, u_k) + Q^*(x_{k+1}, \mu^*(x_{k+1})). \tag{2.103}$$

Thus, (2.101) serves as a fixed point equation or the 'Bellman equation' in terms of the Q-function, similar to (2.80). With this, any online RL method previously discussed can be used as the foundation for realizing AD-HDP, including the policy iteration and value iteration.

2.3.6 Q- LEARNING FOR LINEAR QUADRATIC REGULATOR

We shall now derive a Q-learning based optimal controller for a linear system. Consider the linear quadratic regulator (LQR), where the one-step-cost is defined as the sum of quadratic function of state and control inputs. With this, we shall examine the choice of suitable approximator structures for the QFA.

The Q-function for the LQR is given by equation (2.96)

$$Q_K(x_k, u_k) = x_k^T Q x_k + u_k^T R u_k + x_{k+1}^T P x_{k+1}, \tag{2.104}$$

where P is the solution to an associated Lyapunov equation for the policy K (Lewis et al., 2012b). Therefore, we have

$$Q_K(x_k, u_k) = x_k^T Q x_k + u_k^T R u_k + (Ax_k + Bu_k)^T P (Ax_k + Bu_k), \tag{2.105}$$

which can be rewritten in matrix form as

$$Q_K(x_k, u_k) = \begin{bmatrix} x_k \\ u_k \end{bmatrix}^T \begin{bmatrix} Q + A^T PA & B^T PA \\ A^T PB & R + B^T PB \end{bmatrix} \begin{bmatrix} x_k \\ u_k \end{bmatrix} \equiv z_k^T H z_k. \tag{2.106}$$

This equation represents the Q-function for the LQR case. It is quadratic in (x_k, u_k). Using the Kronecker product, we can rewrite this equation as

$$Q_K(x_k, u_k) = \bar{H}^T \bar{z}_k \tag{2.107}$$

where $\bar{H} = \text{vec}(H)$ and $\bar{z}_k = z_k \otimes z_k = \begin{bmatrix} x_k \\ u_k \end{bmatrix} \otimes \begin{bmatrix} x_k \\ u_k \end{bmatrix}$. The term $\bar{z}_k$ is the quadratic basis set composed of the components of the state and the control input. Then, the fixed point equation (2.101) becomes

$$\bar{H}^T \bar{z}_k = x_k^T Q x_k + u_k^T R u_k + \bar{H}^T \bar{z}_{k+1} \tag{2.108}$$

with $u_k = -Kx_k$.

Define the Q-function in terms of state x_k and control u_k as

$$Q_K(x_k, u_k) = z_k^T H z_k = \begin{bmatrix} x_k \\ u_k \end{bmatrix}^T \begin{bmatrix} H_{xx} & H_{xu} \\ H_{ux} & H_{uu} \end{bmatrix} \begin{bmatrix} x_k \\ u_k \end{bmatrix}. \tag{2.109}$$

This decomposes the matrix H into four submatrices: H_{xx}, H_{xu}, H_{ux}, and H_{uu}. Then equation (2.100) gives us

$$0 = H_{ux}x_k + H_{uu}u_k, \tag{2.110}$$

which can be rearranged to solve for u_k, the control action at step k,

$$u_k = -(H_{uu})^{-1} H_{ux}x_k. \tag{2.111}$$

Here, the matrix H can be acquired or learned through online RL, and this step does not necessitate knowledge of the system dynamics. Interestingly, if we apply (2.100) to (2.106), we get K as

$$K = \left(R + B^T PB\right)^{-1} B^T PA, \tag{2.112}$$

which is the same as a traditional LQR controller (Lewis et al., 2012b).

2.3.7 Q-LEARNING FOR NONLINEAR SYSTEM

In nonlinear systems, we can make informed assumptions about the structure of our Q-function approximation. The Q-function can be perceived as a parametric mapping of state and action variables (x, u), characterized by a set of weights W and a chosen basis function ϕ. This can be implemented using NN or other approximation schemes. The approximated Q-function can therefore be represented as

$$Q(x_k, u_k) = W^T \phi(x_k, u_k) = W^T \phi(z_k), \tag{2.113}$$

where $z_k = [x_k^T \;\; u_k^T]^T$. Building on this approximation, we can calculate the TD error. The TD error can be expressed as

$$e_k = r(x_k, \mu(x_k)) + W^T \phi(z_{k+1}) - W^T \phi(z_k). \tag{2.114}$$

With this TD error, we can apply policy iteration or value iteration to continuously learn the weight vector in an online manner.

Furthermore, with the critic NN defined as in (2.113), our aim is to identify the point at which the derivative of the Q-function with respect to the control action u equals zero

$$\frac{\partial}{\partial u} Q(x_k, u) = \frac{\partial}{\partial u} W^T \phi(x_k, u) = 0. \tag{2.115}$$

Again, due to the nature of the NN structure that inherently includes the control action u (a feature of AD-HDP), these derivatives can be calculated without the knowledge of the system dynamics. Nonetheless, formulating an explicit policy $u_k = \mu(x_k)$ by finding a solution for u is not a straightforward task. This necessitates the application of the implicit function theorem tailored to this specific neural network structure. This framework is flexible and facilitates the use of both policy iteration and value iteration techniques for Q-learning, thus offering diverse pathways to learn optimal solutions.

2.4 TIME-BASED ADP FOR DISCRETE-TIME SYSTEMS WITHOUT ITERATION

In the previous section, the approximate solution to optimal control problems using iterative approaches (policy and value iteration) using fixed-point equations is presented. Although these iterative approaches guarantee optimality at every time instant, one of the limitations is the number of iterations required (to solve policy evaluation and/or policy improvement steps) within a sampling instant to converge to the fixed-point solution. This renders the real-time implementation of these schemes difficult. To address this issue, Dierks and Jagannathan (2012b) presented an optimal control framework for nonlinear discrete-time systems, which learns the Hamilton-Jacobi-Bellman

(HJB) equation and the corresponding optimal control policy truly online and forward in-time using NN without incorporating policy and value iterations.

Consider an affine nonlinear discrete-time system that can be characterized by

$$x_{k+1} = f(x_k) + g(x_k)u(x_k) \tag{2.116}$$

where $x_k \in \mathbb{R}^n$, $f(x_k) \in \mathbb{R}^n$, and $g(x_k) \in \mathbb{R}^{n \times m}$, adhering to the condition $\|g(x_k)\|_F \leq g_M$. Here, $\|\cdot\|_F$ is the Frobenius norm. The control input is represented as $u(x_k) \in \mathbb{R}^m$. The internal dynamics, denoted by $f(x_k)$, are treated as unknown, whereas the input coefficient matrix, $g(x_k)$, is known. An optimal control policy for (2.116) should result in a control sequence $u(x_k)$ that minimizes the infinite horizon cost function defined by

$$J(x_k) = \sum_{i=0}^{\infty} r(x_{k+i}, u(x_{k+i})) \tag{2.117}$$

for all x_k, where $r(x_k, u(x_k)) = Q(x_k) + u(x_k)^T R u(x_k)$, and $Q(x_k) \geq 0$ and $R \in \mathbb{R}^{m \times m}$ is a symmetric positive definite matrix. Here $Q(x_k)$ is a penalty function on the state and is not related to the Q-function.

The Bellman equation (2.80), using the value function, can be written as

$$V(x_k) = r(x_k, u(x_k)) + V(x_{k+1}) = r(x_k, u(x_k)) + V(f(x_k) + g(x_k)u(x_k)) \tag{2.118}$$

It is necessary for $J(x_k) = 0$ for $x_k = 0$, which allows $J(x_k)$ to serve as a Lyapunov function. Furthermore, the control policy $u(x_k)$ must assure that (2.117) is finite, making $u(x_k)$ admissible. By leveraging the Bellman's principle of optimality (2.63), it can be established that the infinite horizon optimal cost function, denoted by $V^*(x_k)$, is time-invariant and satisfies the discrete-time Hamilton-Jacobi-Bellman (HJB) equation (Lewis et al., 2012b)

$$V^*(x_k) = \min_{u(x_k)} \left(r(x_k, u(x_k)) + V^*(f(x_k) + g(x_k)u(x_k)) \right). \tag{2.119}$$

By invoking the stationarity condition (Lewis et al., 2012b), the optimal control $u^*(x_k)$ that minimizes $V^*(x_k)$ can be computed. The stationarity condition can be expressed as

$$\frac{\partial V^*(x_k)}{\partial u(x_k)} = 2Ru(x_k) + g(x_k)^T \left(\frac{\partial V^*(x_{k+1})}{\partial x_{k+1}} \right) = 0, \tag{2.120}$$

which leads to the optimal control expressed as

$$u^*(x_k) = -\frac{1}{2} R^{-1} g(x_k)^T \left(\frac{\partial V^*(x_{k+1})}{\partial x_{k+1}} \right). \tag{2.121}$$

Despite the complete knowledge of the system dynamics, the optimal control (2.121) generally remains inaccessible for nonlinear discrete-time systems due to its reliance on the future state vector x_{k+1} at the current time instant k. As discussed in the previous sections, value and policy iteration-based strategies are often employed to overcome this limitation. The actor-critic approach employs two NNs: a critic NN to learn the HJB equation and an action NN to learn the control policy that minimizes the estimated cost function. Leveraging the approximation property of NNs, Jagannathan (2006), representations for the cost function (2.118) and feedback control policy (2.121) can be expressed using NNs (over a compact set S) as follows

$$V(x_k) = \Phi^T \sigma(x_k) + \varepsilon_{Jk}(x_k) \tag{2.122}$$

and

$$u(x_k) = \Theta^T \vartheta(x_k) + \varepsilon_{uk}(x_k), \tag{2.123}$$

where Φ and Θ represent the constant target NN weights, while $\varepsilon_{Jk}(x_k)$ and $\varepsilon_{uk}(x_k)$ are the bounded state-dependent approximation errors for all $x_k \in S$. The activation function vectors for the critic and action NN are denoted by $\sigma(\bullet)$ and $\vartheta(\bullet)$, respectively, and they are independent. In the time-based ADPs, the authors Dierks and Jagannathan (2012b) defined the upper bounds for the target NN weights are set as $\|\Phi\| \leq \Phi_M$ and $\|\Theta\|_F \leq \Theta_M$, where Φ_M and Θ_M are positive constants. The approximation errors were constrained to be $|\varepsilon_{Jk}| \leq \varepsilon_{JM}$ and $\|\varepsilon_{uk}\| \leq \varepsilon_{uM}$, where ε_{JM} and ε_{uM} are positive constants (Jagannathan, 2006). Lastly, the gradient of the approximation error was also assumed to be bounded above as $\|\partial\varepsilon_{Jk}/(\partial x_{k+1})\|_F \leq \varepsilon'_{JM}$, where ε'_{JM} is another positive constant. These bounds were used to analyze the convergence properties of the time-based ADP algorithm in control applications. See Dierks and Jagannathan (2012b); Xu (2012); Sahoo (2015) for more details.

2.4.1 APPROXIMATION OF VALUE FUNCTION VIA CRITIC NN

Similar to other approximation-based methods, the time-based ADP algorithm also uses the value function approximation using a critic NN and is denoted as

$$\hat{V}_k(x_k) = \hat{\Phi}_k^T \sigma(x_k), \tag{2.124}$$

where $\hat{V}_k(x_k)$ is the approximation of the cost function and $\hat{\Phi}_k$ represents the estimate of the target NN weight vector, Φ. The subscript k indicates the time index, denoting the association between the approximated cost function $\hat{V}_k(x_k)$ and $\hat{\Phi}_k$ within the same time frame. To ensure $\hat{J}(0) = 0$ is satisfied, the basis function must fulfill the condition $\|\sigma(0)\| = 0$ when $\|x\| = 0$.

Next, define the residual or cost-to-go (CTG) error as

$$e_{V_k} = r(x_{k-1}, u(x_{k-1})) + \hat{\Phi}_k^T \Delta\sigma(x_{k-1}), \tag{2.125}$$

where $\Delta\sigma(x_{k-1})$ is $\sigma(x_k) - \sigma(x_{k-1})$. This CTG error (2.125) can be understood as the time-shifted TD error, discussed in the previous section, with its dynamics expressed as

$$e_{V_{k+1}} = r(x_k, u(x_k)) + \hat{\Phi}_{k+1}^T (\sigma(x_{k+1}) - \sigma(x_k)). \tag{2.126}$$

Following this, an auxiliary CTG error vector can be defined as

$$E_{V_k} = Y_{k-1} + \hat{\Phi}_k^T X_{k-1} \in \mathbb{R}^{1\times(1+j)}, \tag{2.127}$$

where Y_{k-1} consists of $r(x_{k-1}, u(x_{k-1}))$ through $r(x_{k-1-j}, u(x_{k-1-j}))$ and X_{k-1} consists of $\Delta\sigma(x_{k-1})$ through $\Delta\sigma(x_{k-1-j})$ with $j < k-1$. The auxiliary vector (2.127) represents the previous $j+1$ CTG errors, recalculated using the most recent $\hat{\Phi}_k$. The parameter j is a design choice, but it must satisfy $j \leq L-1$, where $\sigma(x_k) \in \mathbb{R}^L$. Then the dynamics of the auxiliary vector are defined as

$$E_{V_{k+1}}^T = Y_k^T + X_k^T \hat{\Phi}_{k+1}. \tag{2.128}$$

Now define the cost function NN weight update to be

$$\hat{\Phi}_{k+1} = X_k \left(X_k^T X_k\right)^{-1} \left(\alpha_J E_{V_k}^T - Y_k^T\right), \tag{2.129}$$

where $0 < \alpha_J < 1$, and substituting (2.129) into (2.128) reveals

$$E_{V_{k+1}}^T = \alpha_J E_{V_k}^T. \tag{2.130}$$

It can be observed that the NN weight update reveals that the time-evolution of the CTG error can be controlled by the choice of the parameter α_J.

Remark 2.6. *Observing the definition of the cost function* (2.122) *and its NN approximation* (2.124)*, it is evident that both become zero only when* $x_k = 0$*. Thus, once the system states become zero, the cost function approximation is no longer updated. This can be viewed as a PE requirement for the inputs to the cost function NN wherein the system states must be persistently exiting long enough for the NN to learn the optimal cost function. This PE requirement ensures the existence of a constant* α*, such that* $\alpha \leq \left\|X_k^T X_k\right\|_F$ *(Jagannathan, 2006).*

Remark 2.7. *Implementation of the time-driven ADP-based optimal control scheme does not use policy or value iterations, which are commonly used in offline optimal control training (Al-Tamimi et al., 2008). Instead, online learning and time-based policy updates are used here by using both state measurements and its time history.*

2.4.2 APPROXIMATION OF CONTROL POLICY VIA ACTOR NN

To derive the control policy that minimizes the approximated cost function (2.124), an action NN is employed to approximate (2.121), and is given by

$$\hat{u}(x_k) = \hat{\Theta}_k^T \vartheta(x_k), \tag{2.131}$$

where $\hat{\Theta}_k$ is the estimated value of the ideal weight matrix Θ_k. The basis function, $\vartheta(\bullet)$, is designed to satisfy $\|\vartheta(0)\| = 0$, which guarantees $\|\hat{u}(0)\| = 0$, a requirement for admissibility. Subsequently, the action error, the difference between the feedback control applied to (2.116) and the control signal that minimizes the estimated cost function (2.124), is defined as

$$\tilde{u}(x_k) = \hat{\Theta}_k^T \vartheta(x_k) + \frac{1}{2} R^{-1} g^T(x_k) \left(\frac{\partial \sigma(x_{k+1})}{\partial x_{k+1}}\right)^T \hat{\Phi}_k. \tag{2.132}$$

To drive the action error to zero, the control NN weight update was proposed by Dierks and Jagannathan (2012b) as

$$\hat{\Theta}_{k+1} = \hat{\Theta}_k - \alpha_u \frac{\vartheta(x_k)\, \tilde{u}_k^T}{\vartheta^T(x_k)\, \vartheta(x_k) + 1}, \tag{2.133}$$

where $0 < \alpha_u < 1$ is a positive design parameter, controlling the rate of change of the control NN weight matrix.

Remark 2.8. *To calculate the action error* (2.132) *and implement the NN weight update* (2.133)*, knowledge of the input transformation matrix* $g(x_k)$ *is required. However, knowledge of the internal dynamics* $f(x_k)$ *can be avoided.*

Dierks and Jagannathan (2012b) also derived sufficient condition to warrant the uniform ultimate boundedness of the critic and action NN weight estimation errors using Lyapunov theory. Further, the estimated control input (2.131) was shown to approach the optimal control signal with a small bounded error. This error is expected to be a function of the NN reconstruction errors ε_J and ε_u. If both the NN approximation errors are considered to be negligible (Chen and Jagannathan, 2008; Al-Tamimi et al., 2008) as in the case of standard adaptive control (Jagannathan, 2006) or when the number of hidden-layer neurons is significantly increased (Jagannathan, 2006), the estimated control policy will approach the optimal control asymptotically as shown by Dierks and Jagannathan (2012b). In summary, time-based ADP facilitates real-time online learning of the optimal control policy. It accomplishes this by integrating historical data throughout the system's trajectory.

2.4.3 A SPECIAL CASE OF LINEAR SYSTEM

Consider a linear discrete-time system as the special case of the nonlinear system in (2.116) given by

$$x_{k+1} = Ax_k + Bu(x_k). \tag{2.134}$$

For the infinite horizon cost function (2.117), the Hamiltonion function reveals a discrete algebraic Riccati equation (ARE) given by

$$P = A^T PA + Q - A^T PB\left(R + B^T PB\right)^{-1} B^T PA \tag{2.135}$$

with $J^*(x_k) = x^T Px$ (Lewis et al., 2012b). In addition, the optimal control policy (2.121) is obtained as

$$u^*(x_k) = -K^* x_k = -\left(R + B^T PB\right)^{-1} B^T PAx_k. \tag{2.136}$$

In order to show that the time-driven ADP is useful for linear systems, the cost function $J(x_k) = x_k^T Px_k$ and the feedback control policy (2.136) have NN representations as

$$J(x_k) = \Phi^T \sigma(x_k) = \Phi^T \bar{x}_k \tag{2.137}$$

and

$$u(x_k) = \Theta^T \vartheta(x_k) = \Theta^T x_k \tag{2.138}$$

respectively, where Φ, Θ, $\sigma(\bullet)$, and $\vartheta(\bullet)$ are as defined in (2.122) and (2.123). Further, $\Phi = vec(P)$ and $\Theta = -K^{*T}$ with $vec(\bullet)$ denoting a vector function that transforms an $n \times n$ matrix into a column vector by stacking the columns of the square matrix into a one column with the off-diagonal elements summed as $P_{ij} + P_{ji}$. The term $\bar{x}_k = \left(x_1^2, \ldots, x_1x_n, x_2^2, x_2x_3, \ldots, x_{n-1}x_n, x_n^2\right)$ is the Kronecker product quadratic polynomial basis vector. Note that the NN reconstruction errors, ε_{Jk} and ε_{uk}, are negligible for the case of linear systems as the basis functions are the exact regression functions.

It is demonstrated by Dierks and Jagannathan (2012b) that the NN estimation errors, $\tilde{\Phi}$ and $\tilde{\Theta}$, and the CTG error and action error, e_{Jk} and $\tilde{u}(x_k)$, respectively, converge to zero asymptotically as $k \to \infty$ when ε_{Jk} and ε_{uk} are zero. This implies that there exists a time, k_a, such that for all $k > k_a, \hat{\Phi} = \Phi = vec(P), \hat{\Theta} = \Theta = -K^{*T}$, $\|E_{Jk}\| = 0$, and $\hat{J}(x_k) = \hat{\Phi}^T \bar{x}_k = x^T Px = J(x_k)$. Under these conditions, the NN cost function update (2.129) is rewritten as

$$\hat{\Phi}_{k+1} = \Phi = -X_k\left(X_k^T X_k\right)^{-1} Y_k^T. \tag{2.139}$$

Therefore, multiplying both sides of (2.139) by X_k^T and taking the transpose of both sides yields $\Phi^T X_k = -Y_k$ which can be expanded as

$$\begin{aligned}&\Phi^T \begin{bmatrix}\bar{x}_{k+1} - \bar{x}_k & \bar{x}_k - \bar{x}_{k-1} & \ldots & \bar{x}_{k+1-j} - \bar{x}_{k-j}\end{bmatrix}\\ &= \begin{bmatrix}r(x_k, u(x_k)) & r(x_{k-1}, u(x_{k-1})) & \ldots & r\left(x_{k-j}, u\left(x_{k-j}\right)\right)\end{bmatrix}.\end{aligned} \tag{2.140}$$

Then, by using $\Phi^T \bar{x}_k = x_k^T Px_k$ and $r(x_k, u(x_k)) = x_k^T Qx_k + u^T(x_k) Ru(x_k)$, (2.140) can be rewritten as

$$\begin{bmatrix} x_k^T Px_k \\ x_{k-1}^T Px_{k-1} \\ \vdots \\ x_{k-j}^T Px_{k-j}\end{bmatrix} = \begin{bmatrix} x_k^T Qx_k + u^T(x_k) Ru(x_k) + x_{k+1}^T Px_{k+1} \\ x_{k-1}^T Qx_{k-1} + u^T(x_{k-1}) Ru(x_{k-1}) + x_k^T Px_k \\ \vdots \\ x_{k-j}^T Qx_{k-j} + u^T\left(x_{k-j}\right) Ru\left(x_{k-j}\right) + x_{k+1-j}^T Px_{k+1-j}\end{bmatrix}. \tag{2.141}$$

Now, using (2.134) and $\Theta = -K^{*T}$ allows (2.141) to take the form of the equation (as shown in the equation (2.144)), or $z^T \operatorname{diag}\left\{P - Q - K^{*T}RK^* - \left(A^T - K^{*T}B^T\right)P(A - BK^*)\right\} z = 0$ where $z = \begin{bmatrix} x_k^T & x_{k-1}^T & \cdots & x_{k-j}^T \end{bmatrix}^T$. Since $\|z\| > 0$ by the PE condition, it follows that

$$P - Q - K^{*T}RK^* - \left(A^T - K^{*T}B^T\right)P(A - BK^*) = 0. \tag{2.142}$$

After rearranging this expression and recalling $K^* = \left(R + B^T\ PB\right)^{-1} B^T PA$, (2.142) can be rewritten as

$$\begin{aligned} P &= Q + K^{*T} RK^* + \left(A^T - K^{*T} B^T\right) P \left(A - BK^*\right) \\ &= A^T PA + Q - A^T PB \left(R + B^T PB\right)^{-1} B^T PA, \end{aligned} \tag{2.143}$$

which is nothing but the discrete-time ARE (DARE) shown in (2.135). Therefore, the NN update (2.129) indeed solves the matrix Lyapunov equation for linear systems.

$$\begin{bmatrix} x_k^T P x_k \\ x_{k-1}^T P x_{k-1} \\ \vdots \\ x_{k-j}^T P x_{k-j} \end{bmatrix} = \begin{bmatrix} x_k^T Q x_k + x_k^T K^{*T} RK^* x_k + x_k^T \left(A^T - K^{*T} B^T\right) P \left(A - BK^*\right) x_k \\ x_{k-1}^T Q x_{k-1} + x_{k-1}^T K^{*T} RK^* x_{k-1} + x_{k-1}^T \left(A^T - K^{*T} B^T\right) P \left(A - BK^*\right) x_{k-1} \\ \vdots \\ x_{k-j}^T Q x_{k-j} + x_{k-j}^T K^{*T} RK^* x_{k-j} + x_{k-j}^T \left(A^T - K^{*T} B^T\right) P \left(A - BK^*\right) x_{k-j} \end{bmatrix} \tag{2.144}$$

Example 2.2. *(Dierks and Jagannathan, 2012b) Consider the linear system whose dynamics are given by*

$$x_{k+1} = \begin{bmatrix} x_{1k+1} \\ x_{2k+1} \end{bmatrix} = \begin{bmatrix} 0 & -0.8 \\ 0.8 & 1.8 \end{bmatrix} x_k + \begin{bmatrix} 0 \\ -1 \end{bmatrix} u\left(x_k\right). \tag{2.145}$$

Design and simulate an optimal control policy that minimizes the performance index (2.117)*, where* $Q(x_k) = x_k^T x_k$ *and* $R = 1$ *using time-based ADP.*

Using a quadratic cost function (2.117) with $Q\left(x_k\right) = x_k^T x_k$ and $R = 1$, the optimal control input can be found by solving the associated DARE and revealed to be $u^*\left(x_k\right) = \left[0.6239 \quad 1.2561\right] x_k$ while the optimal cost function is found to be $J^*\left(x_k\right) = 1.5063 x_{1k}^2 + 2.0098 x_{1k} x_{2k} + 3.7879 x_{2k}^2$. To obtain this solution through time-based ADP, we shall begin by selecting the initial stabilizing policy for the algorithm to be $u_0\left(x_k\right) = \left[\ 0.5 \quad 1.4\ \right] x_k$. Generate the basis functions for the critic from a sixth-order polynomial as

$$\left\{x_1^2, x_1 x_2, x_2^2, x_1^4, x_1^3 x_2, \ldots, x_2^6\right\}$$

and the action network basis functions can be chosen as the system states as we are working with a linear system.

The initial critic NN weight estimates may be set to zero at the beginning of the simulation while the initial weight estimates of the action network should reflect the initial stabilizing control. For the results presented in the following, the simulation was run for 240 time steps. The design parameters for the critic and action networks were selected as $a_J = 10^{-6}$, $a_u = 0.1$. With these parameters, the time-based ADP algorithm was implemented to learn the optimal policy and value for the linear quadratic regulation problem and the final values of the critic and actor NN weights are shown as follows

$$\begin{aligned} \hat{\Phi} = [\ & 1.5071 \quad 2.0097 \quad 3.7886 \quad -0.0082 \quad -0.0015 \\ & 0.0025 \quad 0.0030 \quad -0.0014 \quad 0.0020 \quad 0.0000 \cdots \\ & 0.0000 \quad 0.0008 \quad -0.0003 \quad 0.0009 \quad -0.0002\ ] \end{aligned}$$

and

$$\begin{aligned} \hat{\Theta} = [\ & 0.6208 \quad 1.2586 \quad 0.0589 \quad -0.0338 \quad 0.0095 \quad \cdots \\ & 0.0092 \quad -0.0049 \quad 0.0074 \quad 0.0050 \quad 0.0075 \quad -0.0054\ ]. \end{aligned}$$

Examining the final values for the NN weights and comparing them to the target parameters shown above in $u^*\left(x_k\right)$ and $J^*\left(x_k\right)$, it is clear that they have successfully learned the optimal values with small bounded error. Additionally, the difference between the optimal control law obtained from the DARE and the optimal control learned online is shown in Figure 2.7. This figure shows that control input generated by the time-based online ADP scheme converges to the target optimal control scheme. It can be observed that the NN-based adaptive optimal control law converged to the optimal value with a small bounded error within the first 200 time steps. Finally, Figure 2.7 (right panel) illustrates that the system state trajectories for the initial stabilizing control that is not optimal and the final online optimal control law.

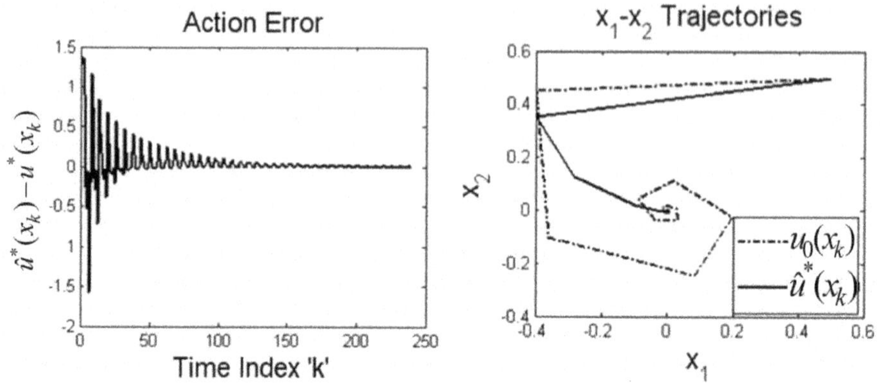

Figure 2.7 Convergence of action errors and state trajectories.

Example 2.3. *(Dierks and Jagannathan, 2012b) Consider a nonlinear system defined by*

$$x_{k+1} = \begin{bmatrix} x_{1k+1} \\ x_{2k+1} \end{bmatrix} = \begin{bmatrix} -x_{1k}x_{2k} \\ x_{1k}^2 + 1.8x_{2k} \end{bmatrix} + \begin{bmatrix} 0 \\ -1 \end{bmatrix} u(x_k). \tag{2.146}$$

Design and simulate an optimal control policy that minimizes the performance index (2.117) *as defined in Example 2.2 using time-based ADP.*

The initial stabilizing policy for the algorithm was selected to be $u_0(x_k) = \begin{bmatrix} -0.4 & 1.24 \end{bmatrix} x_k$, while the basis functions for the cost function approximator were generated as a sixth-order polynomial, and the control network basis functions were generated from the gradient of the cost function basis vector. The design parameters for the cost function and control NN were selected as $a_J = 10^{-6}$ and $a_u = 0.1$, while the cost function approximator NN weights were set to zero at the beginning of the simulation. The initial weights of the action control network were chosen to reflect the initial stabilizing control. The simulation was run for 375 time steps, and the time history of the NN weight estimates are shown in Figure 2.8 (a), and the action error is shown in Figure 2.8 (b). Examining Figure 2.8 (a), it is clear that all NN weights remain bounded while Figure 2.8 (b) shows that the control signal error converges to a small bounded region around the origin.

As a comparison, the SDRE algorithm was implemented along with the offline training algorithm presented in (Chen and Jagannathan, 2008). Figure 2.9 (a) shows the state trajectories when the final optimal control policies learned online, trained offline, and using the discrete SDRE solution, respectively, are applied to the nonlinear system. From the plot shown in Figure 2.9 (a), it is clear that the resulting state trajectories for the online learning and offline training solutions are identical. However, the SDRE solution differs from online and offline HJB-based solutions since SDRE is a suboptimal approximation. Thus, SDRE is an attractive alternative for nonlinear optimal control, however, the resulting control laws are suboptimal even when the exact dynamics are known.

Figure 2.9 (b) displays the cost functions associated with the final optimal control policy learned online, the final optimal control policy found via offline training (Chen and Jagannathan, 2008), and the SDRE control policy, which confirms that the cost associated with the final control policy learned online is on par with the final control policy trained offline as the two curves are indistinguishable

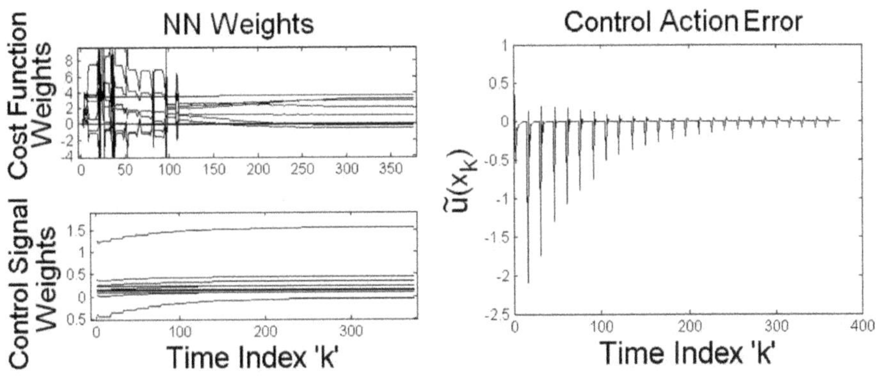

Figure 2.8 (a) NN weights and (b) control signal error for the nonlinear system.

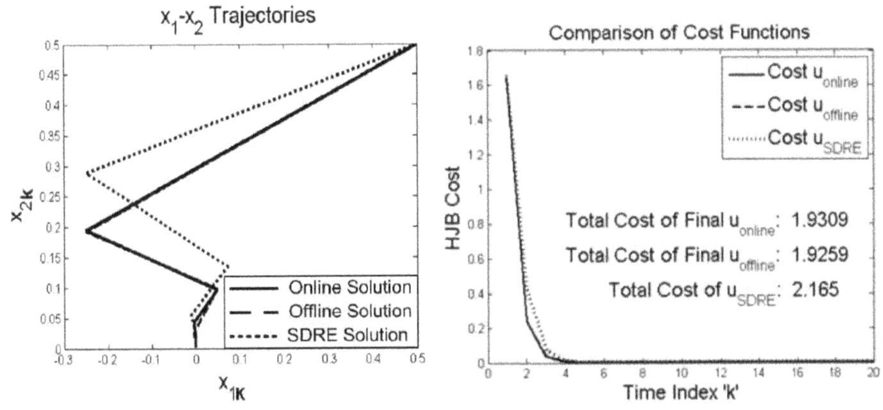

Figure 2.9 (a) Convergence of state trajectories and (b) comparison of near-optimal cost functions.

from each other. In addition, the sub-optimality of the SDRE approach is once again illustrated. Also, this figure indicates the total cost for each policy, which was calculated according to

$$J_{\text{Total}} = \sum_{k=0}^{k_{\text{final}}} J(x_k).$$

Examining the total cost values, the total costs for the online and offline policies are nearly the same, while the total cost of the SDRE approach is higher, as expected.

2.5 ADAPTIVE DYNAMIC PROGRAMMING FOR CONTINUOUS-TIME SYSTEMS

The task of applying RL to continuous-time (CT) systems is a significantly more challenging endeavor compared to its discrete-time counterparts. To understand this, we shall consider a CT nonlinear dynamical system in an affine form

$$\dot{x}(t) = f(x) + g(x)u(t), \quad x(0) = x_0, \tag{2.147}$$

where $x(t) \in \mathbb{R}^n$ is the state vector and the control input is denoted by $u(t) \in \mathbb{R}^m$. To solve an optimal control problem for the CT system, we shall begin by making the standard assumptions to ensure the existence of unique solution to the initial value problem and an equilibrium point at $x = 0$. This includes the requirement for $f(0) = 0$ and the Lipschitz continuity of $f(x) + g(x)u$ on a subset $\Omega \subseteq \mathbb{R}^n$ that includes the origin. We further assume that the system can be stabilized on Ω by a continuous control function $u(t)$, rendering the closed-loop system asymptotically stable on Ω.

We represent the concept of goal-oriented optimal behavior by defining a cost function or performance measure associated with the feedback control policy $u = \mu(x)$ as

$$V(x(t)) = \int_t^{\infty} r(x(\tau), u(\tau))d\tau, \tag{2.148}$$

where the utility function $r(x,u) = Q(x) + u^T Ru$ is employed. The function $Q(x)$ is positive definite, that is, $Q(x) > 0$ for all $x \neq 0$ and $Q(x) = 0$ for $x = 0$. The matrix $R \in \mathbb{R}^{m\times m}$ is also positive definite. Here a control input is said to be an *admissible control* if it stabilizes the system and ensures that the integral (2.148) is well-defined.

If the cost is smooth, it leads to a nonlinear Lyapunov equation, an infinitesimal equivalent to equation (2.148), which can be derived by differentiation as

$$0 = r(x, \mu(x)) + (\nabla V)^T (f(x) + g(x)\mu(x)), V(0) = 0, \tag{2.149}$$

where ∇V (a column vector) represents the gradient of the cost function V with respect to x. The equation (2.149) known as the *CT Bellman equation*, is defined based on the *CT Hamiltonian function*

$$H(x, \mu(x), \nabla V) = r(x, \mu(x)) + (\nabla V)^T (f(x) + g(x)\mu(x)). \tag{2.150}$$

Now using the *stationarity condition*, we may defined the feedback control policy by solving $\frac{\partial H(x,\mu(x),\nabla V)}{\partial \mu(x)} = 0$ for $\mu(x)$ using (2.150). Substituting the $\mu(x)$ back into (2.150) will yield the so-called *Hamilton-Jacobi-Bellman* (HJB) equation.

At this juncture, we can see the immediate challenge with CT systems. When we compare the CT Bellman Hamiltonian (2.150) to the discrete-time Hamiltonian (2.81), we notice that the former includes the full system dynamics $f(x) + g(x)u$, which is not the case with the latter. Therefore, the CT Bellman equation (2.149) cannot be leveraged as the basis for RL unless the full dynamics are available. Observing that

$$0 = r(x, \mu(x)) + (\nabla V)^T (f(x) + g(x)\mu(x)) = r(x, \mu(x)) + \dot{V}. \tag{2.151}$$

Euler's method can be employed (Baird, 1994) to discretize this to obtain

$$0 = r(x_k, u_k) + \frac{V(x_{k+1}) - V(x_k)}{T} \equiv \frac{r_S(x_k, u_k)}{T} + \frac{V(x_{k+1}) - V(x_k)}{T}. \tag{2.152}$$

Here, the sample period is represented by T, such that $t = kT$. The discrete sampled utility is $r_S(x_k, u_k) = r(x_k, u_k)T$, where it is important to multiply the CT utility by the sample period. It is alo noteworthy that the discretized CT Bellman equation (2.152) bears the same structure as the DT Bellman equation (2.80). Consequently, many early RL methods developed for discrete-time systems can be deployed. Baird (1994), based on this, defined *advantage learning* as a way of enhancing the conditioning of RL for sampled CT systems. He observed that if the utility is not discretized appropriately, the discrete-time solutions do not converge to the CT solutions as T approaches zero. However, it's important to recognize this as only an approximation. Alternatively, in many works that followed (Lewis et al., 2012a), the HJB equation was treated as a consistency condition that must be satisfied by the approximated value function and control policy to learn the optimal value function iteratively. Doya (2000) studied the CT RL problem directly using the Hamiltonion expression (2.150). An alternate exact method for CT RL was proposed by Vrabie et al. (2009a). One can write the cost in the integral reinforcement form

$$V(x(t)) = \int_t^{t+T} r(x(\tau), u(\tau))d\tau + V(x(t+T)). \tag{2.153}$$

This equation forms the exact CT analogue of the DT Bellman equation (2.80) for any $T > 0$. Bellman's principle of optimality specifies that the optimal value is structured as follows (Lewis et al., 2012b)

$$V^*(x(t)) = \min_{\bar{u}(t:t+T)} \left(\int_t^{t+T} r(x(\tau),u(\tau))d\tau + V^*(x(t+T)) \right), \tag{2.154}$$

where $\bar{u}(t:t+T)$ signifies the control set $\{u(\tau) : t \leq \tau < t+T\}$. The optimal control can be represented as

$$\mu^*(x(t)) = \arg\min_{\bar{u}(t:t+T)} \left(\int_t^{t+T} r(x(\tau),u(\tau))d\tau + V^*(x(t+T)) \right). \tag{2.155}$$

Vrabie et al. (2009a) demonstrated that the nonlinear Lyapunov equation (2.149) aligns exactly with the integral reinforcement form (2.153). This implies that the positive definite solution to both equations gives the value (2.148) of the policy $u = \mu(x)$. The integral reinforcement form is a manifestation of the Bellman equation for CT systems and functions as a fixed point equation. Accordingly, we can describe the temporal difference error for CT systems as follows

$$e(t:t+T) = \int_t^{t+T} r(x(\tau),u(\tau))d\tau + V(x(t+T)) - V(x(t)). \tag{2.156}$$

This equation is decoupled from the system dynamics. As such, policy iteration and value iteration for CT systems can be formulated directly from this definition.

2.5.1 CONTINUOUS-TIME POLICY ITERATION (PI) ALGORITHM

Similar to the dicrete-time policy iteration, the algorithm in CT demands an initial stabilizing policy and involves the policy evaluation and improvement phases. If the control vector-field or the control coefficient for a nonlinear input-affine system is known, then the PI algorithm can be implemented as described below.

1. **Initialization.** Start with any admissible, i.e., stabilizing, control policy $\mu^{(0)}(x)$.
2. **Policy Evaluation Phase.** Calculate $V^{(i)}(x(t))$ through the following relation:

$$\begin{aligned} V^{(i)}(x(t)) &= \int_t^{t+T} r\left(x(s),\mu^{(i)}(x(s))\right) ds + V^{(i)}(x(t+T)), \\ V^{(i)}(0) &= 0. \end{aligned} \tag{2.157}$$

3. **Policy Improvement Phase.** Find an enhanced policy using

$$\mu^{(i+1)} = \arg\min_u \left[H\left(x,u,\nabla V_x^{(j)}\right)\right], \tag{2.158}$$

which is specifically

$$\mu^{(i+1)}(x) = -\frac{1}{2}R^{-1}g^T(x)\nabla V_x^{(i)}. \tag{2.159}$$

Here the superscript i denotes the iteration index and $\nabla V_x^{(i)}$ is the gradient of the value function with respect to the state.

2.5.2 CONTINUOUS-TIME VALUE ITERATION (VI) ALGORITHM

Similar to the PI, the continuous-time analogue for the value iteration algorithm is summarized as follows:

1. **Initialization.** Begin with any control policy $\mu^{(0)}(x)$, not necessarily a stabilizing one.

2. **Policy Evaluation Phase.** Solve for $V^{(i)}(x(t))$ using the following:

$$
\begin{aligned}
V^{(i)}(x(t)) &= \int_t^{t+T} r\left(x(s), \mu^{(i)}(x(s))\right) ds + V^{(i-1)}(x(t+T)), \\
V^{(i)}(0) &= 0.
\end{aligned}
\tag{2.160}
$$

3. **Policy Improvement Phase.** Determine a superior policy using

$$
\mu^{(i+1)} = \arg\min_u \left[H\left(x, u, \nabla V_x^{(i)}\right)\right], \tag{2.161}
$$

which specifically is

$$
\mu^{(i+1)}(x) = -\frac{1}{2} R^{-1} g^T(x) \nabla V_x^{(i)}. \tag{2.162}
$$

Crucially, these algorithms do not demand explicit knowledge about the internal system dynamics function $f(\cdot)$, thus making them suitable for partially unknown systems. The PI and VI algorithms can be executed online by using the value function approximation and the temporal difference error along with the data collected at each time increment $(x(t), x(t+T), \rho(t:t+T))$, where

$$
\rho(t:t+T) = \int_t^{t+T} r(x(\tau), u(\tau)) d\tau \tag{2.163}
$$

represents the reinforcement gathered in each time span. With the TD error defined for the CT case, algorithms including the Q-learning and the actor-critic techniques can be analogously implemented in the CT case. See Lewis et al. (2012a); Kiumarsi et al. (2017) for more information. The RL time interval T is not required to be constant at each iteration. Adjusting T based on the time required to glean meaningful insights from the observations is permissible. We shall see that a time-varying sampling period T_k can designed, wherein the value of T_k is dynamically determined by the event-triggering mechanism in an event-triggering control framework in Chapter 4.

2.6 ADAPTIVE DYNAMIC PROGRAMMING FOR OPTIMAL TRACKING

We shall now revisit the tracking control problem considered in Chapter 1. Unlike the regulation problem, the difficulty for designing closed-loop optimal tracking control lies in solving the time-varying Hamilton-Jacobi-Bellman (HJB) equation, which is usually too hard to solve analytically. The time-varying nature arises due to the dependence of the HJB equation on the desired or reference trajectory. As a consequence, the value function and control policy are typically obtained as time-varying functions (Dierks and Jagannathan, 2010a, 2009b; Zhang et al., 2011a, 2008a). Typical approaches to handle this challenge have been to make assumptions on the desired trajectory, which is usually assumed to be a state of a dynamic system, referred as *generator dynamics*. Additionally, assumptions on the boundedness of the reference trajectory and steady-state stability of the generator dynamics are made inorder to keep the tracking control problem tractable. In this section, we briefly review two popular approaches reported in the literature to address the optimal tracking control problem. Both these methods focus on transforming the nonautonomous tracking error system into an augmented autonomous system, which will result in well-defined infinite horizon performance index. For more information on the methods described in this section, see Zhang et al. (2008b, 2011b); Kamalapurkar et al. (2015); Modares and Lewis (2014b) and the references therein.

2.6.1 OPTIMAL TRACKING FOR CONTINUOUS-TIME SYSTEMS

Consider an affine nonlinear controllable continuous-time system given by

$$
\dot{x}(t) = f(x(t)) + g(x(t))u(t), \quad x(0) = x_0, \tag{2.164}
$$

where $x : [0, \infty) \to \mathbb{R}^n$ and $u : \mathbb{R}^n \to \mathbb{R}^m$ are state and control input vectors, respectively. The nonlinear vector function $f : \mathbb{R}^n \to \mathbb{R}^n$ and matrix function $g : \mathbb{R}^n \to \mathbb{R}^{n\times m}$ are, respectively, the internal dynamics and the input gain function with $f(0) = 0$. The control objective is to track a feasible reference trajectory $x_d(t) \in \mathbb{R}^n$ generated by a reference system represented by

$$\dot{x}_d(t) = \zeta(x_d(t)), \;\; x_d(0) = x_{d0}, \tag{2.165}$$

where $x_d(t) \in \mathbb{R}^n$ is the reference state, and $\zeta : \mathbb{R}^n \to \mathbb{R}^n$ is the internal dynamics with $\zeta(0) = 0$. To address the tracking control problem, the following assumptions characterizing the systems in (2.164) and (2.165) are essential.

Assumption 2.1. *System* (2.164) *is controllable and the system states are available for measurement.*

Assumption 2.2. *The functions $f(x)$ and $g(x)$ are Lipschitz continuous for all $x \in \Omega_x$ where Ω_x is a compact set containing the origin. Further, the function $g(x)$ has a full column rank for all $x \in \Omega_x$ and satisfies $\|g(x)\| \le g_M$ for some constant $g_M > 0$. In addition, $g(x_d)g^+(x_d) = I$ where $g^+ = (g^T g)^{-1} g^T$.*

Assumption 2.3. *The feasible reference trajectory $x_d(t) \in \Omega_{x_d}$, where Ω_{x_d} is a compact set, is bounded such that $\|x_d(t)\| \le b_{x_d}$ where $b_{x_d} > 0$ is a constant.*

Define the error between the system state and the reference state as tracking error, given by $e_r(t) \triangleq x(t) - x_d(t)$. Then, the tracking error system, utilizing (2.164) and (2.165), can be defined by

$$\dot{e}_r(t) = \dot{x}(t) - \dot{x}_d(t) = f(e_r + x_d) + g(e_r + x_d)u - \zeta(x_d), \quad e_r(0) = x(0) - x_d(0). \tag{2.166}$$

Unlike the non-optimal case discussed in Chapter 1, to design optimal tracking controller, a steady-state feed-forward control policy as a function of the reference trajectory is needed (Zhang et al., 2011a). The feed-forward component of the control policy can be expressed as

$$u_d = g^+(x_d)(\zeta(x_d) - f(x_d)), \tag{2.167}$$

where $u_d : \mathbb{R}^n \to \mathbb{R}^m$. By augmenting the tracking error e_r and desired trajectory x_d, the dynamics of the augmented tracking error system can be represented as

$$\dot{\chi}(t) = F(\chi) + G(\chi)w(t), \tag{2.168}$$

where $\chi \triangleq [e_r^T \;\; x_d^T]^T \in \mathbb{R}^{2n}$ is the augmented state with $\chi(0) = [e_r^T(0) \;\; x_d^T(0)]^T = \chi_0$, $F : \mathbb{R}^{2n} \to \mathbb{R}^{2n}$ is given by $F(\chi) \triangleq \begin{bmatrix} f(e_r + x_d) + g(e_r + x_d)u_d - \zeta(x_d) \\ \zeta(x_d) \end{bmatrix}$, $G : \mathbb{R}^{2n} \to \mathbb{R}^{2n\times m}$ given by $G(\chi) \triangleq \begin{bmatrix} g(e_r + x_d) \\ 0 \end{bmatrix}$, and the mismatched control policy $w \triangleq u - u_d \in \mathbb{R}^m$. The infinite horizon performance index with state constraint enforced by the dynamical system in (2.168) can be defined as

$$J(\chi, w) = \int_0^\infty [\chi^T(\tau)\bar{Q}\chi(\tau) + w(\tau)^T R w(\tau)] d\tau \tag{2.169}$$

where $\bar{Q} \triangleq \begin{bmatrix} Q & 0_{n\times n} \\ 0_{n\times n} & 0_{n\times n} \end{bmatrix} \in \mathbb{R}^{2n\times 2n}$ with $Q \in \mathbb{R}^{n\times n}$ and $R \in \mathbb{R}^{m\times m}$ are symmetric positive definite matrices. The matrix $0_{n\times n}$ is a matrix with all elements zero. Note that the performance index is defined using the mismatched policy w and, therefore, the cost functional is finite for any admissible control policy $w \in \Omega_w$, where Ω_w is the set of all admissible policies (Lewis et al., 2012b). With the above-reformulated cost function (2.169), one can design the optimal control policy $w^*(t)$ by treating it as an optimal regulator using methods discussed in Section 2.5.

2.6.1.1 A Special Case of Linear System

Consider a linear continuous-time system given in (1.45). The control objective is to track a feasible reference trajectory $x_d(t) \in \mathbb{R}^n$ generated by a reference system represented by

$$\dot{x}_d(t) = A_d x_d(t), \quad x_d(0) = x_{d0}, \tag{2.170}$$

where $x_d(t) \in \mathbb{R}^n$ is the reference state, and $A_d \in \mathbb{R}^{n\times n}$ is the internal dynamics with $x_d(0) = 0$.

Define the error between the system state and the reference state as the tracking error, given by $e_r(t) \triangleq x(t) - x_d(t)$. Then, the tracking error system, utilizing (1.45) and (2.170), can be defined by

$$\dot{e}_r(t) = \dot{x}(t) - \dot{x}_d(t) = A(e_r + x_d) + Bu - A_d x_d. \tag{2.171}$$

The steady-state feed-forward control policy for the reference trajectory can be expressed as

$$u_d = B^{+}(A_d x_d - A x_d), \tag{2.172}$$

where $u_d : \mathbb{R}^n \to \mathbb{R}^m$ is the steady state control policy corresponding to the reference trajectory. By augmenting the tracking error e_r and desired trajectory x_d, the dynamics of the augmented tracking error system can be represented as

$$\dot{\chi}(t) = G\chi(t) + Hw(t), \tag{2.173}$$

where $\chi \triangleq [e_r^T \ \ x_d^T]^T \in \mathbb{R}^{2n}$ is the augmented state with $\chi(0) = [e_r^T(0) \ \ x_d^T(0)]^T = \chi_0$, $G \in \mathbb{R}^{2n}$ is given by $G \triangleq \begin{bmatrix} A & A - A_d \\ 0 & A_d \end{bmatrix}$, $H \in \mathbb{R}^{2n\times m}$ given by $H \triangleq \begin{bmatrix} B \\ 0 \end{bmatrix}$, and the mismatched control policy $w \triangleq u - u_d \in \mathbb{R}^m$. The augmented error system in (2.173) transforms the tracking problem into a regulation problem, which can then be solved to stabilize the augmented error system using any of the methods described in Section 2.5.

2.6.2 OPTIMAL TRACKING FOR DISCRETE-TIME SYSTEMS

Consider an affine nonlinear controllable discrete-time system given by

$$x_{k+1} = f(x_k) + g(x_k)u_k, \quad x_0 \in \mathbb{R}^n, \tag{2.174}$$

where $x : [0,\infty) \to \mathbb{R}^n$ and $u : \mathbb{R}^n \to \mathbb{R}^m$ are state and control input vectors, respectively. The nonlinear vector function $f : \mathbb{R}^n \to \mathbb{R}^n$ and matrix function $g : \mathbb{R}^n \to \mathbb{R}^{n\times m}$ are, respectively, the internal dynamics and the input gain function. The control objective is to track a feasible reference trajectory $x_{k,d} \in \mathbb{R}^n$ generated by a reference system represented by

$$x_{k+1,d} = \zeta(x_{k,d}), \quad x_{0,d} \in \mathbb{R}^n, \tag{2.175}$$

where $x_{k,d} \in \mathbb{R}^n$ is the reference state, and $\zeta : \mathbb{R}^n \to \mathbb{R}^n$ is the internal dynamics. To address the tracking control problem, the following assumptions characterizing the systems in (2.174) and (2.175) are essential. Similar to the assumptions used for the continuous-time systems, the system (2.174) should be controllable. Further, it is important that the function $g^{-1}(x_{k,d})$ exists, the reference trajectory is feasible and bounded.

Define the error between the system state and the reference state as tracking error, given by $e_{k,r} \triangleq x_k - x_{k,d}$. Then, the tracking error system, utilizing (2.164) and (2.175), can be defined by

$$e_{k+1,r} = x_{k+1} - x_{k+1,d} = f(e_{k,r} + x_{k,d}) + g(e_{k,r} + x_{k,d})u_k - \zeta(x_{k,d}), \quad e_{k,r} = x_0 - x_{k,d}. \tag{2.176}$$

For time-invariant optimal tracking problems in linear systems, the performance index is typically defined as the following quadratic form

$$J(e_{0,r}, u_k) = \sum_{k=0}^{\infty} \{e_{k,r}^T Q e_{k,r} + u_k^T R u_k\}, \tag{2.177}$$

where Q, R are positive definite penalty matrices. Sometimes the control penalty function in the cost is defined as $(u_k - u_{k-1})^T R (u_k - u_{k-1})$ (Zhang et al., 2008a). However, in the case of time-variant tracking problems within a nonlinear environment, the issue becomes considerably more complex. The aforementioned performance index, i.e., $J(e_{0,r}, u_k)$ calculated by (2.177), may become invalid, leading to potential infinity values, as the control u_k depends on the desired trajectory $x_{k,d}$. To solve this problem, several approaches are presented in the literature. In particular, derived from Zhang et al. (2008a) the following performance index can be used

$$J(e_{0,r}, u_k) = \sum_{k=0}^{\infty} \{e_{k,r}^T Q e_{k,r} + w_k^T R w_k\}, \tag{2.178}$$

where $w_k = u_k - u_{k,d}$. To keep the change in controls small, Zhang et al. (2008a) used the penalty term $(w_k - w_{k-1})^T R (w_k - w_{k-1})$ with $w_k = 0$ for $k < 0$. The steady-state feed-forward control policy as a function of the reference trajectory, following (Zhang et al., 2008a), is expressed as

$$u_{k,d} = g^{-1}(x_{k,d})(\zeta(x_{k,d}) - f(x_{k,d})), \tag{2.179}$$

where $u_d : \mathbb{R}^n \to \mathbb{R}^m$. In equation (2.178), the first term represents the tracking error, while the second term corresponds to the difference in feedback and feedforward control components. Nevertheless, a concern persists that if the performance index considers only these two aspects, the system may exhibit oscillations. For instance, the feedback and feedforward control difference may be small, yet a significant error could exist between the these two control components. To address this, Zhang et al. (2008a) introduced an additional penalty term $(u_k - u_{k,d})^T S (u_k - u_{k,d})$ in the cost function to suppress oscillatory transients.

The transformation of the tracking control problem to a regulation problem will be complete if we define the augmented system and the associated cost function based on the previous developments. By augmenting the tracking error e_r and desired trajectory x_d, the dynamics of the augmented tracking error system can be represented as

$$\chi_{k+1} = F(\chi_k) + G(\chi_k) w_k, \tag{2.180}$$

where $\chi \triangleq [e_r^T \;\; x_d^T]^T \in \mathbb{R}^{2n}$ is the augmented state with $\chi_0 = [e_{0,r}^T \;\; x_{0,d}^T]^T$, $F : \mathbb{R}^{2n} \to \mathbb{R}^{2n}$ is given by $F(\chi) \triangleq \begin{bmatrix} f(e_r + x_d) + g(e_r + x_d) u_d - \zeta(x_{k,d}) \\ \zeta(x_{k,d}) \end{bmatrix}$, $G : \mathbb{R}^{2n} \to \mathbb{R}^{2n \times m}$ given by $G(\chi) \triangleq \begin{bmatrix} g(e_r + x_d) \\ 0 \end{bmatrix}$, and the mismatched control policy $w \triangleq u - u_d \in \mathbb{R}^m$. The infinite horizon performance index with state constraint enforced by the dynamical system in (2.168) can be defined as

$$J(\chi, w) = \int_0^{\infty} [\chi^T(\tau) \bar{Q} \chi(\tau) + w(\tau)^T R w(\tau)] d\tau \tag{2.181}$$

where $\bar{Q} \triangleq \begin{bmatrix} Q & 0_{n\times n} \\ 0_{n\times n} & 0_{n\times n} \end{bmatrix} \in \mathbb{R}^{2n\times 2n}$ with $Q \in \mathbb{R}^{n\times n}$ and $R \in \mathbb{R}^{m\times m}$ are symmetric positive definite matrices. The matrix $0_{n\times n}$ is a matrix with all elements zero. Note that the performance index is defined using the mismatched policy w and, therefore, the cost functional is finite for any admissible control policy $w \in \Omega_w$, where Ω_w is the set of all admissible policies (Lewis et al., 2012b). With the above-reformulated cost function (2.181), one can design the optimal control policy $w^*(t)$ by treating it as an optimal regulator using methods discussed in Section 2.5.

2.6.3 OPTIMAL TRACKING FOR CONTINUOUS-TIME SYSTEMS USING DISCOUNTED COST

The conventional tracking control design techniques, including the one presened in Section 2.6.1, find the feedback and feedforward parts of the control input separately using complete knowledge of the system dynamics. In addition, with the augmented system dynamics, they employ ADP methods to learn the control components. An alternative method to learn the tracking control input with both the feedback and feedforward parts of the control input simultaneously was reported in the work by Modares and Lewis (2014a,b). In their approach, they considered the generator model as in (2.165) and constructed an augmented system

$$\dot{\chi}(t) = \begin{bmatrix} \dot{e}_r(t) \\ \dot{x}_d(t) \end{bmatrix} = \begin{bmatrix} f(e_r+x_d)-\zeta(x_d) \\ \zeta(x_d) \end{bmatrix} + \begin{bmatrix} g(e_r+x_d) \\ 0 \end{bmatrix} u(t) \equiv F(\chi)+G(\chi)u(t), \tag{2.182}$$

with the augmented states and their initial conditions defined as in (2.168) and the functions F and G redefined based on (2.182). In this case, the cost function, characterizing the performance of the tracking controller is defined as

$$J(\chi(t),w(t)) = \int_t^{\infty} \exp^{-\lambda(\tau-t)}[\chi^T(\tau)\bar{Q}\chi(\tau)+u(\tau)^T Ru(\tau)]d\tau, \tag{2.183}$$

where $\lambda \geq 0$ is the discount factor. It is important to note that both the steady-state (feed-forward) and feedback components of the control input are obtained simultaneously through the minimization of the discounted performance function (2.183) along the trajectories of the augmented system (2.182). The incorporation of a discount factor in the performance index is crucial. This is due to the presence of a steady-state component in the control input, which typically renders the integral in (2.183) unbounded if a discount factor is not utilized.

In this case, the continuous-time equivalent of the Bellman equation can be obtained as

$$[\chi^T(\tau)\bar{Q}\chi(\tau)+u(\tau)^T Ru(\tau)] - \lambda V + \frac{\partial V^T}{\partial \chi}[F(\chi)+G(\chi)u] = 0, \quad V(0)=0, \tag{2.184}$$

and the Hamiltonian function given by

$$H(\chi,u,\frac{\partial V^T}{\partial \chi}) = [\chi^T(\tau)\bar{Q}\chi(\tau)+u(\tau)^T Ru(\tau)] - \lambda V + \frac{\partial V^T}{\partial \chi}[F(\chi)+G(\chi)u]. \tag{2.185}$$

The optimal control policy is then obtained via stationarity condition and is given by $u^*(t) = -R^-1G^T(\chi)\frac{\partial V^*}{\partial \chi]}$, with V^* denoting the optimal value function for the tracking problem. As described earlier, the augmented error system transforms the tracking problem into a regulation problem, which can then be solved to stabilize the augmented error system using any of the ADP methods described in Section 2.5.

2.7 CONCLUDING REMARKS

In this chapter, a brief introduction to neural networks and their approximation property, dynamic programming-based backward-in-time optimal control, and online iterative and time-based solutions to approximate optimal control using adaptive dynamic programming both in discrete and continuous time domains are presented. The universal approximation property of the NNs is leveraged to approximate the value function (solution to the HJB equation) and optimal control policy using actor-critic architecture. First, an online iterative approach using the policy and value iteration is presented and then a non-iterative approach using the time history of the cost-to-go and system trajectory is presented. This time-based approach is utilized as the backbone for the development of event-based ADP and Q-learning presented in the next chapters (Chapters 3-8).

2.8 PROBLEMS

2.8.1 A neuron with linear activation function is described by $y = v_1x_1 + v_2x_2 + v_0$. Select the weights to design one-layer NN that implement the following Logic operations:

(a) AND

(b) OR

(c) COMPLEMENT

What about the Exclusive-OR (XOR) operation? Plot the decision boundary learned by the NN.

2.8.2 Perform a MATLAB simulation of the Hopfield nets (both continuous and discrete time) using their equations provided in 2.1.2.5. Select $u_i = 0$, $\tau_i, p_i \in (0,1)$, and $w_{ij} \in [0,1]$ for all i, j. Make phase-plane plots for representative initial conditions $x(0)$.

2.8.3 Build and train a two-layer NN that implements the X-OR operation. Begin with random weights and train using backpropagation. The input vectors x are $\{(0\,0)^T, (0\,1)^T, (1\,0)^T, (1\,1)^T\}$, and the associated desired outputs y are given by the definition of X-OR. Plot the decision boundary learned by the network.

2.8.4 Perform a detailed derivation of backpropogation algorithm using matrix techniques.

2.8.5 Let P desired input-output pairs $(X^1, Y^1), (X^2, Y^2), \ldots, (X^P, Y^P)$ be prescribed for the NN. In batch updating, all P pairs are presented to the NN and a cumulative error is computed. At the end of this procedure, the NN weights are updated once using the backpropogation algorithm. Derive this update law by defining the cumulative error for one epoch as

$$E(k) = \sum_{p=1}^{P} E^p(k)$$

with $E^p(k)$ given as the squared difference between network output and the target output. Use matrix calculus for the derivation. Implement the resulting algorithm for the X-OR problem. Alternatively, in a stochastic gradient-based updating, the p pairs are sampled randomly and weights of the NN are updated using the sampled data. Assign uniform probability distribution to the P pairs of data and sample them with equal probability. Implement the resulting algorithm for the X-OR problem. Is there any difference in the convergence time between the two algorithms?

2.8.6 The activation function derivatives are required to implement backpropagation training. Compute the derivatives of the following: (a) sigmoid activation function (b) tanh activation function (c) RBF.

2.8.7 Derive the backpropagation algorithm using: (a) Tanh activation functions. (b) RBF activation functions.

2.8.8 (Lewis et al. (1998)) A modified backpropagation algorithm is obtained by changing the order of the operations in the standard backpropogation algorithm. Thus, suppose the backpropagated error and updated weights are computed in the interleaved fashion

$$\delta_i^2 = y_i(1-y_i)e_i; i = 1,2,\ldots,m$$
$$w_{i\ell} = w_{i\ell} + \eta z_\ell \delta_i^2; \quad i = 1,2,\ldots,m; \quad \ell = 0,1,\ldots,L$$

$$\delta_\ell^1 = z_\ell(1-z_\ell)\sum_{i=1}^{m} w_{i\ell}\delta_i^2.; \quad \ell = 1,2,\ldots,L$$
$$v_{\ell j} = v_{\ell j} + \eta X_j \delta_\ell^1; \quad \ell = 1,2,\ldots,L; j = 0,1,\ldots,n$$

where the new layer-2 weights $w_{i\ell}$ are used to compute the layer-1 backpropagated error δ_ℓ^1. Justify this algorithm (or argue against it) using partial derivative/chain rule arguments. Would you expect this algorithm to perform better or worse than standard backpropagation?

2.8.9 Write a MATLAB M file to implement the modified backpropagation training algorithm given in the previous problem . Using your program, and any example, answer the following questions: Does the modified algorithm converge faster than standard backpropagation? Can this behavior be generalized to any example?

2.8.10 The longitudinal dynamics of an F-16 aircraft in straight and level flight at 502 ft/sec are given by

$$\dot{x} = Ax + Bu = \begin{bmatrix} -2.0244\times10^{-2} & 7.8761 & -3.2169\times10^{1} & -6.502\times10^{-1} \\ -2.5373\times10^{-4} & -1.0189 & 0 & 9.0484\times10^{-1} \\ 0 & 0 & 0 & 1 \\ 7.9472\times10^{-11} & -2.498 & 0 & -1.3861 \end{bmatrix} x \quad (2.186)$$
$$+ \begin{bmatrix} -1\times10^{-2} \\ -2.09\times10^{-3} \\ 0 \\ -1.99\times10^{-1} \end{bmatrix} u$$

The state is $x = \begin{bmatrix} v_T & \alpha & \theta & q \end{bmatrix}^T$, with v_T the forward velocity, α the angle of attack, θ the pitch angle, and q the pitch rate. The control input $u(t)$ is the elevator deflection δ_e.

(a) Try MATLAB function LQR to perform linear quadratic regulator design. Use $Q = I, R = 0.1$.

2.8.11 Consider the scalar bilinear system

$$x_{k+1} = x_k u_k + u_k^2 \quad (2.187)$$

with the cost index

$$J_0 = x_N^2 + \sum_{k=0}^{N-1} x_k u_k. \quad (2.188)$$

Let $N = 2$ and the control is constrained to take values of $u_k = -1, 0, 1$ and the state to take values of $x_k = -2, -1, 0, 1, 2$. Use dynamic programming to find an optimal state feedback control law. Let $x_0 = -2$. Find the optimal cost, control sequence, and state trajectory.

2.8.12 Write a MATLAB program to implement the dynamic programming algorithm to solve the previous problem.

2.8.13 For the system in (2.186), implement the value iteration, policy iteration algorithms to learn the optimal control policy.

2.8.14 For the system in (2.186), implement the time-based ADP algorithm to learn the optimal control policy.

3 Linear Discrete-time and Networked Control Systems

CONTENTS

The resource-aware event-triggered control, discussed in Chapter 1, can considerably save the computational and communication costs for implementing the control schemes in systems that use embedded processors with limited computational capabilities and communication networks in the feedback loop. The primary focus of Chapter 1 is to introduce the traditional event-based controller design techniques (for regulation and tracking problems) via an emulation-based approach, which can guarantee the stability of the systems with less frequent computation of the control input. The event-triggering mechanism or condition for determining the sampling instants is designed using complete knowledge of the system dynamics and Lyapunov stability. On the other hand, in Chapter 2, we focused on optimizing the system performance by minimizing a performance index by exploiting adaptive control, optimal control, and reinforcement learning (RL), referred to as adaptive dynamic programming (ADP). One of the challenges we encountered in Chapter 2 is the requirement of higher computation due to the value function and control policy approximation using neural networks. To alleviate the challenges in deploying the ADP-based near-optimal control schemes due to the computational demand, in this chapter, we shall explore the domain of event-driven ADP for linear systems with state and output feedback. We will also explore networked systems where the feedback data and control input are communicated via a communication network.

In the first part of the chapter, we shall focus on designing near-optimal adaptive regulators for uncertain linear discrete-time systems utilizing ADP (dynamic programming and Q-learning techniques). We shall start with the assumption that the communication channels in the control loop are lossless. In the second part, we shall extend the Q-learning techniques to the networked control system (NCS), where an imperfect communication network closes the feedback loop. In both the cases, we shall utilize the feedback data that are sampled and communicated at event-based aperiodic time instants. To solve the feedback control problem in this setting, we shall incorporate event-driven ADP-based Q-learning technique with both state and output feedback and learn the infinite horizon near-optimal control policy. We shall develop aperiodic or intermittent update laws for tuning the Q-function parameters only at the event-triggering instants. For both the state and the output feedback cases, event-triggering conditions, asymptotic stability and convergence results, and existence of non-trivial minimum inter-event times shall be analyzed. Finally, we shall see that these developments are also useful in the context of developing near-optimal tracking controllers for linear discrete-time systems with unknown models. The techniques and analysis presented in this chapter are based on the developments in (Sahoo, 2015).

3.1 INTRODUCTION

Event-driven sampling and feedback control frameworks (Astrom and Bernhardsson, 2002; Cogill, 2009; Donkers and Heemels, 2010; Eqtami et al., 2010; Garcia and Antsaklis, 2011; Heemels et al., 2008; Lunze and Lehmann, 2010; Mazo and Tabuada, 2011; Molin and Hirche, 2013; Tabuada, 2007; Wang and Lemmon, 2008), called event-triggered control (ETC), have been introduced to reduce the computational burden. The ETC framework is instrumental in the area of networked control systems (NCS) (Xu et al., 2012). It saves bandwidth due to the non-periodic transmission of feedback signals through the communication network included within the loop. The main idea behind the ETC design is determining the aperiodic sampling or event-triggering instants. A state or output-dependent condition called an event-triggering condition is generally employed to determine these triggering instants. Further, the event-triggering condition also ensures the desired performance and closed-loop stability of the physical systems. As discussed in Chapter 1, the initial development of the event-triggered control schemes using state and output feedbacks are designed with the assumption of complete knowledge of system dynamics (Donkers and Heemels, 2010; Eqtami et al., 2010; Heemels et al., 2008; Lunze and Lehmann, 2010) or a model of a physical system with small uncertainties (Garcia and Antsaklis, 2011). Later, Sahoo et al. (2013b) presented an adaptive control scheme in an event-triggered context. The system dynamics were estimated using adaptive control (Narendra and Annaswamy, 2012) techniques with an event-based sampling of state and output measurements.

In the earlier works on event-triggered optimal control, Molin and Hirche (2013) examined traditional optimal control (Lewis et al., 2012b) in the context of event-based transmission of the system states. The Riccati equation (RE), with complete knowledge of the system dynamics, was used to solve the finite horizon Linear Quadratic Regulator (LQR) problem in a backward-in-time manner. In general, the optimal control schemes use Q-learning-based iterative techniques (Bradtke et al., 1994; Watkins, 1989) were proposed for periodically sampled linear systems to obtain iteratively optimal control using dynamic programming in a forward-in-time manner, which also relaxes the assumption of complete knowledge of system dynamics. However, with these iterative techniques (Cheng et al., 2007; Wang et al., 2011), a significant number of iterations are needed within a sampling interval to obtain a solution to the dynamic programming, and therefore limits its applicability (Dierks and Jagannathan, 2009b) in real-world systems. Dierks and Jagannathan (2009b) proposed a time-based approach, discussed in Chapter 2, to obtain the optimal solution forward in time. Although the approach in (Dierks and Jagannathan, 2009b) alleviates the issue of iteration, the approximation of the value function still uses period sampling and control updates, demanding higher computation. In this chapter, we will focus on an approach that alleviates the issue of computational demand called event-driven Q-learning.

In the first part of the chapter, taken from (Sahoo, 2015) (Chapter 1), an event-driven ADP-based state feedback control scheme for uncertain linear discrete-time systems is introduced. The event-driven ADP (Xu et al., 2012; Bradtke et al., 1994; Watkins, 1989) technique solves the infinite horizon optimal control problem under both the state and the output feedback measurements. In event-driven ADP, the cost function is parametrized by introducing the Q-function, and the control input is computed from the learned parameters of the Q-function using the event-based state measurements. This complete data-driven Q-learning technique relaxes the assumption of complete knowledge of system dynamics for both designs. Instead of the iterative approaches (value/policy iterations), the time history of the cost-to-go function at the event-triggering instants is used (Dierks and Jagannathan, 2009b) for Q-function parameter update. A non-periodic parameter tuning law is used to tune the parameters of the Q-function.

However, the state vector is not always available for measurement in many practical applications. Therefore, the above approach is extended for output feedback event-triggered optimal control design. An adaptive observer to estimate the system state vector was included at the sensor and tuned periodically for the output feedback design. The estimated state vector is sampled at the event-triggering instants and used for estimating the Q-function for the output feedback case. The adaptive event-triggering conditions for the state and output feedback are designed as a function of the estimated Q-function parameters and with either measured or estimated state vectors. We will also demonstrate that the adaptive event-triggering condition ensured the convergence of parameters by creating a sufficient number of events during the initial adaptation. The stability of the closed-loop event-triggered system was demonstrated using the Lyapunov direct method, as discussed by the authors in Wang and Lemmon (2008). It is shown in Wang and Lemmon (2008) that the Lyapunov function need not converge monotonically. In the case ETC, as discussed in Wang and Lemmon (2008), it may increase during the inter-event times but remains bounded. Therefore, the convergence of the Lyapunov function is shown using a decrescent function that upper bounds the Lyapunov function, provided the regression vectors satisfy the PE condition (Green and Moore, 1985). Finally, the existence of non-trivial inter-event times for the state feedback case is shown by deriving an explicit formula.

3.2 STATE FEEDBACK DESIGN

In this section, the event-triggered optimal adaptive state feedback-based regulation is presented. The event-based estimation and event-based stability issues are precisely addressed while formulating the problem. Subsequently, a solution is introduced along with the design procedure.

3.2.1 PROBLEM STATEMENT

Consider the linear time-invariant (LTI) discrete-time system

$$\begin{aligned} x_{k+1} &= Ax_k + Bu_k \\ y_k &= Cx_k, \end{aligned} \tag{3.1}$$

where $x_k \in \Omega_x \subseteq \mathbb{R}^n$ and $u_k \in \Omega_u \subseteq \mathbb{R}^m$ represent the state and the control input vectors, respectively, with initial state x_0. The system matrices, $A \in \mathbb{R}^{n\times n}$ and $B \in \mathbb{R}^{n\times m}$, are considered unknown. The system (3.1) satisfies the following assumption.

Assumption 3.1. *The system is considered controllable with the control coefficient matrix satisfying $\|B\| \leq B_{\max}$, where $B_{\max} > 0$ is a known constant. Further, the order of the system is known, and the state vector is considered measurable.*

The system states x_k, in an event-triggered framework (see Figure 3.1), is sent to the controller at the event sampled instants only. Let a subsequence $\{k_i\}_{i=0}^{\infty}$ of time instants $k \in \mathbb{N} \cup \{0\}$ satisfying $k_{i+1} > k_i$ and $k_i \to \infty$ as $i \to \infty$ referred to as event-sampled instants with $k_0 = 0$ as the initial event sampled instant. Alternatively, the system state vector (x_{k_i}) is sent to the controller at the time instant k_i for $i = 0, 1, 2, \cdots$. The controller holds it until the next trigger instant for the controller execution. The state vector at the controller can be defined as

$$\hat{x}_k = \begin{cases} x_k, & k = k_i, \\ x_{k_i}, & k_i < k < k_{i+1}, \end{cases} \tag{3.2}$$

where $\hat{x}_k$ is the state at the controller between two triggering instants with an initial value $\hat{x}_0 = x_0$ due to the initial trigger at k_0.

The event-triggering condition (defined later) is typically a function of the event-triggering error and a state-dependent threshold (Tabuada, 2007). The event-triggering error, e_k, is defined as the difference between the current, x_k, and the last transmitted and held system state vector, $\hat{x}_k$, at the controller, i.e.,

$$e_k = x_k - \hat{x}_k, \; k_i \le k < k_{i+1}. \tag{3.3}$$

The event-based state feedback controller can be written as

$$u_k = \mu\left(\hat{x}_k\right), \; k_i \le k < k_{i+1}, \tag{3.4}$$

where $\mu\left(\hat{x}_k\right)$ is a function of the event-based state (3.2).

The primary objective here is to design an event-based optimal controller u_k with without the knowledge of the system dynamics (A and B) while minimizing the performance index defined as

$$J_k = \sum\nolimits_{j=k}^{\infty} r(x_j, u_j), \tag{3.5}$$

where $r(x_k, u_k) = x_k^T P x_k + u_k^T R u_k$ is a quadratic cost-to-go function at the time instant k where the matrix $P \in \mathbb{R}^{n\times n}$ is positive semi-definite that penalizes the system state (x_k) and the matrix $R \in \mathbb{R}^{m\times m}$ that is positive definite and penalizes the control input. The initial control input u_0 is assumed to be admissible, i.e., the control input u_0 is stabilizing, and the integral in the performance index exists.

According to Bellman's principle of optimality (Bellman, 1966), discussed in Chapter 2, the optimal value function can be defined as

$$V^*(x_k) = \min_{u_k}\left(r(x_k, u_k) + V^*(x_{k+1})\right), \tag{3.6}$$

where $V^*(x_k)$ is the optimal value function at time instant k, and $V^*(x_{k+1})$ is the optimal value function from time $k+1$ onwards. The Hamiltonian is given by

$$H\left(x_k, u_k\right) = r(x_k, u_k) + V\left(x_{k+1}\right) - V\left(x_k\right). \tag{3.7}$$

The state feedback optimal control input u_k^* satisfies the stationarity condition given by $\frac{\partial H(x_k, u_k)}{\partial u_k} = 0$. Using the stationarity condition, the optimal control input with periodic state x_k^T for $\forall k$ can be expressed as

$$u_k^* = \mu^*\left(x_k\right) = -K_k^* x_k, \tag{3.8}$$

Using the emulation-based approach, the event-triggered optimal input u_k^* with the event-sampled state vector at the controller, $\hat{x}_k$, can now be written as

$$u_k^* = \mu^*\left(\hat{x}_k\right) = -K_k^* \hat{x}_k, \tag{3.9}$$

where $K^* = \left(R + B^T S B\right)^{-1} B^T S A$ is the optimal control gain matrix and the matrix S satisfies the algebraic Riccati equation (ARE) (Lewis et al., 2012b) given by

$$S = A^T\left[S - SB\left(B^T S B + R\right)^{-1} B^T S\right]A + P. \tag{3.10}$$

Using the solution, S, to the ARE, the optimal value function can be expressed in a quadratic form (Lewis et al., 2012b) as

$$V^*(x_k) = x_k^T S x_k. \tag{3.11}$$

Note that the computation of optimal control gain matrix K^* in (3.9) requires the system matrices, A and B, which are considered unknown in this case. Hence, the ARE (3.10) cannot be solved to compute the control gain K^*; they must be estimated online. The event-based availability of the state vector precludes the use of periodic time-based approaches for parameter estimation. Therefore, the parameters must be estimated using the state and control input information available and computed, respectively, at the triggering instances k_i for $i = 0,1,2,\cdots$. This requires the adaptive (update) laws or tuning rules for parameters to be aperiodic while ensuring the convergence of the parameter estimation error. Therefore, the main objective is to design an adaptive event-triggering condition under unknown system dynamics to reduce computation and facilitate the optimal control gain matrix estimation.

As a solution, the event-driven Q-learning-based technique is presented for designing the near-optimal adaptive regulator whose structure is illustrated in Figure 3.1.

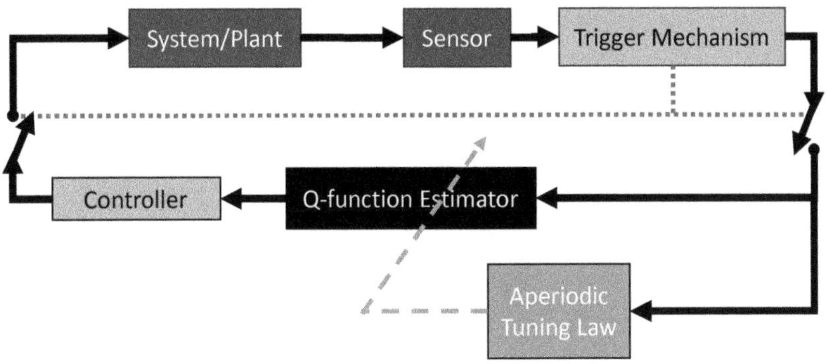

Figure 3.1 Event-triggered optimal state feedback regulator.

In the Q-learning approach (Starr and Ho, 1969), the control gain matrix K^* can be computed from the action-dependent value function, usually referred to as the Q-function. Therefore, in this approach, an event-driven adaptive Q-function estimator (QFE) is utilized at the controller to learn the Q-function online. An aperiodic tuning law, which updates only at the event-triggering instances, is used to tune the estimated Q-function parameters. A smart sensor and a triggering mechanism are included near the plant to determine the event-triggering instants. At the triggering mechanism, the event-triggering condition is evaluated at every sampling instant k, and a decision is made to release the system state vector both for time instant k_i and $k_i - 1$ (x_{k_i} and x_{k_i-1}, $i = 1,2,\ldots$) to the controller only at the violation of the triggering condition. Note that the threshold in the event-triggering condition becomes a function of both the estimated Q-function parameters and the system state. Therefore, the event-triggering condition becomes adaptive, unlike the ZOH and model-based triggering conditions discussed in Chapter 1 for known system dynamics (Tabuada, 2007; Garcia and Antsaklis, 2011; Wang and Lemmon, 2008). The adaptive triggering condition not only ensures stability but facilitates the estimation process.

The Q-function parameters are also estimated locally at the triggering mechanism using a mirror QFE to evaluate the triggering condition. This will save transmissions of Q-function parameters between the QFE at the controller and the triggering mechanism in case of an NCS (discussed in the second part of this chapter). The mirror at the triggering mechanism and the actual QFE at the controller operate in synchronism and are initialized with the same initial conditions. It is to be noted that the mirror QFE at the triggering mechanism demands additional computational power.

However, the overall computational power required for the execution of the event-driven Q-leaning-based controller is found to be lesser than its traditional counterpart (Barto et al., 2004) with one QFE.

Table 3.1
State feedback control scheme

System dynamics	$x_{k+1} = Ax_k + Bu_k$
Event-triggering error	$e_k = x_k - \hat{x}_k,\ k_i \leq k < k_{i+1}$
Q-function estimator (QFE)	$Q(x_k, u_k) = z_k^T G z_k = \Theta^T \xi_k$
QFE residual error	$e_k^V = \begin{cases} r(x_k, u_k) + \hat{\Theta}_k^T \Delta\xi_k, & k = k_i, \\ r(\hat{x}_k, u_k) + \hat{\Theta}_k^T \Delta\hat{\xi}_k, & k_i < k < k_{i+1}, \end{cases}$
Auxilary QFE error	$\Xi_k^V = \Pi_k + \hat{\Theta}_k^T Z_k,\ k = k_i$
Event-based update law	$\hat{\Theta}_k = \begin{cases} \hat{\Theta}_{k-1} - \dfrac{W_{k-1} Z_{k-1} \Xi_{k-1}^{V^T}}{\lVert I + Z_{k-1}^T W_{k-1} Z_{k-1} \rVert}, & k = k_i \\ \hat{\Theta}_{k-1},\ k_{i-1} < k < k_i, \end{cases}$ $W_k = \begin{cases} W_{k-1} - \dfrac{W_{k-1} Z_{k-1} Z_{k-1}^T W_{k-1}}{\lVert I + Z_k^T W_k Z_k \rVert}, & k = k_i \\ W_k,\ k_{i-1} < k < k_i \end{cases}$
Control input	$u_k = -\hat{K}_k \hat{x}_k,\ k_i \leq k < k_{i+1}$ $\hat{K}_k = (\hat{G}_k^{uu})^{-1} \hat{G}_k^{ux}$
Event-triggering Condition	$\lVert e_k \rVert \leq \sigma_k^{ETC} \lVert x_k \rVert$ $\sigma_k^{ETC} = \sqrt{\Gamma(1 - 3\bar{\mu})/3B_{\max}^2 \lVert \hat{K}_k \rVert^2}$

3.2.2 THE Q-FUNCTION SETUP

The action-dependent value function or the Q-function as a function of the system state vector and control input can be represented as

$$Q(x_k, u_k) = r(x_k, u_k) + V^*(x_{k+1}). \tag{3.12}$$

The value function for the time instant $k+1$, taken from (3.11), can be expressed as $V^*(x_{k+1}) = x_{k+1}^T S x_{k+1}$. Substituting $V^*(x_{k+1})$ along with the system dynamics from (3.1) into (3.12) generates the following

$$\begin{bmatrix} x_k^T & u_k^T \end{bmatrix} G \begin{bmatrix} x_k^T & u_k^T \end{bmatrix}^T = \begin{bmatrix} x_k \\ u_k \end{bmatrix}^T \begin{bmatrix} P + A^T SA & A^T SB \\ B^T SA & R + B^T SB \end{bmatrix} \begin{bmatrix} x_k \\ u_k \end{bmatrix}. \tag{3.13}$$

Defining

$$G = \begin{bmatrix} P + A^T SA & A^T SB \\ B^T SA & R + B^T SB \end{bmatrix} = \begin{bmatrix} G^{xx} & G^{xu} \\ G^{ux} & G^{uu} \end{bmatrix}, \tag{3.14}$$

where $G^{xx} = P + A^T SA$, $G^{xu} = A^T SB$, $G^{ux} = B^T SA$, and $G^{uu} = R + B^T SB$ are the block matrices, we can express the Q-function in a compact form as

$$Q(x_k, u_k) = \begin{bmatrix} x_k^T & u_k^T \end{bmatrix} G \begin{bmatrix} x_k^T & u_k^T \end{bmatrix}^T. \tag{3.15}$$

The optimal action dependent value function or the Q-function $Q^*(x_k, u_k^*)$ in (3.12) is equal to the optimal value function $V^*(x_k)$ in (3.6) when the control policy, $u_k = u_k^*$. i.e., optimal. Thus,

$$V^*(x_k) = \min_{u_k}\{Q(x_k, u_k)\} = \min_{u_k}\{[x_k^T \quad u_k^T]G[x_k^T \quad u_k^T]^T\} = Q^*(x_k, u_k^*). \tag{3.16}$$

The action-dependent value function or the Q-function using (3.16) can be expressed as

$$Q(x_k, u_k) = r(x_k, u_k) + Q^*(x_{k+1}, u_k^*). \tag{3.17}$$

The equation (3.17) is the action-dependent version of the Bellman equation of optimality in (3.6). Therefore, the last row of the G matrix in (3.14) can be used to express the optimal control gain as

$$K^* = (R + B^T SB)^{-1} B^T SA = (G^{uu})^{-1} G^{ux}. \tag{3.18}$$

Therefore, the estimation of matrix G in the action-dependent value function or Q-function will include all the information needed to compute the optimal control gain matrix, K^*. Alternatively, the estimation of the G matrix using data is equivalent to solving the ARE (3.10) without information of A and B matrics. This allows the computation of the optimal control input online in a forward-in-time manner without explicit knowledge of the system dynamics. The next subsection details the procedure for the computation of the optimal control policy using the event-based Q-learning scheme.

3.2.3 PARAMETRIC FORM AND LEARNING OF OPTIMAL GAIN

In this subsection, we express the action-dependent value function or Q-function (3.12) in a parametric form. The Q-function parameters are learned using the time history of the system state and input at triggering instants.

Rewriting the optimal Q-function (3.13) in a parametric form as

$$Q(x_k, u_k) = z_k^T G z_k = \Theta^T \xi_k, \tag{3.19}$$

where $z_k = \begin{bmatrix} x_k^T & u_k^T \end{bmatrix}^T \in \mathbb{R}^{n+m=l}$ is the column vector obtained through concatenation of x_k and u_k. The regression vector

$$\xi_k = z_k \otimes z_k = [z_{k1}^2, \cdots, z_{k1}z_{kl}, z_{k2}^2, \cdots, z_{kl-1}z_{kl}, z_{kl}^2)] \in \mathbb{R}^{l_g}$$

is a quadratic polynomial vector and $\otimes$ denotes the Kronecker product. The vector $\Theta \in \mathbb{R}^{l(l+1)/2=l_g}$ is a vector representation of the Q-function parameter matrix G. The vector Θ is formed by stacking the columns of the square matrix G as a column vector with the off-diagonal elements summed as $G_{ab} + G_{ba}$. The subscript represents the ath row and the bth column where $a \neq b$ and $a, b = 1, \cdots, l$.

Now, to estimate the Q-function (3.19), the QFE with the event-based availability of the system state vector can be defined as

$$\hat{Q}(\hat{x}_k, u_k) = \hat{z}_k^T \hat{G}_k \hat{z}_k = \hat{\Theta}_k^T \hat{\xi}_k, \quad k_i \leq k < k_{i+1}, \tag{3.20}$$

where $\hat{\Theta}_k \in \mathbb{R}^{l_g}$ is the estimate of the target parameter Θ, and $\hat{\xi}_k = \hat{z}_k \otimes \hat{z}_k$ is the event-based regression vector with $\hat{z}_k = [\hat{x}_k^T \quad u_k^T]^T$ constructed at the controller.

We can express the QFE explicitly at the triggering instants (k_i) and between two triggers ($k_i < k < k_{i+1}$) using the event-based state vector at the controller (3.2) as

$$\hat{Q}(\hat{x}_k, u_k) = \begin{cases} z_k^T \hat{G}_k z_k = \hat{\Theta}_k^T \xi_k, \ k = k_i, \\ \hat{z}_k^T \hat{G}_k \hat{z}_k = \hat{\Theta}_k^T \hat{\xi}_k, \ k_i < k < k_{i+1}. \end{cases} \tag{3.21}$$

One can reconstruct the estimated Q-function matrix $\hat{G}_k = \begin{bmatrix} \hat{G}_k^{xx} & \hat{G}_k^{xu} \\ \hat{G}_k^{ux} & \hat{G}_k^{uu} \end{bmatrix}$ using $\hat{\Theta}$. The estimated gain matrix $\hat{K}_k$ can be obtained from the Q-function estimated parameter vector $\hat{\Theta}_k$ or, alternatively, $\hat{G}_k$. The estimated event-based control input can now be written as

$$u_k = -\hat{K}_k \hat{x}_k, \ k_i \leq k < k_{i+1}, \tag{3.22}$$

where the estimated control gain $\hat{K}_k$ can be expressed as

$$\hat{K}_k = \left(\hat{G}_k^{uu}\right)^{-1} \hat{G}_k^{ux}. \tag{3.23}$$

The Bellman equation of Q-function in (3.17) with (3.19), can be rewritten as

$$0 = r(x_k, u_k) + Q^*(x_{k+1}, u_{k+1}) - Q^*(x_k, u_k) = r(x_k, u_k) + \Theta^T \Delta\xi_k, \tag{3.24}$$

where $Q^*(x_{k+1}, u_{k+1}) = \Theta^T \xi_{k+1}$ and $\Delta\xi_k = \xi_{k+1} - \xi_k$.

The estimated QFE in (3.21) is not optimal. Thus, Bellman equation (3.24) does not hold and leads to an error referred to as Q-function estimation error (QFE error). It is denoted by

$$e_k^V = \begin{cases} r(x_k, u_k) + \hat{\Theta}_k^T \Delta\xi_k, \ k = k_i, \\ r(\hat{x}_k, u_k) + \hat{\Theta}_k^T \Delta\hat{\xi}_k, \ k_i < k < k_{i+1}, \end{cases} \tag{3.25}$$

where $\Delta\hat{\xi}_k = \hat{\xi}_{k+1} - \hat{\xi}_k$ and $r(\hat{x}_k, u_k) = \hat{x}_k^T P \hat{x}_k^T + u_k^T R u_k$. This error is similar to the temporal difference (TD) error used for the iteration-based Q-learning schemes. Therefore, minimization of the QFE error online will ensure the estimated control input converges to the optimal value.

Define an auxiliary QFE error vector as

$$\Xi_k^V = \Pi_k + \hat{\Theta}_k^T Z_k, \ k = k_i \tag{3.26}$$

where

$$\Pi_k = \left[r(x_{k_i}, u_{k_i}) \ r(x_{k_{i-1}}, u_{k_{i-1}}) \ \cdots \ r(x_{k_{i-1-j}}, u_{k_{i-j}})\right]$$

and

$$Z_k = \left[\Delta\xi_{k_i} \ \Delta\xi_{k_{i-1}} \ \cdots \ \Delta\xi_{k_{i-1-j}}\right]$$

with $0 < j < k_i$.

Remark 3.1. *The auxiliary QFE error is formed by using the aperiodic time history of the system state and control input and the current Q-function parameter vector $\hat{\Theta}_k$. The auxiliary error eliminates the use of policy iteration, and a near-optimal control gain can be achieved by updating the Q-function parameters at the aperiodic sampling instants.*

The QFE parameters are tuned only at the sampling instants (k_i, $i = 0, 1, \cdots$) with the updated state information and held during the inter-sampling times, $k_{i-1} < k < k_i$, $i = 0, 1, \cdots$ as follows

$$\hat{\Theta}_k = \begin{cases} \hat{\Theta}_{k-1} - \dfrac{W_{k-1} Z_{k-1} \Xi_{k-1}^{V^T}}{\left\| I + Z_{k-1}^T W_{k-1} Z_{k-1} \right\|}, \ k = k_i, \\ \hat{\Theta}_{k-1}, \ k_{i-1} < k < k_i, \end{cases} \tag{3.27}$$

$$W_k = \begin{cases} W_{k-1} - \dfrac{W_{k-1} Z_{k-1} Z_{k-1}^T W_{k-1}}{\left\| I + Z_k^T W_k Z_k \right\|}, & k = k_i \\ W_{k-1}, \; k_{i-1} < k < k_i \end{cases}, \tag{3.28}$$

where $W_0 = \beta I$ with $\beta > 0$ a larger positive value and I is the identity matrix.

Remark 3.2. *The Q-function parameters tuning law* (3.27) *requires the state vectors x_{k_i} and x_{k_i-1} for the computation of $\Delta\xi_{k_i-1}$ defined in* (3.26). *Thus, the system state vectors x_{k_i} and x_{k_i-1}, together, are sent to the controller at the aperiodic sampling instants, as proposed. This tuning rule saves the computation when compared to a traditional adaptive control technique (Narendra and Annaswamy, 2012).*

Remark 3.3. *The estimation stops as the QFE in* (3.21) *becomes zero when the system state vector converges to zero before the Q-function parameters $\hat{\Theta}_k$ converge to the target parameters Θ. Hence, the regression vector ξ_k must satisfy the PE condition (Green and Moore, 1985) for the Q-function parameters to converge to its target values. The PE condition is a necessary condition for parameter convergence in traditional adaptive control (Narendra and Annaswamy, 2012). The definition of the PE condition (Green and Moore, 1985) is presented next for completeness.*

Definition 3.1. *A vector $\varphi(x_k)$ is said to be persistently exciting over an interval if there exist positive constants δ, $\underline{\alpha}$, $\bar{\alpha}$ and $k_d \geq 1$, such that*

$$\underline{\alpha} I \leq \sum_{k=k_d}^{k+\delta} \varphi(x_k)\, \varphi^T(x_k) \leq \bar{\alpha} I, \tag{3.29}$$

where I is the identity matrix of the appropriate dimension.

A PE-like condition can be achieved by adding an exploration noise to the control input u_k during the estimation process (Xu et al., 2012).

The Q-function parameter estimation error dynamics from (3.27), by forwarding one time step, can be represented as

$$\tilde{\Theta}_{k+1} = \begin{cases} \tilde{\Theta}_k + \dfrac{W_k Z_k \Xi_k^{V^T}}{\left\| I + Z_k^T W_k Z_k \right\|}, & k = k_i, \\ \tilde{\Theta}_k, \; k_i < k \leq k_{i+1}, \end{cases} \tag{3.30}$$

where $\tilde{\Theta}_k = \Theta - \hat{\Theta}_k$ is the Q-function parameter estimation error.

Since we only update the QFE parameters at the triggering instants, the QFE error e_k^V for $k = k_i$ can expressed in terms of the Q-function parameter estimation error $\tilde{\Theta}_k$, by subtracting (3.24) from (3.25), as

$$e_k^V = -\tilde{\Theta}_k^T \Delta\xi_k, \; k = k_i. \tag{3.31}$$

The auxiliary QFE error (3.26) in terms of the Q-function parameter estimation error can be represented by

$$\Xi_k^V = -\tilde{\Theta}_k^T Z_k, \; k = k_i. \tag{3.32}$$

Next, the lemma guarantees the boundedness of the Q-function parameter estimation error.

Lemma 3.1. *Consider both the QFE* (3.21) *and the tuning law* (3.27) *and* (3.28) *with an initial admissible control policy $u_0 \in \mathbb{R}^m$. Let Q-function parameter vector $\hat{\Theta}_0$ is initialized with nonzero and finite value in a compact set. Then, the Q-function parameter estimation error $\tilde{\Theta}_k$ is bounded during inter-event times and converges to zero asymptotically when the triggering instants $k_i \to \infty$ as $i \to \infty$.*

Sketch of Proof: We will analyze the convergence of Q-function parameter estimation error using Lyapunov stability theory. The proof is carried out by considering both the cases of triggering condition, i.e., at the event sampled instants $(k = k_i)$ and inter-event times $(k_i < k < k_{i+1})$, because of the aperiodic tuning of the QFE parameters. A common Lyapunov function is used to evaluate both cases, and the asymptotic stability is shown by combining both cases.

Select a Lyapunov function candidate given as

$$L_{\tilde{\Theta}k} = \tilde{\Theta}_k^T W_k^{-1} \tilde{\Theta}_k \tag{3.33}$$

where W_k is a positive definite matrix as defined in (3.28).

Case I: *At the event sampled instants* $(k = k_i)$. In this case, the QFE parameters are tuned by using (3.27) and (3.28) for the case $k = k_i$. The QFE parameter estimation error dynamics (3.30) with the augmented Bellman error (3.32), can be written as

$$\tilde{\Theta}_{k+1} = \left(I - \frac{W_k Z_k Z_k^T}{\left\| I + Z_k^T W_k Z_k \right\|} \right) \tilde{\Theta}_k. \tag{3.34}$$

The equation (3.28) can also be expressed as

$$W_{k+1} W_k^{-1} = I - \frac{W_k Z_k Z_k^T}{\left\| I + Z_k^T W_k Z_k \right\|}. \tag{3.35}$$

Substituting (3.35) in (3.34), the QFE parameter estimation error dynamics become

$$\tilde{\Theta}_{k+1} = W_{k+1} W_k^{-1} \tilde{\Theta}_k. \tag{3.36}$$

With the above results the first difference $\Delta L_{\tilde{\Theta},k}$ along (3.36) and using (3.34), is upper bounded as

$$\Delta L_{\tilde{\Theta},k} \leq -\bar{Z}_{\min}^2 \left\| \tilde{\Theta}_k \right\|^2 < 0. \tag{3.37}$$

Since the regression vector Z_k satisfies the PE condition, it holds that $0 < \bar{Z}_{\min} \leq \frac{\left\| Z_k Z_k^T \right\|}{\left\| I + Z_k^T W_k Z_k \right\|} < 1$. This implies, the Lyapunov function $L_{\tilde{\Theta},k}$ decreases i.e., $L_{\tilde{\Theta},k_i+1} < L_{\tilde{\Theta},k_i}$.

Case II: *During the inter-event times* $(k_i < k < k_{i+1})$. In this case, the QFE parameters are not tuned and held at their previous values. Consider the same Lyapunov function in (3.33). The first difference along (3.28) and (3.34) for $k_i < k < k_{i+1}$ is given by

$$\Delta L_{\tilde{\Theta},k} = \tilde{\Theta}_{k+1}^T W_{k+1}^{-1} \tilde{\Theta}_{k+1} - \tilde{\Theta}_k^T W_k^{-1} \tilde{\Theta}_k = 0, k_i < k < k_{i+1}. \tag{3.38}$$

By Lyapunov theorem, the QFE parameter estimation error $\tilde{\Theta}_k$ remains constant during the inter-event times.

By combining both the cases for the interval $k_i \leq k < k_{i+1}$, the QFE parameter estimation error remains constant during the inter-event intervals and decreases at the triggering instant. Note that the Lyapunov function is positive definite and lower bounded by zero. Therefore the Lyapunov function decreases to to zero as the triggering instants $k_i \to \infty$, $i \to \infty$, i.e., asymptotically. For the detailed steps of the proof, refer to (Sahoo, 2015) Proof of Lemma 4.4. The convergence of the estimated control input u_k to near-optimal value and closed-loop stability is presented in the next subsection.

3.2.4 CLOSED-LOOP STABILITY ANALYSIS

The closed-loop system dynamics, using the system in (3.1) and the control input in(3.22), can be expressed as

$$\begin{aligned} x_{k+1} &= Ax_k - B\hat{K}_k \hat{x}_k \\ &= Ax_k - B\hat{K}_k x_k + B\hat{K}_k e_k, \; k \leq k_i < k_{i+1}. \end{aligned} \tag{3.39}$$

To ensure the closed-loop system is stable, the condition

$$\|e_k\| \le \sigma_k^{ETC} \|x_k\|, \tag{3.40}$$

is selected as the event-triggering condition, where $\sigma_k^{ETC} = \sqrt{\frac{\Gamma(1-3\bar{\mu})}{3B_{\max}^2 \|\hat{K}_k\|^2}}$ is the threshold coefficient, $0 < \Gamma < 1$, and $\bar{\mu} < 1/3$. The event-triggering instants are decided at the violation of the inequality (3.40). The threshold coefficient σ_k^{ETC} uses the estimated control gain matrix $\hat{K}_k$. Thus, the event-triggering condition (3.40) is adaptive in nature, as proposed earlier. This adaptive nature of the triggering condition helps estimate the Q-function parameters by generating a suitable number of events during the initial learning phase.

The adaptive event-triggering condition (3.40) becomes equal to the traditional triggering condition (Tabuada, 2007; Garcia and Antsaklis, 2011; Wang and Lemmon, 2008), discussed in Chapter 1, for systems with known dynamics once the Q-function parameters converge to their target values.

Now we are ready to show the stability of the closed-loop system. We will use the following lemma to prove the stability.

Lemma 3.2. *Consider the controllable linear discrete-time system* (3.1). *Then there exists an optimal control input, u_k^*, such that the closed-loop dynamics are expressed as*

$$\|Ax_k + Bu_k^*\|^2 \le \bar{\nu}\|x_k\|^2, \tag{3.41}$$

where $0 < \bar{\nu} < 1$ is a constant.

Proof. This can be seen by selecting a Lyapunov function $L(x_k) = x_k^T x_k$. The first difference along the system dynamics (3.1) can be expressed as $\Delta L(x_k) \le \|Ax_k + Bu_k^*\|^2 - \|x_k\|^2 \le -(1-\bar{\nu})\|x_k\|^2$. Since the system is controllable and the optimal control input u_k^* is stabilizing (Lewis et al., 2012b), the first difference $\Delta L(x_k) < 0$ provided the parameter $\bar{\nu}$ satisfies $0 < \bar{\nu} < 1$. □

Theorem 3.1. *Consider the closed-loop event-triggered system* (3.39), *Q-function parameter estimation error dynamics* (3.30) *and assume Assumption 3.1 holds. Let $u_0 \in \Omega_u \subseteq \mathbb{R}^m$ is an initial admissible control policy and the Q-function parameter estimate $\hat{\Theta}_0$ initialized in a compact set. Suppose the last held state vector, $\hat{x}_k$, and the Q-function parameter vector, $\hat{\Theta}_k$ are updated by using* (3.2), (3.27) *and* (3.28), *respectively, at the violation of the event-triggering condition* (3.40). *Then, the control input* (3.22) *ensures the closed-loop event-triggered system state vector x_k and the Q-function parameter estimation error $\tilde{\Theta}_k$ converges to zero asymptotically, provided the regression vector ξ_k satisfies PE condition and the following inequality*

$$\|\tilde{K}_k x_k\|^2 \le l_{\tilde{\Theta}} \frac{\|\tilde{\Theta}_k^T Z_k Z_k^T \tilde{\Theta}_k\|}{\|I + Z_k^T W_k Z_k\|} \tag{3.42}$$

holds where $l_{\tilde{\Theta}} > 0$ is a positive constant. Moreover, the estimated control input converges to its optimal value, i.e., $u_k \to u_k^*$ as $k \to \infty$.

Sketch of the Proof. Note that in an event-based control framework, the Lyapunov function need not decrease monotonically during both the events and inter-event times (Wang and Lemmon, 2008). The Lyapunov function may increase during the inter-event times, as shown in Figure 3.2. We only need to show the existence of a piecewise continuous function $h(k) \in \mathbb{R}_{>0}$, such that

$$h(k) \ge L_k^s \text{ for all } k \in \mathbb{N} \text{ and } \lim_{k\to\infty} h(k) = 0, \tag{3.43}$$

where L_k^s is a common Lyapunov function from both the event and inter-event times.

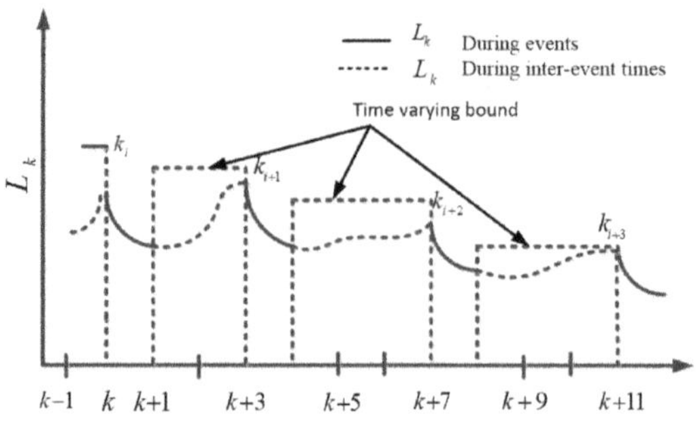

Figure 3.2 Evolution of the Lyapunov function during event and inter-event times

Consider the Lyapunov function candidate given by

$$L_k^s = \Lambda_1 L_{x,k} + \Lambda_2 L_{\tilde{\Theta},k}, \tag{3.44}$$

where $L_{x,k} = x_k^T x_k$ and $L_{\tilde{\Theta},k} = \tilde{\Theta}_k^T W_k^{-1} \tilde{\Theta}_k$ with $\Lambda_1 = \frac{\pi}{2B_{\max}^2 l_{\tilde{\Theta}}}$ and $\Lambda_2 = 2\pi$ with $0 < \pi < 1$ and $l_{\tilde{\Theta}}$ is a positive constant.

Case 1. *At the sampled instants* $(k = k_i)$. For simplicity, we will evaluate each term in the Lyapunov function candidate (3.44) and combine them to get the overall first difference.

At the event-sampled instants with $e_k = 0$, along the closed-loop system dynamics $x_{k+1} = Ax_k - B\hat{K}_k x_k$, $k = k_i$, the first difference of the first term, $\Delta L_{x,k} = x_{k+1}^T x_{k+1} - x_k^T x_k$ with the relation $\tilde{K}_k = K^* - \hat{K}_k$ and Cauchy-Schwartz (C-S) inequality, can be expressed as

$$\Delta L_{x,k} \le -(1-2\bar{v}) \left\|x_k\right\|^2 + 2B_{\max}^2 \left\|\tilde{K}_k x_k\right\|^2. \tag{3.45}$$

The first difference of the second term, $L_{\tilde{\Theta},k}$, in (3.44), the first difference is the same as in (3.37) of Lemma 3.1. Combining the individual first differences (3.45) and (3.37), the overall first difference $\Delta L_k^s = \Lambda_1 \Delta L_{x,k} + \Lambda_2 \Delta L_{\tilde{\Theta},k}$ as

$$\Delta L^s{}_k \le -(1-2\bar{v}) \left\|x_k\right\|^2 + 2B_{\max}^2 \left\|\tilde{K}_k x_k\right\|^2 - \frac{\tilde{\Theta}_k^T Z_k Z_k^T \tilde{\Theta}_k}{\left\|I + Z_k^T W_k Z_k\right\|}. \tag{3.46}$$

From the hypothesis of the theorem $\left\|\tilde{K}_k x_k\right\|^2 \le l_{\tilde{\Theta}} \frac{\left\|\tilde{\Theta}_k^T Z_k Z_k^T \tilde{\Theta}_k\right\|}{\left\|I + Z_k^T W_k Z_k\right\|}$, and the definitions of Λ_1 and Λ_2 in (3.44), the overall first difference can be written as

$$\Delta L_k^s \le -(1-2\bar{v})\Lambda_1 \left\|x_k\right\|^2 - \pi \bar{Z}_{\min}^2 \left\|\tilde{\Theta}_k\right\|^2 < 0, \tag{3.47}$$

where $0 < \pi < 1, 0 < \bar{v} < \frac{1}{2}$. By Lyapunov theorem, the Lyapunov function is a decreasing function, i.e., $L_{k_i+1}^s < L_{k_i}^s$.

Case 2. *During the inter-event times* $(k_i < k < k_{i+1})$. Consider the same Lyapunov function (3.44) as in Case 1. The system dynamics during the inter-event times become

$$x_{k+1} = Ax_k - B\hat{K}_k x_k + B\hat{K}_k e_k, \;\; k_i < k < k_{i+1}. \tag{3.48}$$

The first difference of the first term, with system dynamics (3.48), Lemma 3.2, and Cauchy-Swartz inequality, can be expressed as

$$\Delta L_{x,k} \le -(1-3\bar{v}) \left\|x_k\right\|^2 + 3B_{\max}^2 \left\|\tilde{K}_k x_k\right\|^2 + 3B_{\max}^2 \left\|\hat{K}_k\right\|^2 \left\|e_k\right\|^2. \tag{3.49}$$

Recalling the triggering condition (3.40) with $\bar{\mu} = \bar{\nu}$, one can reach at

$$\Delta L_{x,k} \leq -(1-\Gamma)(1-3\bar{\nu})\left\|x_k\right\|^2 + 3B_{\max}^2 l_{\tilde{\Theta}} \frac{\left\|\tilde{\Theta}_k^T Z_k Z_k^T \tilde{\Theta}_k\right\|}{\left\|I + Z_k^T W_k Z_k\right\|}. \tag{3.50}$$

The first difference of the second term for $k_i < k < k_{i+1}$ remains the same as in (3.34) in Lemma 3.1. Combing the individual first differences (3.50) and (3.34), the overall first difference $\Delta L_k^s = \Lambda_1 \Delta L_{x,k} + \Lambda_2 \Delta L_{\tilde{\Theta},k}$, using the fact $\frac{\left\|\tilde{\Theta}_k^T Z_k Z_k^T \tilde{\Theta}_k\right\|}{\left\|I+Z_k^T W_k Z_k\right\|} \leq \|\tilde{\Theta}_k\|^2$, is expressed as

$$\Delta L_k^s \leq -(1-\Gamma)(1-3\bar{\nu})\Lambda_1 \left\|x_k\right\|^2 + 3\Lambda_1 B_{\max}^2 l_{\tilde{\Theta}} \left\|\tilde{\Theta}_k\right\|^2. \tag{3.51}$$

From (3.34) in Lemma 3.1, $\tilde{\Theta}_k$ remains constant for $k_i < k < k_{i+1}$. Thus, $\left\|\tilde{\Theta}_k\right\|^2 = \left\|\tilde{\Theta}_{k_i+1}\right\|^2 \leq B_{\tilde{\Theta},k_i+1}$ for $k_i < k < k_{i+1}$. Substituting the inequality in (3.51), the first difference

$$\Delta L_k^s \leq -(1-\Gamma)(1-3\bar{\nu})\Lambda_1 \left\|x_k\right\|^2 + B_{\tilde{\Theta},k_i+1}^s, \tag{3.52}$$

where $B_{\tilde{\Theta},k_i+1}^s = 3\Lambda_1 B_{\max}^2 l_{\tilde{\Theta}} B_{\tilde{\Theta},k_i+1}$. From (3.52), the first difference of the Lyapunov function $\Delta L_k^s < 0$, as long as

$$\left\|x_k\right\| > \sqrt{B_{\tilde{\Theta},k_i+1}^s/(1-\Gamma)(1-3\bar{\nu})\Lambda_1} = B_{x,k_i+1}^c. \tag{3.53}$$

By Lyapunov theorem, the system state, x_k and QFE parameter error $\tilde{\Theta}_k$ are bounded. Further, system state x_k converges to the ball of radius B_{x,k_i+1}^c in a finite time and $\tilde{\Theta}_k$ remains bounded.

The bound for the Lyapunov function (3.44) for $k_i < k < k_{i+1}$ can obtained by using the bounds for x_k and $\tilde{\Theta}_k$ as

$$B_{L,k} = \Lambda_1 \left(B_{x,k_i+1}^c\right)^2 + \Lambda_2 \left(B_{\tilde{\Theta},k_i+1}\right)^2 \text{ for } k_i < k < k_{i+1}. \tag{3.54}$$

It follows that the Lyapunov function L_k^s for $k_i < k < k_{i+1}$ converges to the bound $B_{L,k}$ in a finite time and stay within $B_{L,k}$.

Now, from Case I and Case II, we will show the existence of a function $h(k)$ such that (31) holds to prove the asymptotic convergence of x_k and $\tilde{\Theta}_k$. With this effect, define a piecewise continuous function

$$h(k) = \max\left\{L_k^s, B_{L,k}\right\}, k \in \mathbb{N}. \tag{3.55}$$

It is clear that $h(k) \geq L_k^s$ for all $k \in \mathbb{N}$. From Lemma 3.1 $B_{\tilde{\Theta},k_i+1} \to 0$ with event sampled instants $k_i \to \infty$. Therefore, from (3.53), $B_{x,k_i+1}^c \to 0$ as $k_i \to \infty$. It follows that the bound $B_{L,k} \to 0$ as $k_i \to \infty$. Since, the Lyapunov function $L_{k_i+1}^s < L_{k_i}^s$ for $k = k_i$ and $L_k^s \to B_{L,k}$, $k_i < k < k_{i+1}, L_k^s \to 0$ as $k_i \to \infty$. Consequently, the upper bound functions $h(k) \to 0$ as $k_i \to \infty$. Since k_i is a subsequence of $k \in \mathbb{N}$, by extension $h(k) \to 0$ as $k \to \infty$. Finally, since the QFE error converges to zero as $k_i \to \infty$, $u(t) \to u^*(t)$ as $k_i \to \infty$.

The event-triggering condition can also be represented alternatively as a function of the last held state $(\hat{x}_k)$ by the ZOH. It is given in the following corollary.

Corollary 3.1. *Consider the closed-loop event-triggered system* (3.39)*, Q-function parameter estimation error dynamics* (3.30) *and assume Assumption 3.1 holds. Let $u_0 \in \Omega_u \subseteq \mathbb{R}^m$ is an initial admissible control policy and the Q-function parameter estimate $\hat{\Theta}_0$ initialized in a compact set. Suppose the event-triggering condition is rewritten as*

$$\left\|e_k\right\| \leq \frac{\sigma_k^{ETC}}{1+\sigma_k^{ETC}} \left\|\hat{x}_k\right\|, \tag{3.56}$$

where threshold σ_k^{ETC} is defined in (3.40)*. Then, the closed-loop event-triggered system state vector x_k and the Q-function parameter estimation error $\tilde{\Theta}_k$ converge to zero asymptotically provided the regression vector ξ_k satisfies PE condition.*

Proof Sketch: It is routine to check that the triggering threshold in (3.56) is smaller than that in (3.40). Therefore, Theorem 3.1 holds.

The minimum inter-event time, implicitly defined by either the event-triggering condition (3.40) or, alternatively, (3.56), is the minimum time required for the event-triggering error to reach the threshold value over all inter-trigger intervals ($k_i < k < k_{i+1}$), $i \in \mathbb{N}$. In a discrete-time system the minimum inter-event time is trivial and is equal to the sampling time (T_s) or, alternatively, $\delta k_{\min} = \min_{i\in\mathbb{N}} \{\delta k_i\} = 1$ where $\delta k_i = k_{i+1} - k_i$, $i \in \mathbb{N}$ are the inter-event times. Hence, to demonstrate the efficacy of the event-triggered control of a discrete-time system, the inter-event times must be non-trivial, i.e., $\delta k_i > 1, \forall i \in \mathbb{N}$).

Proposition 3.1. *Consider the linear discrete-time system in* (3.1), *the controller* (3.22), *the event-triggering condition in* (3.56). *Let the initial Q-function parameter estimate* $\hat{\Theta}_0$ *be initialized in a compact set. Then, the inter-event times* (δk_i) *implicitly defined by* (3.56), *are given as*

$$\delta k_i \geq \frac{\ln\left(1 + \frac{1}{M_i}(F-1)\sigma_i\right)}{\ln(F)}, \tag{3.57}$$

where $\sigma_i = \frac{\sigma_{k_i}^{ETC}}{1+\sigma_{k_i}^{ETC}}$ *is the event-trigger threshold for* i^{th} *inter-event time,* $\sigma_{k_i}^{ETC} = \sqrt{\frac{\Gamma(1-3\bar{\mu})}{3B_{\max}}}\left\|\hat{K}_{k_i}\right\|^2$, $F = \sqrt{\bar{\mu}} + B_{\max}K_M$, $M_i = (\sqrt{\bar{\mu}} + B_{\max}\left\|\tilde{K}_{k_i}\right\| + 1)$, $\left\|K_k^*\right\| \leq K_M$, *and* $\tilde{K}_k = K^* - \hat{K}_k$. *The inter-event times becomes non-trivial when* $\frac{\sigma_i}{M_i} > 1$.

Sketch of the Proof: The formula for the inter-trigger times can be derived by solving for the dynamics of e_k within an inter-trigger period of $k_i < k < k_{i+1}$ and comparing the solution with the threshold.

Remark 3.4. *The threshold* $\sigma_{k_i}^{ETC}$ *is dependent on upon the estimated control gain* $\hat{K}_k$ *(i.e., implicitly on the control gain estimation error* $\tilde{K}_k$ *via the relation* $\hat{K}_k = K^* - \tilde{K}_k$ *and* M_i, *which is also a function of* $\tilde{K}_k$*). Thus, the inter-event times* (δk_i) *in* (3.57) *is a function of the parameter estimation error* $\tilde{K}_k$. *Alternatively, the convergence of the Q-function parameter estimation error to its ultimate bound, as proven in Lemma* (3.1), *will increase the threshold value* $\sigma_{k_i}^{ETC}$ *and reduce* M_i *in* (3.57). *This will increase the inter-event times* δk_i *and leads to non-trivial values, i.e.,* $\delta k_i > 1$, $k \in \mathbb{N}$.

Example 3.1. *Consider the benchmark example of the batch reactor whose discrete-time with a sampling interval of* $T_s = 0.01$ *s is given as*

$$x_{k+1} = Ax_k + Bu_k, \quad y_k = Cx_k, \tag{3.58}$$

where $A = \begin{bmatrix} 1.0142 & -0.0018 & 0.0651 & -0.0546 \\ -0.0057 & 0.9582 & -0.0001 & 0.0067 \\ 0.0103 & 0.0417 & 0.9363 & 0.0563 \\ 0.0004 & 0.0417 & 0.0129 & 0.9797 \end{bmatrix}$, $B = \begin{bmatrix} 4.7798\times10^{-6} & -0.0010 \\ 0.0556 & 1.5316\times10^{6} \\ 0.0125 & -0.0304 \\ 0.0125 & -0.0002 \end{bmatrix}$ *and* $C = \begin{bmatrix} 1 & 0 & 1 & -1 \\ 0 & 1 & 0 & 0 \end{bmatrix}$. *Assume the system states are available for measurement and design and simulate a near-optimal controller and associated parameter update laws using the event-triggered Q-learning approach in Tables 3.1.*

Solution: We can use Table 3.1 for the controller and update laws. The quadratic cost function was chosen as in (3.5) with the penalty matrices $P = I_{4\times4}$ and $R = I_{2\times2}$ where I denotes the identity matrix. The initial system states were selected $x_0 = \begin{bmatrix} 0.1 & -0.1 & 0.3 & -0.5 \end{bmatrix}^T$. The initial parameter vector $\hat{\Theta}_0 \in \mathbb{R}^{l_g=21}$ was chosen at random from a uniform distribution in the interval $[0, \ 1]$.

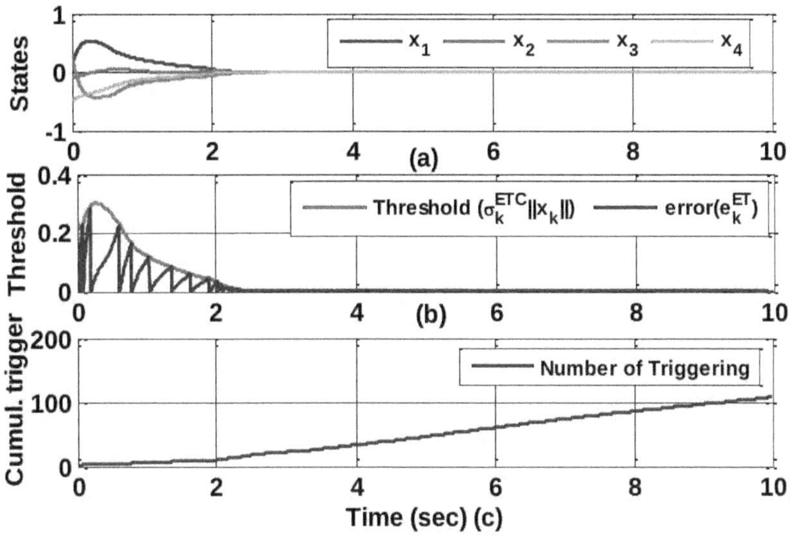

Figure 3.3 Performance of the event-based controller with state feedback: (a) convergence of state vector, (b) evolution of the event-trigger threshold and the event-trigger error, and (c) the total number of trigger instants.

The design parameters were $\beta = 2 \times 10^5$, $\bar{\mu} = 0.3$, and $\Gamma = 0.1$. The PE condition was satisfied by adding a zero mean Gaussian noise with the control input. The simulation was conducted for 10 sec with a sampling time of 0.01 sec or 1000 sampling instants.

The event-based optimal controller's performance is illustrated in Figure 3.3. The convergence of the system state close to zero and the event-trigger threshold are depicted in Figure 3.3 (a) and (b), respectively. The threshold converged as the state converged. The event-trigger error shown in Figure 3.3(b) evolved during the inter-event times; it resets to zero at the triggered instants. The cumulative number of trigger instants plotted in Figure 3.3 (c) was found to be 108 out of 1000 sampling instants. This implies the controller and the Q-function parameters were updated only 108 times. Thus, the computation was reduced when compared to the traditional discrete-time systems. The inter-event times plotted in Figure 3.3(d) shows the aperiodic occurrence of events validated by the design. The QFE error is illustrated in Figure 3.4 (b). The QFE error converged close to zero. This implies the near optimality of the adaptive controller is achieved in finite time.

3.3 OUTPUT FEEDBACK DESIGN

This section extends the state-feedback event-triggered optimal control design to the output feedback design.

Assumption 3.2. *The system* (3.1) *is observable and the output matrix* $C \in \mathbb{R}^{p_o \times n}$ *is considered known.*

The performance index can be redefined as a function of the system output, given by

$$J_k = \sum_{j=k}^{\infty} r^y(y_j, u_j), \tag{3.59}$$

where $r^y(y_j, u_j) = y_j^T P^y y_j + u_j^T R u_j$ and u_j is the sequence of event-based control input that minimizes the value function. The performance index can be rewritten by using the output equation

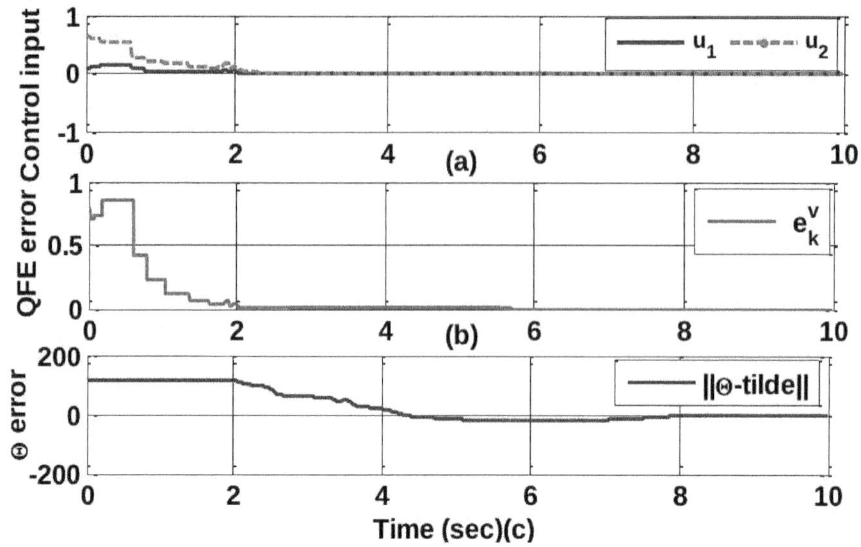

Figure 3.4 (a) Control policy, (b) QFE errors, and (c) parameter estimation error.

as

$$J_k = \sum_{j=k}^{\infty} x_j^T C^T P^y C x_j + u_j^T R u_j = \sum_{j=k}^{\infty} x_j^T P x_j + u_j^T R u_j, \tag{3.60}$$

where $P = C^T P^y C$. Note that if the system state vector can be reconstructed, then the state feedback design can be used for the output feedback case. Hence, an adaptive observer-based approach is proposed next.

3.3.1 ADAPTIVE OBSERVER DESIGN

An adaptive observer is included at the sensor node to estimate the system states. The observer has access to the system output (y_k) at every periodic time instant k. Therefore, the adaptive observer parameters can be tuned using a traditional time-triggered tuning law at every time instant k, unlike the QFE tuning law, as discussed in the previous section. This architecture needs additional computational power at the sensor node when compared to the state feedback design and can be considered as a trade-off.

3.3.1.1 Adaptive Observer Design

Consider the adaptive observer dynamics given by

$$\begin{aligned} x_{k+1}^o &= \hat{A}_k x_k^o + \hat{B}_k u_k + \hat{L}_k (y_k - y_k^o), \\ y_k^o &= C x_k^o, \end{aligned} \tag{3.61}$$

where $x_k^o \in \mathbb{R}^n$ and $y_k^o \in \mathbb{R}^{p_o}$ are the observer state and the output vectors, respectively. The matrices $\hat{A}_k \in \mathbb{R}^{n\times n}$ and $\hat{B}_k \in \mathbb{R}^{n\times m}$ are the estimated observer system matrices, and $\hat{L}_k \in \mathbb{R}^{n\times p_o}$ is the estimated observer gain matrix.

In a parametric form, the observer dynamics can be represented as

$$x_{k+1}^o = \hat{\psi}_k^T \phi_k, \tag{3.62}$$

where $\hat{\psi}_k = [\hat{A}_k \quad \hat{B}_k \quad \hat{L}_k]^T \in \mathbb{R}^{(n+m+p_o)\times n}$ is the estimated observer parameter matrix. The regression vector for the observer is denoted as $\phi_k = [x_k^{oT} \quad u_k^T \quad e_k^{yT}]^T \in \mathbb{R}^{(n+m+p_o)}$, where $e_k^y = y_k - y_k^o$ is the output error vector. The observer state estimation error can be defined as

$$e_k^x = x_k - x_k^o, \tag{3.63}$$

and the state estimation error dynamics from (3.63) and (3.61) become

$$e_{k+1}^x = Ax_k + Bu_k - \hat{A}_k x_k^o - \hat{B}_k u_k - \hat{L}_k (y_k - y_k^o) = (A - LC) e_k^x + \tilde{\psi}_k^T \phi_k, \tag{3.64}$$

where $\tilde{\psi}_k = [\tilde{A}_k \quad \tilde{B}_k \quad \tilde{L}_k]^T \in \mathbb{R}^{(n+m+p_o)\times n}$ is the observer parameter estimation error with $\tilde{\psi}_k = \psi - \hat{\psi}_k$, $\tilde{A}_k = A - \hat{A}_k$, $\tilde{B}_k = B - \hat{B}_k$, and $\tilde{L}_k = L - \hat{L}_k$. The observer ideal target parameters $\psi = \begin{bmatrix} A & B & L \end{bmatrix}^T \in \mathbb{R}^{(n+m+p)\times n}$ and L is the ideal observer gain matrix. The observability of the system in Assumption 3.2 guarantees the existence of an ideal observer gain matrix L such that $A - LC$ is Schur stable.

The observer output error dynamics can be written by using (3.64) as

$$e_{k+1}^y = C(A - LC) e_k^x + C\tilde{\psi}_k^T \phi_k. \tag{3.65}$$

A time-triggered periodic tuning law

$$\hat{\psi}_{k+1} = \hat{\psi}_k + \alpha_\psi^o \frac{\phi_k e_{k+1}^{y^T} X}{1 + \phi_k^T \phi_k}, \tag{3.66}$$

can be selected to estimate the observer parameters, thereby guaranteeing that the observer state estimation error converges to zero asymptotically. The learning gain$\alpha_\psi^o > 0$ and $X \in \mathbb{R}^{p_o \times n}$ is a constant matrix to match the dimension and selected such that $\left\|X^T C\right\| \leq 1$. The observer parameter estimation error dynamics can be computed from (3.66) as

$$\tilde{\psi}_{k+1} = \tilde{\psi}_k - \alpha_\psi^o \frac{\phi_k e_{k+1}^{y^T} X}{1 + \phi_k^T \phi_k}, \forall k. \tag{3.67}$$

The boundedness of the observer parameter estimation error is presented in the following lemma.

Lemma 3.3. *Consider the adaptive observer* (3.61) *in a parametric form* (3.62) *and let Assumption 3.2 holds. Assume the initial observer parameters $\hat{\psi}_0$ are initialized in a compact set Ω_ψ. Suppose the observer parameters are updated by the tuning law* (3.66). *Then, the observer state estimation error e_k^x and the parameter estimation error $\tilde{\psi}_k$ converge asymptotically to zero provided the regression vector ϕ_k satisfies PE condition and the learning gain satisfies* $0 < \alpha_\psi^o < \frac{c_{\min}}{2\left(1+\|\phi_k\|^2\right)}$.

Proof. The proof is similar to the proof of Lemma 3.1. For a detailed proof, refer to (Sahoo, 2015) (Chapter 1, proof of Lemma 5.1). □

3.3.2 OBSERVER-BASED CONTROLLER DESIGN AND CLOSED-LOOP STABILITY

The event-based observer state vector will be used to design the near-optimal control input. Therefore, the observer states are sent to the controller at the triggered instants, similar to the state feedback case. The event-triggering error now can be redefined as the difference between the current observer state and the last released observer state as

$$e_k^{o,ET} = x_k^o - x_k^{o,c}, \quad k_i \leq k < k_{i+1}. \tag{3.68}$$

Table 3.2
Observer-based feedback controller design

System dynamics	$x_{k+1} = Ax_k + Bu_k, \ y_k = Cx_k$
Observer dynamics	$x_{k+1}^o = \hat{A}_k x_k^o + \hat{B}_k u_k + \hat{L}_k\left(y_k - y_k^o\right), \ y_k^o = Cx_k^o$
Adaptive observer update	$\hat{\psi}_{k+1} = \hat{\psi}_k + \alpha_\psi^o \frac{\phi_k e_{k+1}^{y^T} X}{1+\phi_k^T \phi_k},$
Event-triggering error	$e_k^{o,ET} = x_k^o - x_k^{o,c}, \ k_i \le k < k_{i+1}.$
Q-function estimator (QFE)	$\hat{Q}(x_k^{o,c}, u_k) = \begin{cases} z_k^{o^T} \hat{G} z z_k^o = \hat{\Theta}_k^T \xi_k^o, & k = k_i, \\ z_k^{o,c^T} \hat{G}_k z_k^{o,c} = \hat{\Theta}_k^T \xi_k^{o,c}, & k_i < k < k_{i+1}, \end{cases}$
QFE residual error	$e_k^{o,V} = \begin{cases} x_k^{o^T} P x_k^o + u_k^T R u_k + \hat{\Theta}_k^T \Delta \xi_k^o, & k = k_i, \\ x_k^{o,c^T} P x_k^{o,c} + u_k^T R u_k + \hat{\Theta}_k^T \Delta \xi_k^{o,c}, & k_i < k < k_{i+1}, \end{cases}$
Auxilary QFE error	$\Xi_k^{o,V} = \Pi_k^o + \hat{\Theta}_k^T Z_k^o, \ k = k_i$
Q-function estimator update	$\hat{\Theta}_k = \begin{cases} \hat{\Theta}_{k-1} - \dfrac{\alpha_V^o Z_{k-1}^o \Xi_{k-1}^{o,V^T}}{\left\| I + Z_{k-1}^{o^T} Z_{k-1}^o \right\|}, & k = k_i, \\ \hat{\Theta}_{k-1}, \ k_{i-1} < k < k_i. \end{cases}$
Control input	$u_k = -\hat{K}_k x_k^{o,c} = -\left(\hat{G}_k^{uu}\right)^T \hat{G}_k^{ux} x_k^{o,c}, \ k_i \le k < k_{i+1}$
Event-triggering condition	$\left\| e_k^{0,ET} \right\| \le \sigma_k^{o,ETC} \left\| x_k^o \right\|, \ \sigma_k^{o,ETC} = \sqrt{\Gamma_{ET}^o (1 - 4\bar{\mu})/4B_{\max}^2 \left\| \hat{K}_k \right\|^2}$

The event-sampled observer state vector at the controller $x_k^{o,c}$ can be redefined as

$$x_k^{o,c} = \begin{cases} x_k^o, & k{=}k_i, \\ x_{k_i}^o, & k_i < k < k_{i+1}. \end{cases} \tag{3.69}$$

The action-dependent value function or the Q-function for the output feedback design with value function (3.60) is the same as that in the state feedback case. Therefore, the optimal control input can be computed by estimating the Q-function parameter matrix G or, alternatively, the parameter vector Θ defined in (3.19). The event-based QFE with observer's state can be written as

$$\hat{Q}(x_k^{o,c}, u_k) = \begin{cases} z_k^{o^T} \hat{G} z z_k^o = \hat{\Theta}_k^T \xi_k^o, & k = k_i, \\ z_k^{o,c^T} \hat{G}_k z_k^{o,c} = \hat{\Theta}_k^T \xi_k^{o,c}, & k_i < k < k_{i+1}, \end{cases} \tag{3.70}$$

where the event-based regression vectors $\xi_k^o = z_k^o \otimes z_k^o$, $\xi_k^{o,c} = z_k^{o,c} \otimes z_k^{o,c}$, $z_k^o = [x_k^{o^T} \quad u_k^T]^T$ and $z_k^{o,c} =$

$[x_k^{o,c^T} \quad u_k^T]^T$.

The Q-function estimation error, based on the observer states, becomes

$$e_k^{o,V} = \begin{cases} x_k^{o^T} P x_k^o + u_k^T R u_k + \hat{\Theta}_k^T \Delta\xi_k^o, & k = k_i, \\ x_k^{o,c^T} P x_k^{o,c} + u_k^T R u_k + \hat{\Theta}_k^T \Delta\xi_k^{o,c}, & k_i < k < k_{i+1}, \end{cases} \tag{3.71}$$

where $\Delta\xi_k^o = \xi_{k+1}^o - \xi_k^o$ and $\Delta\xi_k^{o,c} = \xi_{k+1}^{o,c} - \xi_k^{o,c}$.

Similar to the state feedback case, the augmented error using the time history of the observer states and the control input at the trigger instant can be defined as

$$\Xi_k^{o,V} = \Pi_k^o + \hat{\Theta}_k^T Z_k^o, \quad k = k_i \tag{3.72}$$

where $\Pi_k^o = [r(x_{k_i}^o, u_{k_i}) \ r(x_{k_{i-1}}^o, u_{k_{i-1}}) \ \cdots \ r(x_{k_{i-1-j}}^o, u_{k_{i-j}}]$ and $Z_k^o = [\Delta\xi_{k_i}^o \ \Delta\xi_{k_{i-1}}^o \ \cdots \ \Delta\xi_{k_{i-1}}^o]$ for $k = k_i$ with $0 < j < k_i$. A tuning law can be defined to tune the Q-function parameter estimates as

$$\hat{\Theta}_k = \begin{cases} \hat{\Theta}_{k-1} - \dfrac{\alpha_V^o Z_{k-1}^o \Xi_{k-1}^{o,V^T}}{\left\| I + Z_{k-1}^{o^T} Z_{k-1}^o \right\|}, & k = k_i, \\ \hat{\Theta}_{k-1}, \quad k_{i-1} < k < k_i. \end{cases} \tag{3.73}$$

The parameter estimation error dynamics by using (3.73) with a forwarded time step can be represented as

$$\tilde{\Theta}_{k+1} = \begin{cases} \tilde{\Theta}_k + \dfrac{\alpha_V^o Z_k^o \Xi_k^{0,V^T}}{\left\| I + Z_k^{o^T} Z_k^o \right\|}, & k = k_i, \\ \tilde{\Theta}_k, \quad k_i < k < k_{i+1}, \end{cases} \tag{3.74}$$

The observer-based QFE error ($e_k^{o,V}$) from (3.72) and (3.24) at the triggering instants $k = k_i$ is expressed in terms of the parameter estimation error $\tilde{\Theta}_k$ as

$$e_k^{o,V} = -\tilde{\Theta}_k^T \Delta\xi_k^o + \Theta^T (\Delta\xi_k^o - \Delta\xi_k) + f(x_k^o) - f(x_k), \quad k = k_i \tag{3.75}$$

where $f(x_k^o) = x_k^{o^T} P_k x_k^o$ and $f(x_k) = x_k^T P_k x_k$. The function $f(\centerdot)$ is a continuous function. Therefore it satisfies the Lipschitz continuity given as $\left\| f(x_k^o) - f(x_k) \right\| \leq L_f e_k^x$. The observer-based augmented QFE error (3.72) using (3.75) can be rewritten as

$$\Xi_k^{o,V} = -\tilde{\Theta}_k^T Z_k^o + \Theta^T (Z_k^o - Z_k) + F_k^o - F_k, \quad k = k_i, \tag{3.76}$$

where $F_k^o = [x_{k_i}^{o^T} P x_{k_i}^o, x_{k_{i-1}}^{o^T} P x_{k_{i-1}}^o, \cdots, x_{k_{i-j-1}}^{o^T} P x_{k_{i-j-1}}^o]$ and $F_k = [x_{k_i}^T P x_{k_i}, x_{k_{i-1}}^T P x_{k_{i-1}}, \cdots, x_{k_{i-j-1}}^T P x_{k_{i-j-1}}]$.

The estimated control (3.22) with the event-based observer state vector and the Q-function estimated parameters can be written as

$$u_k = -\hat{K}_k x_k^{o,c} = -\left(\hat{G}_k^{uu}\right)^T \hat{G}_k^{ux} x_k^{o,c}, \quad k_i \leq k < k_{i+1}. \tag{3.77}$$

The closed-loop dynamics of the observer-based event-triggered system from (3.1) and control input (3.77) can be described as

$$\begin{aligned} x_{k+1} &= A x_k - B\hat{K}_k x_k^{o,c} = A x_k - B\hat{K}_k x_k^o + B\hat{K}_k e_k^{o,ET} \\ &= (A - B\hat{K}_k) x_k + B\hat{K}_k e_k^x + B\hat{K}_k e_k^{o,ET}, \quad k \leq k < k_{i+1}. \end{aligned} \tag{3.78}$$

Consider the event-triggering error (3.68). The event-triggering condition as a function of the event-triggering error, the Q-function estimated parameter, and the observer state vector is selected as

$$\left\| e_k^{0,ET} \right\| \leq \sigma_k^{o,ETC} \left\| x_k^o \right\|, \tag{3.79}$$

where $\sigma_k^{o,ETC} = \sqrt{\frac{\Gamma_{ET}^o(1-4\bar{\mu})}{4B_{\max}^2 \left\| \hat{K}_k \right\|^2}}$ is the event-trigger threshold, $0 < \Gamma_{ET}^o < 1$, $\bar{\mu} < 1/4$. The main results of the output feedback design are claimed in the next theorem.

Theorem 3.2. *Consider the uncertain LTI discrete-time system* (3.1), *the adaptive observer* (3.61), *and the observer-based controller* (3.77) *represented as a closed-loop event-triggered system* (3.78). *Let the Assumption 3.2 holds and the regression vectors ϕ_k and ξ_k^o satisfy the PE condition. Suppose $u_0 \in \Omega_u \subset \mathbb{R}^m$is the initial admissible control policy and the initial parameters $\hat{\Theta}_0$ and $\hat{\psi}_0$ initialized in compact sets. Let the state vector ($x_k^{o,c}$) and the Q-function parameter vector ($\hat{\Theta}_k$) are updated, respectively, by* (3.69) *and* (3.73) *at the violation of the triggering condition* (3.79). *Then, the closed-loop event-triggered system state vector x_k , the Q-function parameter estimation error $\tilde{\Theta}_k$, the observer state estimation error e_k^x, and the observer parameter estimation error $\tilde{\psi}_k$ converge to zero asymptotically. Further, the estimated control input converge to the optimal control input, i.e., $u_k \to u_k^*$, as $k \to \infty$ provided the design parameters satisfy $0 < \alpha_V^o < 1/3$ and $0 < \alpha_\psi^o < c_{\min}/2\left(1 + \left\|\phi_k\right\|^2\right)$.*

Proof. The proof is similar to the proof of Theorem 3.1 in the state feedback case. The detailed proof of the theorem can be found in (Sahoo, 2015) (Chapter 1, Theorem 5.2) □

Example 3.2. *Consider the benchmark example of the batch reactor as given in* (3.58). *Assume the system states are not available for measurement, and the only available signal to measure is the output of the system. Design and simulate a near-optimal controller using the output measurement and associated parameter update laws using the event-triggered Q-learning approach in Tables 3.2. Select the parameters of the performance index, learning gains, and initial values of the state and parameters. Plot all the signals, including event-trigger condition, state, and parameter estimation errors. Comment on the convergence of the system states and QFE error convergence.*

Solution: The simulation parameters were chosen as follows. The adaptive gains for the observer were $\alpha_\Psi^0 = 0.01$, $\alpha_V^o = 0.01$, $\bar{\mu} = 0.2$, and $\Gamma_{ET}^o = 0.1$. The observer parameters were initialized randomly from the uniform distribution in the interval $[0, 0.5]$. The initial observer states were given as $x_0^o = [.02,\ -.02,\ .03,\ -0.1]^T$. The penalty matrices were $P = I_{4\times 4}$ and $R = I_{2\times 2}$. The remaining parameters for the state feedback in Example 3.1 are used here as well.

The observer-based output feedback controller performance is illustrated in Figures 3.5 and 3.6. The system states, and the event-triggering threshold are converged close to zero, as shown in Figure 3.5 (a) and (b). It was observed that the number of cumulative trigger instants was increased to 115, as shown in Figure 3.5 (c) when compared to the state feedback case. This is due to the additional uncertainty introduced by the adaptive observer. The inter-event times are plotted in Figure 3.5 (d). The QFE and the TC errors are converged to zero (shown in Figure 3.6 (a) and (b)), implying optimality was achieved in the final time. The convergence observer state estimation error is shown in Figure 3.6.

3.4 EVENT-SAMPLED NETWORKED CONTROL SYSTEMS

In the previous event-based state and output feedback schemes, the communication network is not considered. This section introduces an event-triggered design for networked control systems (NCS) (Walsh et al., 2002; Xu et al., 2012) consisting of a communication network enclosed within the

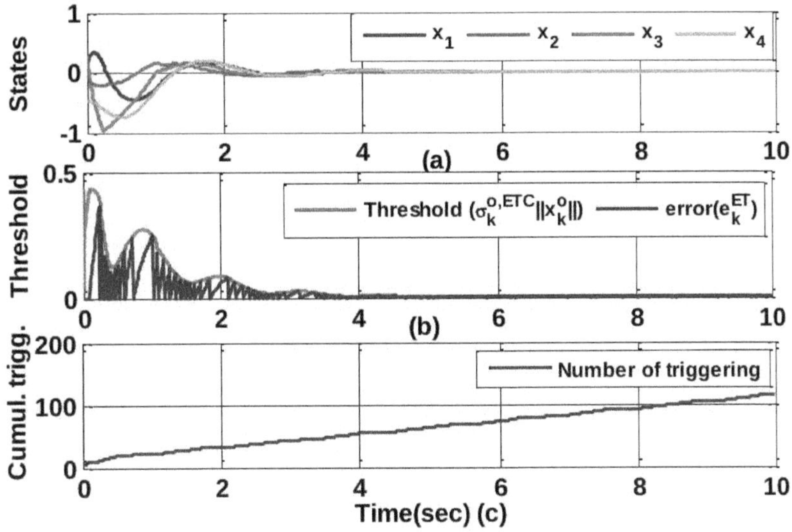

Figure 3.5 The event-based controller performance of output feedback design: (a) Convergence of the system states, (b) evolution of both the event-trigger threshold and the error, (c) the cumulative number of triggers.

feedback loop. Despite the advantages, such as flexibility in remote control and spatial distribution of the systems, the communication network introduces imperfections, such as time-varying delays, random packet losses, and quantization errors (Walsh et al., 2002) that significantly affect the system's stability and performance. Traditional control design approaches use a fixed sampling interval to transmit the feedback information (Walsh et al., 2002; Xu et al., 2012) and execute the control policy. This periodic transmission requires a large bandwidth, which is often challenging when shared communication networks are employed for control applications.

In the past decade, various stable (Åström and Bernhardsson, 1999; Wang and Lemmon, 2011b) and optimal (Narayanan and Jagannathan, 2016b) event-triggered control schemes have been proposed for linear and nonlinear systems in the presence of delays and packet losses (Wang and Lemmon, 2011b) for systems with known and unknown dynamics. Since the randomness of delays and packet losses are encountered in NCS, the optimal controller design for uncertain NCS is presented using stochastic control theory in (Xu et al., 2012, 2014b). In this section, a co-design approach from (Sahoo et al., 2017a), to optimize both the transmission instants and the control policy for uncertain NCS, is proposed to regulate the system optimally. The NCS is represented as a stochastic time-varying discrete-time system by including random delays and packet losses. A stochastic cost function is defined to co-optimize the control input and transmission intervals. The problem is represented as a discrete-time min-max problem (Basar and Bernhard, 2008) where the optimal control policy minimizes the cost function, and the control input error maximizes it.

3.4.1 NCS REFORMULATION AND PROBLEM STATEMENT

Consider an NCS represented by a continuous time linear time-invariant (LTI) system given by

$$\dot{x}(t) = Ax(t) + \alpha(t)Bu(t-\tau(t)), \;\; x(0) = x_0, \tag{3.80}$$

where $x(t) \in \mathbb{R}^n$ and $u(t) \in \mathbb{R}^m$ are the system state and control input vectors and $A \in \mathbb{R}^{n\times n}$ and $B \in \mathbb{R}^{n\times m}$, are uncertain time-invariant system and input matrices, respectively. The random time delay $\tau(t) = \tau_{sc}(t) + \tau_{ca}(t)$ where $\tau_{sc}(t)$ and $\tau_{ca}(t)$ are mutually independent delays from the sensors to controller (S-C) and controller to actuator (C-A) channels, respectively. The random packet losses

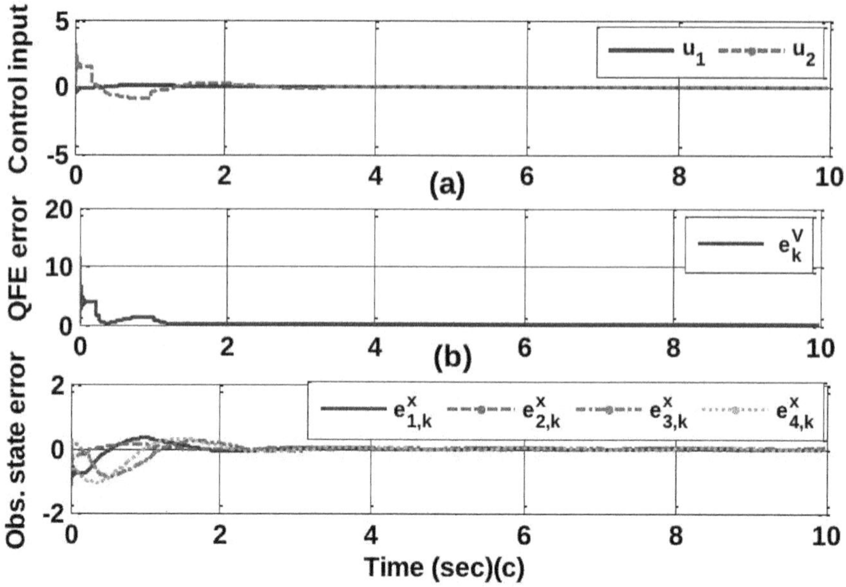

Figure 3.6 The performance of the optimal controller: (a) Convergence of observer state error; (b) optimal control input; (c) value function estimation error.

$\alpha(t) = \alpha_{sc}(t)\alpha_{ca}(t)$ is the packet loss indicator defined as

$$\alpha(t) = \begin{cases} 1, \text{ control input received at } t; \\ 0, \text{ control input not received at } t. \end{cases} \tag{3.81}$$

where $\alpha_{sc}(t)$ and $\alpha_{ca}(t)$ are the S-C channel and C-A channel mutually independent packet loss indicators.

Assumption 3.3. *The pair (A,B) is controllable and the state vector is measurable. Further, the order of the system is known.*

Since a packet switch communication network is used in the feedback loop, as shown in Fig. 3.7, the controller is implemented in a sampled data framework, i.e., the sensor samples the system state at time instants kT_s, where $k \in \mathbb{N}$ and T_s is the fixed sampling period. The control input remains constant between two consecutive sampling instants. To make the design tractable, the following standard properties of the communication network are assumed (Liou and Ray, 1991).

Assumption 3.4. *(Liou and Ray, 1991) (i) the initial value of the system states are deterministic; (ii) The time-varying random delays are bounded satisfying $\tau_{sc}^k \leq \Delta_s$ and $\tau_{ca}^k \leq dT_s$ where $\Delta_s < T_s$ is a fixed skew between the sensor and controller sampling instants, d is a positive integer and superscript k denotes the variable at time instant k. Further τ_{sc}^k and τ_{ca}^k are mutually independent process with known statistics; and (iii) The random packet losses α_{sc}^k and α_{ca}^k are i.i.d and follows Bernoulli distribution with $\mathbb{P}(\alpha^k = 1) = \mathbb{P}(\alpha_{sc}^k = 1)\mathbb{P}(\alpha_{ca}^k = 1) = \alpha_p$ with $\mathbb{P}(\cdot)$ is the probability of the random variable.*

From Assumption 3.4 (ii), the upper bound of the C-A channel delays τ_{ca}^k is d. Therefore, a maximum of $d+1$ delayed control inputs can be received at the actuator within a sampling interval $[kT_s, (k+1)T_s]$, without any packet loss, i.e., $\alpha_k = 1$. The control inputs are applied to the plant

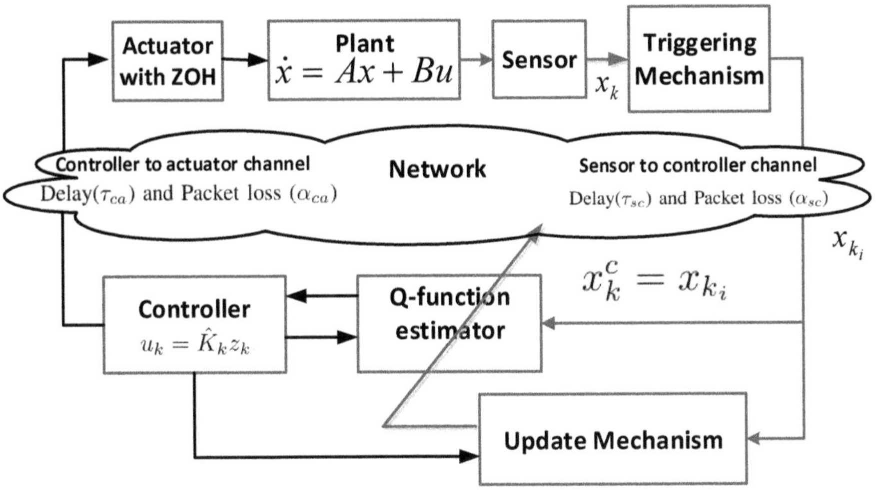

Figure 3.7 Block diagram of event-triggered NCS.

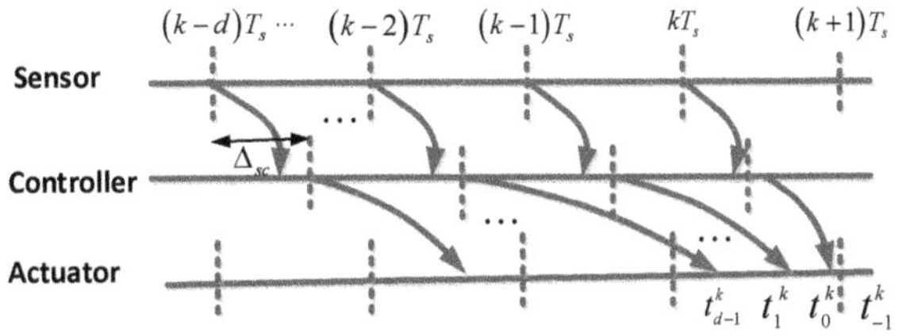

Figure 3.8 Timing diagram of transmission with time-varying delay.

instantly once they are received. A packet reordering mechanism is used such that the latest control input is held at the actuator till the next is available and applied to the system at time $kT_s + t_l^k$ where t_l^k, $l = 0,1,2,\cdots,d$ is the time after kT_s satisfying $t_l^k > t_{l+1}^k$ and $t_{-1}^k = T_s$ and $T_d^k = 0$, as shown in Fig. 3.8. In case of multiple packets arriving simultaneously, the one with the latest timestamp is used, and old ones are discarded.

A discrete time version of system in (3.80), by incorporating the delays τ_k and packet losses α_k, can be obtained by integrating (3.80) (Liou and Ray, 1991) and is given by

$$x_{k+1} = A^s x_k + \sum_{l=0}^{d} \alpha_{k-l} B_l^k u_{k-l}, \tag{3.82}$$

where $x_k = x(kT_s)$, $A_s = e^{AT_s}$, $B_l^k = \int_{t_l^k}^{t_{l-1}^k} e^{A(T_s-w)} dwB$ with $t_{-1}^k = T_s$ and $t_d^k = 0$.

In the event-based control framework, the state vector received at the controller time instants is given by

$$x_k^c = x_{k_i}, \quad k_i \leq k < k_{i+1}, i = 1,2,\cdots. \tag{3.83}$$

where x_k^c is the event-based received state at the controller.

Remark 3.5. *Since the delay $\tau_{sc}^k < \Delta_s$, the system states are available at the controller before the skewed controller sampling instants for controller execution when no packet loss occurs in the S-*

C channel. Therefore, the mirror estimator at the triggering mechanism, discussed in the previous sections, is synchronized to evaluate the triggering condition and execute the controller.

The event-based control input, with state x_k^c at the controller, can be expressed as

$$u_k^s = \mu(x_k^c) = \mu(x_{k_i}), \;\; k_i \leq k < k_{i+1}, i = 1, 2, \cdots, \tag{3.84}$$

where $\mu : \mathbb{R}^n \to \mathbb{R}^m$. The error introduced in the control input due to the event-based transmission is defined as

$$e_k^u = u_k^s - u_k = \mu(x_k) - \mu(x_k^c), \tag{3.85}$$

where e_k^u is the control input error. With event-based current and delayed control inputs $u_k^s, \cdots, u_{k-d}^s$ the system (3.82) can be expressed as

$$x_{k+1} = A^s x_k + \sum_{l=0}^{d} \alpha_{k-l} B_l^k u_{k-l}^s. \tag{3.86}$$

Replacing event-based current and delayed control inputs $u_{k-l}^s = u_{k-l} + e_{k-l}^u$, $l = 0, 1, \cdots, d$ from (3.85), the event based system (3.86) can be expressed as

$$x_{k+1} = A^s x_k + \sum_{l=0}^{d} \alpha_{k-l} B_l^k u_{k-l} + \sum_{l=0}^{d} \alpha_{k-l} B_l^k e_{k-l}^u. \tag{3.87}$$

For the co-optimization of control policy and transmission intervals, consider the infinite horizon stochastic cost function

$$J(x_0) = \mathop{\mathbb{E}}_{\tau,\alpha} \left\{ \sum_{k=0}^{\infty} (x_k^T H x_k + u_k^T R u_k - \gamma^2 e_k^{uT} e_k^u) \right\} \tag{3.88}$$

where $H \in \mathbb{R}^{n \times n}$ and $R \in \mathbb{R}^{m \times m}$ are constant symmetric positive definite user defined matrices and $\gamma > \gamma*$ is the penalty for the control input error, where γ^* is the minimum value of γ such that the cost function (3.88) is finite. The operator $\mathop{\mathbb{E}}_{\tau,\alpha}\{.\}$ is the expected value of $(\cdot)$.

Defining the augmented state $z_k = [x_k^T \; u_{k-1}^T \; \cdots \; u_{k-d}^T \; e_{k-1}^{u^T} \; \cdots \; e_{k-d}^{u^T}]^T \in \mathbb{R}^{n+2dm}$, the discretized system in (3.87) can be expressed as

$$z_{k+1} = A_k^{\tau,\alpha} z_k + B_k^{\tau,\alpha} u_k + E_k^{\tau,\alpha} e_k^u \tag{3.89}$$

where $A_k^{\tau,\alpha} \in \mathbb{R}^{(n+2dm)\times(n+2dm)}$, $B_k^{\tau,\alpha} \in \mathbb{R}^{(n+2dm)\times m}$, and $E_k^{\tau,\alpha} \in \mathbb{R}^{(n+2dm)\times m}$, are defined in (3.90).

The cost function for the augmented NCS (3.89) can be defined by redefining the weight matrices in (3.88) [2] as

$$J(z_k) = \mathop{\mathbb{E}}_{\tau,\alpha} \left\{ \sum_{j=k}^{\infty} r(z_j, u_j, e_j^u) \right\} \tag{3.91}$$

where $r(z_k, u_k, e_k^u) = z_k^T H_z z_k + u_k^T R_z u_k - \gamma_z^2 e_k^{u^T} e_k^u$ with $H_z = diag\{H, R/(d+1), \cdots, R/(d+1)\}$, $R_z = R/(d+1)$ are positive definite matrices, and $\gamma_z^2 = \gamma^2/(d+1)$.

The co-optimization of the event-triggered NCS in (3.86) with performance index (3.88) is the same as the co-optimization of the augmented NCS (3.89) with performance index (3.91). Since the objective is to co-optimize the transmission intervals $\delta_{k_i} = k_{i+1} - k_i, i = 1, 2, \cdots$ and the control policy u_k, the problem can be formulated as a two-player zero-sum game where the control input u_k is the player I and the input error e_k^u is the player II. The Player I's objective is to minimize the cost function (3.91) while the player II attempts to maximize it.

Therefore, the optimization problem leads to a min-max problem where the optimal value $V^*(z_k)$ of the cost function (3.91) is given by

$$V^*(z_k) = \min_{u_k} \max_{e_k^u} \mathop{\mathbb{E}}_{\tau,\alpha} \{ r(z_k, u_k, e_k^u) + V(z_{k+1}) \} \tag{3.92}$$

$$A_k^{\tau,\alpha} = \begin{bmatrix} A^s & \alpha_{k-1}B_1^k & \cdots & \alpha_{k-(d-1)}B_d^k & \alpha_{k-d}B_d^k & \alpha_{k-1}B_1^k & \cdots & \alpha_{k-(d-1)}B_d^k & \alpha_{k-d}B_d^k \\ 0 & 0 & \cdots & 0 & 0 & 0 & \cdots & 0 & 0 \\ 0 & I_m & \cdots & 0 & 0 & 0 & \cdots & 0 & 0 \\ \vdots & \vdots & \ddots & \vdots & \vdots & 0 & \cdots & 0 & 0 \\ 0 & 0 & \cdots & I_m & 0 & 0 & \cdots & 0 & 0 \\ 0 & 0 & \cdots & 0 & 0 & 0 & \cdots & 0 & 0 \\ 0 & 0 & \cdots & 0 & 0 & I_m & \cdots & 0 & 0 \\ \vdots & \vdots & \vdots & \vdots & \vdots & 0 & \ddots & 0 & 0 \\ 0 & 0 & \cdots & 0 & 0 & 0 & \cdots & I_m & 0 \end{bmatrix},$$

$$B_k^{\tau,\alpha} = \begin{bmatrix} \alpha_k B_0^k \\ I_m \\ 0 \\ \cdots \\ 0 \\ 0 \\ 0 \\ \cdots \\ 0 \end{bmatrix}, \text{ and } E_k^{\tau,\alpha} = \begin{bmatrix} \alpha_k B_0^k \\ 0 \\ 0 \\ \cdots \\ 0 \\ I_m \\ 0 \\ \cdots \\ 0 \end{bmatrix} \tag{3.90}$$

where $V(z_{k+1})$ is the cost-to-go from time $k+1$ onward. For a given optimal sequence (u_k^*, e_k^{u*}), observable pair $(\mathop{\mathbb{E}}_{\tau,\alpha}\{A_k^{\tau,\alpha}\}, \sqrt{H_z})$, and $\gamma_z > \gamma_z^*$ a saddle point solution exists (Basar and Bernhard, 2008) i.e.,

$$\min_{u_k} \max_{e_k^u} J = \max_{e_k^u} \min_{u_k} J.$$

The solution to the min-max problem can be obtained by solving the stochastic game Ricatti (SGR)-like equation with known system matrices $A_k^{\tau,\alpha}$, $B_k^{\tau,\alpha}$, and $E_k^{\tau,\alpha}$. Since the matrices $A_k^{\tau,\alpha}$, $B_k^{\tau,\alpha}$, and $E_k^{\tau,\alpha}$ are stochastic and uncertain, one needs to develop solution approach that is completely data-driven, as presented in the next section.

3.4.2 CO-OPTIMIZATION UNDER UNCERTAIN NCS DYNAMICS

In this section, a model-free solution to the co-optimization problem for the stochastic uncertain system is presented using event-based stochastic Q-learning.

Define the Hamiltonian for the cost function (3.91) as

$$\mathscr{H}(z_k, u_k, e_k^u, V^*(z_{k+1})) = \mathop{\mathbb{E}}_{\tau,\alpha}\{r(z_k, u_k, e_k^u) + V^*(z_{k+1})\}. \tag{3.93}$$

Assuming the stochastic game has a solution, the stochastic optimal value function (3.92) in a quadratic form (Lewis et al., 2012b) is given by $V^*(z_k) = \mathop{\mathbb{E}}_{\tau,\alpha}(z_k^T S_k z_k)$, where S_k is the time-varying positive definite symmetric matrix solution of the SGR-like equation given by.

$$\mathop{\mathbb{E}}_{\tau,\alpha}(S_k) = \mathop{\mathbb{E}}_{\tau,\alpha}(A_k^{\tau,\alpha^T} P_{k+1} A_k^{\tau,\alpha}) - H_z - \left[\mathop{\mathbb{E}}_{\tau,\alpha}(A_k^{\tau,\alpha^T} P_{k+1} B_k^{\tau,\alpha}) \quad \mathop{\mathbb{E}}_{\tau,\alpha}(A_k^{\tau,\alpha^T} P_{k+1} E_k^{\tau,\alpha})\right]$$
$$\times \begin{bmatrix} R_z + \mathop{\mathbb{E}}_{\tau,\alpha}(B_k^{\tau,\alpha^T} P_{k+1} B_k^{\tau,\alpha}) & \mathop{\mathbb{E}}_{\tau,\alpha}(B_k^{\tau,\alpha^T} P_{k+1} E_k^{\tau,\alpha}) \\ \mathop{\mathbb{E}}_{\tau,\alpha}(E_k^{\tau,\alpha^T} P_{k+1} B_k^{\tau,\alpha}) & \mathop{\mathbb{E}}_{\tau,\alpha}(E_k^{\tau,\alpha^T} P_{k+1} E_k^{\tau,\alpha}) - \gamma_z^2 I \end{bmatrix} \begin{bmatrix} \mathop{\mathbb{E}}_{\tau,\alpha}(B_k^{\tau,\alpha^T} P_{k+1} A_k^{\tau,\alpha}) \\ \mathop{\mathbb{E}}_{\tau,\alpha}(E_k^{\tau,\alpha^T} P_{k+1} A_k^{\tau,\alpha}) \end{bmatrix} \tag{3.94}$$

The optimal control input u_k^* using the stationarity condition can be found as

$$u_k^* = K_k^* z_k, \tag{3.95}$$

where

$$K_k^* = -\left(R_z + \mathop{\mathbb{E}}_{\tau,\alpha}(B_k^{\tau,\alpha^T} S_{k+1} B_k^{\tau,\alpha}) - \mathop{\mathbb{E}}_{\tau,\alpha}(B_k^{\tau,\alpha^T} S_{k+1} E_k^{\tau,\alpha}) \left(\mathop{\mathbb{E}}_{\tau,\alpha}(E_k^{\tau,\alpha^T} S_{k+1} E_k^{\tau,\alpha}) - \gamma_z^2 I\right)^{-1}\right.$$
$$\times \mathop{\mathbb{E}}_{\tau,\alpha}(E_k^{\tau,\alpha^T} S_{k+1} B_k^{\tau,\alpha})\Big)^{-1} \left(\mathop{\mathbb{E}}_{\tau,\alpha}(B_k^{\tau,\alpha^T} S_{k+1} E_k^{\tau,\alpha}) \left(\mathop{\mathbb{E}}_{\tau,\alpha}(E_k^{\tau,\alpha^T} S_{k+1} E_k^{\tau,\alpha}) - \gamma_z^2 I\right)^{-1}\right. \tag{3.96}$$
$$\left.\times \mathop{\mathbb{E}}_{\tau,\alpha}(E_k^{\tau,\alpha^T} S_{k+1} A_k^{\tau,\alpha}) - \mathop{\mathbb{E}}_{\tau,\alpha}(B_k^{\tau,\alpha^T} S_{k+1} A_k^{\tau,\alpha})\right)$$

is the optimal control input gain, and the optimal control input error e_k^{u*} is given by

$$e_k^{u*} = L_k^* z_k, \tag{3.97}$$

where L_k^* the optimal control input gain given by

$$L_k^* = -\left(\mathop{\mathbb{E}}_{\tau,\alpha}(E_k^{\tau,\alpha^T} S_{k+1} E_k^{\tau,\alpha}) - \gamma_z^2 I - \mathop{\mathbb{E}}_{\tau,\alpha}(E_k^{\tau,\alpha^T} S_{k+1} B_k^{\tau,\alpha}) \left(\mathop{\mathbb{E}}_{\tau,\alpha}(B_k^{\tau,\alpha^T} S_{k+1} B_k^{\tau,\alpha}) + R_z\right)^{-1}\right.$$
$$\times \mathop{\mathbb{E}}_{\tau,\alpha}(B_k^{\tau,\alpha^T} S_{k+1} E_k^{\tau,\alpha})\Big)^{-1} \left(\mathop{\mathbb{E}}_{\tau,\alpha}(E_k^{\tau,\alpha^T} S_{k+1} B_k^{\tau,\alpha}) \left(\mathop{\mathbb{E}}_{\tau,\alpha}(B_k^{\tau,\alpha^T} S_{k+1} B_k^{\tau,\alpha}) + R_z\right)^{-1}\right. \tag{3.98}$$
$$\left.\times \mathop{\mathbb{E}}_{\tau,\alpha}(B_k^{\tau,\alpha^T} S_{k+1} A_k^{\tau,\alpha}) - \mathop{\mathbb{E}}_{\tau,\alpha}(E_k^{\tau,\alpha^T} S_{k+1} A_k^{\tau,\alpha})\right).$$

Alternatively, we can state that the optimal control input u_k^* is stabilizing under the worst-case error e_k^{u*}. Therefore, the optimal triggering instants can be determined by using the worst-case control input error $L_k^* z_k$ as a threshold of the triggering condition. Thus, the triggering condition can be defined as

$$e_k^{u^T} e_k^u = \mathop{\mathbb{E}}_{\tau,\alpha}\{z_k^T L_k^{*T} L_k^* z_k\}. \tag{3.99}$$

Further, by emulation-based approach, the event-based optimal control input can be expressed as

$$u_k^{s*} = K_k^* z_k^s, \; k_i \le k < k_{i+1} \tag{3.100}$$

where u_k^{s*} is the event-based optimal control input and $z_k^s = z_{k_i}, k_i \le k < k_{i+1}$ is the event-based augmented state transmitted at the triggering instants. With the NCS dynamics uncertain, the gains K_k^* and L_k^* can not be computed analytically. Therefore, implementing the controller in (3.100) and triggering condition (3.99) is impossible. Therefore, an estimation-based approach using stochastic Q-learning is developed. Similar to the deterministic case in the previous section, the action-dependent value function or the Q-function can be written as

$$Q(z_k, u_k, e_k^u) = \mathop{\mathbb{E}}_{\tau,\alpha}\{(r(z_k, u_k, e_k^u) + V^*(z_{k+1}))\} \tag{3.101}$$

where $Q(z_k, u_k, e_k^u)$ is the Q-function and $V^*(z_{k+1})$ is the optimal cost for $k+1$ onward. The optimal value function for the time instant $k+1$ in a quadratic form can be expressed as $V^*(z_{k+1}) = \mathop{\mathbb{E}}_{\tau,\alpha}\{z_{k+1}^T S_{k+1} z_{k+1}\}$.

Substitute $V^*(z_{k+1})$ in (3.101) to get $Q(z_k, u_k, e_k^u) = \mathop{\mathbb{E}}_{\tau,\alpha}\{z_k^T P_z z_k + u_k^T R_z u_k + z_{k+1}^T S_{k+1} z_{k+1}\}$. Along the system dynamics (3.89), the Q-function,further, leads to

$$Q(z_k, u_k, e_k^u) = \mathop{\mathbb{E}}_{\tau,\alpha}\{[z_k^T \;\; u_k^T \;\; e_k^{u^T}] G_k [z_k^T \;\; u_k^T \;\; e_k^{u^T}]^T\} = \mathop{\mathbb{E}}_{\tau,\alpha}\{w_k^T G_k w_k\}, \forall k \tag{3.102}$$

where $w_k = [z_k^T \ u_k^T \ e_k^{u^T}]^T \in \mathbb{R}^{n+(d+2)m} = l_{mn}$, and $G_k = \begin{bmatrix} G_k^{zz} & G_k^{zu} & G_k^{ze} \\ G_k^{uz} & G_k^{uu} & G_k^{ue} \\ G_k^{ez} & G_k^{eu} & G_k^{ee} \end{bmatrix} \in \mathbb{R}^{l_{mn} \times l_{mn}}$.

$$Q(z_k, u_k, e_k^u) = \mathop{\mathbb{E}}_{\tau,\alpha}\{[z_k^T \ u_k^T \ e_k^{u^T}] G_k [z_k^T \ u_k^T \ e_k^{u^T}]^T\} = \mathop{\mathbb{E}}_{\tau,\alpha}\{w_k^T G_k w_k\}, \forall k \tag{3.103}$$

where $w_k = [z_k^T \ u_k^T \ e_k^{u^T}]^T \in \Re^{n+(d+2)m} = l_{mn}$, and $G_k = \begin{bmatrix} G_k^{zz} & G_k^{zu} & G_k^{ze} \\ G_k^{uz} & G_k^{uu} & G_k^{ue} \\ G_k^{ez} & G_k^{eu} & G_k^{ee} \end{bmatrix} \in \Re^{l_{mn} \times l_{mn}}$ where the sub matrices $G_k^{(\cdot)}$ defined as

$$G_k = \begin{bmatrix} H_z + \mathop{\mathbb{E}}_{\tau,\alpha}(A_k^{\tau,\alpha^T} S_{k+1} A_k^{\tau,\alpha}) & \mathop{\mathbb{E}}_{\tau,\alpha}(A_k^{\tau,\alpha^T} S_{k+1} B_k^{\tau,\alpha}) & \mathop{\mathbb{E}}_{\tau,\alpha}(A_k^{\tau,\alpha^T} S_{k+1} E_k^{\tau,\alpha}) \\ \mathop{\mathbb{E}}_{\tau,\alpha}(B_k^{\tau,\alpha^T} S_{k+1} A_k^{\tau,\alpha}) & R_z + \mathop{\mathbb{E}}_{\tau,\alpha}(B_k^{\tau,\alpha^T} S_{k+1} B_k^{\tau,\alpha}) & \mathop{\mathbb{E}}_{\tau,\alpha}(B_k^{\tau,\alpha^T} S_{k+1} E_k^{\tau,\alpha}) \\ \mathop{\mathbb{E}}_{\tau,\alpha}(E_k^{\tau,\alpha^T} S_{k+1} A_k^{\tau,\alpha}) & \mathop{\mathbb{E}}_{\tau,\alpha}(E_k^{\tau,\alpha^T} S_{k+1} B_k^{\tau,\alpha}) & \mathop{\mathbb{E}}_{\tau,\alpha}(E_k^{\tau,\alpha^T} S_{k+1} E_k^{\tau,\alpha}) - \gamma_z^2 I \end{bmatrix}. \tag{3.104}$$

The optimal Q-function $Q^*(z_k, u_k^*, e_k^{u*})$ is equals the optimal value function $V^*(z_k)$ when both $u_k = u_k^*$ and $e_k^u = e_k^{u*}$, i.e., $\mathop{\mathbb{E}}_{\tau,\alpha}\{Q^*(z_k, u_k^*, e_k^{u*})\} = \mathop{\mathbb{E}}_{\tau,\alpha}\{V^*(z_k)\}$. Therefore, the optimal control input gain K_k^* in terms of the Q-function parameters G_k can be written as

$$K_k^* = (G_k^{uu} - G_k^{ue} G_k^{ee^{-1}} G_k^{eu})^{-1} (G_k^{ue} G_k^{ee^{-1}} G_k^{ez} - G_k^{uz}). \tag{3.105}$$

Similarly, the control input error gain L_k^* is given by

$$L_k^* = (G_k^{ee} - G_k^{eu} G_k^{uu^{-1}} G_k^{ue})^{-1} (G_k^{eu} G_k^{uu^{-1}} G_k^{uz} - G_k^{ez}). \tag{3.106}$$

Remark 3.6. *The gains K_k^* and L_k^* are well defined, i.e., the inverses in (3.105) and (3.106) exist if $\gamma_z^2 I - \mathop{\mathbb{E}}_{\tau,\alpha}\{E_k^{\tau,\alpha^T} S_{k+1} E_k^{\tau,\alpha}\} > 0$. This condition is a required condition for the existence of the saddle point solution (Basar and Bernhard, 2008) and ensures the optimal control input u_k^* is strictly feedback stabilizing in the presence of worst-case control input error e_k^{u*}.*

Assumption 3.5. *Xu et al. (2012) The Q-function is slowly time-varying and can be expressed as linear in the unknown parameters.*

In a parametric form the Q-function can be represented as

$$Q(z_k, u_k, e_k^u) = \mathop{\mathbb{E}}_{\tau,\alpha}\{g_k^T \xi_k\}, \forall k \tag{3.107}$$

The Q-function estimator (QFE) at the controller sampling instants can be represented as

$$\hat{Q}(z_k^s, u_k^s, e_k^u) = \mathop{\mathbb{E}}_{\tau,\alpha}\{\hat{g}_k^T \xi_k^s\}, \ k_i \le k < k_{i+1}, \tag{3.108}$$

where $\hat{Q}(z_k^s, u_k^s, e_k^u)$ is the estimate of Q-function in (3.107), $\hat{g}_k \in \mathbb{R}^{l_g}$ is the estimate of g_k. The event-based regression vector $\xi_k^s = \xi_{k_i}, k_i \le k < k_{i+1}, i = 1, 2, \cdots$; evaluated at the transmission instants. The estimates of the Q-function parameter matrix $\hat{G}_k$ can be reconstructed from $\hat{g}_k$ to compute the estimated control gain matrix $\hat{K}_k$ given by

$$\hat{K}_k = (\hat{G}_k^{uu} - \hat{G}_k^{ue} \hat{G}_k^{ee^{-1}} \hat{G}_k^{eu})^{-1} (\hat{G}_k^{ue} \hat{G}_k^{ee^{-1}} \hat{G}_k^{ez} - \hat{G}_k^{uz}) \tag{3.109}$$

and the estimated control input error gain matrix $\hat{L}_k$ given by

$$\hat{L}_k = (\hat{G}_k^{ee} - \hat{G}_k^{eu}\hat{G}_k^{uu^{-1}}\hat{G}_k^{ud})^{-1}(\hat{G}_k^{eu}\hat{G}_k^{uu^{-1}}\hat{G}_k^{uz} - \hat{G}_k^{ez}). \tag{3.110}$$

where $\hat{G}_k^{(\cdot)}$ is the estimated block matrix element of $\hat{G}_k$.

The event-based estimated control input can be computed as

$$u_k^s = \hat{K}_k z_k^s,\ k_i \leq k < k_{i+1}. \tag{3.111}$$

Similarly, the estimated control input error e_k^u is given by

$$e_k^u = \hat{L}_k z_k,\ k_i \leq k < k_{i+1}. \tag{3.112}$$

The Bellman equation for the stochastic discrete-time system (3.89) satisfies

$$V^*(z_k) = \mathop{\mathbb{E}}_{\tau,\alpha}\{r(z_k, u_k, e_k^u)\} + \mathop{\mathbb{E}}_{\tau,\alpha}\{V^*(z_{k+1})\}. \tag{3.113}$$

With a one-time step backward, the Bellman equation becomes

$$0 = \mathop{\mathbb{E}}_{\tau,\alpha}\{r(z_{k-1}, u_{k-1}, e_{k-1}^u) + \mathop{\mathbb{E}}_{\tau,\alpha}\{V^*(z_k)\} - \mathop{\mathbb{E}}_{\tau,\alpha}\{V^*(z_{k-1})\}. \tag{3.114}$$

Since the optimal Q-function $\mathop{\mathbb{E}}_{\tau,\alpha}\{Q^*(z_k, u_k^*, e_k^{u*})\} = \mathop{\mathbb{E}}_{\tau,\alpha}\{V^*(z_k)\}$, the Bellman equation (3.114) in terms of the Q-function parameters can be expressed as

$$0 = \mathop{\mathbb{E}}_{\tau,\alpha}\{r(z_{k-1}, u_{k-1}, e_{k-1}^u)\} + \mathop{\mathbb{E}}_{\tau,\alpha}\{Q^*(z_k, u_k^*, e_k^{u*})\} - \mathop{\mathbb{E}}_{\tau,\alpha}\{Q^*(z_{k-1}, u_{k-1}^*, e_{k-1}^{u*})\}. \tag{3.115}$$

Using the parametric form (3.107), the Bellman equation is represented as

$$0 = \mathop{\mathbb{E}}_{\tau,\alpha}\{r(z_{k-1}, u_{k-1}, e_{k-1}^u)\} + \mathop{\mathbb{E}}_{\tau,\alpha}\{g_k^T \Delta\xi_{k-1}\}, \tag{3.116}$$

where $\Delta\xi_{k-1} = \xi_k - \xi_{k-1}$. With the estimated Q-function parameters, the resulting Bellman error can be represented as

$$e_k^B = \mathop{\mathbb{E}}_{\tau,\alpha}\{r^s(z_{k-1}, u_{k-1}, e_{k-1}^u) + \mathop{\mathbb{E}}_{\tau,\alpha}\{\hat{g}_k^T \Delta\xi_{k-1}^s, z_{k_i-1}\}, k_i \leq k < k_{i+1}, \tag{3.117}$$

where $r^s(z_{k-1}, u_{k-1}, e_{k-1}^u) = r(z_{k_i-1}, u_{k_i-1}, e_{k_i-1}^u)$ and $\Delta\xi_{k-1}^s = \xi_{k_i}^s - \xi_{k_i-1}^s$, $k_i \leq k < k_{i+1}, i = 1, 2, \cdots$.

Remark 3.7. *The computation of the Bellman error at the controller requires the state information at time k_i and $k_i - 1$ for all $i = 1, 2, \cdots$. Therefore, the trigger mechanism transmits both the state information z_{k_i} and z_{k_i-1} at transmission instants $k_i, i = 1, 2, \cdots$.*

The objective of the Q-function parameter estimation is to drive the Bellman error (3.117) to zero by designing an update law such that the optimal solution is reached. Before defining the update law for the interval $[k_i, k_{i+1})$ the following notations are introduced. The time instants $k \in [k_i, k_{i+1})$ are denoted by $k = k_i + j, j = 0, 1, 2, \cdots, k_{i+1} - k_i - 1$. The recursive least square (Goodwin and Sin, 2014) update law for the estimated Q-function parameter for time instants $k_i + j, j = 0, 1, 2, \cdots, k_{i+1} - k_i - 1$, is

$$\hat{g}_{k_i+j} = \mathop{\mathbb{E}}_{\tau,\alpha}\left\{\hat{g}_{k_i-1+j} - \alpha_g \frac{W_{k_i-2+j}\Delta\xi_{k_i-1}^s e_{k_i-1+j}^{s,B^T}}{1 + \Delta\xi_{k_i-1}^{s^T} W_{k_i-2+j}\Delta\xi_{k_i-1}^s}\right\}, \tag{3.118}$$

for $j = 0,1,2,\cdots,\ k_{i+1}-k_i-1$, where the dynamics of Bellman error (3.117) for $k_i+j, j = 0,1,2,\cdots,k_{i+1}-k_i-1$ are represented as

$$e^{s,B}_{k_i-1+j} = \mathop{\mathbb{E}}_{\tau,\alpha}\{r(z_{k_i-1},u_{k_i-1},e^u_{k_i-1}) + \mathop{\mathbb{E}}_{\tau,\alpha}\{\hat{g}^T_{k_i-1+j}\Delta\xi^s_{k_i-1}\}, \tag{3.119}$$

for $j = 0,1,2,\cdots,\ k_{i+1}-k_i-1$,and the dynamics of the gain matrix are given by

$$W_{k_i+j} = \left(W_{k_i-1+j} - \alpha_w \frac{W_{k_i-1+j}\Delta\xi^s_{k_i-1}\Delta\xi^{s^T}_{k_i-1}W_{k_i-1+j}}{1+\Delta\xi^{s^T}_{k_i-1}W_{k_i-1+j}\Delta\xi^s_{k_i-1}}\right)\mathbf{1}_{\{\|W_{k_i+j}\|\geq W_{min}\}}, \tag{3.120}$$

for $j = 0,1,2,\cdots,k_{i+1}-k_i+1$, where $W_{k_i+j} \in \mathbb{R}^{l_g\times l_g}$ is the positive definite time-varying gain matrix with $W_0 = \beta_w I$ where $\beta_w > 0$ is a constant, W_{min} minimum value of the gain matrix indicated by the indicator function $\mathbf{1}_{(\cdot)}$. The learning gains α_g and α_w are positive constants.

The rationale behind the parameter update law (3.118) with (3.120), defined for all time instants in the interval $[k_i,k_{i+1})$ for all $i = 1,2,\cdots$, is to update the parameters at the trigger instants $k = k_i$ with the new event-based information and, further, utilize the time between the triggering-instants $k_i < k < k_{i+1}$ to accelerate the parameter update using the information available at the previous triggering instants. Thus, the parameter update scheme (3.118) with (3.119) can be considered as a hybrid update scheme (Narayanan and Jagannathan, 2016b). This is different from the parameter update law introduced in the previous sections for systems without a network. This update law is referred to as the hybrid update law.

Remark 3.8. *From (3.120), the gain matrix may converge to zero during the update process. Therefore, the gain matrix W_{k_i+j} resets to W_0 when $\|W_{k_i+j}\| \leq W_{min}$ (Goodwin and Sin, 2014). In the recursive least square approach, this is referred to as covariate resetting (Goodwin and Sin, 2014), and the proof of stability holds when the gain is reset to its initial value.*

Defining the Q-function parameter estimation error $\mathop{\mathbb{E}}_{\tau,\alpha}\{\tilde{g}_k\} = \mathop{\mathbb{E}}_{\tau,\alpha}\{g_k\} - \mathop{\mathbb{E}}_{\tau,\alpha}\{\hat{g}_k\}$, the Bellman error by subtracting (3.116) from (3.117) can be expressed as

$$e^{s,B}_k = \mathop{\mathbb{E}}_{\tau,\alpha}\{\tilde{g}^T_k\Delta\xi^s_{k-1}\}, k = k_i. \tag{3.121}$$

The dynamics of Bellman error for $k = k_i+j, j = 0,1,2,\cdots,k_{i+1}-k_i-1$, from (3.121), can be expressed as

$$e^{s,B}_{k_i-1+j} = \mathop{\mathbb{E}}_{\tau,\alpha}\{\tilde{g}^T_{k_i-1+j}\Delta\xi^s_{k_i-1}\}. \tag{3.122}$$

From (3.119), the Bellman error for time k_i+j becomes

$$e^{s,B}_{k_i+j} = \mathop{\mathbb{E}}_{\tau,\alpha}\{r(z_{k_i-1},u_{k_i-1},e^u_{k_i-1}) + \mathop{\mathbb{E}}_{\tau,\alpha}\{\hat{g}^T_{k_i+j}\Delta\xi^s_{k_i-1}\}, \tag{3.123}$$

for $j = 0,1,2,\cdots,k_{i+1}-k_i-1$. Substitute the update law (3.118) in (3.123) to get

$$e^{s,B}_{k_i+j} = \left(1-\alpha_g\Gamma_{k_i-1}\right)e^{s,B}_{k_i-1+j}. \tag{3.124}$$

where $\Gamma_{k_i-1} = \dfrac{\Delta\xi^{s^T}_{k_i-1}W_{k_i-2+j}\Delta\xi^s_{k_i-1}}{1+\Delta\xi^{s^T}_{k_i-1}W_{k_i-2+j}\Delta\xi^s_{k_i-1}}$. Again, substituting $e^{s,B}_{k_i-1+j}$ from (3.122) in (3.124) leads to

$$e^{s,B}_{k_i+j} = \left(1-\alpha_g\Gamma_{k_i-1}\right)\mathop{\mathbb{E}}_{\tau,\alpha}\{\tilde{g}^T_{k_i-1+j}\Delta\xi^s_{k_i-1}\}. \tag{3.125}$$

Further, from (3.122), the dynamics of Bellman error $e^{s,B}_{k_i+j} = \mathop{\mathbb{E}}_{\tau,\alpha}\{\tilde{g}^T_{k_i+j}\Delta\xi^s_{k_i-1}\}, j = 0,1,\cdots,(k_{i+1}-k_i-1)$. Inserting in (3.125), reveals that

$$\mathop{\mathbb{E}}_{\tau,\alpha}\{\tilde{g}^T_{k_i+j}\Delta\xi^s_{k_i-1}\} = \mathop{\mathbb{E}}_{\tau,\alpha}\{\left(1-\alpha_g\Gamma_{k_i-1}\right)\tilde{g}^T_{k_i-1+j}\Delta\xi^s_{k_i-1}\}. \tag{3.126}$$

The next lemma guarantees the convergence of the parameter estimation error.

Lemma 3.4. *Consider the Q-function in (3.107) and the event-based estimation in (3.108). Let Assumption 3.3 - 3.5 hold and the Q-function parameters $\hat{g}_0$ is initialized with nonzero values in a compact set $\Omega_g \subset \Re^{l_g \times l_g}$ and updated using (3.118) and (3.120). Then, for constants $0 < \alpha_g < 2$, Q-function parameter estimation error $\tilde{g}_k$ converges to zero asymptotically in the mean square provided the regression vector satisfies the PE condition.*

Sketch of the proof. Consider a candidate Lyapunov function given by $L(\tilde{g}_{k_i-1+j}) = \mathbb{E}_{\tau,\alpha}\{\tilde{g}^T_{k_i-1+j}\Delta\xi^s_{k_i-1}\Delta\xi^{s^T}_{k_i-1}\tilde{g}_{k_i-1+j}\}$. The first difference of the Lyapunov function

$$\Delta L(\tilde{g}_{k_i-1+j}) = \mathbb{E}_{\tau,\alpha}\{\tilde{g}^T_{k_i+j}\Delta\xi^s_{k_i-1}\Delta\xi^{s^T}_{k_i-1}\tilde{g}_{k_i+j}\} - \mathbb{E}_{\tau,\alpha}\{\tilde{g}^T_{k_i-1+j}\Delta\xi^s_{k_i-1}\Delta\xi^{s^T}_{k_i-1}\tilde{g}_{k_i-1+j}\}. \tag{3.127}$$

Substituting (3.126) in the first difference leads to

$$\Delta L(\tilde{g}_{k_i-1+j}) = -\mathbb{E}_{\tau,\alpha}\{\left(\alpha_g\Gamma_{k_i-1}(2-\alpha_g\Gamma_{k_i-1})\right)\tilde{g}^T_{k_i-1+j}\Delta\xi^s_{k_i-1}\Delta\xi^{s^T}_{k_i-1}\tilde{g}_{k_i-1+j}\}. \tag{3.128}$$

By definition of Γ_{k_i-1} in (3.124) and persistency of excitation condition (Green and Moore, 1985) of the regression vector, it is clear that $0 < \xi^2_{min} \leq \Gamma_{k_i-1} < 1$ where $\xi_{min} > 0$ is a constant. Utilizing the above fact, the first difference is upper bounded by

$$\Delta L(\tilde{g}_{k_i-1+j}) \leq -\mathbb{E}_{\tau,\alpha}\{\left(\alpha_g\xi^2_{min}(2-\alpha_g)\right)\tilde{g}^T_{k_i-1+j}\Delta\xi^s_{k_i-1}\Delta\xi^{s^T}_{k_i-1}\tilde{g}_{k_i-1+j}\}. \tag{3.129}$$

The Lyapunov first difference (3.129) $\Delta L(\tilde{g}_{k_i-1+j}) < 0$ by selecting $0 < \alpha_g < 2$. Therefore, the Lyapunov function decreases in the interval $k_i \leq k < k_{i+1}$, $i = 0, 1, \cdots$. Consequently, $\lim_{k_i\to\infty}\mathbb{E}_{\tau,\alpha}\{\tilde{g}^T_{k_i-1+j}\Delta\xi^s_{k_i-1}\Delta\xi^{s^T}_{k_i-1}\tilde{g}_{k_i-1+j}\} = 0$. Since the regression vector $\Delta\xi^s_{k_i-1}$ satisfies PE condition (Green and Moore, 1985), the Q- function parameter estimation error $\tilde{g}_k$ converges to zero asymptotically in the mean square, i.e, $\lim_{k_i\to\infty}\mathbb{E}_{\tau,\alpha}\{\tilde{g}^T_{k_i-1+j}\tilde{g}_{k_i-1+j}\} = 0$ or alternatively, $\lim_{k\to\infty}\mathbb{E}_{\tau,\alpha}\{\tilde{g}^T_k\tilde{g}_k\} = 0$ since k_i is a subsequence of $k \in \Re$.

Next, the main results are presented by designing the event-triggering condition to decide the transmission instants.

3.4.3 MAIN RESULTS AND STABILITY ANALYSIS

The closed-loop dynamics of the system (3.89) with estimated control input (3.111) both at trigger instants and during inter-event times are given by

$$z_{k+1} = A^{\tau,\alpha}_k z_k + B^{\tau,\alpha}_k \hat{K} z^s_k, k = k_i, \tag{3.130}$$

and

$$z_{k+1} = A^{\tau,\alpha}_k z_k + B^{\tau,\alpha}_k \hat{K} z_k + E^{\tau,\alpha}_k \hat{L} z_k, k_i < k < k_{i+1} \tag{3.131}$$

Since $\hat{K}_k$ and $\hat{L}_k$ are computed from the estimated $\hat{G}_k$, the following assumption is necessary to ensure the estimated control gain matrix is well defined.

Assumption 3.6. *The estimated Q-function submatrices $\hat{G}^{uu}_k$ and $\hat{G}^{ee}_k$ are full rank during the estimation process.*

This assumption can be satisfied by initializing the Q-function parameters with non-zero values in a compact set and observed heuristically with numerical simulation. Before presenting the theorem, the following technical lemma is necessary.

Lemma 3.5. *Consider the augmented NCS (3.89) and estimated Q-function (3.108) along with the estimated control input (3.111) and control input error (3.112). Let the Q-function parameter laws be as given in (3.120) and (3.122). Then, the inequalities*

$$W_{min}\|\underset{\tau,\gamma}{\mathbb{E}}\{z_k^T\tilde{K}_k^T R_z \tilde{K}_k z_k\}\| \leq \varpi_K \lambda_{max}(R_z)\alpha_w \|\underset{\tau,\gamma}{\mathbb{E}}\{\tilde{g}_k\}\|^2, \tag{3.132}$$

and

$$W_{min}\|\underset{\tau,\gamma}{\mathbb{E}}\{z_k^T\tilde{L}_k^T \tilde{L}_k z_k\}\| \leq \varpi_L \alpha_w \|\underset{\tau,\gamma}{\mathbb{E}}\{\tilde{g}_k\}\|^2 \tag{3.133}$$

hold, where $\underset{\tau,\alpha}{\mathbb{E}}\{\tilde{K}_k\} = \underset{\tau,\alpha}{\mathbb{E}}\{K_k^* - \hat{K}_k\}$, $\underset{\tau,\alpha}{\mathbb{E}}\{\tilde{L}_k\} = \underset{\tau,\alpha}{\mathbb{E}}\{L_k^* - \hat{L}_k\}$ *are the errors in gain matrices,* $\varpi_K = C_g^2\bar{\xi}_c^2 > 0$ *and* $\varpi_L = C_L^2\bar{\xi}_c^2 > 0$ *with* $C_g > 0$*,* $C_L > 0$ *and* $\bar{\xi}_c > 0$ *are constants,* W_{min} *defined in (3.120), and* $\lambda_{max}(R_z)$ *is the maximum eigenvalue of* R_z*.*

Sketch of Proof: By definition $\|\underset{\tau,\gamma}{\mathbb{E}}\{z_k\}\| \leq \|\underset{\tau,\gamma}{\mathbb{E}}\{\xi_k\}\|$. Therefore, there exists a constant $\bar{\xi}_c > 0$ such that $\|\underset{\tau,\gamma}{\mathbb{E}}\{z_k\}\| \leq \bar{\xi}_c\|\underset{\tau,\gamma}{\mathbb{E}}\{\Delta\xi_{k_i-1}^s\}\|$ holds.

Further, defining $\tilde{G}_k = G_k - \hat{G}_k$ and using Frobenius norm for matrices, it is clear that the block matrices $\|\tilde{G}_k^{(\cdot)}\| \leq \|\tilde{G}_k\|$. Further, from (3.105), (3.106), (3.109) and (3.110), $\tilde{K}_k = K_k^* - \hat{K}_k = f(\tilde{G}_k^{eu}, \tilde{G}_k^{uu}, \tilde{G}_k^{ud}, \tilde{G}_k^{uz}, \tilde{G}_k^{ez})$. Since the inverse of the estimated block matrices $\hat{G}_k^{uu}$ and $\hat{G}_k^{ee}$ exists from Assumption 3.6, it holds that

$$\|\tilde{K}_k\| = \|f(\tilde{G}_k^{eu}, \tilde{G}_k^{uu}, \tilde{G}_k^{ud}, \tilde{G}_k^{uz}, \tilde{G}_k^{ez})\| \leq C_g\|\tilde{G}_k\| = C_g\|\tilde{g}_k\|$$

where $C_g > 0$ is a constant. With similar arguments the matrix $\tilde{L}_k$ satisfies $\|\tilde{L}_k\| \leq C_L\|\tilde{G}_k\| = C_L\|\tilde{g}_k\|$ where $C_L > 0$ is a constant.

With the above results, consider the left side term in (3.132)

$$W_{min}\|\underset{\tau,\gamma}{\mathbb{E}}\{z_k^T\tilde{K}_k^T R_z \tilde{K}_k z_k\}\| \leq W_{min}\lambda_{max}(R_z)\|\underset{\tau,\gamma}{\mathbb{E}}\{z_k\}\|^2\|\underset{\tau,\gamma}{\mathbb{E}}\{\tilde{K}_k\}\|^2. \tag{3.134}$$

From update law for the gain matrix W_{k_i+j} in (3.120) $W_{min} \leq \|W_{k_i+j}\|$. By matrix inverse lemma Goodwin and Sin (2014), it holds that

$$W_{k_i+j} = \alpha_w \frac{W_{k_i-1+j}}{1 + \Delta\xi_{k_i-1}^{sT} W_{k_i-1+j}\Delta\xi_{k_i-1}^s}. \tag{3.135}$$

By generalizing the equation (3.135) for time instants k and $j = 1$, it holds that $W_{min} \leq \alpha_w \frac{\|W_k\|}{1 + \Delta\xi_{k_i-1}^{sT} W_k \Delta\xi_{k_i-1}^s}$. Substituting the inequality in (3.134) leads to

$$W_{min}\|\underset{\tau,\gamma}{\mathbb{E}}\{z_k^T\tilde{K}_k^T R_z \tilde{K}_k z_k\}\| \leq C_g^2\bar{\xi}_c^2\lambda_{max}(R_z)\alpha_w\|\underset{\tau,\gamma}{\mathbb{E}}\{\tilde{g}_k\}\|^2, \tag{3.136}$$

where $\frac{\|W_k\|\|\underset{\tau,\gamma}{\mathbb{E}}\{\Delta\xi_{k_i-1}^s\}\|^2}{1 + \Delta\xi_{k_i-1}^{sT} W_k \Delta\xi_{k_i-1}^s}\| < 1$. Replacing $\varpi_K = C_g^2\bar{\xi}_c^2$ one can reach the inequality in (3.132). Further, with the similar argument, it can also be shown that the inequality in (3.133) also holds.

Remark 3.9. *The constants* $\varpi_K > 0$ *and* $\varpi_L > 0$ *in inequality (3.132) and (3.133) are not necessary for the implementation of the controller and only used for stability proof.*

Theorem 3.3. *Consider the continuous time system (3.80) represented as a sampled data system (3.86) and an augmented NCS (3.89) along with the estimated control input (3.111) and control* *input error (3.112). Let the Assumptions 1 to 4 hold, the Q-function parameters are initialized with non-zero values in a compact set* $\Omega_g \subset \mathbb{R}^{l_g \times l_g}$*, and the parameters are updated using (3.118) and (3.120). Then, the closed-loop event-triggered NCS is asymptotically stable in the mean square provided the regression vector satisfies PE, the inequality*

$$e_k^{u^T} e_k^u \leq \mathop{\mathbb{E}}_{\tau,\alpha}\{z_k^T \hat{L}_k^T \hat{L}_k z_k\},\ k_i \leq k < k_{i+1} \tag{3.137}$$

holds, and the parameters satisfy $0 < \alpha_g < 2$, $0 < c_1 < 1$ *and* $\sqrt{2}\gamma_z > \gamma_z^*$*. Further, the estimated control input* u_k^s *converges to it optimal value* u_k^{s*} *and the set of transmission instants determined by the equality condition in (3.137), i.e.,* $\{k_i | i \in \mathbb{N}, e_k^{u^T} e_k^u = z_k^T \hat{L}_k^T \hat{L}_k z_k$ *converges to the optimal sampling set* $\{k_i | i \in \mathbb{N}, e_k^{u^T} e_k^u = \mathop{\mathbb{E}}_{\tau,\alpha}\{z_k^T L_k^{*T} L_k^* z_k\}\}$.

Sketch of the Proof. The closed-loop stability of the event-triggered NCS is demonstrated by proving the Lyapunov function $L \in \mathbb{R}_+$ decreases for $k_i \leq k < k_{i+1}$ for $i = 1, 2, \cdots$. Since the interval $[k_i, k_{i+1}) = [k_i, k_i + 1) \cup [k_i + 1, k_{i+1})$ it suffices to demonstrate that the first difference of the Lyapunov function $\Delta L_k < 0, k = k_i$ and $\Delta L_k < 0, k_i < k < k_{i+1}$.

With this effect, we can select a Lyapunov function candidate given by

$$L(z_k, \tilde{g}_k) = \mathop{\mathbb{E}}_{\tau,\alpha}\{\tilde{g}_k^T \Delta\xi_{k_i-1}^s \Delta\xi_{k_i-1}^{s^T} \tilde{g}_k\} + v_x W_{min} \mathop{\mathbb{E}}_{\tau,\gamma}\{V^*(z_k)\} = L(z_k) + L(\tilde{g}_k). \tag{3.138}$$

Note that the first term in the Lyapunov function is the Q-function parameter estimation error term in Lemma 3.5, and the second term is the optimal value function. Since the Optimal value function is positive definite, we can use it as the Lyapunov function. By using the results from Lemma 3.5 and evaluating the second both at the triggering instant $k = k_i$ and inter-triggering times $k_i < k < k_{i+1}$ (in two cases) along the NCS dynamics, update law, and event-triggering condition, we can show that $\Delta L_k < 0$ for both the cases.

Example 3.3. *The benchmark example of batch reactor Xu et al. (2014b) is selected for simulation whose continuous-time dynamics are represented by* $\dot{x} = Ax + Bu$*, where A and B matrices are defined in Xu et al. (2014b).*

Solution: Select the following parameters for the simulation. The initial state vector of the NCS was taken as $[2\ \ -2\ \ 6\ \ -10]^T$. The delay bound $d = 2$ with a mean of 0.1s, and the packet loss follows the Bernoulli distribution. The sensor sampling time is selected to be $T_s = 0.1$ sec. A quadratic cost function is selected with $H_z = 0.2I$ and $R_z = 0.2I$, where I is the identity matrix. The penalty for the control input error $\gamma_z = 5$. The learning gains were $\alpha_g = 0.5$ and $\alpha_w = 1$. Initial value of the gain matrix $W_0 = 9999I$. To ensure the initial value of the Q-function parameters are non-zero and in a compact set, the values are selected as 60% of the actual values. An exploration noise of small magnitude was added to the regression vector to satisfy the PE condition, and a Monte Carlo simulation was run for 5 sec or sampling instants.

First, the performance of the event-based optimal regulator is studied. The state vector is regulated to zero by the proposed event-based optimal regulator, as shown in Fig. 3.9(a). It is clear that this event-based regulator is able to handle random delays and packet losses in the presence of uncertain system dynamics. The optimal control input, shown in Fig. 3.9(b), also converges to zero as the system state converges. The convergence Bellman error to zero shown in Fig. 3.9(c) implies the optimal control is attained.

Second, the event-based regulator performance to save the bandwidth and computation is shown in Fig. 3.10. The events or the transmission instants are illustrated in 3.10 (a). The cumulative number of events that occurred during the simulation time is shown in Fig. 3.10 (b). The horizontal axis indicates the total number of sampling instants. This shows that a fewer number of times the data is being transmitted when compared to the traditional periodic transmission.

Table 3.3
Co-optimization of sampling and control for NCS

System dynamics	$\dot{x}(t) = Ax(t) + \alpha(t)Bu(t-\tau(t)),\ x(0) = x_0,$
Event-triggering error	$e_k^u = u_k^s - u_k = \mu(x_k) - \mu(x_k^c)$
Q-function estimator (QFE)	$\hat{Q}(z_k^s, u_k^s, e_k^u) = \mathbb{E}_{\tau,\alpha}\{\hat{g}_k^T \xi_k^s\},\ k_i \le k < k_{i+1}$
QFE residual error	$e_k^{s,B} = \mathbb{E}_{\tau,\alpha}\{\tilde{g}_k^T \Delta\xi_{k-1}^s\}, k = k_i$
Auxilary QFE error	$\Xi_k^{o,V} = \Pi_k^o + \hat{\Theta}_k^T Z_k^o,\ k = k_i$
Q-function estimator update	$\hat{g}_{k_i+j} = \mathbb{E}_{\tau,\alpha}\left\{ \hat{g}_{k_i-1+j} - \alpha_g \frac{W_{k_i-2+j}\Delta\xi_{k_i-1}^s e_{k_i-1+j}^{s,B^T}}{1+\Delta\xi_{k_i-1}^{s^T} W_{k_i-2+j}\Delta\xi_{k_i-1}^s} \right\}$ $W_{k_i+j} = \left(W_{k_i-1+j} - \alpha_w \frac{W_{k_i-1+j}\Delta\xi_{k_i-1}^s \Delta\xi_{k_i-1}^{s^T} W_{k_i-1+j}}{1+\Delta\xi_{k_i-1}^{s^T} W_{k_i-1+j}\Delta\xi_{k_i-1}^s} \right) \mathbf{1}_{\{\lVert W_{k_i+j}\rVert \ge W_{min}\}}$ $j = 0, 1, 2, \cdots, k_{i+1} - k_i - 1$
Control input	$u_k^s = \hat{K}_k z_k^s,\ k_i \le k < k_{i+1}$
Event-triggering condition	$e_k^{u^T} e_k^u \le \mathbb{E}_{\tau,\alpha}\{z_k^T \hat{L}_k^T \hat{L}_k z_k\},\ k_i \le k < k_{i+1}$

3.5 OPTIMAL TRACKING CONTROL

Consider a linear continuous-time system given in (3.80). The control objective is to track a feasible reference trajectory $x_d(t) \in \mathbb{R}^n$ generated by a reference system represented by

$$\dot{x}_d(t) = A_d x_d(t),\ x_d(0) = x_{d0} \tag{3.139}$$

where $x_d(t) \in \mathbb{R}^n$ is the reference state, and $A_d \in \mathbb{R}^{n \times n}$ is the internal dynamics with $x_d(0) = 0$. Following standard characteristics of the systems in (3.80) and (3.139) are assumed.

Assumption 3.7. *System* (3.80) *is stabilizable, and the system states are available for measurement.*

Assumption 3.8. *The feasible reference trajectory* $x_d(t) \in \Omega_{x_d}$*, where* Ω_{x_d} *is a compact set, is bounded such that* $\lVert x_d(t) \rVert \le b_{x_d}$ *where* $b_{x_d} > 0$ *is a constant. The control coefficient matrix B has full column rank.*

Define the error between the system state and the reference state as the tracking error, given by $e_r(t) \triangleq x(t) - x_d(t)$. Then, the tracking error system, utilizing (3.80) and (3.139), can be defined by

$$\dot{e}_r(t) = \dot{x}(t) - \dot{x}_d(t) = A(e_r(t) + x_d(t)) + \alpha(t)Bu(t-\tau) - A_d x_d(t). \tag{3.140}$$

Following the derivations in Section 2.6, the steady-state feed-forward control policy for the reference trajectory can be expressed as

$$u_d = B^+(A_d x_d - A x_d) \tag{3.141}$$

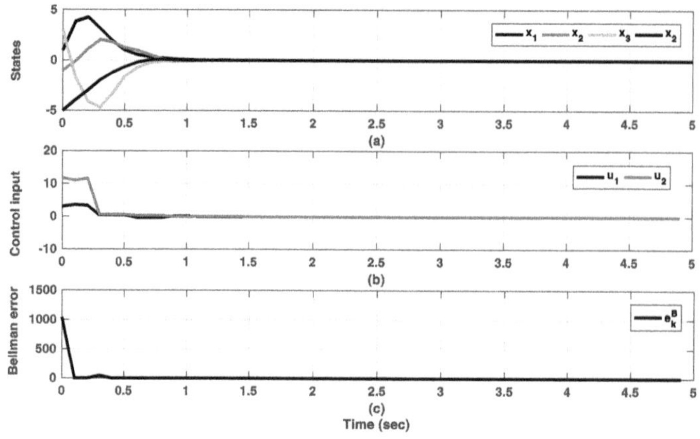

Figure 3.9 Convergence of (a) closed-loop event-triggered state vector; (b) event-based optimal control input; and (c) Bellman error.

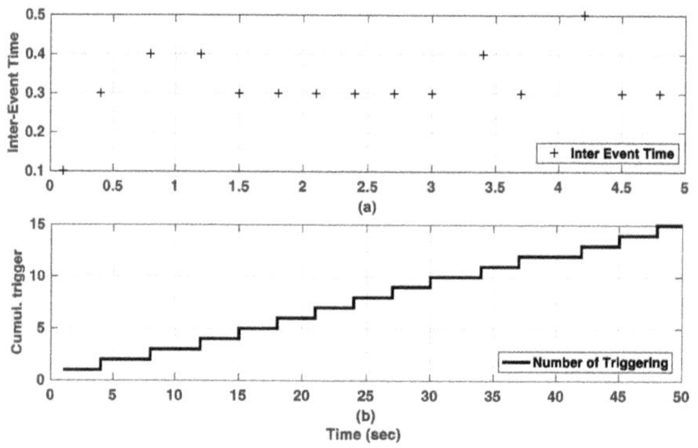

Figure 3.10 (a) Transmission instants and inter-event times; and (b) cumulative number of triggering instants

where $u_d : \mathbb{R}^n \to \mathbb{R}^m$ is the steady state control policy corresponding to the reference trajectory and B^+ is the (left) pseudoinverse of B. Note that here we use the assumption that B has full column rank, and therefore, the pseudoinverse we need, exists (Strang, 2022). By augmenting the tracking error e_r and desired trajectory x_d, the dynamics of the augmented tracking error system can be represented as

$$\dot{\chi}(t) = G\chi(t) + \alpha(t)Hw(t-\tau) \tag{3.142}$$

where $\chi \triangleq [e_r^T \;\; x_d^T]^T \in \mathbb{R}^{2n}$ is the augmented state with $\chi(0) = [e_r^T(0) \;\; x_d^T(0)]^T = \chi_0$, $G \in \mathbb{R}^{2n}$ is given by $G \triangleq \begin{bmatrix} A & A - A_d \\ 0 & A_d \end{bmatrix}$, $H \in \mathbb{R}^{2n\times m}$ given by $H \triangleq \begin{bmatrix} B \\ \mathbf{0} \end{bmatrix}$, and the mismatched control policy $w(t-\tau) \triangleq u(t-\tau) - u_d(t) \in \mathbb{R}^m$.

The augmented error system in (3.142) transforms the tracking problem into a regulation problem. We can then follow the discretization procedure and the control synthesis technique developed in Section 3.4.

3.6 CONCLUDING REMARKS

This chapter presents three event-based infinite-time horizon near-optimal control techniques for uncertain linear discrete-time systems with and without communication networks in the feedback loop. Both the state and the output feedback-based near-optimal controllers for the system without a communication network are designed using the system state and output vectors without needing the system dynamics. The event-triggering conditions are designed as a function of the estimated Q-function parameters and the measured or observer system state vector, making it adaptive in nature. In both cases, these triggering conditions ensured sufficient events to estimate the Q-function parameters. The aperiodic tuning laws guaranteed the convergence of the Q-function parameter estimation errors; the Lyapunov technique was used to prove them. For NCS, the delays and packet losses are integrated to reformulate the system, and Q-learning-based design is extended to the stochastic domain. The simulation results using benchmark examples also corroborated the analytical results by revealing the convergence of the closed-loop parameters and the reduction in the computation. It was observed that the cumulative number of triggers was dependent on the initial Q-function parameters.

3.7 PROBLEMS

3.7.1 The longitudinal dynamics of an F-16 aircraft in straight and level flight at 502 ft/sec are given by

$$\dot{x} = Ax + Bu = \begin{bmatrix} -2.0244\times10^{-2} & 7.8761 & -3.2169\times10^{1} & -6.502\times10^{-1} \\ -2.5373\times10^{-4} & -1.0189 & 0 & 9.0484\times10^{-1} \\ 0 & 0 & 0 & 1 \\ 7.9472\times10^{-11} & -2.498 & 0 & -1.3861 \end{bmatrix} x \tag{3.143}$$

$$+ \begin{bmatrix} -1\times10^{-2} \\ -2.09\times10^{-3} \\ 0 \\ -1.99\times10^{-1} \end{bmatrix} u \tag{3.144}$$

The state is $x = \begin{bmatrix} v_T & \alpha & \theta & q \end{bmatrix}^T$, with v_T the forward velocity, α the angle of attack, θ the pitch angle, and q the pitch rate. The control input $u(t)$ is the elevator deflection δ_e.

(a) Plot the response of the open-loop system to initial conditions of $x_0 = \begin{bmatrix} 0 & 0.1 & 0 & 1 \end{bmatrix}^T$ (note that the angular units are in radians).

(b) Try MATLAB function lqr to perform linear quadratic regulator design. Use $Q = I, R = 0.1$.

(c) Use the Q-learning algorithm (Table 3.1) with $\tau = 0$ and $\gamma_{ca} = 1$ to learn the control inputs for $Q = I, R = 0.1$.

3.7.2 Consider a of linear dynamical system given by

$$\frac{d}{dt}x(t) = Ax(t) + Bu(t), \tag{3.145}$$

where $A = \begin{pmatrix} 0 & -1 \\ 1 & 0 \end{pmatrix}$ and $B = \begin{pmatrix} 1 & 0 \\ 0 & 1 \end{pmatrix}$.

(a) Use the Q-learning algorithm (Table 3.1) with $\tau = 0$ and $\gamma_{ca} = 1$ to learn the control inputs for $Q = I, R = 0.1$.

(b) Now consider the channel losses. The new dynamics will take the form $\frac{d}{dt}x(t) = Ax(t) + \gamma_{ca}Bu(t-\tau)$, $\tau = 0.1$ and γ_{ca} is a random variable characterized by Bernoulli distribution with the probability of data lost is 10%. Use the Q-learning algorithm (3.3) to learn the control inputs for $Q = I, R = 0.1I$.

(c) What happens when τ is a random variable following a Gaussian distribution with mean 10ms and 1ms standard deviation?

3.7.3 Consider the system of an inverted pendulum. The dynamics are

$$\dot{x}(t) = \begin{bmatrix} 0 & 1 \\ \frac{g}{l} - \frac{a_j k}{ml^2} & 0 \end{bmatrix} x_i(t) + \gamma_{ca} \begin{bmatrix} 0 \\ \frac{1}{ml^2} \end{bmatrix} u_i(t-\tau),$$

where $l = 5$, $g = 10$, $m = 5$, $k = 5$ and $h_{ij} = 1$ for $\forall j \in \{1, 2, .., N\}$. The system is open loop unstable.

(a) Use the Q-learning algorithm (Table 3.3) with τ being a random variable following a Gaussian distribution with mean 100ms and 20ms standard deviation and γ is a random variable characterized by Bernoulli distribution with the probability of data lost is 10% to learn the control inputs for $Q = 10 \times I, R = 0.001$.

(b) What if the cost function is defined with $R = 10$ and $Q = 0.1 \times I$.

3.7.4 Use the system defined in the Problems 3.7.1-3. Consider the first state as the only measured quantity (output) of the system. Use the Q-learning algorithm (Table 3.2) to design feedback control inputs to steer the system to the equilibrum point at origin.

3.7.5 Use the system defined in the previous problem and do not use the data history in the state-feedback-based Q-learning algorithm described in this chapter. Does the Q-function parameters converge? Try using the gradient descent algorithm in place of RLS-based parameter updates. Does the Q-function parameters converge?

3.7.6 Consider a linear discrete-time system given by

$$\begin{aligned} x_{k+1} &= \begin{bmatrix} -1 & 2 \\ 2.2 & 1.7 \end{bmatrix} x_k + \begin{bmatrix} 2 \\ 1.6 \end{bmatrix} u_k \\ y_k &= \begin{bmatrix} 1 & 2 \end{bmatrix} x_k \end{aligned} \tag{3.146}$$

The open-loop poles are $z_1 = -2.1445$ and $z_2 = 2.8445$, so the system is unstable. Use the Q-learning algorithm in Table 3.1, with $Q = 6$ and $R = 1$, to design a feedback control to optimally stabilize the system.

3.7.7 For the system described in the previous problem, consider the trajectory tracking control task. Design a Q-learning-based trajectory tracking controller to track the reference trajectory generated by the command generator dynamics given by $r_{k+1} = -r_k$, with $r(0) = -1$.

3.7.8 For the system used in the previous two examples, use the output matrix to $C = [0 \quad 1]$ and implement the learning algorithm in Table 3.1. What is the minimum value for the weighting parameter Q for $R = 1$ for which the learning algorithm converges.

3.7.9 For the Example 3.1, select the parameters of the performance index, learning gains, and initial values of the state and parameters. Use the equations in Table 3.1 to design feedback controller. Plot all the signals, including event-trigger condition, state, and parameter estimation errors. Comment on the convergence of the system states and QFE error convergence with PE signal selected as

a. Sinusoid signal.

b. Pulse train with 50% duty cycle.

3.7.10 For the Example 3.1, select the parameters of the performance index, learning gains, and initial values of the state and parameters. Use the equations in Table 3.2 to design feedback controller. Start with $\tau = 0$ and use the Bernoulli distribution to characterize γ_{ca} with a probability of packet loss set at 10% and increase the τ by 0.05. Plot the parameter estimation error convergence time versus τ. Repeat the experiments with a τ fixed at 0.1 and vary the probability of packet loss with 5% increments. Comment on the convergence of the system states and QFE error convergence with respect to channel losses.

4 Nonlinear Continuous-time Systems

CONTENTS

In the previous chapter, we studied Q-learning-based optimal control synthesis techniques suitable for uncertain linear discrete-time systems using state and output feedback when the communication network in the feedback loop is lossless as well as when it is lossy. On the other hand, in the first part of this chapter, based on the work in (Sahoo et al., 2016), we shall consider multi-input-multi-output (MIMO) uncertain nonlinear continuous-time (CT) systems in affine form. In particular, we shall develop an approximation-based event-triggered controller suitable for MIMO nonlinear CT systems whose dynamics are represented in affine form. The controller utilizes a linearly parameterized neural network (NN) whose weights are tuned using data that are sampled based on aperiodic events. In this context, we shall revisit the NN approximation property with event-based sampling, develop an event-triggering condition by using the Lyapunov technique to reduce the network resource utilization, and generate the required number of events for the NN approximation. In the second part of this chapter, based on the work in (Sahoo et al., 2017b), we shall develop approximate optimal controllers for the uncertain nonlinear CT systems using adaptive dynamic programming (ADP) with event-sampled state and input vectors. In this case, we shall incorporate NNs to not only mitigate the need for an accurate model of the system dynamics but also learn the optimal value function, which becomes an approximate solution to the Hamilton-Jacobi-Bellman (HJB) equation associated with the optimal control problem. For both the non-optimal and optimal controllers presented in this chapter, we shall also develop weight tuning rules to train the NNs online with aperiodic feedback data, design event-triggering conditions, derive sufficient conditions for closed-loop stability, and develop arguments to compute a positive lower bound on the minimum inter-sample time.

4.1 INTRODUCTION

Among the earlier works on event-triggered control, Tabuada (2007) presented an event-triggered control for nonlinear systems by assuming the input-to-state stability (ISS) of the system with respect to measurement error. Further, an event-triggering condition is developed for deciding the triggering instants to execute the controller with a desired closed-loop performance. A lower bound on the inter-triggering times is also guaranteed to avoid the accumulation point. In these early works (Tabuada, 2007; Donkers and Heemels, 2012; Postoyan et al., 2011; Heemels and Donkers, 2013; Lunze and Lehmann, 2010; Stöcker and Lunze, 2011), the complete knowledge system dynamics have been considered for the ETC design both for linear and nonlinear systems with a few exceptions (Garcia and Antsaklis, 2013; Wang and Hovakimyan, 2010). In (Garcia and Antsaklis, 2013), the authors considered known uncertainty for the system and developed a model-based event-triggered control scheme. Further, in (Wang and Hovakimyan, 2010), an L1 adaptive control scheme is proposed where the nominal system dynamics are considered known, and uncertainties are compensated for by using an adaptive term tuned with a projection-based tuning law. On the other hand, in (Sahoo et al., 2013a), the complete knowledge of the system dynamics was relaxed by approximating the dynamics using a neural network (NN)-based approximations for SISO systems, while a zero-order hold (ZOH) was used for the controller implementation.

On the other hand, as discussed in Chapter 2, optimal control (Lewis et al., 2012b; Bertsekas, 2012) of nonlinear dynamic systems in continuous time is a challenging problem due to the difficulty involved in obtaining a closed-form solution to the Hamilton-Jacobi-Bellman (HJB) (Bertsekas, 2012) equation. Adaptive dynamic programming (ADP) (Lewis et al., 2012a; Bertsekas, 2012; Chen and Jagannathan, 2008; Si et al., 2004; Vrabie et al., 2009b; Jiang and Jiang, 2015; Prokhorov and Wunsch, 1997; Liu and Wei, 2013; Zhang et al., 2009; Dierks and Jagannathan, 2010b; Xu et al., 2012; Dierks and Jagannathan, 2012b; Zhang et al., 2008a) techniques are used to solve the optimal control of uncertain dynamic systems online by finding an approximated value function, which becomes a solution to the HJB equation.

The first section of the chapter, taken from (Sahoo et al., 2016), introduces the development of event-triggered control (ETC) of MIMO nonlinear continuous-time systems in affine form when the system and the controller are separated by an ideal communication network with no delays and packet losses. Instead of approximating the unknown nonlinear functions of the system dynamics by using two NNs (Sahoo et al., 2013a), the controller is approximated by using a linearly parameterized NN in the event-triggered context under the assumption that the system states are measurable. An event-triggering condition based on the system state and estimated NN weight is designed to orchestrate the transmission of the state vector and control input between the plant and controller. Since the approximation is carried out using the event-based state vector, the event-triggering condition is made adaptive to attain a tradeoff between resource utilization and function approximation. In addition, the NN weights and the control inputs are only updated at the triggering instants, which are aperiodic in nature and held until the next update. Consequently, the proposed scheme reduces the overall computation when compared to the traditional NN schemes (Lewis et al., 1998), where weights are updated periodically. In addition, to analyze the system stability and design the event-triggering condition, the nonlinear impulsive dynamical model of the closed-loop dynamics is considered. The well-developed Lyapunov approach for the nonlinear impulsive dynamical system (Michel, 2008; Hayakawa and Haddad, 2005) is utilized to study inter-event and event time behavior and used to prove the local ultimate boundedness (UB) of the system state and the NN weight estimation errors.

In the second part of the paper, the event-triggered stabilizing controller design in the first part is extended to event-based optimal control design and taken from (Sahoo et al., 2016) using event-sampled actor-critic NN. Here, the NN weights are updated at the event-sampled instants and, hence, aperiodic in nature to save computation. The event-triggering conditions are also made adaptive to orchestrate the sampling instants, such that the approximation accuracy is maintained along with the system performance. The closed-loop stability and convergence are guaranteed by using the extension of the Lyapunov approach for switched systems.

4.2 CONTROL OF UNCERTAIN NONLINEAR SYSTEM USING EVENT-BASED APPROXIMATION

Consider the multi-input-multi-output (MIMO) nonlinear uncertain continuous-time system represented in the affine form as

$$\dot{x} = f(x) + g(x)u, \; x(0) = x_0, \tag{4.1}$$

where $x = \begin{bmatrix} x_1 & x_2 & \cdots & x_n \end{bmatrix}^T \in \mathbb{R}^{n_x}$ and $u \in \mathbb{R}^{m_u}$ are the state and input vectors of the system (4.1), respectively. The nonlinear vector function, $f(x) \in \mathbb{R}^{n_x}$, and the matrix function, $g(x) \in \mathbb{R}^{n_x \times m_u}$, represent the internal dynamics and control coefficient function, respectively. We assume the system satisfies the properties as stated below.

Assumption 4.1. *The system* (4.1) *is controllable and input-to-state linearizable. The internal dynamics, $f(x)$ and control coefficient $g(x)$ are considered unknown with the control coefficient matrix, $g(x)$, bounded above in a compact set for all $x \in \Omega_x \subset \mathbb{R}^{n_x}$, satisfying $\|g(x)\| \leq g_{\max}$ with $g_{\max} > 0$ being a known positive constant (Lewis et al., 1998).*

The input-to-state linearizable assumption is satisfied by a wide variety of practical systems such as a robot manipulator, mass damper system, and many others. For these classes of controllable nonlinear systems in affine form (4.1) with complete knowledge of system dynamics, $f(x)$ and $g(x)$, there exists an ideal feedback linearizable controller u_d, given by

$$u_d = K(x), \tag{4.2}$$

which renders the closed-loop system asymptotically stable, where $K(x)$ is a function of the system state vector. The linear closed-loop dynamics can be represented by

$$\dot{x} = Ax, \tag{4.3}$$

where A is a Hurwitz matrix and can be designed as per the closed-loop performance requirement. By converse Lyapunov theorem (Drazin and Drazin, 1992), an asymptotically stable system admits a Lyapunov function, $V(x) : \Omega_x \to \mathbb{R}$, which satisfies the following inequalities

$$\alpha_1(\|x\|) \leq V(x) \leq \alpha_2(\|x\|), \tag{4.4}$$

$$\dot{V}(x) \leq -\alpha_3(\|x\|), \tag{4.5}$$

where α_1, α_2 and α_3 are class $\mathcal{K}$ functions.

Moreover, considering a standard quadratic Lyapunov function, $V(x) = x^T Px$, for the closed-loop system (4.3), the class $\mathcal{K}$ functions are expressed as $\alpha_1(\|x\|) = \lambda_{\min}(P)\|x\|^2$, $\alpha_2(\|x\|) = \lambda_{\max}(P)\|x\|^2$ and $\alpha_3(\|x\|) = \lambda_{\min}(Q)\|x\|^2$. The matrices $P \in \mathbb{R}^{n_x \times n_x}$ and $Q \in \mathbb{R}^{n_x \times n_x}$ are symmetric, positive definite, and satisfy the Lyapunov equation given by

$$A^T P + PA = -Q. \tag{4.6}$$

In the case of a traditional NCS, the state vector, x, and the control input, u, are transmitted with a fixed sampling interval T_s. On the other hand, in an event-triggering context, the system state vector is sampled and transmitted at the triggering instants only.

Let $\{t_k\}$, for $k = 0, 2, \cdots$ be a monotonically increasing sequence of time instants with $t_0 = 0$ such that $t_{k+1} > t_k$ and $t_k \to \infty$ as $k \to \infty$ represent the event-triggering instants. The system states, $x(t_k)$, and control inputs, $u(t_k)$, are transmitted at these time instants, rather continuously. The event-based transmitted state and the control input vectors are held, respectively, at the controller and plant by the zero-order-holds (ZOH). It is important to note that t_k is a function of current system state x and the last transmitted system state, $\breve{x} = x(t_k)$, $t_k < t \leq t_{k+1}$, and is aperiodic in nature.

Define the event-triggering error, $e_s \in \mathbb{R}^{n_x}$, as

$$e_s = x - \breve{x}, t_k < t \leq t_{k+1}. \tag{4.7}$$

The triggering instants, t_k, $k = 1, 2, 3, \cdots$, are determined by an event-triggering condition consisting of the event-triggering error (4.7) and a state-dependent threshold. Once the event-triggering error exceeds the threshold (time instant, $t = t_k$), the sensor and triggering mechanism initiates the transmission of the current state vector x. The last held event-based state vector $\breve{x}$ updated to the new value, i.e., $\breve{x}^+ = x$, for $t = t_k$ and held for $t_k < t \leq t_{k+1}$ where $\breve{x}^+ = \breve{x}\left(t_k^+\right)$ and t_k^+ is the time instant just after t_k. The event-triggering error is then reset to zero for the next event to occur, i.e.,

$$e_s^+ = 0, \quad t = t_k. \tag{4.8}$$

Since the system dynamics $f(x)$ and $g(x)$ are considered unknown, the implementation of the controller (4.2) is not possible. Further, in the event-based sampling and transmission context, the intermittent availability of the system state vector at the controller precludes the traditional neural network (NN)-based approximation with a periodic update of the NN weights. Therefore, the NN function approximation property is revisited under the event-based sampling and transmission next.

4.2.1 FUNCTION APPROXIMATION

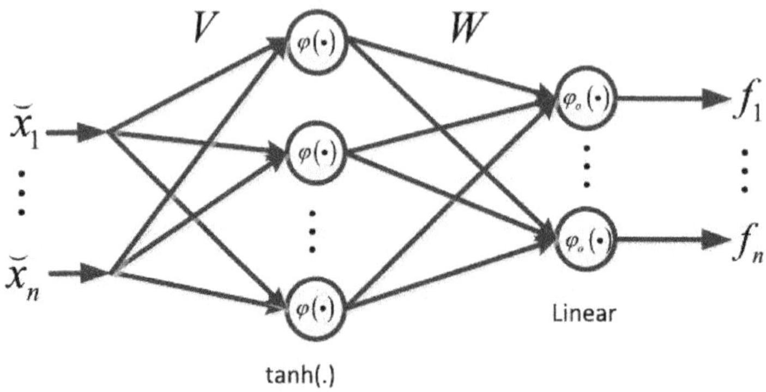

Figure 4.1 NN structure with an event-based activation function.

As discussed in Chapter 2 Section 2.1.3.1, by the universal approximation property of NN, any continuous function $f(x)$ can be approximated over a compact set for all $x \in \Omega_x \subset \mathbb{R}^{n_x}$ up to a desired level of accuracy ε_f by the selection of suitable activation functions and an adequate number of hidden layer neurons. Alternatively, there exists an unknown target weight matrix W such that $f(x)$ in a compact set can be written as

$$f(x) = W^T \varphi(V^T x) + \varepsilon_f(x), \tag{4.9}$$

where $W \in \mathbb{R}^{l \times b}$ and $V \in \mathbb{R}^{a \times l}$ represent the target NN weight matrix for the output and input layers, respectively, and defined as

$$(W, V) = \arg \min_{(W,\, V)} \left[\sup_{x \in \Omega_x} \left\| W^T \varphi(V^T x) - f(x) \right\| \right]. \tag{4.10}$$

where the activation function is denoted by $\varphi(.) : \mathbb{R}^a \to \mathbb{R}^l$ and $\varepsilon_f(x) \in \mathbb{R}^{n_x}$ denotes the traditional reconstruction error. The constants $l,\ a,$ and b are the number of neurons in the hidden layer, number of input and output of the NN, respectively.

We will consider the linearly parameterized (Lewis et al., 1998) NNs, as shown in Figure 4.1, for approximating the unknown function as in (4.9) where the output layer weights $W \in \mathbb{R}^{l\times b}$ are updated while the input layer weight matrix $V \in \mathbb{R}^{a\times l}$ is initialized at random and held. This linearly parameterized NN is also known as random vector functional link networks (RVFL) (Lewis et al., 1998). The activation function $\varphi(.) : \mathbb{R}^a \to \mathbb{R}^l$ is a hyperbolic tangent activation function and given by $\varphi(.) = e^{2\bar{x}} - 1/e^{2\bar{x}} + 1$ with $\bar{x} = V^T x$. The activation function $\varphi(V^T x)$ forms a basis for the unknown function, and the universal approximation property is retained. The output layer activation functions, $\varphi_o(.)$, are selected to be purely linear.

Recall the universal approximation property of the NN under intermittent event-based transmission of the system states, as discussed in Chapter 2 Section 2.1.3.4. The approximation error is a function of the event-triggering error. Therefore, it must be handled effectively to ensure that the NNs approximate the desired functions at the controller using aperiodic feedback data. Next, the adaptive event triggered control (ETC) scheme development is introduced.

4.2.2 ADAPTIVE EVENT-TRIGGERED STATE FEEDBACK CONTROL

This section proposes a state-feedback design of the NN-based adaptive ETC. The structure of the proposed adaptive ETC scheme with a communication network between the plant and the controller is depicted in Figure 4.2. Further, for simplicity, the following assumption regarding the network is considered.

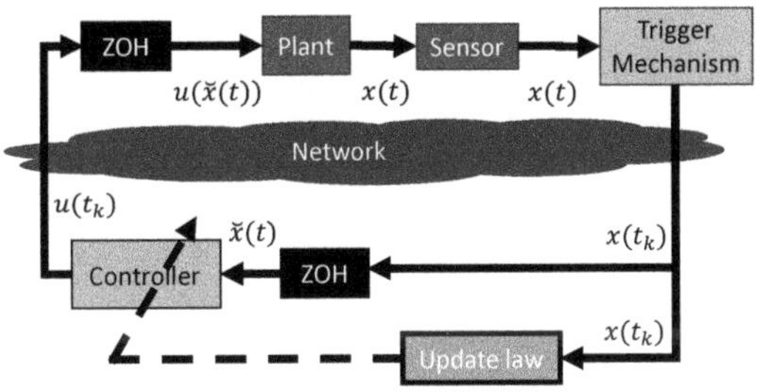

Figure 4.2 Structure of the adaptive state feedback ETC system.

Assumption 4.2. *The communication network between the plant and the controller is ideal (Donkers and Heemels, 2012), i.e., the networked induced delays, including the computational delay and the packet losses, are not present.*

In the proposed scheme, a smart sensor and triggering mechanism are included at the plant to decide the event-triggering instants by evaluating the event-triggering condition continuously. At the violation of the event-triggering condition, the state vector is transmitted first, and then the controller is updated and transmitted to the plant. The ZOHs are used to hold the last transmitted state and control input, respectively, at the controller and the plant until the next transmission is received.

Since the system dynamics are considered unknown, the control input is approximated by using a NN in an event-sampling context. Further, the NN weights are updated in an aperiodic manner at every triggering instant only and held during the inter-event durations. In order to achieve the desired approximation accuracy, an adaptive event-triggering condition is designed to generate the required number of events during the learning phase. Thus, the event-triggering condition becomes a function of the NN weight estimates and the system state vector, whereas, in the traditional ETC design, it is a function of system state only (Tabuada, 2007; Donkers and Heemels, 2012) with a constant threshold. Therefore, to evaluate the event-triggering condition locally, the NN weights are updated at both the triggering mechanism and controller in synchronism without transmitting the estimated NN weights. This increases the computation, but the overall computation reduces due to the event-based aperiodic update at both places.

By the universal approximation property of the NNs, the ideal control input (4.2) is written as

$$u_d = W_u^T \varphi_u(\bar{x}) + \varepsilon_u(x), \tag{4.11}$$

where $W_u \in \mathbb{R}^{l_u \times m_u}$ is the output layer unknown ideal NN weight matrix, and $\varphi_u(\bar{x}) \in \mathbb{R}^{l_u}$ is the tangent hyperbolic activation function with $\bar{x} = V_u^T x$. The function $\varepsilon_u(x) \in \mathbb{R}^{m_u}$ is the traditional NN reconstruction error, $V_u \in \mathbb{R}^{n_x \times l_u}$ is the input layer weight matrix and $l = l_u$, $a = n_x$, and $b = m_u$ are the number of neurons in the hidden layer, number of inputs and outputs of the NN, respectively.

Before presenting the approximation-based controller design, the following standard assumptions are introduced for the NN.

Assumption 4.3. *The target weights, W_u, the activation function, $\varphi_u(\cdot)$, and the reconstruction error $\varepsilon_u(\cdot)$ of the NN are upper bounded in compact set such that $\|W_u\| \le W_{u,\max}$, $\|\varphi_u(\cdot)\| \le \varphi_{u,\max}$ and $\|\varepsilon_u(\cdot)\| \le \varepsilon_{u,\max}$ where $W_{u,\max}$, $\varphi_{u,\max}$, and $\varepsilon_{u,\max}$ are positive constants.*

Assumption 4.4. *The NN activation function, $\varphi_u(\bar{x})$, is considered Lipschitz continuous in a compact set for all $x \in \Omega_x \subset \mathbb{R}^{n_x}$. Alternatively, for every $x \in \Omega_x \subset \mathbb{R}^{n_x}$, there exists a constant $L_{\varphi_u} > 0$ such that $\left\|\varphi_u(\bar{x}) - \varphi_u\left(\bar{\breve{x}}\right)\right\| \le L_{\varphi_u}\left\|x - \breve{x}\right\|$ is satisfied.*

In the event-triggered control context, the actual controller uses the event-based state vector $\breve{x}$ held at the ZOH. Hence, by Theorem 1, the actual event-based control input is represented as

$$u = \hat{W}_u^T \varphi_u(\bar{\breve{x}}), \; t_k < t \le t_{k+1}, \tag{4.12}$$

where $\hat{W}_u \in \mathbb{R}^{l_u \times m_u}$ is the estimated NN weight matrix, $\varphi_u\left(\bar{\breve{x}}\right) \in \mathbb{R}^{l_u}$ is the event-based NN activation function where $\bar{\breve{x}} = V_u^T \breve{x}$ is the scaled input to the NN. Since the last held state, $\breve{x}$ and the NN weights are updated at the event-triggering instants, $t = t_k$, the control input is also updated at the triggering instants, and, then, transmitted to the plant and held by the ZOH until the next update is received.

Further, as proposed, the estimated NN weights, $\hat{W}_u \in \mathbb{R}^{l_u \times m_u}$, are held during inter-event durations $t_k < t \le t_{k+1}$ and updated at the triggering instants or referred to as jumps at $t = t_k$. Therefore, the NN update law during inter-event durations is defined as

$$\dot{\hat{W}}_u = 0, \;\; t_k < t \le t_{k+1}. \tag{4.13}$$

Further, at the event-triggering instants, the update law is selected as

$$\hat{W}_u^+ = \hat{W}_u - \frac{\alpha_u}{c + \|e_s\|^2} \varphi_u(\bar{x}) e_s^T L - \kappa \hat{W}_u, t = t_k, \tag{4.14}$$

where $\hat{W}_u^+ \in \mathbb{R}^{l_u \times m_u}$ is the updated NN weight estimate just after the triggering instant with $\alpha_u > 0$ being the NN learning rate, $c > 0$ is a positive constant, $L \in \mathbb{R}^{n_x \times m_u}$ is a design matrix to match the dimension, and $\kappa > 0$ is a positive constant serving the same role as the sigma-modification (Ioannou and Fidan, 2006) in the traditional adaptive control. Note that the update law (4.14) uses traditional activation $\varphi_u(\bar{x})$ since the system state vector, x, is available for the update at the triggering instants.

Next, define the NN weight estimation error as $\tilde{W}_u = W_u - \hat{W}_u$. The weight estimation error dynamics during the flow, by using (4.13), can be written as

$$\dot{\tilde{W}}_u = \dot{W}_u - \dot{\hat{W}}_u = 0, \;\; t_k < t \leq t_{k+1}, \tag{4.15}$$

while for the jump instant, $t = t_k$, the NN weight estimation error dynamics derived from (4.14) becomes

$$\tilde{W}_u^+ = W_u - \hat{W}_u^+ = \tilde{W}_u + \alpha_u \chi_s \varphi_u(\bar{x}) e_s^T L + \kappa \hat{W}_u, \;\; t = t_k, \tag{4.16}$$

with $\chi_s = 1/\left(c + \|e_s\|^2\right)$.

As per the proposed scheme, the last transmitted state and the NN weights are updated at the triggering instants only. Hence, the closed-loop event-triggered system behaves as an impulsive dynamical system. Assuming the event instants are distinct, i.e., there exists a non-zero lower bound on the inter-event times, $\delta t_k = t_{k+1} - t_k > 0$, which is proven later in Section 4.2.3, the closed loop dynamics can be formulated in two steps.

The first step towards impulsive system modeling is to formulate the flow dynamics. The closed-loop system dynamics during the flow interval for $t \in (t_k, t_{k+1}]$ can be derived by using both (4.1) and (4.12), and represented as

$$\dot{x} = f(x) + g(x)\hat{W}_u^T \varphi_u(\bar{\breve{x}}), \;\; t \in (t_k, t_{k+1}]. \tag{4.17}$$

Adding and subtracting the ideal control input u_d yields

$$\dot{x} = f(x) + g(x)\left(\hat{W}_u^T \varphi_u(\bar{\breve{x}}) + u_d - u_d\right), \;\; t \in (t_k, t_{k+1}]. \tag{4.18}$$

Recalling the NN approximation of the ideal controller (4.12) and the ideal closed-loop dynamics (4.3), (4.18) becomes

$$\dot{x} = Ax + g(x)\left(\hat{W}_u^T \varphi_u\left(\bar{\breve{x}}\right) - W_u^T \varphi_u(\bar{x}) - \varepsilon_u(x)\right), \;\; t \in (t_k, t_{k+1}]. \tag{4.19}$$

From the definition, $W_u = \hat{W}_u + \tilde{W}_u$, the closed loop dynamics (4.19) can be written as

$$\dot{x} = Ax - g(x)\left(\tilde{W}_u^T \varphi_u(\bar{x}) + \varepsilon_u(x)\right) + g(x)\left(\hat{W}_u^T \varphi_u\left(\bar{\breve{x}}\right) - \hat{W}_u^T \varphi_u(\bar{x})\right), \; t \in (t_k, t_{k+1}]. \tag{4.20}$$

Similarly, the dynamics of the last transmitted state vector, $\breve{x}$, held by the ZOH, during the flow interval becomes

$$\dot{\breve{x}} = 0, \;\; t \in (t_k, \;\; t_{k+1}]. \tag{4.21}$$

Further, the flow dynamics of the NN weight estimation error is given by (4.15).

In the second and final step, it only remains to formulate the reset dynamics to complete the impulsive modeling of the event-triggered system. This consists of the jumps in the system state, i.e.,

$$x^+ = x, \;\; t = t_k, \tag{4.22}$$

the last transmitted state held by the ZOH,

$$\breve{x}^+ = x, \;\; t = t_k, \tag{4.23}$$

and NN weight estimation error dynamics (4.16).

From (4.22), (4.23) and (4.16), the reset dynamics for the system are given by

$$\Delta x = x^+ - x = 0, \;\; t = t_k, \tag{4.24}$$

$$\Delta\breve{x} = \breve{x}^{+} - \breve{x} = x - \breve{x} = e_s, \quad t = t_k, \tag{4.25}$$

and

$$\Delta\tilde{W}_u = \tilde{W}_u^{+} - \tilde{W}_u = \alpha_u \chi_s \varphi_u(\bar{x}) e_s^T L + \kappa \hat{W}_u, \quad t = t_k. \tag{4.26}$$

For formulating the impulsive dynamical system, we consider $\xi_s = \begin{bmatrix} x^T & \breve{x}^T & \mathbf{vec}(\tilde{W}_u)^T \end{bmatrix} \in \mathbb{R}^{n_{\xi_s}}$ as the augmented states where $\mathbf{vec}(\tilde{W}_u) \in \mathbb{R}^{l_u m_u}$ is the vector form of the NN weight estimation error matrix and $n_{\xi_s} = n_x + n_x + l_u m_u$.

Now combine (4.20), (4.21) and (4.15) to obtain the flow dynamics as

$$\dot{\xi}_s = F_c^s(\xi_s), \quad \xi_s \in C \subset D_s, \quad \xi_s \notin Z_s. \tag{4.27}$$

Next combine (4.24), (4.25) and (4.26) to get the reset dynamics as

$$\Delta\xi_s = F_d^s(\xi_s), \quad \xi_s \in D_s, \quad \xi_s \in Z_s, \tag{4.28}$$

for the impulsive dynamical nonlinear system where the nonlinear functions, $F_c^s(\xi_s)$ and $F_d^s(\xi_s)$, are defined as $F_c^s(\xi_s) = \begin{bmatrix} H(\xi_s) \\ 0 \\ 0 \end{bmatrix}$ and $F_d^s(\xi_s) = \begin{bmatrix} 0 \\ e_s \\ \mathbf{vec}\left(\alpha_u \chi_s \varphi_u(\bar{x}) e_s^T L + \kappa \hat{W}_u\right) \end{bmatrix}$ with $H(\xi_s) = Ax - g(x)\left(\tilde{W}_u^T \varphi_u(\bar{x}) + \varepsilon_u(x)\right) + g(x)\left(\hat{W}_u^T \varphi_u\left(\breve{x}\right) - \hat{W}_u^T \varphi_u(\bar{x})\right)$ and $\Delta\xi_s = \xi_s^{+} - \xi_s$. The set $D_s \subset \mathbb{R}^{n_\xi}$ is an open set with $0 \in D_s$. The flow set $C_s \subset D_s$ is defined as $C_s = \{\xi_s \in D_s : \|e_s\| \le \sigma_s \|x\|\}$, $Z_s \subset D_s$ is the jump set and defined as $Z_s = \{\xi_s \in D_s : \|e_s\| > \sigma_s \|x\|\}$ where $\sigma_s \|x\|$ is the event-triggering threshold to be designed next.

The following lemma guarantees the boundedness of the NN weight estimation error both during the flow and the jump instants.

Lemma 4.1. *(Boundedness of the NN weight estimation error): Consider the nonlinear continuous-time system* (4.1) *and the controller* (4.12) *expressed as a nonlinear impulsive dynamical system* (4.27) *and* (4.28). *Let Assumptions 4.1 through 4.4 be satisfied while the initial NN weights, $\hat{W}_u(0)$, are initialized in the compact set Ω_{W_u}. Under the assumption that a non-zero positive lower bound on the inter-event times, $\delta t_k = t_{k+1} - t_k > 0$, $k \in \mathbb{N}$ exists, there exist positive constants $\alpha_u > 0$, $0 < \kappa < 1/2$, $\bar{T}$ and T such that the weight estimation error, $\tilde{W}_u$, is bounded during the flow period and ultimately bounded for all $t_k > \bar{T}$ or, alternatively $t > T$ when the NN weights are updated by using* (4.13) *and* (4.14).

Proof: Refer to (Sahoo et al., 2016).

The event-triggering condition, given by

$$D(\|e_s\|) \le \sigma_s \|x\|, \tag{4.29}$$

where

$$\sigma_s = \frac{\Gamma_s q_{\min}}{4 g_{\max} L_{\varphi_u} \|\hat{W}_u\| \|P\|}, \tag{4.30}$$

is the threshold coefficient with $0 < \Gamma_s < 1$ and L_{φ_u} is the Lipschitz constants for the activation functions, $q_{\min}$ is the minimum eigenvalue of Q, P is a symmetric positive definite matrix with P and Q satisfying (4.6), and $\mathscr{D}(.)$ is a dead-zone operator defined as

$$\mathscr{D}(\|e_s\|) = \begin{cases} \|e_s\|, & \text{if } \|x\| > B_{s,\max}^x, \\ 0, & \text{otherwise,} \end{cases} \tag{4.31}$$

where $B^x_{s,\max}$ is the bound for the system state vector x. The system state vector is transmitted to the controller, and the updated control input is transmitted to the plant by the violation of the event-triggering condition (4.29). The adaptive event-triggering condition (4.29) guarantees the stability of the equilibrium points of the closed-loop impulsive dynamical system, as stated in the theorem below.

Theorem 4.1. *(Closed-loop stability): Consider the nonlinear system* (4.1)*, the control input* (4.12)*, NN update laws* (4.13) *and* (4.14)*, expressed as an impulsive dynamical system* (4.27) *and* (4.28)*. Let Assumptions 4.1 through 4.4 hold. Assume there exists a non-zero positive lower bound on the inter-event times given by $\delta t_k = t_{k+1} - t_k > 0$, $k \in \mathbb{N}$ and the initial NN weight, $\hat{W}_u(0)$, is initialized in the compact set Ω_{W_u}. Then, the closed-loop system state vector ξ_s for any initial condition $\xi_s(0) \in D_s \subset \mathbb{R}^{n_\xi}$ is locally ultimately bounded with a bound $\|\xi_s\| \leq \Xi$ provided the events are triggered at the violation of the condition* (4.29)*. Further, the ultimate bound is given by*

$$\Xi = \sqrt{\eta/\lambda_{\min}(\bar{P})}, \tag{4.32}$$

where $\bar{P} = diag\{P,P,I\}$ is a positive definite matrix where I is the identity matrix with appropriate dimension and $\eta = \max\{\lambda_{\max}(\bar{P})\mu_s^2, \theta\}$ with $\theta = \sup_{\xi_s \in \bar{B}_{\mu_s} \cap Z_s} V_s\left(\xi_s + F_d^s(\xi_s)\right)$, $\mu_s = \max\left\{B^x_{s,\max}, B^{\breve{x}}_{s,\max}, B^{\tilde{W}}_{s,\max}\right\}$ where $B^x_{s,\max}$, $B^{\breve{x}}_{s,\max}$, and $B^{\tilde{W}}_{s,\max}$ are the bounds for the system state, x, the last transmitted state, $\breve{x}$, and the NN weight estimation error, $\tilde{W}_u$, respectively.

Proof: For detailed proof, refer to (Sahoo et al., 2016).

Remark 4.1. *The threshold coefficient σ_s of the event-triggering condition* (4.29) *is a function of the norm of NN weight estimates $\|\hat{W}_u\|$ and, hence, adaptive in nature. Since the weights are updated only at the triggering instants, $\|\hat{W}_u\|$ is piecewise constant and jumps at the triggering instants $t = t_k$, according to the update law* (4.14)*. This implies that σ_s is also a piecewise constant function and changes at the triggering instants. This variation in σ_s, implicitly depends on the NN weight estimation error, $\tilde{W}_u$, which generates the required number of triggers for the NN approximation of the control input during the learning phase. Once the NN weight matrix, $\hat{W}_u$, converges close to the unknown constant target weight matrix, W_u, the weight estimates, $\hat{W}_u$ becomes steady; in turn, σ_s becomes a constant like the traditional event-triggered control with known knowledge of the system dynamics Tabuada (2007); Tallapragada and Chopra (2013).*

Remark 4.2. *The dead-zone operator $\mathscr{D}(.)$ is used to stop the unnecessary triggering of events due to the NN reconstruction error once the state vector reaches and stays within the ultimately bounded (UB) region. This implies that, for an event to trigger, the following two conditions need to be satisfied:*

1) The system state vector is outside the bound, i.e. $\|x\| > B^x_{s,\max}$, and

2) the event-trigger condition (4.29) *is violated, i.e., $\|e_s\| > \sigma_s \|x\|$.*

Remark 4.3. *The assumption on the non-zero positive lower bound on inter-event times in Theorem 4.1 is relaxed by guaranteeing a non-zero positive value in Theorem 4.2, which is discussed in detail in Section 4.2.3. In addition, an explicit formula for analyzing the lower bound on the inter-event times when the system state vector $\|x\| > B^x_{s,\max}$ to avoid accumulation point is also derived.*

Remark 4.4. *From the proof, the system state vector, x, and NN weight estimation error, $\tilde{W}_u$, remain locally ultimately bounded (UB) for all $t_k > \bar{T}$ or alternatively, for all $t > T$ where the time T depends on $\bar{T}$. This implies that the control input and the event-triggering error are also locally UB. Consequently, all the closed-loop system parameters remain UB for all time $t > T$.*

4.2.3 LOWER BOUND ON INTER-EVENT TIMES

In this section, the existence of non-zero positive lower bound on inter-event times is presented in the following theorem. In addition, an explicit formula for the s is derived.

Theorem 4.2. *Consider the event-triggered system* (4.1) *along with the controller* (4.12) *represented as an impulsive dynamical system* (4.27) *and* (4.28). *Let Assumptions 4.1 through 4.4 hold and NN weights,* $\hat{W}_u(0)$*is initialized in a compact set* Ω_{W_u}*and updated using* (4.13) *and* (4.14) *by the violation of event-triggering condition* (4.29). *Then, the lower bound on the inter-event times* $\delta t_k = t_{k+1} - t_k$ *for all* $k \in \mathbb{N}$ *implicitly defined by* (4.29) *is bounded away from zero and is given by*

$$\delta t_k \geq \frac{1}{\|A\|} \ln\left(1 + \frac{\|A\|}{\nu_{1,k}} \sigma_{s,\min} B^x_{s,\max}\right) > 0, \tag{4.33}$$

where $\sigma_{s,\min}$ *is the minimum value of the threshold coefficient over all inter-trigger times. Further,* $\nu_{1,k} = g_{\max}\left(\left\|\tilde{W}_{u,k}\right\| \varphi_{u,\max} + \varepsilon_{u,\max}\right) + 2g_{\max} L_{\varphi_u} \varphi_{u,\max} \left\|\hat{W}_{u,k}\right\|$ *with* $\tilde{W}_{u,k}$ *and* $\hat{W}_{u,k}$ *are the NN weight estimation error and weight estimate for* k^{th} *flow interval.*

Proof. For detailed proof, refer to (Sahoo et al., 2016). □

Furthermore, it is interesting to study the effect of NN weight estimation error $\tilde{W}_u$ on the inter-event times. The following proposition defines a relation between the lower bound on inter-event times δt_k and the NN weight estimation error, $\tilde{W}_u$.

Proposition 4.1. *Assume the hypothesis in Theorem 4.2 holds. Then, the lower bound on inter-event times also satisfies*

$$\delta t_k \geq \frac{1}{\|A\|} \ln\left(1 + \frac{\|A\|}{\nu_{M,k}} \sigma_{s,\min} B^x_{s,\max}\right), \tag{4.34}$$

where $\nu_{M,k} = g_{\max}\left(\varphi_{u,\max}(1 + 2L_{\varphi_u})\left\|\tilde{W}_{u,k}\right\| + \varepsilon_{u,\max}\right) + 2g_{\max} L_{\varphi_u} \varphi_{u,\max} W_{u,\max}$.

Proof. For detailed proof, refer to (Sahoo et al., 2016). □

Remark 4.5. *It is clear from* (4.34) *that the lower bound on inter-event times depends on* $\nu_{M,k}$ *which is a function of NN weight estimation error* $\tilde{W}_u$. *During the initial learning phase of the NN, the term* $\nu_{M,k}$ *in* (4.34) *might become larger for certain initial value* $\hat{W}_u(0)$ *and lead to smaller inter-event times closer to zero. A proper initialization of the NN weights,* $\hat{W}_u(0)$, *close to the target will reduce the weight estimation error,* $\tilde{W}_u$, *and in turn* $\nu_{M,k}$ *in* (4.34). *This will keep the inter-event times away from zero and reduce the number of transmissions in the initial phase. In addition, as per Lemma 4.1, the convergence of the NN weight estimation errors to the bound will further increase the inter-event times, leading to less resource utilization.*

We will now consider some examples to implement the control algorithms. The first example considers a second-order system and is an academic example providing an intuitive idea of the analytical design. Tthe second example emphasizes the practical application point of view by considering a practical industrial example of a two-link robot manipulator.

Example 4.1. *Consider the single-input second-order nonlinear dynamics given by*

$$\begin{aligned} \dot{x}_1 &= x_2, \\ \dot{x}_2 &= -x_1^3 - x_2 + u. \end{aligned} \tag{4.35}$$

The simulation parameters include the initial state vector as $[5 \;\; -1]^T$ *whereas the closed-loop system matrix is given by* $A = [0 \;\; 1; -3 \;\; -4]$ *and the positive definite matrix,* $Q = diag\{0.1,\, 0.1\}$.

Table 4.1
Event-triggered control of nonlinear system

System dynamics	$\dot{x} = f(x) + g(x)u,\ x(0) = x_0$
Event-triggering error	$e_s = x - \breve{x},\ t_k < t \le t_{k+1}$
Control input	$u = \hat{W}_u^T \varphi_u(\breve{\bar{x}}),\ t_k < t \le t_{k+1}$
NN weight update law	$\dot{\hat{W}}_u = 0,\ \text{for}\ t_k < t \le t_{k+1}$
	$\hat{W}_u^+ = \hat{W}_u - \frac{\alpha_u}{c + \lVert e_s \rVert^2} \varphi_u(\bar{x}) e_s^T L - \kappa \hat{W}_u, t = t_k,$
Event-triggering condition	$\mathscr{D}(\lVert e_s \rVert) \le \sigma_s \lVert x \rVert$
	$\mathscr{D}(\lVert e_s \rVert) = \begin{cases} \lVert e_s \rVert, & \text{if}\ \lVert x \rVert > B_{s,\max}^x, \\ 0, & \text{otherwise,} \end{cases}$
	$\sigma_s = \frac{\Gamma_s q_{\min}}{4 g_{\max} L_{\varphi_u} \lVert \hat{W}_u \rVert \lVert P \rVert}$

The learning gain, $\alpha_u = 0.001$, $\kappa = 0.001 \Gamma_s = 0.9$, $c = 1$ and $L \in \mathbb{R}^{2\times 1}$ with elements are all one. The ultimate bound for the system state vector was chosen as 0.001. The tangent hyperbolic activation function, $\tanh\left(V_u^T x\right)$, was used in the NN hidden layer with a randomly initialized fixed input weight, V_u, from the uniform distribution in the interval $[0,\ 1]$. The Lipschitz constant for the activation function was computed to be $L_{\varphi_u =} \lVert V_u \rVert = 4.13$. The number of neurons in the hidden layer was chosen as $l_u = 15$. The NN weight $\hat{W}_u(0)$ was initialized at random from the uniform distribution in the interval $[0,\ 0.01]$. The sampling time chosen for simulation was 0.001 s.

Figure 4.3 (a) illustrates the evolution of the state-dependent event error and threshold, and in Figure 4.3 (b), the cumulative number of events occurred. The total number of events triggered is found to be 645, and the events frequently occurred during the initial NN learning phase. This is due to a large initial NN weight estimation error, $\tilde{W}_u$ as discussed in Remark 4.5. Alternatively, the event-triggering condition generates the required number of triggers for the NN to approximate the control input. A proper selection of the initial weights, $\hat{W}_u(0)$, will further reduce the number of initial triggers.

Furthermore, the lower bound on the inter-event times is observed to be 0.002 s, as shown in Figure 4.4, implying the existence of a non-zero lower bound on the inter-event times to avoid accumulation points. It is clear from Figure 4.4 that the inter-event times are gradually increasing along with the convergence of the weight estimation error, $\tilde{W}_u$, to its ultimate bound, as presented in Proposition 4.1 and discussed in Remark 4.5. This elongated inter-event time reduces resource utilization, which is one of the primary objectives of the design.

Figures 4.5 (a) and (b) depict the convergence of the closed-loop ETC system state vector and approximated control input. This implies the event-based control input with reduced computation can regulate the system state close to zero. Figure 4.6 shows the convergence of the estimated NN weights with an aperiodic weight update.

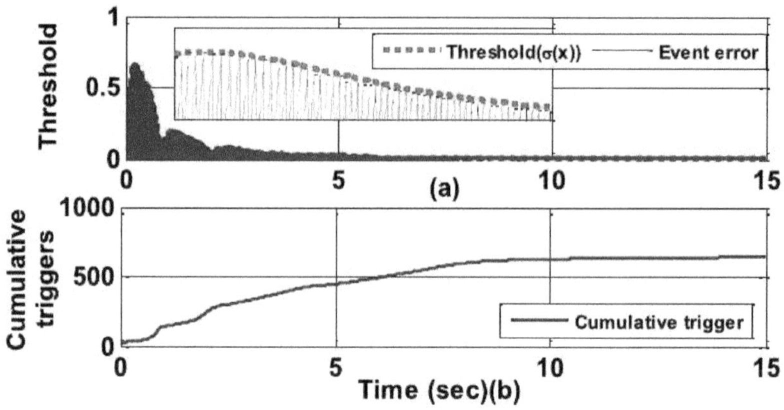

Figure 4.3 (a) Evolution of the event-trigger threshold. (b) Cumulative number of events.

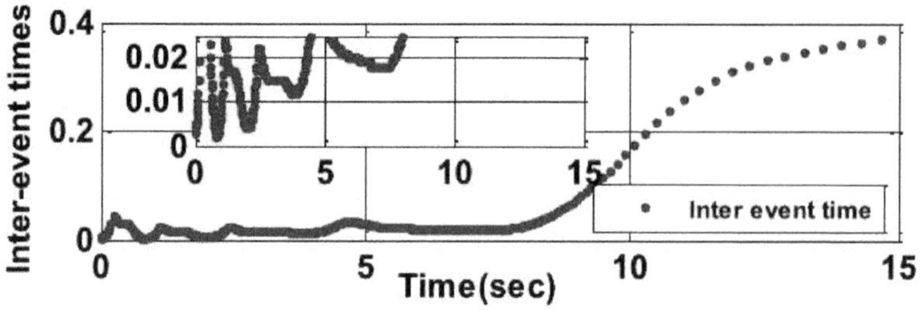

Figure 4.4 Existence of a nonzero positive lower bound on inter-event times.

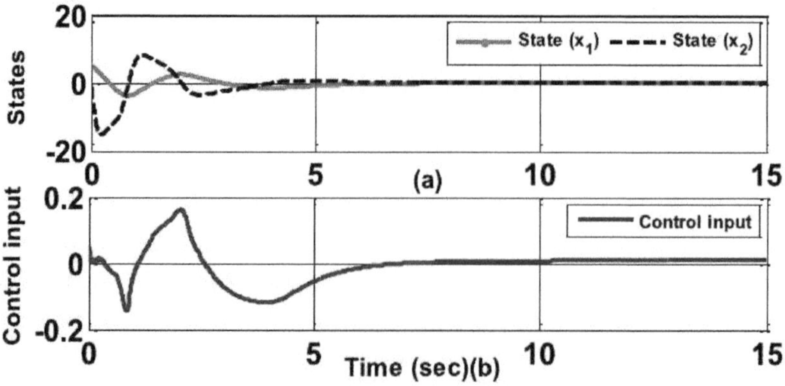

Figure 4.5 Convergence of (a) system states and (b) approximated control input.

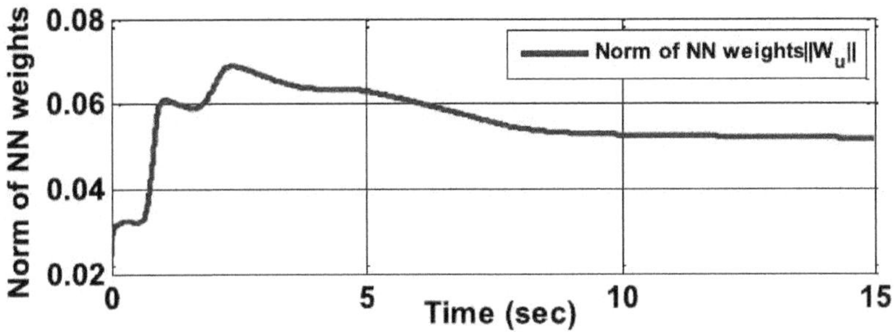

Figure 4.6 Convergence of the NN weight estimates.

Next, we consider the benchmark example of a MIMO system to evaluate the design.

Example 4.2. *A two-link robot manipulator is considered whose dynamics are given by*

$$\dot{x} = f(x) + g(x)u, \tag{4.36}$$

where $f(x) = \begin{bmatrix} x_3 \\ x_4 \\ \dfrac{\begin{pmatrix} -(2x_3x_4 + x_4^2 - x_3^2 - x_3^2\cos x_2)\sin x_2 \\ +20\cos x_1 - 10\cos(x_1+x_2)\cos x_2 \end{pmatrix}}{\cos^2 x_2 - 2} \\ \dfrac{\begin{pmatrix} (2x_3x_4 + x_4^2 + 2x_3x_4\cos x_2 + x_4^2\cos x_2 + 3x_3^2 \\ +2x_3^2\cos x_2 + 20(\cos(x_1+x_2) - \cos x_1)\times \\ (1+\cos x_2) - 10\cos x_2\cos(x_1+x_2) \end{pmatrix}}{\cos^2 x_2 - 2} \end{bmatrix}$

and $g(x) = \begin{bmatrix} 0 & 0 \\ 0 & 0 \\ \frac{1}{2-\cos^2 x_2} & \frac{-1-\cos x_2}{2-\cos^2 x_2} \\ \frac{-1-\cos x_2}{2-\cos^2 x_2} & \frac{3+2\cos x_2}{2-\cos^2 x_2} \end{bmatrix}.$

The following simulation parameters were selected for the simulation. The initial state vector is given by $x = \begin{bmatrix} \pi/3 & -\pi/10 & 0 & 0 \end{bmatrix}^T$ while the closed-loop matrix $A = \text{diag}\{-3,\ -4,\ -6,\ -8\}$ and the positive definite matrix was chosen as $Q = \text{diag}\{0.1,\ 0.1,\ 0.1,\ 0.1\}$. The learning gain was selected as $\alpha_u = 0.5$, $\Gamma_s = 0.9$, $\kappa = 0.0015$, $L \in \mathbb{R}^{4\times 2}$ with elements all one, $g_{\max} = 3$ and $c = 1$. The bound for system state vector was chosen as 0.001. The tangent hyperbolic activation function was used in the hidden layer of the NN with a randomly initialized fixed input weight V_u from the uniform distribution in the interval$[0,\ 1]$. The Lipschitz constant for the activation function was computed to be $L_{\varphi_u} = \|V_u\| = 3.42$. The number of neurons in the hidden layer was selected as $l = 15$. The NN weight $\hat{W}_u(0)$ was initialized at random from the uniform distribution in the interval $[0,\ 0.01]$. The sampling time chosen for simulation was 0.001 sec.

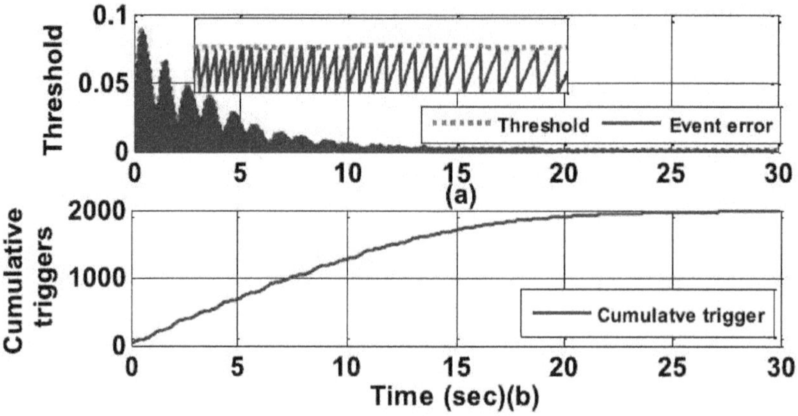

Figure 4.7 (a) Evolution of the event-trigger threshold. (b) Cumulative number of events.

The event-triggering threshold is shown in Figure 4.7 (a), along with the event-triggering error. The cumulative number of triggered events is illustrated in Figure 4.7(b), which shows the state vector is only transmitted 2000 times, indicating the reduction in communication bandwidth usage when compared to a continuous transmission. Further, the lower bound on the inter-event times is found to be 0.002 sec, proven in Theorem 4.2. In addition, as per Proposition 4.1, the inter-event times increase with the convergence of the NN weight estimates to the target, as shown in Figure 4.8.

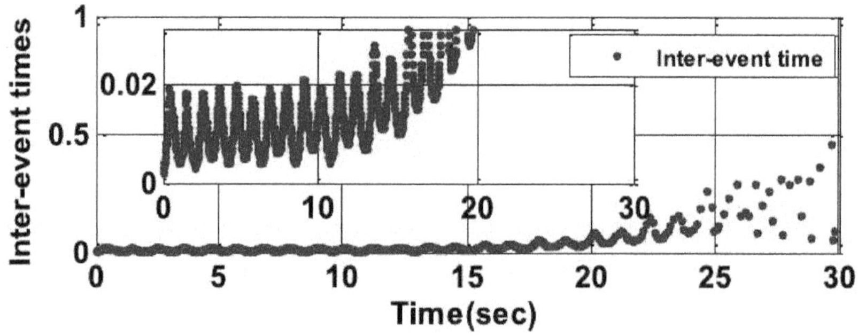

Figure 4.8 Existence of a nonzero positive lower bound on inter-event times and gradual increase with the convergence of NN weight estimates to target.

Further, from Theorem 4.1, the cumulative number of events depends upon the initial NN weights. The histogram in Figure 4.9 shows the plot between the norm of initial weights and the cumulative number of events. The cumulative number of events varies with weight initialization.

Convergence of the system state and control input is shown in Figures 4.10 (a) and (b), respectively, implying the event-based controller-regulated system states close to zero. Further, the convergence of the estimated NN weights to the target value with aperiodic event-based update law is shown in Figure 4.11.

Finally, comparison results in terms of computation and the network traffic between a sampled-data system with a fixed periodic sampling and event-based sampling are presented in Table 4.2 and Figure 4.12, respectively.

Table 4.2 gives the number of computations observed in terms of addition and multiplications that are needed for realizing both methods. It is evident that with the event-based system, a 48%

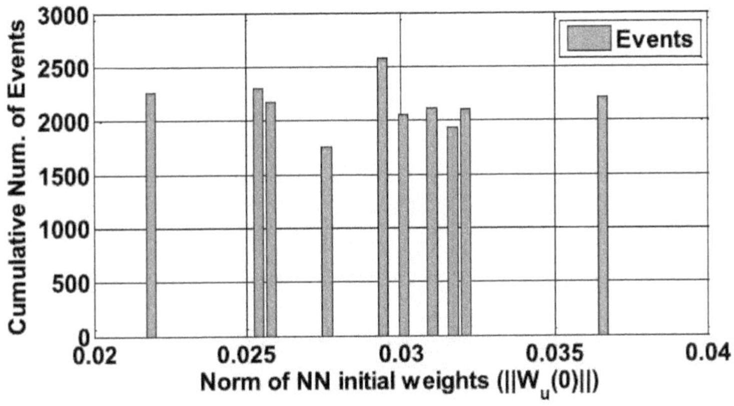

Figure 4.9 Cumulative number of events with different NN initial weights.

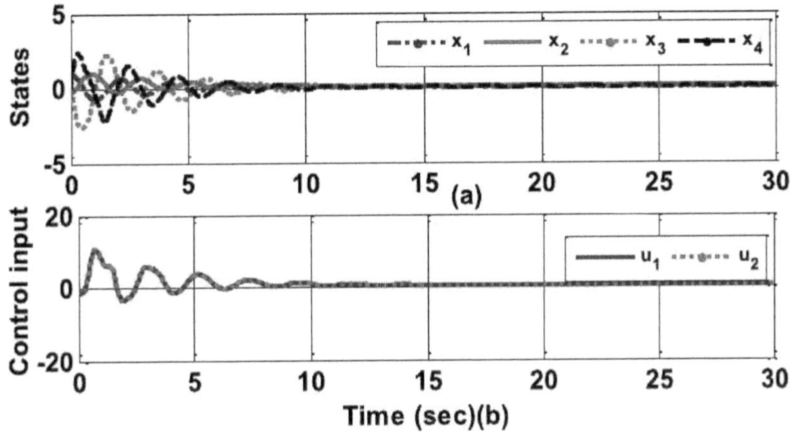

Figure 4.10 Convergence of (a) system state vectors and (b) control input.

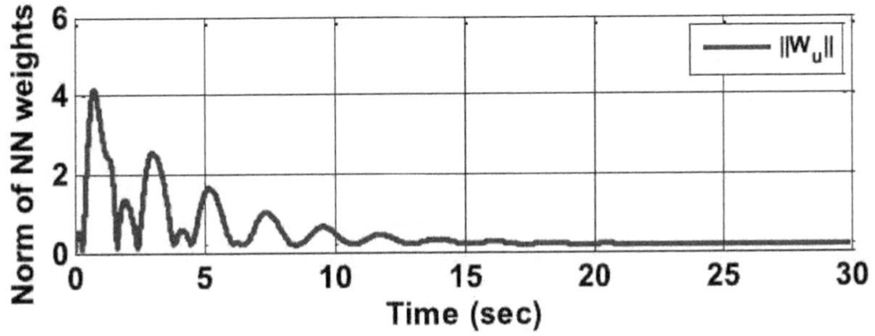

Figure 4.11 Convergence of the NN weight estimates.

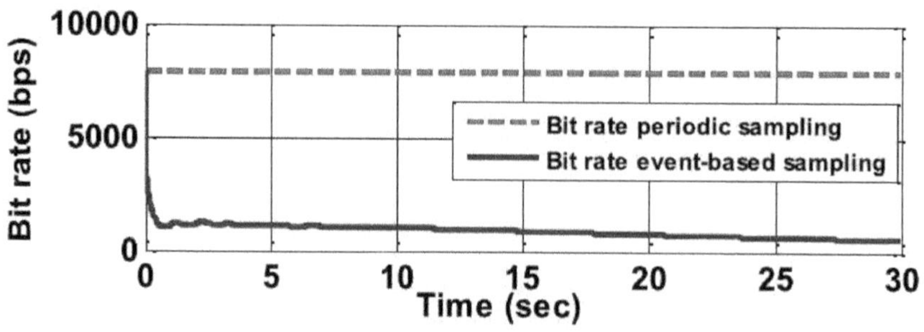

Figure 4.12 Data rates with periodic as well as event-based sampling.

Table 4.2
Comparison of computational load between periodic and event-sampled system.

System		Traditional periodic sampled data system	Event-based non-periodic sampled
Samping instants		30,000	2000
Number of additions and Multiplications at every sampling instant	NN update law at the controller	10	10
	Update law at the trigger mechanism	0	10
	Trig. Condition executed at every periodic sampled instant	0	6
Total number of Computation		226000	

reduction in computation when compared to the sample data approach is observed. Further, considering each packetized transmission is of 8-bit data through the ideal network, Figure 4.12 compares the data rates in both the cases. It is clear that the data rate in the case of event-based sampling is lower, implying that the needed network bandwidth is less. This verifies the resourcefulness of the event-triggered control design.

4.3 OPTIMAL CONTROL USING EVENT-BASED NEURO-DYNAMIC PROGRAMMING

In the previous sections, an event-based approximation of the controller using NN is presented to design a stabilizing controller with less computation and communication. In this section, we will discuss an ADP-based optimal control scheme for nonlinear continuous-time systems with completely uncertain dynamics and event-based sampling. The ADP scheme uses two NNs, one for approximating the uncertain system dynamics and the other for the value function. Similar to the stable controller design in the previous section, an adaptive sampling condition is derived via Lyapunov techniques, the NN weight estimates are tuned at the event sampled instants, and the closed-loop system is formulated as a nonlinear impulsive dynamical system (Haddad et al., 2006; Goebel et al., 2009; Hayakawa and Haddad, 2005) to leverage the extension of the Lyapunov direct method (Haddad et al., 2006) for guaranteeing the locally UB of all signals.

4.3.1 BACKGROUND AND PROBLEM STATEMENT

Consider the controllable nonlinear continuous-time systems given in (4.1) satisfying the following assumption.

Assumption 4.5. *(Dierks and Jagannathan, 2010b) The nonlinear system is controllable and observable. The nonlinear matrix function $g(x)$ for all $x \in \Omega_x$ satisfies $g_m \leq \|g(x)\| \leq g_M$, where g_M and g_m are the known positive constants, with Ω_x is a compact set.*

In an optimal control setting, the goal is to design a control input that minimizes the value function given by

$$V(t) = \int_t^{\infty} r(x(t), u(t))dt \tag{4.37}$$

where $r(x,u) = Q(x) + u^T Ru$ is the cost-to-go function, $Q(x) \in \mathbb{R}$ and $R \in \mathbb{R}^{m\times m}$ represent positive definite quadratic function and matrix, respectively, to penalize the system state vector and the control input. The initial control input u_0 must be admissible to keep the infinite horizon value function (4.37) finite.

The Hamiltonian for the cost function (4.37) can be given by

$$H(x,u) = Q(x) + u^T Ru + \nabla_x V^T [f(x) + g(x)u],$$

where $\nabla_x V = \frac{\partial V}{\partial x}$. The optimal control policy $u^*(x)$ that minimizes the value function (4.37) can be obtained using the stationarity condition as

$$u^*(x) = -\frac{1}{2} R^{-1} g^T(x) \frac{\partial V^*}{\partial x} \tag{4.38}$$

where $V^* \in \mathbb{R}$ is the optimal value function. Then, substituting the optimal control input into the Hamiltonian, the HJB equation becomes

$$H^*(x,u^*) = Q(x) + \nabla_x V^*(x) f(x) - \frac{1}{4} \nabla_x V^{*T}(x) g(x) R^{-1} g^T(x) \nabla_x V^*(x) = 0 \tag{4.39}$$

where $\nabla_x V^*(x) = \frac{\partial V^*}{\partial x}$. It is extremely difficult to obtain an analytical solution to the HJB (4.39). Therefore, the ADP techniques (Dierks and Jagannathan, 2010b) are utilized to generate an approximate solution in a forward-in-time manner by using periodically sampled state vectors with the assumption that the system state or output vectors are available continuously for measurement.

For optimal policy generation using ADP in an event-sampled framework, the value function and the system dynamics need to be approximated with intermittently available system state vector. The optimal value function using NN-based approximation with an event-sampled state vector, as discussed in the previous section, can be written as

$$V^*(x) = W_V^T \phi(\breve{x}) + \varepsilon_{e,V}(\breve{x}, e_s), \quad t_k < t \leq t_{k+1} \tag{4.40}$$

where $W_V \in \mathbb{R}^{l_V}$ is the unknown constant target NN weights, $\phi(\breve{x}) \in \mathbb{R}^{l_V}$ is the event-sampled activation function, and $\varepsilon_{e,V}(\breve{x}, e_s) = W_V^T(\phi(x) - \phi(\breve{x})) + \varepsilon_V(\breve{x} + e_s)$ is the eventbased reconstruction error, where $\varepsilon_V(\breve{x} + e_s) = \varepsilon_V(x) \in \mathbb{R}$ is the traditional reconstruction error.

The HJB equation (4.39) with event-sampled approximation of the value function (4.40) can be expressed as

$$H^*(x,u^*) = Q(x) + \left(W_V^T \nabla_x \phi(\breve{x}) + \nabla_x \varepsilon_{e,V}(\breve{x},e_s)\right) f(x) - \frac{1}{4}\left(W_V^T \nabla_x \phi(\breve{x}) + \nabla_x \varepsilon_{e,V}(\breve{x},e_s)\right) \times D(x)\left(\nabla_x \phi^T(\breve{x}) W_V + \nabla_x \varepsilon_{e,V}(\breve{x},e_s)\right) \tag{4.41}$$

where $D(x) = g(x)R^{-1}g^T(x), \nabla_x \phi(\breve{x}) = \frac{\partial \phi(\breve{x})}{\partial x}$, and $\nabla_x \varepsilon_{e,V}(\breve{x},e_s) = \frac{\partial \varepsilon_{e,V}(\breve{x},e_s)}{\partial x}$. It is clear from (4.41) that similar to the NN approximation, the HJB equation is also a function of the event sampling error e_s. In other words, the optimal controller performance is governed by the design of the event sampling condition.

Thus, the event-sampled optimal control problem in an approximate optimal control framework can be defined more precisely as follows.

1. Approximate the unknown system dynamics $f(x)$ and $g(x)$, and the value function, V, in an event-sampled context with a desired level of accuracy.
2. Design the event sampling condition not only to reduce computation but also to minimize approximation error.
3. Guarantee a positive lower bound on the inter-sample times.

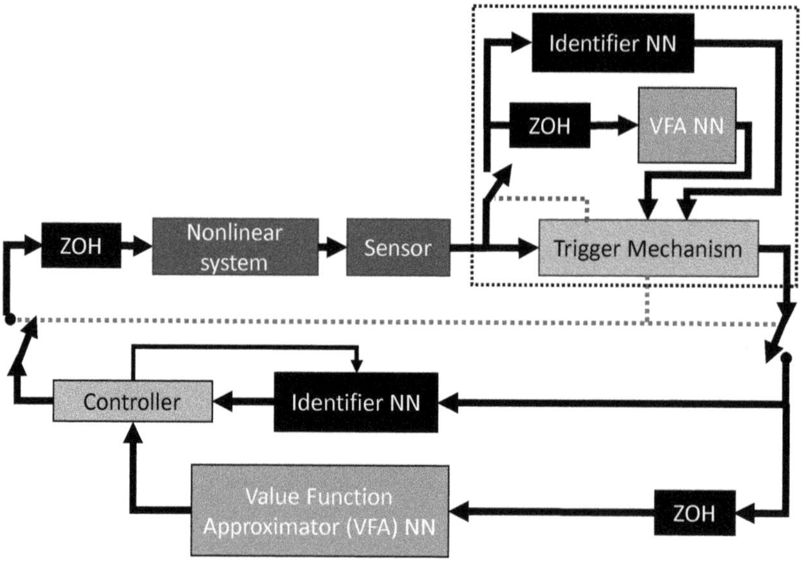

Figure 4.13 Near-optimal event-sampled control system.

4.3.2 APPROXIMATE OPTIMAL CONTROLLER DESIGN

The structure of the event-sampled approximate optimal controller is shown in Fig. 4.13, and the design will be carried out using two NNs with an event-sampled state vector. One NN is used as an identifier to approximate the unknown system dynamics, and the second one is used to approximate the solution of the HJB equation, which is the value function. Now, to reduce the computation and ensure the accuracy of the approximation, we propose an adaptive event-triggering or sampling condition as a function of event-sampling error, the estimated NN weights, and the system state vector (defined later). The system state is sent to the controller at the event-sampled instants and used to tune the NN weights. The weights are held during the inter-sample times, so the tuning scheme becomes aperiodic.

Remark 4.6. *To evaluate the proposed adaptive event sampling condition at the triggering mechanism, in the case of networked control systems (NCSs) Xu et al. (2012), it will require the transmission of the NN weight estimates from the controller. To mitigate this additional transmission cost, mirror identifier and value function approximator NNs are used at the triggering mechanism to estimate the NN weights locally. Both the actual and mirror NNs operate in synchronism. Thus, this design can be considered as an event-sampled NCS with negligible delays and packet losses.*

4.3.3 IDENTIFIER DESIGN

The knowledge of the system dynamics, $f(x)$ and $g(x)$, is needed for the computation of the optimal control policy (4.38). To relax this, an event-sampled NN-based identifier design is presented in this section. By using the event-based approximation (Sahoo et al., 2015), the nonlinear continuous-time system in (3) can be represented as

$$\dot{x} = f(x) + g(x)u = W_I^T \sigma_I(\breve{x})\bar{u} + \varepsilon_{e,I} \tag{4.42}$$

where $W_I = \begin{bmatrix} W_f^T & W_g^T \end{bmatrix}^T \in \mathbb{R}^{(l_f+ml_g)\times n}$, where $W_f \in \mathbb{R}^{l_f\times n}$ and $W_g \in \mathbb{R}^{ml_g\times n}$ are the unknown target NN weight matrices, and $\sigma_I(\breve{x}) = \begin{bmatrix} \sigma_f(\breve{x}) & 0 \\ 0 & \sigma_g(\breve{x}) \end{bmatrix}$, where $\sigma_f(\breve{x}) \in \mathbb{R}^{l_f}$ and $\sigma_g(\breve{x}) \in \mathbb{R}^{ml_g\times m}$ are the event-sampled activation functions. The error $\varepsilon_{e,I} = \left[\varepsilon_{e,f}(\breve{x},e_s)\, \varepsilon_{e,g}(\breve{x},e_s)\right]\bar{u}$ is the eventbased reconstruction error with $\varepsilon_{e,f}(\breve{x},e_s) = W_f^T(\sigma_f(x) - \sigma_f(\breve{x})) + \varepsilon_f(\breve{x}+e_s), \varepsilon_{e,g}(\breve{x},e_s) = W_g^T(\sigma_g(x) - \sigma_g(\breve{x})) + \varepsilon_g(\breve{x}+e_s)$, and $\bar{u} = \begin{bmatrix} 1 & u^T \end{bmatrix}^T$. The subscripts f and g denote the parameters corresponding to the functions $f(\cdot)$ and $g(\cdot)$, respectively. The event-sampled reconstruction error $\varepsilon_{e,I}$ can also be written as $\varepsilon_{e,I} = W_I^T\tilde{\sigma}_I(x,\breve{x})\bar{u} + \varepsilon_I$, where $\tilde{\sigma}_I(x,\breve{x}) = \sigma_I(x) - \sigma_I(\breve{x})$ is the activation function error and $\varepsilon_I = \begin{bmatrix} \varepsilon_f & \varepsilon_g u \end{bmatrix}$ is the augmented traditional reconstruction error. The constants l_f and l_g denote the number of neurons of the NNs. The following assumption holds for the NN (Jagannathan, 2006).

Assumption 4.6. *The target weight vector, W_I, the activation function, $\sigma_I(\cdot)$, and the augmented reconstruction error $\varepsilon_I(\cdot)$ are bounded above in a compact set, such that $\|W_I\| \le W_{I,M}$, $\|\sigma_I(\cdot)\| \le \sigma_{I,M}$, and $\|\varepsilon_I(\cdot)\| \le \varepsilon_{I,M}$ satisfied, where $W_{I,M}, \sigma_{I,M}, \varepsilon_{I,M}$ are positive constants. Furthermore, it is assumed that the activation function $\sigma_I(x)$ is Lipschitz continuous in the compact set for all $x \in \Omega_x$ and satisfies $\|\sigma_I(x) - \sigma_I(\breve{x})\| \le C_{\sigma_I}\|x - \breve{x}\|$, where $C_{\sigma_I} > 0$ being a constant.*

Since the system state vector is only available at event sampled instants, the identifier dynamics is defined as

$$\dot{\hat{x}} = A(\hat{x} - \breve{x}) + \hat{f}(\breve{x}) + \hat{g}(\breve{x})u, \quad t_k < t \le t_{k+1} \tag{4.43}$$

where $\hat{x} \in \mathbb{R}^n$ is the identifier estimated state vector, A is a user-defined Hurwitz matrix and satisfies the Lyapunov equation $A^TP + PA = -\Pi$, where P and Π are positive definite matrices. The matrix A ensures the stability of the identifier. The functions $\hat{f}(\breve{x}) \in \mathbb{R}^n$ and $\hat{g}(\breve{x}) \in \mathbb{R}^{n\times m}$ are the estimated system dynamics. By using the event-sampled NN approximation for the system as in (4.42), the estimated value of the identifier dynamics is represented as

$$\dot{\hat{x}} = A(\hat{x} - \breve{x}) + \hat{W}_I^T(t)\sigma_I(\breve{x})\bar{u}, \quad t_k < t \le t_{k+1} \tag{4.44}$$

where $\hat{W}_I(t)$ is the estimated NN weight matrices and $\sigma_I(\breve{x})$ being event sampled the activation function.

Defining $e_I = x - \hat{x}$ as the identification error, the identifier error dynamics, from (4.42) and (4.44) can be expressed as

$$\dot{e}_I = Ae_I - Ae_s + \tilde{W}_I^T \sigma_I(\breve{x})\bar{u} + \hat{W}_I^T \tilde{\sigma}_I(x,\breve{x})\bar{u} + \varepsilon_I \tag{4.45}$$

where $\tilde{W}_I = W_I - \hat{W}_I$ is the NN identifier weight estimation error. Since e_I can only be computed at the event-sampled instants with the current sampled state at the identifier, the NN identifier weight matrices are tuned at the event-sampled instants only. This can be considered as a jump in the identifier NN weights, which is given by

$$\hat{W}_I^+ = \hat{W}_I + \frac{\alpha_I \sigma_I(x)\bar{u}e_I^T}{\left(c + \|\bar{u}\|^2 \|e_I\|^2\right)} - \alpha_I \hat{W}_I, \quad t = t_k \tag{4.46}$$

where $\alpha_I > 0$ denotes the learning rate, and $c > 0$ is a positive constant. During the inter-sample times referred as flow duration, i.e., $t_k < t \leq t_{k+1}$, the weights are held at the previously tuned values. Therefore, the tuning law for the flow duration is given by

$$\dot{\hat{W}}_I = 0, \quad t_k < t \leq t_{k+1}. \tag{4.47}$$

From (4.46) and (4.47), it is clear that the NN weights are tuned at aperiodic instants saving computation when compared with the traditional NN [10], [19] control. The approximated control coefficient function in (4.43) is held to ensure the ultimate boundedness of the closed-loop system parameters once it becomes less than equal to the lower bound. It can be expressed as

$$\|\hat{g}(\cdot)\| = \begin{cases} g_{\min}, & \text{if } \|\hat{g}(x)\| \leq g_{\min} \\ \|\hat{g}(\cdot)\|, & \text{otherwise.} \end{cases} \tag{4.48}$$

The NN identifier weight estimation error dynamics from (4.46) and (4.47) at both jump and flow durations can be expressed as

$$\tilde{W}_I^+ = \tilde{W}_I - \frac{\alpha_I \sigma_I(x)\bar{u}e_I^T}{c + \|\bar{u}\|^2 \|e_I\|^2} + \alpha_I \hat{W}_I, \quad t = t_k \tag{4.49}$$

$$\dot{\tilde{W}}_I = \dot{W}_I - \dot{\hat{W}}_I = 0, \quad t_k < t \leq t_{k+1}. \tag{4.50}$$

We will use the identifier dynamics to design an event-sampled near-optimal controller.

4.3.4 CONTROLLER DESIGN

In this section, the solution to the HJB equation, essentially the value function, is approximated by using a second NN with an event-sampled state vector. The approximated value function is utilized to obtain the near-optimal control input. Consider the event-sampled approximation of the optimal value function in (4.40). The following assumptions hold in a compact set.

Assumption 4.7. *The target NN weights, activation functions, and the traditional reconstruction errors of the value function approximation* NN *are bounded above satisfying* $\|W_V\| \leq W_{V,M}$, $\|\phi(\cdot)\| \leq \phi_M$, *and* $|\varepsilon_V(\cdot)| \leq \varepsilon_{V,M}$, *where* $W_{V,M}, \phi_M$, *and* $\varepsilon_{V,M}$ *are the positive constants. It is further assumed that the gradient of the activation function and the reconstruction error is bounded by a positive constant, i.e.,* $\nabla_x \phi(\cdot) = \partial\phi(\cdot)/\partial x \leq \phi_M'$ *and* $\|\nabla_x \varepsilon_V(\cdot)\| = \partial\varepsilon_V(\cdot)/\partial x \leq \varepsilon_{V,M}'$.

The activation function and its gradient are Lipschitz continuous in a compact set, such that for $x \in \Omega_x$, *there exist positive constants* $C_\phi > 0$ *and* $C_{\nabla\phi} > 0$, *satisfying* $\|\phi(x) - \phi(\breve{x})\| \leq C_\phi \|x - \breve{x}\|$ *and* $\|\nabla_x \phi(x) - \nabla_x \phi(\breve{x})\| \leq C_{\nabla\phi} \|x - \breve{x}\|$.

The optimal control policy (4.38) in terms of event-sampled NN approximation of the value function becomes

$$u^* = -\frac{1}{2}R^{-1}g^T(x)\left(\nabla_x\phi^T(\breve{x})W_V + \nabla_x\varepsilon_{e,V}(\breve{x},e_s)\right). \tag{4.51}$$

The estimated value function in the context of an event-sampled state can be represented as

$$\hat{V}(\breve{x}) = \hat{W}_V^T\phi(\breve{x}), \quad t_k < t \le t_{k+1}. \tag{4.52}$$

Therefore, the actual control policy by using the estimated value function (4.52) and the identifier dynamics is given by

$$\begin{aligned} u(x) &= -\frac{1}{2}R^{-1}\hat{g}^T(\breve{x})\nabla_x\phi^T(\breve{x})\hat{W}_V \\ &= -\frac{1}{2}R^{-1}\left(\hat{W}_g^T\sigma_g(\breve{x})\right)^T\nabla_x\phi^T(\breve{x})\hat{W}_V, \quad t_k < t \le t_{k+1}. \end{aligned} \tag{4.53}$$

Now, with the estimated value function (4.52) and approximated system dynamics (4.43), the error introduced in the HJB equation (4.41), referred to as temporal difference (TD) or HJB equation error, can be expressed as

$$\hat{H}(\breve{x},u) = Q(\breve{x}) + u^TRu + \nabla_x\hat{V}^T(\breve{x})[\hat{f}(\breve{x}) + g(\breve{x})u] \tag{4.54}$$

for $t_k < t \le t_{k+1}$, where $\nabla_x\hat{V}(\breve{x}) = \partial\hat{V}(\breve{x})/\partial x$. Substituting the actual control policy (4.53) in (4.54), the TD or HJB equation error can further be expressed as

$$\hat{H}\left(\breve{x},\hat{W}_V\right) = Q(\breve{x}) + \hat{W}_V^T\nabla_x\phi(\breve{x})\hat{f}(\breve{x}) - \frac{1}{4}\hat{W}_V^T\nabla_x\phi(\breve{x})D(\breve{x})\nabla_x^T\phi(\breve{x})\hat{W}_V, \tag{4.55}$$

for $t_k < t \le t_{k+1}$, where $\hat{D}(\breve{x}) = \hat{g}(\breve{x})R^{-1}\hat{g}^T(\breve{x})$.

Similar to the NN identifier, the value function NN weight is updated at the event-sampled instants with the updated HJB error. The HJB error (4.55) with event-sampled state at the sampled instants with $\breve{x}^+ = x, t = t_k$ can be written as

$$\hat{H}^+\left(x,\hat{W}_V\right) = Q(x) + \hat{W}_V^T\nabla_x\phi(x)\hat{f}(x) - \frac{1}{4}\hat{W}_V^T\nabla_x\phi(x)D(x)\nabla_x^T\phi(x)\hat{W}_V, \quad t = t_k. \tag{4.56}$$

The NN tuning law at the event-sampled instants is selected as

$$\hat{W}_V^+ = \hat{W}_V - \alpha_V\frac{\hat{\omega}\hat{H}^{+T}\left(x,\hat{W}_V\right)}{\left(1+\hat{\omega}^T\hat{\omega}\right)^2}, \quad t = t_k \tag{4.57}$$

where $\alpha_1 > 0$ is the NN learning gain parameter and

$$\hat{\omega} = \nabla_x\phi(x)\hat{f}(x) - \frac{1}{2}\nabla_x\phi(x)\hat{D}(x)\nabla_x^T\phi(x)\hat{W}_V. \tag{4.58}$$

During the inter-sample times or flow period, the tuning law for the value function NN is given as

$$\dot{\hat{W}}_V = 0, \quad t_k < t \le t_{k+1}. \tag{4.59}$$

Define the value function NN weight estimation error as $\tilde{W}_V = W_V - \hat{W}_V$. The NN weight estimation error dynamics by using (4.57) and (4.59) can be expressed as

$$\tilde{W}_V^+ = \tilde{W}_V + \left(\alpha_V\hat{\omega}\hat{H}^{+T}\left(x,\hat{W}_V\right)\left(1+\hat{\omega}^T\hat{\omega}\right)^2\right), \quad t = t_k, \tag{4.60}$$

$$\dot{\tilde{W}}_V = 0, \quad t_k < t \le t_{k+1}. \tag{4.61}$$

The HJB or TD error in terms of the value function NN weight estimation error $\tilde{W}_V$, using (4.41) and (4.55) can be expressed as

$$\hat{H}\left(\breve{x},\hat{W}_V\right) = Q(\breve{x}) - Q(x) + \hat{W}_V^T\nabla_x\phi(\breve{x})\hat{f}(\breve{x}) - W_V^T\nabla_x\phi(x)f(x) - (1/4)\hat{W}_V^T\nabla_x\phi(\breve{x})D(\breve{x})\nabla_x^T\phi(\breve{x})\hat{W}_V \\ - (1/4)W_V^T\nabla_x\phi(x)D(x)\nabla_x\phi^T(x)W_V - \varepsilon_H, \quad t_k < t \leq t_{k+1} \tag{4.62}$$

where $\varepsilon_H = \nabla_x^T\varepsilon_V(x)\left(f(x)+g(x)u^*\right) - (1/4)\nabla_x^T\varepsilon_V(x)\ D(x)\nabla_x\varepsilon_V(x)$. It is routine to check that $\|\varepsilon_H\| \leq \varepsilon_{H,M}$, where $\varepsilon_{H,M}$ is a positive constant.

Similarly, the HJB equation error at the event-sampled instants with $\breve{x}^+ = x$ can be computed from (4.62) as

$$\hat{H}^+\left(x,\hat{W}_V\right) = -\tilde{W}_V^T\nabla_x\phi(x)\hat{f}(x) - W_V^T\nabla_x\phi(x)\tilde{f}(x) + \frac{1}{2}\tilde{W}_V^T\nabla_x\phi(x)D(x)\nabla_x^T\phi(x)\hat{W}_V \\ + \frac{1}{4}\tilde{W}_V^T\nabla_x\phi(x)D(x)\nabla_x^T\phi(x)\tilde{W}_V + (1/4)W_V^T\nabla_x\phi(x)D(x)\nabla_x\phi^T(x)W_V - \varepsilon_H \quad t = t_k. \tag{4.63}$$

4.3.5 STABILITY OF THE CLOSED-LOOP SYSTEM

Now, consider the augmented state vector $\zeta = \begin{bmatrix} x^T & e_I^T & \breve{x}^T & vec(\tilde{W}_I)^T & \tilde{W}_V^T \end{bmatrix}$.

Flow Dynamics: The closed-loop system dynamics during the flow, $t_k < t \leq t_{k+1}$, can be represented by

$$\dot{x} = f(x) + g(x)\left(-\frac{1}{2}R^{-1}\hat{g}^T(\breve{x})\nabla_x\phi^T(\breve{x})\hat{W}_V\right). \tag{4.64}$$

Adding and subtracting $g(x)u^*$ in (4.64) and with some simple mathematical operations, the closed-loop dynamics during the flow can be written as

$$\dot{x} = f(x) + g(x)u^* + (1/2)g(x)R^{-1}\tilde{g}^T(x)\nabla_x\phi^T(x)W_V + (1/2)g(x)R^{-1}\hat{g}^T(x)\nabla_x\phi^T(x)\tilde{W}_V \\ + (1/2)g(x)R^{-1}\hat{g}^T(\breve{x}) \times \left(\nabla_x\phi^T(x) - \nabla_x\phi^T(\breve{x})\right)\hat{W}_V + (1/2)g(x)R^{-1}g^T(x)\nabla_x\varepsilon_V(x) \tag{4.65}$$

for $t_k < t \leq t_{k+1}$.

The flow dynamics for the identification error e_I is the same as in (4.45). The last held state, $\breve{x}$, during the flow period remains constant. Thus, the dynamics can be represented as

$$\dot{\breve{x}} = 0, \quad t_k < t \leq t_{k+1}. \tag{4.66}$$

Finally, the dynamics of the NN weight estimation errors vec $\left(\tilde{W}_I\right)$ and $\tilde{W}_V$ during the flow are as in (4.50) and (4.61) represented in vector form. Combining (4.45), (4.50), (4.61), (4.65), and (4.66), the flow dynamics of the impulsive dynamical system as

$$\dot{\zeta} = F_c(\zeta), \quad \zeta \in \Omega_\zeta, \quad \zeta \in \mathscr{C}, \quad \zeta \notin \mathbb{Z} \tag{4.67}$$

where $F_c(\zeta) = \begin{bmatrix} F_c^{sT} & F_c^{e_I^T} & 0^T & 0^T & 0^T \end{bmatrix}^T$ with

$$F_c^s = f(x) + g(x)u^* + \frac{1}{2}g(x)R^{-1}\tilde{g}^T(x)\nabla_x\phi^T(x)W_V + \frac{1}{2}g(x)R^{-1}\hat{g}^T(x)\nabla_x\phi^T(x)\left(W_V - \tilde{W}_V\right) \\ + \frac{1}{2}g(x)R^{-1}\hat{g}^T(\breve{x})\left(\nabla_x\phi^T(x) - \nabla_x\phi^T(\breve{x})\right)\left(W_V - \tilde{W}_V\right) + \frac{1}{2}g(x)R^{-1}g^T(x)\nabla_x\varepsilon_V(x), F_c^{e_I} \\ = Ae_I - Ae_s + \tilde{W}_I^T\sigma_I(\breve{x})\bar{u} + \hat{W}_I^T\tilde{\sigma}_I(x,\breve{x})\bar{u} + \varepsilon_I$$

and 0^T s are the null vectors of appropriate dimensions.

Jump Dynamics: The jump dynamics of the system state vector and the identification error are given by

$$x^+ = x, \quad t = t_k \tag{4.68}$$

$$e_I^+ = x^+ - \hat{x}^+ = x - \hat{x} = e_I, \quad t = t_k. \tag{4.69}$$

The jump dynamics of the last held state, $\breve{x}$, is given by

$$\breve{x}^+ = x, \quad t = t_k. \tag{4.70}$$

Furthermore, the jumps in the NN weight estimation errors are given by (4.49) and (4.60).

Defining the first difference $\Delta\zeta = \zeta^+ - \zeta$ and using (4.49), (4.60), and (4.68)-(4.70), the difference equation for the reset/jump dynamics can be written as

$$\Delta\zeta = F_d(\zeta), \quad \zeta \in \Omega_\zeta, \quad \zeta \in Z \tag{4.71}$$

where $F_d(\zeta) = \begin{bmatrix} 0^T & 0^T & e_s^T & \text{vec}\left(\Delta\tilde{W}_I\right)^T \left(\Delta\tilde{W}_V\right)^T \end{bmatrix}^T$ with

$$\Delta\tilde{W}_I = -\frac{\alpha_I}{c + \|\bar{u}\|^2 \|e_I\|^2}\sigma_I(x)\bar{u}e_I^T + \alpha_I\left(W_I - \tilde{W}_I\right)$$

and

$$\Delta\tilde{W}_V = \alpha_V \frac{\hat{\omega}\hat{H}^+\left(x, \hat{W}_V\right)}{\left(1 + \hat{\omega}^T\hat{\omega}\right)^2}.$$

The set $\mathscr{C} \subset \Omega_\zeta$ is the flow set, $Z \subset \Omega_\zeta$ is the jump set, and $\Omega_\zeta \subset \mathbb{R}^{n_\zeta}$ is an open set with $0 \in \Omega_\zeta, n_\zeta = n + n + n + l_I + l_V$ and $l_I = \left(l_f + ml_g\right)n$. The event sampling condition decides the flow and jump sets introduced next.

Consider the event sampling error in (4.7). Define a condition given by

$$\mathscr{D}\left(\|e_s\|\right) > \sigma_{\text{ETC}}\left(x, \left\|\hat{W}_V\right\|, \left\|\hat{W}_I\right\|\right) \tag{4.72}$$

where $\sigma_{\text{ETC}}\left(x, \left\|\hat{W}_V\right\|, \left\|\hat{W}_I\right\|\right) = \min\left\{\frac{\Gamma Q(x)}{\eta_1}, \sqrt{\frac{2\Gamma Q(x)}{\eta_2}}\right\}$ is the threshold with $\left\|\hat{W}_V\right\| \geq \kappa$, $\left\|\hat{W}_I\right\| \geq \kappa, \eta_1 = g_M\lambda_{\max}\left(R^{-1}\right)\sigma_{I,M}\phi_M'\left\|\hat{W}_V\right\|\left\|\hat{W}_I\right\|C_{\nabla\phi}$ and $\eta_2 = C_{\nabla\phi}g_M\lambda_{\max}\left(R^{-1}\right)\sigma_{I,M}\phi_M'\left\|\hat{W}_I\right\| + \frac{32}{\Pi_{\min}}\left(C_{\sigma_I}\left\|\hat{W}_I\right\|^2\|\bar{u}\|^2\|P\|^2 + \|AP\|^2\right)$. The constant κ is a small positive constant to ensure that the threshold is well-defined. The previous value of the NN weight estimates is used to compute (4.72) of the estimated values $\left\|\hat{W}_V\right\| < \kappa$ or $\left\|\hat{W}_I\right\| < \kappa$. The design parameter Γ satisfies $0 < \Gamma < 1$, the constants $C_{\nabla\phi}$ and C_{σ_I} are the Lipschitz constants, and $\Pi_{\min} = \lambda_{\min}(\Pi)$. The dead-zone operator $\mathscr{D}(\cdot)$ is defined as

$$\mathscr{D}(\cdot) = \begin{cases} \cdot, & \|x\| > B_{\text{ub}}^x \\ 0 \end{cases} \tag{4.73}$$

where B_{ub}^x is the desired ultimate bound for the closed-loop system and can be selected arbitrarily close to zero. The event-sampled instants are decided when the condition (4.72) is satisfied.

Remark 4.7. *The main advantage of the adaptive event sampling condition* (4.72) *is that the threshold* $\sigma_{\text{ETC}}(\cdot)$ *gets tuned with* NN *weight estimates in addition to the system state. Therefore, the system states will be sampled based on the NN weight estimation errors and the system performance, ensuring the accuracy of approximation and stability. Once the NN weights converged close to their target values and became constant, the threshold became similar to those used in the traditional event sampling conditions (Tabuada, 2007; Postoyan et al., 2011).*

Remark 4.8. *The dead-zone operator $\mathscr{D}(\cdot)$ prevents unnecessary triggering of events due to the NN reconstruction error once the system state is inside the ultimate bound.*

To show the locally ultimately boundedness of the closed-loop event-sampled system, we will use the extension of the Lyapunov direct method of stability from (Haddad et al., 2006) for the nonlinear impulsive dynamical systems. Before claiming the main results, the following technical results are necessary.

Lemma 4.2. *Consider the definition of $\hat{\omega}$ given in* (4.58). *For any positive number $N > 0$, the following inequality holds:*

$$
\begin{aligned}
-\frac{\tilde{W}_V^T \hat{\omega}\hat{\omega}^T \tilde{W}_V}{(1+\hat{\omega}^T\hat{\omega})^2} \leq & \left(\frac{1}{N(1+\hat{\omega}^T\hat{\omega})^2}\right) \tilde{W}_V^T \left(\frac{1}{2}\nabla_x\phi(x)\hat{D}(x)\nabla_x^T\phi(x)W_V - \nabla_x\phi(x)\hat{f}(x)\right) \\
& \times \left(\frac{1}{2}\nabla_x\phi(x)\hat{D}(x)\nabla_x^T\phi(x)W_V - \nabla_x\phi(x)\hat{f}(x)\right)^T \tilde{W}_V - \frac{1}{\left(4(N+1)(1+\hat{\omega}^T\hat{\omega})^2\right)} \\
& \times \left(\tilde{W}_V^T\nabla_x\phi(x)\hat{D}(x)\nabla_x^T\phi(x)\tilde{W}_V\right)\left(\tilde{W}_V^T\nabla_x\phi(x)\hat{D}(x)\nabla_x^T\phi(x)\tilde{W}_V\right)^T.
\end{aligned}
\tag{4.74}
$$

Proof. Refer to (Sahoo et al., 2017b). □

We will use the above results to show the local UB of the NN weight estimation errors in Lemma 4.3, using which the closed-loop system is shown to be bounded.

Lemma 4.3. *Consider the nonlinear continuous-time system* (4.1) *along with the NN-based identifier* (4.44) *and the value function approximator* (4.52) *with an event-sampled state vector. Let Assumptions 4.5 to 4.7 hold and the initial identifier and value function* NN *weights, $\hat{W}_I(0)$ and $\hat{W}_V(0)$, respectively, be initialized with nonzero finite values. Suppose there exists a nonzero positive inter-sample time between two consecutive event sampling instants, $\delta t_k = t_{k+1} - t_k > 0$, and the value function activation function $\phi(x)$ and its gradient $\nabla_x\phi(x)$ satisfy the persistency of excitation (PE) condition. Then, the weight estimation errors $\tilde{W}_I$ and $\tilde{W}_V$ are locally UB for all event sampling instant $t_k > \bar{T}$ or $t > T$ for $T > \bar{T}$ provided that the NN weights are tuned by using* (4.46) *and* (4.47), *and the learning gains satisfy* $0 < \alpha_I < \frac{1}{3}$, $0 < \alpha_V < \min\{\frac{1}{40}, \frac{2N(1-N)}{2(N+1)(16+N)}\}$ *with* $0 < N < 1$.

Proof. Refer to (Sahoo et al., 2017b). □

Theorem 4.3. *Consider the nonlinear continuous-time system* (4.1), *identifier* (4.44), *and the value function approximator* (4.52) *represented as an impulsive dynamical system* (4.67) *and* (4.71). *Let u_0 be an initial stabilizing control policy for* (4.1). *Let Assumptions 4.5 to 4.7 hold, and assume there exists a minimum inter-sample time* $\min_k\{\delta t_k\} > 0$. *Suppose the value function activation function $\phi(x)$ and its gradient $\nabla_x\phi(x)$ satisfy the PE condition, and the system states are transmitted at the violation of the event sampling condition* (4.72). *Let the initial identifier and value function NN initial weights, $\hat{W}_I(0)$ and $\hat{W}_V(0)$, are nonzero and finite and updated according to* (4.57) *and* (4.59). *Then, the closed-loop impulsive dynamical system is locally* UB *for all event sampling instant $t_k > \bar{T}$ or $t > T$ for $T > \bar{T}$. Furthermore, the estimated value function satisfies $\|V^* - \hat{V}\| \leq B_V$, where B_V is a small positive constant provided that the design parameters are selected as in Lemma 4.3.*

Proof. Refer to (Sahoo et al., 2017b). □

The assumption on the inter-sample time in Theorem 4.3 is relaxed by guaranteeing the existence of a positive minimum inter-sample time in the next section.

4.3.6 MINIMUM INTERSAMPLE TIME

The following theorem guarantees the existence of the nonzero positive minimum inter-sample time $\min_{k\in\mathbb{N}}\{\delta t_k\} = \min_{k\in\mathbb{N}}\{t_{k+1}-t_k\}$.

Theorem 4.4. *Consider the continuous-time system* (4.1) *represented as impulsive dynamical systems* (4.67) *and* (4.71) *along with the event sampling condition* (4.72)*. Then, the minimum inter-sample time* $\min_{k\in\mathbb{N}}\{\delta t_k\}$ *implicitly defined by* (4.72) *is lower bounded by a nonzero positive constant and given by*

$$\delta t_{\min} = \min_{k\in\mathbb{N}}\{\delta t_k\} \geq \min_{k\in\mathbb{N}}\left\{\frac{1}{K}\ln\left(1+\frac{K}{M_k}\sigma_{\mathrm{ETC,min}}\right)\right\} > 0 \tag{4.75}$$

where $\sigma_{\mathrm{ETC,min}}$ *is the minimum threshold coefficient value,* $K > 0$ *is a constant, and*

$$M_k = g_M\lambda_{\max}\left(R^{-1}\right)\sigma_{I,M}\phi_M'\left\|\hat{W}_{I,k}\right\|\left\|\hat{W}_{V,k}\right\| + \frac{1}{2}g_M\lambda_{\max}\left(R^{-1}\right)\phi_M' W_{V,M}\left(\sigma_{I,M}\left\|\tilde{W}_{I,k}\right\| + \bar{\varepsilon}_I\right) + \frac{1}{2}g_M\lambda_{\max}\left(R^{-1}\right)\sigma_{I,M}\phi_M'\left\|\hat{W}_{I,k}\right\|\left\|\tilde{W}_{V,k}\right\| + \frac{1}{2}g_M^2\lambda_{\max}\left(R^{-1}\right)\varepsilon_{V,M}',$$

where the subscript k represents the kth inter-sample time.

Proof. For the proof, refer to (Sahoo et al., 2017b). □

Remark 4.9. *The constant K satisfies the inequality* $\|f(x)+g(x)u^*\| \leq K\|x\|$*. This inequality holds since the ideal optimal control input is stabilizing.*

Remark 4.10. *It is clear from* (4.75) *that the lower bound on inter-sample times depends on* M_k *or, alternatively, on the NN weight estimation errors* $\tilde{W}_V$*, and* $\tilde{W}_I$ *by the definitions* $\hat{W}_I = W - \tilde{W}_I$ *and* $\hat{W}_V = W - \tilde{W}_V$*. During the initial learning phase of the NN, the term* M_k *in* (4.75) *may become large for certain initial values* $\hat{W}_V(0)$ *and* $\hat{W}_I(0)$*, which may lead to shorter nonzero inter-sample times. Hence, proper initialization of the NN weights is necessary to keep the inter-sample time away from zero during the learning phase. In addition, with an update in NN weights, the convergence of the NN weight estimation errors will elongate the inter-sample times, leading to fewer sampled events and less resource utilization.*

We will use the example of a two-link robot manipulator for implementing the optimal control design to investigate its effectiveness via simulation.

Example 4.3. *Consider the two-link robot dynamics given in Example 4.2 and implement the event-based optimal control design presented in the previous sections.*

The following simulation parameters were chosen for simulation. The initial system state vector was chosen as $\begin{bmatrix}\pi/6 & -\pi/6 & 0 & 0\end{bmatrix}^T$. The cost function was selected as in (4.37) with $Q = I_{4\times 4}$ and $R = I_{2\times 2}$. The learning parameters are chosen as $\alpha_V = 0.005$ and $\alpha_I = 0.055$, and other design parameters were $g_M = 3, g_m = 1$, $\Gamma = 0.99, A = -10I$, and $P = I$, where I is the identify matrix satisfying the intervals as in Lemma 1. The basis function for approximating the value function is given by the expansion of $\phi(x) = \left[x_1^2,x_2^2,x_3^2,x_4^2,x_1x_2,\ldots,x_1^4,x_2^4,\ldots,x_1^3x_2,\ldots,x_1^2x_2x_3,\ldots,x_1x_2x_3x_4\right]$. The activation functions for the identifier $\sigma_I(\cdot) = \mathrm{diag}\{\tanh(\cdot),\tanh(\cdot)\}$. A number of hidden layer neurons for identifier and value function NN are selected as 25 and 39, respectively. All the NN weight estimates are initialized at random from a uniform distribution in the interval $(0,1)$. The ultimate bound for the system state is chosen as 0.001.

The performance of the event-sampled control system is shown in Fig. 4.14. The system state is regulated close to zero, as shown in Fig. 4.14(a), along with the control input in Fig. 4.14(b). The

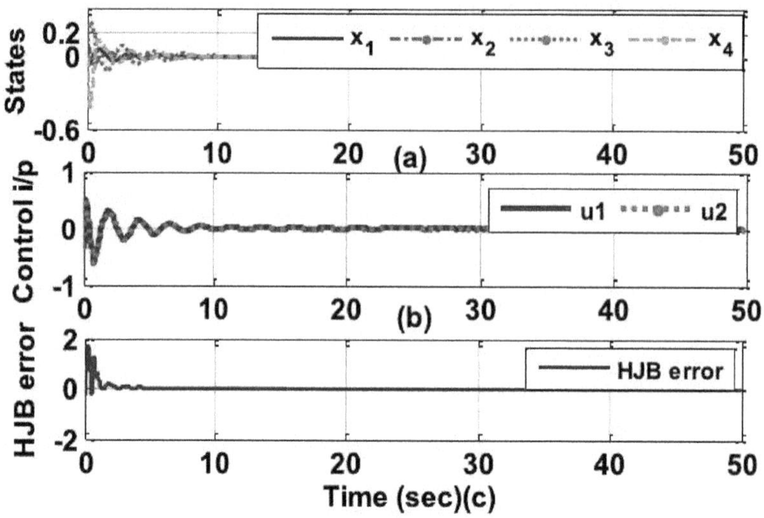

Figure 4.14 Convergence of (a) system state, (b) control input, and (c) HJB error.

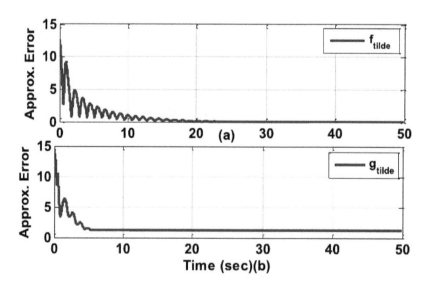

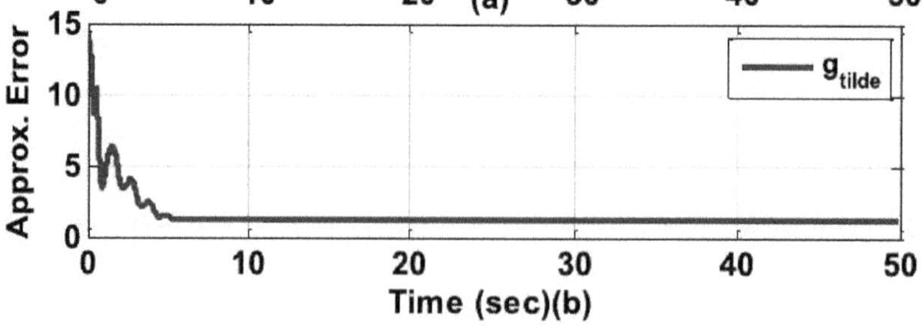

Figure 4.15 NN performance. (a) Approximation error $\tilde{f}$. (b) Approximation error $(\tilde{g})$.

Table 4.3
Event-triggered optimal control of nonlinear system

System dynamics	$\dot{x} = f(x) + g(x)u, \; x(0) = x_0$
Identifier dynamics	$\dot{\hat{x}} = A(\hat{x} - \breve{x}) + \hat{W}_I^T(t)\sigma_I(\breve{x})\bar{u}, \quad t_k < t \leq t_{k+1}$
Value function	$V(t) = \int_t^\infty r(x(\tau), u(\tau))d\tau$
Identifier NN weight update	$\dot{\hat{W}}_I = 0, \quad t_k < t \leq t_{k+1}$ $\hat{W}_I^+ = \hat{W}_I + \frac{\alpha_I \sigma_I(x)\bar{u}e_I^T}{(c+\lVert\bar{u}\rVert^2\lVert e_I\rVert^2)} - \alpha_I \hat{W}_I, \quad t = t_k$
Event-triggering error	$e_s(t) = x(t) - \breve{x}(t), t_k < t \leq t_{k+1} \quad \forall k = 1, 2, \ldots$
Value function approximation	$\hat{V}(\breve{x}) = \hat{W}_V^T \phi(\breve{x}), \quad t_k < t \leq t_{k+1}$
Optimal Control input	$u = -\frac{1}{2}R^{-1}\left(\hat{W}_g^T \sigma_g(\breve{x})\right)^T \nabla_x \phi^T(\breve{x})\hat{W}_V, \quad t_k < t \leq t_{k+1}$
Critic NN weight update law	$\dot{\hat{W}}_V = 0, \quad t_k < t \leq t_{k+1}$ $\hat{W}_V^+ = \hat{W}_V - \left(\alpha_V \hat{\omega} \hat{H}^{+T}(x, \hat{W}_V) / \left(1 + \hat{\omega}^T\hat{\omega}\right)^2\right), \quad t = t_k$
Event-triggering condition	$\mathscr{D}(\lVert e_s \rVert) > \sigma_{\text{ETC}}\left(x, \lVert\hat{W}_V\rVert, \lVert\hat{W}_I\rVert\right)$ $\sigma_{\text{ETC}}\left(x, \lVert\hat{W}_V\rVert, \lVert\hat{W}_I\rVert\right) = \min\left\{\frac{\Gamma Q(x)}{\eta_1}, \sqrt{\frac{2\Gamma Q(x)}{\eta_2}}\right\}$

HJB equation error converges close to zero [shown in Fig. 4.14(c)], confirming that a near-optimal control policy is achieved with an event-sampled implementation. This further implies that the value function is approximated satisfactorily with the event-sampled NN. The approximation error for the system dynamics is shown in Fig. 4.15, which appears to be bounded.

The event sampling threshold's evolution and the event sampling error are shown in Fig. 4.16(a). Cumulative number of event-sampled instants is shown in Fig. 4.16(b), and the inter-sample times are shown in Fig. 4.16(c). From the cumulative number of event-sampled instances, it is evident that fewer sampled instances occurred when compared with the traditional periodic sampled data system. The number of event-sampled instants is found to be 15783 for a simulation duration of 50 s with a sampling interval of 0.001 s or 50000 sampling instants for the traditional sampled data system.

Furthermore, it is clear from Fig. 4.16(b) that the event sampling condition generated a large number of sampled instants at the initial NN online learning phase. This is due to the large weight estimation error and makes the NN learn the unknown system dynamics and the value function to achieve near optimality. Over time, as the NN approximates the system dynamics and value function, the inter-sample times increase, thereby reducing the number of sampled events. The convergence of all the NN weight estimates is shown in Fig. 4.17 (a)-(c).

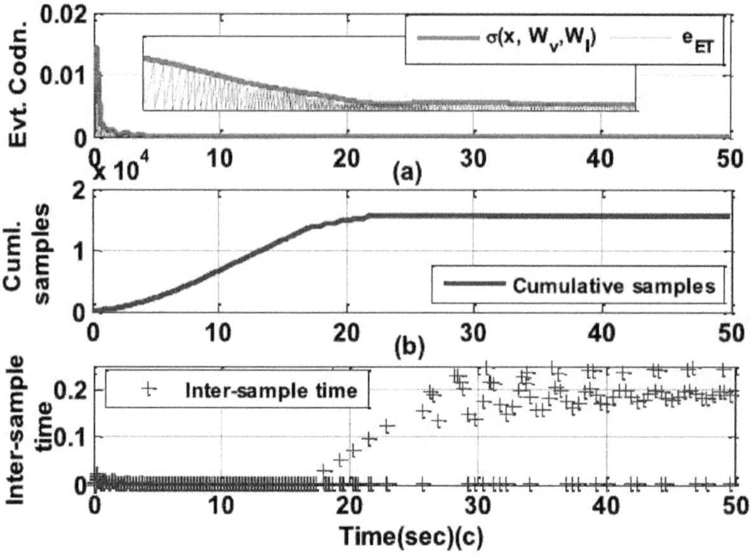

Figure 4.16 Evolution of (a) event sampling condition, (b) cumulative number of event-sampled instants, and (c) inter-sample times.

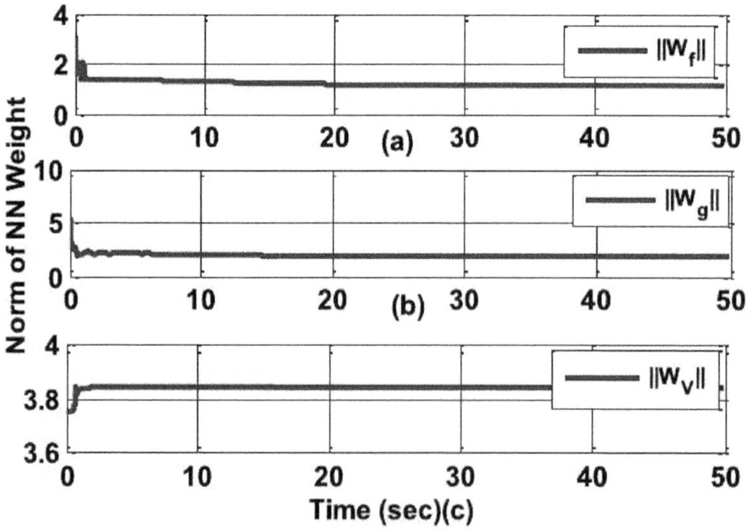

Figure 4.17 Convergence of the norm of the NN weight estimates. (a) $\|\hat{W}_f\|$; (b) $\hat{W}_g\|$ and (c) $\hat{W}_v\|$

4.4 OPTIMAL EVENT-BASED TRACKING CONTROL

Consider an affine nonlinear continuous-time system given in (4.1) The control objective is to track a feasible reference trajectory $x_d(t) \in \mathbb{R}^n$ generated by a reference system represented by

$$\dot{x}_d(t) = \zeta(x_d(t)), \;\; x_d(0) = x_{d0} \tag{4.76}$$

where $x_d(t) \in \mathbb{R}^n$ is the reference state, and $\zeta : \mathbb{R}^n \to \mathbb{R}^n$ is the internal dynamics with $\zeta(\mathbf{0}) = \mathbf{0}$.

Assumption 4.8. *The functions $f(x)$ and $g(x)$ are Lipschitz continuous for all $x \in \Omega_x$ where Ω_x is a compact set containing the origin. Further, the function $g(x)$ has a full column rank for all $x \in \Omega_x$ and satisfies $\|g(x)\| \le g_M$ for some constant $g_M > 0$. In addition, $g(x_d)g^+(x_d) = I$ where $g^+ = (g^T g)^{-1} g^T$.*

Assumption 4.9. *The feasible reference trajectory $x_d(t) \in \Omega_{x_d}$, where Ω_{x_d} is a compact set, is bounded such that $\|x_d(t)\| \le b_{x_d}$ where $b_{x_d} > 0$ is a constant.*

Define the error between the system state and the reference state as tracking error, given by $e_r(t) \triangleq x(t) - x_d(t)$. Then, the tracking error system, utilizing (4.1) and (4.76), can be defined by

$$\dot{e}_r = \dot{x} - \dot{x}_d = f(e_r + x_d) + g(e_r + x_d)u - \zeta(x_d). \tag{4.77}$$

The steady-state feed-forward control policy for the reference trajectory (Kamalapurkar et al., 2015) can be expressed as

$$u_d = g^+(x_d)(\zeta(x_d) - f(x_d)) \tag{4.78}$$

where $u_d : \mathbb{R}^n \to \mathbb{R}^m$ is the steady state control policy corresponding to the reference trajectory. By augmenting the tracking error e_r and desired trajectory x_d, the dynamics of the augmented tracking error system can be represented as

$$\dot{\chi} = F(\chi) + G(\chi)w \tag{4.79}$$

where $\chi \triangleq [e_r^T \;\; x_d^T]^T \in \mathbb{R}^{2n}$ is the augmented state with $\chi(0) = [e_r^T(0) \;\; x_d^T(0)]^T = \chi_0$, $F : \mathbb{R}^{2n} \to \mathbb{R}^{2n}$ is given by $F(\chi) \triangleq \begin{bmatrix} f(e_r + x_d) + g(e_r + x_d)u_d - \zeta(x_d) \\ \zeta(x_d) \end{bmatrix}$, $G : \mathbb{R}^{2n} \to \mathbb{R}^{2n \times m}$ given by $G(\chi) \triangleq \begin{bmatrix} g(e_r + x_d) \\ \mathbf{0} \end{bmatrix}$, and the mismatched control policy $w \triangleq u - u_d \in \mathbb{R}^m$. It is routine to check that $F(\mathbf{0}) = \mathbf{0}$.

The infinite horizon performance index with state constraint enforced by the dynamical system in (4.79) can be defined as

$$J(\chi, w) = \int_0^\infty [\chi^T(\tau)\bar{Q}\chi(\tau) + w(\tau)^T R w(\tau)] d\tau \tag{4.80}$$

where $\bar{Q} \triangleq \begin{bmatrix} Q & \mathbf{0}_{n\times n} \\ \mathbf{0}_{n\times n} & \mathbf{0}_{n\times n} \end{bmatrix} \in \mathbb{R}^{2n\times 2n}$ with $Q \in \mathbb{R}^{n\times n}$ and $R \in \mathbb{R}^{m\times m}$ are symmetric positive definite matrices. The matrix $\mathbf{0}_{n\times n}$ is a matrix with all elements zero. Note that the performance index is defined using the mismatched policy w in Kamalapurkar et al. (2015) and, therefore, the cost functional is finite for any admissible control policy $w \in \Omega_w$ where Ω_w is the set of all admissible policies Lewis et al. (2012b).

Observe that the augmented system dynamics in (4.79) and the performance index (4.80) are in a similar form as in (4.1) and (4.37). Therefore, we can use Table 4.3, *mutatis mutandis*, for designing the optimal event-based tracking controller for the nonlinear system (4.79).

4.5 CONCLUDING REMARKS

This chapter presented an event-triggered stabilization of MIMO uncertain nonlinear continuous-time systems. The control input was directly approximated by using an NN in the context of event-based transmission. A novel event-triggering condition was developed based on the system state vector and NN weight estimate to ensure the reduction in transmission of the feedback control signal. The weights were updated in a non-periodic manner at the triggering instants. The controller design guaranteed the desired performance while relaxing the need for system dynamics. Lyapunov analysis confirmed the closed-loop stability. Simulation results confirmed the validity of the control design and reduction in resource utilization.

The second part of the chapter presented an event-sampled near-optimal control of an uncertain continuous-time system. A near-optimal solution of the HJB equation was achieved with event sampled approximation of the value function and system dynamics. The NN weight tuning at the event-sampled instants with adaptive event sampling conditions was found to ensure the convergence of the NN weight estimates to their respective target values. It was observed that the inter-sample times depend upon the initial values of the NN weight estimates. Furthermore, the inter-sample times were found to increase with the convergence of the parameters. The simulation results validated the analytical design. The cost function considered in this paper only optimizes the control policy. Finally, a framework for extending the optimal regulator design for event-based trajectory tracking control is presented.

4.6 PROBLEMS

4.6.1 Consider an inverted pendulum (Spooner and Passino, 1999), which can be represented as an input-affine nonlinear dynamical system. The dynamics of the system are given by

$$\dot{x}_1 = x_2,$$
$$\dot{x}_2 = (\frac{mgr}{J} - \frac{kr^2}{4}J)\sin x_1 + \frac{kr}{2J}(l-b) + \frac{u}{J}. \tag{4.81}$$

Design feedback control policies based on the control algorithm using equations in Table 4.1.

4.6.2 Design near-optimal control policies based on the learning algorithm using equations in Table 4.3 for the Problem 4.6.1.

4.6.3 For the same system as in Problem 4.6.1., consider the linearized dynamics as in (Guinaldo et al., 2011). The parameters in the system dynamics are $m_1 = 2$, $m_2 = 2.5$, $J_1 = 5$, $J_2 = 6.25, k = 10, r = 0.5, l = 0.5$, and $g = 9.8, b = 0.5$. Pick the initial conditions of the system states in the interval $[0,1]$ and the initial weights of the NN from $[-1,1]$, randomly. Design control policies based on the algorithms using equations in Table 4.1.

4.6.4 For the linearized system used in Problem 4.6.3., select the parameters in the system dynamics as $m_1 = 20$, $m_2 = 25$, $J_1 = 5$, $J_2 = 6.25, k = 10, r = 0.5, l = 0.5$, and $g = 9.8, b = 0.5$. Pick the initial conditions of the system states in the interval $[0,1]$ and the initial weights of the NN from $[-1,1]$, randomly. Design control policies based on the algorithms using equations in Table 4.3.

4.6.5 Design feedback control policies based on the learning algorithm using equations in Table 4.3 for the Example 4.1. Use RVFL network with sigmoid activation function.

4.6.6 Design feedback control policies based on the learning algorithm using equations in Table 4.1 for the Example 4.2. Choose the event-triggering condition with $\Gamma_s \in (0,1)$ and comment on the performance of the event-triggering mechanism.

4.6.7 Design feedback control policies based on the learning algorithm using equations in Table 4.3 for the Example 4.2. Choose $Q = 0.4I$ and vary the parameter values for R. The penalty on control torques and the events generated are interdependent. Comment on the number of events generated versus the control penalty function.

4.6.8 Design feedback control policies based on the learning algorithm using equations in Table 4.3 for the Example 4.2. What if the regulation task is replaced with tracking problem, where the goal is to track a sinusoidal reference trajectory?

4.6.9 Consider the nonlinear system represented by

$$\begin{aligned} \dot{x}_1 &= -x_1 + x_2 \\ \dot{x}_2 &= -\frac{1}{2}(x_1 + x_2) + \frac{1}{2}x_2 \sin^2(x_1) + (\sin(x_1))\,u \end{aligned} \tag{4.82}$$

Using the controller equations in Table 4.1 to design an event-based feedback control policy.

4.6.10 For the system given in the previous problem, design a learning-based controller using equations given in Table 4.3. Select the infinite horizon cost function as $V^u(x(t)) = \int_t^\infty \left(Q(x) + u^2\right) d\tau$ with $Q(x) = x_1^2 + x_2^2$ to be minimized.

5 Co-optimization of Sampling and Control

CONTENTS

In Chapters 3 and 4, we covered ADP-based controllers for linear and nonlinear systems in the event-triggered control framework. In both these chapters, we have seen that the event-triggering conditions can be derived using Lyapunov stability analysis. By contrast, in this chapter, we shall see that the design of event-triggering condition can be coupled with the control synthesis by utilizing game-theoretic techniqes. To this end, this chapter presents an event and a self-triggered sampling and regulation scheme for linear and nonlinear continuous-time dynamic systems, as well as tracking control problems. We shall develop these schemes based on a zero-sum game formulation, wherein the control policy is treated as the first player, and the threshold for control input error due to aperiodic dynamic feedback is treated as the second player. The optimal control policy and sampling intervals are generated using the saddle point or Nash equilibrium solution, which is obtained from the corresponding game algebraic Riccati equation. The event- and self-triggering control schemes presented in this chapter are based on Sahoo et al. (2018, 2017a) and the second part of the chapter dealing with nonlinear systems is based on Narayanan et al. (2018b) with the last part on tracking control is based on Sahoo and Narayanan (2019).

5.1 LINEAR SYSTEMS

In this section, a co-optimization approach for both the control policy and the sampling intervals, taken from (Sahoo et al., 2018), is presented. Unlike the emulation-based methods in previous chapters, which involved designing a control policy to guide the system with continuous feedback and later creating an event-triggering condition based on stability conditions, here, the control policy and event-triggering condition are concurrently designed. The optimal event-based sampling and control problem is formulated as a two-player zero-sum game where the control policy is treated as the first player, and the threshold for the error between continuous and event-triggered control policy due to the aperiodic sampling is viewed as the second player. A performance index is defined using the system state and the players. Player I's objective is to minimize the cost function, while Player II attempts to maximize it. The problem leads to a min-max problem (Basar and Bernhard, 2008) where the objective is to reach a saddle point solution or Nash equilibrium (Basar and Bernhard, 2008). The Nash equilibrium solution is obtained using the game-theoretic algebraic Riccati equation (GARE) (Basar and Bernhard, 2008). The event-based optimal control policy is designed using the solution of GARE and the optimal sampling condition is derived using the worst-case threshold to maximize the sampling periods.

To eliminate the requirement of the additional piece of hardware for triggering mechanisms in the event-based implementation, a self-triggered control scheme is also presented. A weaker triggering condition, derived from the event-based implementation, is utilized to determine the future sampling instants for the self-triggered design. Thus, the self-triggered sampling condition leads to a suboptimal solution. We shall see that these controllers lead to asymptotic stability of the closed-loop system and the Zeno-free behavior of the triggering mechanism is also guaranteed.

The next section briefly describes the background on event-based control and formulates the problem for linear systems.

5.1.1 PROBLEM STATEMENT

Consider a linear continuous-time system given by

$$\dot{x}(t) \quad = \quad Ax(t)+Bu(t), \;\; x(0)=x_0, \tag{5.1}$$

where $x(t) \in \mathbb{R}^n$ and $u(t) \in \mathbb{R}^m$ denote the system state and control input vector, respectively. The matrices $A \in \mathbb{R}^{n\times n}$ and $B \in \mathbb{R}^{n\times m}$ are the internal dynamics and input coefficient matrices, respectively.

Assumption 5.1. *The pair (A,B) is controllable, and the state vector $x(t)$ is measurable.*

Consider a traditional infinite horizon performance index for the system in (5.1) given by

$$J(x(0)) = \int_0^{\infty} (x^T(\tau)Hx(\tau)+u^T(\tau)Ru(\tau))d\tau, \tag{5.2}$$

where $H \in \mathbb{R}^{n\times n}$ and $R \in \mathbb{R}^{m\times m}$ are symmetric positive definite matrices, and $u(t) = \mu(x(t))$, where $\mu : \mathbb{R}^n \to \mathbb{R}^m$ is an admissible control policy. The objective is to minimize the performance index J by designing an optimal control policy $u^*(t) = \mu^*(x(t))$. The solution of the optimal control problem can be obtained by solving the algebraic Riccati equation (ARE) (Lewis et al., 2012b). The inherent assumption of the execution of the optimal control policy is the continuous availability of the system state vector.

As discussed in Chapter 1, in the event-triggered and self-triggered control formalism, the system state vector is sampled, and the controller is executed aperiodically by using a sampling condition. Define the aperiodic sampling instants as $\{t_k\}_{k=0}^{\infty}$ with $t_0 = 0$. The sampled state sent to the controller at the aperiodic sampling instants can be expressed as

$$\hat{x}(t) = x(t_k), \; t_k \leq t < t_{k+1} \tag{5.3}$$

where $\hat{x}(t) \in \mathbb{R}^n$ is the sampled state at the controller for controller execution. The resulting state measurement error can be expressed as

$$e_{s,x}(t) = \hat{x}(t) - x(t) = x(t_k) - x(t), \ t_k \leq t < t_{k+1} \tag{5.4}$$

where $e_{s,x}(t) \in \mathbb{R}^n$ is the state measurement error. Now, the control input with the sampled state $\hat{x}(t)$ is expressed as $\hat{u}(t) = \mu(\hat{x}(t))$, which is held at the actuator by a zero-order-hold (ZOH) and applied to the system till the next update is reached. The system in (5.1) with sampled state based input $\hat{u}(t)$ can be expressed as

$$\dot{x}(t) = Ax(t) + B\hat{u}(t). \tag{5.5}$$

Note that the sampled control input $\hat{u}(t) = \mu(\hat{x}(t)) \in \mathbb{R}^m$ is a piecewise constant input signal due to ZOH. Define the error between the continuous control input, $u(t) = \mu(x(t))$, and the sampled control input, $\hat{u}(t)$, as

$$e_{s,u}(t) = \hat{u}(t) - u(t), \tag{5.6}$$

where $e_{s,u}(t) \in \mathbb{R}^m$, the control input error due to the aperiodic feedback, is a piecewise continuous function. The sampled system (5.5) with (5.6) can be expressed as

$$\dot{x}(t) = Ax(t) + Bu(t) + Be_{s,u}(t). \tag{5.7}$$

The aperiodic sampling and controller execution introduced an error term, $Be_{s,u}(t)$, in the system dynamics (5.1), which can be considered as an exogenous input to the system. It is clear that larger the magnitude of $e_{s,u}(t)$, larger the event-triggering error is allowed to grow, resulting in longer inter-event time.

To obtain an optimal threshold for $e_{s,u}(t)$ such that the sampling intervals can be maximized, we introduce a dynamical system

$$\dot{x}(t) = Ax(t) + Bu(t) + B\hat{e}_{s,u}(t), \tag{5.8}$$

where $\hat{e}_{s,u}$ is an exogenous independent signal, whose optimal value will be used as a threshold for $e_{s,u}$ in (5.7). Therefore, the objective is to, first, design the optimal control policy u^* for the system in (5.8) in the presence of the worst case exogenous signal $e^*_{s,u}$ (worst case value for $\hat{e}_{s,u}$) such that the system in (5.8) mimics the optimal target system, $\dot{x}(t) = Ax(t) + Bu^*(t) + Be^*_{s,u}(t)$. Second, design the sampling instants and the control policy for the system in (5.7) such that the resulting closed-loop system emulates the target system. Therefore, the traditional performance index in (5.2) for the system in (5.8) must be redefined to include the additional term $\hat{e}_{s,u}$, which can be maximized. This clearly leads to a zero-sum min-max game formulation. In the next section, a solution to the dynamic game is presented.

5.1.2 CO-OPTIMIZATION SCHEME

Redefine the infinite horizon performance index (5.2) for an event-based control system (5.8) as

$$J(x(0), u, \hat{e}_{s,u}) = \frac{1}{2}\int_0^\infty \left(x^T(\tau)Hx(\tau) + u(\tau)^T Ru(\tau) - \gamma^2 \hat{e}_{s,u}(\tau)^T \hat{e}_{s,u}(\tau)\right) d\tau, \tag{5.9}$$

where $H \in \mathbb{R}^{n\times n}$ and $R \in \mathbb{R}^{m\times m}$ are constant symmetric positive definite user-defined matrices and $\gamma > \gamma^*$, with γ^* denoting the minimum value of γ, is a constant such that the performance index in (5.9) is finite.

Remark 5.1. *In the traditional H_∞ optimal control (Basar and Bernhard, 2008; Wei and Guo, 2010) approach, solution of the optimal control problem leads to a saddle point optimal control input u^* and worst case exogenous signal $e^*_{s,u}$ (Basar and Bernhard, 2008). In the event-triggered formalism,* *the control input error $e_{s,u}$ is a function of u, unlike the independent disturbance in H_∞ optimal control (Basar and Bernhard, 2008; Wei and Guo, 2010). However, the event-triggering threshold is an independent time-dependent signal. In the co-design scheme, the performance index (5.8) is defined using an independent continuous exogenous signal, $\hat{e}_{s,u}$, based on (5.8). Minimization of (5.9) will lead to the optimal exogenous signal, $e^*_{s,u}$, which is utilized as the threshold for the triggering mechanism (defined in (5.20)).*

To design optimal control policy, u^* and the sampling instants $\{t_k\}_{k=0}^{\infty}$, which will maximize the sampling intervals, $\delta t_k = t_{k+1} - t_k$, a saddle point solution to the min-max optimization problem (Basar and Bernhard, 2008), defined by the cost function (5.9) with dynamic state constraint (5.8), needs to be obtained. This means, we should find the optimal value function given by

$$
\begin{aligned}
V^*(x(t)) &= \min_u \max_{\hat{e}_{s,u}} J(x,u,\hat{e}_{s,u}) \\
&= \min_u \max_{\hat{e}_{s,u}} \int_t^\infty \frac{1}{2}(x^T(\tau)Hx(\tau) + u^T(\tau)Ru(\tau) - \gamma^2 \hat{e}^T_{s,u}(\tau)\hat{e}_{s,u}(\tau))d\tau,
\end{aligned}
\tag{5.10}
$$

such that, given the pair $(u^*, e^*_{s,u})$, the saddle point solution is reached, i.e., $\min_u \max_{\hat{e}_{s,u}} J(x,u,\hat{e}_{s,u}) = \max_{\hat{e}_{s,u}} \min_u J(x,u,\hat{e}_{s,u})$. To solve the optimal control problem, begin by defining the Hamiltonian for the optimal value function (5.10) along the system dynamics (5.8). The Hamiltonian can be expressed as

$$
\mathscr{H}(x,u,\hat{e}_{s,u},\frac{\partial V^*}{\partial x}) = \frac{1}{2}x^T Hx + \frac{1}{2}u^T Ru - \frac{1}{2}\gamma^2 \hat{e}^T_{s,u}\hat{e}_{s,u} + \frac{\partial V^{*T}}{\partial x}(Ax + Bu + B\hat{e}_{s,u}),
\tag{5.11}
$$

where $\frac{\partial V^{*T}}{\partial x} = \frac{\partial V^{*T}(x(t))}{\partial x(t)}$.

The optimal control input can be computed by using the stationarity condition ($\frac{\partial \mathscr{H}(x,u,\hat{e}_{s,u},\frac{\partial V^*}{\partial x})}{\partial u} = 0$) and given by

$$
u^* = \mu^*(x) = \arg\min_u \mathscr{H}(\cdot) = -R^{-1}B^T \frac{\partial V^*}{\partial x},
\tag{5.12}
$$

and the threshold policy, with $\frac{\partial \mathscr{H}(x,u,\hat{e}_{s,u},\frac{\partial V^*}{\partial x})}{\partial \hat{e}_{s,u}} = 0$, is given by

$$
e^*_{s,u} = \arg\max_{\hat{e}_{s,u}} \mathscr{H}(\cdot) = \frac{1}{\gamma^2} B^T \frac{\partial V^*}{\partial x}.
\tag{5.13}
$$

The optimal value for linear systems with quadratic performance index (5.9) can be represented as $V^* = \frac{1}{2}x^T Px$, where $P \in \mathbb{R}^{n \times n}$ is a symmetric positive definite kernel matrix of the GARE (to be derived in (5.17)). Then, the optimal control input (5.12) can be expressed as

$$
u^*(t) = -R^{-1}B^T Px(t),
\tag{5.14}
$$

whereas the threshold policy (5.13) is given by

$$
e^*_{s,u}(t) = \frac{1}{\gamma^2} B^T Px(t).
\tag{5.15}
$$

By substituting the optimal control input (5.14) and the worst-case control-input input error (5.15) or the threshold policy, the Hamilton-Jacobi-Isaacs (HJI) equation can be expressed as

$$
\mathscr{H}(x,u^*,e^*_{s,u},\frac{\partial V^*}{\partial x}) = -\frac{1}{2}x^T Hx - \frac{1}{2}u^{*T} Ru^* + \frac{1}{2}\gamma^2 e^{*T}_{s,u} e^*_{s,u} + \frac{\partial V^{*T}}{\partial x}(Ax + Bu^* + Be^*_{s,u}).
$$

Rearranging the equation reveals

$$\mathscr{H}(x,u^*,e^*_{s,u},\frac{\partial V^*}{\partial x}) = \frac{1}{2}x^T(A^TP+PA+H-PBR^{-1}B^TP+\frac{1}{\gamma^2}PBB^TP)x, \tag{5.16}$$

where the GARE is given by

$$A^TP+PA+H-PBR^{-1}B^TP+\frac{1}{\gamma^2}PBB^TP=0. \tag{5.17}$$

The next theorem states the existence of a unique solution of the GARE in the context of aperiodic sampling.

Theorem 5.1. *(Existence of the solution of GARE) Consider the linear system (5.1). Let Assumption 5.1 holds. Then, there exists a unique symmetric positive definite kernel matrix P satisfying the GARE (5.17) provided the condition* $R^{-1} > \frac{1}{\gamma^2}I$ *is satisfied. Further, the Hamiltonian* $\mathscr{H}(x,u^*,e^*_{s,u},\frac{\partial V^*}{\partial x})=0$.

Proof. The GARE (5.17) can be rewritten as

$$A^TP+PA+H-PB(R^{-1}-\frac{1}{\gamma^2}I)B^TP=0. \tag{5.18}$$

By selecting γ properly one can find a positive definite matrix $\bar{R}$ such that $R^{-1}-(1/\gamma^2)I=\bar{R}^{-1}$. Substituting $\bar{R}^{-1}$, the GARE (5.18) becomes an algebraic Riccati equation (ARE) (Lewis et al., 2012b). Since, the pair $(A,\sqrt{H})$ is detectable, the matrix P is unique symmetric and positive definite solution of (5.17) (Lewis et al., 2012b). Since P satisfies the GARE in (5.17), the Hamiltonian $\mathscr{H}(x,u^*,e^*_{s,u},\frac{\partial V^*}{\partial x})=0$. □

The sampled optimal control input, using the solution of the GARE, with sampled state (5.3) can be expressed as

$$\hat{u}^*(t)=-R^{-1}B^TP\hat{x}(t). \tag{5.19}$$

Next, define the event-triggering condition for the system in (5.7) to determine sampling instants using the threshold policy in (5.15) as

$$e^T_{s,u}(t)e_{s,u}(t) \le \frac{1}{\gamma^4}x^T(t)PBB^TPx(t), \quad \forall t \in \mathbb{R}_{\ge 0}. \tag{5.20}$$

The triggering-mechanism evaluates the condition (5.20) and samples the system state vector when the inequality is violated. The following theorem guarantees the asymptotic stability of the sampled system.

Theorem 5.2. *(Asymptotic stability of optimal event-triggered system) Consider the linear system (5.1) represented as event-sampled system in (5.5). Let Assumption 5.1 holds,* γ *satisfies* $\gamma^2 > \lambda_{max}(R)$ *and the symmetric positive definite matrix P satisfies (5.17). Then, the sampled system (5.5) with control policy (5.19) is asymptotically stable for any initial state* $x_0 \in \mathbb{R}^n$ *if the inequality in (5.20) holds.*

Proof. ■ Let $L:\mathbb{R}^n \to \mathbb{R}_{\ge 0}$ be a continuously differentiable positive definite Lyapunov candidate function given by

$$L(x(t)) = \frac{1}{2}x^T(t)Px(t) = V^*(x),$$

where $V^*(x)$ is the optimal value function and P is a symmetric positive definite matrix that satisfies GARE (5.17).

- The first derivative of $L(x)$ along the system dynamics (5.5) is given by

$$\dot{L}(x) = \frac{\partial V^{*T}}{\partial x}\dot{x}(t) = \frac{\partial V^{*T}}{\partial x}(Ax + Bu_s) = \frac{\partial V^{*T}}{\partial x}(Ax + Bu + Be_{s,u}).$$

- Replacing with the optimal value of control input u^* from (5.14), the first difference leads to

$$\dot{L}(x) = \frac{\partial V^{*T}}{\partial x}[(Ax + Bu^* + Be^*_{s,u}) - B(e^*_{s,u} - e_{s,u})] \tag{5.21}$$

- Given u^* and $e^*_{s,u}$, the HJI equation in (5.16) satisfies $\mathscr{H}(x, u^*, e^*_{s,u}, \frac{\partial V^*}{\partial x}) = 0$. Then, the HJI equation can be rearranged as

$$\frac{\partial V^{*T}}{\partial x}(Ax + Bu^* + Be^*_{s,u}) = -\frac{1}{2}x^T Hx - \frac{1}{2}u^{*T}Ru^* + \frac{1}{2}\gamma^2 e^{*T}_{s,u}e^*_{s,u}.$$

- Further, from (5.13) we have $\gamma^2 e^*_{s,u} = B^T \frac{\partial V^*}{\partial x}$. Utilizing these facts and inserting in (5.21), the first derivative

$$\dot{L}(x) = -\frac{1}{2}x^T Hx - \frac{1}{2}u^{*T}Ru^* + \frac{1}{2}\gamma^2 e^{*T}_{s,u}e^*_{s,u} - \gamma^2 e^{*T}_{s,u}e^*_{s,u} + \gamma^2 e^{*T}_{s,u}e_{s,u}. \tag{5.22}$$

- Applying Young's inequality the first derivative is further simplified as

$$\dot{L}(x) \leq -\frac{1}{2}x^T Hx - \frac{1}{2}u^{*T}Ru^* + \frac{1}{2}\gamma^2 e^{*T}_{s,u}e^*_{s,u} - \gamma^2 e^{*T}_{s,u}e^*_{s,u} + \frac{1}{2}\gamma^2 e^{*T}_{s,u}e^*_{s,u} + \frac{1}{2}\gamma^2 e^{T}_{s,u}e_{s,u}. \tag{5.23}$$

- Recalling the triggering condition (5.20), the condition can be rewritten as $e^T_{s,u}e_{s,u} \leq e^{*T}_{s,u}e^*_{s,u}$. Substituting this triggering condition in (5.23), the first derivative is upper bounded as

$$\dot{L} \leq -\frac{1}{2}x^T Hx - \frac{1}{2}u^{*T}Ru^* + \frac{1}{2}\gamma^2 e^{*T}_{s,u}e^*_{s,u}. \tag{5.24}$$

- Inserting u^* from (5.14) and e^*_u in (5.15), the first derivative of the Lyapunov function can be simplified as

$$\dot{L}(x) \leq -\frac{1}{2}x^T Hx - \frac{1}{2}x^T PBR^{-1}B^T Px + \frac{1}{2}\gamma^2(\frac{1}{\gamma^4}x^T PBB^T Px) = -\frac{1}{2}x^T Mx, \tag{5.25}$$

  where $M = H + PBR^{-1}B^T P - \frac{1}{\gamma^2}PBB^T P$ is a positive definite matrix since H is positive definite and by selecting γ such that $\gamma^2 > \lambda_{max}(R)$, the matrix $R^{-1} - \frac{1}{\gamma^2}I$ will also be positive definite.
- From (5.25), the Lyapunov first derivative $\dot{L}(x)$ is negative definite. By the Lyapunov stability theorem, the system states $x(t) \to 0$ as $t \to \infty$.

□

Remark 5.2. *Note that the set of sampling instants is determined using the equality condition in (5.20), i.e.,* $\{t_k\}_{k=0}^{\infty} = \{t \in \mathbb{R}_{\geq 0} | e^T_{s,u}e_{s,u} = \frac{1}{\gamma^4}x^T PBB^T Px\}$. *Since the threshold for the sampled policy error is selected as its worst-case value, the sampling intervals* $\delta t_k = t_{k+1} - t_k$ *are maximized with respect to the performance index* (5.9)

The optimal event-triggering condition (5.20) is a function of the control input error and the state vector of the original system. The following corollary presents a traditional triggering condition (Tabuada, 2007) using the state error (5.4) and the sampled state vector (5.3).

Corollary 5.1. *Let the hypothesis of Theorem 5.2 hold. Then, the sampled system (5.5) with control policy (5.19) is asymptomatically stable for any initial state* $x_0 \in \mathbb{R}^n$ *if the inequality*

$$e_{s,x}^T \Pi e_{s,x} \leq \frac{1}{2}\hat{x}^T \Omega \hat{x}, \forall t \in [t_k, t_{k+1}), k \in \mathbb{N}, \tag{5.26}$$

holds, where $\Pi = \psi_\pi I + \Omega + K^T K \in \mathbb{R}^{n\times n}$ *with* $\Omega = \frac{1}{\gamma^4} PBB^T P \in \mathbb{R}^{n\times n}$, $K = R^{-1}B^T P \in \mathbb{R}^{m\times n}$, $\psi_\pi > 0$ *is a constant and* I *is the identity matrix with appropriate dimension.*

Proof. ■ To complete the proof, it suffices to show that given the inequality (5.26) the sampling condition (5.20) holds. By the definition of Ω in (5.26), the inequality (5.20) can be rewritten as $e_{s,u}^T e_{s,u} \leq x^T \Omega x$. Further, the control input error

$$e_{s,u} = \hat{u} - u = K\hat{x} - Kx = K(\hat{x} - x) = Ke_{s,x}.$$

■ Expansion of the expression in (5.26) leads to

$$\begin{aligned} e_{s,x}^T \Pi e_{s,x} &= \psi_\pi e_{s,x}^T e_{s,x} + e_{s,x}^T \Omega e_{s,x} + e_{s,x}^T K^T K e_{s,x} \\ &= \psi_\pi e_{s,x}^T e_{s,x} + e_{s,x}^T \Omega e_{s,x} + e_{s,u}^T e_{s,u} \leq \frac{1}{2}\hat{x}^T \Omega \hat{x}. \end{aligned} \tag{5.27}$$

■ Rearrangement of the equation (5.27) reveals that

$$e_{s,u}^T e_{s,u} \leq \frac{1}{2}\hat{x}^T \Omega \hat{x} - e_{s,x}^T \Omega e_{s,x} - \psi_\pi e_{s,x}^T e_{s,x}.$$

■ Adding and subtracting similar terms and rearranging the equation again, we get

$$e_{s,u}^T e_{s,u} \leq \hat{x}_s^T \Omega \hat{x}_s + e_{s,x}^T \Omega e_{s,x} - 2\hat{x}_s^T \Omega e_{s,x} - \left(\frac{1}{2}\hat{x}^T \Omega \hat{x} + 2e_{s,x}^T \Omega e_{s,x} - 2\hat{x}^T \Omega e_{s,x}\right) - \psi_\pi e_{s,x}^T e_{s,x}.$$

■ By completion of the square, we have

$$\begin{aligned} e_{s,u}^T e_{s,u} &\leq (\hat{x} - e_{s,x})^T \Omega (\hat{x} - e_{s,x}) - (\frac{1}{\sqrt{2}}\hat{x} - \sqrt{2}e_{s,x})^T \Omega (\frac{1}{\sqrt{2}}\hat{x} - \sqrt{2}e_{s,x}) - \psi_\pi e_{s,x}^T e_{s,x} \\ &\leq x^T \Omega x. \end{aligned} \tag{5.28}$$

■ From (5.28) it is clear that given (5.26) the inequality (5.20) holds. Consequently, by Theorem 5.2, the event-sampled system (5.5) is asymptotically stable.

□

Remark 5.3. *The condition in (5.26) uses the sampled state vector* $\hat{x}$ *and can also be used as an event-triggering condition. The sampling instants can be determined by the violation of the inequality. However, the condition in (5.26) is a weaker condition and results in sub-optimal triggering. The main advantage of the inequality in (5.26) is that it only uses sampled signals and can be used to predict the next sampling instants at the controller using the current sampled state without any triggering mechanism as presented in the next section.*

5.1.3 SELF-TRIGGERED IMPLEMENTATION

In this section, we shall extend the event-based design to the self-triggered case by deriving a sampling condition with current states to determine the sampling instants.

The inequality in (5.26) can be equivalently written as

$$\|\sqrt{\Pi}e_{s,x}\| \leq \frac{1}{\sqrt{2}}\|\sqrt{\Omega}\hat{x}\|, \quad \forall t \in [t_k, t_{k+1}), \quad k \in \mathbb{N}, \tag{5.29}$$

where $\sqrt{\Pi}$ and $\sqrt{\Omega}$ are the matrix square roots of the matrices Π and Ω, respectively. By definition, the inverse of Π and, hence, $\sqrt{\Pi}$ exists by properly selecting the value of ψ_π.

The most important condition for developing the self-triggered scheme is that the sampling periods must be bounded from below by a nonzero positive constant (Wang and Lemmon, 2009b). The following lemma states the lower boundedness of the sampling period or the inter-event time.

Lemma 5.1. *Consider the linear system (5.1) represented as sampled data system in (5.5) along with the sampled optimal control input (5.19). Let γ satisfies $\gamma^2 > \lambda_{max}(R)$, Π is invertible, and there exists a symmetric positive definite matrix P satisfy (5.17). Then, the sampled system is asymptotically stable if the sampling is carried out when the condition in (5.29) is violated. Further, the inter-sample times δt_k are lower bounded by a non-zero positive constant.*

Proof.
- From Corollary 5.1, the inequality in (5.26) or equivalently in (5.29) is weaker than (5.20). Consequently, by Theorem 5.2, the sampled system is asymptotically stable.
- It only remains to show the lower boundedness inter-sample times. Since the inequality in (5.29) is a weaker condition of (5.20), it suffices to show that the inter-sample times δt_k determined by (5.29) are lower bounded.
- Define an error $\bar{e}_{s,x} = \sqrt{\Pi}e_{s,x}$. The inter-sampling period $\delta t_k = t_{k+1} - t_k$ is implicitly defined by the equality in (5.29). The error $\|\bar{e}_{s,x}(t)\|$ evolves from zero at time t_k for $k \in \mathbb{N}$ to the threshold value of $\frac{1}{\sqrt{2}}\|\sqrt{\Omega}x_s\|$ at time t_{k+1}.
- The time derivative of the measurement error $\|\bar{e}_{s,x}\|$ becomes

$$\begin{aligned}\frac{d}{dt}\|\bar{e}_{s,x}(t)\| &\leq \|\dot{\bar{e}}_{s,x}(t)\| = \|\sqrt{\Pi}(\dot{\hat{x}}(t) - \dot{x}(t))\| = \|\sqrt{\Pi}\dot{x}(t)\| = \|\sqrt{\Pi}(Ax + B\hat{u})\| \\ &= \|\sqrt{\Pi}(A(\hat{x} - e_{s,x}) + BK\hat{x})\| \\ &\leq \|\sqrt{\Pi}(A+BK)\hat{x}\| + \|\sqrt{\Pi}Ae_{s,x}\| \leq \|\sqrt{\Pi}A\sqrt{\Pi}^{-1}\sqrt{\Pi}e_{s,x}\| + \|\sqrt{\Pi}(A+BK)\hat{x}\|.\end{aligned}$$

- Defining $\alpha_s = \|\sqrt{\Pi}A\sqrt{\Pi}^{-1}\|$ and $\beta_s = \|\sqrt{\Pi}(A+BK)\|$, we have.

$$\frac{d}{dt}\|\bar{e}_{s,x}\| \leq \alpha_s\|\bar{e}_{s,x}\| + \beta_s\|\hat{x}\|. \tag{5.30}$$

- By comparison lemma (Khalil, 2002), the solution of the differential inequality in (5.30) is upper bounded by

$$\begin{aligned}\|\bar{e}_{s,x}(t)\| &\leq \|\bar{e}_{s,x}(t_k)\|e^{\alpha_s(t-t_k)} + \int_{t_k}^{t} \beta_s\|\hat{x}(t)\|e^{\alpha_s(t-\tau)}d\tau \\ &= \frac{\beta_s\|\hat{x}(t)\|}{\alpha_s}\left(e^{\alpha_s(t-t_k)} - 1\right).\end{aligned} \tag{5.31}$$

- With $\|\bar{e}_{s,x}(t_k)\| = 0, \forall k \in \mathbb{N}$, at the next sampling instant $t_{k+1}, \forall k \in \mathbb{N}$, the error $\|\bar{e}_{s,x}(t_{k+1})\| = \frac{1}{\sqrt{2}}\|\sqrt{\Omega}\hat{x}\|$.
- From (5.31) it holds that $\frac{1}{\sqrt{2}}\|\sqrt{\Omega}\hat{x}\| = \|\bar{e}_{s,x}(t_{k+1})\| \leq \frac{\beta_s\|\hat{x}\|}{\alpha_s}(e^{\alpha_s(t_{k+1}-t_k)} - 1)$, which leads to $\frac{\beta_s\|\hat{x}\|}{\alpha_s}(e^{\alpha_s(t_{k+1}-t_k)} - 1) > \frac{1}{\sqrt{2}}\|\sqrt{\Omega}\hat{x}\|$.
- Solving for the $\delta t_k = t_{k+1} - t_k$ reveals

$$\delta t_k > \frac{1}{\alpha_s}\ln\left(1 + \frac{\alpha_s}{\sqrt{2}\beta_s\|\hat{x}\|}\|\sqrt{\Omega}\hat{x}\|\right). \tag{5.32}$$

- From (5.32), the inter-sample duration $\delta t_k = t_{k+1} - t_k > 0,\ \forall k \in \mathbb{N}$ and, hence, the sampling periods are bounded from below by a non-zero positive constant.

□

With the guarantee of lower boundedness of the sampling periods, the following theorem consolildates the stability results for the sub-optimal self-triggered control scheme.

Theorem 5.3. *Consider the linear continuous-time system (5.1) represented as a sampled data system in (5.5). Let the Assumption 5.1 hold, γ satisfies $\gamma^2 > \lambda_{max}(R)$, and the symmetric positive definite matrix P satisfies (5.17). Then the self-triggered system (5.5) with optimal control policy (5.19) is asymptomatically stable for any initial state $x_0 \in \mathbb{R}^n$ if systems states are sampled, and the controller is executed at the time-instants determined by the following inequality*

$$t_{k+1} \geq t_k + \frac{1}{\alpha_s} \ln\left(1 + \frac{\alpha_s}{\sqrt{2}\beta_s \|\hat{x}\|} \|\sqrt{\Omega}\hat{x}\|\right). \tag{5.33}$$

Further, the self-triggered system is Zeno-free.

Sketch of proof:

- The next sampling instant t_{k+1} for the self-triggered condition (5.33) uses the expression of inter-sample time δt_k in (5.32). Alternatively, enforcing the self-triggered sampling condition (5.33) ensures the event-triggering condition (5.29) is satisfied. Therefore, by Lemma 5.1, the self-triggered system is asymptotically stable.
- Further, from (5.32) of Lemma 5.1, $\delta t_k \geq \frac{1}{\alpha_s} \ln\left(1 + \frac{\alpha_s}{\sqrt{2}\beta_s \|\hat{x}\|} \|\sqrt{\Omega}\hat{x}\|\right) > 0$. This implies $t_{k+1} - t_k > 0$, i.e., the sampling periods are bounded from below by a non-zero positive number, and the self-triggered system does not exhibit Zeno behavior.

Remark 5.4. *The sampling intervals determined by the self-triggering scheme use a weaker condition* (5.29) *when compared to the event-triggering condition* (5.20)*. Therefore, the self-triggered control results have a known degree of sub-optimality from the sampling period point of view.*

Example 5.1. *The unstable batch reactor example (Walsh et al., 2002; Heemels et al., 2010) is considered for simulation whose dynamics are given by*

$$\dot{x}(t) = \begin{bmatrix} 1.38 & -0.207 & 6.715 & -5.676 \\ -0.581 & -4.29 & 0 & 0.675 \\ 1.067 & 4.273 & -6.654 & 5.893 \\ 0.048 & 4.273 & 1.343 & -2.104 \end{bmatrix} x(t) + \begin{bmatrix} 0 & 0 \\ 5.679 & 0 \\ 1.136 & -3.146 \\ 1.136 & 0 \end{bmatrix} u(t).$$

The simulation parameters were selected as follows: initial state vector $x_0 = [1.8, -2.4, -4.6, 4]^T$, the matrices for the cost function $H = I_{4\times4}$ and $R = 0.05 I_{2\times2}$. The value of $\gamma = 0.25$ was selected such that $\gamma^2 > \lambda_{max}(R)$, as in Theorem 5.1. The simulation is run for 5 seconds and the results are shown in Figure 5.1 through Figure 5.5.

Event-triggered control: The evolution of the system state vector and the control inputs are shown in Figures 5.1 (a) and (b). The optimal event-sampled control input in Figure 5.1 (b) is a piecewise constant function due to the event-based aperiodic execution of the control input. The control input error $e_{s,u}$ used as the event-triggering error is plotted in Figure 5.1 (c) along with the threshold. The plot is zoomed out for clarity of the evolution of the control input error, which resets at every sampling instants. A total of 123 sampling instants occurred during the simulation time of 5 sec for $\gamma = 0.25$, as shown in Fig. 5.1 (d). A minimum sampling time of $0.011s$ is observed, and the aperiodic sampling instants during the simulation are plotted in Figure 5.2.

Table 5.1
Co-optimization of sampling instants and control policy of linear systems

System dynamics	$\dot{x}(t) = Ax(t) + Bu(t), \;\; x(0) = x_0$
Event-triggering error	$e_{s,u}(t) = \hat{u}(t) - u(t),$
Performance index	$J(x(0), u, \hat{e}_{s,u}) = \frac{1}{2}\int_0^\infty \left(x^T(\tau)Hx(\tau) + u(\tau)^T Ru(\tau) - \gamma^2 \hat{e}_{s,u}(\tau)^T \hat{e}_{s,u}(\tau)\right) d\tau$
Game Riccati equation	$A^T P + PA + H - PBR^{-1}B^T P + \frac{1}{\gamma^2} PBB^T P = 0$
Control input	$\hat{u}^* = -R^{-1}B^T P\hat{x}$
Event-triggering condition	$e_{s,u}^T e_{s,u} \leq \frac{1}{\gamma^4} x^T PBB^T Px, \forall t$
Self-triggering condition	$t_{k+1} \geq t_k + \frac{1}{\alpha_s} \ln\left(1 + \frac{\alpha_s}{\sqrt{2}\beta_s \lVert\hat{x}\rVert} \lVert\sqrt{\Omega}\hat{x}\rVert\right)$

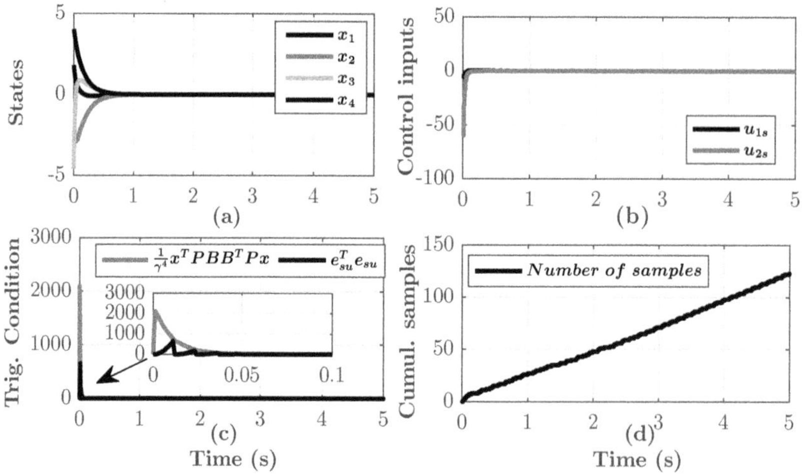

Figure 5.1 Evolution of (a) the state trajectory; (b) optimal event-based control policy; (c) control input error and sampling threshold; and (d) cumulative number of sampling instants.

Next, the comparison results with the traditional scheme developed by Wang and Lemmon (2009b) is presented. Note that a direct comparison is not possible due to the difference between the approaches and performance requirements. Therefore, to have a fair comparison in terms of the cost, same value of $\gamma = 0.25$ is used for both the approaches, and $\beta = 0.76$ was selected for evaluating the triggering condition (5.20) developed by Wang and Lemmon (2009b) such that equal numbers of triggering occurs for both the methods. This results in 122 events which is close to the game-based method, i.e., 123. The optimal cost trajectory for both the approaches are computed as $V^*(x) = x^T Px$ with the same P matrix, which is the solution of the GARE in (5.17). The cumulative optimal costs are computed by integrating the current values.

The optimal cost surface and the optimal cost trajectory for the game-based and a classical method (Wang and Lemmon, 2009b) are plotted in Figure 5.3. Since the batch reactor is a fourth-order system, only the first two states are considered at a time for plotting the costs, while the other

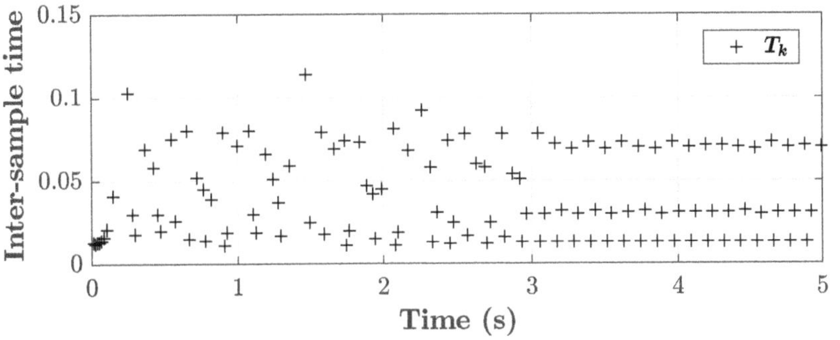

Figure 5.2 Aperiodic inter-sample times with a minimum inter-sample time of 0.011 s for $\gamma = 0.25$.

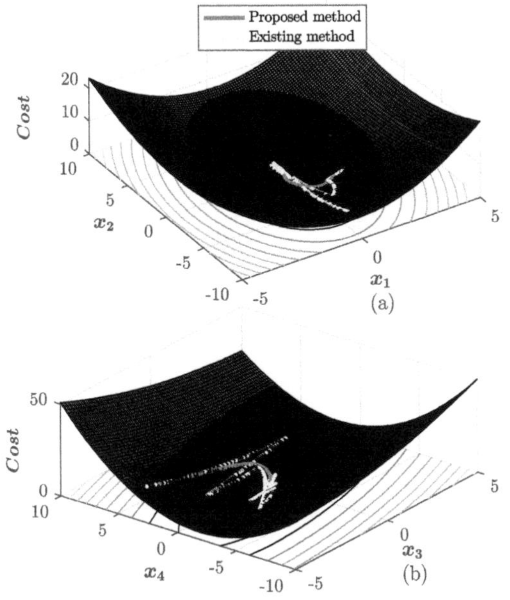

Figure 5.3 Optimal cost surface and comparison of optimal cost trajectory between the game-based method (Sahoo et al., 2018) and existing method (Wang and Lemmon, 2009b) (a) for state x_1 and x_2 with $x_3 = x_4 = 0$.; and (b) for state x_3 and x_4 with $x_1 = x_2 = 0$.

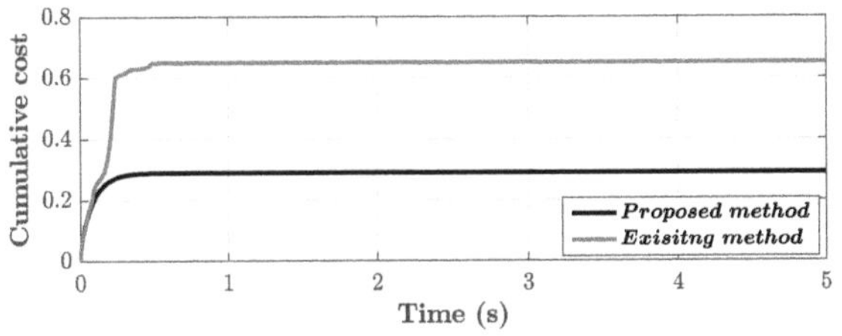

Figure 5.4 Comparison of cumulative cost between game-based method presented in this section based on (Sahoo et al., 2018) and the method presented by Wang and Lemmon (2009b).

two are made zero. The optimal cost in the game-based method uses the shortest path resulting in lower cumulative cost, which, compared to the existing method (Wang and Lemmon, 2009b), is shown in Figure 5.4.

Self-triggered control: The sampling instants are determined by the controller using the self-triggering condition in (5.33) with $\psi_\pi = 0.001$ and all other parameters are the same as in the case of event-triggered control. The convergence of the system states and control input are shown in Figures

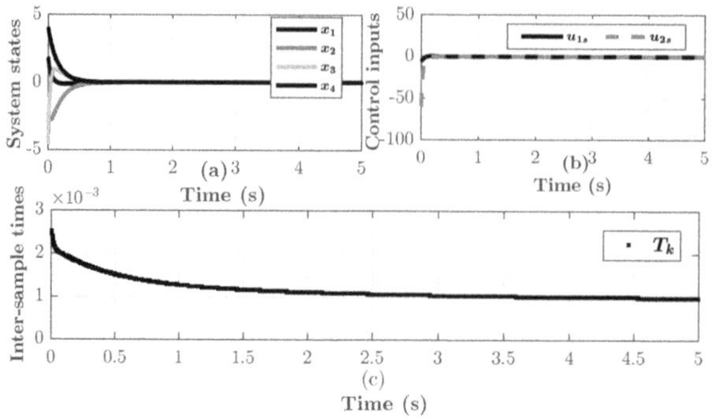

Figure 5.5 Self-triggered implementation: (a) evolution of the state trajectory; (b) optimal event-based control policy; and (c) inter-sample time with $\gamma = 0.25$.

5.5 (a) and (b). The inter-sample times are shown in Figure 5.5 (c). Recall that the self-triggering condition (5.33) is derived using a weaker condition than the event-triggering condition given by (5.20). Therefore, inter-sample times are small when compared to the event-based inter-sample times. A minimum inter-sample time of $0.001s$ is observed with an averaged sampling interval of $0.0011s$.

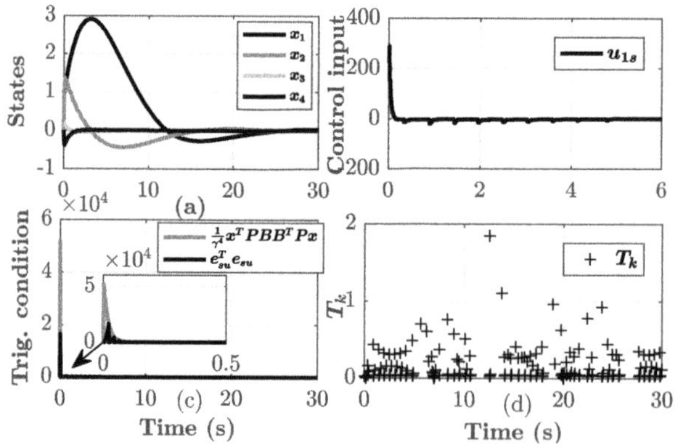

Figure 5.6 (a) Evolution of the state trajectory; (b) optimal event-based control policy; (c) triggering condition; and (d) inter-sample times

Example 5.2. *In this example, the inverted pendulum on a cart with dynamics as described by Wang and Lemmon (2009b) is considered. The parameters used for the simulation were* $m = 1$, $g = 10$, $M = 10$, *and* $l = 3$ *with initial state* $x_0 = [0.98,\ 0,\ 0.2,\ 0]^T$, $H = I$, *and* $R = 0.05$.

All other parameters are selected as in Example 5.1 to show the efficacy of the design for both sampling intervals and cost. The convergence of the system states and the optimal control input are shown in Figures 5.6 (a) and (b), respectively. The evolution of the triggering condition is shown in Figure 5.6 (c), and inter-sample times with an average inter-sample time of 0.156 s are shown in Figure 5.6 (d). The comparison results for the number of samples and cumulative cost are shown in Figures 5.7 (a) and (b), respectively.

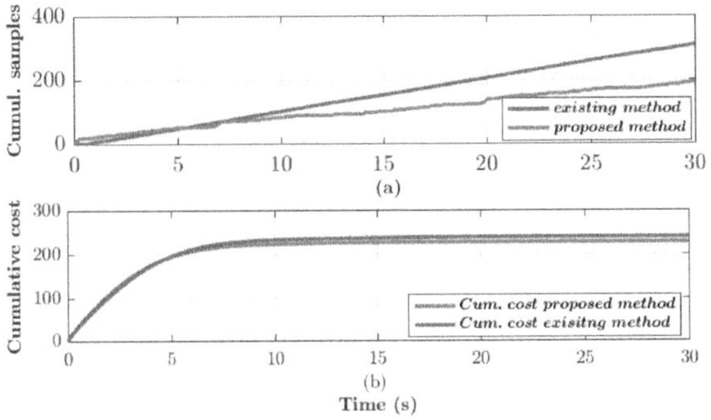

Figure 5.7 Comparison of (a) cumulative sampling instants; and (b) cumulative cost between the method in (Sahoo et al., 2018) and the method in (Wang and Lemmon, 2009b)

5.2 NONLINEAR SYSTEMS

In this section, the co-design approach is extended to control systems governed by nonlinear continuous-time systems. First, the performance index is redefined as a two-player zero-sum game where the control policy is one player and the threshold policy to bound the event-triggering error is the second. The solution to this game is obtained as the saddle point solution to the min-max optimization problem (Basar and Bernhard, 2008). The maximizing policy obtained as a solution to the game is utilized as the dynamic threshold to determine the sampling instants, which optimizes the sampling intervals, while the minimizing control policy, which accounts for the lack of continuous feedback is applied to the system.

Since the solution to the optimization problem is difficult to obtain, an approximate solution using ADP and RL techniques is presented. A functional-link linearly-parametrized artificial NN is employed to learn the optimal value function and, further, used to determine the optimal control policy and worst-case error in control policy for designing the threshold in the event-triggering mechanism. We shall use a forward-in-time hybrid learning scheme from Narayanan and Jagannathan (2016a), which is elaborated in Chapters 6-8, to estimate the NN weights online. We shall use Lyapunov stability analysis to guarantee the local ultimate boundedness of the state vector and the NN weight estimation errors.

5.2.1 PROBLEM STATEMENT

Consider a continuous time nonlinear dynamical system represented in an input affine form given by

$$\dot{x}(t) = f(x) + g(x)u(t), \quad x(0) = x_0, \tag{5.34}$$

where $x(t) \in \Omega_x \subset \mathbb{R}^n$ and $u(t) \in \mathbb{R}^m$ are, respectively, the state and the control input; Ω_x is a compact set in the n-dimensional Euclidean space. The maps $f : \Omega_x \to \mathbb{R}^n$, and $g : \Omega_x \to \mathbb{R}^{n\times m}$ are the internal dynamics and input gain functions with $f(0) = 0$. The feedback control input for (5.34) is of the form

$$u(t) = \mu(x(t)), \tag{5.35}$$

where $\mu : \Omega_u \to \mathbb{R}^m$ is a nonlinear map satisfying $\mu(0) = 0^m$ and Ω_u is a compact subset of Ω_x. The vector 0^m denotes the zero vector in $\mathbb{R}^m$.

In an event-triggered control framework the system states are sampled, and the control policies are updated at the instant t_k for $k = 0, 1, \cdots$. The control policy is held at the actuator using a zero-order hold and satisfies

$$u_e(t) = \mu(x_e(t)), \forall t \in [t_k, t_{k+1}), \tag{5.36}$$

where $u_e(t)$ is the event-sampled control policy and $x_e(t) = x(t_k)$, $\forall t \in [t_k, t_{k+1})$ is the event-sampled state received at the controller. Hence, the control input $u_e(t)$ applied to the system is a piecewise constant function. The error between the continuous state $x(t)$ and the intermittently available state $x_e(t)$, referred to as event-triggering error (or measurement error), is given by

$$e(t) = x_e(t) - x(t), \ \forall t \in [t_k, t_{k+1}). \tag{5.37}$$

Note that, with the newly received state information at the sampling instants, the error (5.37) resets to zero, i.e., $e(t_k) = 0$. The event-triggering error leads to an error in the control input. Define the error between the continuous control input (5.35) and the event-sampled control control input $u_e(t)$ in (5.36), referred to as sampling error policy $e_{s,u}(t)$, given as

$$e_{s,u}(t) = u_e(t) - u(t) = \mu(x_e) - \mu(x). \tag{5.38}$$

Remark 5.5. *Unlike the linear case, in the case of nonlinear systems, the policy (5.35) cannot be represented as a linear function of the event-triggering error. Therefore, for clarity of exposition, the error $e_{s,u}(t)$ in (5.38), is defined as a sampling error policy.*

The nonlinear system given by (5.34) with event-based control policy (5.36) can be re-written as

$$\dot{x}(t) = f(x) + g(x)u_e(t). \tag{5.39}$$

Define the performance measure $\zeta(t)$ for the system (5.34) as

$$\|\zeta(t)\|^2 = Q(x(t)) + u^T(t)Ru(t) \tag{5.40}$$

where $Q(\bullet)$ is a positive definite function satisfying $Q(0) = 0$ and R is a positive definite matrix. The function Q and the matrix R penalize the states and the control policy, respectively. A block diagram

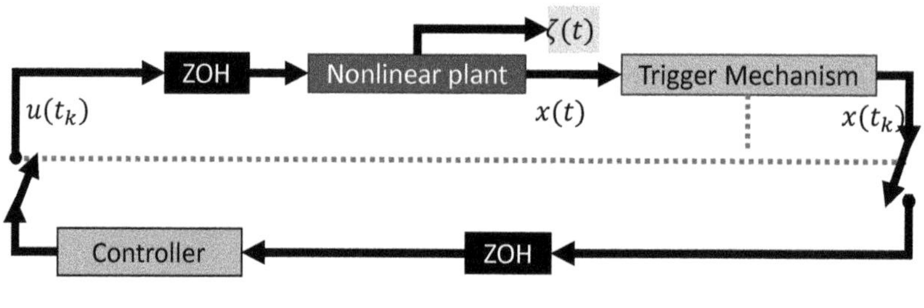

Figure 5.8 Networked control system and event-triggered feedback.

for the traditional optimal state feedback control with event-based availability of the state vector is shown in Figure 5.8. The control policy in (5.35) is designed by minimizing the performance index (5.40) and the triggering condition is designed to retain the stability by forming an upper bound to the measurement error (5.37). The event-triggering mechanism monitors the sensor measurements and evaluates the triggering condition and dynamically determines the time-instants $\{t_k\}$, $\forall k = 1, 2, \cdots$ to close the feedback loop.

Although the control policy minimizes the cost when continuously implemented, the event-triggering instants are not optimal. Therefore, the problem at hand is to design an optimal control policy that minimizes (5.40) and an event-triggering condition that maximizes the inter-sampling interval. In the next section, a min-max optimization problem is presented to achieve this design objective.

5.2.2 CO-OPTIMIZATION METHODOLOGY

In this section, similar to the linear case, a min-max optimization problem is developed for the nonlinear system and the saddle-point solution to the min-max co-optimization problem is derived.

Further, the resulting worst-case sampling error policy is utilized to design the event-triggering condition.

Utilizing the definition of the sampling error policy (5.38), one can express the system dynamics (5.39) as

$$\dot{x}(t) = f(x) + g(x)u(x(t)) + g(x)e_{s,u}(t). \tag{5.41}$$

To optimize the ever-triggering instants, the sampling error policy $e_{s,u}(t)$ must be maximized. Keeping this in mind, redefine the infinite horizon performance index using (5.40) as

$$J(x, e_{s,u}, u) = \int_t^{\infty} [\|\zeta(\tau)\|^2 - \sigma^2 e_{s,u}^T e_{s,u}] d\tau, \tag{5.42}$$

where $\sigma > 0$ represents the attenuation constant (Basar and Bernhard, 2008). The above optimal control problem is clearly a two-player zero-sum game-based min-max problem, where the control policy $u(t)$ is the minimizing player, and the sampling error policy is the maximizing player. The objective here is to find a saddle-point solution $(u^*, e_{s,u}^*)$ such that these policies yield an optimal value satisfying

$$V^*(x(t)) = \min_u \max_{e_{s,u}} J(u, e_{s,u}) = \max_{e_{s,u}} \min_u J(u, e_{s,u}). \tag{5.43}$$

For a reachable and zero-state observable system (Basar and Bernhard, 2008) with $Q(x) = C(x)^T C(x)$, with a nonlinear map C, there exists a minimum positive definite solution, the optimal value function (5.43), for the associated HJI equation when $\sigma > \sigma^*$, where σ^* is the H_∞ gain as described earlier for the case of linear systems using the variable γ^* (Basar and Bernhard, 2008).

To solve this optimal control problem, define the Hamiltonian function using the infinitesimal version of the cost function. For an admissible control policy (Dierks and Jagannathan, 2010b), consider the cost function defined using (5.42) and the dynamic state constraint in (5.41) as

$$H(x, u, e_{s,u}) = Q(x) + u^T R u - \sigma^2 e_{s,u}^T e_{s,u} + V_x^{*T} [f(x) + g(x)u(t) + g(x)e_{s,u}(t)], \tag{5.44}$$

where $V_x^* = \frac{\partial V^*}{\partial x}$ with $V^*(x)$ denoting the value-function defined in (5.43). The optimal control policies, by using the stationarity condition $\frac{\partial H(x,u,e_{s,u})}{\partial u} = 0$, is given by

$$u^*(x(t)) = -\frac{1}{2} R^{-1} g^T(x) V_x^*. \tag{5.45}$$

Similarly, the worst-case sampling error policy, with $\frac{\partial H(x,u,e_{s,u})}{\partial e_{s,u}} = 0$, is given by

$$e_{s,u}^*(x(t)) = \frac{1}{2\sigma^2} g^T(x) V_x^*. \tag{5.46}$$

The event-sampled optimal control policy $u_e^*(t) = \mu^*(x_e)$ is given by

$$u_e^*(t) = -\frac{1}{2} R^{-1} g^T(x_e) V_{x_e}^*, \tag{5.47}$$

where $V_{x_e}^* = \frac{\partial V^*(x)}{\partial x}|_{x=x_e}$.

Inserting the optimal control policy (5.45) and worst-case sampling error policy (5.46) in the Hamiltonian (5.44) results in the HJI equation given by

$$H = Q(x) + V_x^{*T} f(x) - \frac{1}{4} V_x^{*T} g(x) R^{-1} g^T(x) V_x^* + \frac{1}{4\sigma^2} V_x^{*T} g(x) g^T(x) V_x^*. \tag{5.48}$$

Assumption 5.2. *The functions $f(x)$ and $g(x)$ are Lipschitz continuous in the compact set Ω_x and the function $g(x)$ satisfies $\|g(x)\| \leq g_M$, where $g_M > 0$ is a constant.*

Assumption 5.3. *The control policy $u(t)$ is locally Lipschitz continuous and satisfies $\|e_{s,u}(t)\| = \|\mu(x_e) - \mu(x)\| = \|u_e(t) - u(t)\| \leq L_u \|e(t)\|$, where $L_u > 0$ is the Lipschitz constant.*

A solution to the HJI equation (5.48), i.e., the optimal value function V^*, exists for $\sigma > \sigma^*$ and is positive definite when the system and the performance function satisfy certain properties related to the controllability and observability of the system (Basar and Bernhard (2008)). If we assume that such a solution exists in the domain of interest and that it is smooth, the resulting optimal cost (5.42) will be finite and the optimal control policy (5.45) will be asymptotically stabilizing in the presence of the worst-case sampling error policy (5.46).

The following lemma establishes the ISS of the system (5.41) with respect to the ever-triggering error.

Lemma 5.2. *(Narayanan et al., 2018b) Consider the nonlinear system (5.41) and the performance index (5.42). Let V^* be the positive definite solution for the HJI equation (5.48) and Assumptions 5.2 and 5.3 hold. Then the optimal policy (5.45) renders the closed-loop system (5.41) is locally ISS with respect to the event-triggering error $e(t)$.*

Next, the main results of this section are presented.

Theorem 5.4. *(Narayanan et al., 2018b) Consider the affine nonlinear system dynamics (5.41) along with the infinite horizon performance index (5.42). Suppose the Assumptions 5.2 and 5.3 hold. Let V^* be the positive definite solution for the HJI equation (5.48) and there exists a $\sigma > 0$ such that the inequality*

$$\delta_1(\|x\|) > (\delta_2(\|x\|))^2$$

holds, where

$$\delta_1(\|x\|) = Q(x) + \frac{1}{2}V_x^{*T} g(x) R^{-1} g^T(x) V_x^* + \frac{1}{4\sigma^2} V_x^{*T} g(x) g^T(x) V_x^* > 0$$

and $\delta_2(\|x\|) = V_x^{*T} g$. Then the event-sampled optimal control policy in (5.47) with the event-triggering condition given by

$$\|e_{s,u}(t)\| \leq \left\|e_{s,u}^*(t)\right\|, \quad t \in [t_k, t_{k+1}), \quad \forall k \in \{0, \mathbb{N}\} \tag{5.49}$$

renders the closed-loop system asymptotically stable when $Q, R,$ and σ are selected such that $\delta_3(\|x\|) = \delta_1(\|x\|) - (\delta_2(\|x\|))^2 > 0$.

From the triggering condition (5.49) the events are triggered when the sampling error reaches the worst case sampling error policy with respect to the performance index (5.42). Consequently, the sequence of sampling instant is optimal.

Corollary 5.2. *(Narayanan et al., 2018b) Let the hypothesis of the Theorem 5.4 hold. Then, if the following inequality given by*

$$L_u \|e(t)\| \leq \frac{1}{2} \|e_{s,u}^*(t_k)\| \tag{5.50}$$

holds, the system (5.41) is asymptotically stable. Further, the minimum inter-sampling time $\delta t_m = \inf_{k \in \{0, \mathbb{N}\}} (\delta t_k) = \inf_{k \in \{0, \mathbb{N}\}} (t_{k+1} - t_k) > 0$ where δt_k is given by

$$\delta t_k = t_{k+1} - t_k \geq \frac{1}{\|g\|} \ln\left(\frac{\|g\|}{X_M} \|e_{s,u}^*(t_k)\| + 1\right) > 0. \tag{5.51}$$

is lower bounded by a nonzero positive constant with $X_M > 0$ such that $\|f(x) + g(x)u^*\| \leq X_M$.

Remark 5.6. *The expression for inter-event times (5.51) is a function of the previous sampling instant. Therefore, can be utilized to determine the next sampling instant without using the event-triggering mechanism. The sensor sampling instants can be pre-scheduled which will save the additional computation power required at the sensor. This autonomous sampling scheme is leads to the self-triggering scheme for the case of nonlinear systems considered in this section.*

As discussed earlier, a closed-form solution to the HJI equation is almost impossible to compute analytically even with the complete knowledge of the system dynamics. Hence, we shall utilize ADP methods to obtain an approximate solution with NN-based approximation and a learning scheme.

5.2.3 NEURAL NETWORK CONTROLLER DESIGN

In this section, an approximate solution to the HJI equation is obtained by approximating the value function with the help of a NN-based value function approximator (VFA), which is the solution of the HJI equation. The control policy and the event-triggering condition is designed using the approximate value. Thus, the saddle point solution to the min-max problem is learned online and in a forward-in-time manner.

A schematic of the NN-based learning scheme is given in Figure 5.9. Since, the estimated solution is utilized for designing the event-triggering condition, the event-trigger mechanism is equipped with a VFA as the one at the controller. This is similar to the mirror estimators introduced in Chapter 4. Both the value function approximators are synchronized by initializing with equal NN weight matrices and subsequent updates.

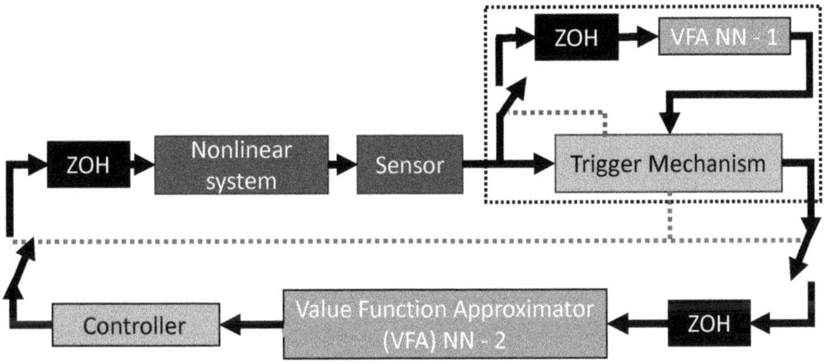

Figure 5.9 Approximate optimal event sampled control system.

In an event-based sampling framework the value function (5.42) can be expressed as

$$V(x(0)) = \sum_{k=0}^{\infty}\left(\frac{1}{2}\int_{t_k}^{t+T_k}(Q(x)+u^T Ru - \sigma^2 e_{s,u}^T e_{s,u})d\tau\right).$$

Using the infinitesimal version of the cost function (5.42), we can write

$$\dot{V}(\tau) = -Q(x) - u^T(\tau)Ru(\tau) + \sigma^2 e_{s,u}^T(\tau)e_{s,u}(\tau). \tag{5.52}$$

By integrating (5.52) in the interval $[t_k, t_{k+1})$, the Bellman equation in the integral form is obtained as

$$V^*(t_{k+1}) - V^*(t_k) = \int_{t_k}^{t_{k+1}}(-Q(x(\tau)) - u^T(\tau)Ru(\tau) + \sigma^2 e_{s,u}^T(\tau)e_{s,u}(\tau))d\tau. \tag{5.53}$$

Assuming that the solution to the HJI equation is a smooth function, a two-layer linearly parameterized NN with a fixed input layer can be used to approximate the optimal value function. This means, there exist constant weight matrices W and ω such that the value function in parametric form can be represented as

$$V^*(x) = W^T\phi(\omega^T x) + \varepsilon(x) \tag{5.54}$$

where $W \in \Omega_W \subset \mathbb{R}^{N_o \times 1}$ is the unknown target weight matrix, $\phi(\omega^T x) \in \mathbb{R}^{N_o}$ is the smooth activation function satisfying $\phi(0) = 0$ and ω is the randomly selected constant input layer weight matrix. Recall from Chapter 2 that the random selection of the input layer weights form a stochastic basis (Lewis et al. (1998)). The function $\varepsilon(x)$ is the reconstruction error and N_o is the number of hidden layer neurons. Since ω is not updated online, for brevity we express $\phi(\omega^T x) = \phi(x)$ in the rest of this section.

To approximate the optimal value function using a NN, the following standard assumptions are needed.

Assumption 5.4. *The optimal value function $V^*(x)$ exists and is smooth in Ω_x. The target weight vector W satisfies the bound $\|W\| \le W_M$. The set of activation functions $[\phi_1\ \phi_2 \ldots \phi_{N_o}]^T$ form a basis on the compact set Ω_x with $\|\phi(x)\| \le N_o$. The reconstruction error satisfies $\|\varepsilon(x)\| \le \varepsilon_M$.*

The Bellman equation (5.53) in terms of the NN approximation, by inserting (5.54), yields

$$W^T\Delta\phi(\tau) + \Delta\varepsilon(\tau) = \int_{t_k}^{t_{k+1}} (-Q(x) - u^T(\tau)Ru(\tau) + \sigma^2 e_{s,u}^T(\tau)e_{s,u}(\tau))d\tau \tag{5.55}$$

where $\Delta\phi(\tau) = \phi(t_{k+1}) - \phi(t_k)$ and $\Delta\varepsilon(\tau) = \varepsilon(x(t_{k+1})) - \varepsilon(x(t_k))$. Defining the optimal value function estimate as $\hat{V}$ and substituting it in the Bellman equation (5.53), the Bellman error/TD error can be expressed as

$$\chi_{k+1} = \int_{t_k}^{t_{k+1}} (Q(x) + u^T(\tau)Ru(\tau) - \sigma^2 e_{s,u}^T(\tau)e_{s,u}(\tau))d\tau + \hat{V}(t_{k+1}) - \hat{V}(t_k), \tag{5.56}$$

where χ_{k+1} is calculated at the occurrence of $k+1$ event. The estimated value function in a parametric form using NN weights, $\hat{W} \in \mathbb{R}^{N_o}$ is given by

$$\hat{V}(x) = \hat{W}^T\phi(x). \tag{5.57}$$

Substituting the estimate of the approximated optimal value function from (5.57) in (5.56) yields

$$\chi_{k+1} = \int_{t_k}^{t_{k+1}} (Q(x) + u^T(\tau)Ru(\tau) - \sigma^2 e_{s,u}^T(\tau)e_{s,u}(\tau))d\tau + \hat{W}^T\Delta\phi(\tau), \tag{5.58}$$

where $\Delta\phi(\tau) = \phi(t_{k+1}) - \phi(t_k)$ and χ_{k+1} is the residual error calculated at the event-sampling instant t_{k+1}. Define the NN weight estimation error as $\tilde{W} = W - \hat{W}$. Then, substituting for the right hand side of (5.55) in (5.58), we shall get

$$-\chi_{k+1} = W^T(t)\Delta\phi(\tau) - \hat{W}^T(t)\Delta\phi(\tau) + \Delta\varepsilon = \tilde{W}^T(t)\Delta\phi(\tau) + \Delta\varepsilon. \tag{5.59}$$

Note that, TD error (5.59) is expressed as a function of NN weight estimation error and used for demonstrating the stability of the system.

Now, with the estimated value function, the control policy can be expressed as

$$u(t) = -\frac{1}{2}R^{-1}g^T(x)\hat{V}_x = -\frac{1}{2}R^{-1}g^T(x)\nabla^T\phi(x)\hat{W}, \tag{5.60}$$

where $\hat{V}_x = \frac{\partial \hat{V}(x)}{\partial x}$, $\nabla\phi$ is the partial derivative of ϕ with respect to x. The event-sampled control input with event-based state x_e can be written from (5.60) as

$$u_e(t) = -\frac{1}{2}R^{-1}g^T(x_e)\hat{V}_{x_e} = -\frac{1}{2}R^{-1}g^T(x_e)\nabla^T\phi(x_e)\hat{W}, \tag{5.61}$$

where $\hat{V}_{x_e} = \frac{\partial \hat{V}(x)}{\partial x}|_{x_e}$. Similarly, the event-triggering condition using the estimated values is expressed as

$$\|e_{s,u}(t)\| \leq \|\hat{e}_{s,u}(t)\|, \quad t \in [t_k, t_{k+1}), \quad \forall k \in \{0, \mathbb{N}\}, \tag{5.62}$$

where the estimated worst-case sampled error or the threshold policy $\hat{e}_{s,u} = \frac{1}{2\sigma^2} g^T(x)\hat{V}_x(t)$. Since the objective is to estimate the optimal value function online, this can be achieved by minimizing the TD error (5.58). Thus, the following NN weight adaptation rule can be used.

$$\dot{\hat{W}} = \begin{cases} -\alpha \frac{[\Delta\phi(\tau)]}{(1+[\Delta\phi(\tau)]^T[\Delta\phi(\tau)])^2} \chi_k^T, & t = t_k \\ -\alpha \frac{[\Delta\phi(\tau)]}{(1+[\Delta\phi(\tau)]^T[\Delta\phi(\tau)])^2} \chi^T(t_k), & t \in (t_k, t_{k+1}). \end{cases} \tag{5.63}$$

The derivative of $\hat{W}$ represent the right derivative at $\{t_k\}$ for $k = 0, 1, \ldots$.

Remark 5.7. *In contrast to the traditional policy or value iteration schemes described earlier in Chapter 2, the parameter tuning rule presented in (5.63) is a hybrid learning scheme developed by Narayanan and Jagannathan (2016a), which can be implemented online. The Bellman error, χ_k, is calculated at every event-triggering instant, t_k, and the parameters are updated continuously using (5.63) both at the event-sampling and inter-event intervals. The update rule utilizes the new information obtained at the event-triggering instant to calculate the Bellman error, $\chi_k(t)$, and this error is reduced by weight updates in the inter-event period, $[t_k, t_{k+1})$.*

Next the main result of the section is summarized.

Theorem 5.5. *(Narayanan et al., 2018b) Consider the nonlinear input affine system dynamics (5.41) along with the performance index (5.42), control policy (5.61) and NN weight update rule (5.63) with a persistently exciting regression vector. With the Assumptions 5.2-5.4 satisfied, let the NN initial weights $\hat{W}(0)$ be defined in a compact set Ω_W and let the initial control policy be admissible. Then, there exists an $N > 0$ such that the closed-loop state vector and the NN weight estimation error are locally ultimately bounded with the event-triggering instants $k > N$, provided the event-triggering condition given in (5.62) is satisfied and the design parameters α, Q, R, and σ are chosen such that $\bar{\delta}_x > L_u^2$, $\frac{\alpha}{\rho} > \frac{1}{2} + \frac{g_M^2}{2}$, where $\rho = (1 + [\Delta\phi(\tau)]^T[\Delta\phi(\tau)])^2$ and $\bar{\delta}_x = \|Q(x) + u^{*T}Ru^* - \sigma^2 e_{s,u}^{*T} e_{s,u}\|$ with the learning rate $\alpha > 0$. The bounds for states and NN weight estimation error are $\mathscr{B}_x = \sqrt{\frac{\frac{1}{2}g_M^2\nabla\varepsilon_M^2 + \alpha^2\varepsilon_M^2}{(\bar{\delta}_x - L_u^2)}}$ and $\mathscr{B}_W = \sqrt{\frac{\frac{1}{2}g_M^2\nabla\varepsilon_M^2 + \alpha^2\varepsilon_M^2}{(\frac{\alpha}{\rho} - \frac{g_M^2}{2} - \frac{1}{2})}}$, respectively, as defined in the proof with $\|g(x)\| \leq g_M$, $\|\nabla\varepsilon\| \leq \nabla\varepsilon_M$, $\|\varepsilon\| \leq \varepsilon_M$ where $\nabla\varepsilon_M, g_M, \varepsilon_M$ are positive constants.*

Sketch of proof:

- Consider a continuously differentiable candidate Lyapunov function $L : B_x \times \Omega_W \to \mathbb{R}_+$ given by

$$L(x, \tilde{W}) = L_x(t) + L_W(t) \tag{5.64}$$

where $L_x(t) = V^*(x)$ and $L_W(t) = \frac{1}{2}\tilde{W}^T\tilde{W}$ with $\tilde{W} = W - \hat{W}$.
- The directional derivative of the Lyapunov can be expressed as

$$\dot{L}(x, \tilde{W}) = \dot{L}_x(t) + \dot{L}_W(t). \tag{5.65}$$

- Substituting the system dynamics and the weight estimation error dynamics using the update rule, we obtain the expression for the slope of the Lyapunov candidate function.

- Using the optimal Hamiltonian $H(x,u^*,e^*_{s,u}) = 0$ and simplification using standard vector norm inequalities, the bounds $\mathscr{B}_x$ and $\mathscr{B}_W$ can be obtained.

Remark 5.8. *Note that the bounds on the closed loop signals are obtained as a function of the NN reconstruction error. It is known that as the number of hidden layer neurons are increased, the reconstruction error converges to zero. In this special case, by appropriate design of the NN approximator, one can bring the state vector and the NN weight estimation error arbitrarily close to zero asymptotically.*

Table 5.2
Co-optimization of sampling instants and control policy for nonlinear systems

System dynamics	$\dot{x}(t) = f(x(t)) + g(x(t))u(t), x(0) = x_0$
Event-triggering error	$e_{s,u}(t) = u_e(t) - u(t)$
Performance index	$J(x, e_{s,u}, u) = \int_t^\infty [\|\zeta(\tau)\|^2 - \sigma^2 e^T_{s,u} e_{s,u}] d\tau$
Value function approximation	$\hat{V}(x) = \hat{W}^T \phi(x)$
Critic NN update law	$\dot{\hat{W}} = \begin{cases} -\alpha \frac{[\Delta\phi(\tau)]}{(1+[\Delta\phi(\tau)]^T[\Delta\phi(\tau)])^2} \chi_k^T, \ t = t_k \\ -\alpha \frac{[\Delta\phi(\tau)]}{(1+[\Delta\phi(\tau)]^T[\Delta\phi(\tau)])^2} \chi^T(t_k), \ t \in (t_k, t_{k+1}). \end{cases}$
Optimal control input	$u_e(t) = -\frac{1}{2} R^{-1} g^T(x_e) \hat{V}_{x_e} = -\frac{1}{2} R^{-1} g^T(x_e) \nabla^T \phi(x_e) \hat{W}$
Event-triggering condition	$\|e_{s,u}(t)\| \leq \|\hat{e}_{s,u}(t)\|, \ t \in [t_k, t_{k+1}), \forall k \in \{0, \mathbb{N}\}$

Example 5.3. *Consider the unstable continuous-time nonlinear system dynamics as in Dierks and Jagannathan (2010b) given by*

$$\begin{aligned} \dot{x}_1 &= -(29x_1 + 87x_1x_2^2)/8 - (2x_2 + 3x_2x_1^2)/4 + u_1 \\ \dot{x}_2 &= -(x_1 + 3x_1x_2^2)/4 + 3u_2. \end{aligned}$$

The analytical solution to the HJI equation (optimal value function) was calculated as $V^*(x) = x_1^2 + 2x_2^2 + 3x_1x_2$ by Dierks and Jagannathan (2010b). For the example results presented here, the simulation parameters were selected as described by Dierks and Jagannathan (2010b), with $\sigma = 0.7$. The NN weights are initialized with random values in the interval [-2, 2]. The first layer weights are fixed at the random values and sigmoid activation function is utilized in the hidden layer neurons.

To verify if the game-theoretic method developed in this section offers any advantage, the results obtained with this method are compared with that of an event-triggered optimal approximate controller with the event-triggering condition developed by Narayanan and Jagannathan (2016a).

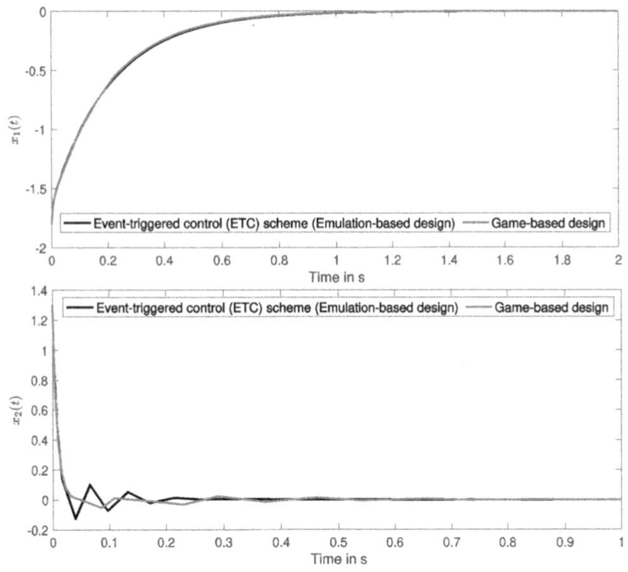

Figure 5.10 Comparison of state trajectories

The convergence of the closed-loop system state is shown in Figure 5.10 and control inputs in Figure 5.11. It can be observed that the state trajectories are satisfactory with similar control efforts. The comparison between the inter-sampling times is shown in Figure 5.12 (top). Further, the lower bound on the inter-event times is observed to be 1 ms. It is clear from Figure 5.12 (top) that the inter-event times are elongated, reducing resource utilization, which is one of the primary objectives of the design. Further, it is observed that the average inter-event time is increased considerably. The comparison of the cumulative cost function in Figure 5.12 (bottom) reveals the benefit of using the game-theoretic scheme resulting in lower cost.

5.3 CO-OPTIMIZED TRACKING CONTROL OF NONLINEAR SYSTEMS

We shall now expand the game-theoretic co-design technique for designing a tracking controller for nonlinear dynamical systems. Trajectory tracking control (Tallapragada and Chopra, 2013; Postoyan et al., 2015; Cheng and Ugrinovskii, 2016; Peng et al., 2016; Gao and Chen, 2008), which concerns with the problem of steering the system state or the output of a system along a desired trajectory, has a wide range of practical applications. Examples include leader-follower architecture of mobile robots (Cheng and Ugrinovskii, 2016; Han et al., 2015), autonomous systems employed for surveillance (Postoyan et al., 2015), and target tracking radars. In a trajectory tracking control, the control policy is, in general, time-varying which leads to a continuous control effort to keep the tracking error minimum. Therefore, a time-based periodic implementation of a tracking control policy requires significantly higher computations when compared to a state regulation problem. We have reviewed the event-based tracking controllers (Tallapragada and Chopra, 2013; Cheng and Ugrinovskii, 2016; Postoyan et al., 2015) in Chapter 1 while their optimal counterpart was discussed in Chapter 2.

This section, based on the work by Sahoo and Narayanan (2019), presents a performance-based sampling scheme for trajectory tracking control. A performance index is introduced, which aids in designing the optimal triggering threshold. The event-based tracking error system is formulated by incorporating the error between the continuous control policy and the event-based control policy, referred to as *sampled error policy* or the *threshold policy*. An augmented tracking error system,

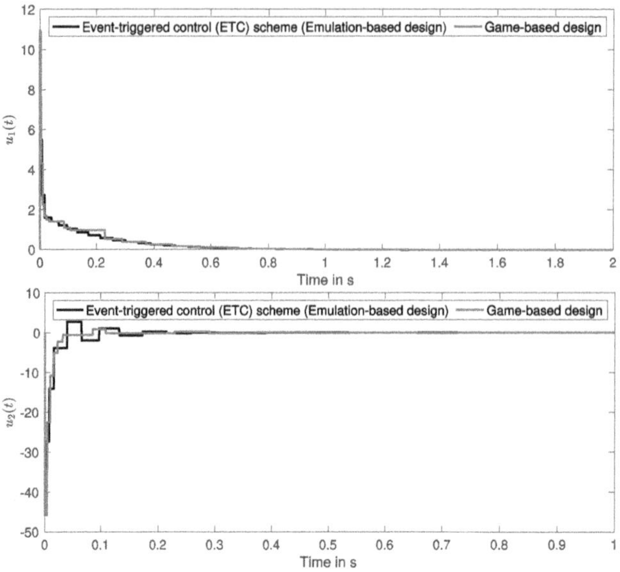

Figure 5.11 Comparison of control policies

similar to the one developed in Chapter 2, in an event-based formalism, is defined.

The solution to the HJI equation, i.e., the optimal value function, is approximated using a functional link critic neural network. Event-based intermittently available state information is used as the input of the NN. The estimated optimal control policy and the triggering threshold are computed from the approximated value function. Since the triggering threshold is a function of the estimated NN weights, which are updated with an impulsive update scheme, the triggering condition becomes adaptive. To avoid the Zeno behavior of the closed-loop system during the learning period, a lower bound on the adaptive threshold is enforced. We shall see that for the event-based tracking problem, the tracking error and the NN weight estimation errors are ultimately bounded.

5.3.1 BACKGROUND AND PROBLEM DEFINITION

Recall the problem setup for a tracking control design task from Chapter 2. We begin with an affine nonlinear continuous-time system given in (5.34). The control objective is to track a *feasible* reference trajectory $x_d(t) \in \mathbb{R}^n$ generated by a reference system

$$\dot{x}_d(t) = \zeta(x_d(t)), \ \ x_d(0) = x_{d0}, \tag{5.66}$$

where $x_d(t) \in \mathbb{R}^n$ is the reference state and $\zeta : \mathbb{R}^n \to \mathbb{R}^n$ is the internal dynamics with $\zeta(0) = 0$. Following standard characteristics of the systems in (5.34) and (5.66) are assumed.

Assumption 5.5. *The system described by* (5.34) *is controllable and its states are available for measurement.*

Assumption 5.6. *The functions $f(x)$ and $g(x)$ are Lipschitz continuous for all $x \in \Omega_x$, where Ω_x is a compact set containing the origin. Further, the function $g(x)$ has a full column rank for all $x \in \Omega_x$ and satisfies $\|g(x)\| \leq g_M$ for some constant $g_M > 0$. In addition, $g(x_d)g^+(x_d) = I$, where $g^+ = (g^T g)^{-1} g^T$.*

Assumption 5.7. *The feasible reference trajectory $x_d(t) \in \Omega_{x_d}$, where Ω_{x_d} is a compact set, is bounded such that $\|x_d(t)\| \leq b_{x_d}$, where $b_{x_d} > 0$ is a constant.*

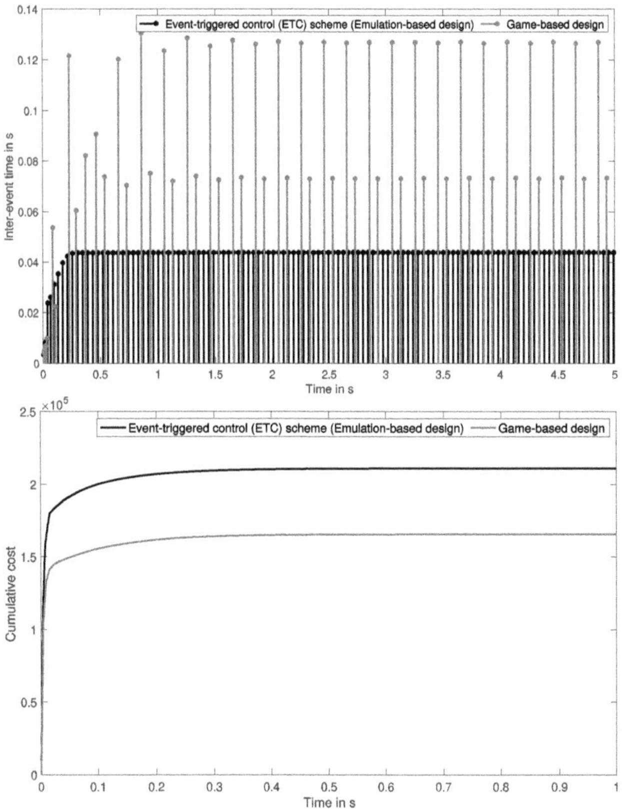

Figure 5.12 Comparison of (top) inter-event time; and (bottom) cumulative cost.

Define the error between the system state and the reference state as the tracking error, given by $e_r(t) \triangleq x(t) - x_d(t)$. Then, the tracking error system, utilizing (2.164) and (5.66), can be defined by

$$\dot{e}_r(t) = \dot{x}(t) - \dot{x}_d(t) = f(e_r + x_d) + g(e_r + x_d)u(t) - \zeta(x_d). \tag{5.67}$$

The steady-state feed-forward control policy for the given reference trajectory (see Chapter 2) can be expressed as

$$u_d(t) = g^+(x_d)(\zeta(x_d)) - f(x_d), \tag{5.68}$$

where $u_d : \mathbb{R}^n \to \mathbb{R}^m$ is the steady state control policy corresponding to the reference trajectory. By augmenting the tracking error e_r and desired trajectory x_d, the dynamics of the augmented tracking error system can be represented as

$$\dot{\chi}(t) = F(\chi(t)) + G(\chi(t))w(t), \tag{5.69}$$

where $\chi(t) \triangleq [e_r^T(t) \;\; x_d^T(t)]^T \in \mathbb{R}^{2n}$ is the augmented state with $\chi(0) = [e_r^T(0) \;\; x_d^T(0)]^T = \chi_0$, $F : \mathbb{R}^{2n} \to \mathbb{R}^{2n}$ is given by $F(\chi) \triangleq \begin{bmatrix} f(e_r + x_d) + g(e_r + x_d)u_d - \zeta(x_d) \\ \zeta(x_d) \end{bmatrix}$, $G : \mathbb{R}^{2n} \to \mathbb{R}^{2n \times m}$ given by $G(\chi) \triangleq \begin{bmatrix} g(e_r + x_d) \\ 0 \end{bmatrix}$, and the mismatched control policy $w(t) \triangleq u(t) - u_d(t) \in \mathbb{R}^m$. Further, we require that $F(0) = 0$.

The infinite horizon performance index with state constraint enforced by the dynamical system in (5.69) can be defined as

$$J(\chi(0), w(0)) = \int_0^\infty [\chi^T(\tau)\bar{Q}\chi(\tau) + w(\tau)^T R w(\tau)] d\tau \tag{5.70}$$

where $\bar{Q} \triangleq \begin{bmatrix} Q & \mathbf{0}_{n\times n} \\ \mathbf{0}_{n\times n} & \mathbf{0}_{n\times n} \end{bmatrix} \in \mathbb{R}^{2n\times 2n}$ with $Q \in \mathbb{R}^{n\times n}$ and $R \in \mathbb{R}^{m\times m}$ are symmetric positive definite matrices. The matrix $\mathbf{0}_{n\times n}$ is a matrix with all elements zero. Note that the performance index is defined using the mismatched policy w (Sahoo and Narayanan, 2019; Kamalapurkar et al., 2015) and, therefore, the cost functional is finite for any admissible control policy $w \in \Omega_w$, where Ω_w is the set of all admissible policies.

5.3.2 EVENT-BASED TRACKING PROBLEM

In an ETC formalism, the system state $x(t_k)$ is sent to the controller at the time instants $t_k, \forall k \in \{0, \mathbb{N}\}$. The sampled state at the controller can be written as

$$x_s(t) = x(t_k), \quad \forall t \in [t_k, t_{k+1}). \tag{5.71}$$

In this section, note that we use a different notation (x_s) to represent event-triggered state feedback information. This is to prevent any potential ambiguity with notations related to reference trajectory (indicated by subscript notation) and NN estimates (denoted by the $\hat{(\cdot)}$ notation).

The event-based control policy, executed at the sampling instants $t_k, \forall k \in \{0, \mathbb{N}\}$ with the state information $x_s(t)$ and reference trajectory $x_{ds} = x_d(t_k), \forall t \in [t_k, t_{k+1})$, can be represented as

$$u_s(t) = \mu(x_s(t) - x_{ds}(t)) = \mu(e_r(t), t_k), \quad \forall t \in [t_k, t_{k+1}), \tag{5.72}$$

where $\mu : \mathbb{R}^n \times \mathbb{R}_{\geq 0} \to \mathbb{R}^m$. The control policy $u_s(t)$ is held at the actuator using a zero-order hold and applied to the system till the next update. Therefore, the event-based control policy is a piece-wise constant function.

The event-based nonlinear system can be rewritten with event-based control policy u_s as

$$\dot{x}(t) = f(x) + g(x)u_s(t). \tag{5.73}$$

We define the error between the continuous control input $u(t) \triangleq \mu(x(t), x_d(t)) = \mu(e_r(t), t)$ and the event-based control input $u_s(t)$ in (5.72) as sampled error policy, $e_u(t) \in \mathbb{R}^m$, which is given by

$$e_u(t) = u_s(t) - u(t). \tag{5.74}$$

The event-triggered system dynamics in (5.73), with sampled error policy in (5.74), lead to

$$\dot{x}(t) = f(x) + g(x)u(t) + g(x)e_u(t). \tag{5.75}$$

The tracking error dynamics, with the event-triggered system (5.75) and the reference system (5.66), becomes

$$\dot{e}_r(t) = f(e_r + x_d) + g(e_r + x_d)u(t) + g(e_r + x_d)e_u(t) - \zeta(x_d). \tag{5.76}$$

The event-based augmented tracking error system, from (5.76) and (5.66), can be represented as

$$\dot{\chi}(t) = F(\chi) + G(\chi)w(t) + G(\chi)e_u(t). \tag{5.77}$$

Our main objective is to develop a unified design scheme by minimizing a performance index such that both the sampling intervals and the control policy are optimized. Therefore the problem in hand is threefold: 1) redefinition of the time-invariant performance index in (5.70) to obtain the worst case threshold for the sampled error policy, e_u in (5.77), which in turn determines the event-based sampling intervals; 2) design of the event-based sampling condition such that the sampling intervals are maximized; and 3) design of the NN weight update law for approximation of the solution of the corresponding HJI equation in an ETC framework. While at this point, one may follow the developments from Section 5.2.2, there are subtle differences in developing a tracking controller. We shall develop the solution to the tracking control problem next.

5.3.3 PERFORMANCE INDEX AND SOLUTION TO THE MIN-MAX OPTIMIZATION

In this section, the co-design problem is formulated as a min-max optimization problem by introducing a performance index. A saddle point solution to the optimization problem is obtained by solving the associated HJI equation.

Reformulation of Performance Index

The event-based sampling instants can be designed by triggering the events when the sampled error policy, e_u, in (5.74) reaches a maximum value without jeopardizing the stability. Alternatively, the design is to obtain an optimal threshold for $e_u(t)$, to determine the triggering instants with respect to the desired performance of the system. With this effect, redefine the cost functional (5.70) with the dynamic constraint (5.77) as

$$J(\chi, w, \hat{e}_u) = \int_0^\infty [\chi^T(\tau)\bar{Q}\chi(\tau) + w(\tau)^T Rw(\tau) - \gamma^2 \hat{e}_u^T(\tau)\hat{e}_u(\tau)]d\tau, \tag{5.78}$$

where $\gamma > \gamma^*$ represents the penalizing factor for the threshold $\hat{e}_u$ of sampled error policy e_u with $\gamma^* > 0$ such that the performance index is finite for all admissible w.

Note that the performance index (5.78) is minimized by maximizing the threshold $\hat{e}_u$ and minimizing the control policy w. Therefore, the optimization problem leads to a min-max problem having two players. The mismatch control policy, w, acts as player 1, i.e., the minimizing player, and the threshold, $\hat{e}_u$, as player 2, i.e., the maximizing player. The objective, now, can be redefined as solving the two-player zero-sum-game (Basar and Bernhard, 2008) to reach at the saddle-point optimal value, $V^* : \mathbb{R}^{2n} \to \mathbb{R}_{\geq 0}$, i.e., the optimal value where $\min_{w} \max_{\hat{e}_u} J(\chi, w, \hat{e}_u) = \max_{\hat{e}_u} \min_{w} J(\chi, w, \hat{e}_u)$.

Remark 5.9. *The traditional min-max problem (Basar and Bernhard, 2008) optimizes the control policy in the presence of an independent disturbance, explicitly added to the system dynamics, by using a performance index similar to* (5.78)*. However, the threshold $\hat{e}_u$ in* (5.78) *is implied in the system dynamics* (5.76)*. The main advantage of the proposed performance index is to obtain the worst case value of $\hat{e}_u$ in terms of system state χ, which can be used as the threshold for sampled error policy e_u. Note that this is a function of the reference trajectory.*

From (5.78) the saddle-point optimal value, V^*, can be written as

$$V^*(\chi) = \min_{w(\tau)|\tau \in \mathbb{R}_{\geq t}} \; \max_{\hat{e}_u(\tau)|\tau \in \mathbb{R}_{\geq t}} \int_t^\infty \left[\chi^T(\tau)\bar{Q}\chi(\tau) + w(\tau)^T Rw(\tau) - \gamma^2 \hat{e}_u^T(\tau)\hat{e}_u(\tau)\right] d\tau. \tag{5.79}$$

Define the Hamiltonian, with the admissible control policy and dynamic constraint (5.77), as

$$\mathscr{H}(\chi, w, \hat{e}_u) = \chi^T(t)\bar{Q}\chi(t) + w^T(t)Rw(t) - \gamma^2 \hat{e}_u^T(t)\hat{e}_u(t) + V_\chi^{*T}[F(\chi) + G(\chi)w(t) + Ge_u(t)], \tag{5.80}$$

where $V_\chi^* = \partial V^*/\partial \chi$. By using the stationarity conditions, $\frac{\partial \mathscr{H}(\chi, w, \hat{e}_u)}{\partial w} = 0$ and $\frac{\partial \mathscr{H}(\chi, w, \hat{e}_u)}{\partial \hat{e}_u} = 0$, the optimal mismatch control policy

$$w^*(\chi) = -\frac{1}{2}R^{-1}G^T(\chi)V_\chi^*(\chi) \tag{5.81}$$

and the worst-case threshold value

$$e_u^*(\chi) = \frac{1}{2\gamma^2}G^T(\chi)V_\chi^*(\chi). \tag{5.82}$$

From (5.81) and (5.68) the continuous optimal control policy u^* is given by

$$u^*(t) = -\frac{1}{2}R^{-1}G^T(\chi)V_\chi^*(\chi) + g^+(x_d)(\zeta(x_d) - f(x_d)). \tag{5.83}$$

To implement the control policy (5.83) in the ETC framework, the augmented state at the controller can be expressed as

$$\chi_s(t) = \chi(t_k),\ \forall t \in [t_k, t_{k+1}), \tag{5.84}$$

where $\chi(t_k) = [e_r^T(t_k), x_d^T(t_k)]^T, \forall k \in \{0, \mathbb{N}\}$. The event-sampled optimal control policy u_s^* with the augmented sampled state can be expressed as

$$u_s^*(t) = -\frac{1}{2}R^{-1}G^T(\chi_s)V_{\chi_s}^* + g^+(x_{ds})(\zeta(x_{ds}) - f(x_{ds})). \tag{5.85}$$

where $V_{\chi_s}^* = \frac{\partial V^*(\chi)}{\partial \chi}|_{\chi=\chi_s}$. The HJI equation with optimal policies (5.81) and (5.82) is given by

$$\mathscr{H}^* = \chi^T(t)\bar{Q}\chi(t) + w^{*T}(t)Rw^*(t) - \gamma^2 e_u^{*T}(t)e_u^*(t) + V_\chi^{*T}[F(\chi) + G(\chi)w^*(t) + G(\chi)e_u^*(t)] = 0 \tag{5.86}$$

for all χ with $V^*(0) = 0$. The following assumption regarding the HJI equation is essential to proceed further.

Assumption 5.8. *The solution to the HJI equation, i.e., the optimal value function V^*, exists and is continuously differentiable.*

Remark 5.10. *Note that the solution of the HJI equation* (5.86), *i.e., the optimal value function, V^*, exists for a reachable and zero-state observable system for $\gamma > \gamma^*$, where γ^* is the H_∞ gain (Basar and Bernhard, 2008).*

5.3.4 OPTIMAL EVENT-SAMPLING CONDITION AND STABILITY ANALYSIS

The sampling condition for the triggering mechanism can be defined using worst-case sampled error e_u^* as the threshold. Define the sampling condition as

$$t_{k+1} = \inf\{t > t_k | e_u(t)^T e_u(t) = \max\{r^2, \frac{1}{4\gamma^4}V_\chi^{*T}GG^TV_\chi^*\}\} \tag{5.87}$$

with $t_0 = 0$. The parameter $r > 0$ is a design choice.

Remark 5.11. *The parameter $r > 0$ is introduced in the triggering condition to enforce the positive minimum inter-sample time, i.e., Zeno-free behavior of the system, and can be arbitrarily selected close to zero. However, this minimum threshold on triggering condition leads to bounded stability of the ETC system.*

Next, the stability results of the optimal event-triggered system are presented in the theorem. The transformation of the time-varying tracking control problem to a time-invariant problem results in a positive semidefinite optimal value function (5.79) (Kamalapurkar et al., 2015), rendering it unsuitable to be treated as a Lyapunov candidate function. This shortcoming is overcome by considering the time-variant counterpart of the time-invariant optimal value function V^* given by $V_t^* : \mathbb{R}^n \times \mathbb{R}_{\geq 0} \to \mathbb{R}$, where $V_t^*(e_r, t) = V^*([e_r^T,\ x_d^T(t)]^T)$ for all $e_r \in \mathbb{R}^n$ and for all $t \in \mathbb{R}_{\geq 0}$. It was shown by Kamalapurkar et al. (2015) that $V_t^* : \mathbb{R}^n \times \mathbb{R}_{\geq 0} \to \mathbb{R}$ is a valid candidate Lyapunov function.

Before presenting the stability results, the following technical lemma, which also establishes the ISS of the system (5.77) with respect to the sampled error policy, is presented.

Lemma 5.3. *(Sahoo and Narayanan, 2019) Consider the augmented tracking error system* (5.77) *and the performance index* (5.78). *Let the solution to the HJI equation (5.86) be V^*, and the Assumptions 5.5-5.8 hold. Then the mismatch optimal policy* (5.81) *renders the augmented system* (5.77) *local ISS with respect to $e_u(t)$.*

Theorem 5.6. *(Sahoo and Narayanan, 2019) Consider the affine nonlinear system (2.164) and the reference system* (5.66), *reformulated as event-sampled augmented tracking error system* (5.77). *Let V^* be the solution of the HJI equation (5.86), and the Assumptions 5.5 - 5.8 hold. Then, with the event-based optimal control policy* (5.85) *and event-based sampling condition* (5.87), *the tracking error is ultimately bounded provided γ satisfies $\gamma^2 > \lambda_{max}(R)$.*

From the optimal value perspective, the next corollary quantifies the degree of optimality by computing the optimal value for the event-triggered implementation when compared to the continuous saddle point optimal value.

Corollary 5.3. *(Sahoo and Narayanan, 2019) Let the hypothesis of Theorem 5.6 hold. Then, the optimal cost for the event-triggered implementation with policy w_s^* is given by*

$$J(;, w_s^*) = V^*(\chi) + \int_t^{\infty} [e_u^T(R - \gamma^2 I)e_u - \gamma^2 e_u^{*T} e_u^*] d\tau. \tag{5.88}$$

Note that the cost due to event-triggering introduces the second term in (5.88). Although not surprising, the event-based implementation can perform no better than the continuous implementation in terms of the performance cost. This also indicates that the cost can be adjusted by parameters R and γ.

Remark 5.12. *The performance index in* (5.78) *provides an extra degree of freedom, in terms of the parameter γ, in optimizing the value when compared to the optimal value in (Vamvoudakis et al., 2017b). In addition, when compared to the threshold coefficient parameter σ in the traditional event-triggering condition in (Tabuada, 2007), this penalizing term γ as threshold coefficient in the sampling condition* (5.87) *also determines the degree of optimality.*

5.3.5 ZENO-FREE BEHAVIOR OF SYSTEM

To show the sampling instants are not accumulated, i.e., Zeno-free behavior of the system, we will use a more conservative event-sampling condition. Define the augmented state sampling error e_s as the error between the continuous augmented state $\chi(t)$ and the sampled augmented state $\chi_s(t)$. It can be expressed as

$$e_s(t) = \chi_s(t) - \chi(t), \quad \forall t \in [t_k, t_{k+1}). \tag{5.89}$$

The following standard assumption and the technical lemma are necessary to proceed.

Assumption 5.9. *The optimal policies u^* and e_u^* are locally Lipschitz in a compact set, such that, $\|u_s^* - u^*\| = \|e_u\| \le L_u \|e_s\|$ and $\|e_u^*(\chi) - e_u^*(\chi_s)\| \le L_u \|e_s\|$ where $L_u > 0$ is the Lipschitz constant.*

Lemma 5.4. *If the inequality $L_u\|e_s(t)\| \le (1/4\gamma^2)\|G^T(\chi_s)V_{\chi_s}^*\|$ holds, then the inequality $e_u^T(t)e_u(t) \le (1/4\gamma^4)V_\chi^{*T} G(\chi)G^T(\chi)V_\chi^*$ also holds.*

Proof. ■ By definition we have $\frac{1}{4\gamma^2}\|G^T(\chi_s)V_{\chi_s}^*\| = \frac{1}{2}\|e_u^*(t_k)\|$ and, therefore, the expression

$$L_u\|e_s(t)\| \le (1/4\gamma^2)\|G^T(\chi_s)V_{\chi_s}^*\|$$

can be rewritten as

$$2L_u\|e_s(t)\| \le \|e_u^*(t_k)\| = \|e_u^*(t) + e_u^*(t_k) - e_u^*(t)\| \le \|e_u^*(t)\| + \|e_u^*(t_k) - e_u^*(t)\| \le \|e_u^*(t)\| + L_u\|e_s(t)\|.$$

■ Rearranging the expression leads to

$$L_u\|e_s(t)\| \le \|e_u^*(t)\|. \tag{5.90}$$

- By Assumption 5.9, $\|e_u(t)\| < L_u\|e_s(t)\|$, comparing with (5.90), it holds that $\|e_u(t)\| \leq \|e_u^*(t)\|$. Squaring both side it holds that

$$e_u^T(t)e_u(t) \leq (1/4\gamma^4)V_\chi^{*T}G(\chi)G^T(\chi)V_\chi^*.$$

□

Corollary 5.4. *(Sahoo and Narayanan, 2019) Let the hypothesis of the Theorem 5.6 holds. Then, the sampling condition defined by*

$$t_{k+1} = \inf\{t > t_k \mid L_u\|e_s(t)\| = \max\{r, \frac{1}{4\gamma^2}\|G^T(\chi_s)V_{\chi_s}^*\|\}, \tag{5.91}$$

ensures the tracking error convergence to it's ultimate bound. Further, the minimum inter-sample time $\tau_m = \inf_{k\in\{0,\mathbb{N}\}}(\tau_k) = \inf_{k\in\{0,\mathbb{N}\}}(t_{k+1} - t_k) > 0$ *where* τ_k *is given by*

$$\tau_k > \frac{1}{\kappa_1}\ln\left(\frac{\kappa_1 r}{\kappa_2} + 1\right), \tag{5.92}$$

where $\kappa_1 = G_M L_u + L_u\rho$ and $\kappa_3 = L_u\rho\|\chi_s\|$.

Since, an analytical closed-form solution to the HJI equation (5.86) is difficult to compute (Bellman, 1966), the solution is approximated using a NN and is presented in the next section.

5.3.6 APPROXIMATE SOLUTION FOR THE MIN-MAX OPTIMIZATION PROBLEM

In this section, the optimal value function, which is the solution of the HJI equation is approximated using a functional link NN to design the optimal control policy and the sampling condition.

Value Function Approximation and Event-sampled Bellman Error. Recalling the Assumption 5.8, the solution to the HJI equation, i.e., the optimal value function $V^*(\chi)$ is smooth and continuous. By the universal approximation property (Lewis et al., 1998), the value function can be approximated using neural network, referred to as *critic NN*, in a compact set $\Omega_\chi \subset \mathbb{R}^{2n}$. Alternatively, in a compact set Ω_χ, there exists an ideal weight vector W and a basis function $\phi(\chi)$ such that the value function can be expressed as

$$V^*(\chi) = W^T\phi(\chi) + \varepsilon(\chi) \tag{5.93}$$

where $W \in \mathbb{R}^{l_o}$ is the target weight vector, which is unknown, $\phi : \mathbb{R}^{2n} \to \mathbb{R}^{l_o}$ is the activation function, and $\varepsilon : \mathbb{R}^{2n} \to \mathbb{R}$ is the approximation error. Further, the activation function satisfy $\phi(0) = 0$ and l_o is the number of neurons in the hidden layer. The following standard assumption for the NN is used for analysis.

Assumption 5.10. *The unknown target weight vector W, the activation function* ϕ*, and the reconstruction error* ε *are bounded in the compact sets. This means, there exists constants* $W_M > 0$, $\phi_M > 0$ *and* $\varepsilon_M > 0$ *such that,* $\|W\| \leq W_M$, $\sup_{\chi\in\Omega_\chi}\|\phi(\chi)\| \leq \phi_M$, *and* $\sup_{\chi\in\Omega_\chi}\|\varepsilon(\chi)\| \leq \varepsilon_M$. *Further, the gradient of approximation error satisfies* $\sup_{\chi\in\Omega_\chi}\|\nabla\varepsilon(\chi)\| \leq \bar{\varepsilon}_M$, *where* $\bar{\varepsilon}_M > 0$ *is a constant and* $\nabla\varepsilon(\chi) = \frac{\partial\varepsilon(\chi)}{\partial\chi}$.

The optimal mismatch control policy in a parametric form using NN approximation can be computed as

$$w^*(\chi) = -(1/2)R^{-1}G^T(\chi)(\nabla\phi^T(\chi)W + \nabla\varepsilon(\chi)), \tag{5.94}$$

and, similarly, the worst case threshold becomes

$$e_u^*(\chi) = -(1/2\gamma^2)G^T(\chi)(\nabla\phi^T(\chi)W + \nabla\varepsilon(\chi)), \tag{5.95}$$

where $\nabla\phi(\chi) = \frac{\partial\phi(\chi)}{\partial\chi}$. The estimated value function $\hat{V}(\chi)$ is given by

$$\hat{V}(\chi) = \hat{W}^T\phi(\chi_s), \ \ \forall t \in [t_k, t_{k+1}), \tag{5.96}$$

where $\hat{W} \in \mathbb{R}^{l_o}$ is NN weight estimates and $\phi(\chi_s) \in \mathbb{R}^{l_o}$ is the activation function with sampled augmented state χ_s as input. Then, estimated mismatch control policy

$$w(\chi) = -(1/2)R^{-1}G^T(\chi)(\nabla\phi^T(\chi_s)\hat{W}) \tag{5.97}$$

and the estimated control input can be expressed as

$$u(t) = -\frac{1}{2}R^{-1}G^T(\chi)\nabla\phi^T(\chi_s)\hat{W} + g^+(x_d)(\zeta(x_d) - f(x_d)). \tag{5.98}$$

The estimated sampled control policy now can be expressed as

$$u_s(t) = -(1/2)R^{-1}G^T(\chi_s)\nabla\phi^T(\chi_s)\hat{W} + g^+(x_{ds})(\zeta(x_{ds}) - f(x_{ds})), \forall t \in [t_k, t_{k+1}). \tag{5.99}$$

Further, the estimated threshold is given by

$$\hat{e}_u(t) = (1/2\gamma^2)G^T(\chi)\nabla\phi^T(\chi_s)\hat{W}. \tag{5.100}$$

To update the weights of the critic NN we will use the Bellman principle of optimality. Note that, the value function (5.78) in the ETC frame work can equivalently be expressed as

$$J(\chi(0)) = \sum_{k=0}^{\infty}\left(\int_{t_k}^{t_k+\tau_k}(\chi^T\bar{Q}\chi + w^TRw - \gamma^2\hat{e}_u^T\hat{e}_u)d\tau\right).$$

By Bellman principle of optimality, the Bellman equation in an integral from is given by

$$V^*(t_{k+1}) - V^*(t_k) = \int_{t_k}^{t_{k+1}}\left(-\chi^T\bar{Q}\chi - w^TRw + \gamma^2\hat{e}_u^T\hat{e}_u\right)d\tau, \tag{5.101}$$

where $t_{k+1} = t_k + \tau_k$. The event-based integral Bellman equation (5.101), with the critic NN (5.93), yields

$$W^T\Delta\phi(\tau_k) + \Delta\varepsilon(\tau_k) = \textstyle\int_{t_k}^{t_{k+1}}(-\chi^T\bar{Q}\chi - w^TRw + \gamma^2\hat{e}_u^T\hat{e}_u)d\tau, \tag{5.102}$$

where $\Delta\phi(\tau_k) = \phi(\chi(t_{k+1})) - \phi(\chi(t_k))$ and $\Delta\varepsilon(\tau_k) = \varepsilon(\chi(t_{k+1})) - \varepsilon(\chi(t_k))$. With estimated critic NN weights (5.96), the Bellman error can be expressed as

$$\begin{aligned}\delta_{k+1} &= \textstyle\int_{t_k}^{t_{k+1}}(\chi^T\bar{Q}\chi + w^TRw - \gamma^2\hat{e}_u^T\hat{e}_u)d\tau + \hat{V}(t_{k+1}) - \hat{V}(t_k)\\ &= \textstyle\int_{t_k}^{t_{k+1}}(\chi^T\bar{Q}\chi + w^TRw - \gamma^2\hat{e}_u^T\hat{e}_u)d\tau + \hat{W}^T\Delta\phi(\tau_k),\end{aligned} \tag{5.103}$$

where δ_{k+1} is the Bellman residual error or temporal difference error calculated at the occurrence of $k+1$ event.

The critic NN weights are learned online such that the Bellman residual error (5.103) is minimized. Since the augmented system states at the controller are updated only at the sampling instants, the Bellman residual error (5.103) can only be computed at the sampling instants. Therefore, the NN weights are updated as a jump in the weight at the triggering instants $t_k, \forall k \in \{0, \mathbb{N}\}$ with the new state feedback information, given as

$$\hat{W}^+ = \hat{W} - \alpha_2\frac{\Delta\phi(\tau_{k-1})}{(1+\Delta\phi^T(\tau_{k-1})\Delta\phi(\tau_{k-1}))^2}\delta_k^T, \ t = t_k, \tag{5.104}$$

where $\hat{W}^+ = \hat{W}(t_k^+)$ and t_k^+ is the time instant just after t_k. Further, to utilize the inter-sample times and accelerate the convergence of NN weights, the Bellman residual error computed at the previous sampling instants t_k is used to update the critic NN weight estimates. The continuous update (flow) during the inter-sample times is defined as

$$\dot{\hat{W}} = -\alpha_1 \frac{\Delta\phi(\tau_{k-1})}{(1+\Delta\phi^T(\tau_{k-1})\Delta\phi(\tau_{k-1}))^2}\delta_k^T,\; t \in (t_k, t_{k+1}), \tag{5.105}$$

where $\delta_k = \int_{t_{k-1}}^{t_k}(\chi^T\bar{Q}\chi + w^T Rw - \gamma^2\hat{e}_u^T\hat{e}_u)d\tau + \hat{W}^T\Delta\phi(\tau_{k-1})$ is the Bellman residual error at t_k, derived from (5.103) with $\alpha_1 > 0$, and $\alpha_2 > 0$ are learning gains.

Remark 5.13. *Note that the integration $\int_{t_{k-1}}^{t_k}(\cdot)d\tau$ and the difference $\Delta\phi(\tau_k)$ can be computed using the augmented state χ and mismatch control input w information at two consecutive sampling instants t_k and t_{k-1}, which are available at the controller at the kth-time instant.*

Remark 5.14. *The update laws in* (5.104) *and* (5.105) *can be referred to as impulsive parameter update scheme with* (5.104) *as jump and* (5.105) *as flow dynamics. Further, the update during the inter-sample times is motivated by the traditional value/policy iteration based ADP schemes (Bertsekas, 2012). This ensures boundedness of the closed-loop system parameters during the flow periods when the control policy is not updated.*

5.3.7 ADAPTIVE EVENT-SAMPLING CONDITION AND STABILITY

The event-based sampling condition with estimated $\hat{e}_u$ in (5.100) can be defined as

$$t_{k+1} = \inf\{t > t_k \mid e_u(t)^T e_u(t) = \max(r^2, \frac{1}{4\gamma^4}\hat{W}^T\nabla\phi(\chi_s)G(\chi)G^T(\chi)\nabla\phi^T(\chi_s)\hat{W})\}. \tag{5.106}$$

Defining the NN weight estimation error $\tilde{W} = W - \hat{W}$, the Bellman residual error, by subtracting (5.103) from (5.102) with a event-step backward, can be represented as

$$\delta_k = -\tilde{W}^T\Delta\phi(\tau_{k-1}) - \Delta\varepsilon(\tau_{k-1}). \tag{5.107}$$

The Bellman residual error δ_k using (5.107) is not computable since the target NN weight W is unknown and will only be used for demonstrating the stability; presented in the next theorem.

The event-sampled augmented tracking error system, by defining a concatenated state vector $\xi = [\chi^T, \tilde{W}^T]^T \in \mathbb{R}^{2n+l_o}$, can be expressed as a nonlinear impulsive dynamical system as

$$\dot{\xi}(t) = \begin{bmatrix} F(\chi) + G(\chi)w(t) + G(\chi)e_u(t) \\ \alpha_1 \frac{\Delta\phi(\tau_{k-1})}{(1+\Delta\phi^T(\tau_{k-1})\Delta\phi(\tau_{k-1}))^2}\delta_k^T \end{bmatrix},\; \xi \in \mathscr{C},\; t \in (t_k, t_{k+1}) \tag{5.108}$$

and

$$\xi^+ = \begin{bmatrix} \chi \\ \tilde{W} + \alpha_2 \frac{\Delta\phi(\tau_{k-1})}{(1+\Delta\phi^T(\tau_{k-1})\Delta\phi(\tau_{k-1}))^2}\delta_k^T \end{bmatrix},\; \xi \in \mathscr{D},\; t = t_k, \tag{5.109}$$

where (5.108) are the dynamics of the system during the inter-sample times, referred to as flow dynamics, and (5.109) are the dynamics at the sampling instants referred to as jump dynamics. The sets

$$\mathscr{C} \triangleq \{\xi \in \mathbb{R}^{2n+l_o} \mid e_u(t)^T e_u(t) < \max(r^2, \frac{1}{4\gamma^4}\hat{W}^T\nabla\phi(\chi_s)G(\chi)G^T(\chi)\nabla\phi^T(\chi_s)\hat{W})\}$$

and

$$\mathscr{D} \triangleq \{\xi \in \mathbb{R}^{2n+l_o} \mid e_u(t)^T e_u(t) \geq \max(r^2, \frac{1}{4\gamma^4}\hat{W}^T\nabla\phi(\chi_s)G(\chi)G^T(\chi)\nabla\phi^T(\chi_s)\hat{W})\}$$

are the flow and jump sets, respectively.

For brevity and to facilitate the proof of the theorem, presented next, the following variables are defined.

$$g_r = GR^{-1}G^T, \quad g_\phi = \nabla\phi GR^{-1}G^T\nabla^T\phi, \quad g_\gamma = \nabla\phi GG^T\nabla^T\phi. \tag{5.110}$$

Further, using the Assumptions 5.6 and 5.10, the following bounds are are developed in compact set Ω_χ:

$$\begin{aligned}
&\|\tfrac{1}{2}W^T g_\phi + \tfrac{1}{2}\nabla\varepsilon^T g_r \nabla\phi^T\| = \iota_1, \ \|g_\gamma\| = \iota_2,\\
&\tfrac{1}{2}\|W^T\nabla\phi g_r \nabla\varepsilon\| + \tfrac{1}{2}\|\nabla\varepsilon^T g_r \nabla\varepsilon\| = \iota_3, \|g_r\| = \iota_4,\\
&\|g_\phi\| = \iota_5, \ (\iota_1 + \tfrac{\iota_2}{2\gamma^2}) = \varpi_1, \tfrac{\iota_2}{2\gamma^2}\|W\|^2 + \iota_3 = \varpi_2,\\
&\varpi_3 = \varpi_2 + \tfrac{\alpha}{4}\Delta\varepsilon_M^2, \ \varpi_5 = \tfrac{1}{2}\alpha^2\Delta\varepsilon_M^2 + \tfrac{1}{2}\alpha\Delta\varepsilon_M^2 + \tfrac{1}{2}\alpha^2\Delta\phi_M\Delta\varepsilon_M^2.
\end{aligned} \tag{5.111}$$

Moreover, the inequalities

$$\left\|\frac{\Delta\phi(\tau_{k-1})}{1+\Delta\phi^T(\tau_{k-1})\Delta\phi(\tau_{k-1})}\right\| \le \frac{1}{2}, \frac{1}{1+\Delta\phi^T(\tau_{k-1})\Delta\phi(\tau_{k-1})} \le 1 \tag{5.112}$$

for every vector $\Delta\phi$ are also utilized to claim the practical stability using Lyapunov analysis by the authors Sahoo and Narayanan (2019).

Before presenting the main results, the following standard assumption on the PE condition for parameter estimation is presented for completeness.

Assumption 5.11. *The vector* $\varphi(\tau) \triangleq \frac{\Delta\phi(\tau)}{1+\Delta\phi^T(\tau)\Delta\phi(\tau)} \in \mathbb{R}^{l_o}$ *is persistently exciting, i.e., there exist a time period* $T > 0$ *and a constant* $\varphi_\delta > 0$ *such that over the interval* $[t, t+T]$ *the regressor vector satisfies* $\int_t^{t+T}\varphi(\tau)\varphi^T(\tau)d\tau \ge \varphi_\delta I$, *where* I *is the identity matrix of appropriate dimensions.*

Theorem 5.7. *(Sahoo and Narayanan, 2019) Consider the event-triggered system represented as a nonlinear impulsive hybrid dynamical system in* (5.108) *and* (5.109) *with control policy (5.99). Suppose the Assumptions 5.5-5.11 hold, the NN initial weights* $\hat{W}(0)$ *initialized in a compact set* Ω_W *and the initial control policy be admissible. Then, there exists a positive integer* $N > 0$, *such that, the tracking error* e_r *and the NN weight estimation error* $\tilde{W}$, *is locally ultimately bounded for all sampling instants* $t_k > t_N$, *provided event-based sampling instants are obtained using (5.106) and the weight tuning gains are selected as* $0 < \alpha_1 < 1$ *and* $0 < \alpha_2 < \frac{1}{2}$. *Further,* $\|V^* - \hat{V}\|$ *and* $\|w_s - w_s^*\|$ *are also ultimately bounded.*

Corollary 5.5. *Let the hypothesis of Theorem 5.7 hold. Then, the set of the sequence of event sampling instants* $\{t_k \mid k \in \{0,\mathbb{N}\}, e_u^T e_u = \max(r^2, \frac{1}{4\gamma^4}\hat{W}^T\nabla\phi(\chi_s)GG^T(\chi)$
$\nabla^T\phi(\chi_s)\hat{W})\}$ *determined by (5.106) converges the closed neighborhood of the actual sampling sequence* $\{t_k \mid k \in \{0,\mathbb{N}\}, e_u(t)^T e_u(t) = \max\{r^2, (1/4\gamma^4)V_\chi^{*T}GG^TV_\chi^*\}\}$ *determined in* (5.87).

Corollary 5.6. *(Sahoo and Narayanan, 2019) Let the hypothesis of the Theorem 5.7 hold. Then, with the event-based sampling condition*

$$t_{k+1} = \inf\{t > t_k \mid L_u\|e_s(t)\| = \max\{r, \frac{1}{4\gamma^2}\|G^T(\chi_s)\hat{V}_{\chi_s}\|\}\} \tag{5.113}$$

the tracking error e_r *and NN weight estimation error* $\tilde{W}$ *are locally ultimately bounded. Further, the minimum inter-sample time* $\delta t_m = \inf_{k\in\{0,\mathbb{N}\}}(\delta t_k) > 0$, *where* δt_k *is given by*

$$\delta t_k > \frac{1}{\kappa_1}\ln\left(\frac{\kappa_1 r}{\kappa_2} + 1\right). \tag{5.114}$$

The implementation of the proposed analytical design is detailed in the flow chart shown in Figure 5.13.

Table 5.3
Co-optimization of sampling instants and control policy for trajectory tracking

System dynamics	$\dot{x}(t) = f(x(t)) + g(x(t))u(t), x(0) = x_0$
Reference system dynamics	$\dot{x}_d(t) = \zeta(x_d(t)),\ x_d(0) = x_{d0}$
Augmented error system	$\dot{\chi} = F(\chi) + G(\chi)w$
Event-triggering error	$e_u(t) = u_s(t) - u(t),$
Performance index	$J(\chi, w, \hat{e}_u) = \int_0^{\infty} [\chi^T(\tau)\bar{Q}\chi(\tau) + w(\tau)^T R w(\tau) - \gamma^2 \hat{e}_u^T(\tau)\hat{e}_u(\tau)] d\tau$
Value function approximation	$\hat{V}(\chi) = \hat{W}^T \phi(\chi_s),\ \forall t \in [t_k, t_{k+1})$
Critic NN update law	$\dot{\hat{W}} = -\alpha_1 \frac{\Delta\phi(\tau_{k-1})}{(1+\Delta\phi^T(\tau_{k-1})\Delta\phi(\tau_{k-1}))^2}\delta_k^T,\ t \in (t_k, t_{k+1})$ $\hat{W}^+ = \hat{W} - \alpha_2 \frac{\Delta\phi(\tau_{k-1})}{(1+\Delta\phi^T(\tau_{k-1})\Delta\phi(\tau_{k-1}))^2}\delta_k^T,\ t = t_k$
Optimal control input	$u_s(t) = -(1/2)R^{-1}G^T(\chi_s)\nabla\phi^T(\chi_s)\hat{W}$ $+ g^+(x_{ds})(\zeta(x_{ds}) - f(x_{ds})), \forall t \in [t_k, t_{k+1}).$
Event-triggering condition	$t_{k+1} = \inf\{t > t_k \vert e_u(t)^T e_u(t) = \max\{r^2, \frac{1}{4\gamma^4} V_\chi^{*T} G G^T V_\chi^*\}\}$

Example 5.4. *A numerical example of Van-der-Pol oscillator, whose dynamics is given by*

$$\dot{x}(t) = f(x) + g(x)u(t),$$

with $f = \left[x_2,\ x_2(x_1^2 - 1) + x_1\right]^T$ *and* $g = [0,\ 1]^T$, *is considered for the validation using simulation.*

The reference trajectory considered is given by $x_d = [0.5cos(2t),\ -sin(2t)]^T$ with $\zeta(x_d) = [x_{d2},\ -4x_{d1}]^T$. The penalty matrices in the performance index (5.78) are selected as $Q = 50 \times diag[1, 0.1], R = 0.1, \gamma = 0.35$. The NN weights are initialized randomly from a uniform distribution in the interval $[0,\ 2]$. The learning gains are selected as $\alpha_1 = 0.045$, and $\alpha_2 = 0.08$. A polynomial regression vector $\phi(\chi) = (1/8)[\chi_1^2, \chi_1\chi_2, \chi_1\chi_3, \chi_1\chi_4, \chi_2^2, \chi_2\chi_3, \chi_2\chi_4, \chi_3^2, \chi_3\chi_4, \chi_1^2\chi_2, \chi_1^2\chi_3, \chi_1^2\chi_4, \chi_2^2, \chi_2^2\chi_3, \chi_2^2\chi_4, \chi_3^2\chi_4, \chi_1^2\chi_2^2, \chi_1^2\chi_3^2, \chi_1^2\chi_4^2, \chi_2^2\chi_3^2, \chi_2^2\chi_4^2, \chi_3^2\chi_4^2, \chi_4^2]^T$ is used for approximating the solution of the HJI equation. A normally distributed probing noise in the interval $[0, 1]$ is added to the regressor vector to satisfy PE condition to ensure the convergence of the NN weights. The simulation is run for 35 s with initial states $x_0 = [2,\ 1.5]^T$.

The results of the proposed near-optimal event-based ADP-based scheme is compared with sampled data implementation of the scheme, where the feedback signals are sampled and the controller is executed periodically. The plots are superimposed to verify the effectiveness of the proposed approach. The notation (e) and (c) next to the simulation variables in the figures indicate event-based implementation and sampled data implementation, respectively. All simulation parameters, including the initial conditions, are kept the same for both cases. Learning gain for the NN weight update during the flow period, which is not available in the sampled data case, is adjusted to obtain

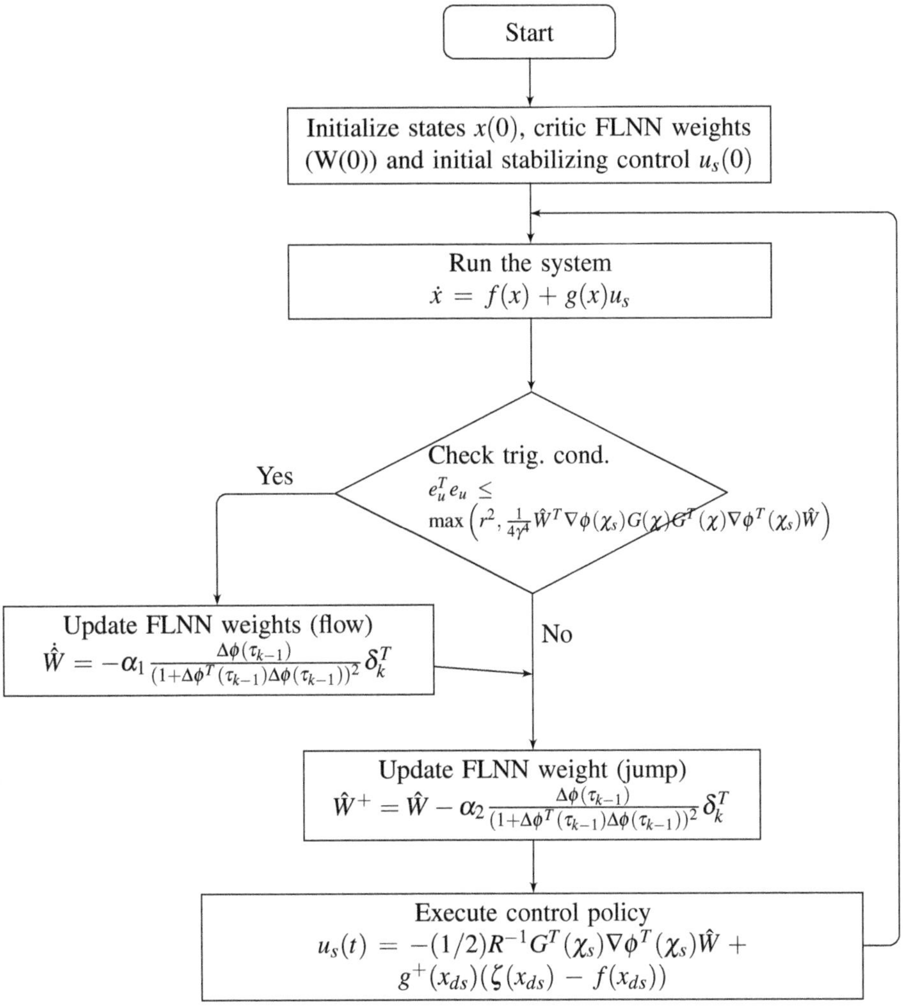

Figure 5.13 Implementation of the game-based algorithm presented in this section.

a comparable state convergence rate for fair comparison in terms of computation and performance cost.

The event-sampling condition in (5.104) with $r = 0.005$ is utilized for the sampling and controller execution. The states and the desired trajectory are shown in Figure 5.14. It clear from the figure that with the event based implementation of the control input closely follows the sampled data implementation with less frequent control execution. The system states converge arbitrarily close to the desired states in about 20 second. The large initial tracking error is due to the approximated controller with randomly initialized NN weights. As the NN weight estimates converge close to the target values, the system states converge close to the desired trajectories. The convergence of the tracking errors for both event-based and sampled data implementation to their respective bounds are shown in Figure 5.15. Note that the event-based tracking error closely follows the sampled-data tracking error. This is achieved by selecting the NN weight tuning gain during the flow period appropriately, which accelerate the convergence rate of the weight updates.

The convergence of the event-based Bellman residual error close to zero is shown in Figure 5.16. Note that the Bellman error converges earlier than the state convergence in both cases. This implies

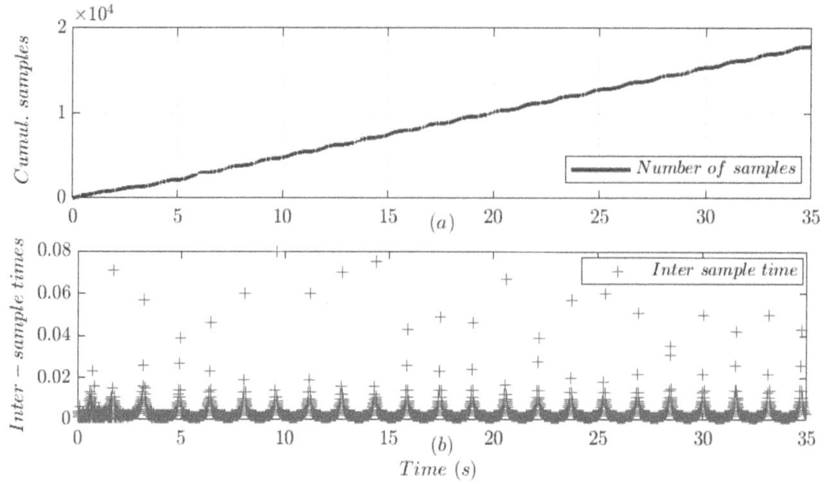

Figure 5.14 Plot showing trajectories of (a) cumulative events and (b) inter-sample time.

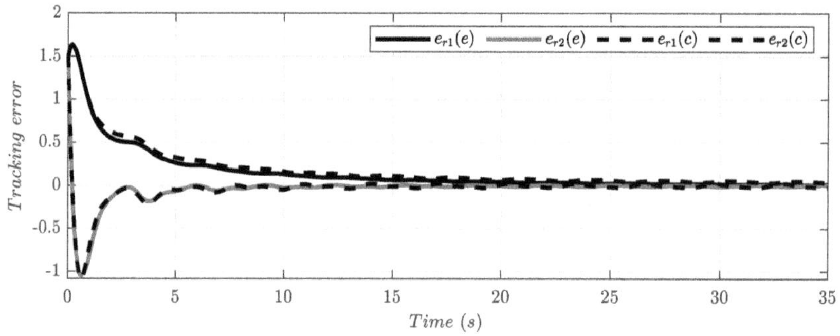

Figure 5.15 Convergence of tracking errors.

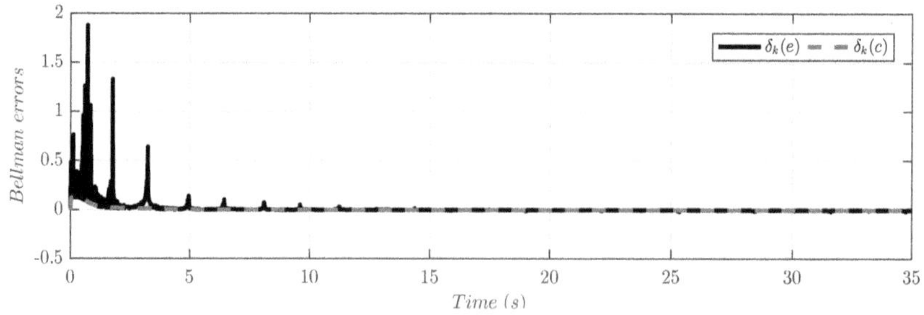

Figure 5.16 Convergence of event-based Bellman errors.

the approximate value function converges to arbitrarily close neighborhood of their optimal values before the states converge to their respective desired states. It is observed that the Bellman error for the event-based implementation case spikes before convergence when compared to the smooth plot of sampled data implementation. This is due to the aperiodic control execution. However, the Bellman error converges close to zero as in the case of sampled data implementation. The cost comparison is shown in Figure 5.17. The cumulative cost for the event-based approach is close to each other. Note that the penalty factor γ in (5.76) determines the degree of optimality and different

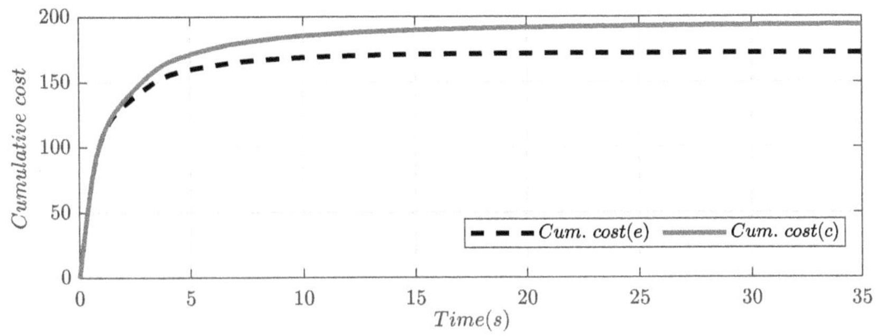

Figure 5.17 Comparison of cumulative costs

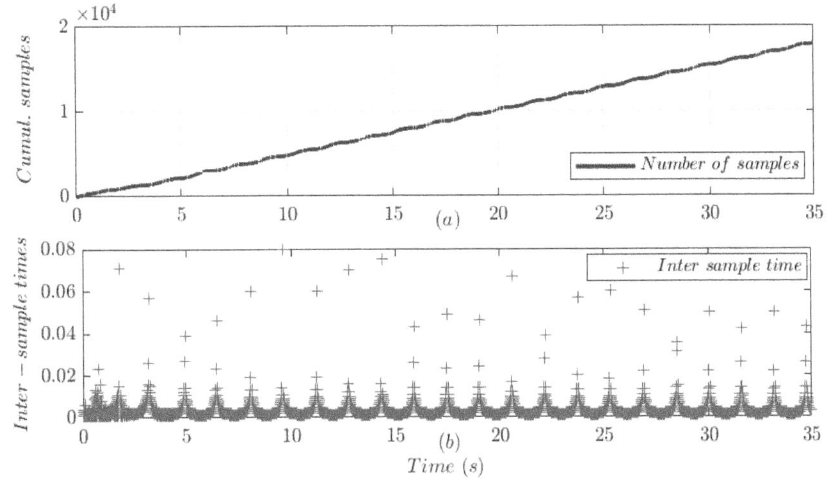

Figure 5.18 Cumulative number of sampling instants and inter-sample times.

values of γ will lead to different costs.

From the reduction of computation point of view, the cumulative number of sampling instants and the inter-sampling times are shown in Figure 5.18 (a) and (b). It is observed that the control is executed 51.18% of times when compared to the periodic sampled data execution for $\gamma = 0.35$ during the simulation time of 35 s. This shows a 48.82% reduction of feedback communication and computational load. Note that γ is selected such that $\gamma^2 > \lambda_{max}(R)$ where $\lambda_{max} = 0.1$. Different value of γ and r will result in different number of sampling. From Figure 5.18 (b) it is evident that the sampling instants are aperiodic and the events are crowded till 2.5 secs. This is due to the high initial tracking error in the learning phase of the NN. Once the NN estimated weights converge close to the target values, shown in Figure 5.19, the sampling instants are reduced.

Since the ideal NN weights are unknown, it is not possible to show convergence of the NN estimated weight to the target values. However, from Figure 5.19 (a) and (b), it can be observed that the NN weight estimates reaches their steady state, i.e., become constant, approximately about 18 seconds for both cases. Therefore, it can be concluded that the NN weights converge to a close neighborhood of the target weights. Alternatively, the NN weight estimation error is ultimately bounded. Note that the target values for both cases are different since the optimal value function for sampled data case is different from the proposed event-based case.

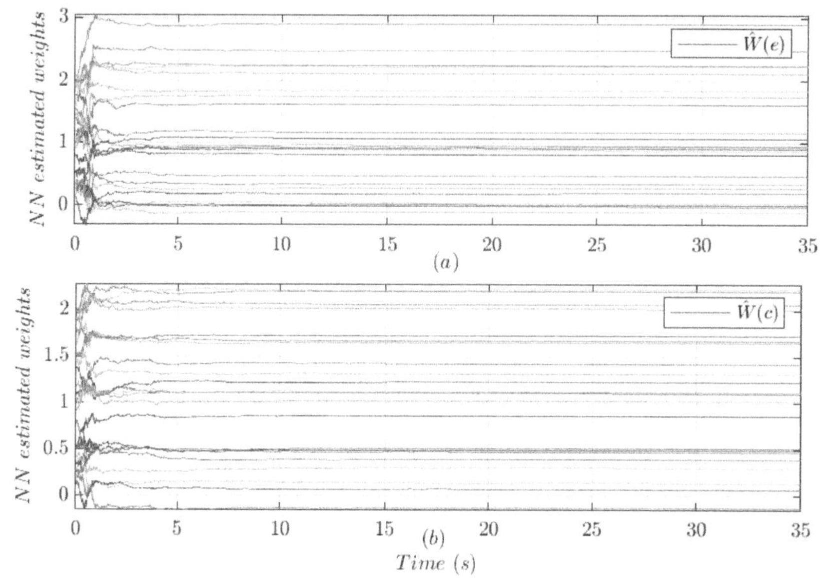

Figure 5.19 Convergence of estimated NN weights.

5.4 CONCLUDING REMARKS

In conclusion, this chapter presents event-based control strategies, each tailored to optimize system performance based on game-theoretic techniques. First, we looked at an event-triggered and self-triggered controllers for linear dynamical systems to co-design the optimal control policy and trigger conditions. The second part extended this co-design approach, leveraging game theory to jointly optimize sampling instants and control policy for nonlinear dynamical system. Finally, we focused on near-optimal adaptive sampling for state trajectory tracking, with significant reductions in control execution. The key takeaway from these techniques is that the co-design method using the zero-sum game formulation offers an extra design variable to optimize the performance cost. This degree of freedom can be leveraged to optimize event-triggered controllers.

5.5 PROBLEMS

5.5.1 Consider an inverted pendulum (Spooner and Passino, 1999), which can be represented as an input-affine nonlinear dynamical system. The dynamics of the system are given by

$$\dot{x}_1 = x_2,$$
$$\dot{x}_2 = (\frac{mgr}{J} - \frac{kr^2}{4}J)\sin x_1 + \frac{kr}{2J}(l-b) + \frac{u}{J}. \tag{5.115}$$

Design feedback control policies based on the control algorithm using equations in Table 5.2.

5.5.2 Design near-optimal control policies based on the learning algorithm using equations in Table 5.3 for the Problem 5.5.1.

5.5.3 For the same system as in Problem 5.5.1., consider the linearized dynamics as in (Guinaldo et al., 2011). The parameters in the system dynamics are m_1= 2,m_2= 2.5, J_1= 5,J_2= 6.25, $k = 10, r = 0.5, l = 0.5$, and $g = 9.8, b = 0.5$. Pick the initial conditions of the system states in the interval [0,1] and the initial weights of the NN from [-1,1], randomly. Design event- and self-triggered control policies based on the algorithms using equations in Table 5.1.

5.5.4 Consider the system of an inverted pendulum. The dynamics are

$$\dot{x}(t) = \begin{bmatrix} 0 & 1 \\ \frac{g}{l} - \frac{a_i k}{ml^2} & 0 \end{bmatrix} x_i(t) + \gamma_{ca} \begin{bmatrix} 0 \\ \frac{1}{ml^2} \end{bmatrix} u_i(t-\tau),$$

where $l = 5$, $g = 10$, $m = 5$, $k = 5$ and $h_{ij} = 1$ for $\forall j \in \{1,2,..,N\}$. The system is open loop unstable. Design event- and self-triggered control policies based on the algorithms using equations in Table 5.1.

5.5.5 For the system described in the previous problem, design feedback control policies using equations in Table 5.2. Compare results with the solution obtained using 5.1.

5.5.6 Design feedback control policies using equations in Table 5.1 for the Problem 2.8.1.

5.5.7 Consider the nonlinear system represented by

$$\begin{aligned} \dot{x}_1 &= -x_1 + x_2 \\ \dot{x}_2 &= -\frac{1}{2}(x_1 + x_2) + \frac{1}{2} x_2 \sin^2(x_1) + (\sin(x_1))\,u \end{aligned} \tag{5.116}$$

Design feedback control policies using equations in Table 5.2.

5.5.8 Consider the two-link robot manipulator system with the dynamics described in Example 4.3. Design feedback control policies using equations in Table 5.2.

5.5.9 For the system defined in the previous problem, Design feedback control policies using equations in Table 5.3. Use the generator system with dynamics $\dot{x}_d(t) = 0$, with initial conditions $(0.1, 0.1)$.

5.5.10 Consider the two-link robot manipulator system with the dynamics described in Example 4.3. Design feedback control policies using equations in Table 5.3. Compare the performance of the event-triggering mechanisms with that given in Example 4.3.

6 Linear Interconnected Systems

CONTENTS

So far in the book, we have focused on isolated dynamical systems. We have considered the design of control inputs for these systems along with an event-triggering scheme to specify the sampling and communication instants and determine when the sensor data and the control inputs are transmitted from the sensor to the controller and the controller to the actuator, respectively. In this chapter, we shall expand our focus to large-scale interconnected systems govered by linear dynamics. These systems are composed of multiple subsystems each of which is governed by the drift dynamics, dynamics due to control inputs, and an interconnection dynamics that model the effect of interactions/coupling between the subsystems. For such large-scale systems, we shall first extend the Q-learning algorithm described in Chapter 3 to develop a distributed learning algorithm for synthesizing distributed control policies. The distributed learning algorithm, called the *hybrid Q-learning* algorithm introduced in (Narayanan and Jagannathan, 2016b, 2015), shall be used for the design of a linear adaptive optimal regulator for a large-scale interconnected system with event-sampled input and state vector. We shall see that the extension of Q-learning-based controllers to such large-scale systems with event-triggered distributed control execution introduces significant challenges in data sampling and communication protocol design due to network losses. To accommodate these losses, we shall utilize a stochastic dynamic modelling approach (Xu et al., 2012) for the large-scale system and use this model to design the Q-learning algorithm. We shall see that by embedding iterative parameter learning updates within the event-sampled instants along with the time-driven Q-learning algorithm introduced in Chapter 3, the efficiency of the optimal regulator is improved considerably.

6.1 INTRODUCTION

The control of large-scale interconnected systems has been a prominent research area for the past five decades (Jamshidi, 1996). These systems are characterized by their complexity, comprising geographically distributed subsystems connected with each other through either structural interactions (e.g., power grid, Venkat et al., 2008), communication network (e.g., wireless sensor networks, Mazo and Tabuada, 2011), or through control inputs in applications modeled as ensemble control systems (Li and Khaneja, 2006; Yu et al., 2023). Traditional centralized controller design techniques for such systems often face challenges related to computational limitations, control integrity (Ioannou, 1986), demands high communication cost, is prone to single-point-of-failure, and requires an accurate model of the structural interconnections (Siljak, 2011). To address these issues, decentralized and distributed control schemes have been extensively explored in the literature, empowering each subsystem with an independent local controller (Ioannou, 1986; Siljak and Zecevic, 2005; Mehraeen and Jagannathan, 2011; Liu et al., 2014; Narendra and Mukhopadhyay, 2010; Venkat et al., 2008; Camponogara and de Lima, 2012; Song and Fang, 2014; Zhou et al., 2015; Zheng et al., 2012; Wang et al., 2010; Chen et al., 2015; Wang and Lemmon, 2011b; Guinaldo et al., 2012). The design of local controllers in these schemes becomes complex due to constraints imposed by the interconnections, specifically the coupling matrix (Jamshidi, 1996; Ioannou, 1986; Siljak and Zecevic, 2005; Mehraeen and Jagannathan, 2011; Liu et al., 2014; Narendra and Mukhopadhyay, 2010; Venkat et al., 2008; Camponogara and de Lima, 2012; Song and Fang, 2014; Zhou et al., 2015; Zheng et al., 2012; Wang et al., 2010; Chen et al., 2015) in systems with linear dynamics. This matrix determines how the states and/or the control of one subsystem influence the dynamics of the other subsystems.

In a decentralized control scheme, each subsystem is equipped with independent controllers and are controlled using locally available feedback information (Siljak, 2011; Bakule, 2008; Antonelli, 2013). In other words, in these schemes, the control feedback loop at each subsystem is closed locally, and hence, a dedicated communication network to share information among the subsystems is not required. However, decentralized controllers may lead to unsatisfactory performance, and even instability, especially either if the interconnection strength is strong (Antonelli, 2013; Gusrialdi and Hirche, 2011) or in the presence of unstable fixed modes (Wang and Davison, 1973). To systematically deal with the stability issues arising in decentralized controllers, robust control approaches based on small-gain theorem were introduced in a series of works by Jiang et al. (1994, 1996); Liu and Jiang (2015); Dashkovskiy et al. (2010). In these approaches, an ISS gain operator was derived, and conditions were imposed on this ISS gain operator to guarantee the existence of an ISS Lyapunov function for the overall system. However, they did not consider the task of optimizing the transient response performance of the subsystems. Optimality was later included as a design criterion in the decentralized control framework (Bakule, 2008; Liu et al., 2014; Jiang and Jiang, 2012; Gao et al., 2016).

Over the years, significant advancements have been made in the design of controllers for large-scale systems to ensure the stabilization of subsystems despite uncertain interconnection matrices and limited communication (Ioannou, 1986; Jamshidi, 1996; Siljak and Zecevic, 2005). Prominently, adaptive controllers were introduced with the aim of learning the interconnection terms and providing appropriate compensation (Ioannou, 1986; Siljak and Zecevic, 2005; Mehraeen and Jagannathan, 2011; Liu et al., 2014), although their effectiveness was found to be limited when dealing with strong interconnections. As an alternative, the utilization of reference models emerged as a method to gather information about other subsystems, but it was reported by Narendra and Mukhopadhyay (2010) that relying solely on reference models without direct communication of state information leads to unsatisfactory transient performance. Furthermore, leveraging the communication network that connects subsystems, several distributed control algorithms have been proposed (e.g., Venkat et al. (2008); Hirche et al. (2009); Camponogara and de Lima (2012); Song and Fang (2014); Zhou et al. (2015); Zheng et al. (2012), and the references therein).

Alternatively, works employing model-predictive control (MPC) to effectively address optimization problems for large-scale systems while leveraging the network have been popular. MPC-based algorithms typically rely on accurate system models to predict future outputs and iteratively minimize a cost function over a limited time horizon (Venkat et al., 2008; Camponogara and de Lima, 2012; Song and Fang, 2014; Zhou et al., 2015; Zheng et al., 2012). In contrast, we shall see that the Q-function-based distributed control algorithm developed in this chapter offers distinct advantages.

It does not necessitate an accurate system model and avoids extensive iterations for optimization.

As demonstrated in previous chapters, the utilization of aperiodic event-triggered control offers significant advantages in reducing communication and computational overhead, making it particularly well-suited for large-scale interconnected systems. This is relevant when considering systems that share a communication network with limited bandwidth, where minimizing network usage becomes crucial. Event-triggered control has been extensively studied in the context of large-scale interconnected systems, as evident in various works (Wang and Lemmon, 2011b; Guinaldo et al., 2012; Chen et al., 2015). Notably, these advancements often incorporate assumptions on interconnection strengths (Wang and Lemmon, 2011b; Chen et al., 2015) or control coefficients (Guinaldo et al., 2012) to achieve subsystem decoupling. Moreover, the presence of a communication network among subsystems and within the feedback loop introduces random time delays and data dropouts (Halevi and Ray, 1988; Zhang et al., 2001; Shousong and Qixin, 2003), which can significantly degrade control performance. Therefore, it is essential to incorporate these network losses in the control design process to ensure realistic control signals for controlling large-scale systems. In the approach presented in this chapter, we incorporate these network losses using a well-established sampled-data modeling approach based on the developments outlined in Xu et al. (2012) and Halevi and Ray (1988).

Learning control signals for isolated system when the dynamics are not fully known is already challenging. In the event-triggered framework with aperiodic feedback, we have seen that the learning process is slowed down considerably. We have also seen in the previous chapters that the inter-event time was dependent on the learning error and the use of mirror estimator in the event-triggering mechanism resulted in frequent events when the learning errors were large. We shall see that a hybrid model-free Q-learning scheme, introduced in this chapter, uses event-sampled state and input vector to improve the learning time. This hybrid algorithm embeds a finite number of Q-function parameter updates within the inter-event period to facilitate faster learning without explicitly increasing the events as discussed in Chapter 3. In the hybrid algorithm, we shall also see that the temporal-difference based ADP schemes (Xu et al., 2012; Sahoo and Jagannathan, 2014) and the policy/value iterations based ADP schemes (Lewis et al., 2012a; Zhong et al., 2014) become special cases. Since the Q-function parameters at each subsystem are estimated online with event-sampled input, state information along with past history, and the data obtained from other subsystems through the communication network, an overall system model is not required. This makes the control scheme data-driven (Hou and Wang, 2013). In this chapter, we will cover the development of a hybrid Q-learning scheme from (Narayanan and Jagannathan, 2016b) using event-sampled states, input vectors, and their history. Additionally, we will discuss the derivation of a time-driven and hybrid Q-learning scheme for an uncertain large-scale interconnected system governed by linear dynamics and enclosed by a communication network.

6.2 LARGE-SCALE SYSTEMS AND PERIODIC CONTROLLERS

In this section, we shall develop a time-driven Q-learning scheme for large-scale interconnected systems with periodic feedback.

6.2.1 LARGE-SCALE SYSTEMS WITH LINEAR DYNAMICS

Consider a linear time-invariant continuous-time system having N interconnected subsystems as shown in Figure 6.1 with subsystem dynamics described by

$$\dot{x}_i(t) = A_i x_i(t) + B_i u_i(t) + \sum_{\substack{j=1 \\ j\neq i}}^{N} A_{ij} x_j(t), \quad x_i(0) = x_{i0}, \tag{6.1}$$

where $x_i(t), \dot{x}_i(t) \in \mathbb{R}^{n_i \times 1}$ represent the state vector and state derivatives, respectively, $u_i(t) \in \mathbb{R}^{m_i}$, $A_i \in \mathbb{R}^{n_i \times n_i}$, and $B_i \in \mathbb{R}^{n_i \times m_i}$ denote control input, internal dynamics, and control gain ma-

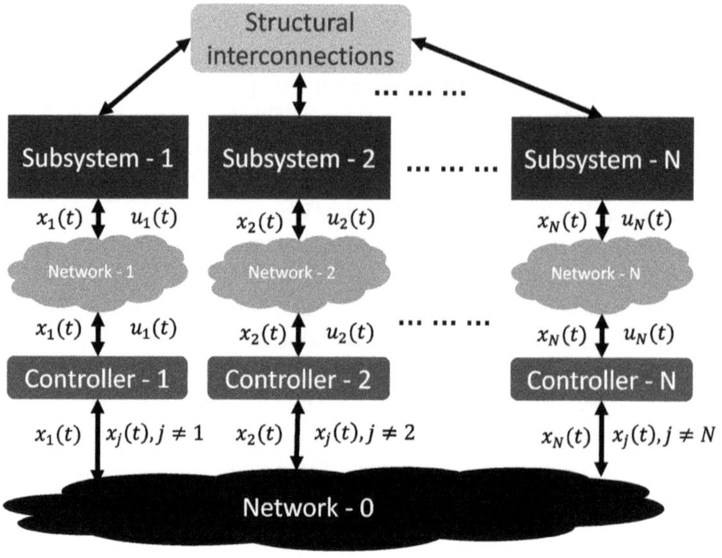

Figure 6.1 Block diagram illustrating distributed control scheme in a large-scale interconnected system.

trices of the ith subsystem, $A_{ij} \in \mathbb{R}^{n_i \times n_j}$ represents the interconnection matrix between the ith and j^{th} subsystem for $i \in 1,2,..N$. The system matrices A_i, B_i, and the interconnection matrix A_{ij} are considered uncertain, which implies that the entries in these matrices are not accurately known. The overall system description can be expressed in a compact form as

$$\dot{X}(t) = AX(t) + BU(t), \quad X(0) = X_0, \tag{6.2}$$

where $X(t) \in \mathbb{R}^n$, $U(t) \in \mathbb{R}^m$, $B \in \mathbb{R}^{n \times m}$, $A \in \mathbb{R}^{n \times n}$, $\dot{X} = [\dot{x}_1^T, \ldots, \dot{x}_N^T]^T$, $A = \begin{pmatrix} A_1 & \ldots & A_{1N} \\ : & \ldots & : \\ A_{N1} & \ldots & A_N \end{pmatrix}$, $B = diag[B_1,..,B_N]$ (block diagonal matrix), and $U = [u_1^T, \ldots, u_N^T]^T$. In the large-scale interconnected system, the subsystems communicate with each other via Network-0 (shown in Figure 6.1), while each subsystem is also enclosed by their local networks. Effects of the network-induced losses can be modeled along with the system dynamics by utilizing the discretization technique previously seen in Chapter 3. Detailed exposition on the assumptions and the modeling approach can be seen in works by Halevi and Ray (1988); Xu et al. (2012). The assumptions in this context cover various aspects related to traffic patterns, message lengths, data latencies, sampling intervals, time skew, control signal processing delay, network conditions, and queue capacity.

They can be summarized as follows: The communication network traffic follows a periodic pattern with deterministic (time-dependent) queueing delays and data latencies. The message lengths for sensor and control signals are identical, indicating that their latencies share similar characteristics. The sampling intervals for the sensor and controller are the same. A constant time skew exists between the sampling instants of the sensor and controller over a finite time window. The control signal processing delay is constant and shorter than the sampling interval. The network is assumed to be non-overloaded and free from transmission errors. Additionally, the receiver queue at the controller has a capacity of one (Halevi and Ray, 1988; Xu et al., 2012). These assumptions provide specific conditions for analyzing and designing controls in the context of CPS with communication networks in their feedback loops.

Assumption 6.1. *The system (6.2) is considered controllable and the states are measurable. Further, the order of subsystems is considered known.*

With the network-induced delays and data-dropout, the dynamics of the plant can be rewritten as

$$\dot{X}(t) = AX(t) + \gamma_{ca}(t)BU(t-\tau(t)), \quad X(0) = X_0, \tag{6.3}$$

where $\gamma_{ca}(t)$ is the data-dropout indicator, which becomes $I^{n\times n}$ when the control input is received at the actuator and $0^{n\times n}$ when the control input is lost at time t. This only includes the data loss in Network 2 and $\tau(t)$ is the total delay. Now, integrating the system dynamics with network parameters over the sampling interval (Halevi and Ray, 1988; Xu et al., 2012), we get

$$X_{k+1} = A_d X_k + \gamma_{ca,k} B_0^k U_k + \gamma_{ca,k-1} B_1^k U_{k-1} + \ldots + \gamma_{ca,k-\bar{d}} B_{\bar{d}}^k U_{k-\bar{d}}, \quad X(0) = X_0, \tag{6.4}$$

where $X_k = X(kT_s)$, $A_d = e^{AT_s}$, $\bar{d}$ is the delay bound, U_k is the control input. The matrices B_0^k and B_i^k for $i = \{1, 2, \ldots \bar{d}\}$ are all defined as in (Xu et al., 2012). From the discretized system representation, we can define an augmented state vector consisting of state and past control inputs as $\bar{X}(k) = [X_k^T \; U_{k-1}^T \ldots U_{k-\bar{d}}^T]^T \in \mathbb{R}^{n+\bar{d}m}$. The new augmented system representation is given by

$$\bar{X}_{k+1} = A_{\bar{x}k}\bar{X}_k + B_{\bar{x}k}U_k, \quad \bar{X}(0) = \bar{X}_0, \tag{6.5}$$

with the system matrices given by $A_{\bar{x}k} = \begin{bmatrix} A_d & \gamma_{ca,k-1}B_1^k & \cdots & \gamma_{ca,k-\bar{d}}B_{\bar{d}}^k \\ 0 & \cdots & 0 & 0 \\ \vdots & I_m & \vdots & \vdots \\ 0 & \cdots & I_m & 0 \end{bmatrix}$ and $B_{\bar{x}k} = \begin{bmatrix} \gamma_{ca,k}B_0^k \\ I_m \\ \vdots \\ 0 \end{bmatrix}$.

Note that the system dynamics in (6.5) are stochastic due to the network-induced delays and data-dropouts. The assumptions regarding the controllability, observability, and the existence of unique solution for the stochastic Riccati equation (SRE) are now dependent on the Grammian functions associated with this stochastic system (Lewis et al., 2012b). Hence, inorder to proceed further toward developing a Q-learning-based control scheme, the following assumption is needed.

Assumption 6.2. *We need the system defined in* (6.5) *to be both uniformly completely observable and controllable (Lewis et al., 2012b).*

The time-driven Q-learning and adaptive optimal regulation of such stochastic linear time-varying interconnected system is presented next. We shall begin by considering the case when the feedback is periodic.

6.2.2 PERIODICALLY-SAMPLED TIME-DRIVEN Q-LEARNING

For the system dynamics (6.5), we can define an infinite horizon cost function as

$$J_k = \underset{\tau,\gamma}{\mathbb{E}}\left[\frac{1}{2}\sum\nolimits_{t=k}^{\infty} \bar{X}_k^T P_{\bar{x}} \bar{X}_k + U_k^T R_{\bar{x}} U_k\right], \tag{6.6}$$

where $P_{\bar{x}} = diag(P, \frac{R}{\bar{d}}, \ldots, \frac{R}{\bar{d}})$ and $R_{\bar{x}} = \frac{R}{\bar{d}}$. The penalty matrices P and R are positive semidefinite and positive definite, respectively. $\mathbb{E}$ denotes the expected value operator. The cost function (6.6) can also be represented as

$$J_k = \underset{\tau,\gamma}{\mathbb{E}}[\bar{X}_k^T S_k \bar{X}_k]$$

with S_k being the symmetric positive semi-definite solution of the SRE (Lewis et al., 2012b). The next step is to define the action-dependent Q-function for the stochastic system (6.5) with the cost-to-go function (6.6) as

$$Q(\bar{X}_k, U_k) = \underset{\tau,\gamma}{\mathbb{E}}[r(\bar{X}_k, U_k) + J_{k+1}|\bar{X}_k] = \underset{\tau,\gamma}{\mathbb{E}}\{[\bar{X}_k^T \quad U_k^T]G_k[\bar{X}_k^T \quad U_k^T]^T\}, \tag{6.7}$$

where $r(\bar{X}_k, U_k) = \bar{X}_k^T P_{\bar{x}} \bar{X}_k + U_k^T R_{\bar{x}} U_k$ and G_k is a time-varying matrix. In the Bellman equation, we have the matrix

$$\underset{\tau,\gamma}{\mathbb{E}}(G_k) = \begin{bmatrix} P_{\bar{x}} + \underset{\tau,\gamma}{\mathbb{E}}(A_{\bar{x}k}^T S_{k+1} A_{\bar{x}k}) & \underset{\tau,\gamma}{\mathbb{E}}(A_{\bar{x}k}^T S_{k+1} B_{\bar{x}k}) \\ \underset{\tau,\gamma}{\mathbb{E}}(B_{\bar{x}k}^T S_{k+1} A_{\bar{x}k}) & R_{\bar{x}} + \underset{\tau,\gamma}{\mathbb{E}}(B_{\bar{x}k}^T S_{k+1} B_{\bar{x}k}) \end{bmatrix}$$
$$= \begin{bmatrix} \underset{\tau,\gamma}{\mathbb{E}}(G_k^{\bar{x}\bar{x}}) & \underset{\tau,\gamma}{\mathbb{E}}(G_k^{\bar{x}U}) \\ \underset{\tau,\gamma}{\mathbb{E}}(G_k^{U\bar{x}}) & \underset{\tau,\gamma}{\mathbb{E}}(G_k^{UU}) \end{bmatrix}. \tag{6.8}$$

From the matrix equation (6.8), the time-varying control gain can be expressed as

$$K_k = \underset{\tau,\gamma}{\mathbb{E}}\{[R_{\bar{x}} + B_{\bar{x}k}^T S_{k+1} B_{\bar{x}k}]^{-1} B_{\bar{x}k}^T S_{k+1} A_{\bar{x}k}\} = \underset{\tau,\gamma}{\mathbb{E}}\{(G_k^{UU})^{-1} G_k^{U\bar{x}}\}. \tag{6.9}$$

The Q-function (6.7) in parametric form is given by

$$Q(\bar{X}_k, U_k) = \underset{\tau,\gamma}{\mathbb{E}}(z_k^T G_k z_k) = \underset{\tau,\gamma}{\mathbb{E}}(\Theta_k^T \xi_k), \tag{6.10}$$

where $z_k = [(\gamma_{sc,k}\bar{X}_k)^T \quad U_k^T]^T \in \mathbb{R}^{\bar{l}}$ with $\bar{l} = m + n + m\bar{d}$ and $\xi_k = z_k^T \otimes z_k$ is the regression vector. The symbol $\otimes$ denotes the Kronecker product, $\Theta_k \in \Omega_\Theta \subset \mathbb{R}^{l_g}$ is formed by vectorization of the parameter matrix G_k, and $\gamma_{sc,k}$ is a packet loss indicator, defined similar to $\gamma_{ca,k}$. The estimate of the optimal Q-function is expressed as

$$\hat{Q}(\bar{X}_k, U_k) = \underset{\tau,\gamma}{\mathbb{E}}(z_k^T \hat{G}_k z_k) = \underset{\tau,\gamma}{\mathbb{E}}(\hat{\Theta}_k^T \xi_k), \tag{6.11}$$

where $\hat{\Theta}_k \in \mathbb{R}^{l_g}$ is the estimate of expected target parameter Θ_k. By Bellman's principle of optimality, the optimal value function satisfies

$$0 = \underset{\tau,\gamma}{\mathbb{E}}(J_{k+1}^* | \bar{X}_k) - \underset{\tau,\gamma}{\mathbb{E}}(J_k^*) + \underset{\tau,\gamma}{\mathbb{E}}(r(\bar{X}_k, U_k)) = \underset{\tau,\gamma}{\mathbb{E}}(r(\bar{X}_k, U_k)) + \underset{\tau,\gamma}{\mathbb{E}}(\Theta_k^T \Delta\xi_k), \tag{6.12}$$

where $\Delta\xi_k = \xi_{k+1} - \xi_k$ and $\underset{\tau,\gamma}{\mathbb{E}}(J_{k+1}^* | \bar{X}_k)$ is the expected cost-to-go at $k+1^{st}$ instant given the state information at the kth instant. Since the estimated Q-function does not satisfy (6.12), the temporal difference (TD) error will be observed as

$$e_B(k) = \underset{\tau,\gamma}{\mathbb{E}}(r(\bar{X}_k, U_k) + \hat{\Theta}_k^T \Delta\xi_k). \tag{6.13}$$

Remark 6.1. *In the iterative learning schemes (Bradtke et al., 1994; Lewis et al., 2012a) the parameters of the Q-function estimator (QFE) are updated to minimize the error in (6.13) until the error converges to a small value for every time step k. On the contrary, time-driven ADP schemes (Xu et al., 2012; Sahoo and Jagannathan, 2014; Dierks and Jagannathan, 2009a) calculate the Bellman error at each step and update once at the sampling instant and the stability of the closed-loop system is established under certain mild assumptions on the estimated control policy.*

The overall cost function (6.6) for the large-scale system (6.5), can be represented as the sum of the individual cost of all the subsystems as, $J_k = \sum_{i=1}^N J_{i,k}$, where $J_{i,k} = \underset{\tau,\gamma}{\mathbb{E}}\{\frac{1}{2}\sum_{s=k}^{\infty} \bar{x}_{i,k}^T P_{\bar{x},i} \bar{x}_{i,k} + u_{i,k}^T R_{\bar{x},i} u_{i,k}\}$ is the quadratic cost function for i^{th} subsystem with $\bar{x}_i$ representing the augmented states of the ith subsystem, $P_{\bar{x}} = diag\{P_{\bar{x},1} \cdots P_{\bar{x},N}\}$ and $R_{\bar{x}} = diag\{R_{\bar{x},1} \cdots R_{\bar{x},N}\}$.

The optimal control sequence to minimize the quadratic cost function (6.6) in a decentralized framework is not straightforward because of the interconnection dynamics. Alternatively, the distributed optimal control policy for each subsystem, which minimizes the cost function (6.6), is obtained by using the SRE of the overall system given the system dynamics $A_{\bar{x}k}$ and $B_{\bar{x}k}$. It is given by

$$u^*_{i,k} = \underset{\tau,\gamma}{\mathbb{E}}\{-K^*_{i,k}\bar{x}_{i,k} - \sum_{j=1,j\neq i}^{N} K^*_{ij,k}\bar{x}_{j,k}\}, \tag{6.14}$$

where $K^*_{i,k}$ are the diagonal elements and $K^*_{ij,k}$ are the off-diagonal elements of K^*_k in (6.9). In the following lemma, we shall see that with the control law (6.14) designed at each subsystem, the overall system is asymptotically stabilized in the mean square.

Lemma 6.1. *Consider the ith subsystem of the large-scale interconnected system (6.5). Let Assumption 6.2 hold and let the system matrices $A_{\bar{x}k}$ and $B_{\bar{x}k}$ be known. The optimal control policy obtained as in (6.14) renders the individual subsystems asymptotically stable in the mean square.*

Proof:

- By definition, the optimal control input is stabilizing. The closed-loop system matrix $(A_{\bar{x}k} - B_{\bar{x}k}K^*_k)$ is Schur stable (Kailath, 1980). Therefore, the Lyapunov equation $(A_{\bar{x}k} - B_{\bar{x}k}K^*_k)^T\bar{P}(A_{\bar{x}k} - B_{\bar{x}k}K^*_k) - \bar{P} = -\bar{F}$, has a positive definite solution $\bar{F}$.
- Consider the Lyapunov function candidate $L_k = \underset{\tau,\gamma}{\mathbb{E}}(\bar{X}_k^T\bar{P}\bar{X}_k)$, with $\bar{P}$ being positive definite.
- The first difference, using the overall system dynamics with optimal control input is $\Delta L_k = -\underset{\tau,\gamma}{\mathbb{E}}(\bar{X}_k^T\bar{F}\bar{X}_k)$. Since, $\bar{F}$ can be chosen as a diagonal matrix, the first difference in terms of the subsystems can be expressed as

$$\Delta L_k = -\sum_{i=1}^{N}\underset{\tau,\gamma}{\mathbb{E}}(\bar{x}_{i,k}^T\bar{F}_i\bar{x}_{i,k}) \leq -\sum_{i=1}^{N}\bar{q}_{\min}\underset{\tau,\gamma}{\mathbb{E}}\left\|\bar{x}_{i,k}\right\|^2, \tag{6.15}$$

  where $\bar{q}_{\min}$ is the minimum singular value of $\bar{F}$.
- This implies the subsystems are asymptotically stable in the mean square. The results of this lemma plays a key role in the stability analysis of the interconnected system, where the need for the accurate knowledge of $A_{\bar{x}k}$ and $B_{\bar{x}k}$ can be relaxed.

The controller design using a hybrid Q-learning based ADP approach for such large-scale interconnected system in the presence of network-induced losses and with intermittent feedback is discussed next.

6.3 EVENT-BASED HYBRID Q-LEARNING SCHEME

In this section, we present the distributed hybrid learning scheme reported in (Narayanan and Jagannathan, 2016b), which builds upon the time-driven Q-learning-based ADP approach for the control of large-scale interconnected system to improve the convergence time with event-sampled state and input vectors. In the hybrid algorithm, the idle-time between any two successive events are utilized to perform limited parameter updates iteratively in order to minimize the Bellman error. The finite number of iterations between any two events may vary, and hence, the resulting control policy need not necessarily converge to an admissible policy. In this case, the stability of the closed-loop system cannot be established following the arguments used in traditional iterative ADP schemes (Lewis et al., 2012a) or the time-driven Q-learning schemes (Sahoo and Jagannathan, 2014; Xu et al., 2012).

An additional challenge is to estimate the Q-function parameters in (6.11) for the system defined in (6.5) with intermittent feedback and in the presence of network-induced losses. Since subsystems broadcast their states via the communication network, each local subsystem can estimate the Q-function of the overall system so that a predefined reference model is not needed. Subsequently, the optimal control gains and the decoupling gains for each subsystem can be computed without using the complete knowledge of the system dynamics and interconnection matrix. Although, the estimation of the Q-function at each subsystem increases the computation, this additional computation overhead can be considered as trade-off for relaxing the assumption on the strength of interconnection terms and estimating optimal control policy.

Assumption 6.3. *The target parameters are assumed to be slowly-varying (Goodwin and Sin, 2014).*

In adaptive identification, the estimation of unknown parameters is carried out adaptively. When these parameters exhibit time-dependent behavior, the adaptive learning scheme must track a moving target. Consequently, the assumption sets the constraints on the target parameters that enable an adaptive scheme to learn them in real-time.

6.3.1 TIME-DRIVEN Q-LEARNING WITH INTERMITTENT FEEDBACK

In the case of an event-sampled system, the system state vector $\bar{X}_k$ is sent to the controller at event-sampled instants. To denote the event-sampling instants, we define a sub-sequence $\{k_l\}_{l\in\mathbb{N}}$, $k = 0,1,\ldots,$ with $k_0 = 0$ being the initial sampling instant and $\mathbb{N}$ is the set of natural numbers. The system state vector $\bar{X}_{k_l}$ sent to the controller is held by ZOH until the next sampling instant, and it is expressed as $\bar{X}_k^e = \bar{X}_{k_l}$, $k_l \le k < k_{l+1}$. The error in measurements due to this aperiodic feedback transmission is referred to as the *event-sampling error.* Precisely, this error can be expressed as

$$e_{ET}(k) = \bar{X}_k - \bar{X}_k^e, \quad k_l \le k < k_{l+1}, \quad l = 1,2,\cdots. \tag{6.16}$$

Since the estimation of expected value of the parameter matrix G_k must use $\bar{X}_k^e$, the Q-function estimate can be expressed as

$$\hat{Q}(\bar{X}_k^e, U_k) = \mathop{\mathbb{E}}_{\tau,\gamma}(z_k^{e,T}\hat{G}_k z_k^e) = \mathop{\mathbb{E}}_{\tau,\gamma}(\hat{\Theta}_k^T\xi_k^e), \quad k_l \le k < k_{l+1}, \tag{6.17}$$

where $z_k^e = [(\gamma_{sc,k}\bar{X}_k^e)^T \quad U_k^T]^T \in \mathbb{R}^{\bar{l}}$, $\xi_k^e = z_k^{e,T} \otimes z_k^e$ being the event-sampled regression vector, and $\hat{\Theta}$ is the result of vectorization of the matrix $\hat{G}_k$. The Bellman error with event-sampled state is given by

$$e_B(k) = \mathop{\mathbb{E}}_{\tau,\gamma}\left[r(\bar{X}_k^e, U_k) + \hat{\Theta}_k^T\Delta\xi_k^e\right], \quad k_l \le k < k_{l+1}. \tag{6.18}$$

Here $r(\bar{X}_k^e, U_k) = \bar{X}_k^{e,T}P_{\bar{x}}\bar{X}_k^e + U_k^T R_{\bar{x}} U_k$ and $\Delta\xi_k^e = \xi_{k+1}^e - \xi_k^e$. The Bellman error in (6.18) can be rewritten as

$$e_B(k) = \mathop{\mathbb{E}}_{\tau,\gamma}\{r(\bar{X}_k, U_k) + \hat{\Theta}_k^T\Delta\xi_k + \Xi_s(\bar{X}_k, e_{ET}(k), \hat{\Theta}_k)\}, \tag{6.19}$$

where $\Xi_s\left(\bar{X}_k, e_{ET}(k), \hat{\Theta}_k\right) = r(\bar{X}_k - e_{ET}(k), U_k) - r(\bar{X}_k, U_k) + \hat{\Theta}_k^T(\Delta\xi_k^e - \Delta\xi_k)$.

Remark 6.2. *By comparing (6.19) with (6.13), one can see that the Bellman error in (6.19) has an additional error term, $\Xi_s\left(\bar{X}_k, e_{ET}(k), \hat{\Theta}_k\right)$. This additional error consists of errors in cost-to-go and the regression vector, which are driven by $e_{ET}(k)$. Hence, the estimation of QFE parameters depends upon the frequency of the event-sampling instants. We have seen this in Chapters 3-5. One of the consequence of this was that the learning process was tied with the event-triggering, and often, faster parameter convergence required frequent events.*

The parameter vector estimated via the QFE, $\hat{\Theta}_k^i$, is tuned only at the event-sampling instants. The superscript i denotes the overall system parameters at the ith subsystem. Using these parameters, the estimated control policy at each subsystem can be computed as

$$U_k^i = -\hat{K}_k^i\bar{X}_k^{i,e} = -(\hat{G}_k^{i,uu})^{-1}(\hat{G}_k^{i,ux})\bar{X}_k^{i,e}. \tag{6.20}$$

By using (6.20), the event-based estimated control input for the ith subsystem is given by

$$u_{i,k} = -\hat{K}_{i,k}\bar{x}_{i,k}^e - \sum\nolimits_{j=1,j\neq i}^{N}\hat{K}_{ij,k}\bar{x}_{j,k}^e, \quad k_l \le k < k_{l+1}, \quad \forall i \in \{1,2,..N\}. \tag{6.21}$$

Remark 6.3. *It should be noted that the optimal controllers designed at each subsystem takes into account the structural constraint that are present in the form of the interconnection matrix. However, the consideration of input, state, and time constraints (Lewis et al., 2012b) as a part of the optimal control problem is not dealt with in this book.*

With the following assumption, the parameter update rule for the Q-function estimator is presented.

Assumption 6.4. *The target parameter vector Θ_k is assumed to be bounded by positive constant such that $\|\Theta_k\| \leq \Theta_M$. The regression function $Z^i(\bar{X}_k)$ is locally Lipschitz for all $\bar{X}_k \in \Omega_x$.*

6.3.2 HYBRID Q-LEARNING WITH INTERMITTENT FEEDBACK

In the time-driven Q-learning scheme (Sahoo and Jagannathan, 2014) discussed in Chapter 3, the parameters of the QFE are not updated during the inter-event time interval. On the contrary, in the hybrid learning algorithm, the parameters are also tuned during the inter-event interval thus making the Q-function to converge faster and the actual control input to attain optimality quicker.

6.3.2.1 Parameter update at event-sampling instants

The QFE parameter vector $\hat{\Theta}_k^i$ is tuned by using the past data of the Bellman error (6.19) that is available at the event-sampling instants. Therefore, the auxiliary Bellman error at the event-sampling instants is expressed as

$$\Xi_B{}^{i,e}(k) = \Pi_k^{i,e} + \hat{\Theta}_k^{i,T} Z_k^{i,e}, \quad \text{for} \quad k = k_l,$$

where

$$\Pi_k^{i,e} = [r(\bar{X}_{k_l^i}^i, U_{k_l^i}^i) \;\; r(\bar{X}_{k_{l-1}^i}^i, U_{k_{l-1}^i}^i \;\; \cdots \;\; r(\bar{X}_{k_{l-v-1}^i}^i, U_{k_{l-v-1}^i}^i)] \in \mathbb{R}^{1\times v}$$

and

$$Z_k^{i,e} = [\Delta\xi_{k_l^i}^i, \;\; \Delta\xi_{k_{l-1}^i}^i, \;\; \cdots \;\; \Delta\xi_{k_{l-v-1}^i}^i] \in \mathbb{R}^{l_g \times v}.$$

Remark 6.4. *A larger time history may lead to faster convergence but results in higher computation. The (optimal or minimum) number of historic states and input values v is not fixed is a design choice.*

Next, to reduce this error, select the update law (Goodwin and Sin, 2014) for the QFE parameter vector $\hat{\Theta}_k^i$ tuned only at the event-sampling instants, as

$$\hat{\Theta}_k^i = \hat{\Theta}_{k-1}^i + \frac{W_{k-2}^i Z_{k-1}^{i,e} \Xi_B^{i,e^T}(k-1)}{1 + Z_{k-1}^{i,e^T} W_{k-2}^i Z_{k-1}^{i,e}}, \quad k = k_l, \tag{6.22}$$

where

$$W_k^i = W_{k-1}^i - \frac{W_{k-1}^i Z_{k-1}^{i,e} Z_{k-1}^{i,e^T} W_{k-1}^i}{1 + Z_{k-1}^{i,e^T} W_{k-1}^i Z_{k-1}^{i,e}}, \quad k = k_l. \tag{6.23}$$

Here $W_0^i = \beta I$, with $\beta > 0$, a large positive value. The aperiodic execution of (6.22), saves computation, when compared to the traditional adaptive Q-learning techniques. The superscript i indicating the overall system parameters at the ith subsystem, will be dropped from hereon. The update rules for tuning the parameters within the inter-event periods are presented next.

6.3.2.2 Iterative parameter update

The Recursive Least Squares (RLS) algorithm was employed in the work presented in (Bradtke et al., 1994; Lewis et al., 2012a) to iteratively update the parameters of the Q-function within periodic sampling instants for performing the *policy evaluation*, i.e., to estimate the value function satisfying the Bellman equation for the given policy. The update equations aim to minimize the Bellman error, and analytical findings in (Bradtke et al., 1994; Lewis et al., 2012a) demonstrate that each iteration produces a control policy that is at least as good as the existing policy in minimizing the Bellman error.

However, performing a large number of iterative updates in real-time control is not practical. To address this, the time-driven Q-learning approach (Xu et al., 2012; Sahoo and Jagannathan, 2014) was developed. To compensate for the lack of sufficent updates in the time-driven learning, Dierks and Jagannathan (2009b) proposed update rules that included data batches consisting of historic data. Studies in (Xu et al., 2012; Sahoo and Jagannathan, 2014) reveal that as the sampling instants increase, the parameter estimation error converges to zero. To enhance the convergence rate of the estimation error, the RLS update equations (6.22) and (6.23) were applied at the sampling instants and additional iterative parameter updates were introduced by Narayanan and Jagannathan (2016b) between two event-triggering instants.

In other words, to utilize the time between two event-sampling instants, Narayanan and Jagannathan (2016b) proposed to update the parameters iteratively to minimize the error that was calculated during the previous event, which is expressed as $\Xi_B{}^{j,e}(k) = \Pi_k^{j,e} + \hat{\Theta}_k^{j,T} Z_k^{j,e},\ k = k_l$, where j is the iteration index. In this scheme, the Q-function parameters are updated using the equations

$$\hat{\Theta}(k_l^j) = \hat{\Theta}(k_l^{j-1}) + \frac{W(k_{l-2}^{j-2})Z(k_{l-1}^{j-1})\Xi_B^T(k_{l-1}^{j-1})}{1+Z^T(k_{l-1}^{j-1})W(k_{l-2}^{j-1})Z(k_{l-1}^{j-1})}, \tag{6.24}$$

$$W(k_l^j) = W(k_{l-1}^{j-1}) - \frac{W(k_{l-1}^{j-1})Z(k_{l-1}^{j-1})Z^T(k_{l-1}^{j-1})W(k_{l-1}^{j-1})}{1+Z^T(k_{l-1}^{j-1})W(k_{l-1}^{j-1})Z(k_{l-1}^{j-1})}, j = 0, 1, \ldots. \tag{6.25}$$

These updates start at k_l^j with $j = 0$ and ends at k_{l+1}^j for some $j > 0$ for every $l > 0$. Hence, whenever there is an event, the Q-function parameter vector, which is updated iteratively using (6.24) and (6.25) is passed on to the QFE to calculate the new Bellman error. The estimated control gain matrix can be obtained from the estimated parameter vector $\hat{\Theta}_k$ in (6.22) at each event-sampled instants. In terms of the estimated parameters, the control gains are given by (6.20), where

$$\hat{K}_k = (\hat{G}_k^{uu})^{-1}\hat{G}_k^{ux} = \begin{bmatrix} \hat{K}_1 & \cdots & \hat{K}_{1N} \\ \vdots & \ddots & \vdots \\ \hat{K}_{N1} & \cdots & \hat{K}_N \end{bmatrix} \tag{6.26}$$

is the estimated control gain. It is important to note that this control gain is obtained directly from the Q-function parameters, which are constructed with the past data and the current feedback information, and without using the system dynamics.

In the hybrid algorithm, the update equations (6.24) and (6.25) together with (6.18) search for an improved Q-function during every inter-event period. This is done by utilizing the Bellman error equation (6.18) to evaluate the existing control policy, the Q-function is iteratively updated between two event-sampling instants. However, in contrast to the algorithms in (Bradtke et al., 1994; Lewis et al., 2012a), the iteration index j in (6.24) and (6.25) depends on the event-sampling mechanism, resulting in finite, varying number of iterative updates between any two events.

Remark 6.5. *The control policy for the individual subsystem is given by (6.21). Since it is possible that $\hat{G}_k^{uu}$ might be rank-deficient during the learning phase, Narayanan and Jagannathan (2016b)* *proposed the following conditions to check before the control law is updated. If $\hat{G}^{uu}_{k-1}$ is singular or if $\hat{G}^{uu}_{k-1} - R_{\bar{x}}$ is not positive definite, then, $\hat{G}^{uu}_{k-1}$ is replaced by $R_{\bar{x}}$ in the control policy. The conditions can be checked easily by calculating the eigenvalues of $\hat{G}^{uu}_{k-1}$.*

Remark 6.6. *The QFE parameter update rules given by (6.22) and (6.23) requires the state vectors X_{k_l} to $X_{k_{l-v-1}}$ for the computation of regression vector at $k = k_l$. Therefore, the past values are required to be stored at the QFE.*

With the update rules presented in this section and the control gains selected from (6.23), the assumption in (Xu et al., 2012; Sahoo and Jagannathan, 2014) that the inverse of $\hat{G}^{uu}_k$ exists when the updates utilize the time history of the regression function and Bellman error is no longer needed. The analytical results for the learning algorithm are summarized next.

6.3.2.3 Stability Analysis

Defining the QFE's parameter estimation error $\underset{\tau,\gamma}{\mathbb{E}}(\tilde{\Theta}_k) = \underset{\tau,\gamma}{\mathbb{E}}(\Theta_k - \hat{\Theta}_k)$, the error dynamics for the parameters at event-triggering instants and the inter-event times can be represented using (6.22) and (6.24) as

$$\underset{\tau,\gamma}{\mathbb{E}}(\tilde{\Theta}^0_{k_{l+1}}) = \underset{\tau,\gamma}{\mathbb{E}}(\tilde{\Theta}^j_k + \frac{W^j_k Z^{j,e}_k \Xi^{j,e^T}_B(k)}{1 + Z^{ej,T}_k W^j_k Z^{j,e}_k}), \quad k = k^0_l, \tag{6.27}$$

$$\underset{\tau,\gamma}{\mathbb{E}}(\tilde{\Theta}^{j+1}_{k_l}) = \underset{\tau,\gamma}{\mathbb{E}}(\tilde{\Theta}^j_k + \frac{W^j_k Z^{j,e}_k \Xi^{j,e^T}_B(k)}{1 + Z^{ej,T}_k W^j_k Z^{j,e}_k}), \quad k^0_l < k < k^0_{l+1}. \tag{6.28}$$

Remark 6.7. *When there is no data loss, the Q-function estimator is updated and the control policy is updated as soon as it is computed. This requires the broadcast scheme to generate an acknowledgment signal whenever the packets are successfully received at the subsystems (Guinaldo et al., 2012). A suitable scheduling protocol has to ensure that the data lost in the network is kept minimal.*

Next, an event-sampling condition is selected for the Q-learning scheme to work execute these parameter and control updates and sampling instants. We can develop event-triggering conditions as in Chapters 3 and 4. The hybrid learning algorithm introduced in this chapter is independent of the event-sampling condition. Here, we consider a quadratic function $f^i(k) = \bar{x}_i(k)^T \Gamma_i \bar{x}_i(k)$, with $\Gamma_i > 0$, for the ith subsystem. The event-sampling condition should satisfy

$$f^i(k) \leq \lambda f^i(k_l + 1), \forall k \in [k_l + 1, k_{l+1}), \tag{6.29}$$

for stability, when $\lambda < 1$, as shown in the next section.

Remark 6.8. *The event-sampling condition presented here depends only on the local subsystem state information. The function $f^i(k)$ can be selected as the Lyapunov function and such an event-sampling condition is also presented in (Meng and Chen, 2013) for a single system.*

The following technical lemma will be used to prove the stability of the closed-loop system during the learning period. Detailed proofs for the Lemmas and Theorems presented in this chapter are available in (Narayanan and Jagannathan, 2016b).

Lemma 6.2. *Consider the system in (6.5) and the QFE (6.17). Define $\tilde{U}(k_{l-1}) = U(k_{l-1}) - \hat{U}(k_{l-1})$ and $\tilde{G}^{ux}_{k_{l-1}} = G^{ux}_{k_{l-1}} - \hat{G}^{ux}_{k_{l-1}}$. If the control policy is updated such that, whenever $\hat{G}^{uu}_{k_{l-1}} - R_{\bar{x}}$ is not positive definite or $\hat{G}^{uu}_{k_{l-1}}$ is singular, $\hat{G}^{uu}_{k_{l-1}}$ is replaced by $R_{\bar{x}}$ in the control policy, then*

$$\underset{\tau,\gamma}{\mathbb{E}}(\tilde{U}(k_{l-1})) \leq \underset{\tau,\gamma}{\mathbb{E}}\{2\|R^{-1}_{\bar{x}}\| \left\|G^{ux}_{k_{l-1}}\right\| \|\bar{X}_{k_{l-1}}\| + \|R^{-1}_{\bar{x}}\| \left\|\tilde{G}^{ux}_{k_{l-1}}\right\| \|\bar{X}_{k_{l-1}}\|\} \tag{6.30}$$

Key Ideas of the Proof:

- This Lemma establishes an upper bound for the error in the control inputs applied to the system based on the QFE.
- In particular, this bound holds for the cases when $\hat{G}^{uu}_{k_{l-1}}$ is either singular or nonsingular. The upper bound is used in the main Theorem to demonstrate the closed-loop stability of the controlled system.
- The proof is a straight-forward application of the given definitions, the use of triangle inequality, and basic properties of norm operators given in Chapter 1.
- Together with the requirement of *persistency of excitation*, conditions for stability of the closed loop system can be derived.

Recall the definition of a persistently exciting (PE) signal from Chapter 3. A regression vector $\varphi(x_k)$ is said to be PE if there exists positive constants $\delta, \underline{\alpha}, \bar{\alpha}$, and $k_d \geq 1$ such that

$$\underline{\alpha} I \leq \sum_{k=k_d}^{k+\delta} \varphi(x_k)\varphi^T(x_k) \leq \bar{\alpha} I,$$

where I is the identity matrix of appropriate dimension.

Lemma 6.3. *Consider the QFE in (6.17) with an initial admissible control policy $U_0 \in \mathbb{R}^m$. Let all the aforementioned Assumptions (3.1-3.4) hold, and the QFE parameter vector $\hat{\Theta}(0)$ be initialized in a compact set Ω_Θ. When the QFE is updated at the event-sampling instants using (6.22) and (6.23) and during the inter-sampling period using (6.24) and (6.25), the QFE parameter estimation error $\underset{\tau,\gamma}{\mathbb{E}}(\tilde{\Theta}^j_{k_l})$ is bounded. Under the assumption that the regression vector $\xi^j_{k_l}$ is PE, the QFE parameter estimation error $\tilde{\Theta}^j_{k_l}$ for all $\hat{\Theta}(0) \in \Omega_\Theta$ converges to zero asymptotically in the mean square as the event instants $k_l \to \infty$.*

Sketch of Proof:

- The proof is composed of two parts. The first part considers the event-sampling instants and the second part considers the inter-event time. A common Lyapunov function for both the cases are considered to show that this function values decrease as the events increases.
- The Lyapunov candidate function is chosen to be

$$L_{i,\tilde{\Theta}}(k_l^j) = \underset{\tau,\gamma}{\mathbb{E}} \tilde{\Theta}^T(k_l^j) W^{-1}(k_{l-1}^j)\tilde{\Theta}(k_l^j) \tag{6.31}$$

  where j is the iteration index.
- Using the definition of $\tilde{\Theta}$ and matrix inversion lemma (Goodwin and Sin, 2014), the first difference for all the Q function estimators can be obtained as

$$\sum_{i=1}^{N} \Delta L_{i,\tilde{\Theta}}(k_l^j) \leq -N \underset{\tau,\gamma}{\mathbb{E}} \frac{\tilde{\Theta}^T(k_{l-1}^j) Z(k_{l-1}^j) Z^T(k_{l-1}^j)\tilde{\Theta}(k_{l-1}^j)}{1 + Z^T(k_{l-1}^j) W(k_{l-1}^j) Z(k_{l-1}^j)}. \tag{6.32}$$

- Similarly, during the inter-sampling instants, since the parameters are updated iteratively using (6.24) and (6.25). The first difference of the Lyapunov candidate function, using similar arguments as in the previous case, can be shown to be negative semi-definite.
- If the regression vector satisfies PE condition, we can show that the Lyapunov first differences satisfies the following bound

$$\sum_{i=1}^{N} \Delta L_{i,\tilde{\Theta}}(k_l^j) \leq -N \kappa_{min} \underset{\tau,\gamma}{\mathbb{E}} \left\| \tilde{\Theta}^T(k_{l-1}^j) \right\|^2 \tag{6.33}$$

  with $0 < \kappa_{min} \leq 1$.

- Thus, with the regression vector satisfying PE condition, the parameter estimation error is strictly decreasing both during the event-sampling instants and the inter-event period. This implies that as $k_l^j \to \infty$, the QFE parameter estimation error converges to zero asymptotically in the mean-square.

Remark 6.9. *Covariance resetting technique (Goodwin and Sin, 2014) can be used to reset W whenever $W \leq W_{min}$. This condition was also used in the Lyapunov analysis to ensure stability of the closed-loop system (Narayanan and Jagannathan, 2016b). With the covariance resetting, the parameter convergence proof in Lemma 6.3 will still be valid (Goodwin and Sin, 2014).*

Next, the Lyapunov analysis is used to derive the conditions for the stability of the closed-loop system, with the controller designed in this section.

Theorem 6.1. *Consider the closed-loop system (6.5), parameter estimation error dynamics (6.23) along with the control input (6.20). Let the Assumptions 6.1-6.4 hold, and let $U(0) \in \Omega_u$ be an initial admissible control policy. Suppose the last held state vector, $\bar{X}_{k_l}^{e,j}$, and the QFE parameter vector, $\hat{\Theta}_{k_l}^j$ are updated by using, (6.22),(6.23) at the event-sampled instants, and (6.24),(6.25) during the inter-sampling period. Then, there exists a constant $\gamma_{\min} > 0$ such that the closed-loop system state vector $\bar{X}_{k_l}^j$ for all $\bar{X}(0) \in \Omega_x$ converges to zero asymptotically in the mean square and the QFE parameter estimation error $\tilde{\Theta}_{k_l}^j$ for all $\hat{\Theta}(0) \in \Omega_\Theta$ remains bounded. Further, under the assumption that the regression vector $\xi_{k_l}^j$ satisfies the PE condition, the QFE parameter estimation error $\tilde{\Theta}_{k_l}^j$ for all $\hat{\Theta}(0) \in \Omega_\Theta$ converges to zero asymptotically in the mean square, with event-sampled instants $k_l \to \infty$, provided the inequality $\gamma_{\min} > \mu + \rho_1$ is satisfied. Further, the estimated Q-function $\hat{Q}(\bar{X}(k), U(k)) \to \underset{\tau,\gamma}{\mathbb{E}}\{Q^*(\bar{X}(k), U(k))\}$ and estimated control input $U(k) \to \underset{\tau,\gamma}{\mathbb{E}}\{U^*(k)\}$. μ, ρ_1 are positive constants.*

Sketch of Proof: The proof step considers two cases. In the first case, the periodic feedback case is be analysed. In the second case, the aperiodic feedback is considered.

- Case 1: The Lyapunov function considered is

$$L(\bar{X}, \tilde{\Theta}) = \underset{\tau,\gamma}{\mathbb{E}} \bar{X}_{k-1}^T \Gamma \bar{X}_{k-1} + \underset{\tau,\gamma}{\mathbb{E}} \bar{\Pi} \sum_{i=1}^N L_{i,\tilde{\Theta}} \tag{6.34}$$

$\bar{\Pi} = \eta \frac{\|W_0\| \rho_2}{N}$ with $\eta > 1$.

- For the first term, the first difference can be obtained as

$$\Delta L_x \leq -(\gamma_{\min} - \mu - \rho_1) \underset{\tau,\gamma}{\mathbb{E}} \|\bar{X}_{k-1}\|^2 + \rho_2 \|\Gamma\| \underset{\tau,\gamma}{\mathbb{E}} \left\|\tilde{\Theta}_{k-1}\right\|^2 \|\bar{X}_{k-1}\|^2, \tag{6.35}$$

where $\rho_1 = \left\|(\Gamma + \frac{\Gamma^2}{\varepsilon_2}) B_{\max}\right\|^2 (4G_M \|R_{\bar{x}}^{-1}\|^2 + 2\varepsilon)$, $\rho_2 = \|\Gamma\| \left\|(1 + \frac{\Gamma}{\varepsilon_2}) B_{\max}\right\|^2 (\|R_{\bar{x}}^{-1}\|^2 + \frac{2G_M^2 \|R_{\bar{x}}^{-1}\|^4}{\varepsilon})$, $\mu = \|\varepsilon_2 A_c\|^2$. To obtain this inequality, the results of Lemma 6.2, Assumption 6.4, and the bounds G_M are used along with the Young's inequality (Young, 1912).

- For the second term in the Lyapunov function, we use Lemma 6.3, when $0 < \|\Gamma\| \leq W_{min}$ (from *Remark* 6.9), and since the history values are used, $\|Z_{k-1}\|^2 \geq \|\bar{X}_{k-1}\|^2$, then the first difference becomes

$$\Delta L \leq -(\gamma_{\min} - \mu - \rho_1) \underset{\tau,\gamma}{\mathbb{E}} \|\bar{X}(k-1)\|^2 - (\bar{\Pi} N - \|W_0\| \rho_2) \kappa_{min} \underset{\tau,\gamma}{\mathbb{E}} \left\|\tilde{\Theta}(k-1)\right\|^2, \tag{6.36}$$

with $0 \leq \alpha \leq 1$. Substituting the value of $\bar{\Pi}$, the second term is always negative. Therefore, $L(k+1) < L(k), \forall k \in \mathbb{N}$.

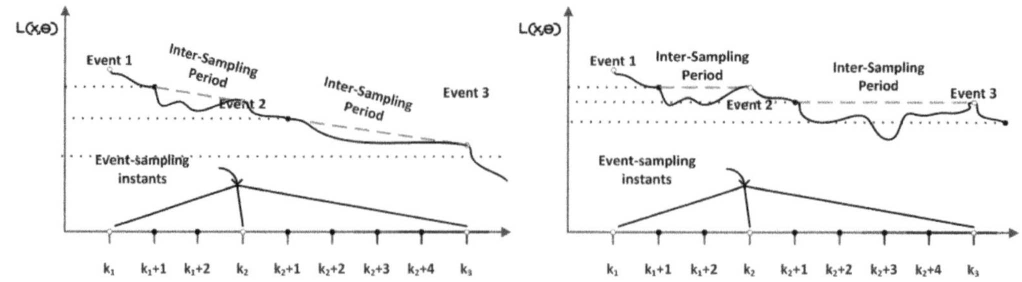

Figure 6.2 Evolution of the Lyapunov function (a) with Hybrid learning scheme. (b) without Hybrid learning scheme.

- Case 2: To extend the stability results for the event-based control scheme, it is required to prove that between any two aperiodic sampling instants, the Lyapunov function is non-increasing. Let the Lyapunov function be given by (6.34). Taking the first difference to get

$$\Delta L_k = \mathop{\mathbb{E}}_{\tau,\gamma}\{\bar{X}_k^T\Gamma\bar{X}_k - \bar{X}_{k-1}^T\Gamma\bar{X}_{k-1} + \bar{\Pi}\sum_{i=1}^{N}\Delta L_{i,\tilde{\Theta}}\} \quad k_l \le k < k_{l+1}, \forall l \in \mathbb{N} \tag{6.37}$$

- When the events occurring at k_l and $k_{l+1} = k_l + 1$, the Lyapunov function is decreasing due to (6.36).
- When the event-sampling does not occur consecutively at $k_l, k_l + 1$, the interval $[k_l, k_{l+1}) = [k_l, k_l + 1) \cup [k_l + 1, k_{l+1})$. During $[k_l, k_l + 1)$, the Lyapunov function is decreasing because of the control policy updated at k_l. In the interval $[k_l + 1, k_{l+1})$ due to the event-sampling algorithm the inequality in (6.29) is satisfied. Therefore, $\Delta L(\bar{X}, \tilde{\Theta}) = \mathop{\mathbb{E}}_{\tau,\gamma}\{\bar{X}_k^T\Gamma\bar{X}_k - \lambda\bar{X}_{k_l+1}^T\Gamma\bar{X}_{k_l+1}\} + \Delta L_{i,\tilde{\Theta}}$. Using the results from Lemma 6.3 and for $\bar{\lambda} < 1$, we get

$$\Delta L_k = -(1-\bar{\lambda})\mathop{\mathbb{E}}_{\tau,\gamma}\{\bar{X}_{k_l}^T\Gamma\bar{X}_{k_l}\} - N\kappa_{min}\mathop{\mathbb{E}}_{\tau,\gamma}\left\|\tilde{\Theta}^T(k_{l-1}^j)\right\|^2 \tag{6.38}$$

- Therefore, $\Delta L(\bar{x}, \tilde{\Theta}) < 0$ during the inter-sampling period. From Lemma 6.1, $\sum_{i=1}^{N}\Delta L(\bar{x}_i, \tilde{\Theta}^i) < 0$. Combining Case 1 and Case 2, the Lyapunov equation satisfies the following inequality,

$$L(k_{l+1}) < L(k_l + 1) < L(k_l), \forall\{k_l\}_{l\in\mathbb{N}} \tag{6.39}$$

The evolution of the Lyapunov function is depicted in Figure 6.2. During the event-sampling instant, due to the updated control policy (6.21), the Lyapunov function decreases. Due to the event-sampling condition (6.29) and the iterative learning within the event-sampling instants, the Lyapunov function decreases during the inter-sampling period. Since the iterative learning does not take place in the time-driven Q-learning (Sahoo and Jagannathan, 2014), the first difference of the parameter estimation error is zero for the inter-event period. This makes the Lyapunov function negative semi-definite during this period.

Remark 6.10. *The design constants $R_{\bar{x}}, W_{min}$, and W_0 are selected based on the inequalities that are analytically derived in the Theorem 6.1 using the bounds on $A_{\bar{x}k}, B_{\bar{x}k}, S_k$ (see Proof). Then, the constants Γ and $\bar{\Pi}$ can be found to ensure closed-loop system stability. The requirement of PE condition is necessary so that the regression vector is non-zero until the parameter error goes to zero. By satisfying the PE condition in the regression vector, the expected value of the parameter estimation error $\tilde{\Theta}_k$ will converge to zero. This PE signal is viewed as the exploration signal in the reinforcement learning literature (Lewis et al., 2012a).*

Remark 6.11. *An initial identification process can be used to obtain the nominal values of $A_{\bar{x}k}, B_{\bar{x}k}$ which can be used to initialize the Q-function parameters. The algorithm presented in this section*

Table 6.1
Distributed hybrid Q-Learning

Subsystem dynamics	$\dot{x}_i(t) = A_i x_i(t) + B_i u_i(t) + \sum_{\substack{j=1 \\ j\neq i}}^{N} A_{ij} x_j(t), \quad x_i(0) = x_{i0},$
Overall system dynamics	$\dot{X}(t) = AX(t) + \gamma_{ca} BU(t-\tau)$
Sampled stochastic dynamics	$\bar{X}_{k+1} = A_{\bar{x}k}\bar{X}_k + B_{\bar{x}k}U_k, \quad \bar{X}(0) = \bar{X}_0$
Temporal difference (TD) error	$e_B(k) = \underset{\tau,\gamma}{\mathbb{E}}\left(r(\bar{X}_k, U_k) + \hat{\Theta}_k^T \Delta\xi_k\right)$
Event-driven TD error	$e_B(k) = \underset{\tau,\gamma}{\mathbb{E}}\left[r(\bar{X}_k^e, U_k) + \hat{\Theta}_k^T \Delta\xi_k^e\right], \quad k_l \le k < k_{l+1}$
TD Learning	$\hat{\Theta}_k^i = \hat{\Theta}_{k-1}^i + \frac{W_{k-2}^i Z_{k-1}^{i,e} \Xi_B^{i,e^T}(k-1)}{1 + Z_{k-1}^{i,e^T} W_{k-2}^i Z_{k-1}^{i,e}}, \quad k = k_l$
	$W_k^i = W_{k-1}^i - \frac{W_{k-1}^i Z_{k-1}^{i,e} Z_{k-1}^{i,e^T} W_{k-1}^i}{1 + Z_{k-1}^{i,e^T} W_{k-1}^i Z_{k-1}^{i,e}}, k = k_l$
Hybrid learning	$\hat{\Theta}(k_l^j) = \hat{\Theta}(k_l^{j-1}) + \frac{W(k_{l-2}^{j-2}) Z(k_{l-1}^{j-1}) \Xi_B^T(k_{l-1}^{j-1})}{1 + Z^T(k_{l-1}^{j-1}) W(k_{l-2}^{j-1}) Z(k_{l-1}^{j-1})}$
	$W(k_l^j) = W(k_{l-1}^{j-1}) - \frac{W(k_{l-1}^{j-1}) Z(k_{l-1}^{j-1}) Z^T(k_{l-1}^{j-1}) W(k_{l-1}^{j-1})}{1 + Z^T(k_{l-1}^{j-1}) W(k_{l-1}^{j-1}) Z(k_{l-1}^{j-1})}$
Distributed control law	$u_{i,k} = -\hat{K}_{i,k}\bar{x}_{i,k}^e - \sum_{j=1, j\neq i}^{N} \hat{K}_{ij,k}\bar{x}_{j,k}^e, \quad k_l \le k < k_{l+1}, \quad \forall i \in \{1,2,..N\}$

can be used as a time-driven Q-learning scheme by not performing the iterative learning between the event-sampling instants. Also, if the iteration index, $j \to \infty$, for each k_l, the algorithm becomes the traditional value iteration-based ADP scheme.

The event-sampling and broadcast algorithm for the subsystems followed by the hybrid learning algorithm is summarized next.

6.3.2.4 Hybrid Q-learning Algorithm

For estimating the overall Q-function locally, we shall use the following request-based event-sampling algorithm. Consider an event occurring at the ith subsystem at the sampling instant k_l. This subsystem generates a request signal and broadcasts it with its state information to the other subsystems. Upon receiving the broadcast request, the other subsystems broadcast their respective state information to all the subsystems. This can be considered as a forced event at the other subsystems.

Remark 6.12. *The events at all the subsystem occur asynchronously based on the local event-sampling condition, whereas the Q-function estimator and control policy remain synchronized at* *each subsystem due to the forced event. The request signal is considered to be broadcasted without any delay in Network-0 in Figure 6.1.*

The algorithm for the hybrid learning scheme is summarized as Algorithm 6.1.

Algorithm 6.1 Hybrid Q-Learning for Intermittent feedback

1: Initialize $\hat{\Theta}_0^j, W_0^j, U_0$
2: **for** Event-sampling instants: $l = 0 \rightarrow \infty$ **do**
3:     **if** Event = Yes **then**
4:         Calculate Bellman Error $e_B(k_l^j)$
5:         Update $\hat{\Theta}_{k_l}^j, W_{k_l}^j$
6:         Update the control input at the actuator U_{k_l}
7:         Pass the parameters $\hat{\Theta}_{k_l}^0, W_{k_l}^0, e_B(k_l^0)$ for iterations
8:     **else**
9:         **for** Iterative Index: $j = 0 \rightarrow \infty$ **do**
10:             Update $\hat{\Theta}_{k_l}^j, W_{k_l}^j$ with $e_B(k_l^j)$
11:             Calculate $e_B(k_l^{j+1})$
12:             **if** $e_B(k_l^{j+1})$-$e_B(k_l^j) < \varepsilon$ or Event = Yes **then**
13:                 Pass the Parameters $\hat{\Theta}_{k_l}^j, W_{k_l}^j$ to QFE
14:                 Goto 4:
15:             **end if**
16:             $j = j+1$
17:         **end for**
18:     **end if**
19:     **if** $e_B(k_{l+1}^0)$-$e_B(k_l^0) < \varepsilon$ **then**
20:         Stop PE Condition
21:     **end if**
22:     $l = l+1$
23: **end for**

6.3.3 TRACKING CONTROL PROBLEM FOR LINEAR INTERCONNECTED SYSTEMS.

Converting a tracking problem into a regulation problem with augmented system dynamics is a common approach used in control theory to simplify the control design process. An overview of this conversion process is given in Chapters 1 and 2. Here we shall briefly look at this conversion for the interconnected system so that the Q-learning algorithm developed in this chapter can be used to address the tracking problem for linear interconnected systems. In a tracking problem, the goal is to make the system output (or states) follow a desired reference trajectory or signal. We begin with the definition of a feasible reference trajectory for the ith subsystem as $x_{i,d}(t) \in \mathbb{R}_i^n$. Assume that the feasible reference trajectory $x_{i,d}(t) \in \mathbb{R}_i^n$ for the ith subsystem is generated by a reference system represented by

$$\dot{x}_{i,d}(t) = A_{i,d}x_{i,d}(t) + \sum_{j=1, j \neq i}^{N} A_{ij,d}x_{j,d}(t), \quad x_{i,d}(0) = x_{id0}, \tag{6.40}$$

where $x_{i,d}(t) \in \mathbb{R}^{n_i}$ is the reference state of the ith subsystem, $A_{ij,d} \in \mathbb{R}^{n_i \times n_j}$ is the coupling matrix, and $A_{i,d} \in \mathbb{R}^{n_i \times n_i}$ is the internal dynamics with $x_{i,d}(0) = 0$ for the generator system.

Define the error between the system state and the reference state as the tracking error, given by $e_{i,r}(t) \triangleq x_i(t) - x_{i,d}(t)$. Then, the tracking error system, utilizing (6.1) and (6.40), can be defined by

$$\dot{e}_{i,r}(t) = \dot{x}_i(t) - \dot{x}_{i,d}(t) = A_i x_i(t) + B_i u_i(t) + \sum_{\substack{j=1\\ j\neq i}}^{N} A_{ij} x_j(t) - A_{i,d} x_{i,d}(t) - \sum_{j=1, j\neq i}^{N} A_{ij,d} x_{j,d}(t). \tag{6.41}$$

The steady-state control inputs corresponding to the desired trajectory is given by

$$u_{i,d}(t) = B_i^{+}(A_{i,d} x_{id} + \sum_j A_{ij,d} x_{j,d} - A_i x_{i,d} - \sum_j A_{ij} x_{j,d}),$$

where B_i^{+} is defined as $(B_i^T B_i)^{-1} B_i^T$ and is assumed to have full-column rank. By augmenting the tracking error $e_{i,r}$ and desired trajectory $x_{i,d}$, the dynamics of the augmented tracking error system can be represented as

$$\dot{\chi}_i(t) = \mathscr{G}_i \chi_i(t) + \mathscr{H}_i u_{i,d}(t) + \mathscr{H}_i \omega_i(t) + \sum_{j=1, j\neq i}^{N} \mathscr{K}_{ij} \chi_j(t), \tag{6.42}$$

where $\chi_i \triangleq [e_{i,r}^T \quad x_{i,d}^T]^T \in \mathbb{R}^{2n_i}$ is the augmented state with $\chi_i(0) = [e_{i,r}^T(0) \quad x_{i,d}^T(0)]^T = \chi_{i0}$, $\mathscr{G}_i \in \mathbb{R}^{2n_i \times 2n_i}$ is given by $\begin{bmatrix} A_i & A_i - A_{i,d} \\ 0 & A_{i,d} \end{bmatrix}$, $\mathscr{H}_i \in \mathbb{R}^{2n_i \times m_i}$ given by $\begin{bmatrix} B_i \\ \mathbf{0} \end{bmatrix}$, and $\mathscr{K}_{ij}$ is given by $\begin{bmatrix} A_{ij} & A_{ij} - A_{ij,d} \\ \mathbf{0} & A_{ij,d} \end{bmatrix}$.

The augmented error system in (6.42) transforms the tracking problem into a regulation problem. We can follow the steps discussed earlier in this chapter to introduce the network losses and derive a sampled data system, which can then be used to synthesize the tracking control using the Q-learning-based control scheme presented in this chapter. With the augmented system, we can design a feedback controller that stabilizes the augmented system at the desired operating point. This controller will implicitly regulate the original system to track the reference trajectory. The gains of the controller need to be tuned to achieve the desired tracking performance and stability.

Next, we shall see some examples where the hybrid learning algorithm is used in the event-based Q-learning framework online to synthesize distributed control policies.

Example 6.1. *A system of N interconnected inverted pendulums coupled by a spring is considered for the verification of the analytical design presented in this chapter. The dynamics are*

$$\dot{x}_i(t) = \begin{bmatrix} 0 & 1 \\ \frac{g}{l} - \frac{a_i k}{ml^2} & 0 \end{bmatrix} x_i(t) + \begin{bmatrix} 0 \\ \frac{1}{ml^2} \end{bmatrix} u_i(t) + \sum_{j\in N_i} \begin{bmatrix} 0 & 0 \\ \frac{h_{ij} k}{ml^2} & 0 \end{bmatrix} x_j(t),$$

where $l = 2$, $g = 10$, $m = 1$, $k = 5$ and $h_{ij} = 1$ for $\forall j \in \{1, 2, .., N\}$. The system is open loop unstable.

Ideal network: The system is discretized with a sampling time of 0.1s. With $P_i = I_{2\times 2}$ and $R_i = 1$, $\forall i = 1,2,3$, the initial states for the system was selected as $x_1 = [2 \ -3]^T$, $x_2 = [-1 \ 2]^T$ and $x_3 = [-1 \ 1]^T$ and $W(0) = 500, \lambda = 0.6, W_{min} = 250$. For the PE condition, Gaussian white noise with zero mean and 0.2 standard deviation was added to the control inputs. The initial parameters of the QFE is obtained by solving the SRE of the nominal model of the system by introducing a multiplicative uncertainity factor (e.g., $A_i = \varepsilon A_i$ and $B_i = \varepsilon B_i$ for all i) with $\varepsilon = (0.2, 1)$. Under the ideal case, without network-induced losses, the comparisons between the Q-learning using PI versus hybrid learning scheme and time-driven Q-learning versus the hybrid learning scheme are shown in Figures 6.3, respectively. Both these comparisons demonstrate that the convergence rate

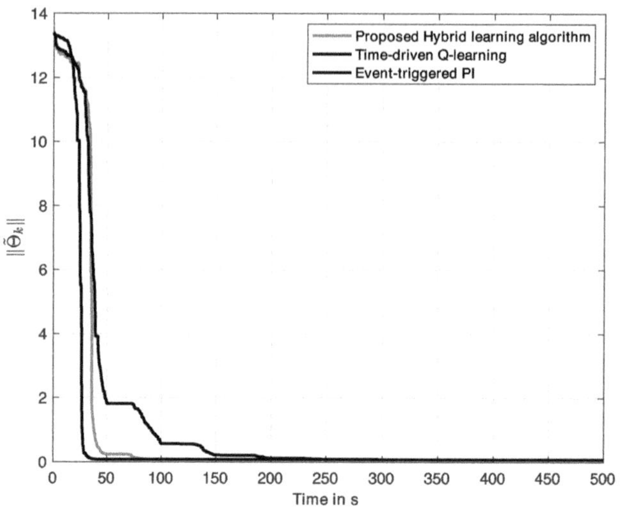

Figure 6.3 Estimation error comparison between event-triggered PI, hybrid learning, and event-triggered TD algorithms when the network is lossless.

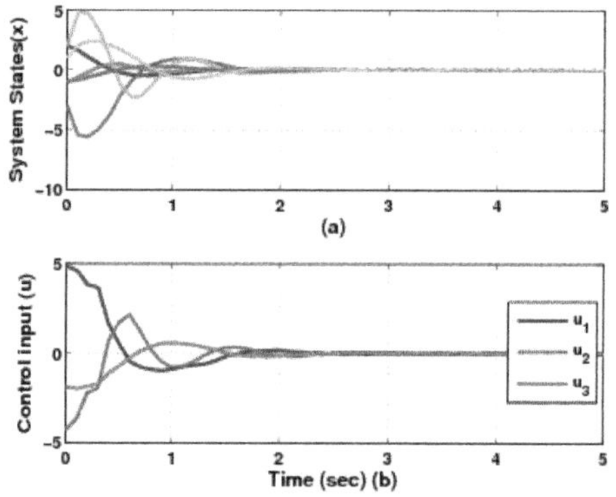

Figure 6.4 Controller performance with delays.

is fastest for the PI while the hybrid learning scheme with event-sampled feedback is faster when compared with the time-driven Q-learning. The advantage of hybrid algorithm over the time-driven Q-learning is due to the iterative parameter updates embedded within the inter-event period. On the other hand, unlike hybrid learning scheme, the PI cannot be implemented in real-time.

Monte-Carlo analysis: The simulation is carried out with random delays ($\bar{d} = 2$) introduced by the network. The delay is characterized by normal distribution with 80 ms mean and 10 ms standard deviation and a Monte-Carlo analysis is carried out for 500 iterations. In the case where the random delays are considered, the state and control trajectories are stable during the learning period as seen in Figure 6.4. The comparison between the time-driven Q-learning and the hybrid learning schemes as seen in Figure 6.5(b) shows that parameter error convergence in the hybrid scheme is much faster, which shows that the hybrid learning algorithm is more robust than the time-driven Q-learning in the presence of delays. This is partly due to augmented state vector and iterative parameter learning within the event-sampled instants.

Random packet-losses characterized with Bernoulli distribution is introduced keeping the probability of data lost at 10%. All design parameters are kept the same. Table 6.2, lists the convergence

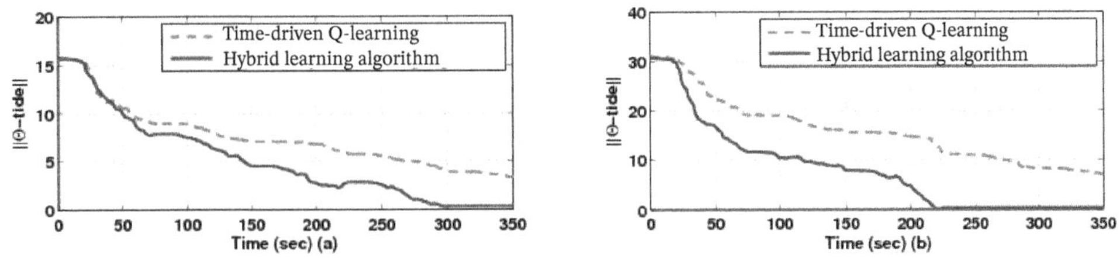

Figure 6.5 Estimation error comparison (a) with 10% packet loss. (b) without packet loss.

Table 6.2
Comparison of parameter error convergence time

Mean-delay (in ms)	% Data-drop out	Convergence time (in sec)	
		Time-driven Q-learning	Hybrid Learning algorithm
0	0	13.7	10.6
30	10	61.0	36.9
	25	246	190.0
80	10	632.0	317.0
	25	486.5	269.0
100	10	239.0	198.0
	25	637.3	239.8

time for the parameter estimation error for the existing time-driven Q-learning algorithm and the hybrid learning algorithm. The error threshold was defined as 10^{-2} and the design parameters were unchanged. In the ideal case, when there are no network losses, the difference in the convergence time for the two algorithms is small. As the network losses are increased, the parameter error converges to the threshold much faster with the hybrid learning algorithm. It is clear that with the hybrid learning scheme the estimation error converges much quicker than the time-driven Q-learning scheme per the information given in the Table 6.2. The total number of events, the state, and the control policy during the learning period are shown in Figures 6.6(a) and 6.6(b) respectively. With the hybrid learning algorithm, the stability of the system is not affected during the learning period. As the events are spaced out, more number of iterative parameter updates take place within the inter-event period.

6.4 CLOSING REMARKS

The hybrid Q-learning-based scheme for a large-scale interconnected system guarantees a desired performance. The stability conditions for the closed-loop system during the learning period is derived using the Lyapunov stability analysis and the asymptotic results hold when we move from isolated systems (Chapter 3) to large-scale systems with event-triggered Q-learning-based online control scheme. The Q-function parameters for the entire system are estimated at each subsystem with the event-sampled inputs, states, and past state vectors, which is computationally not very efficient. This control scheme does not impose any assumptions on the interconnection strengths. The mirror estimator is not used in the event-sampling mechanism and reference models for each subsystems are also not needed. Finally, with embedded iterative updates for parameters in the hybrid

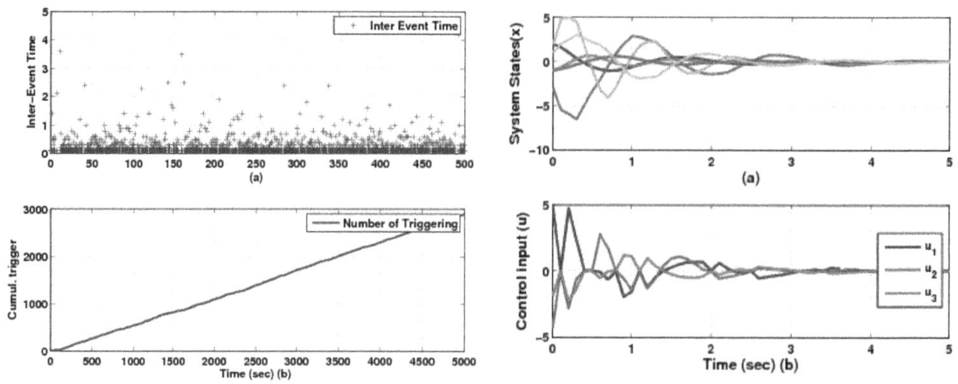

Figure 6.6 (Left panel)(a) Inter-event time and (b) cumulative trigger instants (Right panel) Controller performance with packet-loss. (a) State trajectories and (b) control inputs

learning scheme, the learning process is decoupled from the event-triggering instants.

6.5 PROBLEMS

6.5.1 (Lewis et al., 2012b) The longitudinal dynamics of an F-16 aircraft in straight and level flight at 502 ft/sec are given by

$$\dot{x}(t) = Ax(t) + Bu(t) = \begin{bmatrix} -2.0244\times10^{-2} & 7.8761 & -3.2169\times10^{1} & -6.502\times10^{-1} \\ -2.5373\times10^{-4} & -1.0189 & 0 & 9.0484\times10^{-1} \\ 0 & 0 & 0 & 1 \\ 7.9472\times10^{-11} & -2.498 & 0 & -1.3861 \end{bmatrix} x \tag{6.43}$$

$$+ \begin{bmatrix} -1\times10^{-2} \\ -2.09\times10^{-3} \\ 0 \\ -1.99\times10^{-1} \end{bmatrix} u \tag{6.44}$$

The state is $x = \begin{bmatrix} v_T & \alpha & \theta & q \end{bmatrix}^T$, with v_T the forward velocity, α the angle of attack, θ the pitch angle, and q the pitch rate. The control input $u(t)$ is the elevator deflection δ_e.

(a) Plot the response of the open-loop system to initial conditions of $x_0 = \begin{bmatrix} 0 & 0.1 & 0 & 1 \end{bmatrix}^T$ (note that the angular units are in radians).

(b) Try MATLAB function lqr to perform linear quadratic regulator design. Use $Q = I, R = 0.1$.

6.5.2 For the system described in the previous problem, use the Q-learning algorithm (Algorithm 6.1) with $\tau = 0$ and $\gamma_{ca} = 1$ to learn the control inputs for $Q = I, R = 0.1$. Compare the performance of the controlled system with the event-triggered control algorithm given in Table 3.3.

6.5.3 Consider a of linear dynamical system given by

$$\dot{x}(t) = Ax(t) + Bu(t), \tag{6.45}$$

where $A = \begin{pmatrix} 0 & -1 \\ 1 & 0 \end{pmatrix}$ and $B = \begin{pmatrix} 1 & 0 \\ 0 & 1 \end{pmatrix}$. Use the Q-learning algorithm (Algorithm 6.1) with $\tau = 0$ and $\gamma_{ca} = 1$ to learn the control inputs for $Q = I, R = 0.1$.

6.5.4 For a linear system taking the form $\frac{d}{dt}x(t) = Ax(t) + \gamma_{ca}Bu(t-\tau)$, where $\tau = 0.05$ and γ_{ca} is a random variable characterized by Bernoulli distribution with the probability of data lost is 5%. Use the Q-learning algorithm (Algorithm 6.1) to learn the control inputs for $Q = I, R = 0.1I$. Use the matrices A and B as given in Problem 6.5.1.

6.5.5 Now consider the channel losses for the system described in 6.5.3. The new dynamics will take the form $\frac{d}{dt}x(t) = Ax(t) + \gamma_{ca}Bu(t-\tau)$, where τ and γ_{ca} are random variables characterized by Gaussian distribution with mean 10 ms and 1 ms standard deviation, and Bernoulli distribution with the probability of data lost is 10%, respectively. Use the Q-learning algorithm (Algorithm 6.1) to learn the control inputs for $Q = I, R = 0.1I$. What happens when τ is a random variable following a Gaussian distribution with mean 30 ms and 1 ms standard deviation?

6.5.6 Consider the large-scale system composed of N interconnected inverted pendulums coupled by a spring. The dynamics are

$$\dot{x}(t) = \begin{bmatrix} 0 & 1 \\ \frac{g}{l} - \frac{a_i k}{ml^2} & 0 \end{bmatrix} x_i(t) + \gamma_{ca} \begin{bmatrix} 0 \\ \frac{1}{ml^2} \end{bmatrix} u_i(t-\tau) + \sum_{j \in N_i} \begin{bmatrix} 0 & 0 \\ \frac{h_{ij}k}{ml^2} & 0 \end{bmatrix} x_j(t),$$

where $l = 5$, $g = 10$, $m = 5$, $k = 5$ and $h_{ij} = 1$ for $\forall j \in \{1, 2, .., N\}$. The system is open-loop unstable.

(a) Use the Q-learning algorithm (Algorithm 6.1) with τ being a random variable following a Gaussian distribution with mean 100ms and 20ms standard deviation and γ is a random variable characterized by Bernoulli distribution with the probability of data lost is 10% to learn the control inputs for $Q = 10 \times I, R = 0.001$.

(b) Analyze the performance when the cost function is redefined with $R = 10$ and $Q = 0.1 \times I$.

6.5.7 Use the system defined in the previous problem and do not use the data history in the hybrid Q-learning algorithm described in this chapter. Do the Q-function parameters converge? Try using the gradient descent algorithm in place of RLS-based parameter updates. Do the Q-function parameters converge?

6.5.8 Use the system defined in the Example 6.1. Do not use the covariance resetting technique to reset the learning gain in the hybrid Q-learning algorithm described in this chapter. Does the Q-function parameters converge?

6.5.9 Consider a three-area interconnected power system with HVDC links described in Pham et al. (2019). This system can be represented as

$$\begin{aligned} \dot{x}(t) &= Ax(t) + \sum_{i=1}^{3} A_i x(t-h_i) + \sum_{i=1}^{2} B_i u(t-d_i) + \Gamma w(t), \\ y(t) &= Cx(t), \end{aligned} \tag{6.46}$$

where $x(t) = [x_1^T, x_2^T, x_3^T]^T \in \mathbb{R}^n$, $u(t) = [u_1^T, u_2^T]^T \in \mathbb{R}^m$, $w(t) = [w_1^T, w_2^T, w_3^T]^T \in \mathbb{R}^q$, and $y(t) = [y_1^T, y_2^T, y_3^T]^T \in \mathbb{R}^p$ with

$$A = \begin{bmatrix} A_{11} & A_{12} & A_{13} \\ A_{21} & A_{22} & A_{23} \\ A_{31} & A_{32} & A_{33} \end{bmatrix}, \quad C = \text{diag}(C_1,\ C_2\ C_3),$$

$$B_1 = \begin{bmatrix} B_{d_1} & 0_{n_1 \times m_2} \\ 0_{n_2 \times m_1} & 0_{n_2 \times m_2} \\ 0_{n_3 \times m_1} & 0_{n_3 \times m_2} \end{bmatrix}, \quad B_2 = \begin{bmatrix} 0_{n_1 \times m_1} & 0_{n_1 \times m_2} \\ 0_{n_2 \times m_1} & B_{d_2} \\ 0_{n_3 \times m_1} & 0_{n_3 \times m_2} \end{bmatrix},$$

$$A_1 = \text{diag}(A_{11_h},\ 0_{n_2 \times n_2},\ 0_{n_3 \times n_3}),\ \ A_2 = \text{diag}(0_{n_1 \times n_1},\ A_{22_h},\ 0_{n_3 \times n_3}),$$

and $A_3 = \text{diag}(0_{n_1 \times n_1},\ 0_{n_2 \times n_2},\ A_{33_h})$. The system matrices are defined as

$$A_{ii} = \begin{bmatrix} \frac{-D_i}{M_i} & 0 & \frac{1}{M_i} & \frac{1}{M_i} & \frac{-1}{M_i} & 0 \\ \frac{-1}{R_{gi}T_{gi}} & \frac{-1}{T_{gi}} & 0 & 0 & 0 & 0 \\ 0 & \frac{1}{T_{ti}} & \frac{-1}{T_{ti}} & 0 & 0 & 0 \\ 0 & 0 & 0 & \frac{-1}{T_{ei}} & 0 & 0 \\ 0 & 0 & 0 & 0 & \frac{-1}{T_{dci}} & 0 \\ 1 & 0 & 0 & 0 & 0 & 0 \end{bmatrix}, \quad i = 1, 2, \quad A_{12} = A_{21} = [0],$$

$$A_{i3} = \begin{bmatrix} 0_{5\times1} & 0_{5\times3} \\ -1 & 0_{1\times3} \end{bmatrix}, \quad A_{iih} = \begin{bmatrix} 0_{3\times1} & 0_{3\times5} \\ -\frac{K_{ei}}{T_{ei}}\rho_{ei} & 0_{1\times5} \\ 0_{2\times1} & 0_{2\times5} \end{bmatrix}, \quad B_{d_i} = \begin{bmatrix} 0_{1\times4} & \frac{K_{dci}}{T_{dci}} & 0 \end{bmatrix}^T, \quad i = 1,2,$$

$$C_i = \begin{bmatrix} 1 & 0_{1\times3} & 0 & 0 \\ 0 & 0_{1\times3} & 1 & 0 \\ 0 & 0_{1\times3} & 0 & 1 \end{bmatrix}, \quad i = 1,2, \quad A_{31} = A_{32} = \begin{bmatrix} 0_{1\times4} & \frac{1}{M_3} & 0 \\ 0_{3\times4} & 0_{3\times1} & 0_{3\times1} \end{bmatrix},$$

$$A_{33} = \begin{bmatrix} \frac{-D_3}{M_3} & 0 & \frac{1}{M_3} & \frac{1}{M_3} \\ \frac{-1}{R_{g3}T_{g3}} & \frac{-1}{T_{g3}} & 0 & 0 \\ 0 & \frac{1}{T_{t3}} & \frac{-1}{T_{t3}} & 0 \\ 0 & 0 & 0 & \frac{-1}{T_{e3}} \end{bmatrix}, \quad C_3 = \begin{bmatrix} 1 & 0_{1\times(n_3-1)} \end{bmatrix}, \quad \Gamma_i = \begin{bmatrix} \frac{-1}{M_i} & 0_{1\times(n_i-1)} \end{bmatrix}^T,$$

$$A_{33h} = \begin{bmatrix} 0_{3\times1} & 0_{3\times3} \\ -\frac{K_{e3}}{T_{e3}}\rho_{e3} & 0_{1\times3} \end{bmatrix}, \quad \Gamma_3 = \begin{bmatrix} \frac{-1}{M_3} & 0_{1\times(n_3-1)} \end{bmatrix}^T.$$

For this system, select the system parameters as $T_{ti} = 0.3$, $T_{gi} = 0.08$, $R_{gi} = 2.4$, $\rho_{e1} = 0.9/2.4$, $\rho_{e2} = 1.1/2.4$, $\rho_{e3} = 1/2.4$, $M_i = 0.1667$, $T_{dci} = 0.1$, $T_{ei} = 1$, $K_{ei} = 1$, $K_{dc1} = 0.0191$, $K_{dc2} = 0.0164$, $D_i = 0.0083$, $\alpha_{ij} = 1$, the rated power is 2000 MW, and design a Q-learning-based control policy using Algorithm 6.1. Assume $h_i = 0$ and d_i is a random variable sampled from Gaussian distribution with mean 0.1 and variance 0.05.

6.5.10 For the system described in the previous problem, can the Algorithm 6.1 be applied to the system defined in (6.46) when the delays modeled by h_i are given by Gaussian distribution?

7 Nonlinear Interconnected Systems

CONTENTS

This chapter, based on the work presented in Narayanan and Jagannathan (2017) and Narayanan et al. (2018c), introduces approximate optimal distributed control schemes for large-scale interconnected systems governed by nonlinear dynamcis. We shall leverage event-triggered state feedback control scheme and the hybrid learning approach introduced in Chapter 6 to design distributed nonlinear controllers that learn optimal policies online. Here we shall explore the learning-based synthesis of distributed optimal adaptive controllers with both state and output feedback. To alleviate the need for complete state measurements, an extended nonlinear observer is introduced at each subsystem to estimate the system's internal states using measurable feedback data. We shall also see that the optimal control design for the interconnected system can be reformulated as an N-player dynamic game. The game-theoretic formulation for large-scale interconnected systems, presented in Narayanan et al. (2018c), introduces a systematic way to optimize local (subsystem level) as well as global (overall system level) objectives. An ADP-based approach with critic NNs is introduced to approximate the Nash equilibrium solution of the game by learning the solution to the coupled Hamilton-Jacobi (HJ) equations for the continuous and the event-sampled closed-loop systems. We shall see that modeling the distributed optimal control in a game-theoretic setting offers additional flexibility in terms of fine-tuning the performance of the interconnected systems.

7.1 INTRODUCTION

In this chapter, we shall investigate the learning-based control problem for nonlinear interconnected systems, an area of active research in the control community (Mehraeen and Jagannathan, 2011; Wang et al., 2014; Liu et al., 2014; Spooner and Passino, 1999; Huang et al., 2003; Narendra and Mukhopadhyay, 2010). As we navigate the realm of cyber-physical systems (CPS) and internet-of-things (IoT), we encounter intricate networks of interacting dynamic units in diverse applications. Controlling these interconnected subsystems presents unique challenges in designing distributed control algorithms, which we will continue to explore in this chapter, for nonlinear interconnected systems. When the interconnection or the coupling dynamics are modeled by nonlinear functions, distributed control policies using adaptive terms have been reported in the literature (Huang et al., 2003; Narendra and Mukhopadhyay, 2010). These control policies incorporate additional compensation terms in the control input, finely tuned to learn interconnection dynamics and effectively cancel their effects.

One of the impediments common to these approaches is in implementing the distributed control algorithm, as it introduces communication overhead due to sharing of measurement (outputs or states) information among subsystems. As we have seen in the earlier chapters, to mitigate these costs, event-triggered controllers are proposed (Guinaldo et al., 2011; Wang and Lemmon, 2011a; Tallapragada and Chopra, 2013; Mazo and Tabuada, 2011; Garcia and Antsaklis, 2013; Sahoo et al., 2016; Zhong and He, 2016). In order to extend the learning-based optimal control scheme presented for linear interconnected system in Chapter 6 to the nonlinear setting, we should consider the (coupled) Hamilton-Jacobi-Bellman (HJB) equation associated with the nonlinear interconnected system. When the system dynamics are nonlinear, since the HJB equation does not have a closed-form solution (Werbos, 1995), inspired by the reinforcement RL techniques (Sutton and Barto, 1998), a suite of learning algorithms based on dynamic programming have been proposed, which we have reviewed in Chapter 2. These learning ADP algorithms generate an approximation of the optimal value function and an approximate optimal control policy (Werbos, 1995; Liu et al., 2014; Mehraeen and Jagannathan, 2011; Wang et al., 2014; Prokhorov et al., 1995; Xu and Jagannathan, 2013; Lewis et al., 2012a; Barto et al., 2004; Dierks and Jagannathan, 2010a; Sahoo et al., 2016; Chen and Jagannathan, 2008; Wang et al., 2015; Zhong and He, 2016; Vignesh and Jagannathan, 2016; Liu et al., 2012; Xu et al., 2014a).

Typically, as discussed in Chapter 4, the optimal value function is approximated by using an artificial NN without solving the HJB equation directly. In order to learn the NN weights, the *HJB residual error*, which is a continuous time equivalent of the Bellman error, is used. The RL-based online ADP methods (Liu et al., 2014; Mehraeen and Jagannathan, 2011) applied to interconnected systems typically requires extensive computations and exchange of feedback information among subsystems through a communication network. Comparing with the traditional ADP design, we have seen in the earlier chapters that the event-based method samples the state and updates the controller only when it is necessary.

On the other hand, in the realm of RL theory, the Generalized Policy Iteration (GPI) algorithm, inspired by classical dynamic programming, was introduced to mitigate the requirement for precise knowledge of state transition probabilities and reward distributions, as outlined by Sutton (1998) (Sutton and Barto, 1998). In the GPI algorithm, policy evaluation and improvement are two iterative steps. Various RL schemes are developed based on the number of iterations in each step, aimed at generating a sequence of control actions to maximize a specific reward function. In Chapter 2, we reviewed examples of these algorithms, such as policy and value iteration schemes. The policy evaluation step learns the optimal value function and the policy improvement step learns the greedy action. For online control algorithms, the temporal difference learning (TDL)-based RL schemes with one-step policy evaluation are more suitable. In TDL methods, using the one step feedback and the estimated future cost (bootstrapping), the value function parameters are updated (Sutton and Barto, 1998). Inspired by the TD ADP design in (Dierks and Jagannathan, 2010a) and based on the developments in (Narayanan and Jagannathan, 2017), in the first part of this chapter, we shall develop an online learning framework for interconnected systems by using event-triggered state and output information. Several NNs (Lewis et al., 1998) will be used for estimating the optimal value functions by minimizing the HJB error (Sutton and Barto, 1998). To overcome the requirement of larger inter-event time as demanded by the event-based PI or VI algorithm, and to reduce the convergence time of the event-based TD learning algorithm, a TD-ADP scheme combined with iterative learning between two event sampling instants is developed, which is similar to the hybrid algorithm in Chapter 6.

As the event-triggering instants are decided based on a dynamic condition, the time between any consecutive events is not fixed. Therefore, embedding finite number of iterations to tune the NN weights while assuring stable operation is non-trivial, especially due to the fact that the initial NN parameters and the initial control policy play a vital part in determining the stability during the learning phase. We shall first see the design of learning-based controllers when the state vector of each subsystem is communicated to others. Next, to relax the requirement of measuring the entire state vector, we will design nonlinear observers at each subsystem to estimate the overall system state vector using outputs that are communicated only at event-based sampling instants from the other subsystems. In the second part of the chapter, we will revisit the design of the objective function for the subsystems based on which the local as well as the global system objectives are specified to the learning mechanism.

7.2 NONLINEAR INTERCONNECTED SYSTEMS

7.2.1 SYSTEM DYNAMICS

Consider a nonlinear input-affine system composed of N interconnected subsystems. Let the dynamics of each subsystem be represented as

$$\begin{aligned}\dot{x}_i(t) &= f_i(x_i) + g_i(x_i)u_i(t) + \sum\nolimits_{j=1, j\neq i}^{N} \Delta_{ij}(x_i, x_j),\\ x_i(0) &= x_{i0},\ \ y_i(t) = C_i x_i(t),\end{aligned} \tag{7.1}$$

where $x_i(t) \in S_i \subseteq \mathbb{R}^{n_i \times 1}$ represents the state vector, $\dot{x}_i(t) \in \mathbb{R}^{n_i \times 1}$ represents the state derivative with respect to time for the ith subsystem, $u_i(t) \in \mathbb{R}^{m_i}$ represents the control action, $f_i : \mathbb{R}^{n_i} \to \mathbb{R}^{n_i}$, $g_i : \mathbb{R}^{n_i} \to \mathbb{R}^{n_i \times m_i}$, and $\Delta_{ij} : \mathbb{R}^{n_i \times n_j} \to \mathbb{R}^{n_i}$, represents the nonlinear dynamics, input gain function, and the interconnection map between the ith and j^{th} subsystems, respectively; $y_i(t) \in \mathbb{R}^{p_i}$ is the output vector with $C_i \in \mathbb{R}^{p_i \times n_i}$, a constant matrix and S_i is a compact set. The dynamics of the augmented system are expressed as

$$\dot{X}(t) = F(X) + G(X)U(t),\ X(0) = X_0, \tag{7.2}$$

where $X(t) \in S \subseteq \mathbb{R}^{n \times 1}$, $U(t) \in \mathbb{R}^m$, $G : \mathbb{R}^n \to \mathbb{R}^{n \times m}$, $F : \mathbb{R}^n \to \mathbb{R}^n$, $U = [u_1{}^T, .., u_N{}^T]^T$, $m = \sum_{i=1}^N m_i$, $n = \sum_{i=1}^N n_i$, $\dot{X} = [\dot{x}_1^T, .., \dot{x}_N^T]^T$, $G(X) = diag(g_1(x_1), .., g_N(x_N))$, $F(X) = [(f_1(x_1) + \sum_{j=2}^N \Delta_{1j})^T, .., (f_N(x_N) + \sum_{j=1}^{N-1} \Delta_{Nj})^T]^T$, and S is a compact set obtained as a result of finite union of S_i. The following assumptions on the system dynamics will be made in the analysis presented in this section.

Assumption 7.1. *Each subsystem described by (7.1) and the interconnected system (7.2) are controllable.*

Assumption 7.2. *The nonlinear maps $F(X)$ and $G(X)$ are Lipschitz continuous functions in the compact set S.*

Assumption 7.3. *There exists g_{im} and $g_{iM} > 0$ such that $g_{im} < \|g_i(x_i)\| \leq g_{iM}$, $\forall i \in \{1, .., N\}$.*

Assumption 7.4. *We shall begin with the assumption that the states are measurable. This will be relaxed in the subsequent design using outputs and extended nonlinear observers. Delay and packet loss in the communication network are assumed to be absent.*

Define a subsequence $\{t_k\}_{k\in\mathbb{N}} \subset t$ to represent the event-triggering time-instants. The state of the ith subsystem at the sampling instant t_k^i is denoted as $x_i(t_k^i)$. During the inter-event period, latest sensor measurements are not updated at the controller. The difference between the actual state and the states available at the controller results in an event-sampling error given by

$$e_i(t) = x_i(t) - x_i(t_k^i),\ t_k^i \le t < t_{k+1}^i. \tag{7.3}$$

This error is reset to zero at the sampling instants due to the feedback update. A brief background on the design of optimal controller using aperiodic, event-triggered feedback is presented in the next subsection.

7.2.2 EVENT-BASED OPTIMAL CONTROL POLICY

Let the performance of the interconnected system (7.2), be evaluated using the following function

$$V(X(t),U(t)) = \int_t^{\infty} [Q(X) + U^T(\tau)RU(\tau)]d\tau, \tag{7.4}$$

where $R \in \mathbb{R}^{m\times m}$ is a positive definite penalty matrix, penalizing control actions and $Q : \mathbb{R}^n \to \mathbb{R}$ with $Q(0) = 0$, represent positive definite functions that penalize the states. Use the integral in (7.4) to denote the infinite horizon value function $V(X(t))$ defined in S. If $V(X(t))$ and its derivative are continuous in its domain, the time-derivative of the $V(X(t))$ can be obtained as described in (Bertsekas, 2012; Dierks and Jagannathan, 2010a) and it is given by

$$\dot{V}(X(t)) = -\left[Q(X) + U^T(t)RU(t)\right] = \frac{\partial V^T(t)}{\partial X(t)}\dot{X}(t). \tag{7.5}$$

Assuming that a minimum of the value function exists and it is unique (Lewis et al., 2012a), the optimal control policy can be obtained as

$$U^*(t) = -\frac{R^{-1}}{2} G^T(X(t)) \frac{\partial V(t)^*}{\partial X(t)}. \tag{7.6}$$

Substituting (7.6) in (7.5), the HJB equation is obtained as

$$H = Q(X) + \frac{\partial V^{*T}}{\partial X} F(X) - \frac{1}{4}\frac{\partial V^{*T}}{\partial X} G(X)R^{-1}G^T(X)\frac{\partial V^*}{\partial X}. \tag{7.7}$$

When the feedback is aperiodic and event-based, the Hamiltonian in (7.7) between events can be represented using a piecewise continuous control input as

$$H = \left(Q(X) + U^{*^T}(t_k)RU^*(t_k)\right) + \left(\frac{\partial V^*}{\partial X}\right)^T \dot{X}(t). \tag{7.8}$$

The piecewise continuous control policy that minimizes the Hamiltonian in (7.8) is defined as

$$U^*(t_k) = -\frac{R^{-1}}{2} G^T(X_e) \frac{\partial V^*}{\partial X_e}, \tag{7.9}$$

with $X_e = X(t_k)$, the state held at the actuator using a ZOH circuit between t_k and t_{k+1} for all $k \in \mathbb{N}$.

The function approximation property of NNs with with event-triggered feedback is recalled next.

Neural network approximation using event-based feedback

With the following standard assumption, recall the effect of the aperiodic event-based feedback on the approximation property of the NN from Chapter 4.

Assumption 7.5. *The NN reconstruction error and its derivative, $\varepsilon_i(x), \nabla_x \varepsilon_i(x)$, the constant target weights θ_i^*, and the activation function $\phi(x)$, which satisfies $\phi(0) = 0$, are all bounded.*

Remark 7.1. *The NN approximation with state vector sampled at event-triggering instants as input is a function of event-sampling error. Since the reconstruction error ε_e depends on the error due to event sampling, a direct relationship between approximation accuracy and the frequency of events is revealed. One of the motivations behind the hybrid learning algorithm is to decouple the relationship between the accuracy of approximation and the sampling frequency. In chapter 4, this trade-off is handled by designing the event-triggering condition based on the estimated weights and the states of the system. This resulted in an inverse relationship between the inter-event time and the weight estimation error, thereby forcing more events when the difference between the estimated NN weight and the target weights is large.*

7.3 DISTRIBUTED CONTROLLER DESIGN USING STATE AND OUTPUT FEEDBACK

In this section, we shall begin with the design of distributed approximately optimal controller with state feedback using a hybrid learning scheme. Later, we shall derive nonlinear observers to relax the requirement of full state measurements. Before learning an optimal value function, it is important to assess the existence of such a function, which is related to the existence of solution to an associated partial differential (HJB) equation. Therefore, the following assumption is needed to proceed further.

Assumption 7.6. *$V^*(X) \in C^1(S)$ is a unique solution to the HJB equation introduced in the previous section, where $C^1(S)$ represents the class of continuous functions defined in a closed and bounded set S and have continuous derivatives in S.*

Proposition 7.1 (Vignesh and Jagannathan (2016)). *Consider the augmented system dynamics in (7.2) with the individual subsystems (7.1), $\forall i \in \{1,2,..,N\}$, $\exists u_i^*(t)$ for $t \in [0,\infty)$, which is a function of $X(t)$, such that the cost function (7.4) is minimized.*

Proof: First, consider the infinite horizon value function defined by (7.4) for the augmented system in (7.2). Define

$$R = diag(R_1, R_2, .., R_N), \quad Q(X) = \sum_{i=1}^{N} Q_i(X),$$
$$U(X(t)) = [u_1^T, .., u_N^T]^T, \quad \frac{\partial V^T}{\partial X} = \left[\frac{\partial V_1^T}{\partial x_1}, \frac{\partial V_2^T}{\partial x_2} \ldots\ldots \frac{\partial V_N^T}{\partial x_N}\right],$$

and

$$V(X(t)) = \int_t^\infty \left(\sum_{i=1}^{N} [Q_i(X) + u_i{}^T R_i u_i]\right) d\tau = \int_t^\infty \sum_{i=1}^{N} V_i(X(\tau)) d\tau. \tag{7.10}$$

The Hamiltonian (7.8) becomes

$$H(X,U,\frac{\partial V}{\partial X}) = \left[\frac{\partial V_1^T}{\partial x_1}, \ldots, \frac{\partial V_N^T}{\partial x_N}\right] [\dot{x}_1^T(t), \ldots, \dot{x}_N^T(t)]^T + \left(\sum_{i=1}^{N} [Q_i(X) + u_i{}^T R_i u_i]\right)$$
$$= \sum_{i=1}^{N} H_i(X, u_i, \frac{\partial V_i^T}{\partial x_i}), \text{ where } H_i(X, u_i, \frac{\partial V_i^T}{\partial x_i}) = \left(\frac{\partial V_i^T}{\partial x_i} \dot{x}_i + Q_i(X) + u_i{}^T R_i u_i\right). \tag{7.11}$$

For optimality, each subsystem should generate a control policy from $H_i(X, u_i, \frac{\partial V_i^T}{\partial x_i})$ as

$$u_i{}^*(t) = -\frac{1}{2} R_i{}^{-1} g_i{}^T(x_i) \frac{\partial V_i{}^*}{\partial x_i}, \quad \forall i \in 1, 2, ..N. \tag{7.12}$$

By designing controllers at each subsystem to generate (7.12), the cost function (7.4) of the augmented system is minimized.

Remark 7.2. *A strictly decentralized controller can be realized by designing (7.12) as a function of $x_i(t)$. Despite the simplicity of such controller, the work by Narendra and Mukhopadhyay (2010) highlighted the unacceptable performance observed, especially in the transient period, as a result of such design approach. Therefore, (7.12) is desired to be a function of $X(t)$ and it can be considered as*

$$u_i{}^*(t) = -\frac{1}{2} R_i{}^{-1} g_i{}^T(x_i) \frac{\partial V_{i,i}^*}{\partial x_i} - \frac{1}{2} R_i{}^{-1} g_i{}^T(x_i) \sum_{\substack{j=1 \\ j \neq i}}^{N} \frac{\partial V_{i,j}^*}{\partial x_i}, \tag{7.13}$$

where $V_{i,j}^*$ is the cost due to interconnections and $V_{i,i}^*$ is the optimal cost of the ith subsystem when the interconnections are absent and $V_i^* = V_{i,i}^* + V_{i,j}^*$. The control policy as expressed in (7.13) is composed of two parts. The first part denotes the optimal control policy for a decoupled subsystem wherein the interconnections are absent while the second part compensates for the interconnections.

Remark 7.3. *Note that the control policy (7.12) is considered to be distributed and it is equivalent to (7.13). In the decentralized control policy, the second term in (7.13) is zero (Mehraeen and Jagannathan, 2011). This term explicitly takes into account the interconnection terms in the subsystem dynamics and it is expected to compensate for the interconnections. An equivalent control policy for the linear interconnected system using Riccati solution can be obtained as*

$$u_i^*(t) = -k_{ii} x_i(t) - \sum_{\substack{i=1 \\ i \neq j}}^{N} k_{ij} x_j(t).$$

Here, k_{ii} and k_{ij} are the diagonal and off-diagonal entries of the Kalman gain matrix corresponding to the optimal controller for the interconnected system (7.2) with linear dynamics.

7.3.1 STATE FEEDBACK CONTROLLER DESIGN

We shall use the artificial NNs to represent the optimal value function in a parametric form using NN weights and a set of basis function with a bounded approximation error. Using the parameterized representation, the value function can be represented as

$$V_i(X) = \theta_i^T \phi(X) + \varepsilon_i(X),$$

where $\phi(X)$ is a basis function and $\varepsilon_i(X)$ is the bounded approximation/reconstruction error. Let the target NN weights be θ_i^* and the estimated NN weights be $\hat{\theta}_i$ at the ith subsystem. The parameterized HJB equation with approximate optimal value function can be obtained as

$$Q_i(X) + \theta_i^{*T} \nabla_x \phi(x) \dot{f}_i(x) - \frac{1}{4} \theta_i^{*T} \nabla_x \phi(x) D_i \nabla^T{}_x \phi(x) \theta_i^* + \varepsilon_{iHJB} = 0, \tag{7.14}$$

where

$$\varepsilon_{iHJB} = \nabla_x \varepsilon_i{}^T (\dot{f}_i(x) - \frac{D_i}{2} (\nabla^T{}_x \phi(x) \theta_i^* + \nabla_x \varepsilon_i)) + \frac{1}{4} \nabla_x \varepsilon_i{}^T D_i \nabla_x \varepsilon_i,$$

$$\dot{f}_i(x) = f_i(x_i) + \sum_{\substack{j=1 \\ j \neq i}}^{N} \Delta_{ij}(x_i, x_j),$$

the partial derivative of the optimal cost function V_i^{*T} with respect to x_i is $\nabla^T{}_x\phi(x)\theta_i^*$, and $D_i = D_i(x_i) = g_i(x_i)R_i{}^{-1}g_i{}^T(x_i)$. Let $\|\nabla^T{}_x\phi(x)\theta_i^*\| \leq V_{xiM}$ and $\|D_i\| \leq D_{iM}$. Now, using the estimated weights $\hat{\theta}_i$, the control input (7.12), can be written as

$$\hat{u}_i(t) = -\frac{1}{2}R_i^{-1}g_i^T\hat{\theta}_i^T\nabla_x\phi(x)$$

and the parameterized Hamiltonian equation is

$$\hat{H}_i = Q_i(X) + \hat{\theta}_i^T\nabla_x\phi(x)f_i(x) - \frac{1}{4}\hat{\theta}_i^T\nabla_x\phi(x)D_i\nabla^T{}_x\phi(x)\hat{\theta}_i. \tag{7.15}$$

Equation (7.15) can be used to evaluate the value function for the given policy. Since it is a consistency condition, if the estimated value function is the true optimal value function for the control policy (7.12), then $\hat{H}_i = 0$. Due to the estimated quantity $\hat{\theta}_i$, the value function calculated using the estimated weights is not equal to the optimal value function. This will result in a HJB residual error and $\hat{H}_i = 0$ is no longer true. The estimates $\hat{\theta}_i$ are now updated such that the HJB residual error is minimized. Consider the Levenberg-Marquardt algorithm (Lewis et al., 2012a) to update the NN weights. In this case, the weight estimates evolve based on the dynamic equation given by

$$\dot{\hat{\theta}}_i(t) = \frac{-\alpha_{i1}\sigma_i\hat{H}_i}{(\sigma_i^T\sigma_i + 1)^2},$$

where α_{i1} is the learning step and $\sigma_i = \nabla_x\phi(x)f_i(x) - \frac{1}{2}\nabla_x\phi(x)D_i\nabla_x^T\phi(x)\hat{\theta}_i$. This weight tuning rule ensures the HJB residual error convergence while stability of the closed-loop system when the estimated weights are used in the control policy is not a given, especially, if the initial control policy is not stabilizing. Therefore, to relax the dependence on the initial control policy in dictating the stability of the closed-loop system, a conditional stabilizing term was appended in the weight update rule proposed by Dierks and Jagannathan (2010a). Together with this term, we may use the following weight update rule

$$\dot{\hat{\theta}}_i(t) = -\frac{\alpha_{i1}}{(\sigma_i^T\sigma_i + 1)^2}\sigma_i\hat{H}_i + \frac{1}{2}\beta_i\nabla_x\phi(x)D_iL_{ix}(x_i) - \kappa_i\hat{\theta}_i, \tag{7.16}$$

where κ_i, β_i are positive design parameters and $L_{ix}(x_i)$ is the partial derivative of a positive definite Lyapunov function for the ith subsystem with respect to the state. Since the controller has access to the feedback information only when an event is triggered, (7.16) will have to be slightly modified and this will be presented in the next subsection.

Remark 7.4. *By utilizing the nonlinear maps g_i, the stabilizing term in (7.16) is appended to the NN weight tuning rule to relax the requirement of initial stabilizing control (Dierks and Jagannathan, 2010a). In the event-triggered implementation of the controller, the stabilizing term in the update rule ensures stability of the closed-loop system at the event-based sampling instants and the sigma-modification term ensures that the weights are bounded.*

The event-triggered state feedback controller design is introduced next.

7.3.1.1 Event-triggered state feedback controller

For the near optimal distributed control design with event-triggered state feedback, the error (7.3) introduced due to aperiodic feedback will drive the control policy between two event-based sampling instants. With the estimated optimal value function and the estimated optimal control policy, the Hamiltonian is represented as

$$\hat{H}_i(X, \hat{u}_{i,e}, \frac{\partial\hat{V}_i^T}{\partial x_i}) = \frac{\partial\hat{V}_i^T}{\partial x_i}\dot{x}_{i,e}(t) + [Q_i(X_e) + \hat{u}_{i,e}^T(t)R_i\hat{u}_{i,e}(t)], \tag{7.17}$$

Table 7.1
State feedback controller design equations

Subsystem dynamics	$\dot{x}_i(t) = f_i(x_i) + g_i(x_i)u_i(t) + \sum_{j=1,j\neq i}^{N} \Delta_{ij}(x_i,x_j),\ x_i(0) = x_{i0}$
HJB residual error	$\hat{H}_i = Q_i(X) + \hat{\theta}_i^T \nabla_x \phi(x) f_i(x) - \frac{1}{4}\hat{\theta}_i^T \nabla_x \phi(x) D_i \nabla^T{}_x \phi(x)\hat{\theta}_i$
TD Learning	$\dot{\hat{\theta}}_i(t) = -\frac{\alpha_{i1}}{(\sigma_i^T\sigma_i+1)^2}\sigma_i\hat{H}_i + \frac{1}{2}\beta_i\nabla_x\phi(x)D_iL_{ix}(x_i) - \kappa_i\hat{\theta}_i$
Value function	$\hat{V}(X) = \hat{\theta}^T\phi(X),$
Distributed control law	$u_i = -\frac{1}{2}R_i{}^{-1}g_i{}^T(x_i)\frac{\partial\hat{V}_{i,i}}{\partial x_i} - \frac{1}{2}R_i{}^{-1}g_i{}^T(x_i)\sum_{\substack{j=1\\ j\neq i}}^{N}\frac{\partial\hat{V}_{i,j}}{\partial x_i}$

where $(.)_e$ denotes the influence of (7.3) due to event-based feedback and this notation will be followed henceforth. Using the parameterized representation of the approximate value function, we get

$$\hat{H}_i = Q_i(X_e) + \hat{\theta}_i^T \nabla_x \phi(x_e) f_i(x_e) - \frac{1}{4}\hat{\theta}_i^T \nabla_x \phi(x_e) D_{i,\varepsilon} \nabla^T{}_x \phi(x_e)\hat{\theta}_i, \tag{7.18}$$

where $D_{i,\varepsilon} = D_i(x_{i,e})$. Finally, we can use a NN weight tuning rule to minimize the HJB residual error. For instance,

$$\dot{\hat{\theta}}_i(t) = \begin{cases} -\frac{\alpha_{i1}}{\rho^2}\sigma_i\hat{H}_i + \frac{1}{2}\beta_i\nabla_x\phi(x)D_iL_{ix}(x_i) - \kappa_i\hat{\theta}_i, & t = t_k^i \\ 0, & t \in (t_k^i, t_{k+1}^i), \end{cases} \tag{7.19}$$

where $\rho = (\sigma_{i,e}^T\sigma_{i,e} + 1)$. The estimated NN weights, $\hat{\theta}_i$, at each subsystem are not updated between events. To determine the time instants t_k, a decentralized event-triggering condition is required. Define a locally Lipschitz Lyapunov candidate function, $L_i(x_i)$ for the ith subsystem such that $L_i(x_i) > 0$ for all $x_i \in S\backslash\{0\}$, with $\{0\}$ denoting the singleton set containing zero vector. Events are generated such that the following condition is satisfied

$$L_i(x_i(t)) \leq (1 + t_k - t)\Gamma_i L_i(x_i(t_k)), \quad t_k \leq t < t_{k+1}, \tag{7.20}$$

with $0 < \Gamma_i < 1$. Note that the event-triggering condition (7.20) requires only the local states. Also note that the kth event sampling instant at any two subsystems need not be the same and t_k^i used in the equations above represents the time instant of the occurrence of the kth event at the ith subsystem. Since the estimated weights are not used in (7.20) a mirror estimator is not required (Sahoo et al., 2016). Next, the nonlinear observer which utilizes the output from the subsystems obtained at event-based sampling instants to reconstruct the internal state information is presented, which requires the following standard assumption.

Assumption 7.7. *The subsystems are assumed to be observable. This is required to enable reconstruction of the states from the measured outputs.*

Table 7.2
Event-triggered state feedback controller design equations

Subsystem dynamics	$\dot{x}_i(t) = f_i(x_i) + g_i(x_i)u_{i,e}(t) + \sum_{j=1,j\neq i}^{N} \Delta_{ij}(x_i, x_j),\ x_i(0) = x_{i0}$
HJB residual error	$\hat{H}_i = Q_i(X_e) + \hat{\theta}_i^T \nabla_x \phi(x_e) f_i(x_e) - \frac{1}{4}\hat{\theta}_i^T \nabla_x \phi(x_e) D_{i,\varepsilon} \nabla^T{}_x \phi(x_e)\hat{\theta}_i$
TD Learning	$\dot{\hat{\theta}}_i(t) = \begin{cases} -\frac{\alpha_{i1}}{\rho^2}\sigma_i \hat{H}_i + \frac{1}{2}\beta_i \nabla_x \phi(x) D_i L_{ix}(x_i) - \kappa_i \hat{\theta}_i,\ t = t_k^i \\ 0,\quad t \in (t_k^i, t_{k+1}^i). \end{cases}$
Value function	$\hat{V}(X) = \hat{\theta}^T \phi(X),$
Distributed control law	$u_{i,e}(t) = -\frac{1}{2}R_i{}^{-1} g_i{}^T(x_{i,e}) \frac{\partial \hat{V}_{i,i}}{\partial x_{i,e}} - \frac{1}{2}R_i{}^{-1} g_i{}^T(x_{i,e}) \sum_{\substack{j=1 \\ j\neq i}}^{N} \frac{\partial \hat{V}_{i,j}}{\partial x_{i,e}}$

7.3.2 EVENT-TRIGGERED OUTPUT FEEDBACK CONTROLLER

Output feedback controllers use the measured quantity to estimate the internal system states using observers. The estimated states are then utilized to design the controllers. Since it is desired that the outputs be communicated among subsystems, the observers at each subsystem are designed so that they estimate the state vector of all the subsystems using the event-triggered outputs. To avoid redundancy, all the equations for the controller are not explicitly presented for output feedback-based design. For the implementation of output feedback controller, estimated states will replace the actual states in the design equations presented in the previous subsection. In order to develop an event-triggering condition, we could substitute the outputs in place of the states in (7.20). In the analysis, the event-triggering condition can be represented in terms of the state vector using the linear map C_i. In order to estimate the system state vector using the output information obtained at the event-based sampling instants, consider the observer at i^{th} subsystem with dynamics

$$\dot{\hat{X}}_i(t) = F(\hat{X}_i) + G(\hat{X}_i)U_{i,e}(t) + \mu_i[Y_{i,e}(t) - C\hat{X}_i(t)], \tag{7.21}$$

where $\hat{X}_i, \mu_i$, and $Y_{i,e}$ represent the overall estimated state vector, observer gain matrix, and event-triggered output vector of the overall system, respectively, at the ith subsystem, C is the augmented matrix composed of C_i, each with appropriate dimensions. The output vector is a function of the measurement error since the output from each subsystem is shared only when an event is triggered.

Defining the difference between the actual state and the estimated state vectors at the ith subsystem as the state estimation error

$$\tilde{X}_i(t) = X_i(t) - \hat{X}_i(t),$$

the evolution of the state estimation error is described by the differential equation

$$\dot{\tilde{X}}_i(t) = F(X_i) + G(X_i)U_{i,e}(t) - [F(\hat{X}_i) + G(\hat{X}_i)U_{i,e}(t)] - \mu_i[Y_{i,e}(t) - C\hat{X}_i(t)]. \tag{7.22}$$

Next, the boundedness of the state estimation error with event-triggered output feedback is presented assuming the distributed control policy is admissible. The detailed proofs for the results presented next are available in (Narayanan and Jagannathan, 2017).

Lemma 7.1. *For the augmented system given in (7.2) composed of interconnected subsystems given in (7.1), consider the observer (7.21) at each subsystem with the error dynamics (7.22), and let the measurement error (7.3) be bounded. The observer estimation error is locally UUB, provided the control policy is optimal and the observer gains are chosen such that $\eta_{i,o1}, \eta_{i,o2} > 0$, where the design variables $\eta_{i,o1}, \eta_{i,o2}$ are defined in the proof.*

Sketch of Proof:

- Since the separation principle does not hold for nonlinear systems, the stability of the controllers together with the observers, operating online, should be analyzed.
- The Lyapunov candidate function used in this proof is

$$L_i(\tilde{X}_i(t)) = \frac{1}{2}\tilde{X}_i^T(t)\gamma_i\tilde{X}_i(t) + \frac{1}{4}(\tilde{X}_i^T(t)\gamma_i\tilde{X}_i(t))^2.$$

- Using the estimation error dynamics (7.22) and Assumptions 7.3-7.4, the time-derivative of the Lyapunov function can be obtained to as

$$\dot{L}_i(t) \leq -\eta_{i,o1}\|\tilde{X}_i(t)\|^2 - \eta_{i,o2}\|\tilde{X}_i(t)\|^4 + \xi_{i1,obs}, \tag{7.23}$$

where $\eta_{i,o1} = \|\gamma_i\|\,\|\mu_i\|\,\|C\| - \|\gamma_i\|L_f - 1.5$, $\eta_{i,o2} = \|\gamma_i\|^2\,\|\mu_i\|\,\|C\| - \|\gamma_i\|^2 L_f - 3$, and $\xi_{i1,obs} = \frac{1}{8}G_M^4\|\gamma_i\|^8\|U_i^*\|^4 + \frac{1}{2}G_M^2\|\gamma_i\|^2\|U_i^*\|^2$.
- Note that these bounds are only valid if the control policy is optimal. Further, the constants γ_i, μ_i, and C, are all design variables that can be independently chosen to ensure that these bounds hold.

Recall that the convergence of the NN weights is coupled with the number of events when the weight update rule (7.19) is used. This significantly reduces the convergence time (Sahoo et al., 2016). To decouple this relationship between the number of events and the learning time, a hybrid NN weight adaption rule, from Narayanan and Jagannathan (2017), is introduced in the next subsection.

7.3.2.1 Hybrid learning algorithm

The results of event-based function approximation shows that the approximation error in the optimal value function and the optimal control action generated will depend on the frequency of events. The TD ADP scheme developed by Sahoo et al. (2016) presents an NN approximator wherein the NN weight updates occur only at the event triggering instants t_k^i. In contrast, classical ADP schemes (e.g., PI and VI) performs iterative learning, assuming significant iterations could be carried out during the inter-event period.

Following the hybrid algorithm in Chapter 6, the learning scheme presented here is inspired by the GPI and introduced in (Narayanan and Jagannathan, 2017). Specifically, the NN weights are tuned using the tuning rule

$$\dot{\hat{\theta}}_i(t) = \begin{cases} -\frac{\alpha_{i1}}{\hat{\rho}^2}\hat{\sigma}_i\hat{H}_i + \frac{1}{2}\beta_i\nabla_x\phi(\hat{x})\hat{D}_iL_{ix}(\hat{x}_i) - \kappa_i\hat{\theta}_i, & t = t_k^i \\ -\frac{\alpha_{i1}}{\hat{\rho}^2(t_k^i)}\hat{\sigma}_{i,e}(t_k^i)\hat{H}_{i,e}(\hat{\theta}_i(t)) - \kappa_i\hat{\theta}_i(t), & t_k^i < t < t_{k+1}^i. \end{cases} \tag{7.24}$$

To denote the use of estimated states from the observer, $(\hat{\cdot})$ notation is used for the functions D_i, ρ_i, and σ_i. Whenever an event occurs, new feedback information is updated at the controller and broadcast to the neighboring subsystems. The weights are tuned with the new feedback information and the updated weights are used to generate the control action, which is applied at the actuator. In the inter-event period, past feedback values are used to evaluate the value function and the policy using the HJB equation. This is done by adjusting the estimated weights in the inter-event period according to (7.24) so that $\hat{\theta}_i$ moves towards θ_i^*. It was shown in (Narayanan and Jagannathan, 2017) that

Table 7.3
Design equations for hybrid learning with output feedback

Observer dynamics	$\dot{\hat{X}}_i(t) = F(\hat{X}_i) + G(\hat{X}_i)U_{i,e}(t) + \mu_i[Y_{i,e}(t) - C\hat{X}_i(t)]$
HJB residual error	$\hat{H}_i = Q_i(\hat{X}_e) + \hat{\theta}_i^T \nabla_x \phi(\hat{x}_e) f_i(\hat{x}_e) - \frac{1}{4}\hat{\theta}_i^T \nabla_x \phi(\hat{x}_e) D_{i,\varepsilon} \nabla^T{}_x \phi(\hat{x}_e)\hat{\theta}_i$
Hybrid learning	$\dot{\hat{\theta}}_i(t) = \begin{cases} -\frac{\alpha_{i1}}{\rho^2}\hat{\sigma}_i\hat{H}_i + \frac{1}{2}\beta_i \nabla_x \phi(\hat{x})\hat{D}_i L_{ix}(\hat{x}_i) - \kappa_i\hat{\theta}_i, \; t = t_k^i \\ -\frac{\alpha_{i1}}{\rho^2(t_k^i)}\hat{\sigma}_{i,e}(t_k^i)\hat{H}_{i,e}(\hat{\theta}_i(t)) - \kappa_i\hat{\theta}_i(t), \; t_k^i < t < t_{k+1}^i. \end{cases}$
Value function	$\hat{V}(\hat{X}) = \hat{\theta}^T \phi(\hat{X}),$
Distributed control law	$u_{i,e} = -\frac{1}{2}R_i{}^{-1} g_i{}^T(\hat{x}_{i,e})\frac{\partial \hat{V}_{i,i}}{\partial \hat{x}_{i,e}} - \frac{1}{2}R_i{}^{-1} g_i{}^T(\hat{x}_{i,e})\sum_{\substack{j=1 \\ j\neq i}}^N \frac{\partial \hat{V}_{i,j}}{\partial \hat{x}_{i,e}}$

the stability of the system is preserved as a consequence of the additional stabilizing term in (7.24). Using the actual states in place of the estimated states, the update rules for the hybrid learning scheme can be derived for the state feedback controller.

Remark 7.5. *As the time between two successive events increases, more time is available for the iterative weight updates. Therefore, HJB residual error is reduced considerably resulting in an approximately optimal control action at every event-triggering instant.*

Remark 7.6. *In the traditional RL literature, the GPI is used and a family of TD algorithms are presented, such as TD(0), n-TD, TD(λ) (Sutton and Barto, 1998). All these learning algorithms have a fixed number of iterative weight updates for policy evaluation. In contrast, the event-triggered control framework cannot ensure fixed inter-event time. Hence, the hybrid algorithm is most relevant and applicable in the event-based online learning control framework.*

For the stability analysis, first, using the fact that the optimal control policy results in a stable closed-loop system, a time-varying bound on the closed-loop dynamics can be defined as $\|F(X) + G(X)U^*(t)\| \leq \psi \|X(t)\|$, with $\psi > 0$. It was also shown by Dierks and Jagannathan (2010a) that there exists positive constant ζ_1 such that $\|L_x(X)\| \|f(X) + g(X)U^*(t)\| \leq -\zeta_1 \|L_x(X)\|^2$, with the Lyapunov function $L(X)$, its gradient $L_x(X)$ with respect to the state vector.

Example 7.1. *We can consider the $L(X(t)) = \frac{1}{2}(X^T(t)X(t))$ and linear system dynamics $\dot{X}(t) = AX(t) + BU^*(t)$, where $U^*(t) = -KX(t)$. Computing the time derivative of this function and using the system dynamics, we get $\|X^T(t)\| \|AX(t) + BU^*(t)\| \leq -\zeta_1 \|X(t)\|^2$, where ζ_1 can be selected as the spectral-radius of the closed-loop system matrix.*

With these results, the stability analysis of the state-feedback controller and the output feedback controller with event-triggered feedback are summarized in the next section.

7.3.3 STABILITY ANALYSIS

For the analysis of the event-triggered controller, first, we shall prove that the distributed controller admits a Lyapunov function for the closed loop system which satisfies a local input-to-state stability-like condition, resulting in local UUB of all the states, weight estimation error, and state estimation error. Let the error in the NN weight estimate be defined as $\tilde{\theta}_i = \theta_i^* - \hat{\theta}_i$ and the target weights be constants and bounded by θ_{iM}. Consider the Hamiltonian (7.18), and the ideal HJB equation given in (7.14), adding and subtracting $Q_i(X)$ in (7.18) and rewriting the Hamiltonian in terms of $\tilde{\theta}_i$, we get the following equations:

$$\begin{aligned}\hat{H}_{i,e} &= -\tilde{\theta}_i^T \sigma_{i,e} + \frac{1}{4}\tilde{\theta}_i^T \nabla_x \phi(x_e) D_{i,\varepsilon} \nabla^T{}_x \phi(x_e) \tilde{\theta}_i + Q_i(x_e) \\ &+ \theta_i^{*T}[\nabla_x \phi(x_e) f_i(x_e) - \nabla_x \phi(x) \bar{f}_i(x)] - \varepsilon_{iHJB} - Q_i(X) \\ &+ \frac{1}{4}\theta_i^{*T}[\nabla_x \phi(x) D_i \nabla_x^T \phi(x) - \nabla_x \phi(x_e) D_{i,\varepsilon} \nabla^T{}_x \phi(x_e)]\theta_i^*\end{aligned} \tag{7.25}$$

and, for the case of output feedback, we have

$$\begin{aligned}\hat{H}_i &= -\tilde{\theta}_i^T \hat{\sigma}_{i,e} + \frac{1}{4}\tilde{\theta}_i^T \nabla_x \phi(\hat{x}_e) \hat{D}_{i,\varepsilon} \nabla^T{}_x \phi(\hat{x}_e) \tilde{\theta}_i + Q_i(\hat{X}_e) \\ &+ \frac{1}{4}\theta_i^{*T}[\nabla_x \phi(x) D_i \nabla^T{}_x \phi(x) - \nabla_x \phi(\hat{x}_e) \hat{D}_{i,\varepsilon} \nabla^T{}_x \phi(\hat{x}_e)]\theta_i^* \\ &- \varepsilon_{iHJB} + \theta_i^{*T}(\nabla_x \phi(\hat{x}_e) f_i(\hat{x}_e) - \nabla_x \phi(x) f_i(x)) - Q_i(X).\end{aligned} \tag{7.26}$$

For all the stability results presented in this section, detailed proofs are available in (Narayanan and Jagannathan, 2017).

Theorem 7.1. *Consider the nonlinear dynamics of the augmented system (7.2) with the equilibrium point at origin. Let the initial states $x_{i0}, \hat{X}_{i0} \in S$ and let $\hat{\theta}_i(0)$ be defined in a compact set $\Omega_{i\theta}$. Use the update rule defined in (7.16), with the estimated states, to tune the NN weights. With the estimated states evolving according to the observer dynamics given by (7.21) and measurement error set to zero, there exists $\eta_{i's} > 0$ such that $\tilde{\theta}_i$, $X(t)$ and the observer error dynamics are locally uniformly ultimately bounded (UUB) by ξ_{icl} in the presence of a bounded external input. The constants, $\eta_{i's}$ and the bound, ξ_{icl}, are defined in the proof.*

Sketch of Proof:

- In this proof, the Lyapunov function for the closed-loop system is selected as

$$L_i(x_i, \tilde{\theta}_i, \tilde{X}_i) = L_{i1}(x_i) + L_{i2}(\tilde{\theta}_i) + L_{i3}(\tilde{X}_i). \tag{7.27}$$

- The proof involdes demonstrating that each term in the Lyapunov function has a negative time-derivative outside of the bound defined by certain constants.
- This bound is defined as $\xi_{icl} = \xi_{i1,obs} + \frac{1}{16} R_i^{-4} G_M^4$, where $\xi_{i1,obs}$ is the bound contributed by the observer (Lemma 7.1). Note here that this bound will increase when the measurement error is nonzero. Since the magnitude of the measurement error is kept under a pre-defined threshold, we shall see that the closed-loop system is locally UUB.

This analytical result in Theorem 7.1 is equivalent to the local ISS condition (Khalil, 2002). The reconstruction and the measurement errors can be considered as external inputs to the system. However, the boundedness of the event-based measurement error is summarized in the next theorem using the decentralized event-triggering condition introduced earlier in the section.

Theorem 7.2. *Consider the nonlinear interconnected system described by (7.2) wherein the initial states* $x_{i0}, \hat{X}_{i0} \in S$*. Let the NN weights be initialized in a compact set* $\Omega_{i\theta}$*. Consider the weight tuning rule defined in (7.24) using the estimated states and the event-triggering mechanism satisfying (7.20) with the measured outputs at each subsystem. With the estimated states evolving according to the observer dynamics given by (7.21), there exists* $\eta_{i's} > 0$ *such that* $\tilde{\theta}_i$*,* $X(t)$*, and the observer error dynamics are locally uniformly ultimately bounded by* ξ_{icl} *wherein the bound is obtained independent of the measurement error. The constants,* $\eta_{i's}$ *and the bound,* ξ_{icl}*, are defined in the proof.*

Sketch of Proof:

■ Recall that the results from the previous theorem, it can be observed that when the event-sampling error is zero, the bounds can obtained as in Theorem 7.1. To establish similar results with event-triggered feedback, the event-triggering condition is used to bound this error.

Corollary 7.1. *Consider the nonlinear interconnected system given by (7.2) with origin being the equilibrium point and the initial states* $x_{i0}, \hat{X}_{i0} \in S$*. Let* $\hat{\theta}_i(0)$ *be defined in a compact set* $\Omega_{i\theta}$*. Use the update rule defined in (7.16) to tune the NN weights at each subsystem. Then, there exists computable positive constants* $\alpha_{i1}, \beta_i, \kappa_i$ *such that* $\tilde{\theta}_i$ *and* $X(t)$ *are locally uniformly ultimately bounded with the bounds* ξ_θ, ξ_x*, respectively, when there is a non-zero bounded measurement error. Further, using the event-sampling condition (7.20), it can be shown that the closed-loop system is locally UUB when the NN weights are tuned using (7.19) and (7.24).*

Sketch of Proof:

■ Since the stability results for the state feedback controller can be obtained from Theorem 7.1 and Theorem 7.2 by setting the observer estimation error to zero.

Remark 7.7. *Results from Theorems 7.1 and 7.2 can be used along with Assumption 7.2 to establish the non-zero minimum inter-event time (Wang and Lemmon, 2011a; Guinaldo et al., 2011). However, since the inter-event time is dynamically changing, ensuring sufficient time availability to carry out significantly large number of weight updates between any successive events is not feasible. Therefore, algorithms like PI and VI are restrictive for event-based control implementation. Redundant events can be prevented by using a dead-zone operator as soon as the states of each subsystem converge to their respective bounds. The learning algorithm and the corresponding stability results derived for the closed-loop nonlinear system can be easily extended for linear interconnected system. The event-sampling mechanism at each subsystem operates asynchronously, resulting in lower network congestion. However, suitable communication protocol is required to be utilized along with the controller to minimize the packet losses due to collision and other undesired network performance (Guinaldo et al., 2011).*

Remark 7.8. *The weight tuning rules for the online approximator in (7.24) are used for event-triggered implementation of state and output feedback controllers. The bounds* ξ_{icl} *can be made arbitrarily small by appropriate choice of* α_{i1}, β_i*, and* κ_i *in the weight update rule satisfying the Lyapunov stability results. The iterative learning, presented in (Liu et al., 2014; Zhong and He, 2016; Lewis et al., 2012a), results in the value function approximate that yield approximately optimal, hence, stabilizing control input at each time step. This yields* $\tilde{\theta}_i = 0$ *for each of the algorithms (Liu et al., 2014; Zhong and He, 2016; Lewis et al., 2012a), at each event-triggering instant, which reduces the complexity of analysis. The stabilizing term* $\frac{1}{2}\beta_i \nabla_x \phi(\hat{x}) \hat{D}_i L_{ix}(\hat{x}_i)$ *in the weight tuning rule (7.24) ensures stability of the closed loop system in the presence of non-zero* $\tilde{\theta}_i$*.*

Remark 7.9. *In the adaptive control theory, the sigma/epsilon modification (Narendra and Annaswamy, 2012) terms in the adaptation rule ensures that the actual weights are bounded in the presence of bounded disturbances. It also helps in avoiding the parameter drift and relaxes the PE condition. In all the ADP designs (Lewis et al., 2012a), the PE condition is required for convergence of the weight estimation errors and it is achieved by adding random signal to the control policy (Dierks and Jagannathan, 2010a; Xu and Jagannathan, 2013; Sahoo et al., 2016). This also has an additional benefit of being an exploratory signal. In RL literature, the dilemma of exploration versus exploitation is greatly discussed (Sutton and Barto, 1998). For a learning problem, the exploratory noise signal helps the learning mechanism to explore the search space to find the exact solution and ensures observability conditions while learning (Lewis et al., 2012a). However, for the online control problem, stability is more important and is given priority. Therefore, explicitly adding random exploratory signal to the control policy is undesirable.*

Remark 7.10. *In the RL literature, the one step TD algorithm is proven to have convergence issues (Sutton and Barto, 1998) due to bootstrapping. This occurs as the parameter values that approximate the value function grow unbounded (Sutton and Barto, 1998). However, convergence results for online one-step TD algorithms are presented in (Dierks and Jagannathan, 2010a; Xu and Jagannathan, 2013; Sahoo et al., 2016) under certain conditions. These algorithms utilize the stabilizing terms in the parameter update rule and present local convergence.*

Remark 7.11. *For the output feedback controller, an additional uncertainty due to estimated states is introduced during the learning period. Moreover, the computations are increased due the observer present at each subsystem. The state estimation error forces frequent events when compared to the state feedback controller, where the state estimation error is absent. However, for practical applications, all the states are not measured and with output feedback, only the output vector is broadcast through the network when compared to the entire state vector. The location of the observer is crucial and there are several locations which are feasible to place an observer operating with event-triggered feedback, as discussed in the literature (Tallapragada and Chopra, 2013; Zhong and He, 2016). For the interconnected system, the extended observers discussed here are placed along with the controller for the following reasons – a) only the output from each subsystem is broadcast through the network; b) using the outputs from all the subsystem, the overall state vector can be reconstructed at each subsystem, as required by the distributed controllers. These advantages are lost when the observers are placed along with the sensors at each subsystem. In order to eliminate an additional event-sampling mechanism at each subsystem, the observer states are held constant between the event sampling instants. We shall, nevertheless, explore these design configurations in much more detail in Chapter 9.*

In this section, two examples are discussed in the context of the analytical design presented thus far in this chapter. The first example includes a system of two inverted pendulums connected by spring. We first consider a linear system and then a system with nonlinear dynamics is considered. In the second example, a more practical nonlinear system with three interconnected subsystems is considered.

Example 7.2. *The example used here has two inverted pendulum connected by spring (Spooner and Passino, 1999), which can be represented of the form (7.2). A NN with one layer and 5 neurons together with polynomial basis set wherein the control variables $\alpha_1 = 25, \beta = 0.01$, $L_i(x) = \frac{1}{2} x_i^T \beta x_i$ and $\phi(x) = \left[x_{1,1}{}^2, x_{1,2}{}^2, x_{2,1}{}^2, x_{2,2}{}^2, x^T x\right]^T$; the initial conditions are defined in the interval [0,1] and the initial weights of the NN are chosen randomly from [-1,1]. The dynamics of the system are given by*

$$\dot{x}_{i1}(t) = x_{i2},\ \dot{x}_{i2}(t) = \left(\frac{m_i g r}{J_i} - \frac{kr^2}{4J_i}\right)\sin x_{i1} + \frac{kr}{2J_i}(l-b) + \frac{u_i}{J_i} + \frac{kr^2}{4J_i}\sin x_{j1}.$$

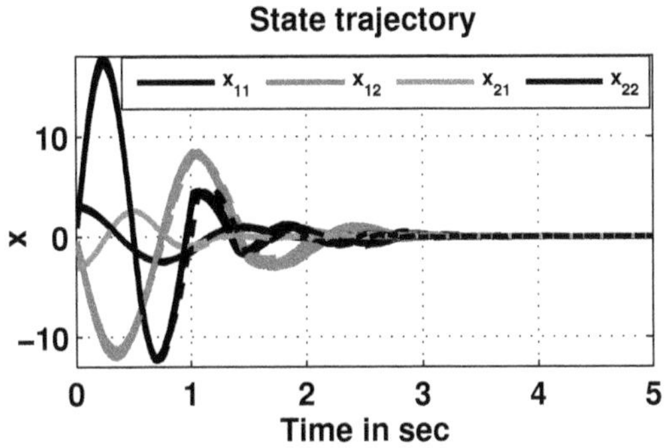

Figure 7.1 State trajectories (Linear example).

For the linear dynamics, refer (Guinaldo et al., 2011). The parameters in the system dynamics are $m_1 = 2$, $m_2 = 2.5$, $J_1 = 5$, $J_2 = 6.25$, $k = 10$, $r = 0.5$, $l = 0.5$, *and* $g = 9.8$, $b = 0.5$. *The controller design parameters are chosen as* $R_1 = .03$, $R_2 = 0.03$, $Q_i = 0.1X^TX$.

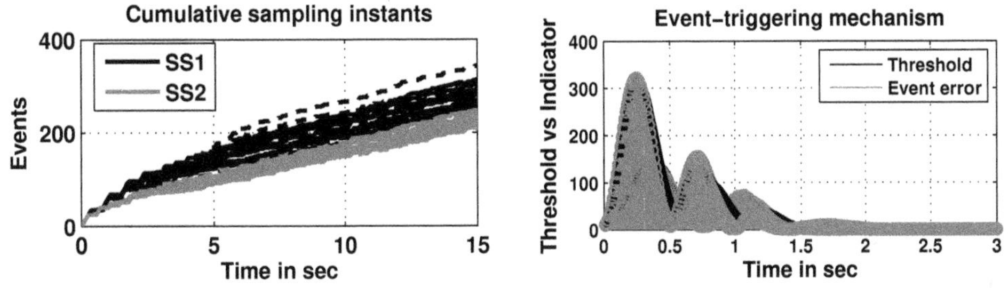

Figure 7.2 Event-triggering mechanism.

The results in Figure 7.1 shows the distributed controller performance for the linear system for various initial conditions. Figure 7.2 shows the cumulative events, event-triggering error, and its threshold for the linear interconnected system, which demonstrates the sparsity of events in the event-based feedback. Next, the results for the event-triggered controller are presented with the distributed control scheme for the nonlinear dynamical system. For the event-triggered controller, the initial states and the weights are chosen as in the previous case. The design parameters are $\Gamma = 0.95, \alpha_1 = 20, \beta = 0.01, R_i = 0.03, Q = 2X^TX$.

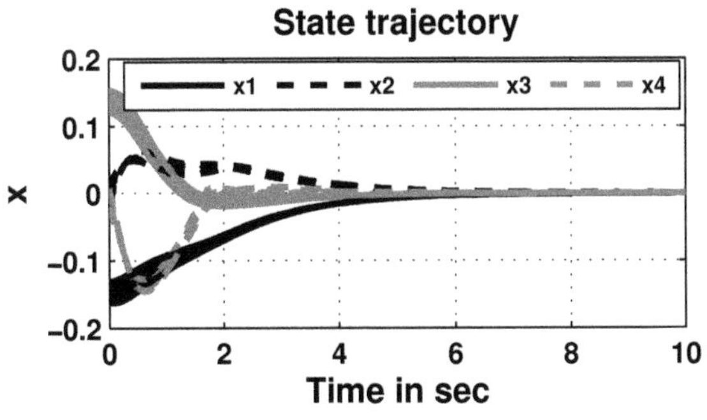

Figure 7.3 State trajectories (Example - 7.2).

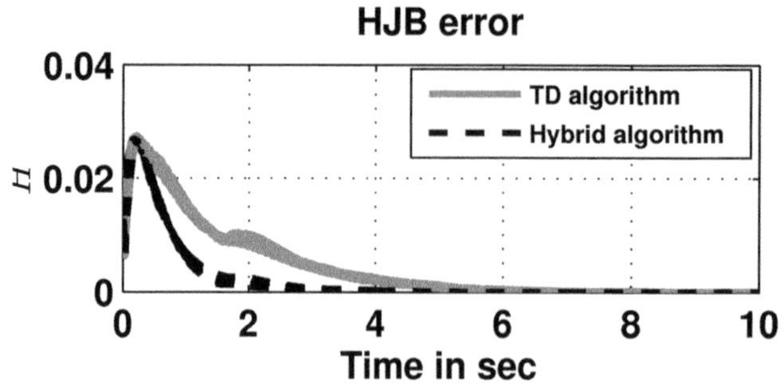

Figure 7.4 HJB error (Example - 7.2).

The system state trajectories with event-triggered controller are stable during the learning phase. This can be verified from Figure 7.3 for both the subsystems. The results in Figure 7.3 include the state trajectories for various initial states. The HJB residual error for the TD ADP-based controller and the hybrid learning based controller are compared. It is evident from the results in Figure 7.4 that the iterative weight updates between event-triggering instants seems to reduce the learning time. The observer performance is presented in Figure 7.5. The plots of estimated and actual outputs with the event-triggered feedback are compared when the hybrid learning algorithm is employed to generate the control policy online. The event triggered feedback and aperiodic update of the observer results in a piecewise continuous estimate of the actual states. The observer error convergence is essential for the stability of the controlled system. Efficiency of the event-triggering condition designed for the two subsystems, SS1 for subsystem 1 and SS2 for subsystem 2; the convergence time for the observer estimation error and the HJB error for various initial conditions are recorded in Table 7.4.

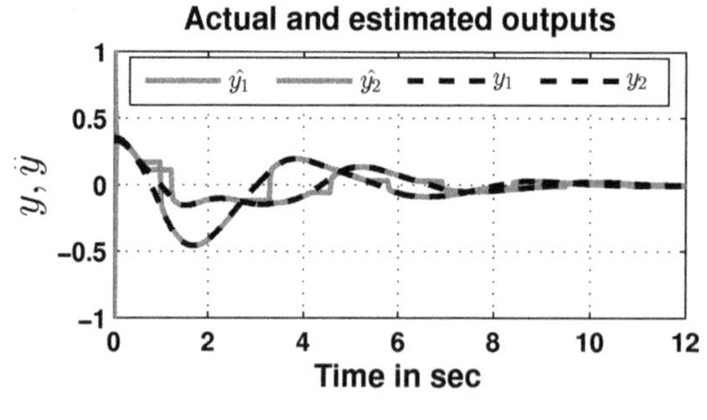

Figure 7.5 Observer performance: Example 7.2.

Example 7.3. *For the second example, a system composed of three interconnected subsystems is considered. The three subsystems describe the dynamics of knee and thigh in a walking robot (Dunbar, 2007). Let $\gamma_1(t)$ be the relative angle between the two thighs, $\gamma_2(t)$ and $\gamma_3(t)$ be the right and left knee angles relative to the right and the left thigh. The dynamical equations of motion (in rad/sec) are*

$$\ddot{\gamma}_1(t) = 0.1[1 - 5.25\gamma_1^2(t)]\dot{\gamma}_1(t) - \gamma_1(t) + u_1(t)$$

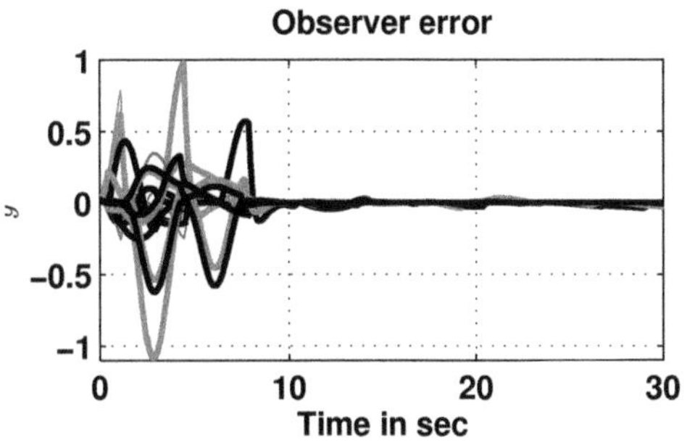

Figure 7.6 Observer performance: Example 7.3.

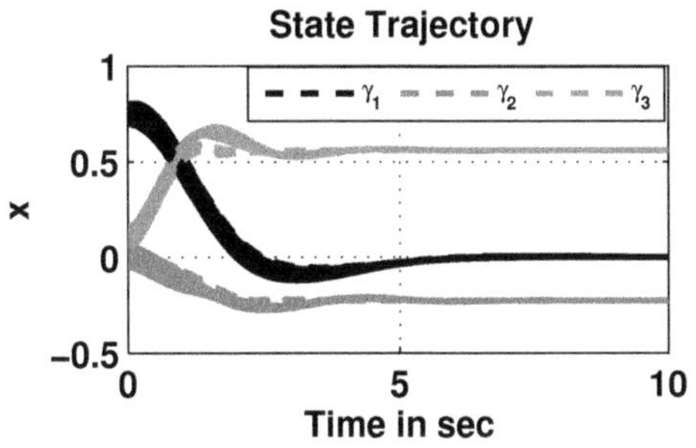

Figure 7.7 State trajectory of walking robot.

$$\ddot{\gamma}_2(t) = 0.01\left[1 - p_2(\gamma_2(t) - \gamma_{2e})^2\right]\dot{\gamma}_2(t) - 4(\gamma_2(t) - \gamma_{2e})$$
$$+0.057\gamma_1(t)\dot{\gamma}_1(t) + 0.1(\dot{\gamma}_2(t) - \dot{\gamma}_3(t)) + u_2(t)$$
$$\ddot{\gamma}_3(t) = 0.01\left[1 - p_3(\gamma_3(t) - \gamma_{3e})^2\right]\dot{\gamma}_3(t) - 4(\gamma_3(t) - \gamma_{3e})$$
$$+0.057\gamma_1(t)\dot{\gamma}_1(t) + 0.1(\dot{\gamma}_3(t) - \dot{\gamma}_2(t)) + u_3(t).$$

The parameter values used to generate the figures given in this example are $(\gamma_{2e}, \gamma_{3e}, p_2 p_3) = (-0.227, 0.559, 6070, 192)$. *The control objective is to design torque commands and bring the robot to a halt.*

The distributed control scheme with an NN to approximate $V_i^*(X)$ at each subsystem is designed. The angles were initialized as $40^\circ \pm 3^\circ, 3^\circ \pm 1^\circ, -3^\circ \pm 1^\circ$ and the angular velocities were initialized at random to take values between 0 and 1. Two layer NNs with 12 neurons in the hidden layer are used at each subsystem. The NN weights of the input layer were initialized at random to form random vector functional link network (Lewis et al., 1998) and the second layer weights are initialized to take values between 0 and 1. The states of each subsystem generated using the hybird learning approach for different initial conditions are recorded. It can be observed that the states reach their equilibrium point (0,-0.227,0.559) every time, ensuring stable operation, for both state and output feedback control implementation (Figure 7.7). The convergence of the observer estimation error can be verified from Figure 7.6. The hybrid algorithm converges faster and reaches steady state before the time driven ADP. The observer estimation error converged to a neighborhood of origin. In the analysis, different initial values for $x_i(0)$ and $\hat{X}_i(0)$ were chosen to test the algorithm and the results are tabulated. It is observed that whenever the observer error persists, performing iterative weight updates did not improve the learning rate. Therefore, the observer should be designed in such a way that the observer error converges faster and in this case the hybrid algorithm with output feedback

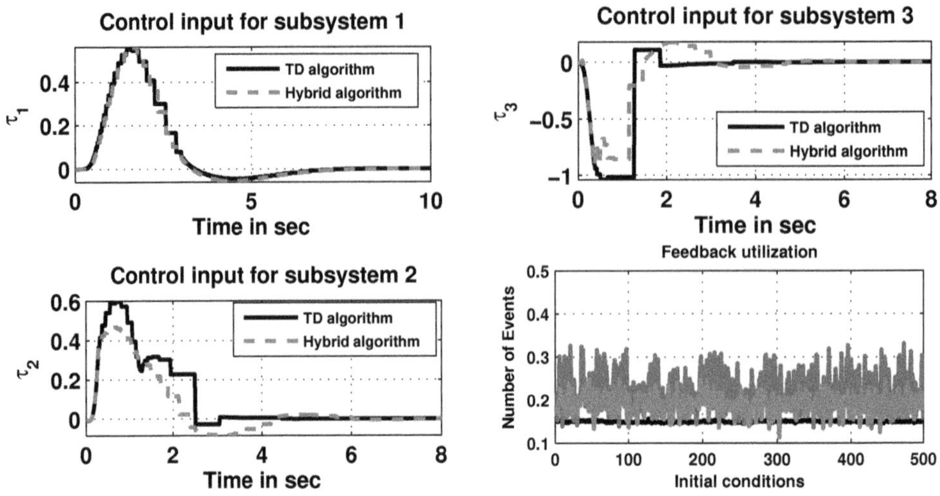

Figure 7.8 Event-triggered control.

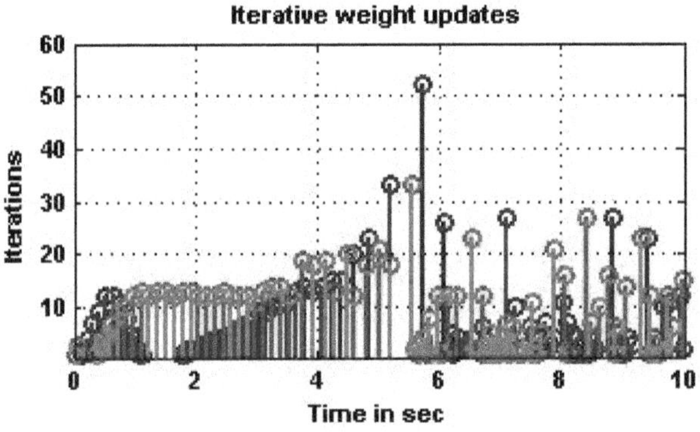

Figure 7.9 Number of iterations in the inter-event period.

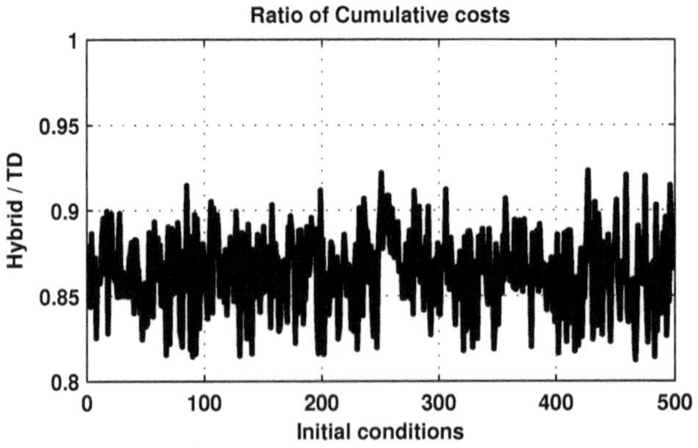

Figure 7.10 Cost comparison (Example 7.3).

controller outperformed the time driven ADP (Table 7.4).

The control torques generated using the hybrid learning algorithm with event-triggered feedback

Table 7.4
Numerical analysis

Example	Algorithm	Cumulative cost (Normalized)		Convergence time in sec			Feedback utilization	
		State feedback (SF)	Output feedback (OF)	HJB error		Observer error	SF	OF
				SF	OF			
1	TD	1	1	10.13	12.89	3.13	0.3716	0.8
	Hybrid	0.988	0.912	6.35	10.74	2.90	0.398	0.7824
2	TD	1	1	4.8	37.20	30.654	0.2	0.4825
	Hybrid	0.86	0.5916	4.1	31.62	27.13	0.3	0.55

and TD ADP are presented in Figure 7.8. Also, the feedback utilization (ratio the event-triggered feedback instants and the sensor samples) are presented for simulations carried out for 500 different initial conditions (Figure 7.8). The cumulative cost is calculated using the cost function defined in (7.4). The comparison of the cumulative cost calculated for the hybrid learning approach with that of the TD ADP reveals that the hybrid scheme results in a lower cumulative cost. Figure 7.10 shows the ratio of costs due to hybrid algorithm over TD algorithm for different initial conditions. For the output feedback case, due to the presence of the observer estimation error, the convergence of the HJB error takes more time when compared to state feedback. The improvement in the learning scheme is due to the learning process in the inter-sampling period. For analysis, the sensor sampling time was fixed at 10ms and the control scheme was simulated to record the number of times the weight update rule was executed in the inter-event period (Figure 7.9). It can be seen that the inter-event time is not uniform and hence, the number of weight updates are varying. Initially, the events are not spaced out and therefore, the iterative updates do not take place, but with time, the events become spaced out, but still with varying intervals. This results in a varying number of iterative weight updates. The comparison of HJB residual error for TD ADP and the learning scheme reveals that the hybrid learning scheme requires less time for convergence. Table 7.4 summarizes the comparison of the two learning algorithms. Feedback utilization is the ratio of events with respect to the sensor samples, when the sensor operates with a sampling period of 10 ms.

So far, this chapter presents an approximation based distributed controller with event triggered state and output feedback that seeks optimality for a class of nonlinear interconnected system. In the next section, we will present dynamic game formulation of the distributed optimal control problem.

7.4 DISTRIBUTED CONTROLLER DESIGN USING NONZERO SUM GAMES

As we have seen in Chapter 3 to 5, the performance of an isolated system, i.e., without interconnection with other systems, can be optimized by solving the associated Riccati equation (RE) or the HJB equation with linear or nonlinear dynamics, respectively. For the nonlinear system, obtaining a closed-form analytical solution for the HJB partial differential equation is involved (Lewis et al., 2012a), and hence, earlier in this chapter, we have sought an ADP-based near optimal solution using a data-driven control scheme. In addition to the network related constraints, designing optimal distributed control for interconnected systems is a challenging problem due to the difficulty involved in determining a trade-off between the performance of the overall system and the subsystems.

On the one hand, the decentralized optimal control techniques optimize local subsystem performance and the resulting control policies may not optimize the overall system performance since all the local controllers are designed independently. On the other hand, the distributed optimal control scheme discussed in the earlier section lumps the overall system objective and the control policies at each subsystem strive to optimize a distributed cost with little flexibility over the control synthesis at each subsystem. In a nutshell, the optimal control problems for interconnected systems are formulated either based on a global objective (Mehraeen and Jagannathan, 2011; Narayanan and Jagannathan, 2017) function or a bunch of independent local objective functions (Liu et al., 2014). This leads to optimization of either the local subsystem or the overall system performance. In practice, the control scheme for a large-scale interconnected system needs to be flexible such that different performance criterion for individual subsystems are met to achieve a global objective. The theory of nonzero-sum (NZS) differential games (Starr and Ho, 1969), where each player has different performance index, is apt to meet the control design requirements for an interconnected system.

In recent times, several *multi-player game theory* (Starr and Ho, 1969) based online control design schemes are presented in the literature (Vamvoudakis and Lewis, 2011; Johnson et al., 2015; Vamvoudakis et al., 2017a) using ADP/RL for isolated systems. In these approaches (Vamvoudakis and Lewis, 2011; Johnson et al., 2015; Vamvoudakis et al., 2017a), each player strives to optimize a performance index such that a *Nash-equilibrium* is achieved. Vamvoudakis and Lewis (2011) proposed an online approximate optimal control scheme for both linear and nonlinear systems. Policy iteration based ADP scheme (Bertsekas, 2012) with actor-critic network is utilized to approximate the Nash equilibrium solution of the coupled Hamilton-Jacobi (HJ) equation. It was shown that the resulting approximate optimal controller guarantees UUB of all closed-loop system signals with the convergence of the ADP algorithm. The requirement of complete knowledge of the system dynamics for implementing the algorithm developed by Vamvoudakis and Lewis (2011) was relaxed by Johnson et al. (2015). Further, Song et al. (2017) presented an off-policy integral RL method to solve the multi-player game problem with an assumption that the control coefficient maps for all the players are same, limiting its applicability. All the above multi-player game based optimal control designs (Vamvoudakis and Lewis, 2011; Johnson et al., 2015; Vamvoudakis et al., 2017a) are presented for multi-input isolated systems.

In the rest of this chapter, we shall focus on the multi-player game-theoretic method, based on (Narayanan et al., 2018c), for designing distributed optimal controllers to attain optimal performance both at the subsystem and the overall system levels, i.e., Nash-equilibrium, with limited and intermittent communication among the subsystems. For the ease of exposition, the distributed optimal control design with continuous transmission of state information among the subsystems is presented first, and then extended to the case of event-based sampling, transmission, and control execution. The interconnected system is first reformulated and treated as an N-player NZS game. A multi-player cost function, utilizing the control inputs as players, is defined at each subsystem. ADP based approximate solution for the game is presented for both continuous and event-based system wherein NNs introduced at each subsystem learn the solution to the coupled HJ equation online.

7.4.1 PROBLEM REFORMULATION

Consider an interconnected system consisting of N subsystems. The dynamics of the ith subsystem, represented in a nonlinear affine form, are given by

$$\dot{x}_i(t) = \bar{f}_i(x_i) + \bar{g}_i(x_i)u_i(t) + \sum\nolimits_{\substack{j=1 \\ j\neq i}}^{N} \Delta_{ij}(x_i, x_j), \tag{7.28}$$

for $i = 1, 2, \cdots, N$, where $x_i(t) \in \mathbb{R}^{n_i}$ with $x_i(0) \in \mathbb{R}^{n_i}$, and $u_i(t) \in \mathbb{R}^{m_i}$ are the state and control input vectors of ith subsystem, respectively. The functions $\bar{f}_i : \mathbb{R}^{n_i} \to \mathbb{R}^{n_i}$ and $\bar{g}_i : \mathbb{R}^{n_i} \to \mathbb{R}^{n_i \times m_i}$ are the internal dynamics and control coefficient of the ith subsystem, respectively, with $\bar{f}(0) = 0$. The function $\Delta_{ij} : \mathbb{R}^{n_i} \times \mathbb{R}^{n_j} \to \mathbb{R}^{n_i}$ represents the interconnection between the ith and the jth subsystem.

As we have seen earlier, to stabilize the ith subsystem effectively, the control policy $u_i(t)$ is desired to be a function of both $x_i(t)$ and $x_j(t)$, $\forall i, j = \{1, \cdots, N\}$, i.e., *distributed control policy*. Therefore, the control objective is to design N distributed optimal control policies $(u_1^*, u_2^*, \cdots, u_N^*)$

at each subsystem such that the following performance index is optimized.

$$J_i(X(t)) = \int_t^{\infty} (Q_i(X) + \Sigma_{j=1}^{N} u_j^T(\tau) R_{ij} u_j(\tau)) d\tau, \tag{7.29}$$

where $X = [x_1^T, ..., x_N^T]^T$ is the overall system state vector, $Q_i(\cdot) \in \mathbb{R}$, $i = 1, 2, \cdots, N$ is a positive definite function with $Q_i(0) = 0$, $R_{ii} \in \mathbb{R}^{m_i \times m_i}$, and $R_{ij} \in \mathbb{R}^{m_j \times m_j}$ are symmetric postive definite matrices.

The rationale behind the performance index (7.29) is to obtain an optimal equilibrium solution for each subsystem while ensuring the Nash equilibrium solution to the overall system (Starr and Ho, 1969). This is different from the traditionally considered decentralized local cost function (Liu et al., 2014), i.e., $J_i(x_i) = \int_t^{\infty}(Q(x_i) + u_i^T(\tau) R_i u_i(\tau)) d\tau$ with local system states x_i and control policy u_i, or the overall system cost function (7.4). A major limitation of these local or global performance indices is that the influence of the neighboring subsystem's control policies are not included while designing the distributed control policy. Although the performance index (7.29) at each subsystem is well defined in the sense that it accounts for the overall system state vector and neighboring control policies, it requires a reformulation for the interconnected system dynamics to derive the corresponding HJ equations.

Moreover, the solution to the HJ equation at each subsystem requires continuous availability of the state information from local and neighboring subsystems. In an event-based control paradigm, recall that each subsystem determines the aperiodic sampling and transmission instants to broadcast the state information asynchronously. With this effect, define the sequences of time instants, $\{t_k^i\}_{k=0}^{\infty}$ and $\{t_k^j\}_{k=0}^{\infty}$, for all $i = 1, 2, \cdots, N$ with $t_0^i = 0$ and $t_0^j = 0$ as event-sampling instants at the ith and j^{th} subsystem, respectively. The states $x_i(t_k^i)$ and $x_j(t_k^j)$ of ith and j^{th} subsystems are transmitted to their respective local controller and broadcasted to neighboring subsystems at time instant t_k^i and t_k^j, respectively. Therefore, for solving the HJ equation and to obtain the optimal control policies at each subsystem, the state information $x_i(t_k^i)$ and $x_j(t_k^j)$ are available at each subsystem which are intermittent and asynchronous.

7.4.2 GAME-THEORETIC SOLUTION

In this section, first, the subsystem dynamics as in (7.28) are reformulated to represent an N-player interconnected system and the corresponding HJ equation for (7.29) is derived. Then, we shall develop the solution to the resulting optimal control problem using game theory and ADP techniques.

The interconnected system, by augmenting the subsystem dynamics, can be represented as an N-player interconnected system given by

$$\dot{X}(t) = f(X) + \sum_{j=1}^{N} g_j(x_j) u_j(t), \; X(0) = X_0, \tag{7.30}$$

where $X(t) = [x_1^T(t), \cdots, x_N^T(t)]^T \in B_x \subseteq \mathbb{R}^n$ with $n = \Sigma_{i=1}^{N} n_i$ is the augmented state of the large-scale system and B_x is a compact set. The map $f(X) = [(\bar{f}_1(x_1) + \Sigma_{j=2}^{N} \Delta_{1j}(x_2))^T, \cdots, (\bar{f}_N(x_N) + \Sigma_{j=1}^{N-1} \Delta_{Nj}(x))^T]^T$ with $f(0) = 0$ and $g_j(x_j) = [0, \cdots, \bar{g}_j^T(x_j), \cdots, 0]^T \in \mathbb{R}^{n \times m_j}$, $j = 1, \cdots, N$ are the known overall internal dynamics and the control coefficient function where 0's are matrices with all elements zero of appropriate dimensions.

Assumption 7.8. *The individual subsystems (7.28) and augmented system in (7.30) are stabilizable and the state vector, $x(t)$, is available for measurement. In addition, the control coefficient matrix $g_i(x_i)$ satisfies $0 < g_{im} < \|g_i(x_i)\| \le g_{iM}$, $i = 1, 2, \cdots, N$ for some constants $g_{im} > 0$ and $g_{iM} > 0$.*

Assumption 7.9. *The functions $\bar{f}_i(x_i)$, $\Delta_{ij}(x_i, x_j)$, and $\bar{g}_i(x_i)$ are locally Lipschitz continuous in their respective domains.*

The optimal value function, V_i^*, is given by

$$V_i^*(X(t)) = \min_{u_i} J_i(X(t)) = \min_{u_i} \int_t^{\infty} (Q_i(X) + \sum_{j=1}^{N} u_j^T(\tau) R_{ij} u_j(\tau)) d\tau, \tag{7.31}$$

for $i = 1,..,N$. As per the Nash equilibrium strategy (Starr and Ho, 1969), given the optimal N-tuple $\{u_1^*, \cdots, u_N^*\}$, the optimal value at each subsystem satisfies

$$V_i^* = V_i^*(u_1^*, u_2^*, \ldots, u_N^*) \leq V_i^*(u_1^*, \ldots, u_i, \ldots, u_N^*), \text{ for } i \in \{1, \ldots, N\}.$$

Using the infinitesimal version of (7.29), the Hamiltonian function H_i is defined as

$$H_i(X, u_1, \cdots, u_N, V_{ix}^*) = Q_i(X) + \sum_{j=1}^{N} u_j^T(t) R_{ij} u_j(t) + V_{ix}^{*T}[f(X) + \sum_{j=1}^{N} g_j(x_j) u_j], \tag{7.32}$$

where $V_{ix} = \partial V_i / \partial X$ and $i = 1, 2, \cdots, N$. Applying the stationarity condition $\partial H_i / \partial u_i = 0$, $i = 1, 2, \cdots, N$, reveals the greedy distributed optimal control policy u_i^* given by

$$u_i^*(t) = -\frac{1}{2} R_{ii}^{-1} g_i^T V_{ix}^*, \ \forall i = \{1, 2, \cdots, N\}. \tag{7.33}$$

Inserting the optimal control policy (7.33) into the Hamiltonian function (7.32), the HJ equation is given by

$$\begin{aligned} H_i(X, u_1^*, \cdots, u_N^*, V_{ix}^*) &= Q_i(X) + V_{ix}^{*T}[f(X) - \frac{1}{2} \sum_{j=1}^{N} g_j R_{jj}^{-1} g_j^T V_{jx}^*] \\ &+ \frac{1}{4} \sum_{j=1}^{N} V_{jx}^* g_j R_{jj}^{-1} R_{ij} R_{jj}^{-1} g_j^T V_{jx}^{*T} = 0, \ \forall i = \{1, 2, \cdots, N\}. \end{aligned} \tag{7.34}$$

Note that the HJ equation (7.34) includes the interconnection dynamics, neighboring subsystem control policy, and hence, coupled. The optimal control policy for the large-scale system (7.30) can be obtained using (7.33) at each subsystem, given the system dynamics and the optimal value function. However, with complete information of the system dynamics in (7.30), a closed form solution of the coupled HJ partial differential equation (7.34), i.e., the optimal value function, is difficult to compute (Vamvoudakis et al., 2017a). In general, approximate solution to the HJ equation is sought using the ADP-based approach by approximating the optimal value function using NNs. Therefore, in the next two sections, solutions for the N-player cooperative game based optimal controller using ADP is presented. The continuous ADP based solution with overall system state is presented in the next followed by the event-based solution.

7.4.3 APPROXIMATE SOLUTION TO THE NZS GAME

In this section, an approximate solution to the N-player game is presented using ADP based approach. Continuous availability of the subsystem state information at every subsystem is assumed, which is relaxed in the next section.

7.4.3.1 Value Function Approximation (critic design)

The optimal value function, which is the solution to the coupled HJ equation (7.34), is approximated using a linearly parametrized dynamic NN at each subsystem. The following standard assumption is required for the universal approximation property of the NN to hold.

Assumption 7.10. *The solution to the HJ equation* (7.34), *i.e., the optimal value function,* $V_i^*(\cdot)$, *exists and is unique, real-valued, and continuously differentiable on the compact set* $B_x \subseteq \mathbb{R}^n$.

By the universal approximation property of the NNs (Lewis et al., 1998), there exists an ideal weight matrix $\theta_i^* \in \mathbb{R}^{l_\theta}$ and a basis function $\phi(X) \in \mathbb{R}^{l_\theta}$ such that the smooth optimal value function $V_i^*(X)$ can be represented as

$$V_i^*(X) = \theta_i^{*^T} \phi(X) + \varepsilon_i(X), \ \forall i = \{1,2,\cdots,N\}, \tag{7.35}$$

where $\theta_i^* \in \mathbb{R}^{l_\theta}$ is the unknown target constant weight matrix, $\phi(X) \in \mathbb{R}^{l_\theta}$ is the activation function and $\varepsilon_i(X)$ is the approximation error. Note that, each subsystem has a value function approximator (critic NN) to approximate the solution of HJ equation using the augmented state X. The optimal control policy in a parametric form using (7.35) can be expressed as

$$u_i^*(t) = -\frac{1}{2}R_{ii}^{-1}g_i^T(\nabla_x^T \phi(X)\theta_i^* + \nabla_x^T \varepsilon_i(X)) \tag{7.36}$$

for $i = 1,2,\cdots,N$, where $\nabla_x = \partial(\cdot)/\partial X$ denotes the gradient with respect to X. The standard assumptions that are used in the analysis are stated next.

Assumption 7.11. *(Lewis et al., 1998) NN target weight matrix θ_i^*, activation function $\phi(\cdot)$, gradient of activation function $\nabla_x \phi(\cdot)$, reconstruction error $\varepsilon_i(\cdot)$, and the gradient of the reconstruction error $\nabla_x \varepsilon_i(\cdot)$, $\forall i = \{1,\cdots,N\}$ are bounded satisfying $\|\theta_i^*\| \le \theta_{iM}$, $\phi_{(\cdot)} \le \phi_M$, $\nabla_x \phi_{(\cdot)} \le \nabla\phi_M$, $\|\varepsilon_i(\cdot)\| \le \varepsilon_{iM}$, and $\nabla_x \varepsilon_i(\cdot) \le \nabla\varepsilon_{iM}$ where θ_{iM}, ϕ_M, $\nabla\phi_M$, and ε_{iM} and $\nabla\varepsilon_{iM}$ are positive constants.*

Since the target weight of the NN approximation in (7.35) is unknown, one needs to estimate the NN weights online. The estimate of the optimal value function can be expressed as

$$\hat{V}_i(X) = \hat{\theta}_i^T(t)\phi(X), \ \forall i = \{1,\cdots,N\}, \tag{7.37}$$

where $\hat{\theta}_i(t) \in \mathbb{R}^{l_\theta}$ is the estimate of the target weight θ_i^*. The estimated control policy using (7.37) is represented as

$$\hat{u}_i(t) = -\frac{1}{2}R_{ii}^{-1}g_i^T\hat{V}_{ix} = -\frac{1}{2}R_{ii}^{-1}g_i^T\nabla_x^T\phi(X)\hat{\theta}_i. \tag{7.38}$$

To update the weights of the NN, we shall avail the Bellman optimality principle. From (7.31), and for $T > 0$, we have the recursive Bellman equation,

$$V_i^*(X(t)) = \int_t^{t+T} (Q_i(X) + \sum_{j=1}^{N} u_j^T(\tau)R_{ij}u_j(\tau))d\tau + V_i^*(X(t+T)). \tag{7.39}$$

Taking one step backwards, we can rewrite (7.39) using the estimated value as

$$\hat{V}_i(X(t-T)) = \int_{t-T}^{t} (Q_i(X) + \sum_{j=1}^{N} u_j^T(\tau)R_{ij}u_j(\tau))d\tau + \hat{V}_i(X(t)) - E_{ib}, \tag{7.40}$$

where E_{ib} is the temporal difference/ Bellman residual error due to the estimated values. The NN weights can then be updated using a gradient based algorithm for minimizing the function $E_{i_{HJ}} = \frac{1}{2}E_{ib}^2$. For example, the NN weight update law is given by

$$\dot{\hat{\theta}}_i(t) = -\alpha_{i1}(\partial E_{ib}/\partial\hat{\theta}_i)E_{ib}, \tag{7.41}$$

where $\alpha_{i1} = \alpha_i/\rho_i^2$ with $\alpha_i > 0$ is the learning gain and $\rho_i = 1 + (\partial E_{ib}/\partial\hat{\theta}_i)^T(\partial E_{ib}/\partial\hat{\theta}_i)$ is the normalization term. To facilitate the stability proof presented in the next subsection, define the NN weight estimation error $\tilde{\theta}_i(t) = \theta_i^* - \hat{\theta}_i$. The weight estimation error dynamics from (7.41) can be expressed as

$$\dot{\tilde{\theta}}_i(t) = \alpha_{i1}(\partial E_{ib}/\partial\hat{\theta}_i)E_{ib}. \tag{7.42}$$

Next, the stability results for the closed-loop system are summarized from (Narayanan et al., 2018c).

Table 7.5
Design equations based on distributed Nash games

Integral Bellman error	$E_{ib} = \int_{t-T}^{t} (Q_i(X) + \sum_{j=1}^{N} u_j^T R_{ij} u_j) d\tau + \hat{V}_i(X(t)) - \hat{V}_i(X(t-T))$
Update rule	$\dot{\hat{\theta}}_i = -\alpha_{i1} (\partial E_{ib} / \partial \hat{\theta}_i) E_{ib}$
Value function	$\hat{V}_i(\hat{X}) = \hat{\theta}_i^T \phi(\hat{X}),$
Distributed control law	$\hat{u}_i(t) = -\frac{1}{2} R_{ii}^{-1} g_i^T \hat{V}_{ix} = -\frac{1}{2} R_{ii}^{-1} g_i^T \nabla_x^T \phi(X) \hat{\theta}_i$

7.4.3.2 Stability Analysis

To claim UUB of the closed-loop parameters, the following technical lemmas are required.

Lemma 7.2. *Consider the NN tuning rule* (7.41) *and the weight estimation error dynamics* (7.42). *With the Bellman equation* (7.40), *the weight estimation error dynamics satisfies*

$$\dot{L}_i(\tilde{\theta}_i) \leq -\frac{\alpha_{i1}}{2} \tilde{\theta}_i^T(t) \Delta\phi(X(t)) \Delta\phi^T(X(t)) \tilde{\theta}_i(t) + \frac{\alpha_{i1}}{2} \varepsilon_{ib}^T(X) \varepsilon_{ib}(X), \tag{7.43}$$

where, $i = \{1, \cdots, N\}$ *and* $L_i(\tilde{\theta}_i(t)) = \frac{1}{2} \tilde{\theta}_i^T(t) \tilde{\theta}_i(t)$.

Sketch of Proof:

- Consider the smooth, positive definite function $L_i(\tilde{\theta}_i(t)) = \frac{1}{2} \tilde{\theta}_i^T(t) \tilde{\theta}_i(t)$. Substituting the parameter error dynamics in the time-derivative of the Lyapunov function and using the Young's inequality will lead to (7.43).

Note that as the number of hidden layer neurons, l, is increased, the approximation error ε_{ib} will approach zero (Lewis et al., 1998).

Lemma 7.3. *Given the interconnected system (7.28) with the optimal control policy* u_j^*, $j = 1, 2, \cdots, N$ *in (7.33). Let Assumptions 7.8 and 7.9 hold. Then, for continuously differentiable, radially unbounded Lyapunov candidate functions* $L_i(x_i)$ *for the subsystem (7.28), there exist constants* $C_{i2} > 0$ *such that the inequality*

$$L_{ix_i}^T(x_i)(\bar{\bar{f}}_i(X) + g_i u_i^*(t)) \leq -C_{i2} \left\| L_{ix_i}(x_i) \right\|^2 \tag{7.44}$$

holds; where $\bar{\bar{f}}_i(X) = \bar{f}_i(x_i) + \sum_{j=1, i \neq j}^{N} \Delta_{ij}(x_i, x_j)$ *and* $L_{ix_i}(x_i) = \partial L_i(x_i) / \partial x_i$.

Proof. The proof is a direct result of the stabilizing property of the optimal policies $u_i^*(x)$ and for details refer to (Dierks and Jagannathan, 2012a, 2010b).

Recall the PE condition (Ioannou and Fidan, 2006), which is used for ensuring the stability of the closed-loop system presented in the theorem. A signal $\frac{\Delta\phi(x,T)}{1+\Delta^T\phi(x,T)\Delta\phi(x,T)}$ is said to be persistently exciting over an interval $[t-T, t]$, if $\forall t \in \mathbb{R}^+$, there exists a $T > 0, \tau_1 > 0, \tau_2 > 0$ such that

$$\tau_1 I \leq \int_{t-T}^{t} \frac{\Delta\phi(x,T)\Delta^T\phi(x,T)}{(1+\Delta^T\phi(x,T)\Delta\phi(x,T))^2} d\tau \leq \tau_2 I,$$

where I is the identity matrix of appropriate dimension.

Theorem 7.3. *Consider the interconnected system with the ith subsystem dynamics given by (7.28) and represented as a N-player large-scale system in (7.30). Let the Assumptions 7.8 to 7.11 hold, the value function approximator NN weights are initialized in a compact set $\Omega_\theta \subseteq \mathbb{R}^{l_\theta}$ and updated according to (7.41). Then the estimated control input (7.38) renders the closed-loop system locally uniformly ultimately bounded provided the design parameters $\beta_i > \frac{D_{iM}^2}{2C_{i2}}$, $\alpha_i > \frac{\nabla\phi_M \beta_i^2}{2}$, and the regression vector is persistently exciting, where D_{iM}, β_i are positive constants.*

Sketch of Proof:

- Since the control policy is continuously updated, we only have to consider one case, where we pick a continuously differentiable positive definite candidate Lyapunov function $L : \mathbb{R}^{l_\theta} \times B_x \to \mathbb{R}$, given as
$$L(\tilde{\theta}, X) = \sum_{i=1}^{N} L_i(\tilde{\theta}_i, x_i), \tag{7.45}$$
where $L_i(\tilde{\theta}_i, x_i) = \beta_i L_i(x_i) + L_i(\tilde{\theta}_i)$ is the Lyapunov function of ith subsystem with $\beta_i > 0$ and $L_i(\tilde{\theta}_i) = (1/2)\tilde{\theta}_i^T \tilde{\theta}_i$.
- The Lyapunov function is a sum of Lyapunov functions corresponding to the N subsystems and each of the subsystem Lyapunov function is composed of two terms, each of which accounts for the NN weight estimation error at a subsystem and the subsystem states, respectively.
- Substituting the time derivatives of the weight estimation errors and the subsystem dynamics, we arrive at the desired bounds. Here β_i and α_i are independent design parameters that can be chosen to satisfy the (sufficiency) conditions defined in the Theorem statement.

Corollary 7.2. *Let the hypothesis of Theorem 7.3 holds. Then the estimated value function (7.37) and control policy (7.38) converge to an arbitrarily close neighborhood of the optimal value function (7.35) and control policy (7.36), respectively.*

Sketch of Proof:

- The proof constitutes considering the error between the estimated value function and the optimal value function and the the error between the optimal control policy and the estimated control policy.
- From the proof of Theorem 7.3, the NN weight estimation error $\tilde{\theta}_i$ is bounded and with Assumption 7.11, $\|\tilde{V}_i\|$ and $\|\tilde{u}_i\|$ are UUB. Since the bound can be made smaller by increasing the number of neurons, the estimated value and the estimated Nash solution converge to the neighborhood of their optimal values, respectively.

Next, the Nash solution in the context of an event-based sampling scheme to reduce the usage of computation and communication bandwidth is presented.

7.4.4 EVENT-BASED APPROXIMATE NASH SOLUTION

In this section, the assumption of continuous availability of the system state vector is relaxed by introducing an asynchronous event-based sampling and transmission scheme among the subsystems. Before presenting the event-sampled formulation, the following property of the communication network is assumed.

Assumption 7.12. *The communication network used for the exchange of feedback information is ideal, i.e., there are no delays and packet losses occurring during transmission.*

7.4.4.1 Event-sampled Optimal Control Policy

Define the local state information received at the ith controller at the occurrence of an event as

$$x_{ie}(t) = x_i(t_k^i), \quad t_k^i \leq t < t_{k+1}^i, \ \forall k \in \mathbb{N}, \tag{7.46}$$

where $x_{ie}(t)$ is the event-sampled state vector of ith subsystem. This intermittent transmission of the system state vector introduces an error, referred to as event-sampling error, and is defined as

$$e_i(t) = x_i(t) - x_{ie}(t), \ t_k^i \leq t < t_{k+1}^i, \ \forall k \in \mathbb{N}, \tag{7.47}$$

where $e_i(t)$ is the event-sampling error of the ith subsystem. The sampling instants t_k^i and t_k^j are asynchronous and solely governed by local event-sampling condition at each subsystem defined later in (7.55). To implement the distributed controller in the event-based sampling context, the broadcasted state information are stored at each subsystem controller and updated as soon as new state information is received. However, each subsystem controller is executed only at the local subsystem sampling instants with the latest information available from the local and neighboring subsystems. The optimal control policy in the event-sampling context can be rewritten from (7.33) using the event-based states as

$$u_{ie}^*(t) = -\frac{1}{2}R_{ii}^{-1}g_i^T(x_{ie})V_{ix_e}^*, \quad \forall i = 1,2,\cdots,N, \tag{7.48}$$

where $X_e = [x_{1e}^T, \cdots, x_{Ne}^T]^T$ is event-based states of the large-scale system received at the controller of each sub-system and $V_{ix_e}^* = \partial V_i^*(X)/\partial X\,|_{X=X_e}$ is the gradient evaluated at X_e. Event-sampled approximation (Sahoo et al., 2013a) of the optimal value function $V_i^*(X)$ using the NNs can be represented as

$$V_i^*(X) = \theta_i^{*T}\phi(X_e) + \varepsilon_{ie}(X_e, e), \ i = 1,2,\cdots,N, \tag{7.49}$$

where $\phi(X_e) \in \mathbb{R}^{l_\theta}$ is the event-sampled activation function and $\varepsilon_{ie}(X_e,e) = \theta_i^{*T}(\phi(X_e+e) - \phi(X_e)) + \varepsilon_i(X_e+e)$, $i = 1,2,\cdots,N$ is the event-sampled approximation error with $e = [e_1^T, \cdots, e_N^T]^T$ is the event-sampling error of the large-scale system.

The optimal control policy with event-based state information in a parametric form can be expressed as

$$u_{ie}^*(t) = -\frac{1}{2}R_{ii}^{-1}g_{ie}^T[\nabla_{x_e}^T\phi(X_e)\theta_i^* + \nabla_{x_e}^T\varepsilon_{ie}(X_e,e)], \tag{7.50}$$

for $i = 1,2,\cdots,N$, where $g_{je} = g_j(x_{je})$ and $\nabla_{x_e} = \partial(\cdot)/\partial X\,|_{X=X_e}$. The estimation of the optimal value function in an event-sampling context can be expressed as

$$\hat{V}_i(X) = \hat{\theta}_i^T(t)\phi(X_e), \ i = 1,2,\cdots,N. \tag{7.51}$$

The estimated control policy $\hat{u}_{ie}$, $i = 1,2,\cdots,N$, from (7.51) is represented as

$$\hat{u}_{ie}(t) = -\frac{1}{2}R_{ii}^{-1}g_{ie}^T\hat{V}_{ix_e} = -\frac{1}{2}R_{ii}^{-1}g_{ie}^T\nabla_{x_e}^T\phi(X_e)\hat{\theta}_i, \tag{7.52}$$

for $i = 1,2,\cdots,N$. To derive the NN learning rule, rewrite the Bellman equation (7.40) in the event-driven framework as

$$\hat{V}_i(X(t_{k-1}^i)) = \int_{t_{k-1}^i}^{t_k^i}(Q_i(X) + \sum_{j=1}^{N}\hat{u}_{je}^T(\tau)R_{ij}\hat{u}_{je}(\tau))d\tau + \hat{V}_i(X(t_k^i)) - E_{ib,e}, \tag{7.53}$$

where $E_{ib,e}$ is the event-driven temporal difference error/Bellman residual error.

Table 7.6
Design equations based on distributed Nash games using event-triggered feedback

Integral Bellman error	$E_{ib,e} = \int_{t_{k-1}^i}^{t_k^i} (Q_i(X) + \sum_{j=1}^{N} u_j^T R_{ij} u_j) d\tau + \hat{V}_i(X(t_k^i)) - \hat{V}_i(X(t_{k-1}^i))$
Update rules	$\hat{\theta}_i^+(t) = \hat{\theta}_i(t) - \alpha_{i1}(\partial E_{ib,e}/\partial \hat{\theta}_i)E_{ib,e},\ t = t_k^i,$ $\dot{\hat{\theta}}_i(t) = -\alpha_{i1}(\partial E_{ib,e}/\partial \hat{\theta}_i)E_{ib,e},\ t_k^i < t < t_{k+1}^i,$
Value function	$\hat{V}_i(\hat{X}) = \hat{\theta}_i^T \phi(\hat{X}_e),$
Distributed control law	$\hat{u}_{ie}(t) = -\frac{1}{2} R_{ii}^{-1} g_{ie}^T \hat{V}_{ix_e} = -\frac{1}{2} R_{ii}^{-1} g_{ie}^T \nabla_{x_e}^T \phi(X_e) \hat{\theta}_i$

Remark 7.12. *Note that the states of the ith subsystem are accessed by the controller located at the ith subsystem at event-triggering instants t_k^i only, therefore, it is natural to consider calculating the temporal difference/Bellman residual error at the event-triggering instants, i.e., the fixed T in (7.39) becomes time-varying $T_k^i = t_{k+1}^i - t_k^i$. This requires that the event-triggering mechanism is Zeno free, i.e., the inter-event times T_k^i is positive. Furthermore, at the triggering instant t_k^i only the local states, x_i, are updated, and the last received states of the jth subsystem should be used. This requires the Bellman error to be redefined as the event-driven Bellman error, $E_{ib,e}$.*

The NN weight update law with event-driven Bellman equation (7.53) is given by

$$\begin{aligned} \hat{\theta}_i^+(t) &= \hat{\theta}_i(t) - \alpha_{i1}(\partial E_{ib,e}/\partial \hat{\theta}_i)E_{ib,e},\ t = t_k^i, \\ \dot{\hat{\theta}}_i(t) &= -\alpha_{i1}(\partial E_{ib,e}/\partial \hat{\theta}_i)E_{ib,e},\ t_k^i < t < t_{k+1}^i, \end{aligned} \tag{7.54}$$

for $i = 1, 2, \cdots, N$ and $k \in \mathbb{N}$, where $\alpha_{i1} = \alpha_i/\rho_{ie}^2$ with $\alpha_i > 0$ is the learning gain and $\rho_{ie} = 1 + (\partial E_{ib,e}/\partial \hat{\theta}_i)^T (\partial E_{ib,e}/\partial \hat{\theta}_i)$ is the normalization term and the notation $\hat{\theta}_i^+(t) = \hat{\theta}_i(t^+)$ evaluated at time $t = t_k^i, k \in \mathbb{N}$, and defined as $\lim_{s \to t} \hat{\theta}_i(s)$. The event-triggering condition for the asynchronous sampling and broadcasting is discussed next.

7.4.4.2 Event-triggering Condition and Stability

An event-sampling mechanism is required at each sub-system to determine the broadcast instants for the system states. Consider a positive definite, locally Lipschitz continuous function $L_i(x_i) \in \mathbb{R}$ as the Lyapunov function of ith subsystem (7.28). The event-triggering condition using the Lyapunov function can be selected as

$$\|\bar{e}_i(t)\| \le ((2 - e^{L_{if\Delta}(t - t_k^i)})\beta_i - 1)L_i(x_i(t_k^i)),\ t \in [t_k^i, t_{k+1}^i), \tag{7.55}$$

where $\beta_i > 1$, $\|\bar{e}_i(t)\| = P_{iL}\|e_i(t)\|$, and $L_{f\Delta} = P_{iL}P_{if\Delta}$ with $P_{iL} > 0$ and $P_{f\Delta} > 0$ being the Lipschitz constants satisfying $\left|L_i(x_i(t_k^i)) - L_i(x_i(t))\right| \le P_{iL}\|e_i(t)\|$ and $\left|\bar{\bar{f}}_i(X) - \bar{\bar{f}}_i(X_e)\right| \le P_{if\Delta}\|e_i(t)\|$. The states are sampled using the equality condition in (7.55).

Remark 7.13. *The event-sampling condition in (7.55) is decentralized and a function of local subsystem information and can be evaluated independently at each subsystem. This leads to an asynchronous sampling and transmission scheme.*

Lemma 7.4. *If the inequality in (7.55) hold, then*

$$L_i(x_i(t)) \leq (2 - e^{L_{if\Delta}(t-t_k^i)})\beta_i L_i(x_i(t_k^i)), \ t \in [t_k^i, t_{k+1}^i). \tag{7.56}$$

Sketch of Proof:

- By Lipschitz continuity of the Lyapunov function $L_i(x_i(t))$, it holds that $\left|L_i(x_i(t)) - L_i(x_i(t_k^i))\right| \leq P_{iL}\left\|x_i(t) - x_i(t_k^i)\right\| = P_{iL}\left\|e_i(t)\right\|, \ t \in [t_k^i, t_{k+1}^i)$.
- As per the Lemma statement, since the inequality (7.55) holds, the above inequality satisfies $\left|L_i(x_i(t)) - L_i(x_i(t_k^i))\right| \leq (2 - e^{L_{f\Delta}(t-t_k^i)})\beta_i L_i(x_i(t_k^i)) - L_i(x_i(t_k^i))$.
- Adding $L_i(x_i(t_k^i))$ on the right hand side, we get the desired bounds.

Define the augmented states $\chi_i = [x_i^T \ x_{ie}^T \ \tilde{\theta}_i^T]^T$ for the closed-loop system. The closed-loop event-triggered system can be formulated as a nonlinear impulsive hybrid dynamical system due to involved flow dynamics during inter event-times $t_k^i < t < t_{k+1}^i$ and the jump dynamics at triggering instants $t = t_k^i$, $\forall k, i$. Using (7.28), (7.46), and (7.54), the closed-loop impulsive dynamics can be obtained as

$$\dot{\chi}_i(t) = \begin{bmatrix} \bar{f}_i(x_i) + \bar{g}_i(x_i)\hat{u}_{ie}(t) + \sum_{\substack{j=1 \\ j\neq i}}^{N} \Delta_{ij}(x_i, x_j), \\ 0 \\ \alpha_{i1}(\partial E_{ib,e}/\partial \hat{\theta}_i)E_{ib,e} \end{bmatrix} \tag{7.57}$$

for $t_k^i < t < t_{k+1}^i$ and

$$\chi_i^{+}(t) = \begin{bmatrix} x_i(t) \\ x_i(t) \\ \tilde{\theta}_i(t) + \alpha_{i1}(\partial E_{ib,e}/\partial \hat{\theta}_i)E_{ib,e} \end{bmatrix} \tag{7.58}$$

for $t = t_k^i$, $\forall k, i$. The closed-loop stability results are summarized next.

Theorem 7.4. *Consider the nonlinear continuous-time interconnected system (7.30), with event-based impulsive dynamics (7.57) and (7.58). Let the Assumptions 7.8 to 7.12 hold, the initial control policy $u_i(0)$ be admissible, the critic NN weights initialized in a compact set, and updated according to (7.54). Suppose the initial event occurs at $t_0^i = 0$ and there exists a positive minimum inter-event time between the triggering instants. Then, the event-sampled control policy (7.52) renders the closed-loop impulsive dynamical system locally UB provided activation function and its gradient satisfy the PE condition and the system states are transmitted at the violation of the event sampling condition (7.55) with the design parameter $0 < \alpha_i < 1$.*

Sketch of Proof:

- The proof constitutes considering two cases corresponding to the flow dynamics and the jump dynamics and demonstrating that the first derivative of the Lyapunov function is ultimately bounds.
- *Flow dynamics:* A continuously differentiable positive definite candidate Lyapunov function is chosen to demonstrate the results as stated. Specifically, the Lyapunov candidate function, $L(\chi)$, is chosen as

$$L(\chi) = \sum_{i=1}^{N} L_i(\chi_i), \tag{7.59}$$

where $L_i(\chi_i) = L_i(\tilde{\theta}_i) + \beta_i L_i(x_i) + \beta_i L_i(x_{i,e})$ is the Lyapunov function of ith subsystem with $L_i(\tilde{\theta}_i) = (1/2)\tilde{\theta}_i^T\tilde{\theta}_i$, $L_i(x_i) = x_i^T x_i$, $L_i(x_{i,e}) = x_{i,e}^T x_{i,e}$, and $\beta_i > 1$.

- *Jump dynamics:* The same Lyapunov function from the flow period is chosen as a candidate for analyzing the jump dynamics as well.
- The time-derivative of the Lyapunov candidate function during the flow and the first-difference of the Lyapunov candidate function during jump dynamics can be computed by using weight estimation error dynamics and the system dynamics during both the event-triggering and inter-event times. Furthermore, by appropriate choice of the learning parameter α_i and NN design, the bounds can be reduced when the regression function is persistently exciting. The overall states and weight estimation error bounds can be obtained similar to Theorem 7.3.

Corollary 7.3. *Let the hypothesis of Theorem 7.4 holds. Then the estimated value function (7.51) and control policy (7.52), respectively, converge arbitrarily close neighborhood of the optimal value function (7.49) and control policy (7.50).*

Proof: The proof follows arguments similar to that of Corollary 7.2. In addition to the Assumptions stated in Corollary 7.2, in the case of event-triggered control scheme considered here, the estimated value function (7.51) and control policy (7.52), respectively, converge arbitrarily close neighborhood of the optimal value function (7.49) and control policy (7.50) as number of event-triggering instant increases. The assumption for the minimum inter-event time between the events is guaranteed in Theorem presented next.

Theorem 7.5. *Let the hypothesis of Theorem 7.4 holds. Then the inter-event times $T_k^i = t_{k+1}^i - t_k^i$, $i = 1,2,\cdots,N$, $\forall k \in \mathbb{N}$ are lower bounded by a non-zero positive number and*

$$T_k^i = t_{k+1}^i - t_k^i \geq \frac{1}{L_{f\Delta}} \ln \frac{\left(1 + \frac{L_{f\Delta}}{\kappa}(2\beta_i - 1)L_i(x_i(t_k^i))\right)}{\left((1 + \frac{L_{f\Delta}}{\kappa}\beta_i L_i(x_i(t_k^i))\right)} > 0, \tag{7.60}$$

where $\kappa > 0$ is defined in the proof.

Proof:

- The dynamics of the event-trigger error satisfies

$$\begin{aligned}\frac{d\,\|\bar{e}_i(t)\|}{dt} &\leq \|\dot{\bar{e}}_i(t)\| = \|P_{iL}\dot{x}_i(t)\| \\ &= \left\| P_{iL}\bar{\bar{f}}_i(X) - (1/2)P_{iL}\bar{D}_i\nabla_x^T\phi(X_e)\hat{\theta}_i \right\| \leq L_{f\Delta}\,\|\bar{e}_i\| + \kappa,\end{aligned}$$

  where $L_{f\Delta} = P_{iL}P_{if\Delta}$, $\kappa = \|\bar{\bar{f}}(X_e)\| + (1/2)P_{iL}\bar{D}_{iM}\nabla_x^T\phi_M\hat{\theta}_{iM}$. The above inequality is reached using the Lipschitz continuity of the function $\bar{\bar{f}}_i(X)$.
- By comparison lemma, the solution of $\|\dot{\bar{e}}_i(t)\|$ with $\left\|\bar{e}_i(t_k^i)\right\| = 0$ is upper bounded by

$$\|\bar{e}_i(t)\| \leq \int_{t_k^i}^t \kappa e^{L_{f\Delta}(t-\tau)}d\tau = (\kappa/L_{f\Delta})(e^{L_{f\Delta}(t-t_k^i)} - 1). \tag{7.61}$$

- At the next sampling instant $\left\|e_i(t_{k+1}^i)\right\| = ((1 - e^{L_{f\Delta}(t_{k+1}^i - t_k^i)})\beta_i - 1)L_i(x_i(t_k^i))$. Comparing both the equations

$$\begin{aligned}\left\|e_i(t_{k+1}^i)\right\| &= ((2 - e^{L_{f\Delta}(t_{k+1}^i - t_k^i)})\beta_i - 1)L_i(x_i(t_k^i)) \\ &\leq (\kappa/L_{f\Delta})(e^{L_{f\Delta}(t_{k+1}^i - t_k^i)} - 1).\end{aligned}$$

■ Solving the equation for the inter-sample time leads to (7.60).

$$T_k^i = t_{k+1}^i - t_k^i =$$
$$\frac{1}{L_{f\Delta}} \ln\left(1 + \frac{L_{f\Delta}}{\kappa}(2\beta_i - 1)L_i(x_i(t_k^i))\right) / \left((1 + \frac{L_{f\Delta}}{\kappa}\beta_i L_i(x_i(t_k^i))\right).$$

The inter-sample times $T_k^i > 0, i = 1, 2, \cdots, N$ by selecting $\beta_i > 1$, implies the sampling instants are distinct and not accumulated. Next, the approximate Nash solution for linear system is presented.

7.4.5 DISTRIBUTED CONTROL OF LINEAR INTERCONNECTED SYSTEMS

In this section, we extended the results to linear systems. The dynamics of ith subsystem, represented in a continuous time with linear dynamics, are given by

$$\dot{x}_i(t) = \bar{A}_i x_i(t) + \bar{B}_i u_i(t) + \Sigma_{\substack{j=1 \\ j \neq i}}^{N} A_{ij} x_j(t), \tag{7.62}$$

for $i = 1, 2, \cdots, N$, where the linear map $A_i : \mathbb{R}^{n_i} \to \mathbb{R}^{n_i}$ and $\bar{B}_i : \mathbb{R}^{n_i} \to \mathbb{R}^{n_i \times m_i}$ are the internal dynamics and input gain of the ith subsystem, respectively. The matrix function $A_{ij} : \mathbb{R}^{n_i} \to \mathbb{R}^{n_i \times n_j}$ represents the interconnection between i^{th} and j^{th} subsystem. The interconnected system can be represented as a N-player large scale system given by

$$\dot{X}(t) = AX(t) + \Sigma_{j=1}^{N} B_j u_j(t), \quad X(0) = X_0, \tag{7.63}$$

where the map $A = [\bar{A}_i, A_{i2}, ..., A_{iN}]$ for $i = 1, .., N$ and $B_j = [0, ..., \bar{B}_j^T, ..., 0]^T \in \mathbb{R}^{n \times m_j}$, $j = 1, .., N$ are the known overall internal dynamics and the control coefficient function with 0's representing the zero matrices of appropriate dimensions. The cost functional J_i associated with each subsystem for the admissible policies $u_i(t)$, $i = 1, 2, \cdots, N$ is defined as

$$J_i(X) = \int_t^{\infty} (X^T(\tau) Q_i X(\tau) + \sum_{j=1}^{N} u_j^T(\tau) R_{ij} u_j(\tau)) d\tau,$$

where $Q_i > 0$, $i = 1, 2, \cdots, N$ is a positive definite matrix. The optimal value V_i^* at each subsystem is given by

$$V_i^*(X) = \min_{u_i} J_i(X) = \min_{u_i} \int_t^{\infty} (X^T(\tau) Q_i X(\tau) + \sum_{j=1}^{N} u_j^T(\tau) R_{ij} u_j(\tau)) d\tau.$$

Let the candidate optimal value function be of the form $V_i^*(x) = \frac{1}{2} x^T(t) P_i^* x(t)$, $i = 1, 2, \cdots, N$, where $P_i^* > 0$ is a symmetric positive definite matrix. The Hamiltonian function H_i is defined as

$$H_i(X, u_1, \cdots, u_N, V_{ix}^*) = X^T Q_i X + \sum_{j=1}^{N} u_j^T R_{ij} u_j + V_{ix}^{*T} [AX(t) + \sum_{j=1}^{N} B_j u_j], \tag{7.64}$$

where $V_{ix}^* = \partial V_i / \partial X = P_i^* X$, $i = 1, 2, \cdots, N$. Applying the stationarity condition $\partial H_i / \partial u_i = 0$, $i = 1, 2, \cdots, N$ reveals the greedy optimal control policy u_i^* given by

$$u_i^*(t) = -\frac{1}{2} R_{ii}^{-1} B_i^T P_i^* X(t), \quad i = 1, 2, \cdots, N. \tag{7.65}$$

Inserting the optimal control policy (7.65) in the Hamiltonian function (7.64), reveals the coupled Riccati equation (Song et al., 2017). Using an approach similar to the approximation used in the previous section, forward-in-time solution to the coupled Riccati equation can be adaptively learnt online using the ADP-based approach by representing the optimal value function as

$$V_i^*(X) = \theta_i^{*T} \bar{\phi}(X), \tag{7.66}$$

where $\theta_i^* = vec(P_i^*)$ is obtained using vectorization of the matrix P_i^* and $\bar{\phi}(X) = vec(X^T \otimes X)$, where $\otimes$ is the Kronecker product.

Remark 7.14. *Note that the regression vector is formed using Kronecker product of the system states, and, therefore, different than the bounded activation functions. Further, the approximation error is not present.*

Example 7.4. *Consider three coupled nonlinear subsystems, where the three subsystems represent are the thigh and knee dynamics of a walking robot experiment (Dunbar, 2007). In the following,* $x_1(t)$ *is the relative angle between the two thighs,* $x_2(t)$ *is the right knee angle (relative to the right thigh), and* $x_3(t)$ *is the left knee angle (relative to left thigh). The controlled equations of motion in units of (rad/s) are*

$$\begin{aligned}\ddot{x}_1(t) &= 0.1[1-5.25x_1^2(t)]\dot{x}_1(t) - x_1(t) + u_1(t)\\ \ddot{x}_2(t) &= 0.01\left[1-p_2(x_2(t)-x_{2eq})^2\right]\dot{x}_2(t) - 4(x_2(t)-x_{2eq})\\ &\quad +0.057x_1(t)\dot{x}_1(t) + 0.1(\dot{x}_2(t)-\dot{x}_3(t)) + u_2(t)\\ \ddot{x}_3(t) &= 0.01[1-p_3(x_3(t)-x_{3eq})^2]\dot{x}_3(t) - 4(x_3(t)-x_{3eq})\\ &\quad +0.057x_1(t)\dot{x}_1(t) + 0.1(\dot{x}_3(t)-\dot{x}_2(t)) + u_3(t),\end{aligned}$$

where $\ddot{x}_i$ *correspond to the dynamics of the* i^{th} *subsystem. The control objective is to bring the robot to a stop in a stable manner* ($x_i \to x_{ieq}$)*, where* x_{ieq} *are the equilibrium points with* $x_{1eq} = 0, x_{2eq} = -0.227, x_{3eq} = 0.559$.

The parameters p_2 and p_3 are 6070, and 192, respectively. The NN to approximate V_i^* were designed with 6 hidden layer neurons. The initial conditions $x_i(0)$ and $\hat{\theta}_i(0)$ were selected randomly in the intervals $[-1,1]$ and $[0,1]$, respectively. The learning gains were selected for continuous time simulations as $\alpha_1 = 25$, $\alpha_2 = 35$, $\alpha_3 = 35$, and for the event-triggering case, $\alpha_1 = 0.4$, $\alpha_2 = 0.85$, and $\alpha_3 = 0.85$, $\beta_i = 1.086, \forall i \in \{1,2,3\}$. A quadratic performance index with $Q_i(X) = X^T\bar{Q}_iX$ is selected, where the parameters $\bar{Q}_1 = 0.02$, $\bar{Q}_2 = 0.075$, $\bar{Q}_3 = 0.075$, $R_{11} = 0.04$, $R_{22} = 0.01$, $R_{33} = 0.01$, and $R_{ij} = R_{jj}$, for $i \neq j$, $i,j \in \{1,2,3\}$. The robotic system is simulated with the torques generated using the control algorithm with hybrid leaning scheme.

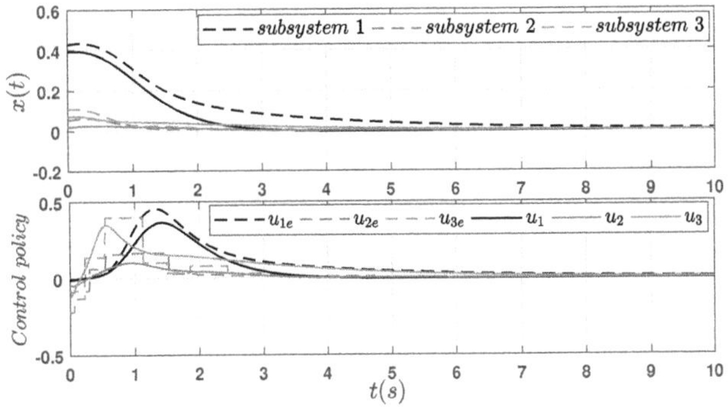

Figure 7.11 Convergence of system states and control inputs for continuous (solid lines) and event-sampled system (dotted lines).

The time history of the large-scale interconnected system states for both continuous (dotted) and event-based (solid) implementation is plotted in Figure 7.11 (top). The system states both for the continuous and event-based designs converge to the equilibrium state with the approximated control policies. The control inputs for both the designs also converge to zero as shown in Figure 7.11 (bottom). The event-triggered control policies (dotted lines) are piecewise constant functions, since they are only updated at the triggering instants, and closely approximates the continuous policies. To show the effectiveness of the event-based implementation in reducing communication and com-

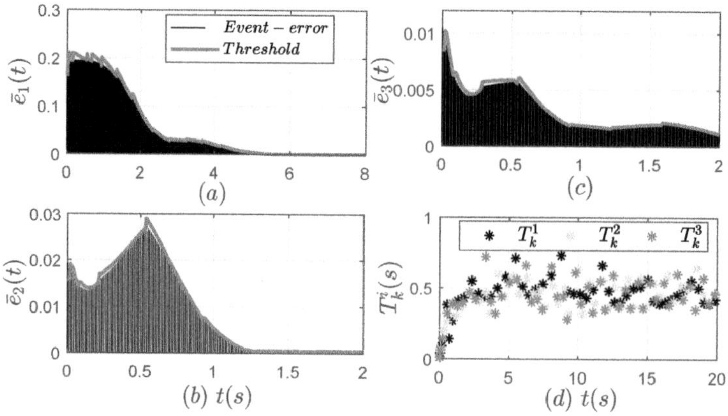

Figure 7.12 Convergence of event-sampled error and threshold and inter-event times showing the asynchronous transmission instants.

putation, the event-trigger error $\bar{e}_i(t)$ and the threshold in condition (7.55) for all the subsystems are shown in Figure 7.12 (a) - (c). Note that the event-triggering conditions are local and decentralized and, therefore, the thresholds are different for each subsystem leading to different number of sampling instants. In terms of number of events, highest number of triggering observed at the subsystem 1 and lowest at subsystem 2; implying asynchronous triggering at subsystems. The inter-event times T_k^i are shown in Figure 7.12 (d). It is clear that the inter-event times are different between two consecutive sampling instants leading to aperiodic sampling. This further implies that the computational and the communication resources are saved by reducing the transmission and controller execution when compared to periodic execution schemes.

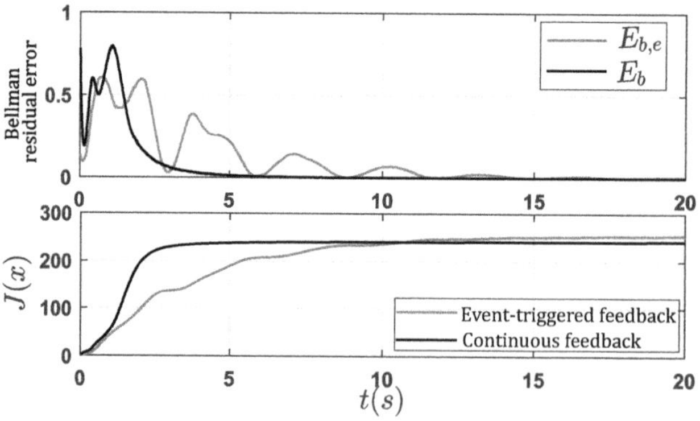

Figure 7.13 Convergence of Bellman error and cumulative cost for continuous and event-sampled designs.

From the optimality perspective, the Bellman residual errors for both continuous and event-based are shown in Figure 7.13 (top) indicating the convergence of the errors to zero at the same time. This implies the estimated value function converged to its optimal value and Nash equilibrium solution is reached for both cases. As expected, the time history of the event-based Bellman residual error is oscillating before convergence. This is due to the NN parameter update using the aperiodic feedback information with event-based sampling and transmission. The comparison between the cumulative cost for continuous and event-triggered solution is shown in Figure 7.13 (bottom). It is clear that the event-based cost is slightly higher than the continuous implementation which demonstrates the trade-off between the system performance and communication resource savings. Finally, to compare the effectiveness of the algorithm with the work in (Narayanan and Jagannathan, 2017), the convergence of Bellman error and cumulative costs for the interconnected system are plotted in Figure

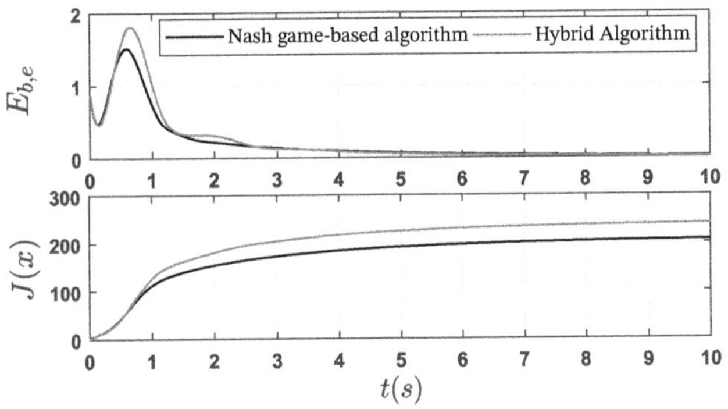

Figure 7.14 Comparison of Bellman error and cumulative cost for the hybrid method with NZS game and existing method (Narayanan and Jagannathan, 2017).

7.14. The parameters in this experiment were chosen as follows: $\alpha_1 = 0.4$, $\alpha_2 = 0.85$, and $\alpha_3 = 0.85$, $\beta_i = 1.086, \forall i \in \{1,2,3\}$. A quadratic performance index with $Q_i(X) = X^T \bar{Q}_i X$ is selected where the parameters $\bar{Q}_1 = 0.05$, $\bar{Q}_2 = 0.085$, $\bar{Q}_3 = 0.085$, $R_{11} = 0.06$, $R_{22} = 0.07$, $R_{33} = 0.04$, and $R_{12} = -0.01$, $R_{13} = -0.002$, $R_{21} = -0.025$, $R_{23} = -0.003$, $R_{31} = -0.025$, $R_{32} = -0.01$. Note that the flexibility of the distributed control framework lies in the additional term $\sum_{j=1,j\neq i}^{3} u_{ij}^T R_{ij} u_{ij}$, that is included in the cost function (7.31) of the ith subsystem, as compared to the results in Section 7.3 based on (Narayanan and Jagannathan, 2017), wherein $R_{ij} = 0$, $\forall i,j \in \{1,2,3\}$. In other words, due to the NZS framework, a trade-off between the performance of different subsystems can be achieved by explicitly accounting for control policies of other neighboring subsystems while computing the control policy. From Figure 7.14, the Bellman residual error for both the designs converge to zero at the same time. Further, it is clear that the method incur in lower cumulative cost when compared to the method in the Section 7.3.

7.5 TRACKING CONTROL OF NONLINEAR INTERCONNECTED SYSTEMS

This section concerns with a brief summary of tracking control problem for nonlinear interconnected systems using the learning-based control algorithms presented in this chapter. In a tracking problem, the goal is to make the system output (or states) follow a desired reference trajectory or signal. We begin with the definition of a feasible reference trajectory for the ith subsystem as $x_{i,d}(t) \in \mathbb{R}^{n_i}$. Assume that the feasible reference trajectory $x_{i,d}(t) \in \mathbb{R}^{n_i}$ for the ith subsystem is generated by a reference system represented by

$$\dot{x}_{i,d}(t) = f_{i,d}(x_{i,d}(t)) + \sum_{j=1,j\neq i}^{N} \Delta_{ij,d}(x_{i,d}, x_{j,d}), \quad x_{i,d}(0) = x_{id0}, \tag{7.67}$$

where $x_{i,d}(t) \in \mathbb{R}^{n_i}$ is the reference state of the ith subsystem, $f_{i,d}$ and $\Delta_{ij,d}$ are nonlinear functions, and $x_{i,d}(0) = 0$. The system in (7.67) is often referred to as the generator system that generates feasible reference trajectories for the system to track.

Define the error between the system state and the reference state as the tracking error, given by $e_{i,r}(t) \triangleq x_i(t) - x_{i,d}(t)$. Then, the tracking error system, utilizing (7.1) and (7.67), can be defined by

$$\begin{aligned}\dot{e}_{i,r}(t) =& \dot{x}_i(t) - \dot{x}_{i,d}(t) = f_i(x_i(t)) + g_i(x_i)u_i(t) + \sum_{\substack{j=1\\ j\neq i}}^{N} \Delta_{ij}(x_i, x_j) - \dot{x}_{i,d}(t), \\ =& f_i(e_{i,r}, x_{i,d}) + g_i(e_{i,r}, x_{i,d})u_i(t) + \sum_{j=1,j\neq i}^{N} \Delta_{ij}(e_{j,r}, e_{i,r}, x_{j,d}, x_{i,d}) - f_{i,d}(x_{i,d}) - \sum_{j=1,j\neq i}^{N} \Delta_{ij,d}(x_{i,d}, x_{j,d}).\end{aligned} \tag{7.68}$$

Recall the following assumptions on the control coefficient and the reference trajectory.

Assumption 7.13. *The function g_i is bounded, the matrix $g_i(x)$ has full column rank for all $x_i(t) \in \mathbb{R}^{n_i}$, the function $g_i^+ : \mathbb{R}^{n_i} \to \mathbb{R}^{m_i \times n_i}$ defined as $g_i^+ \triangleq (g_i^T g_i)^{-1} g_i^T$ is bounded and locally Lipschitz. The reference trajectory is bounded, the functions $f_{i,d}$ and $\Delta_{ij,d}$ are locally Lipschitz functions, and $g_i(x_{i,d}) g_i^+(x_{i,d})(f_{i,d}(x_{i,d}) + \sum_j \Delta_{ij,d}(x_{i,d}, x_{j,d}) - f_i(x_{i,d}) - \sum_j \Delta_{ij}(x_{i,d}, x_{j,d})) = f_{i,d}(x_{i,d}) + \sum_j \Delta_{ij,d}(x_{i,d}, x_{j,d}) - f_i(x_{i,d}) - \sum_j \Delta_{ij}(x_{i,d}, x_{j,d})$.*

The steady-state control policy $u_{i,d} : \mathbb{R}^{n_i} \to \mathbb{R}^{m_i}$ corresponding to the desired trajectory $x_{i,d}$ is

$$u_{i,d}(x_{i,d}) = g_{i,d}^+(x_{i,d})(f_{i,d}(x_{i,d}) + \sum_j \Delta_{ij,d}(x_{i,d}, x_{j,d}) - f_i(x_{i,d}) - \sum_j \Delta_{ij}(x_{i,d}, x_{j,d})). \tag{7.69}$$

By augmenting the tracking error $e_{i,r}$ and desired trajectory $x_{i,d}$, the dynamics of the augmented tracking error system can be represented as

$$\dot{\chi}_i(t) = \mathcal{G}_i(\chi_i(t)) + \mathcal{H}_i(\chi_i(t))\omega_i(t) + \sum_{j=1, j\neq i}^{N} \mathcal{K}_{ij}(\chi_i(t), \chi_j(t)), \tag{7.70}$$

where $\chi_i \triangleq [e_{i,r}^T \; x_{i,d}^T]^T \in \mathbb{R}^{2n_i}$ is the augmented state with $\chi_i(0) = [e_{i,r}^T(0) \; x_{i,d}^T(0)]^T = \chi_{i0}$, $\mathcal{G}_i$ is given by $\begin{bmatrix} f_i(e_{i,r} + x_{i,d}) - f_{i,d}(x_{i,d}) + g_i(e_{i,r} + x_{i,d}) u_{i,d}(x_{i,d}) \\ f_{i,d}(x_{i,d}) \end{bmatrix}$, $\mathcal{H}_i$ given by $\begin{bmatrix} g_i(e_{i,r} + x_{i,d}) \\ \mathbf{0} \end{bmatrix}$, $\mathcal{K}_{ij}$ is given by

$$\begin{bmatrix} \sum_j \Delta_{ij}(e_{i,r} + x_{i,d}, e_{j,r} + x_{j,d}) - \sum_j \Delta_{ij,d}(x_{i,d}, x_{j,d}) \\ \sum_j \Delta_{ij,d}(x_{i,d}, x_{j,d}) \end{bmatrix},$$

and $\omega_i(t) = u_i(t) - u_{i,d}(t)$. The augmented error system in (7.70) associated with the ith subsystem enables transforming the tracking problem into a regulation problem. We can further augment the error subsystems for $i = 1, \ldots, N$ to define the overall tracking error system similar to (7.2).

Further, the cost function for the overall tracking error system can be redefined as

$$V(\chi, \omega) = \int_t^{\infty} [\bar{Q}(\chi) + \omega^T(\tau) \bar{R} \omega(\tau)] d\tau, \tag{7.71}$$

subject to dynamic constraints (7.70) for $i = 1, \ldots, N$. Since the desired trajectories are not controllable with $\omega_i(t)$, the penalty for the desired trajectories are kept as zero. For example, $\bar{Q}(\chi) = [e_r^T x_d^T] \begin{bmatrix} Q & 0 \\ 0 & 0 \end{bmatrix} [e_r^T x_d^T]^T$, where e_r, x_d are the vectors of the overall error, desired trajectories for all the subsystems concatenated into a single vector, respectively, and Q is a positive definite matrix and 0 represent zero matrices of appropriate dimensions. Using (7.70) and (7.71), we can follow the steps discussed earlier in this chapter in Sections 7.3 and 7.4 to design learning-based tracking control schemes for nonlinear interconnected systems.

7.6 CONCLUDING REMARKS

This chapter covered an approximation based distributed controller with event-triggered state and output feedback that seeks optimality for a class of nonlinear interconnected system. The event-triggered control execution significantly reduces the communication and computational resource utilization by reducing the frequency of feedback instants. The hybrid learning scheme accelerates the learning of the NN weights with event-triggered feedback while reducing the communication costs. The event-triggering condition is independent of the estimated parameters and an additional estimator at the event-triggering mechanism is not required. The event-triggering mechanism is decentralized, asynchronous, and ensures that the system is stable during the inter-event period. The requirement of initial stabilizing control policy is relaxed by utilizing the dynamics of the system.

Next a distributed optimal controller design for large-scale interconnected systems is reformulated using N-player NZS game. Nash equilibrium solution is obtained using ADP based scheme for both continuous and event-sampled implementation of the system. Local ultimate boundedness of the system states and NN weight estimation errors are demonstrated analytically. It is observed in the example that the hybrid leaning scheme closely approximates the continuous time solution. From the performance point of view, the event-based implementation closely followed the continuously updated solution while saving the communication bandwidth. The distributed optimization problem when formulated using the NZS game offers flexibility in terms of the achievable trade-off between the performance of various subsystems due to the Nash equilibrium solution.

7.7 PROBLEMS

7.7.1 Consider N inverted pendulum connected by spring (Spooner and Passino, 1999), which can be represented of the form (7.2). The dynamics of the system are given by

$$\begin{aligned} \dot{x}_{i1} &= x_{i2}, \\ \dot{x}_{i2} &= \left(\frac{m_i g r}{J_i} - \frac{kr^2}{4J_i}\right)\sin x_{i1} + \frac{kr}{2J_i}(l-b) + \frac{u_i}{J_i} + \sum_{j=1}^{N}\frac{kr^2}{4J_i}\sin x_{j1}. \end{aligned} \tag{7.72}$$

Treat $x_{i2}(t)$ as the measured variable, $N = 10$, and let all the subsystems be connected such that they form a chain network. Design distributed control policies based on the hybrid learning algorithm using equations in Table 7.2.

7.7.2 For the system described in the previous problem, consider the outputs from each subsystem to defined as $y_i(t) = x_{i1}(t)$. Use the hybrid learning algorithm with distributed observers (see Table 7.3) to design output-feedback controllers.

7.7.3 Design distributed control policies based on the hybrid learning algorithm using equations in Table 7.6 for the Problem 7.7.1.

7.7.4 For the same system as in Problem 7.7.1., consider the linearized dynamics as in (Guinaldo et al., 2011). The parameters in the system dynamics are $m_1 = 2, m_2 = 2.5$, $J_1 = 5, J_2 = 6.25$, $k = 10$, $r = 0.5$, $l = 0.5$, and $g = 9.8$, $b = 0.5$. Pick the initial conditions of the system states in the interval [0,1] and the initial weights of the NN from [-1,1], randomly. Treat $x_{i2}(t)$ as the measured variable, $N = 10$, and let all the subsystems be connected such that they form a ring network. Design distributed control policies based on the hybrid learning algorithm using equations in Table 7.3.

7.7.5 Design distributed control policies based on the hybrid learning algorithm using equations in Table 7.6 for the Problem 7.7.3.

7.7.6 Consider the system of three interconnected systems modeling the robot walking gait. The controlled equations of motion in units of (rad/s) are

$$\begin{aligned} \ddot{x}_1(t) &= 0.1[1-5.25x_1^2(t)]\dot{x}_1(t) - x_1(t) + u_1(t) \\ \ddot{x}_2(t) &= 0.01\left[1 - p_2(x_2(t) - x_{2eq})^2\right]\dot{x}_2(t) - 4(x_2(t) - x_{2eq}) \\ &\quad + 0.057x_1(t)\dot{x}_1(t) + 0.1(\dot{x}_2(t) - \dot{x}_3(t)) + u_2(t) \\ \ddot{x}_3(t) &= 0.01[1 - p_3(x_3(t) - x_{3eq})^2]\dot{x}_3(t) - 4(x_3(t) - x_{3eq}) \\ &\quad + 0.057x_1(t)\dot{x}_1(t) + 0.1(\dot{x}_3(t) - \dot{x}_2(t)) + u_3(t), \end{aligned}$$

where $\ddot{x}_i$ correspond to the dynamics of the ith subsystem. The control objective is to bring the robot to a stop in a stable manner ($x_i \to x_{ieq}$), where x_{ieq} are the equilibrium points with $x_{1eq} = 0, x_{2eq} = -0.227, x_{3eq} = 0.559$. The parameters p_2 and p_3 are 6070, and 192, respectively. Design distributed control policies based on the hybrid learning algorithm using equations in Table 7.3.

7.7.7 Repeat Problem 7.7.5. using Table 7.3 and Table 7.6 with the parameters $x_{1eq} = 0$, $x_{2eq} = 0.559$, $x_{3eq} = 0.226$, $p_2 = 226$, and $p_3 = 5240$.

7.7.8 Consider a nonlinear interconnected system governed by

$$\dot{x}_1 = \begin{bmatrix} -x_{11} + x_{12} \\ -0.5(x_{11} + x_{12}) + 0.5x_{11}^2 x_{12} \end{bmatrix} + \begin{bmatrix} 0 \\ \sin(x_{11}) \end{bmatrix} u_1 \tag{7.73}$$

$$+ \begin{bmatrix} 1 \\ 0 \end{bmatrix} (x_{11} + x_{22}) \sin^2(\rho_1 x_{12}) \cos(0.5x_{21}) \tag{7.74}$$

$$\dot{x}_2 = \begin{bmatrix} 0.5x_{22} \\ -x_{21} - 0.5x_{22} + 0.5x_{21}\cos^2(x_{22}) \end{bmatrix} + \begin{bmatrix} 0 \\ x_{21} \end{bmatrix} u_2 \tag{7.75}$$

$$+ \begin{bmatrix} 1 \\ 0 \end{bmatrix} \left(0.5(x_{12} + x_{22}) \cos\left(\rho_2 e^{x_{21}^2}\right)\right) \tag{7.76}$$

where $x_1 = [x_{11}, x_{12}]^\mathsf{T} \in \mathbb{R}^2$ and $x_2 = [x_{21}, x_{22}]^\mathsf{T} \in \mathbb{R}^2$ are the state vectors of subsystems 1 and 2, respectively, $u_1 \in \mathbb{R}$ and $u_2 \in \mathbb{R}$ are the control inputs of subsystems 1 and 2, respectively, and $\rho_1 \in \mathbb{R}$ and $\rho_2 \in \mathbb{R}$ are the unknown parameters. To simplify discussion, randomly choose$\rho_i \in [-1, 1], i = 1, 2$ as in (Yang and He, 2020). Use the state-feedback based controller with the equations given in Table 7.2.

7.7.9 Use the game-theoretic approach to design control inputs for the system described in the previous problem. Use the equations given in Table 7.6.

7.7.10 Design distributed controls using the equations given in Table 7.5 for the system described in (7.76). Now, what happens if the term $\sum_{j=1}^{2} u_j^T R_{ij} u_j$ used in the equation to compute the integral Bellman error is replaced by $u_i^T R_{ij} u_i - u_j^T R_{ij} u_j$ for the ith subsystem.

8 Exploration and Hybrid Learning for Interconnected Systems

CONTENTS

In this chapter, we shall explore the possibility of systematically improving the distributed control performance using RL techniques. Specifically, we shall develop a distributed control scheme for an interconnected system composed of uncertain input-affine nonlinear subsystems with event-triggered state feedback using an enhanced hybrid learning scheme-based ADP with online exploration. The enhanced hybrid learning scheme was introduced in (Narayanan and Jagannathan, 2017). In this scheme, the NN weight tuning rules for learning the approximate the optimal value function is appended with information from NN identifiers that are used to reconstruct the system dynamics using feedback data. Considering the effects of NN approximation of the system dynamics and the boot-strapping to extrapolate the optimal values, we shall see the the NN weight update rules introduced in this chapter learns the approximate optimal value function faster when compared to the algorithms developed in earlier chapters. Finally, we shall also consider incorporating *exploration* in the online control framework using the NN identifiers to reduce the overall cost at the expense of additional computations during the initial online learning phase.

8.1 INTRODUCTION

Advanced control schemes are necessary for the efficient and cost-effective operation of cyber-physical systems (CPS) in diverse applications, e.g., industrial systems with uncertain dynamics.

As we have seen thus far in this book, the ADP schemes aim to address the problem of optimization over time through learning without needing apriori knowledge of the system dynamics. The event-triggered ADP schemes, while reducing computational and communication burden, are still inefficient due to the following reasons: a) the learning time is increased due to intermittent feedback as the frequency of events decides the approximation accuracy; b) the sampling instants are dynamic, hence, the inter-sampling intervals are time-varying, restricting the use of iterative learning schemes. The flexible hybrid learning framework presented in the Chapters 6 and 7 accelerate the learning process with event-triggered feedback and ensure online, real-time implementation, .

In this chapter, we shall see that the RL techniques together with NN identifiers can be employed to further improve the efficiency of the control scheme for facilitating real-time implementation. An improved weight update rule, based on (Narayanan and Jagannathan, 2017), for learning and enhancing the approximate optimal value function with an online exploration strategy by using the identifiers, is presented in this chapter. We shall see that the cumulative cost during the learning phase can be reduced further with the enhanced learning technique presented in this chapter when compared to the cost incurred with the hybrid learning algorithm at the expense of additional computations.

8.2 BACKGROUND AND PROBLEM STATEMENT

To keep the chapter self-contained, we briefly revisit the system description and optimal control problem for nonlinear interconnected systems.

8.2.1 SYSTEM DESCRIPTION

Consider a nonlinear input-affine continuous-time system composed of N interconnected subsystems, described by the differential equation

$$\dot{x}_i(t) = f_i(x_i) + g_i(x_i)u_i(t) + \sum_{\substack{j=1 \\ j\neq i}}^{N} \Delta_{ij}(x_i, x_j), \qquad x_i(0) = x_{i0}, \tag{8.1}$$

where $x_i(t) \in B_i \subseteq \mathbb{R}^{n_i \times 1}$ represents the state vector of the ith subsystem and $\dot{x}_i(t)$ its time derivative, B_i is a compact set, $u_i(t) \in \mathbb{R}^{m_i}$ is the control input, $f_i : B_i \to \mathbb{R}^{n_i}$, $g_i : B_i \to \mathbb{R}^{n_i \times m_i}$ are uncertain nonlinear maps, and $\Delta_{ij} : \mathbb{R}^{n_i \times n_j} \to \mathbb{R}^{n_i}$ is the uncertain nonlinear interconnection between the ith and the jth subsystems. The augmented system dynamics are

$$\dot{X}(t) = F(X) + G(X)U(t), \qquad x(0) = x_0, \tag{8.2}$$

where $F = [(f_1 + \sum_{j=2}^{N} \Delta_{1j})^T, \cdots, (f_N + \sum_{j=1}^{N-1} \Delta_{Nj})^T]^T$, $X(t) = [x_1^T(t), \cdots, x_N^T(t)]^T \in B \subseteq \mathbb{R}^n$, $B = \bigcup_{i=1}^{N} B_i$, $U(t) = [u_1^T(t), .., u_N^T(t)]^T \in \mathbb{R}^m$, $m = \sum_{i=1}^{N} m_i$, $n = \sum_{i=1}^{N} n_i$, and $G = diag([g_1(x_1)..,g_N(x_N)])$. The following assumptions are needed for the control design.

Assumption 8.1. *The dynamics (8.1) and (8.2) are stabilizable with equilibrium point at the origin. Full-state information is available as measurements. The communication network that facilitates information sharing among subsystems is lossless.*

Assumption 8.2. *The nonlinear map $g_i(x_i)$ is bounded such that $0 < g_{im} < \|g_i(x_i)\| \leq g_{iM}$ in B_i for every subsystem.*

Assumption 8.3. *The functions $f_i(x_i)$, $\Delta_{ij}(x_i, x_j)$, $g_i(x_i)$ are locally Lipschitz continuous on compacts.*

In the next subsection, the notion of event-triggered feedback and greedy policy design with aperiodic event-based feedback is presented.

8.2.2 EVENT-TRIGGERED FEEDBACK AND OPTIMAL CONTROL

Let $x_i(t_k^i)$ be the state of the ith subsystem at time instant t_k^i. Between any successive event-sampling instants t_k^i, t_{k+1}^i, the state vector is denoted as $\breve{x}_i(t) = x_i(t_k^i)$, $\forall k \in \mathbb{N}$. Using the ZOH, the last updated states and control are held at actuators and controllers between events. To denote the difference between the actual system states and the state available at the controller, an event-sampling error is defined as

$$e_i(t) = x_i(t) - x_i(t_k^i),\ t_k^i \le t < t_{k+1}^i. \tag{8.3}$$

By rewriting $\breve{x}_i(t)$ using (8.3), the feedback between events can be defined as $\breve{x}_i(t) = x_i(t) - e_i(t)$. Next, define the infinite horizon cost function of the augmented system (8.2), as

$$V(X(t)) = \int_t^\infty \left[Q(X) + U^T(\tau)RU(\tau)\right]d\tau, \tag{8.4}$$

where $Q(X) > 0$, $\forall X \in B\backslash\{0\}$, $Q(0) = 0$, $R > 0$ are the penalty functions of appropriate dimensions. Let $V(.)$ and its time-derivative be continuous on a compact set B. Then,

$$\dot{V}(X(t)) = -\left[Q(X) + U^T(t)RU(t)\right].$$

Using the infinitesimal version of (8.4), define the Hamiltonian function

$$H(X,U,\frac{\partial V}{\partial X}) = \left[Q(X) + U^T(t)RU(t)\right] + (\partial V^T/\partial X)\dot{X}(t).$$

The optimal control policy which minimizes (8.4) (assuming a unique minimum exists) is obtained by using the stationarity condition as $U^*(t) = -\frac{1}{2}R^{-1}G^T(X)\partial V^*/\partial X$ and it is called greedy policy with respect to (8.4). The Hamiltonian function can be defined between two event-triggering instants, $[t_k, t_{k+1})$, as

$$H(X(t),U(t_k),\frac{\partial V}{\partial X}) = \left[Q(X) + U^T(t)RU(t)\right] + (\partial V^T/\partial X)\dot{X}(t). \tag{8.5}$$

The greedy policy with event-triggered state becomes

$$U^*(t) = -\tfrac{1}{2}R^{-1}G^T(\breve{X})(\partial V^*/\partial \breve{X}) \tag{8.6}$$

with $\breve{X}(t) = X(t_k)$, $t \in [t_k, t_{k+1})$. Now, for the interconnected system (8.2) under consideration, the ith subsystem dynamics (8.1) are influenced by the states of the jth subsystem satisfying $\Delta_{ij}(x_i, x_j) \ne 0$. Consider the ith subsystem in (8.1) and the cost function (8.4) for (8.2), then $\exists u_i^*(t) \in \mathbb{R}^{m_i}$, given by

$$u_i{}^*(t) = -\frac{1}{2}R_i{}^{-1}g_i{}^T(x_i)(\partial V_i{}^*(X)/\partial x_i),\ \forall i \in 1,2,..N. \tag{8.7}$$

as a function of $x_i(t)$, $x_j(t)$, for all $j \in 1,2,..,N,$, where $V_i{}^*(X)$ represent the optimal value function of the ith subsystem, R_i is a positive definite matrix, such that the cost function (8.4) is minimized. Chapter 7 presents a learning algorithm to synthesize this distributed control policy (8.7).

8.2.3 EVENT-SAMPLED NN APPROXIMATION

With the objective of finding the approximate optimal value function as an approximate solution to the HJB using aperiodic event-triggered feedback, we have utilized event-based NN approximation in the prior chapters. To recall, we define a smooth function, $\chi : B \to \mathbb{R}$, in a compact set $B \subseteq \mathbb{R}^n$.

Given $\varepsilon_M > 0$ there exists $\theta^* \in \mathbb{R}^{p\times 1}$ such that $\chi(X) = \theta^{*^T}\phi(X_e) + \varepsilon_e$. The event-triggered approximation error ε_e is defined as $\varepsilon_e = \theta^{*^T}(\phi(X_e+e) - \phi(X_e)) + \varepsilon(X)$, satisfying $\|\varepsilon_e\| < \varepsilon_M$, $\forall X_e \in B$, where X, X_e are continuous and event triggered variables, e is the measurement error due to event sampling, $\varepsilon(X)$ is the bounded NN reconstruction error, and $\phi(X_e)$ is an appropriately chosen basis function. The following assumption is required for the ADP design.

Assumption 8.4. *The solution for the HJB (8.5) is unique, real-valued, smooth and satisfies $V^*(X) = \sum_{i=1}^N V_i^*(X)$. Further, $\phi(X)$ is chosen such that $\phi(0) = 0$, the activation function and its derivative, and the target NN weights are assumed to be bounded.*

The parameterized representation of the optimal value function using NN weights θ^* and basis function $\phi(X_e)$ with event-based inputs is given as

$$V^*(X) = \theta^{*^T}\phi(X_e) + \varepsilon(X_e), \tag{8.8}$$

where $\varepsilon(X_e)$ is the event-driven reconstruction error. Define the target NN weights as θ_i^* at the ith subsystem. Using a parameterized representation (8.8) for $V_i^*(X)$, HJB equation can be derived as

$$\theta_i^{*^T}\nabla_x\phi(X)f_i - \frac{\theta_i^{*^T}\nabla_x\phi(X)D_i\nabla^T{}_x\phi(X)\theta_i^*}{4} + \varepsilon_{iHJB} + Q_i(X) = 0 \tag{8.9}$$

where $Q_i(x) > 0$, $D_i = g_i(x_i)R_i^{-1}g_i^T(x_i)$, $f_i = f_i(x_i) + \sum_{j=1, j\neq i}^N \Delta_{ij}$, and $\varepsilon_{iHJB} = \nabla_x\varepsilon_i^T(f_i - \frac{1}{2}D_i(\nabla^T{}_x\phi(X)\theta_i^* + \nabla_x\varepsilon_i) + \frac{1}{4}D_i\nabla_x\varepsilon_i)$. The estimated value function is given by $\hat{V}_i(X) = \hat{\theta}_i^T\phi(X)$, where $\hat{\theta}_i$ is the NN estimated weights and its gradient along the states is given by $\partial\hat{V}_i/\partial x_i = \hat{\theta}_i^T\nabla_x\phi(X)$ and $\nabla_x\phi(X)$ is the gradient of the activation function $\phi(X)$ along X. The Hamiltonian function using $\hat{V}_i(X_e) = \hat{\theta}_i^T\phi(X_e)$ reveals

$$\hat{H} = Q_i(X_e) + \hat{\theta}_i^T\nabla_x\phi(X_e)f_i - \frac{1}{4}\hat{\theta}_i^T\nabla_x\phi(X_e)D_{i,\varepsilon}\nabla^T{}_x\phi(X_e)\hat{\theta}_i, \tag{8.10}$$

where $D_{i,\varepsilon} = D_{i,\varepsilon}(x_{i,e}) = g_i(x_{i,e})R_i^{-1}g_i^T(x_{i,e})$. The estimated optimal control input is obtained from (8.10) as

$$u_{i,e}(t) = -\frac{1}{2}R_i^{-1}g_i^T(x_{i,e})\hat{\theta}_i^T\nabla_x\phi(X_e),\ \forall i \in 1,2,..N. \tag{8.11}$$

Note that (8.10) is used as the forcing function to tune $\hat{\theta}_i$. The NN identifier design with event-triggered feedback is presented in the next subsection. The identifiers are utilized to generate uncertain nonlinear functions and also for the purpose of exploration, which will be discussed in Section 8.4.

8.3 EVENT-DRIVEN ADAPTIVE DYNAMIC PROGRAMMING

In this section, first, we shall design NN identifiers at each subsystem to approximate the uncertain nonlinear functions in (8.1). These NN identifiers will be used to design an event-triggered hybrid learning algorithm for constructing an approximately optimal control sequence.

8.3.1 IDENTIFIER DESIGN FOR THE INTERCONNECTED SYSTEM

For approximating the subsystem dynamics, consider a distributed identifier at each subsystem, which operates with event-triggered feedback information

$$\dot{\hat{x}}_i(t) = \hat{f}_i(\hat{x}_i) + \hat{g}_i(\hat{x}_i)u_{i,e}(t) + \sum_{j=1, j\neq i}^N \hat{\Delta}_{ij}(\hat{x}_i,\hat{x}_j) - A_i\tilde{x}_{i,e}(t), \tag{8.12}$$

where $\tilde{x}_{i,e}(t) = x_{i,e}(t) - \hat{x}_i(t)$, is the event-driven state estimation error and $A_i > 0$ is a positive definite matrix which stabilizes the NN identifier. To distinguish the identifiers developed in the next section, we use $x(t)$ to denote the states of the overall system instead of $X(t)$. Using NN approximation, the parametric equations for the nonlinear functions in (8.1) are $g_i(x_i) = W_{ig}\sigma_{ig}(x_i) + \varepsilon_{ig}(x_i)$, $\bar{f}_i(x) = W_{if}\sigma_{if}(x) + \varepsilon_{if}(x)$; where $W_{i\bullet}$ denotes the target NN weights, $\sigma_{i\bullet}$ denotes the bounded NN activation functions, and $\varepsilon_{i\bullet}$ denotes the bounded reconstruction errors. Using the estimate of the NN weights, $\hat{W}_{i\bullet}$, define $\hat{\bar{f}}_i(x) = \hat{W}_{if}\sigma_{if}(x)$ and $\hat{g}_i(\hat{x}_i) = \hat{W}_{ig}\sigma_{ig}(\hat{x}_i)$. Now, to analyze the stability of (8.12), define the state estimation error $\tilde{x}_i(t) = x_i(t) - \hat{x}_i(t)$. Using (8.12) and (8.1), the dynamic equation describing the evolution of $\tilde{x}_i(t)$ is revealed as

$$\begin{aligned}\dot{\tilde{x}}_i(t) = \tilde{W}_{if}\sigma_{if}(x) + W_{if}\tilde{\sigma}_{if} - \tilde{W}_{if}\tilde{\sigma}_{if} + [\tilde{W}_{ig}\sigma_{ig}(x_i) + \\ W_{ig}\tilde{\sigma}_{ig} - \tilde{W}_{ig}\tilde{\sigma}_{ig}]u_{i,e}(t) + \varepsilon_{ig}u_{i,e}(t) + \varepsilon_{if} + A_i\tilde{x}_i + A_ie_i(t),\end{aligned} \tag{8.13}$$

with $\tilde{\sigma}_{i\bullet} = \sigma_{i\bullet}(x) - \sigma_{i\bullet}(\hat{x})$ and $\tilde{W}_{i\bullet} = W_{i\bullet} - \hat{W}_{i\bullet}$.

Remark 8.1. *Note that the approximation of $\bar{f}(x)$ requires the states of the ith and j^{th} subsystem satisfying $\Delta_{ij}(x_i, x_j) \neq 0$. Therefore, the inputs to the NN are $\hat{x}_i, x_{j,e}$, and $\tilde{x}_i$. Due to the presence of $x_{j,e}$ as input, the identifier is considered to be distributed.*

With the NN identifiers at each subsystem, the control design equations (8.10) and (8.11) can be re-derived as

$$\hat{H} = Q_i(x_e) + \hat{\theta}_i^T \nabla_x \phi(x_e)\hat{\bar{f}}_i - \frac{1}{4}\hat{\theta}_i^T \nabla_x \phi(x_e)\hat{D}_{i,\varepsilon}\nabla^T{}_x\phi(x_e)\hat{\theta}_i$$

and

$$u_{i,e}(t) = -\frac{1}{2}R_i^{-1}\hat{g}_i^T(x_{i,e})\hat{\theta}_i^T\nabla_x\phi(x_e),$$

with $\hat{D}_{i,\varepsilon} = \hat{g}_i(x_{i,e})R_i^{-1}\hat{g}_i^T(x_{i,e})$. All the design equations to learn the greedy policy $u_i^*(t)$ without requiring the nonlinear functions $\bar{f}_i, g_i$ and V_i^* are presented next.

Lemma 8.1. *Consider the identifier dynamics (8.12). Using the estimation error, $\tilde{x}_i(t)$, as a forcing function, define NN weight tuning using the Levenberg-Marquardt scheme with sigma modification term to avoid parameter drift as*

$$\dot{\hat{W}}_{if}(t) = \frac{\alpha_{if}\sigma_{if}\tilde{x}_{i,e}^T}{c_{if} + \left\|\tilde{x}_{i,e}^T\right\|^2} - \kappa_{if}\hat{W}_{if}, \qquad \dot{\hat{W}}_{ig}(t) = \frac{\alpha_{ig}\sigma_{ig}u_{i,e}\tilde{x}_{i,e}^T}{c_{if} + \left\|\tilde{x}_{i,e}^T\right\|^2\left\|u_{i,e}^T\right\|^2} - \kappa_{ig}\hat{W}_{ig}, \tag{8.14}$$

where $\alpha_{if}, \alpha_{ig}, \kappa_{if}, \kappa_{ig}, c_{if}$ are positive design constants. The error dynamics using (8.14) are obtained as

$$\dot{\tilde{W}}_{if}(t) = \frac{-\alpha_{if}\sigma_{if}\tilde{x}_{i,e}^T}{c_{if} + \left\|\tilde{x}_{i,e}^T\right\|^2} + \kappa_{if}\hat{W}_{if}, \quad \dot{\tilde{W}}_{ig}(t) = \frac{-\alpha_{ig}\sigma_{ig}u_{i,e}\tilde{x}_{i,e}^T}{c_{if} + \left\|\tilde{x}_{i,e}^T\right\|^2\left\|u_{i,e}^T\right\|^2} + \kappa_{ig}\hat{W}_{ig}. \tag{8.15}$$

Let all the assumptions introduced in the previous sections hold. If $u_{i,e}(t) = u_{i,e}^*$, then α_{if}, α_{ig}, κ_{if}, κ_{ig}, $A_i > 0$ can be chosen such that (8.13) and (8.15) are stable and $\tilde{x}_i(t), \tilde{W}_{i\bullet}(t)$ are locally UUB.

Sketch of Proof: The proof considers a Lyapunov candidate function and the result is established by showing that the time-derivative of the function is negative outside a bound.

Table 8.1
Distributed NN identifier design equations

Identifier dynamics	$\dot{\hat{x}}_i(t) = \hat{f}_i(\hat{x}_i) + \hat{g}_i(\hat{x}_i)u_{i,e}(t) + \sum_{\substack{j=1 \\ j\neq i}}^{N} \hat{\Delta}_{ij}(\hat{x}_i,\hat{x}_j) - A_i\tilde{x}_{i,e}$
Event-driven state estimation error	$\tilde{x}_{i,e} = x_{i,e} - \hat{x}_i$
NN approximations	$\hat{\hat{f}}_i(x) = \hat{W}_{if}\sigma_{if}(x)$
	$\hat{g}_i(\hat{x}_i) = \hat{W}_{ig}\sigma_{ig}(\hat{x}_i)$
Weight update rules	$\dot{\hat{W}}_{if}(t) = \frac{\alpha_{if}\sigma_{if}\tilde{x}_{i,e}^T}{c_{if}+\left\|\tilde{x}_{i,e}^T\right\|^2} - \kappa_{if}\hat{W}_{if}$
	$\dot{\hat{W}}_{ig}(t) = \frac{\alpha_{ig}\sigma_{ig}u_{i,e}\tilde{x}_{i,e}^T}{c_{if}+\left\|\tilde{x}_{i,e}^T\right\|^2\left\|u_{i,e}^T\right\|^2} - \kappa_{ig}\hat{W}_{ig}$

- The following Lyapunov candidate function is considered

$$J_{iI}(\tilde{x}_i, \tilde{W}_{if}, \tilde{W}_{ig}) = J_{i\tilde{x}} + J_{i\tilde{f}} + J_{i\tilde{g}},$$

  with $J_{i\tilde{x}} = \frac{1}{2}\mu_{i1}\tilde{x}_i^T P_i\tilde{x}_i$, $J_{i\tilde{f}} = \frac{1}{2}\mu_{i2}\tilde{W}_{if}^T\tilde{W}_{if} + \frac{1}{4}\mu_{i4}(\tilde{W}_{if}^T\tilde{W}_{if})^2$ and $J_{i\tilde{g}} = \frac{1}{2}\mu_{i3}\tilde{W}_{ig}^T\tilde{W}_{ig} + \frac{1}{4}\mu_{i5}(\tilde{W}_{ig}^T\tilde{W}_{ig})^2 + \frac{1}{8}\mu_{i6}(\tilde{W}_{ig}^T\tilde{W}_{ig})^4$. Here the variables $\mu_{ij}, P_i, j = 1,2,..,6$, are positive constants of appropriate dimensions.
- For the optimal control policy, the bounds are obtained as a function of reconstruction error associated with the NNs approximating the unknown functions f_i, g_i, and the upper-bound on the ideal NN weights.
- The bounds can be reduced by tuning the parameters α_{if}, α_{ig}, and the reconstruction error can be reduced with appropriate choice of the NN architecture.

Remark 8.2. *The assumption that the control input is optimal and the measurement error acting as an input $e_i(t)$ is bounded will be relaxed in the closed loop stability analysis. The stability of the identifier in the presence of measurement errors is required to employ the identifiers for the purpose of exploration, wherein the measurement errors in (8.13) are replaced by bounded exploratory signals.*

Recall the Lyapunov function-based event-triggering condition used in Chapter 7. Using similar approach, an event triggering mechanism can be designed at each subsystem to determine the discrete time instants. At these events 1) the ith subsystem controller receives $x_i(t)$, 2) $u_i(t)$ is updated with the latest states at the actuator, and 3) $x_i(t)$ is broadcast to the neighboring subsystems. Define a positive definite, continuous function $J_i(x_i) = x_i^T\Gamma_i x_i$, with $\Gamma_i > 0$. For $0 < \alpha_i < 1$ and $k \in \mathbb{N}$, design the event-triggering mechanism to satisfy the condition

$$J_{ix}(x_i(t)) \leq (1 + t_k^i - t)\alpha_i J_{ix}(x_i(t_k^i)), \;\; t \in [t_k^i, t_{k+1}^i). \tag{8.16}$$

with $t_0^i = 0,\ \forall i \in 1,2,..,N$. The hybrid learning scheme presented in Chapter 7 is best suitable for online implementation. Nevertheless, the hybrid learning scheme does not utilize the feedback information and the reward signal available during the inter-event period. The classical problem of exploration vs exploitation and a modified/enhanced learning algorithm, which strives to exploit the under-utilized information are presented next.

8.4 LEARNING WITH EXPLORATION FOR ONLINE CONTROL

The basic idea behind the enhanced hybrid learning scheme is presented first and the role of the identifiers will be highlighted following that. The identifiers presented in the previous section are used to approximate the subsystem dynamics. Together with these identifiers, the distributed control schemes presented in Chapter 7 can be modified to accommodate uncertainity in the system dynamics. In this section, the NN identifiers that approximate the overall system dynamics at each subsystem will be presented. We shall see that these identifiers aid in the implementation of the enhanced weight update rule presented in this section.

8.4.1 ENHANCED HYBRID LEARNING

The algorithms presented in the previous chapters lack efficiency in learning as they do not utilize the state and control information along the state trajectory during the inter-event period. To address this issue, we may consider storing and using this information to update the weights of the value function NN at the event-sampling instant. However, it should be noted that while the state information during the inter-event period is measured and utilized at the event triggering mechanism, it is not available at the controller/learning mechanism. To overcome this limitation, we may consider storing the state and control information at the trigger mechanism and transmitting it to the controller at the event-sampling instants. This approach requires the transmission of states from the sensor to the controller at each subsystem and broadcasting to other subsystems in the interconnected system. Consequently, this increases the communication overhead, as the packet size will increase due to fewer events. Nevertheless, this approach enhances the learning efficiency and ensures that valuable information is utilized for updating the value function NN.

Building on this basic observation, we may incorporate the identifier located at each subsystem in the controller to generate the data (corresponding to the inter-event time) and can be used in the learning process. However, the use of the online identifier and the controller together will lead to unreliable set of data for the value function estimator. As we shall see later in this chapter, by tuning the identifier weights in such a way that they converge faster that the value function NN, the data generated by the identifier can be utilized for learning the optimal value function. Let the sensor sampling frequency be defined as τ_s. Consider the weight-tuning rule

$$\dot{\hat{\theta}}_i(t) = \begin{cases} -\dfrac{\alpha_{i1v}\hat{\psi}_i\hat{H}_i}{(1+\hat{\psi}_i^T\hat{\psi}_i)^2} - \dfrac{\alpha_{i2v}\hat{\Psi}_i\bar{\eta}_i}{(1+\hat{\Psi}_i^T\hat{\Psi}_i)^2} - \kappa_3\hat{\theta}_i + \dfrac{1}{2}\alpha_{iv}\nabla_x\phi\hat{D}_i x_i \\ \qquad\qquad + \dfrac{1}{2}\mu_{i1}\nabla_x\phi(x)\hat{D}_i^T P_i\tilde{x}_i, \quad t = t_k^i, \\ -(\alpha_{iv}\hat{\psi}_i\hat{H}_i)/(1+\hat{\psi}_i^T\hat{\psi}_i)^2, \quad t_k^i < t < t_{k+1}^i,\ \forall k \in \mathbb{N}, \end{cases} \tag{8.17}$$

with $\bar{\eta}_i, \hat{\Psi}_i$ are the estimated Hamiltonian and its derivative with respect to the NN weights calculated using the estimated states during the inter-event period. Since $\bar{\eta}_i$ is a function of the overall states, a NN identifier that approximates the overall system can provide the overall state estimate at each subsystem and the design of such an identifier is briefly presented next.

Table 8.2
Distributed NN control design equations

Identifier dynamics	$\dot{\hat{X}}_i(t) = \hat{F}_i(\hat{X}_i) + \hat{G}_i(\hat{X}_i)U_{i,e}(t) - A_i\tilde{X}_{i,e}(t)$
HJB error	$\hat{H} = Q_i(x_e) + \hat{\theta}_i^T \nabla_x \phi(x_e) f_i - 0.25\hat{\theta}_i^T \nabla_x \phi(x_e) D_{i,\varepsilon} \nabla^T{}_x \phi(x_e)\hat{\theta}_i$
Estimated value function	$\hat{V}_i(x) = \hat{\theta}_i^T \phi(x), \qquad D_{i,\varepsilon} = D_{i,\varepsilon}(x_{i,e}) = g_i(x_{i,e}) R_i^{-1} g_i^T(x_{i,e})$
Hybrid learning	$\dot{\hat{\theta}}_i(t) = \begin{cases} -(\alpha_{iv}\hat{\psi}_i\hat{H}_i)/(1+\hat{\psi}_i^T\hat{\psi}_i)^2 + 0.5\mu_{i1}\nabla_x\phi\hat{D}_i^T P_i\tilde{x}_i - \kappa_3\hat{\theta}_i + 0.5\alpha_{iv}\nabla_x\phi\hat{D}_i x_i, & t = t_k^i \\ -(\alpha_{iv}\hat{\psi}_i\hat{H}_i)/(1+\hat{\psi}_i^T\hat{\psi}_i)^2, & t_k^i < t < t_{k+1}^i, \ \forall k \in \mathbb{N}. \end{cases}$
Enhanced hybrid learning	$\dot{\hat{\theta}}_i(t) = \begin{cases} -(\alpha_{iv}\hat{\psi}_i\hat{H}_i)/(1+\hat{\psi}_i^T\hat{\psi}_i)^2 + 0.5\mu_{i1}\nabla_x\phi\hat{D}_i^T P_i\tilde{x}_i - \kappa_3\hat{\theta}_i + 0.5\alpha_{iv}\nabla_x\phi\hat{D}_i x_i, & t = t_k^i \\ -(\alpha_{iv}\hat{\psi}_i\hat{H}_i)/(1+\hat{\psi}_i^T\hat{\psi}_i)^2, & t_k^i < t < t_{k+1}^i, \ \forall k \in \mathbb{N}. \end{cases}$

8.4.2 IDENTIFIERS FOR THE ENHANCED HYBRID LEARNING SCHEME

Consider the NN identifier at each subsystem as

$$\dot{\hat{X}}_i(t) = \hat{F}_i(\hat{X}_i) + \hat{G}_i(\hat{X}_i)U_{i,e}(t) - A_i\tilde{X}_{i,e}(t), \tag{8.18}$$

where the subscript i indicates variables available at the ith subsystem, $\hat{F}_i, \hat{G}_i$ are the approximated functions of the overall dynamics F, G, $\hat{X}$ is the estimate of X in (8.2), and U is the augmented control u_i. In contrast to (8.12), the identifier described by (8.18) estimates the states of the interconnected system (8.2) to collect the state information and calculate the reinforcement signal for the inter-event period. The actual and estimated weights for the functions F_i, G_i can be defined as in Section 8.3.1 and equations similar to (8.13)-(8.15) can be derived for the observer in (8.18).

Remark 8.3. *The observer design procedure for (8.18) is similar to that in (8.12). Therefore, all the details are not included. However, there are a few subtle differences in the NN design. Since the observer in (8.18) approximates the nonlinear mapping of the overall system, first, the NN takes as input, the vector* $[\hat{x}_i^T \ \hat{x}_j^T]^T, \forall j = 1,2,..,N$ *instead of* $\hat{x}_i$*. Secondly, the number of neurons in the hidden layer should be increased as the domains of the nonlinear maps being approximated are of higher dimensions.*

The local UUB stability of the identifier presented in the previous section is applicable to the identifier designed in this section as well.

Remark 8.4. *The use of function approximators to learn the optimal value function and system dynamics adds to the uncertainty of bootstrapping in finding the optimal control inputs. In addition, since the learning scheme is based on asynchronous GPI, the initial weights of the function approximators affect the state trajectory and cumulative cost (return).*

8.4.3 ROLE OF IDENTIFIERS AND EXPLORATION IN ONLINE CONTROL

One of the classical problems in the RL literature (Sutton and Barto, 1998; da Silva and Barto, 2012) is the dilemma of exploration vs exploitation. To understand this problem, let us consider the RL decision-making problem. The decision-making process consists of constructing maps of states to expected future rewards using reinforcement signals (Sutton and Barto, 1998). The future actions are influenced by this prediction of future reward, i.e., using the feedback signal, the HJB error is computed and the approximate optimal value function is updated based on the HJB error; the estimated value function is then used to obtain the future control action. If the control action is of the form (8.11), then it is a greedy policy and hence, *exploitative*. This is due to the fact that the control policy exploits the current knowledge of the optimal value function and minimizes the Hamiltonian (8.10). In contrast, if a control policy that is not greedy is applied to the system, then the control policy is said to be *explorative*. One has to ensure stability when such a policy is used in online control. The PE condition is an important requirement for the ADP control methods in (Lewis et al., 2012a) for the convergence of the estimated parameters to its target values. This condition ensures that sufficient data is collected to learn the unknown function before the system states settle at an equilibrium point. Adaptive control theorists developed sigma and epsilon modification techniques (Sastry and Bodson, 2011; Lewis et al., 1998) to prevent parameter drift and relax PE condition requirement. However, from a learning perspective, the sigma and epsilon modification techniques inhibit the learning algorithm from exploring.

To perturb the system and to satisfy the PE condition a control policy of the form $\varpi_e(t) = u(t) + \xi(t)$ was used in the learning algorithms presented in (Lewis et al., 2012a; Dierks and Jagannathan, 2010a) and the references therein, where $\xi(t)$ is seen as an exploratory signal and u is a stabilizing/greedy control policy. For example, random noise signal was used as $\xi(t)$ in the simulations, while (Lee et al., 2015) explicitly considered the control law with $\xi(t)$ to develop an actor-critic based ADP design. To relax the PE condition, sufficient data can be collected to satisfy the rank condition, as indicated in traditional adaptive control (Sastry and Bodson, 2011). It should also be considered that exploration signal $\xi(t)$ is not easy to design. Although several exploration policies are investigated for finite Markov decision processes (Sutton and Barto, 1998) and offline learning schemes (Sutton and Barto, 1998; da Silva and Barto, 2012), an exploration policy that can provide guaranteed time for convergence to a near-optimal policy for an online control problem are not available.

Also, in control, issues of stability and robustness are non-trivial. The system can become unstable in the process of exploration due to the application of $\xi(t)$ in the control action. Inspired by the work on efficient exploration in (da Silva and Barto, 2012), a novel technique to incorporate exploration in the learning controller is developed in (Narayanan and Jagannathan, 2017). This technique is presented next.

8.4.4 EXPLORATION USING IDENTIFIERS

The TD learning (Sutton and Barto, 1998; Dierks and Jagannathan, 2010a; Sahoo et al., 2016) and the hybrid learning schemes (Narayanan and Jagannathan, 2016b,a) reduce the HJB error. But this error is not reduced to zero, $\hat{H}_i(x, u_i) \neq 0$, whenever the control action is updated, i.e., optimality is achieved only in the limit $(t \to \infty, \hat{V} \to V^*)$. Further, in asynchronous learning (Sutton and Barto, 1998), the optimal value function is learned only along the state trajectory and not the entire state space. Therefore, the initial weights of the value function approximator affect the cumulative cost of operating the system. To minimize the cost during the learning period an exploration strategy using identifiers is presented next.

First, consider the identifier described by (8.18). To illustrate the idea, we will consider two sets of initial weights, one of which will be used by the controller to generate the control action $\varpi_{ie}^{(1)}(t) = u_i^{(1)}(t) + \xi_i^{(1)}(t)$, such that $\xi_i^{(1)}(t) = 0$; the other one will be an exploratory policy $\varpi_{ie}^{(2)}(t) = u_i^{(2)}(t) + \xi_i^{(2)}(t)$ with $\xi_i^{(2)}(t) \neq 0$, used with the identifier. Figure 8.1 is a simplified block diagram representation for implementing the exploration strategy. It can be observed that in order to incorporate exploration without affecting the performance of the existing controller, an additional identifier and value function estimator are required.

Let $\hat{\Theta}_{1i}$, $\hat{\Theta}_{2i}$ be the weight vectors at the ith subsystem. Calculate the Hamiltonian as $\hat{H}_i^{(p)}(\hat{x}_e) = Q_i + \hat{\Theta}_{pi}^T \nabla_x \phi(\hat{x}_e) \hat{\hat{f}}_i - \frac{1}{4} \hat{\Theta}_{pi}^T \nabla_x \phi(\hat{x}_e) \hat{D}_i \nabla^T{}_x \phi(\hat{x}_e) \hat{\Theta}_{pi}$, where $p = 1,2$ for each initial weights. We can construct the cost function trajectory with the value function estimator using the NN weights $\hat{\Theta}_{1i}$, $\hat{\Theta}_{2i}$ for both the policies $\varpi_{ie}^{(1)}$, $\varpi_{ie}^{(2)}$. Similar to (8.7), the stationarity condition can provide the $u_{i,e}$ from $\hat{H}_i^{(p)}$. Using the Hamiltonian error, the NN weights are tuned using the weight update rule (8.17). Thus, we can obtain two policies, one exploitative and the other using an exploration policy.

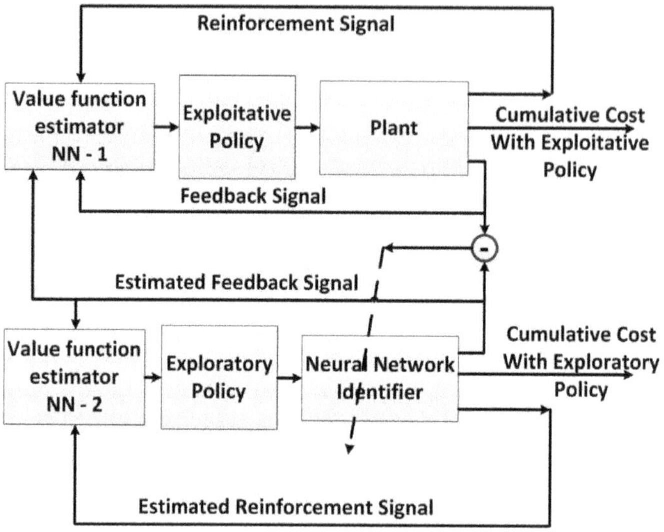

Figure 8.1 Block diagram representation of exploration strategy.

For example, a random exploration policy can be used. For each initial NN weight, a cost function, control policy, Hamiltonian error, and state trajectory are generated. During the learning period, using the performance index, the cumulative cost be calculated, for $p \in \{1,2\}$, using the integral

$$V_i^{(p)}(t) = \int_t^{t_{switch}} \left[Q_i(x) + \varpi_{ie}^{(p)^T}(\tau) R_i \varpi_{ie}^{(p)}(\tau) \right] d\tau. \tag{8.19}$$

Note that the value function trajectories for the two policies start at the same initial cost and evolve based on the function $Q_i(x) + \varpi_{ie}^{(p)^T}(\tau) R_i \varpi_{ie}^{(p)}(\tau)$. Let the time instant $t = t_{switch}$ denote the time at which the difference between the cumulative rewards due to the two control policies start to increase steadily. Define $\hat{V}_i^*(\Theta) = \min\{V_i^1(t), V_i^2(t)\}$. Using the value function approximator NN that corresponds to the estimate $\hat{V}_i^*(\Theta)$ generate the greedy policy at the event-based sampling instants $t_k^i \geq t_{switch}$, $\forall k \in \mathbb{N}$. If both the policies result in the same cumulative cost $V_i^1(t), V_i^2(t)$, the reliability of the cost function estimate can be evaluated by using their HJB error. Choose the estimated value function $\hat{V}_i^*$ such that $\hat{\theta}_i$ satisfies the condition $\hat{\theta}_i = \min(\arg\min_{\Theta_1}(\hat{H}_i^1), \arg\min_{\Theta_2}(\hat{H}_i^2))$. Thus, $\hat{V}_i^*$ which is close to the optimal value function is used to generate the control action and potentially minimize the cost during the learning period. Note that the exploration policy need not necessarily yield a reduced cost function trajectory during the learning period. However, it is observed during the simulation analysis that the appropriate choice of exploration policy can significantly reduce the cost during the learning period.

Remark 8.5. *The sigma/epsilon modification term ($\kappa_3 \hat{\theta}_i$) added in the learning rule (8.17) ensures that the approximated value function reach a neighborhood of the optimal value function without compromising the stability. Further, the control action ϖ_{ie} generated using the learning algorithm* *without the exploration strategy ($\xi_i = 0$) is always exploitative as $\varpi_{ie} = u_{i,e}$, minimizing the cost function (8.4). Therefore, injecting exploratory signal ξ_i, to the identifier and searching for a better policy using the exploration strategy is not going to affect the system performance or stability. In contrast, it can only improve the optimality of the control action. Therefore, it is a very efficient tool for online learning and control applications.*

Using Lyapunov-based analysis, the stability results for the closed-loop system are summarized, from (Narayanan and Jagannathan, 2017), next.

8.5 STABILITY ANALYSIS

In this section, first, a more general result establishes the fact that the continuously updated closed-loop system admits a local input-to-state practically stable Lyapunov function in the presence of bounded external input (measurement error). This result is required to ensure that the event-triggering mechanism does not exhibit Zeno behavior. Further, it is shown using two cases that as the event-sampling instants increase, the states, weight estimation errors, and identifier errors reach a neighborhood of origin. Using the fact that the optimal controller renders the closed-loop dynamics bounded reveals that there exists a function δ and a constant C such that

$$\|f(x)+g(x)u^*(t)\| \le \|\delta(x)\| = C_1\,\|x(t)\|, \tag{8.20}$$

where $\delta(x) \in \mathbb{R}^n$, $C_1 \in \mathbb{R}$. This fact is used in the derivations to demonstrate system stability.

Theorem 8.1. *Consider the subsystem dynamics (8.1). Define the NN weight update rule (8.17) for the value function approximator and (8.14) for the identifiers. Let Assumptions 8.1 to 8.4 hold. Then, α_{iv}, μ_i, $\kappa_3 > 0$ can be designed such that $\tilde{\theta}_i$, $\tilde{W}_{if}$, $\tilde{W}_{ig}$, and x, $\tilde{x}_i$ are locally uniformly ultimately bounded when a bounded measurement error is introduced in the feedback.*

Sketch of Proof: The object of the proof is to establish the local ISS of the subsystems and the overall system.

- Consider the Lyapunov function for the interconnected system

$$J = \sum_{i=1}^{N} J_i(x_i, \tilde{\theta}_i, \tilde{X}_i, \tilde{W}_{if}, \tilde{W}_{ig}),$$

  with the individual terms defined as $J_i = J_{ix} + J_{i\tilde{\theta}} + J_{il}(\tilde{X}_i, \tilde{W}_{if}, \tilde{W}_{ig})$ and $J_{ix} = \frac{1}{2}\alpha_{iv} x_i^T x_i$, $J_{i\tilde{\theta}} = \frac{1}{2}\tilde{\theta}_i^T \gamma_i \tilde{\theta}_i$.
- The time-derivative of the term $J_{il}(\tilde{X}_i, \tilde{W}_{if}, \tilde{W}_{ig})$ can be bounded using arguments from Lemma 8.1.
- The bounds on the time-derivative of the other terms can be computed similarly for Lyapunov functions of each subsystem. However, the error dynamics dues to the state-estimation error and the subsystem dynamics yields a positive term that increases the ultimate bounds.
- The second and fourth terms in the weight update rule (8.17) are used to compensate and cancel these positive terms, leading to reduced bounds on the closed-loop signals.

Theorem 8.2. *Consider the augmented nonlinear system (8.2) and its component subsystems (8.1). Define the NN weight update rule (8.17) for the value function approximator and (8.14), for the identifiers. Let events be generated based on the event-triggering condition defined by (8.16). Then, the control parameters can be designed such that $\tilde{\theta}_i, \tilde{W}_{if}, \tilde{W}_{ig}$ and $x, \tilde{x}_i$ are locally uniformly ultimately bounded.*

The proof of Theorem 8.2 is a special case of Theorem 8.3.

Remark 8.6. *From the results of Theorem 8.1, the closed-loop system admits a Lyapunov function which satisfies the local input-to-state practical stability (ISpS) conditions when the measurement error is bounded. By analyzing the same Lyapunov function during the inter-event period, using the event-triggering condition, the boundedness of the measurement can be established.*

Remark 8.7. *Appropriate choice of design parameters will result in lower bounds on* x, $\tilde{x}_i$ *and* $\tilde{\theta}_i$, $\tilde{W}_{if}$, $\tilde{W}_{ig}$. *Redundant events can be avoided using a dead-zone operator (Sahoo et al., 2016).*

Remark 8.8. *Define the minimum time between two events as* $\delta t_{\min} = \min\{t_{k+1} - t_k\}$, $\forall k \in \mathbb{N}$. *Then* $\delta t_{\min} > 0$ *as a result of Assumption 8.3, Theorems 8.1 and 8.2 (Sahoo et al., 2016).*

Now the close-loop stability results with the enhanced learning algorithm and exploration are presented.

Theorem 8.3. *Consider the augmented nonlinear system (8.2) and its component subsystems (8.1). Define the NN weight update rule (8.14) for the identifiers (8.18). Define the event-triggering condition (8.16), further, let the NN weights of the value function estimator be tuned based on the rule (8.17). Under the assumptions prescribed in the previous sections, the control parameters can be designed such that the NN weight estimation errors* $\tilde{\theta}_i, \tilde{W}_{if}, \tilde{W}_{ig}$, *the interconnected system states, and* $\tilde{x}(t)$ *are locally uniformly ultimately bounded.*

Sketch of Proof: Since local ISS of the subsystems and the overall system are established in Theorem 8.1, we just demonstrate that since the measurement errors are bounded by the event-triggering condition, the UUB results still hold.

- Consider the Lyapunov candidate function

$$J(x,\tilde{\Theta},\tilde{X},\tilde{W}) = \sum_{i=1}^{N} J_i(x_i,\tilde{\theta}_i,\tilde{X}_i,\tilde{W}_{if},\tilde{W}_{ig}),$$

  with $J_i(x_i,\tilde{\theta}_i,\tilde{X}_i,\tilde{W}_{if},\tilde{W}_{ig}) = J_{ix} + J_{i\tilde{\theta}} + J_{il}(\tilde{X}_i,\tilde{W}_{if},\tilde{W}_{ig})$.
- The proof consists of two cases corresponding to measurement error being zero and non-zero. This set of arguments are consistent with the proofs used to demonstrate the closed-loop stability of systems implemented in emulation-based event-triggered control framework, where ISS assumptions are used to ensure that the measurement error does not cause finite-escape time, keeping the closed-loop signals from growing unbounded.

Example 8.1. *In this example, three coupled nonlinear subsystems are considered. The three subsystems are physically meaningful in that they capture the thigh and knee dynamics of a walking robot experiment (Dunbar, 2007). In the following,* $\gamma_1(t)$ *is the relative angle between the two thighs,* $\gamma_2(t)$ *is the right knee angle (relative to the right thigh), and* $\gamma_3(t)$ *is the left knee angle (relative to left thigh). The controlled equations of motion in units of (rad/sec) are*

$$\begin{aligned}
\ddot{\gamma}_1(t) &= 0.1[1 - 5.25\gamma_1^2(t)]\dot{\gamma}_1(t) - \gamma_1(t) + u_1(t),\\
\ddot{\gamma}_2(t) &= 0.01\left[1 - p_2(\gamma_2(t) - \gamma_{2e})^2\right]\dot{\gamma}_2(t) - 4(\gamma_2(t) - \gamma_{2e})\\
&\quad + 0.057\gamma_1(t)\dot{\gamma}_1(t) + 0.1(\dot{\gamma}_2(t) - \dot{\gamma}_3(t)) + u_2(t),\\
\ddot{\gamma}_3(t) &= 0.01\left[1 - p_3(\gamma_3(t) - \gamma_{3e})^2\right]\dot{\gamma}_3(t) - 4(\gamma_3(t) - \gamma_{3e})\\
&\quad + 0.057\gamma_1(t)\dot{\gamma}_1(t) + 0.1(\dot{\gamma}_3(t) - \dot{\gamma}_2(t)) + u_3(t),
\end{aligned}$$

where $\ddot{\gamma}_i(t)$ *correspond to the dynamics of the* i^{th} *subsystem (SSi). The control objective is to bring the robot to a stop in a stable manner. The parameter values* $(\gamma_{2e},\gamma_{3e},p_2,p_3)(t)$ *can be considered in the model taking on the values* $(-0.227, 0.559, 6070, 192)$.

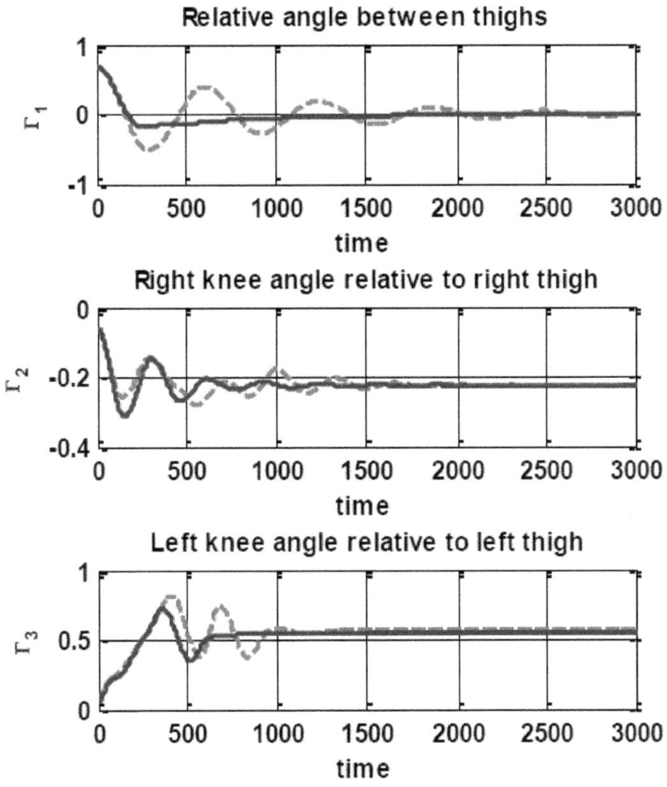

Figure 8.2 State Trajectories (Dotted (red) Lines – Hybrid Algorithm vs Enhanced hybrid algorithm) (Time in 10^{-2}s).

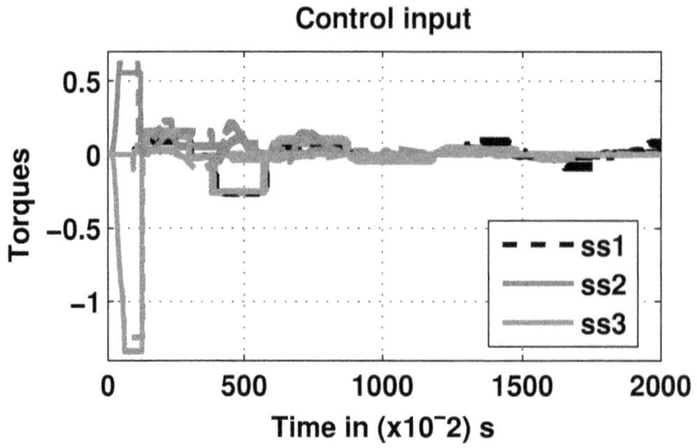

Figure 8.3 Control torques.

The control scheme presented in this chapter requires three NNs at every subsystem. For this example, all the NNs were designed to have two layers and formed random vector functional link networks (Lewis et al., 1998). The NN that approximated $f_i(x) + \Delta_{ij}(x)$, was designed with 25 neurons in the hidden layer. The other two NNs that approximated g_i, V_i^* were designed with 7,6 hidden layer neurons respectively. The following initial conditions were set for the simulation: $x_i(0) \in [-1,1]$, $\hat{x}(0) = 0$, $\hat{\theta}_i(0), \hat{W}_{if}(0), \hat{W}_{ig}(0) \in [0,1]$. The controller parameters are selected as follows: $\alpha_{i1v} = 40$, $\alpha_{i2v} = 0.03$, $\mu_i = 1.95$, $P_i = 2$, $\kappa_3 = 0.001$, $Q_i = 20$, $R_i = 1, A_i = 80$, $C_{if} = 0.5$, $\kappa_{if} = \kappa_{ig} = 0.0001$, $\alpha_{if} = \alpha_{ig} = 100$ and $\Gamma_i = 0.99$.

The robotic system is simulated with the torques generated using the control algorithm with hybrid and enhanced (modified) hybrid approach and exploration. It can be observed that the states reach their equilibrium point faster in the modified hybrid approach (Figure 8.2). The magnitude of the control torque for the hybrid ADP-based learning scheme and the enhanced hybrid approach are compared in Figure 8.3 using the event-triggered feedback. The enhanced hybrid scheme converges faster due to the improved learning as a result of using the reinforcement signals during the inter-event period for tuning the NN weights. Convergence of the identification error ensures that the reinforcement signals used to learn optimal value function and policy are reliable. To test the analytical results for the identifier, 500 different initial conditions and exploration signals like random noise and trigonometric functions of different frequencies but restricted in magnitude to 0.1 were used. The state estimation errors converged on each of these simulations as seen in Figure 8.4.

The optimal value function is learned using the consistency condition dictated by the HJB equation. A lower Hamiltonian/HJB residual error implies that the value function weight estimate is close to the target weights. Evidently, from Figure 8.5, the enhanced/modified weight tuning rule improves the optimality due to faster convergence of the HJB residual error. The cumulative cost calculated for the hybrid learning algorithm and the modified update rule taking into account the states and reinforcement evaluated in the inter-event period are compared in Figure 8.6. For 500 randomly chosen initial values of states of the system and identifier, the ratio of the cumulative cost at the end of 20s for hybrid and the learning algorithm dicussed in this chapter is recorded in Figure 8.6. Due to the dependence of the learning scheme on the identifier, the convergence of the identification errors should precede the convergence of the controller.

The improvement in the learning scheme is a result of the weights updated between events using the past data and the exploration strategy. Finally, four additional NN approximators were utilized, each initialized with the weights randomly selected in [0, 2]. To demonstrate the efficiency of the exploration strategy in off-setting the effects of initial NN weights, each of the randomly picked weights was used to generate a control policy and the cost function over time using additional

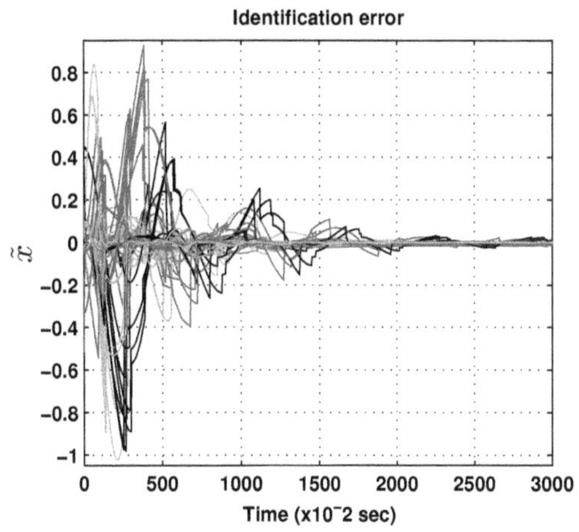

Figure 8.4 Identifier approximation error.

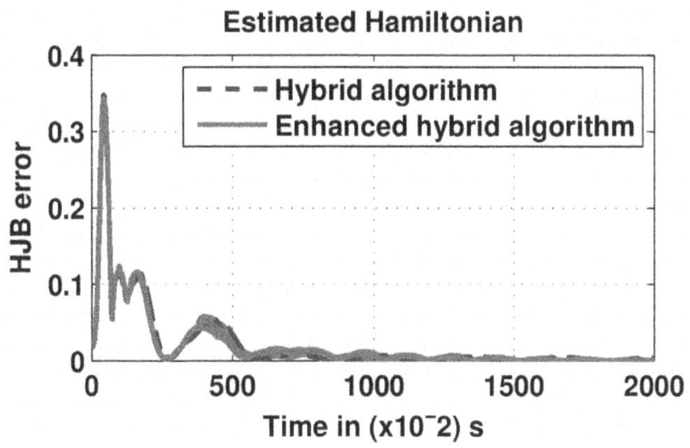

Figure 8.5 Comparison of HJB error.

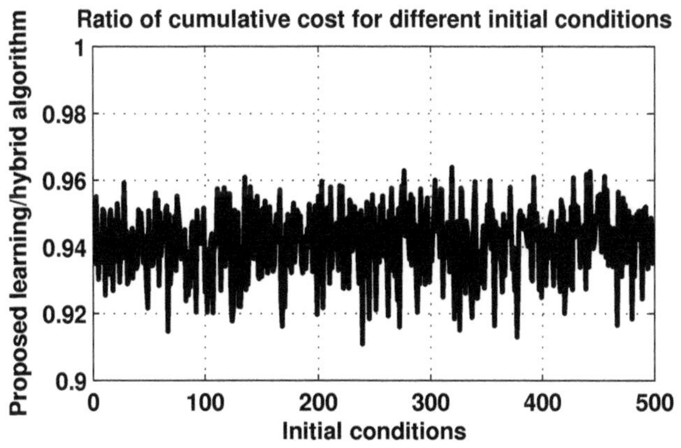

Figure 8.6 Comparison of cost.

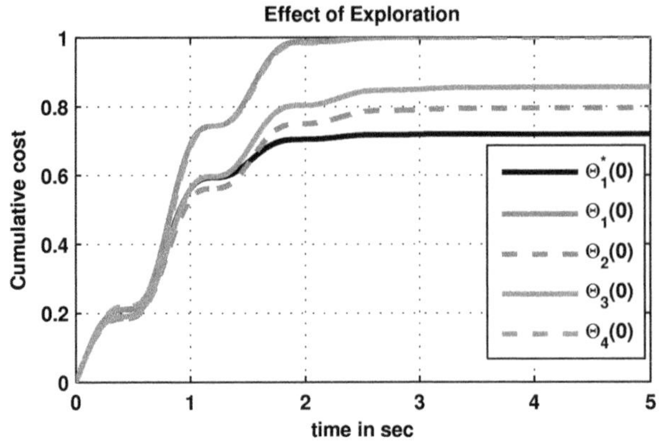

Figure 8.7 Cost function trajectories.

identifiers for each NN weight. These cost trajectories are compared with the cost function trajectory of the system with the exploration strategy presented in the previous section. The variable $\Theta_1^*(t)$ is the estimated NN weights that were used to generate the control action sequence, selected by the exploration strategy, online. This seemed to optimize the performance of the system better than the other policies as seen in Figure 8.7.

Since multiple NNs were used to generate the cost function trajectories using the identifier states, computations increased. However, the effect of the initial weights of the NN approximator on the cost function trajectory is reduced and the learning algorithm eventually used the optimal approximated value function, which yields the best sequence of control policy, when compared in terms of the resulting cost functions. To test the event-triggering mechanism, the sensors were sampled at 1 ms and the number of events generated are recorded. The ratio of the total number of events from the 3 subsystems with the total number of sensor samples collected is computed as 0.5108 for the enhanced hybrid learning scheme and 0.4981 for the hybrid learning scheme. This demonstrates the benefits of the enhanced NN weight update rule when compared with the hybrid learning rule as almost 51% of the sensor information sampled at the event-triggering mechanism is not used by the learning algorithm in the hybrid learning scheme.

Remark 8.9 (Tracking control tasks)**.** *Recall that converting a tracking control problem into a regulation problem with augmented system dynamics, presented in Chapter 7 in Section 7.5, for nonlinear interconnected system required that the system dynamics are accurately know. We can follow the steps discussed earlier in Section 8.4.2 to learn the unknown dynamics $\mathscr{G}_i, \mathscr{F}_i$, and $\mathscr{K}_{ij}$ in the tracking error dynamics* (7.70)*, which can then be used to synthesize the tracking control using the enhanced hybrid-learning-based control scheme presented in this chapter. With the augmented system, we can design a feedback controller that stabilizes the augmented system at the desired operating point. This controller will implicitly regulate the original system to track the reference trajectory. The gains of the controller need to be tuned to achieve the desired tracking performance and stability.*

8.6 SUMMARY AND CONCLUDING REMARKS

The enhanced hybrid learning scheme with exploration uses a system model, which in turn is reconstructed using NN identifiers. Local UUB stability of the controlled system ensures that the system states, NN weights estimation errors, and identification errors are all bounded. The NN identifiers approximated the system nonlinearities and also aided in evaluating the exploration signals to gather useful information about the system dynamics which improved the optimality of the control actions. This learning scheme seems to match and better the performance of the continuous-time TD-ADP learning scheme with limited feedback information. This is achieved with significantly more computations.

8.7 PROBLEMS

8.7.1 Consider N inverted pendulum connected by spring (Spooner and Passino, 1999). The dynamics of the system are given by

$$\dot{x}_{i1} = x_{i2},$$
$$\dot{x}_{i2} = (\frac{m_i g r}{J_i} - \frac{kr^2}{4J_i})\sin x_{i1} + \frac{kr}{2J_i}(l-b) + \frac{u_i}{J_i} + \sum_{j=1}^{N} \frac{kr^2}{4J_i}\sin x_{j1}. \tag{8.21}$$

Treat $x_{i2}(t)$ as the measured variable, $N = 10$, and let all the subsystems be connected such that they form a chain network.

(a) Design distributed identifiers for the system using equations in Table 8.1 with a simple decentralized control applied with linear negative feedback with gain 0.1.

(b) Design distributed control policies based on the hybrid learning algorithm using equations in Table 8.2.

8.7.2 For the same system, consider the linearized dynamics as in (Guinaldo et al., 2011). The parameters in the system dynamics are $m_1 = 2$, $m_2 = 2.5$, $J_1 = 5$, $J_2 = 6.25$, $k = 10$, $r = 0.5$, $l = 0.5$, and $g = 9.8$, $b = 0.5$. Pick the initial conditions of the system states in the interval [0, 1] and the initial weights of the NN from [-1, 1], randomly. Treat $x_{i2}(t)$ as the measured variable, $N = 10$, and let all the subsystems be connected such that they form a ring network.

(a) Design distributed control policies based on the hybrid learning algorithm using equations in Table 8.2.

8.7.3 Consider the system of three interconnected systems modeling the robot walking gait. The controlled equations of motion in units of (rad/s) are

$$\begin{aligned}
\ddot{x}_1(t) &= 0.1[1-5.25x_1^2(t)]\dot{x}_1(t) - x_1(t) + u_1(t)\\
\ddot{x}_2(t) &= 0.01\left[1 - p_2(x_2(t) - x_{2eq})^2\right]\dot{x}_2(t) - 4(x_2(t) - x_{2eq})\\
&\quad + 0.057x_1(t)\dot{x}_1(t) + 0.1(\dot{x}_2(t) - \dot{x}_3(t)) + u_2(t)\\
\ddot{x}_3(t) &= 0.01[1 - p_3(x_3(t) - x_{3eq})^2]\dot{x}_3(t) - 4(x_3(t) - x_{3eq})\\
&\quad + 0.057x_1(t)\dot{x}_1(t) + 0.1(\dot{x}_3(t) - \dot{x}_2(t)) + u_3(t),
\end{aligned}$$

where $\ddot{x}_i$ correspond to the dynamics of the ith subsystem. The control objective is to bring the robot to a stop in a stable manner ($x_i \to x_{ieq}$), where x_{ieq} are the equilibrium points with $x_{1eq} = 0, x_{2eq} = -0.227, x_{3eq} = 0.559$. The parameters p_2 and p_3 are 6070, and 192, respectively. Design distributed control policies based on the hybrid learning algorithm using equations in Table 8.2.

8.7.4 For the system described in Problems 8.7.3., design NN identifiers using Table 8.1. Use bounded control inputs, e.g., constant, sine, etc.

8.7.5 Repeat the Problems 8.7.3. and 8.7.4. using Table 8.2 and 8.1 with the parameters $x_{1eq} = 0$, $x_{2eq} = 0.559$, $x_{3eq} = 0.226$, $p_2 = 226$, and $p_3 = 5240$.

8.7.6 Consider the system described in Example 3.1. Implement the enhanced hybrid learning algorithm, equations of which are given in Table 8.2, to design feedback control policy to stabilize the system. Compare the transient performance of the system with the hybrid learning algorithm-based control scheme.

8.7.7 Consider the system described in Example 4.3. Implement the enhanced hybrid learning algorithm, equations of which are given in Table 8.2, to design feedback control policy to stabilize the system around origin.

8.7.8 For the two-link robot manipulator system given in Example 4.3, implement an NN identifier using the equations given in Table 8.1 to reconstruct the manipulator dynamics.

8.7.9 Use the exploration strategy described in the Section 8.4.4 and construct 4 independent NN controllers using Table 8.2 for the two link robot manipulator given in Example 4.3. Use the following exploration signals given by $\xi(t)$ as $\sin(2\pi t), \Sigma_{i=0}^{5}\cos(i\pi t)$, (unit) pulse signal with 50% duty cycle, (unit) pulse signal with 30% duty cycle, and Gaussian white noise.

8.7.10 Consider 5 inverted pendulums connected by spring, each with the dynamics given as in (8.21). Assume that they are interconnections, when represented as a graph, forms a ring topology, i.e., subsystem i is connected with subsystems $i+1$ and $i-1$ for $i = 2,3,4$. The subsystem $i = 1$ is connected with subsystems $j = 2,5$ while the subsystem 5 is connected with subsystems $j = 1,4$. Compare the cost of the closed-loop system, whose controllers are designed using the equations given in Table 8.2, for the cases when the system dynamics are known and when the system dynamics are unknown, in which case, NN identifiers Table 8.1 are used to reconstruct the system.

8.7.11 Design a tracking controller using the enhanced hybrid learning scheme so that the two-link robot manipulator system (given in Example 4.3) tracks the reference trajectory $x_d(t) = \sin(5\pi t)$

9 Event-Triggered Control Applications

CONTENTS

In this chapter, we shall first explore the utilization of adaptive NNs within the event-triggered feedback controller framework to achieve precise trajectory tracking in two robotic applications. In the first application, we consider the robotic manipulators and detail the design procedure as presented in (Narayanan et al., 2018a). Specifically, we shall explore the output feedback control scheme that incorporates a nonlinear NN observer to reconstruct the joint velocities of the manipulator using joint position measurements. In addition to the observer NN, a second NN is employed to compensate for nonlinearities in the robot dynamics. We will consider two distinct configurations for the control scheme, depending on whether the observer is co-located with the sensor or the controller within the feedback loop. For both configurations, the controller computes the torque input by leveraging the observer NN and the second NN. We shall derive the event-triggering condition and weight update rules for the controller and observer using the Lyapunov stability method.

In the second application, we shall see the event-sampled output-feedback NN-based controller for steering a quadrotor Unmanned Aerial Vehicle (UAV). The controller design encompasses multiple components to ensure precise flight control. Firstly, an observer is devised to estimate the UAV's state-vector from its outputs. Subsequently, a kinematic controller is developed to determine the desired translational velocity, which is used in conjunction with a virtual controller to establish the desired rotational velocity for the UAV's orientation convergence. The signals generated by the dynamic controller enable the tracking of the desired lift velocity and rotational velocities. Throughout the designs, the impact of sampling errors is emphasized. This part of the chapter is based on the results presented in (Szanto et al., 2017a,b).

Finally, we shall explore the application of event-triggered ADP-based controllers in CPS wherein multiple real-time dynamic systems are connected to their corresponding controllers through a shared communication network. In particular, we shall look at a distributed scheduling protocol design via cross-layer approach to optimize the performance of CPS by maximizing the utility function that is generated by using the information collected from both the application and network layers. We shall see that when compared with traditional scheduling algorithms, the application of event-triggered control synthesis together with a distributed scheduling scheme via the cross-layer approach presented here can not only allocate the network resources efficiently but also improve the performance of the overall real-time dynamic system. This last application is based on the work in Xu (2012); Xu and Jagannathan (2012).

9.1 OUTPUT FEEDBACK CONTROL OF ROBOT MANIPULATOR: INTRODUCTION

The design of torque input for robot manipulators has been one of the widely studied problems among the control researchers (Kim and Lewis, 1999; Lewis et al., 1998; Lee and Harris, 1998). For example, in the areas ranging from nano/micro-scale (Cheah et al., 2014) to large-scale applications (Kermani et al., 2007), and for medical environments (Cheah et al., 2015; Sfakiotakis et al., 2015), the robotic manipulators are extensively used. The computed torque (CT) controllers, one of the basic nonlinear controllers for robotic manipulators, convert the nonlinear robot manipulator dynamics into a linear system via the feedback-linearization technique. In the CT control scheme, a filtered tracking error (Lewis et al., 1998) is defined and the controller design process is restated using the filtered tracking error dynamics under the assumption that the dynamics are accurately known. To obviate the requirement of the complete knowledge of the manipulator dynamics, adaptive controllers (Lewis et al., 1998) are introduced under the assumption that the effects of nonlinear dynamics can be represented as a linear combination of known regression functions (linear in the unknown parameters (Lewis et al., 1998)).

With the incorporation of Neural Networks (NNs) (Kim and Lewis, 1999; Lewis et al., 1998; Ge et al., 2013) as function approximators, adaptive NN controllers have emerged to replace known regression functions with NN activation functions. In these works, continuous or periodic measurements of joint positions and velocities are required for the controllers, although the need for joint velocity measurements is later relaxed (Kim and Lewis, 1999). Literature presents various control schemes for robot manipulators, accounting for factors such as network delays (Liu and Chopra, 2012), finite-time control tasks (Galicki, 2015), learning and adaptation for complex tasks (Visioli et al., 2010; Sun et al., 2006, 2018; Pan et al., 2016; de Jesús Rubio, 2016, 2018), input constraint with saturation nonlinearity (He et al., 2016b), time-varying output constraints (He et al., 2017), and fast adaptation with performance guarantee (Pekarovskiy et al., 2018).

In addition to the application specific requirements, robotic manipulator systems with remote interoperability, enabling network integration is desired in many engineering applications wherein continuous feedback information to compute appropriate torque input is not always desirable. In this context, event-based sampling and control implementation has become relevant (Sahoo et al., 2016; Tabuada, 2007; Tallapragada and Chopra, 2012; Zhong and He, 2016; Wang et al., 2017; Yang et al., 2017). However, event-sampled implementation of observer together with the controller for a robot manipulator with uncertain dynamics using NNs is nontrivial. Furthermore, with the aperiodic estimation of states, we shall see that the location of observers plays an important role in the tracking performance, and therefore, needs a careful consideration.

In the first part of this chapter, we shall study an adaptive NN-based control scheme for a robot manipulator system utilizing event-sampled measurements of joint position vector. An NN observer is utilized to reconstruct the joint velocity vector. The nonlinear uncertainties capturing the effects of inertia, Coriolis/centripetal forces, frictional forces, and gravitational forces on the robotic manipulator are learned by using a second NN for generating the torque input. With these components, we shall look at two controller configurations based on the location of the observer in the feedback loop. The first configuration considers that the NN observer is co-located with the sensor whereas in the second configuration, the NN observer is co-located with the controller. Due to the location of the NN observer, we shall see that the convergence properties of the closed-loop system are not identical for the two configurations, and more, the ETM has to be redesigned for these configurations based on the information available at the ETM.

9.1.1 BACKGROUND AND PROBLEM FORMULATION

9.1.1.1 Event-based sampling and control implementation

To denote the time instants when the controller has access to the sensor samples, a sequence, $\{t_k\}_{k=0}^{\infty}$ with $t_0 = 0$, is defined. These time instants are referred to as the event-sampling or event-triggering instants. At the time instant t_k, the sensor measurement denoted by $\gamma(t_k)$ is updated at the controller and between any two sampling instants, a zero-order-hold (ZOH) is utilized at the controller to hold the feedback information. This is represented as $\breve{\gamma}(t) = \gamma(t_k),\ t_k \leq t < t_k + 1,\ \forall k \in \{0, \mathbb{N}\}$. Lack of current sensor measurement at the controller leads to the measurement error or event-sampling error, $\bar{e}_{ET}(t) = \gamma(t) - \breve{\gamma}(t),\ t_k \leq t < t_{k+1}$, with $\bar{e}_{ET}(t_k) = 0,\ \forall k \in \{0, \mathbb{N}\}$.

Remark 9.1. *Similar to the ZOH use at the controller, the actuator is also equipped with a ZOH so that a piecewise constant control input is applied to the dynamic system.*

As we have seen in this book, the design of controller in the event-triggered feedback framework requires the design of an ETM that constructs the sequence $\{t_k\}$, dynamically, along with the controller. Requirement of an efficient ETM is further reinforced by the introduction of a learning mechanism in the controller. In this case, in addition to considering the stability of the system, the learning mechanism and its efficiency should be taken into account when the ETM is developed. In the following Lemma, the event-sampled NN approximation property (Sahoo et al., 2016) is recalled from Chapter 4.

Lemma 9.1. *Given $\chi : A \rightarrow \mathbb{R}$, a smooth, real-valued function with a compact set, $A \subset \mathbb{R}^n$ and a positive constant ε_M, there exists $W^* \in \mathbb{R}^{p \times 1}$ so that*

$$\chi(x) = W^{*T} \phi(\breve{x}) + \breve{\varepsilon}(x, \breve{x}), \tag{9.1}$$

holds, where $\|\breve{\varepsilon}\| < \varepsilon_M$, $\forall \breve{x} \in A$, x, $\breve{x}$ are the continuous and event-sampled variables, $\phi(\breve{x})$ is the bounded event-sampled activation function, which forms a basis set of functions in A (Lewis et al., 1998) and p is the number of hidden layer neurons, and $\breve{\varepsilon} = W^{*T}(\phi(\breve{x} + \bar{e}_{ET}) - \phi(\breve{x})) + \varepsilon$ is the event-driven reconstruction error with ε function approximation error (Sahoo et al., 2016).

Remark 9.2. *Note that the activation function $\phi(x)$ is used to denote the term $\phi(\omega^T x)$, where ω is the input to hidden layer weights which are randomly set to form a stochastic basis, forming a random vector functional link network (Lewis et al., 1998). Since the values of ω are fixed upon initialization, they are not explicitly stated. The approximation of a nonlinear function using an NN given in (9.1) reveals that when the input to the NN is corrupted by the measurement error, the accuracy of the approximation is affected creating a trade-off between the estimation accuracy and the frequency of events.*

Next the robot manipulator dynamics are introduced followed by a brief background on event-triggered tracking control problem.

9.1.1.2 Robot manipulator system

The $n-$link robot manipulator dynamics with rigid links (Lewis et al., 1998) are expressed as

$$M(q)\ddot{q}(t)+V_m(q,\dot{q})\dot{q}(t)+G(q)+F(\dot{q})+\tau_d(t)=\tau(t) \tag{9.2}$$

where $q(t)\in\mathbb{R}^n$ is the joint variable vector, $V_m(q,\dot{q})$ is the Coriolis/centripetal matrix, $M(q)$ is the inertia matrix, $F(\dot{q})$ models the effects of friction, $G(q)$ is the gravity vector, and $\tau_d(t)$ represents disturbances. The control input vector $\tau(t)$ has components of torque for revolute joints and force for prismatic joints. With the following facts, the tracking control problem for the robot dynamics as in (9.2) is introduced.

Some useful facts regarding the dynamics of the robot manipulator is listed here (Lewis et al., 1998): The matrix $M(q)$ satisfies $B_{m_1}I\leq M(q)\leq B_{m_2}I$, for some known positive constants B_{m_1},B_{m_2}, where I is the identity matrix of appropriate dimension, and the Coriolis/centripetal matrix $V_m(q,\dot{q})$ is bounded such that $\|V_m(q,\dot{q})\|\leq V_b\|\dot{q}\|$ with $V_b>0$. There exists constants $g_B,B_F,B_f>0$ such that $\|G(q)\|\leq g_B$ and $\|F(\dot{q})\|\leq B_F\|\dot{q}\|+B_f$. The matrix $\dot{M}-2V_m$ is skew- symmetric, and finally, there exists a positive constant, $\tau_{dM}>0$, such that $\|\tau_d(t)\|\leq\tau_{dM}$, uniformly for all $t\in\mathbb{R}^+$.

9.1.1.3 Tracking control problem

By defining the joint positions and velocities as the state vector, the robot manipulator system dynamics can be represented in a compact form (Lewis et al., 1998) as

$$\begin{bmatrix}\dot{q}(t)\\ \ddot{q}(t)\end{bmatrix}=\begin{bmatrix}\dot{q}(t)\\ -M^{-1}(q)(V_m(q,\dot{q})\dot{q}(t)+F(\dot{q})+G(q))\end{bmatrix}+ \begin{bmatrix}0\\ M^{-1}(q)\end{bmatrix}\tau(t)+\begin{bmatrix}0\\ -M^{-1}(q)\end{bmatrix}\tau_d(t). \tag{9.3}$$

The objective in a tracking control problem is to design the torque input $\tau(t)$ such that the joint positions track a desired trajectory $q_d(t)$. The desired trajectory is restricted to satisfy the following standard assumption.

Assumption 9.1. *(Kim and Lewis, 1999; Lewis et al., 1998) The desired trajectories $q_d(t)\in\mathbb{R}^n$ satisfy $\|Q_d\|\leq q_B$, with $Q_d(t)=[q_d(t)\ \dot{q}_d(t)\ \ddot{q}_d(t)]^T$, and $q_B>0$.*

In real-world applications, for example in manufacturing plants, the robotic manipulator is expected to perform tasks which are characterized by position, velocity and acceleration that are bounded. Therefore, it is reasonable to make the assumption stated above in the design and analysis. To develop a controller, which enables the robot manipulator to track a desired trajectory, we shall begin by defining the tracking error as

$$e(t)=q_d(t)-q(t), \tag{9.4}$$

and the filtered tracking error (Lewis et al., 1998) as

$$r(t)=\dot{e}(t)+\lambda e(t), \tag{9.5}$$

with a symmetric matrix $\lambda>0$ of compatible dimension.

Observe from (9.5) that a positive choice of λ ensures the stability of $\dot{e}(t)$ if the filtered tracking error is finite and bounded. To design the torque input and to ensure boundedness of the filtered tracking error, differentiate (9.5) with respect to time to reveal, $\dot{r}(t)=\ddot{e}(t)+\lambda\dot{e}(t)$. By incorporating the dynamics of the robotic manipulator (9.2) and utilizing (9.4) and (9.5), the dynamics of the filtered tracking error is obtained (Lewis et al., 1998) as

$$M\dot{r}(t)=-V_mr(t)-\tau(t)+f(z)+\tau_d(t) \tag{9.6}$$

with $f(z) = M(q)(\ddot{q}_d + \lambda\dot{e}) + V_m(q,\dot{q})(\dot{q}_d + \lambda e) + F(\dot{q}) + G(q)$ and $z = [e^T\ \dot{e}^T\ q_d^T\ \dot{q}_d^T\ \ddot{q}_d^T]^T$. If the function $f(z)$ is known, it is straight-forward to generate a control input, $\tau(t) = f(z) + k_v r(t)$, where $k_v \in \mathbb{R}^{n\times n}$ is a positive definite design matrix, such that the filtered tracking error dynamics in (9.6) is stable. This leads to a computed torque controller that assumes complete and accurate knowledge of the robot manipulator dynamics. However, the nonlinear function $f(z)$ is often unknown due to the nonlinearities such as friction, inertia matrix, and so on.

Further, in the event-triggered feedback framework, the torque input using the event-sampled state, is designed as

$$\tau(t) = \hat{f}(\breve{z}) + k_v \breve{r}(t), \qquad t_k \le t < t_{k+1}, \tag{9.7}$$

where $\breve{r}(t) = r(t) - e_{ET}(t)$ is the event-sampled filtered tracking error, e_{ET} is the error due to event-based sampling, and $\hat{f}(\breve{z})$ denotes an estimate of $f(z)$ with $\breve{z}(t) = z(t_k)$ in the interval $[t_k, t_{k+1})$. By using (9.7) in (9.6), we get

$$M\dot{r}(t) = -V_m r(t) - \hat{f}(\breve{z}) - k_v \breve{r}(t) + f(z) + \tau_d(t). \tag{9.8}$$

The filtered tracking error dynamics (9.8) reveals that the tracking performance of the robotic manipulator is influenced by the measurement error due to event-based sampling, the mismatch between $f(z)$, and its estimate. Moreover, all the controller equations (9.4)-(9.8) assume the availability of both the joint position and velocities. In the next section, an observer is designed first to generate the estimate of joint velocities, and then, a controller that utilizes the estimated state vector is developed to design (9.7).

9.1.2 NN OBSERVER AND CONTROLLER DESIGN

Before developing the controller, two output feedback control schemes, which are represented using block diagrams in Figure 9.1, are introduced. In the first architecture (Figure 9.1. (a)), the observer is co-located with the sensor. This ensures that the observer has access to the sensor data continuously, and hence, the convergence of the observer estimation error will be fast. When an event is triggered,

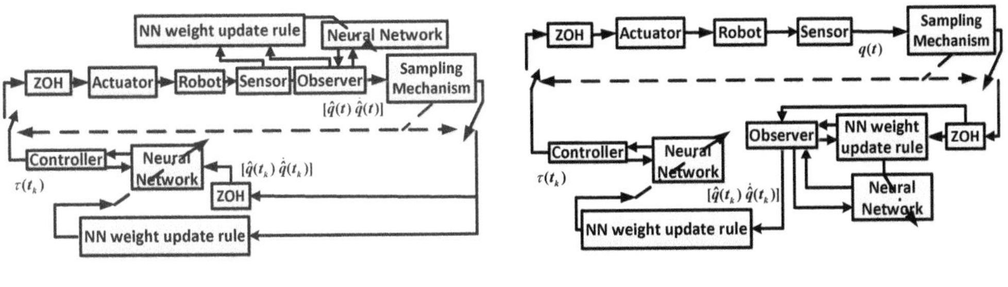

Figure 9.1 Controller block diagram - (a) Configuration 1. (b) Configuration 2.

the estimated joint velocities and the joint positions are fed back to the controller. The controller has access to the event-sampled estimated states to generate the required torque. Moreover, the ETM can be designed as a function of all the estimated states.

In the second architecture (Figure 9.1. (b)), the observer is co-located with the controller. In this configuration, only the output information is transmitted from the sensor to the controller. The observer NN and the controller are updated with current sensor readings only when there is an event. This configuration introduces two issues. Firstly, the observer is injected with an additional error due to event-triggered feedback. Secondly, the event-triggering mechanism now cannot be a function of the estimated state vector as only the outputs are continuously available. Next, the analytical design of the controller and the observer are presented for Configuration 1.

9.1.2.1 Observer and controller dynamics (Configuration 1)

The robot manipulator dynamics (9.3) can be represented as

$$\begin{aligned}\dot{x}_1(t) &= x_2(t)\\ \dot{x}_2(t) &= \bar{f}(x(t),\tau(t)),\end{aligned} \tag{9.9}$$

where x_1, x_2 denote the joint variables and joint velocities, respectively, $x = [x_1^T, x_2^T]^T$, and $\bar{f}(x,\tau) = -M^{-1}(q)(V_m(q,\dot{q})\dot{q} + F(\dot{q}) + G(q) + \tau_d(t) - \tau(t))$. Using the function approximation property of the NN (Lewis et al., 1998), the nonlinear map $\bar{f}(.)$ can be represented as $\bar{f}(x,\tau) = W_o^T\sigma_o(x,\tau) + \varepsilon_o(x)$, where W_o is the unknown, constant NN weights, $\sigma_o(\cdot)$ is the activation function, and $\varepsilon_o(x)$ is the reconstruction error.

Assumption 9.2. *(Lewis et al., 1998) The NN approximation/reconstruction error ($\varepsilon_o(.)$) is bounded such that $\|\varepsilon_o\| \leq \varepsilon_{oM}$ for $\varepsilon_{oM} > 0$. The nonlinear neural network activation function, $\sigma_o(.)$, is chosen such that $\|\sigma_o(\cdot)\| \leq \sqrt{N_o}$, where N_o denotes the number of neurons in the hidden layer. Also, there exists $W_{oM} > 0$ such that $\|W_o\| \leq W_{oM}$, holds. Finally, the nonlinear activation function satisfies, $\|\sigma_o(\alpha) - \sigma_o(\beta)\| \leq L_\sigma \|\alpha - \beta\|$, $\forall \alpha,\beta \in A$, where A is a compact set.*

In the analysis, standard assumptions (Lewis et al., 1998) are made as listed in Assumption 9.2. It is proven in (Lewis et al., 1998) that as the number of hidden layer neurons are increased, i.e., as $N_o \to \infty$, the reconstruction error, $\varepsilon \to 0$. In addition, commonly used activation functions like the sigmoidal function, radial basis functions, and so on, satisfy the bounds and the smoothness properties stated above (Lewis et al., 1998).

Let $\hat{W}_o$ represent the weight estimates of W_o. The approximated nonlinear function is given by $\hat{\bar{f}}(x) = \hat{W}_o^T\sigma_o(\hat{x},\tau)$. Let the estimated joint variable be represented by $\hat{x}_1$ and the estimated joint velocity be represented using the vector $\hat{x}_2$ and let $\hat{x} = [\hat{x}_1^T\ \hat{x}_2^T]^T$. Using $\hat{W}_o$, define the NN observer as

$$\begin{aligned}\dot{\hat{x}}_1(t) &= \hat{x}_2(t) + K_d\tilde{x}_1(t)\\ \dot{z}_2(t) &= \hat{W}_o\sigma_o(\hat{x},\tau) + K\tilde{x}_1(t),\\ \hat{x}_2(t) &= z_2(t) + K_p\tilde{x}_1(t).\end{aligned} \tag{9.10}$$

Now, rewriting (9.10) using the estimated state variables $\hat{x}_1$ and $\hat{x}_2$, one has

$$\begin{aligned}\dot{\hat{x}}_1(t) &= \hat{x}_2(t) + K_d\tilde{x}_1(t)\\ \dot{\hat{x}}_2(t) &= \hat{W}_o\sigma_o(\hat{x},\tau) + K\tilde{x}_1(t) + K_p\dot{\tilde{x}}_1(t),\end{aligned} \tag{9.11}$$

where K_d, K, and K_p are observer gains, the output estimation error $\tilde{x}_1(t) = x_1(t) - \hat{x}_1(t)$, and $\hat{x}(0)$ is the initial state estimate. Note that the dynamics in terms of a new variable $\dot{z}_2(t)$ is introduced in (9.10) and is utilized to get the estimate of x_1 and x_2 as in (Kim and Lewis, 1999). This change of variable enables both the implementation of the observer using (9.10) and facilitates the convergence and stability analysis using (9.11) as was demonstrated in (Lewis et al., 1998).

To analyze the stability of the observer, first, define the state estimation error as $\tilde{x} = [\tilde{x}_1^T\ \tilde{x}_2^T]^T$, where $\tilde{x}_2 = x_2 - \hat{x}_2$. Since the observer is co-located with the sensor, the observer dynamics are not injected with the measurement error and the resulting estimation error dynamics are

$$\begin{aligned}\dot{\tilde{x}}_1 &= \tilde{x}_2 - K_d\tilde{x}_1\\ \dot{\tilde{x}}_2 &= -K_p\tilde{x}_2 - (K - K_pK_d)\tilde{x}_1 + \tilde{W}_o\sigma_o(\hat{x}) + \varepsilon_1(\tilde{x}),\end{aligned} \tag{9.12}$$

where $\varepsilon_1(\tilde{x}) = W_o(\sigma_o(x) - \sigma_o(\hat{x})) + \varepsilon_o(x)$. The stability results of the observer are presented next.

Lemma 9.2. *(Configuration 1): Consider the dynamics of the robotic manipulator* (9.9) *and the observer dynamics* (9.10)*. Let the weight tuning rule for the observer NN be defined as*

$$\dot{\hat{W}}_o(t) = -\Gamma_o K_d \sigma_o(\hat{x})\tilde{x}_1^T(t) - \Gamma_o \kappa_o \hat{W}_o(t) \tag{9.13}$$

where $\Gamma_o, \kappa_o > 0$ *are design parameters. Then the error dynamics* (9.12) *and the weights of the NN observer are locally UUB when* $K_d K > \frac{1}{2}N_o + \frac{1}{2}K_p^2$, $K_p > \frac{1}{2}K_d^2 + \frac{1}{2}N_o + \frac{1}{2}$, $\kappa_o > \frac{1}{2} + \frac{1}{2}K_d^2$, *and the bounds are functions of the approximation error and target NN observer weights given by* $\mathscr{B}_o = \frac{1}{2}\|\varepsilon_1\|^2 + \kappa_o^2 W_{oM}^2$.

Sketch of Proof:

- Consider the Lyapunov candidate function as

$$L_o(\tilde{x}, \tilde{W}_o) = \frac{1}{2}\tilde{x}_1^T(t)K\tilde{x}_1(t) + \frac{1}{2}\tilde{x}_2^T(t)\tilde{x}_2(t) + \frac{1}{2}tr(\tilde{W}_o^T(t)\Gamma_o^{-1}\tilde{W}_o(t)).$$

- Taking the first derivative, we get $\dot{L}_o(\tilde{x}, \tilde{W}_o) = \dot{\tilde{x}}_1^T(t)K\tilde{x}_1(t) + \tilde{x}_2^T(t)\dot{\tilde{x}}_2(t) + tr(\tilde{W}_o^T(t)\Gamma_o^{-1}\dot{\tilde{W}}_o(t))$. Using the error dynamics (9.12) and the weight update rule (9.13) along with the fact that $\dot{\tilde{W}}_o(t) = -\dot{\hat{W}}_o(t)$, we obtain the following inequality

$$\begin{aligned}\dot{L}_o(t) \leq & -K_d K\|\tilde{x}_1\|^2 - K_p\|\tilde{x}_2\|^2 - \kappa_o\left\|\tilde{W}_o\right\|^2 \\ & + \|\tilde{x}_2\|(K_p K_d)\|\tilde{x}_1\| + \|\tilde{x}_2\|\left\|\tilde{W}_o\right\|\sqrt{N_o} + \|\tilde{x}_2\|\|\varepsilon_1\| \\ & + \left\|\tilde{W}_o\right\|K_d\sqrt{N_o}\|\tilde{x}_1\| + \left\|\tilde{W}_o\right\|\kappa_o W_{oM},\end{aligned} \tag{9.14}$$

  with N_o being the number of hidden layer neurons.
- Applying Young's inequality, we get

$$\dot{L}_o(t) \leq -\eta_1\|\tilde{x}_1\|^2 - \eta_2\|\tilde{x}_2\|^2 - \eta_3\|\tilde{W}_o\|^2 + \mathscr{B}_o, \tag{9.15}$$

  where $\eta_1 = (K_d K - \frac{1}{2}N_o - \frac{1}{2}K_p^2)$, $\eta_2 = (K_p - \frac{1}{2}K_d^2 - \frac{1}{2}N_o - \frac{1}{2})$, $\eta_3 = (\kappa_o - \frac{1}{2} - \frac{1}{2}K_d^2)$, and $\mathscr{B}_o = \frac{1}{2}\|\varepsilon_1(\tilde{x})\|^2 + \kappa_o^2 W_{oM}^2$. From (9.15), it can be observed that as long as $\eta_1, \eta_2, \eta_3 > 0$ and $\|\tilde{x}_1\| > \sqrt{\mathscr{B}_o/\eta_1}$ or $\|\tilde{x}_2\| > \sqrt{\mathscr{B}_o/\eta_2}$ or $\|\tilde{W}_o\| > \sqrt{\mathscr{B}_o/\eta_3}$, the Lyapunov function is negative definite. As a consequence, it can be concluded that the observer estimation errors and the observer NN weights are UUB.

To develop the control equations, begin by defining the tracking error using the estimated states as $\hat{e}(t) = x_d(t) - \hat{x}_1(t)$ and $\dot{\hat{e}}(t) = \dot{x}_d(t) - \hat{x}_2(t)$. Now the estimated filtered tracking error can be defined as $\hat{r}(t) = \dot{\hat{e}}(t) + \lambda e(t)$. Note that the filtered tracking error is calculated using the estimated joint velocity tracking error and the actual tracking error (9.4).Next, the nonlinear map in (9.6), is parameterized using an NN as $f(z) = W^T\phi(z) + \varepsilon(z)$, where the NN weights W denotes the target parameter for the learning scheme, the activation function $\phi(.)$, and the reconstruction error $\varepsilon(z)$ with $f(z)$ defined as in (9.6). Using the estimated states, the tracking errors are redefined and the input to the NN is redefined as $\hat{z} = [\hat{e}^T\ \dot{\hat{e}}^T\ q_d^T\ \dot{q}_d^T\ \ddot{q}_d^T]^T$. The estimate of the nonlinear map in the event-triggered feedback framework is given as

$$\hat{f}(\breve{z}) = \hat{W}^T\phi(\breve{z}), \tag{9.16}$$

with the estimated NN weights $\hat{W}$ and $\breve{z} = \hat{z}(t_k)$. Let the weight estimation error be defined as the difference between the target weights and the estimated weights, $\tilde{W}^T = W^T - \hat{W}^T$. Using the estimated states, the estimated filtered tracking error dynamics (Kim and Lewis, 1999) are revealed as

$$M\dot{\hat{r}}(t) = -V_m\hat{r}(t) - \tau(t) + f(z) + \tau_d(t) \tag{9.17}$$

with $f(z) = M(q)(\ddot{q}_d + \dot{\tilde{x}}_2 + \lambda\dot{e}) + V_m(q,\dot{q})(\dot{q}_d + \tilde{x}_2 + \lambda e) + F(\dot{q}) + G(q)$. Using the control torque (9.7), we get

$$M\dot{\hat{r}} = (-V_m - k_v)\hat{r} + \tau_d + \tilde{W}^T\phi(\hat{z}_e) + W^T[\phi(z) - \phi(\hat{z}_e)] + \varepsilon + k_v e_{ET}. \tag{9.18}$$

The subscript $(.)_e$ indicates that the variable is event-sampled. The slope of the filtered tracking error (9.18) reveals that the measurement error introduced by event-based sampling and the error due to the observer affects the tracking performance of the manipulator. The NN is designed by taking into account the standard assumptions as stated in Assumption 9.2. Specifically, there exists positive constants ε_M, $W_M > 0$ so that $\|\varepsilon\| \leq \varepsilon_M$, $\|W\| \leq W_M$ holds. The activation function, $\phi(.)$, satisfies $\|\phi(\bullet)\| \leq \sqrt{N_0}$, $\|\phi(\alpha) - \phi(\beta)\| \leq L_\phi \|\alpha - \beta\|$, $\forall \alpha, \beta \in A$, where N_0 denotes the number of neurons in the hidden layer. The stability results of the closed loop system with continuous feedback is briefly presented next.

Theorem 9.1. *Let the estimated filtered tracking error dynamics for the robot manipulator, using the approximation based torque input* $\tau(t) = \hat{f}(z) + k_v\hat{r}(t)$ *and the NN approximation* (9.16), *be defined as* $M\dot{\hat{r}}(t) = (-V_m - k_v)\hat{r}(t) + \tau_d(t) + \tilde{W}^T\phi(\hat{z}) + W^T[\phi(z) - \phi(\hat{z})] + \varepsilon$. *Let the dynamics of the observer be given by* (9.11). *Select the NN weight tuning rule as*

$$\dot{\hat{W}}(t) = \Gamma\phi(\hat{z})\hat{r}^T(t) - \kappa\Gamma\hat{W}(t), \tag{9.19}$$

with the design parameters $\Gamma > 0, \kappa > \frac{1}{2}$, *and* $\lambda_{min}(k_v) > \frac{1}{2}$. *Let the NN observer weight update rule be given by* (9.13) *with the observer design parameters satisfying the conditions given in Lemma 9.2. Under the Assumptions 9.1 and 9.2, the NN observer, tracking errors, and the error in the NN weight estimates are locally uniformly ultimately bounded.*

Sketch of Proof: Here we just analyze the continuous time implementation of the output feedback controller using Lyapunov stability theory.

- The Lyapunov candidate function $\mathscr{L} = L_o + L$ with $L(\hat{r}, \tilde{W}) = \frac{1}{2}\hat{r}^T M\hat{r} + \frac{1}{2}tr(\tilde{W}^T\Gamma^{-1}\tilde{W})$ consists of two terms. The first term L_o is concernced with the observer variables as defined in Lemma 9.2.
- Taking the first derivative of L and substituting the error dynamics and the weight estimation error dynamics using (9.19), where $\dot{\tilde{W}}(t) = -\dot{\hat{W}}(t)$ and $\tilde{\phi} = \phi(z) - \phi(\hat{z})$, reveals

$$\begin{aligned}\dot{L}(r, \tilde{W}) = &-\hat{r}^T k_v\hat{r} + \hat{r}^T(\varepsilon + \tau_d + W^T(\phi(z) - \phi(\hat{z})))\\ &+ tr(\tilde{W}^T\kappa W - \tilde{W}^T\kappa\tilde{W} + \frac{1}{2}\hat{r}^T(\dot{M} - 2V_m)\hat{r}^T.\end{aligned} \tag{9.20}$$

- Using the skew-symmetry property, $\hat{r}^T(\dot{M} - 2V_m)\hat{r}^T = 0$, applying Young's inequality, and using the results from Lemma 9.2,

$$\begin{aligned}\dot{\mathscr{L}} \leq &-(\lambda_{min}(k_v) - \frac{1}{2})\|\hat{r}\|^2 - (\kappa - \frac{1}{2})\|\tilde{W}^T\|^2\\ &- \eta_1\|\tilde{x}_1\|^2 - \eta_2\|\tilde{x}_2\|^2 - \eta_3\|\tilde{W}_o\|^2 + \mathscr{B}_1,\end{aligned} \tag{9.21}$$

where $\mathscr{B}_1 = \mathscr{B}_{1a} + \mathscr{B}_o$, $\mathscr{B}_o$ is the bounds from Lemma 9.2, and $\mathscr{B}_{1a} = \frac{1}{2}\kappa^2 W_M^2 + \frac{1}{2}\|\varepsilon + \tau_d + W^T(\phi(z) - \phi(\hat{z}))\|^2$. From (9.21), it can be observed that as long as $\eta_1, \eta_2, \eta_3 > 0, \lambda_{min}(k_v) > \frac{1}{2}, \kappa > \frac{1}{2}$, and $\|\tilde{x}_1\| > \sqrt{\mathscr{B}_1/\eta_1}$ or $\|\tilde{x}_2\| > \sqrt{\mathscr{B}_1/\eta_2}$ or $\|\tilde{W}_o\| > \sqrt{\mathscr{B}_1/\eta_3}$ or $\|\tilde{W}\| > \sqrt{\mathscr{B}_1/(\kappa - \frac{1}{2})}$ or $\|\hat{r}\| > \sqrt{\mathscr{B}_1/(\lambda_{min}(k_v) - \frac{1}{2})}$, the Lyapunov function is negative definite. Hence, it can be concluded that the observer estimation errors, the NN weights, and the estimated tracking error are UUB.

In the following theorem, the ETM is designed and the stability results for the event sampled controller will be presented in two cases following an approach similar to (Sahoo et al., 2016).

Theorem 9.2. *(Configuration 1): Consider the estimated filtered tracking error dynamics given by* (9.18) *and the observer dynamics given by* (9.11)*. Define the approximated torque input* (9.7) *and the weight tuning law*

$$\hat{W}^{+} = \hat{W}(t) + \hat{\Gamma}\phi(\hat{z})\hat{r}^{T} - \kappa\Gamma\hat{W}(t), \quad t = t_k, \tag{9.22}$$

for $k \in \mathbb{N}$. Let the Assumptions 9.1-9.2 hold. Let an event be triggered when the following condition is not satisfied in the inter-sampling period

$$\|e_{ET}\|^2 \leq \sigma\mu_k\|\hat{r}\|^2. \tag{9.23}$$

Then the observer estimation error, NN weight estimation error, and the tracking errors are locally ultimately bounded provided the design parameters satisfy $\sigma, \mu_k \in (0,1)$, $\kappa > 0, \Gamma > 0, \lambda_{min}(k_v) \geq \frac{3}{2} + \sigma$, and $\hat{\Gamma} = \frac{\Gamma}{1+\|\hat{r}\|^2}$.

Sketch of Proof:

- The proof can be considered in two cases. Case 1, which involves analysis in the inter-sampling period, is considered first. Consider the Lyapunov function $\mathscr{L} = L(\hat{r}, \tilde{W}) + L_o$, where $L(\hat{r}, \tilde{W}) = \frac{1}{2}\hat{r}^T M\hat{r} + \frac{1}{2}tr(\tilde{W}^T\tilde{W})$.
- Since the NN weights in the controller are not updated during the inter-sampling period, we have $\dot{\hat{W}} = 0$ between event-triggering instants.
- Applying the norm operator, the *facts* stated in Section 9.1.1.2, and using Young's inequality, we get

$$\begin{aligned}\dot{L}(\hat{r}, \tilde{W}) \leq & -\lambda_{\min}(k_v)\|\hat{r}\|^2 + \left\|\hat{r}^T\right\|^2 + \frac{1}{2}\|k_v e_{ET}\|^2 \\ & + \frac{1}{2}\left\|(W^T\phi(z) - \hat{W}^T\phi(\hat{z}_e) + \varepsilon + \tau_d)\right\|^2.\end{aligned} \tag{9.24}$$

  Choose $\|e_{ET}\|^2 \leq \mu_k\|\hat{r}\|^2$ with $\mu_k = 2\sigma/k_v^2$ to get

$$\dot{L}(\hat{r}, \tilde{W}) \leq -(\lambda_{\min}(k_v) - 1 - \sigma)\|\hat{r}\|^2 + \mathscr{B}_{2a}, \tag{9.25}$$

  where $\mathscr{B}_{2a} = \frac{1}{2}\left\|\tilde{W}^T\phi(\hat{z}_e) + W^T(\phi(z) - \phi(\hat{z}_e)) + \varepsilon + \tau_d\right\|^2$.
- Alternatively, choosing $\|e_{ET}\|^2 \leq \mu_k\|\hat{r}\|^2$ with $\mu_k = 2\sigma/[\left\|\hat{W}^T\right\|^2 L_\phi^2 + k_v^2]$ yields

$$\dot{L} \leq -(\lambda_{\min}(k_v) - \frac{3}{2} - \sigma)\|\hat{r}\|^2 + \mathscr{B}_{2b}, \tag{9.26}$$

  with $\mathscr{B}_{2b} = \frac{1}{2}\|W^T\phi(z) - \hat{W}^T\phi(\hat{z}) + \tau_d + \varepsilon\|^2$.
- Finally, the observer Lyapunov function derivative can be combined from Lemma 9.2 to reveal the overall bound.
- For Case 2, we consider the event triggering instants. Consider the Lyapunov function $\mathscr{L}$. The first difference $\Delta\mathscr{L} = \Delta L(\hat{r}, \tilde{W}) + \Delta L_o$. Observe that at $t = t_k$ for all $k \in \{0, \mathbb{N}\}$, $\hat{r}^+ = \hat{r}$ and $\tilde{x}^+ = \tilde{x}$. Therefore, $\Delta\mathscr{L} = \frac{1}{2}tr(\tilde{W}^{+T}\tilde{W}^+) - \frac{1}{2}tr(\tilde{W}^T\tilde{W})$. From the definition $\tilde{W}^+ = W - \hat{W}^+$, we have $\tilde{W}^+ = \tilde{W}(t) - \hat{\Gamma}\phi(z)\hat{r}^T + \kappa\Gamma\hat{W}(t)$. Substituting the error dynamics in the first difference reveals

$$\begin{aligned}\Delta\mathscr{L} =& tr(-\tilde{W}\hat{\Gamma}\phi(z)\hat{r}^T + \frac{1}{2}\hat{r}\phi^T(z)\hat{\Gamma}^T\hat{\Gamma}\phi(z)\hat{r}^T \\ & + \kappa\tilde{W}\Gamma\hat{W}(t) - \kappa\hat{r}\phi^T(z)\hat{\Gamma}^T\Gamma\hat{W} + \frac{1}{2}\kappa^2\hat{W}^T\Gamma^T\Gamma\hat{W}).\end{aligned} \tag{9.27}$$

Table 9.1
Output feedback controller design using Configuration 1

Observer dynamics	$\dot{\hat{x}}_1(t) = \hat{x}_2(t) + K_d\tilde{x}_1(t)$, $\dot{z}_2(t) = \hat{W}_o\sigma_o(\hat{x},\tau) + K\tilde{x}_1(t)$, and $\hat{x}_2(t) = z_2(t) + K_p\tilde{x}_1(t)$.
Filtered tracking error dynamics	$M\dot{r}(t) = -V_m r(t) - \tau(t) + f(z) + \tau_d(t)$
Control torque	$\tau(t) = \hat{f}(\breve{z}) + k_v\breve{r}(t)$
Observer NN weight update rule	$\dot{\hat{W}}_o(t) = -\Gamma_o K_d\sigma_o(\hat{x})\tilde{x}_1^T(t) - \Gamma_o\kappa_o\hat{W}_o(t)$
Controller NN weight update rule	$\hat{W}^+ = \hat{W}(t) + \hat{\Gamma}\phi(\hat{z})\hat{r}^T - \kappa\Gamma\hat{W}(t), \quad t = t_k$
Event-triggering condition - 1	$\|e_{ET}\|^2 \le \mu_k\|\hat{r}\|^2$ with $\mu_k = 2\sigma/k_v^2$
Event-triggering condition - 2	$\|e_{ET}\|^2 \le \mu_k\|\hat{r}\|^2$ with $\mu_k = 2\sigma/[\|\hat{W}^T\|^2 L_\phi^2 + k_v^2]$

Using the fact that $0 \le \frac{\|\hat{r}\|}{1+\|\hat{r}\|^2} \le 1$ and on simplification (Sahoo et al., 2016), we get

$$\Delta\mathscr{L} \le -\frac{1}{8}(\kappa\lambda_{min}(\Gamma) - 8\kappa^2\|\Gamma\|^2)\|\tilde{W}\|^2 + \mathscr{B}_2, \tag{9.28}$$

where $\mathscr{B}_2 = \frac{1}{2\kappa}\|\Gamma\|N_0 + \frac{1}{2}N_0\|\Gamma^T\Gamma\| + \kappa\|\Gamma\|W_M^2 + \kappa\sqrt{N_0}\|\Gamma^T\Gamma\|W_M + 2\kappa N_0\|\Gamma\|^3 + \frac{4}{\kappa}\|\Gamma\|^3 W_M^2 + \frac{1}{2}\kappa^2 {W_M}^2\|\Gamma^T\Gamma\|$. It can be observed from Case 1 and Case 2 that all the errors are UB. Furthermore, as the events increase, the weight estimation errors decrease and converge to their bounds. As a consequence, the bounds calculated for Case 1 decreases.

Remark 9.3. *In Theorem 9.2, two different values for μ_k in (9.23) are derived. In the first condition, $\mu_k = 2\sigma/\|k_v\|^2$ is a constant and it does not require the information regarding the NN weights to determine the event-based sampling instants. In contrast, the second sampling condition uses $\mu_k = 2\sigma/[\|\hat{W}^T\|^2 L_\phi^2 + \|k_v\|^2]$. This condition, similar to (Sahoo et al., 2016), utilizes the NN weights.*

9.1.2.2 Observer and controller dynamics (Configuration 2)

Consider the second control configuration as represented in Figure 9.1 (b). To reconstruct the joint velocities when the observer is co-located with the controller, define event-driven observer dynamics given by

$$\begin{aligned} \dot{\hat{x}}_1(t) &= \hat{x}_2(t) + K_d\tilde{x}_{1,e}(t) \\ \dot{z}_2(t) &= \hat{W}_o\sigma_o(\hat{x}_e,\tau) + K\tilde{x}_{1,e}(t), \quad \text{with} \quad \hat{x}_2(t) = z_2(t) + K_p\tilde{x}_{1,e}(t). \end{aligned} \tag{9.29}$$

Rewriting the observer dynamics (9.29) using the co-ordinate variables $\hat{x}_1(t), \hat{x}_2(t)$, we get

$$\begin{aligned} \dot{\hat{x}}_1(t) &= \hat{x}_2(t) + K_d\tilde{x}_{1,e}(t), \\ \dot{\hat{x}}_2(t) &= \hat{W}_o\sigma_o(\hat{x}_e) + K\tilde{x}_{1,e}(t) + K_p\dot{\tilde{x}}_{1,e}(t). \end{aligned} \tag{9.30}$$

Note that the observer given by (9.29) has access to the outputs only at the event-triggering instants, introducing an error in (9.30). From (9.30), the error dynamics are obtained as

$$\begin{aligned} \dot{\tilde{x}}_1(t) &= \tilde{x}_2(t) - K_d\tilde{x}_{1,e}(t) \\ \dot{\tilde{x}}_2(t) &= \tilde{W}_o\sigma_o(\hat{x}) - K\tilde{x}_{1,e}(t) - K_p\dot{\tilde{x}}_{1,e}(t) + \varepsilon_1(\tilde{x}), \end{aligned} \quad (9.31)$$

where $\varepsilon_1(\tilde{x}) = W_o(\sigma_o(x) - \sigma_o(\hat{x})) + \varepsilon_o(x)$. The stability results of the observer (9.29) are presented next.

Lemma 9.3. *(Configuration 2): Consider the dynamics of the robot manipulator defined by* (9.3) *and the observer dynamics given by* (9.29)*. Let the weight tuning rule for the NN observer be defined as*

$$\hat{W}_o^+ = \hat{W}_o(t) - K_d\hat{\Gamma}_o\sigma_o(\hat{x})\tilde{x}_1^T - \kappa_o\Gamma_o\hat{W}_o(t), \quad t = t_k, \quad (9.32)$$

for $k \in \mathbb{N}$. Then the observer estimation error and the NN observer weights are locally UB when $K_dK > K_p^2, K_p > K_d^2 + 1$, $\hat{\Gamma}_o = \frac{\Gamma_o}{1+\|\tilde{x}_1\|^2}$, $\kappa_o > 0$ with the adjustable bounds defined by $\mathscr{B}_{3oa} + \psi(e_{ET})$, and $\mathscr{B}_{3ob}$ is a function of the ε, the measurement errors, the W_M, and the design constants.

Sketch of Proof: The structure of the proof consists of two parts as in the case of Theorem 9.2. This is because the observer weights are updated only at the event-triggering instants using (9.32).

- The Lyapunov candidate function is chosen as $L_o(\tilde{x}, \tilde{W}_o) = \frac{1}{2}\tilde{x}_1^T K\tilde{x}_1 + \frac{1}{2}\tilde{x}_2^T\tilde{x}_2 + \frac{1}{2}tr(\tilde{W}_o^T\tilde{W}_o)$.
- First, the inter-sampling period is considered. Since the NN weights are not updated in the inter-sampling period, we have $\dot{\hat{W}}_o = 0$. Using this, the Lyapunov time-derivative is given by $\dot{L}_o(\tilde{x}, \tilde{W}_o) = \dot{\tilde{x}}_1^T K\tilde{x}_1 + \tilde{x}_2^T\dot{\tilde{x}}_2$. Using the definition of the event-triggering error and $\dot{\tilde{x}}_1(t)$ in (9.31) reveals

$$\dot{L}_o(\tilde{x}, \tilde{W}_o) \leq -\eta_1\|\tilde{x}_1\|^2 - \eta_2\|\tilde{x}_2\|^2 + \mathscr{B}_{3oa} + \psi(e_{ET}), \quad (9.33)$$

  where $\eta_1 = \frac{1}{2}(K_dK - K_p^2), \eta_2 = \frac{1}{2}(K_p - K_d^2 - 1), \mathscr{B}_{3oa} = \frac{1}{2}\|\tilde{W}_o\sigma_o(\hat{x}) + \varepsilon_1\|^2$, and $\psi(e_{ET}) = \frac{1}{2}K^TK_d\|e_{1,ET}\|^2 + \frac{1}{2}\|(K - K_pK_d)\|^2\|e_{1,ET}\|^2 + \frac{1}{2}K_p\|e_{2,ET}\|^2$. Note that $\tilde{x}_{1,e} = x_{1,e} - \hat{x}_1 = \tilde{x}_1 - e_{1,ET}$. Similarly, $e_{2,ET}(t) = \dot{e}_{1,ET}(t)$.
- Now, for the second case, consider the event-triggering instants. The function $L_o(\tilde{x}, \tilde{W}_o)$ as in the previous case is picked as the Lyapunov candidate function. Taking its first-difference, we get $\Delta L_o = \frac{1}{2}\tilde{x}_1^{+T}K\tilde{x}_1^+ + \frac{1}{2}\tilde{x}_2^{+T}\tilde{x}_2^+ + \frac{1}{2}tr(\tilde{W}_o^{+T}\tilde{W}_o^+) - \frac{1}{2}\tilde{x}_1^TK\tilde{x}_1 - \frac{1}{2}\tilde{x}_2^T\tilde{x}_2 - \frac{1}{2}tr(\tilde{W}_o^T\tilde{W}_o)$. Substituting the jump dynamics and using the fact that $0 \leq \frac{\|\tilde{x}_1\|}{1+\|\tilde{x}_1\|^2} \leq 1$, and on simplification (Sahoo et al., 2016), we get

$$\Delta L_o \leq -\frac{1}{2}\kappa_o\eta_3\|\tilde{W}_o\|^2 + \mathscr{B}_{3ob}, \quad (9.34)$$

  where $\mathscr{B}_{3ob} = \frac{1}{2}\|K_d\Gamma_o\|^2N_o + \frac{1}{2}\kappa_o^2W_{oM}^2\|\Gamma_o^T\Gamma_o\| + \kappa_o\sqrt{N_o}\|\Gamma_o\|^2\|K_d\|W_{oM} + \frac{1}{2}N_o\|\Gamma_o^T\|^2\|K_d^T\|^2 + \frac{1}{2}\kappa_o\Gamma_oW_{oM}^2 + \kappa_o^2\|\Gamma_o\|^2W_{oM}^2 + \frac{1}{2\kappa_o^2}N_oK_d^2$ and $\eta_3 = \lambda_{min}(\Gamma_o) - 4\kappa_o\|\Gamma_o^T\Gamma_o\|$. It can be observed from Cases 1 and 2 that the observer estimation errors and the NN weight estimation errors are UB provided the event-triggering mechanism ensures the boundedness of the measurement errors.

The closed loop results of Configuration 2 are presented next wherein the event-triggering condition is developed with only the joint position vector and event-triggering errors as opposed to the estimated joint positions and velocities in (9.23).

Theorem 9.3. *(Configuration 2): Consider the estimated filtered tracking error for the robot manipulator system defined as* (9.18) *and the observer dynamics from* (9.29)*. Define the torque input* (9.7) *by utilizing the NN approximation* (9.16)*. Consider the weight tuning laws* (9.22) *and* (9.32)*, where* $\Gamma > 0, \kappa > 0, k_v \geq 3$*. If the Assumptions 1-2 are satisfied and when the measurement error satisfies, in the inter-event period,*

$$\|e_{ET}\|^2 \leq \sigma \mu_k \|e\|^2. \tag{9.35}$$

where $\mu_k, \sigma \in (0,1)$*,* $e_{ET} = e(t) - e(t_k)$*. Then, the tracking error, the observer estimation error, and the NN weight estimation errors are locally UB.*

Sketch of Proof: The proof consists of two parts and the arguments are similar to that used in Theorem 9.2.

- Consider the Lyapunov function $\mathscr{L} = L(\hat{r}, \tilde{W}) + L_o$, where $L(\hat{r}, \tilde{W}) = \frac{1}{2}\hat{r}^T M \hat{r} + \frac{1}{2} tr(\tilde{W}^T \tilde{W})$. Since the NN weights are not updated during the inter-sampling period, the derivative $\dot{\hat{W}}(t) = 0$. Therefore, the time-derivative of the Lyapunov function along the estimated filtered tracking error dynamics (9.18) and using the results from (9.33) is given by

$$\begin{aligned}\dot{\mathscr{L}} \leq & -(\lambda_{\min}(k_v) - 1)\|\hat{r}\|^2 + \frac{1}{2}\|k_v\|^2 \|e_{ET}\|^2 \\ & + \mathscr{B}_{3a} - \eta_1 \|\tilde{x}_1\|^2 - \eta_2 \|\tilde{x}_2\|^2 + L_\psi \|e_{ET}\|^2,\end{aligned} \tag{9.36}$$

where $\mathscr{B}_{3a} = \frac{1}{2}\left\|(W^T \phi(z) - \hat{W}^T \phi(\hat{z}_e) + \varepsilon + \tau_d)\right\|^2 + \mathscr{B}_{3oa}$ and $L_\psi > 0$ such that $\|\psi(e_{ET})\| \leq L_\psi \|e_{ET}\|^2$. Using the definition $\hat{r}(t) = \dot{\hat{e}}(t) + \lambda e(t)$ and applying triangle inequality, we have

$$\begin{aligned}\dot{\mathscr{L}} \leq & -2(\lambda_{\min}(k_v) - 1)\left\|\dot{\hat{e}}(t)\right\|^2 - 2(\lambda_{\min}(k_v) - 1)\|\lambda e(t)\|^2 \\ & - \eta_1 \|\tilde{x}_1\|^2 - \eta_2 \|\tilde{x}_2\|^2 + \frac{1}{2}\|k_v\|^2 \|e_{ET}\|^2 + L_\psi \|e_{ET}\|^2 + \mathscr{B}_{3a}.\end{aligned} \tag{9.37}$$

- Choose $\|e_{ET}\|^2 \leq \mu_k \|\lambda e\|^2$ with $\mu_k = \sigma / (\frac{1}{2}\|k_v\|^2 + L_\psi)$, to get

$$\begin{aligned}\dot{\mathscr{L}} \leq & -2(\lambda_{\min}(k_v) - 1)\left\|\dot{\hat{e}}(t)\right\|^2 - 2(\lambda_{\min}(k_v) - 1 - \sigma)\|\lambda e(t)\|^2 \\ & - \eta_1 \|\tilde{x}_1\|^2 - \eta_2 \|\tilde{x}_2\|^2 + \mathscr{B}_{3a}.\end{aligned} \tag{9.38}$$

- Alternatively, another event-sampling condition can be computed by modifying the proof to allow a larger bound. From (9.33), the observer Lyapunov function derivative can be used to obtain

$$\begin{aligned}\dot{\mathscr{L}} \leq & -(\lambda_{\min}(k_v) - \frac{3}{2})\|\hat{r}\|^2 - \eta_1 \|\tilde{x}_1\|^2 - \eta_2 \|\tilde{x}_2\|^2 \\ & + \frac{1}{2}[\left\|\hat{W}^T\right\|^2 L_\phi^2 + \|k_v\|^2 + L_\psi]\|e_{ET}\|^2 + \mathscr{B}_{3b},\end{aligned} \tag{9.39}$$

where $\mathscr{B}_{3b} = \frac{1}{2}\|W^T \phi(z) - \hat{W}^T \phi(\hat{z}) + \tau_d + \varepsilon\|^2 + \mathscr{B}_{3oa}$. Similar to the simplification process preceding (9.38), we get

$$\begin{aligned}\dot{\mathscr{L}} \leq & -(2\lambda_{\min}(k_v) - 3)\left\|\dot{\hat{e}}(t)\right\|^2 - (2\lambda_{\min}(k_v) - 3 - \sigma)\|\lambda e(t)\|^2 \\ & - \eta_1 \|\tilde{x}_1\|^2 - \eta_2 \|\tilde{x}_2\|^2 + \mathscr{B}_{3b}.\end{aligned} \tag{9.40}$$

To obtain (9.40), choose $\|e_{ET}\|^2 \leq \mu_k \|\lambda e\|^2$ with $\mu_k = 2\sigma / [\left\|\hat{W}^T\right\|^2 L_\phi^2 + \|k_v\|^2 + L_\psi]$.

- At the event-triggering instants, consider the Lyapunov function $\mathscr{L}$. The first difference $\Delta\mathscr{L} = \Delta L(\hat{r}, \tilde{W}) + \Delta L_o$. Observe that at $t = t_k$ for all $k \in \{0, \mathbb{N}\}$, $\hat{r}^+ = \hat{r}$ and $\tilde{x}^+ = \tilde{x}$. Therefore, $\Delta\mathscr{L} = \frac{1}{2}tr(\tilde{W}^{+T}\tilde{W}^+) - \frac{1}{2}tr(\tilde{W}^T\tilde{W}) + \Delta L_o$. From the definition $\tilde{W}^+ = W - \hat{W}^+$, we have $\tilde{W}^+ = \tilde{W}(t) - \Gamma\phi(z)\hat{r}^T + \kappa\Gamma\hat{W}(t)$.
- Substituting the first difference of the controller NN weight estimation error from (9.28) and the first difference ΔL_o from Lemma 9.3, reveals $\Delta\mathscr{L} \leq -\frac{\kappa}{8}(\lambda_{min}(\Gamma) - 8\kappa\|\Gamma\|^2)\|\tilde{W}\|^2 - \frac{1}{2}\kappa_o\eta_3\|\tilde{W}_o\|^2 + \mathscr{B}_3$, where $\mathscr{B}_3 = \mathscr{B}_2 + \mathscr{B}_{3ob}$. It can be observed during the event-triggering instants and between events that the estimated tracking errors, the observer estimation errors, and the NN weight estimation errors are UB.

Remark 9.4. *As $\hat{r}$ and $\tilde{x}$ converges to their bounds, the actual filtered tracking error converges to its bound. The proofs of Theorems 9.2-9.3, and Lemma 9.3 consider two cases which correspond to the event-triggering instants and inter-event period to ensure boundedness of the closed loop signals. The event-triggering mechanism presented in this section does not exhibit zeno behavior. This is a consequence of the stability results presented in this section and its proof follows arguments similar to that presented in (Sahoo et al., 2016).*

A brief summary of results for the state feedback case is presented next. As a matter of fact, the derivations for the state-feedback case become simpler since an observer becomes unnecessary and the dynamics that result from one's incorporation vanish from the analysis.

Corollary 9.1. *(State-feedback controller) Consider the filtered tracking error dynamics* (9.8). *In addition to the Assumptions 9.1 and 9.2, let the joint velocities be measured. Generate the torque input* (9.7) *by utilizing the approximated dynamics of the robotic manipulator* (9.6), *where the estimated joint velocities are replaced by the actual joint velocities. Consider the weight tuning law* (9.19), *where $\Gamma > 0$, $\kappa > 0$, and $k_v \geq 3$. Let the trigger condition* (9.23) *be satisfied during the inter-event period with $\mu_k, \sigma \in (0,1)$. The tracking error and the NN weight estimation error are locally UB (Narayanan and Jagannathan, 2016c).*

A detailed presentation for the derivation of the state-feedback controller would be highly redundant. To construct the proof for the Corollary 9.1, the estimated values used in the arguments of the proof to Theorem 9.3 should be replaced with the measured values.

9.1.3 EXAMPLE

In this section, an example involving the event-sampled control of an n-link robotic manipulator (Lewis et al., 1998) are presented. The parameters of the robot manipulator dynamics used in the simulation include (Kim and Lewis, 1999) : $m_1 = 1$, $m_2 = 2.3$, $g = 9.8$, $L_i = 1$ for $i = \{1,2\}$. The controller design variables are selected as $k_v = 30I$, $\lambda = 5$, $\kappa = 0.0001$, $\Gamma = 500$, $L_\phi = 1$, and $\sigma = 0.1$. The observer design parameters are selected as $K = 500$, $K_p = 2$, $K_d = 0.2$, and $\Gamma_o = 6$, $\kappa_o = 0.1$. The initial values of the manipulator system states and the NN weights are chosen at random from $[0,1]$. The trajectory to be tracked by the manipulator system is given by $\sin(\omega t), \cos(\omega t)$ with $\omega = 1$. The NN observer is designed with 26 hidden layer neurons and sigmoid activation and the controller NN is designed with 30 hidden layer neurons with sigmoid activation function. The input to hidden layer weights are randomly selected in the interval $[0, 0.001]$ and held to form an RVFL network. The design parameters for the controller and the observer are similar to those reported in (Kim and Lewis, 1999) and $\tau_d(t) = [8\ \sin(2t)\ 5\ sin(2t)]$.

First, a comparison between the standard event-driven PD control (without the NN compensation in the torque) and the event-driven NN control are presented in Figure 9.2. These can be used to analyze the advantages of the event-sampled NN controller. The Figure 9.2, as expected, demonstrates that the event-driven NN controller improves the performance of the controlled robotic system over

Table 9.2
Output feedback controller design using Configuration 2

Observer dynamics	$\dot{\hat{x}}_1(t) = \hat{x}_2(t) + K_d\tilde{x}_{1,e}(t)$, $\dot{z}_2(t) = \hat{W}_o\sigma_o(\hat{x}_e, \tau) + K\tilde{x}_{1,e}(t)$, and $\hat{x}_2(t) = z_2(t) + K_p\tilde{x}_{1,e}(t)$.
Filtered tracking error dynamics	$M\dot{r}(t) = -V_m r(t) - \tau(t) + f(z) + \tau_d(t)$
Control torque	$\tau(t) = \hat{f}(\breve{z}) + k_v\breve{r}(t)$
Observer NN weight update rule	$\hat{W}_o^+ = \hat{W}_o(t) - K_d\hat{\Gamma}_o\sigma_o(\hat{x})\tilde{x}_1^T - \kappa_o\Gamma_o\hat{W}_o(t), \quad t = t_k$
Controller NN weight update rule	$\hat{W}^+ = \hat{W}(t) + \hat{\Gamma}\phi(\hat{z})\hat{r}^T - \kappa\Gamma\hat{W}(t), \quad t = t_k$
Event-triggering condition - 1	$\|e_{ET}\|^2 \le \mu_k\|\lambda e\|^2$ with $\mu_k = \sigma/(\frac{1}{2}\|k_v\|^2 + L_\psi)$
Event-triggering condition - 2	$\|e_{ET}\|^2 \le \mu_k\|\lambda e\|^2$ with $\mu_k = 2\sigma/[\|\hat{W}^T\|^2 L_\phi^2 + \|k_v\|^2 + L_\psi]$

the event driven PD control similar to the continuous-time NN control as reported in (Lewis et al., 1998).

Case 1: First, the event-triggering condition, which is a function of NN weights is chosen with $\mu_k = 2\sigma/[\|\hat{W}^T\|^2 L_\phi^2 + \|k_v\|^2]$, $\sigma = 0.45$, $L_\phi = 1$, $k_v = 30I$, and the figures correspond to the NN tuning parameters $\Gamma = 0.5$ and $\Gamma_o = 0.6$ with κ, κ_o as chosen above. The initial conditions are same as those stated before. The actual and desired joint variables, and the event-based observer estimation error are plotted in Figure 9.3. Due to the location of the observer, the observer estimation error with event-based feedback remains unaffected. The tracking performance on the other hand converges after the observer error reaches its bound.

Figures 9.3(c) and (d) presents the performance of the event-sampling mechanism. The threshold function, which is defined using the Lyapunov analysis, ensures that the event-triggering error remains bounded. It can also be observed that a total number of events (N_E) is 540 demonstrating the efficacy of the event-sampling and control. The important difference between this ETM with the ETM in Case 2 is that the number of events initially is more in Case 1 and becomes sporadic later, facilitating the NN learning.

Case 2: In the second case, the event-triggering condition, which is not a function of NN weights is evaluated with $\mu_k = 2\sigma/\|k_v\|^2$, $\sigma = 0.0006$, and $k_v = 30I$. In contrast to Case 1, the event-triggering condition does not require an NN at the trigger mechanism, and hence, reduces the computations. The initial conditions were kept the same. The tracking performance and the observer estimation error trajectories are recorded in Figure 9.4. Since the design parameter σ, which affects the event-triggering threshold is adjusted to get a similar cumulative event as in Case 1, similar number of events are recorded. However, it is observed that, in contrast to the Case 1, more events are not triggered in the transient NN learning period. The variation in the number of events with the design parameter σ is summarized in Table 9.3 (Configuration 1). It can be observed that for both the cases, similar cumulative events can result from appropriate choice of σ. The observer convergence time t_o is not affected much, as it has continuous access to the sensor measurements. To avoid redundancy, the results for Configuration 2 are summarized in Table 9.4. In this example, the parameter $L_\psi = 1$ is chosen.

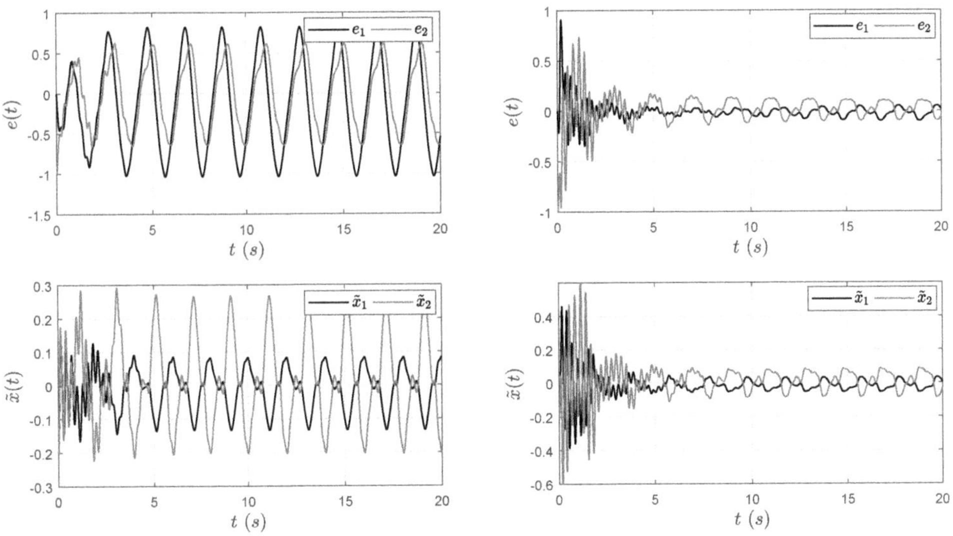

Figure 9.2 Tracking error (a) PD control. (b) NN control. Observer estimation error (c) PD control. (d) NN control.

Table 9.3
Configuration 1: Analysis with σ

$\mu_k = \frac{2\sigma}{[\|\hat{W}^T\|^2 L_\phi^2 + \|k_v\|^2]}$			$\mu_k = \frac{2\sigma}{\|k_v\|^2}$		
σ	N_E	t_o (s)	σ	N_E	t_o (s)
0.05	865	4.257	0.0002	790	4.27
0.1	762	4.244	0.0006	672	4.25
0.3	743	4.466	0.001	636	4.47
0.4	620	4.525	0.003	583	4.54
0.5	513	4.538	0.0045	572	4.321

Thus far we have seen the application of event-triggered control design techniques for robot manipulator. The manipulator dynamics are nonlinear but conform to input-affine structure, which together with the properties of the dyanmics, allowed for designing controllers using a feedback-linearlization using NNs with aperiodic feedback. In the next section, we shall explore the application of event-based NN controller and observer synthesis for an unmanned aerial vehicle. We shall see that this system is governed by nonlinear dynamics and has a strict-feedback form, which requires utilization of backstepping control technique together with NNs and aperiodic feedback data.

9.2 UNMANNED AERIAL VEHICLE: INTRODUCTION

The emergence of quadrotors as unmanned aerial vehicles (UAVs) has resulted in a significant amount of research in efforts to develop effective means by which they can be controlled (Dierks and Jagannathan, 2009c; Voos, 2006; Madani and Benallegue, 2007; Issam and Qingbo, 2014; Lee et al., 2007). In particular, the work in (Dierks and Jagannathan, 2009c) presented a novel output-feedback controller with the use of NNs. The objectives of the proposed controller in (Dierks and

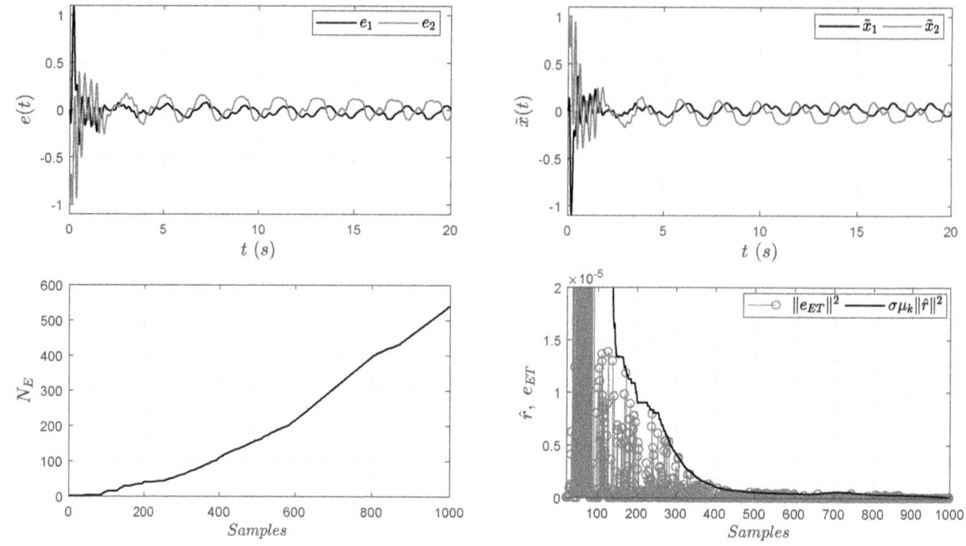

Figure 9.3 Case 1: (a) Tracking error. (b) Observer estimation error. (c) Cumulative number of events. (d) Event-triggering error and threshold.

Table 9.4
Configuration 2: Analysis with σ

$\mu_k = \frac{2\sigma}{[\|\hat{W}^T\|^2 L_\phi^2+\|k_v\|^2+L_\psi]}$			$\mu_k = \frac{\sigma}{(\frac{1}{2}\|k_v\|^2+L_\psi)}$		
σ	N_E	t_o (s)	σ	N_E	t_o (s)
0.05	850	4.240	0.0002	801	4.283
0.1	772	4.242	0.0006	720	4.522
0.3	750	4.457	0.001	663	6.367
0.4	564	6.257	0.003	591	6.518
0.5	525	6.268	0.0045	561	8.576

Jagannathan, 2009c) were to alleviate the need for unnecessary sensors by introducing an observer and to compensate for unknown nonlinear dynamics by making use of the universal approximation property of the NNs. The use of NNs has proven to be a very powerful in the control for a quadrotor UAV. By implementing an NN observer, thereby relaxing the need for full knowledge of the state vector, and by using NNs to compensate for uncertainties, a greater degree of flexibility is made available for engineers. In this section, we shall consider designing such a controller in an event-triggered feedback framework.

In order to do this, we shall revisit the output feedback control design process as presented by Dierks and Jagannathan (2009c). First an observer design is briefly presented, allowing the need for a full knowledge of the state-vector to be avoided. Next, a kinematic controller is designed in order to find a desired translational velocity such that the UAV's position converges to a desired trajectory, which is selected as an external input; additionally, it is in the kinematic controller that the quadrotor's desired orientation is found. Then, the information provided by the kinematic controller is used in the design of a virtual controller wherein a desired rotational velocity is determined such that the UAV's orientation converges to its desired value. In these developments, we shall see that the

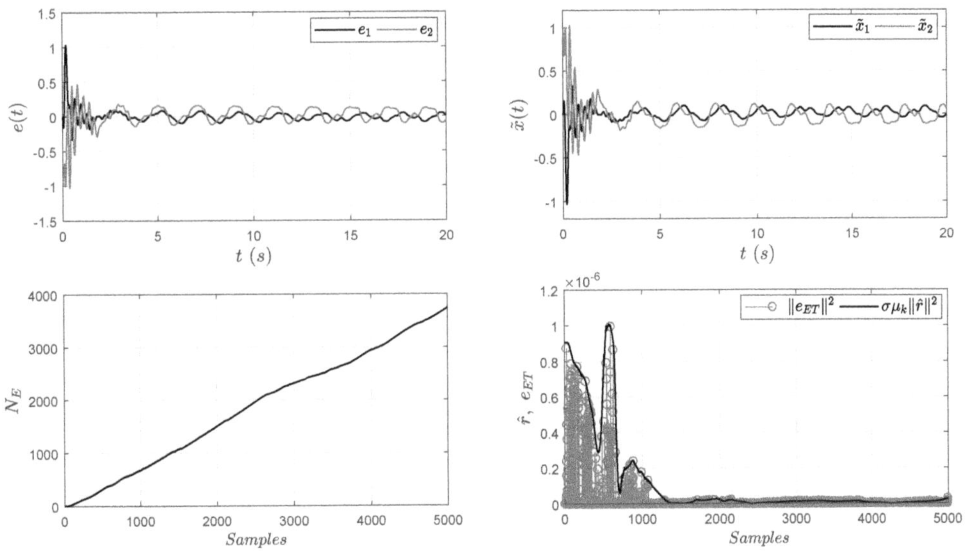

Figure 9.4 Case 2: (a) Tracking error. (b) Observer estimation error. (c) Cumulative number of events. (d) Event-triggering error and threshold.

effects of event-based sampling is injected either implicitly through the NN approximation errors or explicitly through an intermittently updated state-vector.

Finally, we shall see that for a complex quadrotor UAV system, the benefits of event-sampling are two-fold: first, computational costs would be reduced due to aperiodic tuning of NN weights. With fewer computations being performed, battery life and, subsequently, flight time, could be extended. Secondly, event-sampling may also save in communications costs. In a quadrotor UAV system, the regular transmission of data from external sensors, such as GPS and gyro readings, is essential for stable flight and, in these transmissions, packet-losses are inevitable. A reduction in the number of samples being used would minimize the effects of these losses and save in communication costs.

In order to accomplish the incorporation of event-sampling in the control of a quadrotor UAV, first, it is shown how the system exhibits ISS-like behavior with respect to bounded measurement errors; this result is a necessary requirement in order to implement the event-sampled controller because it ensures the existence of nonzero inter-event times. Next, it is necessary to demonstrate that the measurement errors remain bounded for all time. This is demonstrated by considering the dynamics of the system at event-sampling instants as well as during inter-event periods. The boundedness of the measurement errors during inter-event periods is guaranteed by the implementation of an event-execution law, which we shall derive as well.

9.2.1 BACKGROUND AND PROBLEM STATEMENT

In this section, we begin with an introduction on the notations used in the rest of this chapter.

9.2.1.1 Notations and Background

The measurement errors that result from event-sampling is denoted by Ξ. In order to distinguish event-sampled variables with their time-sampled counterparts, this symbol will appear as a subscript; for example, the event-sampled position of the quadrotor is denoted by ρ_Ξ. A formal definition for Ξ is presented in the background section.

The states of the quadrotor UAV are given by its measured coordinate position, $\rho = [x,y,z]^T$; its orientation $\Theta = [\phi, \theta, \psi]^T$ (roll, pitch, yaw), which are measured with respect to the inertial fixed frame; its translational velocity in the body fixed frame, $v = \left[v_{xb}, v_{yb}, v_{zb}\right]^T$; and its rotational velocity in the body fixed frame, $\omega = \left[\omega_{xb}, \omega_{yb}, \omega_{zb}\right]^T$. With these, the kinematics of the quadrotor can be written as (Dierks and Jagannathan, 2009c)

$$\dot{\rho} = Rv \tag{9.41}$$

and

$$\dot{\Theta} = T\omega. \tag{9.42}$$

The translational rotation matrix relating a vector in the body fixed frame to the inertial coordinate frame is defined by

$$R(\Theta) = R = \begin{bmatrix} c_\theta c_\psi & s_\phi s_\theta c_\psi - c_\phi s_\psi & c_\phi s_\theta c_\psi + s_\phi s_\psi \\ c_\theta s_\psi & s_\phi s_\theta s_\psi - c_\phi c_\psi & c_\phi s_\theta s_\psi - s_\phi c_\psi \\ -s_\theta & s_\phi c_\theta & c_\phi c_\theta \end{bmatrix},$$

where $s_{(\bullet)}$ and $c_{(\bullet)}$ are used as abbreviations for $\sin(\bullet)$ and $\cos(\bullet)$, respectively. Moreover, the rotational transformation matrix from the fixed body to the inertial coordinate frame is defined with its inverse as

$$T(\Theta) = T = \begin{bmatrix} 1 & s_\phi t_\theta & c_\phi t_\theta \\ 0 & c_\phi & -s_\phi \\ 0 & \frac{s_\phi}{c_\theta} & \frac{c_\phi}{c_\theta} \end{bmatrix}, \quad T^{-1} = \begin{bmatrix} 1 & 0 & -s_\theta \\ 0 & c_\phi & s_\phi c_\theta \\ 0 & -s_\phi & c_\phi c_\theta \end{bmatrix},$$

where $t_{(\bullet)}$ is used as an abbreviation for $\tan(\bullet)$. Lastly, define the augmented transformation matrix $A = \text{diag}\{R, T\}$.

9.2.1.2 Problem Statement

The dynamics of the quadrotor UAV in the body fixed frame are given by (Dierks and Jagannathan, 2009c)

$$M\begin{bmatrix} \dot{v}(t) \\ \dot{\omega}(t) \end{bmatrix} = \bar{S}(\omega)\begin{bmatrix} v(t) \\ \omega(t) \end{bmatrix} + \begin{bmatrix} N_1(v) \\ N_2(\omega) \end{bmatrix} + \begin{bmatrix} G(R) \\ 0_{3\times 1} \end{bmatrix} + U(t) + \tau_d(t), \tag{9.43}$$

where $M = \text{diag}\{mI_{3\times 3}, J\}$, with m being a positive scalar representing the total mass of the UAV and J being a positive definite inertia matrix; $\bar{S}(\omega) = diag\{-mS(\omega), S(J\omega)\}$, where $S(\bullet)$ is a skew symmetric matrix satisfying $h^T Sh = 0$ for any appropriately dimensioned vector h; $N_1(v)$ and $N_2(\omega)$ are nonlinear aerodynamic effects; $G(R) = mgR^T(\Theta)E_z$ is the gravity vector, with $g = 9.8\,{}^{m}/{}_{s^2}$ and $E_z = [0, 0, 1]^T$; $U = [0, 0, u_1, u_2]^T$ is an augmented vector containing the control inputs corresponding to the total thrust, u_1, and to the rotational torques, $u_2 = [u_{21}, u_{22}, u_{23}]^T$, corresponding to roll, pitch, and yaw, respectively; and $\tau_d = \left[\tau_{d1}^T, \tau_{d2}^T\right]^T$ represents unknown, bounded disturbances such that $\|\tau_d\| \le \tau_M$ for a known positive constant, τ_M.

Before giving the control objective, a definition of the measurement errors that result from event-sampling is introduced. Define the measurement errors to be

$$\Xi_\chi(t) = \chi_\Xi(t_l) - \chi(t), \forall t \in [t_l, t_{l+1}), \tag{9.44}$$

where, in general, $\chi(t)$, represents a time-sampled state variable. Moreover, $\chi_\Xi(t_l)$ denotes the event-sampled state variable that was measured at the event-sampling instant t_l; it is this event-sampled variable that is stored in the controller during the inter-event period $[t_l, t_{l+1})$. Finally, $\Xi_\chi(t)$ is the measurement error that results from intermittent sampling. The introduction of this error presents an additional challenge in the control objective in that it necessitates additional considerations that warrant the controller's stable performance. In particular, it is necessary to design an event-triggering mechanism that ensures that the values that are stored are being updated frequently enough for the controller to be able to achieve acceptable performance while reducing the number of computations.

The control objective is to design an event-sampled output-feedback controller for (9.43) such that the UAV follows a desired trajectory given by $\rho_d = [x_d, y_d, z_d]^T$ and a desired yaw, ψ_d, while maintaining stable flight. This requires knowledge of the quadrotor's dynamics as well as knowledge of the UAV's translational and rotational velocities. However, these requirements are relaxed by utilizing the universal approximation property of NNs (Lewis et al., 1998) in order to estimate the uncertainties and unknown quantities. In particular, in order to avoid the measurement of the UAV's state-vector, an NN observer is implemented to estimate the translational and rotational velocity vector, which are not measured. The estimated values are used in the kinematic controller, the NN virtual controller, and the NN dynamic controller. With these, we shall see that it is possible to design an event-sampled control law that achieves the desired control objective. In order to ensure that the control law is being updated frequently enough for the UAV to achieve its tracking objective, an event-execution law is derived such that the measurement errors remain bounded for all time.

In the analyses, the following assumptions are made.

Assumption 9.3. *The states of the reference trajectory, ρ_d and ψ_d, remain bounded (Dierks and Jagannathan, 2009c). The state-vector corresponding to the UAV's velocity is not available whereas the system (9.43) is observable (Dierks and Jagannathan, 2009c). There are no transmission or computation time delays (Tabuada, 2007). The dynamics of the system (9.43) are locally Lipschitz.*

With these considerations in mind, the derivation of the event-sampled quadrotor UAV controller is presented next. The derivation of the event-sampled controller is presented as two sections: In the first section, the observer design is considered and, in the following section, the controller design is presented.

9.2.2 OBSERVER DESIGN

In order to relax the need for state-vector measurability, an observer is designed to estimate unknown values. Subsequently, the estimated values are used in the controller. Since the stability of the controller relies on accurate sensor readings, the observer's quick convergence is imperative. The introduction of event-sampling only adds to the challenge of designing an observer that performs well enough for the control objectives to be accomplished. Additionally, the implementation of the event-triggering mechanism must also be taken into consideration. For these reasons, the placement of the observer is taken to be at the sensor (similar to the Configuration 1 presented for the case of the robot manuipulator application); practically, this means that, even with event-sampling, the observer can estimate the state-vector continuously, allowing for quicker convergence as well as for sufficient information for the implementation of the event-execution law.

Although the NN observer estimates the state-vector continuously, the NN itself is only updated at event-sampled instants. With a continuously updated state-vector, it would not be correct to directly assign measurement errors to the estimated states. However, since the NN is only being updated intermittently, there is an approximation error due to the event-sampling. Using the fact that the inputs of the NN are only be updated at events, the ideal NN approximation can be manipulated in a manner that allows event-sampling measurement errors to be extracted from the approximation error, resulting from intermittent updates. The measurement errors that are introduced in this section include Ξ_{SX}, $\hat{\Xi}_{SX}$, and $\check{\Xi}_{SV}$, correpsonding to the quadrotor's measured position and orientation, estimated position and orientation, and measured and estimated velocity, respectively. Once the measurement errors are extracted, it is not difficult to account for their effects when the event-execution law is designed.

Begin by defining the augmented vectors $X = \left[\rho^T, \Theta^T\right]^T$ and $V = \left[v^T, \omega^T\right]^T$. Using these augmented vectors, the dynamics (9.41), (9.42), and (9.43) can be rewritten with

$$\begin{aligned} \dot{X}(t) &= AV(t) + \xi_1(t) \\ \dot{V}(t) &= f_o(x_o) + \bar{G} + M^{-1}U(t) + \bar{\tau}_d(t), \end{aligned} \tag{9.45}$$

where ξ_1 represents bounded sensor measurement noise such that $\|\xi_1\| \leq \xi_{1M}$; $\bar{\tau}_d = \left[\tau_{d1}/m, \left[J^{-1}\tau_{d1}\right]^T\right]$ satisfies $\bar{\tau}_d \leq M_M \tau_M$ with $M_M = \left\|M^{-1}\right\|$; $\bar{G} = M^{-1}G(R)$; and $U_\Xi = \left[0, 0, u_{1\Xi}, u_{2\Xi}\right]^T$ is the event-sampled control input which is addressed in later derivations. Note that there is an explicit measurement error present in U_Ξ, however, since this term is canceled out in the observer analysis, it is not considered. Furthermore, by observation of (9.43), $f_o(x_o) = M^{-1}\left[\bar{S}(\omega)V + \left[N_1(v), N_2(\omega)\right]^T\right]$ are unknown dynamics.

Next, introduce the change of variables, $Z = V$, and denote the observer estimates for X and V with hats, specifically $\hat{X}$ and $\hat{V}$, respectively. Finally, the observer estimation error is denoted with a tilde, $\tilde{X} = X - \hat{X}$. With these, the observer takes the form (Dierks and Jagannathan, 2009c)

$$\begin{aligned} \dot{\hat{X}}(t) &= A\hat{Z} + K_{o1}\tilde{X} \\ \dot{\hat{Z}}(t) &= \hat{f}_{o1\Xi} + \bar{G} + K_{o2}A^{-1}\tilde{X} + M^{-1}U_\Xi \\ \hat{V}(t) &= \hat{Z} + K_{o3}A^{-1}\tilde{X}, \end{aligned} \tag{9.46}$$

where K_{o1}, K_{o2}, and K_{o3} are positive design constants. Here A^{-1} is bounded by $\left\|A^{-1}\right\| \leq A_M^I$, where A_M^I is a positive constant. Additionally, $\hat{f}_{o1\Xi}$ is the event-sampled NN estimate of the unknown function, $f_{o1}(x_o) = f_o(x_o) + \left[A^T - K_{o3}\dot{A}^{-1}\right]\tilde{X}$; the second term of the unknown function, $\left[A^T - K_{o3}\dot{A}^{-1}\right]\tilde{X}$, arised in the derivation for the observer estimation error dynamics.

Recalling the *universal approximation property of NNs* (Lewis et al., 1998), for an unknown, smooth function, $f_N(x_N)$, its NN approximation is denoted by $f_N(x_N) = W_N^T\sigma\left(V_N^T x_N\right) + \varepsilon_N$, where W_N is the ideal NN weights matrix that is bounded such that $\|W_N\|_F \leq W_M$; $\sigma(\bullet)$ is the activation function in the hidden layers, which is chosen to be the logarithmic sigmoid function and has the property $\|\sigma\| \leq \sqrt{N}$, with N being the number of hidden layer neurons in the NN; V_N consists of randomly selected constant weights; and ε_N is the NN reconstruction error, which is bounded such that $\|\varepsilon_N\| \leq \varepsilon_M$. Since the ideal NN weights are not available, it becomes necessary to introduce NN weight estimates, $\hat{W}_N$, for which an acceptable tuning law is derived later in this section. Specifically, the ideal, continuousl updated approximation for the unknown function corresponding to the observer is given by $f_{o1}(x_o) = W_o^T\sigma\left(V_o^T x_o\right) + \varepsilon_o = W_o^T\sigma_o + \varepsilon_o$, where the target NN weights are bounded by $\|W_o\| \leq W_{Mo}$ and the approximation error is bounded by $\|\varepsilon_o\| \leq \varepsilon_{Mo}$. Moreover, using estimated weights, the approximation for the unknown function in (9.46) is given by $\hat{f}_{o1\Xi} = \hat{W}_{o\Xi}\sigma_o\left(V_o^T\hat{x}_o\right) = \hat{W}_{o\Xi}\hat{\sigma}_o$ and its input is given with $\hat{x}_o = \left[1, \hat{X}^T, \hat{V}^T, \tilde{X}^T\right]^T$.

In order to account for the effects of intermittent NN updates, begin by adding and subtracting $W_o^T\sigma(x_{o\Xi}) = W_o^T\sigma_{o\Xi}$ to the ideal approximation

$$\begin{aligned} f_{o1}(x_o) =& W_o^T\sigma_{o\Xi} - W_o^T\sigma_{o\Xi} + W_o^T\sigma_o + \varepsilon_o \\ =& W_o^T\sigma_{o\Xi} + W_o^T\left[\sigma_o - \sigma_{o\Xi}\right] + \varepsilon_o. \end{aligned} \tag{9.47}$$

The expression given by (9.47) can be interpreted as the ideal approximation given by an intermittently updated NN and $W_o^T\left[\sigma_o - \sigma_{o\Xi}\right]$ can be viewed as the approximation error that results from the intermittent updating. As the frequency of events increases, the values of the event-sampled variables approach those of their continuously sampled counterparts. As a result, with a very large number of events, the approximation error caused by event-sampling begins to vanish and the ideal

NN approximation is eventually reverted back to its original form. With this, the engineering trade-off is clear: Fewer events will yield more computational efficiency, however, the efficiency comes at the expense of accuracy. With regards to its effects on stability, the approximation error that results from intermittent NN updates is addressed by designing an event-execution law that ensures acceptable behavior in the closed-loop dynamics; the details for this are be shown in Theorem 9.6, Case 2.

Next, by adding and subtracting $\left[A^T - K_{o3}\dot{A}^{-1}\right]\tilde{X}$ and using the information in (9.45) and (9.46), the estimation error dynamics are found to be

$$\begin{aligned}\dot{\tilde{X}}(t) &= A\tilde{V}(t) - [K_{o1} - K_{o3}]\tilde{X}(t) + \xi_1(t)\\ \dot{\tilde{Z}}(t) &= \left[f_o + \left[A^T - K_{o3}\dot{A}^{-1}\right]\tilde{X}(t)\right]\\ &\quad - \hat{f}_{o1\Xi} - K_{o2}A^{-1}\tilde{X}(t) - \left[A^T - K_{o3}\dot{A}^{-1}\right]\tilde{X}(t) - \varepsilon_{o\Xi} + \bar{\tau}_d(t).\end{aligned} \tag{9.48}$$

Next, observe that, from (9.46), $\tilde{V} = V - \hat{V} = \tilde{Z} - K_{o3}A^{-1}\tilde{X}$. The derivative of this expression can be taken and, by adding and subtracting $W_o^T\sigma(\hat{x}_{o\Xi}) = W_o^T\hat{\sigma}_{o\Xi}$ as well as using (9.47) and (9.48), the estimation error dynamics corresponding to V are found to be

$$\begin{aligned}\dot{\tilde{V}} &= \left[f_o + \left[A^T - K_{o3}\dot{A}^{-1}\right]\tilde{X}\right] - W_o^T\sigma\left(V_o^T\hat{x}_{o\Xi}\right) + W_o^T\sigma\left(V_o^T\hat{x}_{o\Xi}\right) - \hat{f}_{o1\Xi} - K_{o2}A^{-1}\tilde{X}\\ &\quad - \left[A^T - K_{o3}\dot{A}^{-1}\right]\tilde{X} + \bar{\tau}_d - K_{o3}\dot{A}^{-1}\tilde{X} - K_{o3}A^{-1}\left[A\tilde{V} - [K_{o1} - K_{o3}]\tilde{X} + \xi_1\right]\\ &= -K_{o3}\tilde{V} + \tilde{f}_{o\Xi} - A^{-1}\left[K_{o2} - K_{o3}\left[K_{o1} - K_{o3}\right]\right]\tilde{X} - A^T\tilde{X} + \varepsilon_{o\Xi} + \xi_2,\end{aligned} \tag{9.49}$$

where $\tilde{f}_{o\Xi} = \left[W_o^T - \hat{W}_{o\Xi}^T\right]\hat{\sigma}_{o\Xi}$ and $\varepsilon_{o\Xi} = W_o^T\left[\sigma_o - \sigma_{o\Xi}\right] + W_o^T\left[\sigma_{o\Xi} - \hat{\sigma}_{o\Xi}\right]$, which is equal to $W_o^T\left[\sigma_o - \hat{\sigma}_{o\Xi}\right]$, contains the approximation error due to event-sampling, and $\xi_2 = \varepsilon_o + \bar{\tau}_d - K_{o3}A^{-1}\xi_1$ is bounded such that $\|\xi_2\| \le \xi_{2M}$, where $\xi_{2M} = \varepsilon_{Mo} + M_M\tau_M + K_{o3}A_M^I\xi_{1M}$. These dynamics given by (9.48) and (9.49) are used in demonstrating the boundedness of the observer subsystem when the NN is updated intermittently.

The following theorem is given in order to demonstrate that the observer described in this section generates an ISS-like Lyapunov function with respect to bounded measurement errors. The results for Theorem 9.4 are needed in order to make conclusions on the inter-event periods being bounded away from zero.

Theorem 9.4. *(NN Observer Boundedness): Consider the observer given by (9.46) with estimation error dynamics described by* (9.48) *and (9.49). Furthermore, let the NN weights be updated with*

$$\dot{\hat{W}}_{o\Xi} = F_o\hat{\sigma}_o\tilde{X}^T - \kappa_{o1}F_o\hat{W}_{o\Xi}, \tag{9.50}$$

where $F_o = F_o^T > 0$ and $\kappa_{o1} > 0$ are constant design parameters, and let the initial weights be in a compact set. Moreover, let the activation function for the NN be Lipschitz. Finally, let the event-sampling measurement errors corresponding to X, $\hat{X}$, and $\dot{X}$ be assumed to be bounded such that $\Xi_{SX} \le \Xi_{X\,max}$, $\hat{\Xi}_{SX} \le \hat{\Xi}_{X\,max}$, and $\check{\Xi}_{SV} \le \check{\Xi}_{V\,max}$, respectively. Then, there exist design constants, K_{o1}, K_{o2}, and K_{o3}, such that the observer estimation errors, $\tilde{X}$ and $\tilde{V}$, as well as the observer NN weight estimation errors, $\tilde{W}_{o\Xi}$, are locally universally ultimately bounded (UUB).

Sketch of Proof:

- We shall consider the positive-definite Lyapunov candidate

$$V_{o\Xi} = \frac{1}{2}\tilde{X}^T\tilde{X} + \frac{1}{2}\tilde{V}^T\tilde{V} + \frac{1}{2}\mathrm{tr}\left\{\tilde{W}_{o\Xi}^T F_o^{-1}\tilde{W}_{o\Xi}\right\}. \tag{9.51}$$

- By invoking known bounding conditions, and by using properties of the matrix trace operation, it is discovered that

$$\dot{V}_{o\Xi} \leq -\left[\frac{[K_{o1} - K_{o3}]}{2} - \frac{N_o}{\kappa_{o1}}\right] \left\|\tilde{X}\right\|^2 - \left[\frac{K_{o3}}{2} - \frac{N_o}{\kappa_{o1}} - \frac{1}{2}\right] \left\|\tilde{V}\right\|^2 - \frac{\kappa_{o1}}{4} \left\|\tilde{W}_{o\Xi}\right\|_F^2$$
$$+ \kappa_{o1} W_{Mo}^2 + \frac{\xi_{1M}^2}{2[K_{o1} - K_{o3}]} + \frac{\xi_{2M}^2}{2K_{o3}} + \frac{1}{2}\varepsilon_{o\Xi}^2 \tag{9.52}$$

after completion of squares with respect to $\left\|\tilde{X}\right\|$, $\left\|\tilde{V}\right\|$, and $\left\|\tilde{W}_{o\Xi}\right\|$.
- It is at this point that the measurement errors are extracted from the approximation error caused by intermittent NN updates. In order to do this, the Lipschitz condition on the NN activation function is to be invoked.
- Additionally, observe that the unknown function that is approximated by the NN is defined in terms of V and $\tilde{X}$. With these in consideration, it is discovered

$$\varepsilon_{o\Xi}^2 \leq \frac{1}{2} W_{Mo}^4 + \frac{1}{2} L_\sigma \left\|\Xi_{SX}\right\|^4 + \frac{1}{2} L_\sigma \left\|\hat{\Xi}_{SX}\right\|^4 + \frac{1}{2} L_\sigma \left\|\check{\Xi}_{SV}\right\|^4, \tag{9.53}$$

where L_σ is the Lipschitz constant and $\check{\Xi}_{SV}$, Ξ_{SX}, and $\hat{\Xi}_{SX}$ are the event-sampling-driven measurement errors corresponding to V, $\hat{V}$ and X, $\hat{X}$, respectively.
- Note that the measurement error corresponding to V is rewritten in terms of $\dot{X}$; this is done because, in practice, the measured velocity is not available and, therefore, it would not be possible to implement an execution law directly for V. This problem can be circumvented by placing a differentiator at the sensor and considering a measurement error in terms of $\dot{X}$. Finally, (9.52) and (9.53) are combined to get

$$\dot{V}_{o\Xi} \leq -K_{\tilde{X}} \left\|\tilde{X}\right\|^2 - K_{\tilde{V}} \left\|\tilde{V}\right\|^2 - K_{Wo} \left\|\tilde{W}_{o\Xi}\right\|_F^2 + B_o, \tag{9.54}$$

where $B_o = \eta_o + \frac{1}{4} L_\sigma \Xi_{X\max}^4 + \frac{1}{4} L_\sigma \hat{\Xi}_{X\max}^4 + \frac{1}{4} L_\sigma \check{\Xi}_{V\max}$ with $\eta_o = \kappa_{o1} W_{Mo}^2 + \frac{1}{4} W_{Mo}^4 + \xi_{1M}^2 / [2[K_{o1} - K_{o3}]] + \xi_{2M}^2 / [2K_{o3}]$; $K_{\tilde{X}} = [K_{o1} - K_{o3}]/2 - N_o/\kappa_{o1}$; $K_{\tilde{V}} = [K_{o1} - 1]/2 - N_o/\kappa_{o1}$; and $K_{Wo} = \kappa_{o1}/4$. Finally, (9.54) is less than zero provided that $K_{o1} > K_{o3} + [2N_o]/\kappa_{o1}$ and $K_{o3} > [2N_o]/\kappa_{o1} + 1$ and the following inequalities hold:

$$\left\|\tilde{X}\right\| > \sqrt{\frac{B_o}{K_{\tilde{X}}}} \quad \text{or} \quad \left\|\tilde{V}\right\| > \sqrt{\frac{B_o}{K_{\tilde{V}}}} \quad \text{or} \left\|\tilde{W}_{o\Xi}\right\|_F > \sqrt{\frac{B_o}{K_{S\max}^2}}. \tag{9.55}$$

- Note that the bounds are primarily dependent on the observer NN. Consequently, by appropriate choice of the observer NN (e.g., number of neurons), the bounds on the observed states will reduce.

Remark 9.5. *The results from Theorem 9.4 can be easily used to demonstrate how the observer generates an ISS-like Lyapunov function with respect to bounded measurement errors. This result, along with the assumption that the dynamics (9.43) are Lipschitz, fulfills the necessary requirements needed to show the existence of nonzero inter-event periods (Tabuada, 2007). However, rather than showing how the observer generates an ISS-like Lyapunov function by itself, (9.54) will be used later when the closed-loop dynamics are considered and it will be demonstrated how the whole system exhibits ISS-like behavior.*

In Theorem 9.4, the measurement errors were assumed to be bounded. However, in order to implement the event-sampled controller, it must be demonstrated that the measurement errors are, in fact, bounded for all time. This can be done by, first, considering the system dynamics when event-sampling measurement errors are zero and, second, considering the system dynamics with nonzero measurement errors. With nonzero measurement errors, an event-execution law can be designed in order to ensure that the system dynamics remain stable. In this chapter, a single event-execution law will be designed when the closed-loop dynamics are considered in Theorem 9.6. However, before proceeding, the following lemma is given in order to show that the observer with an intermittently updated NN is eligible for implementation in the event-sampled controller.

Lemma 9.4. *Consider the observer given by (9.46) with estimation error dynamics described by* (9.48) *and (9.49). Furthermore, let the NN weights be updated with (9.50) with initial weights in a compact set. Then, there exist design constants, K_{o1}, K_{o2}, and K_{o3}, such that the observer estimation errors, $\tilde{X}$ and $\tilde{V}$, as well as the observer NN weight estimation errors, $\tilde{W}_{o\Xi}$, are locally UUB for all time.*

Sketch of Proof: Here the proof is constructed in two steps.

- *Case 1.* In this case, the NN weights are updated using (9.50) and, furthermore, all approximation and measurement errors that are caused by event-sampling are taken to be zero. As a result, $\varepsilon_{o\Xi}$ is absent from the observer estimation error dynamics for $\dot{\tilde{V}}$. Because of this, the coefficient defined in Theorem 9.4 corresponding to $\|\tilde{V}\|^2$ needs to be changed to $K_{\tilde{V}} = [K_{o1}]/2 - N_o/\kappa_{o1}$ and the bounded term needs to be revised to $B_o = \kappa_{o1}W_{Mo}^2 + \xi_{1M}^2/[2[K_{o1} - K_{o3}]] + \xi_{2M}^2/[2K_{o3}]$. Additionally, the event-sampled term that was previously combined with the approximation error due to intermittent updates no longer needs to be considered in the presence of measurement errors. Therefore, the expression for ξ_2 becomes $\xi_2 = \varepsilon_o + \bar{\tau}_d - K_{o3}A^{-1}\xi_1 + W_o^T[\sigma_o - \hat{\sigma}_o]$ with $\|\xi_2\| \leq \xi_{2M}$, where $\xi_{2M} = \varepsilon_{Mo} + M_M\tau_M + K_{o3}A_M^I\xi_{1M} + 2W_{Mo}\sqrt{N_o}$. With these changes in mind, and by selecting gains satisfying $K_{o1} > K_{o3} + [2N_o]/\kappa_{o1}$ and $K_{o3} > [2N_o]/\kappa_{o1}$, it can be concluded that (9.54) is less than zero and that all signals in the observer are locally UUB.
- *Case 2.* In this case, the NN weights are held between events, and therefore, the effects of the third term in (9.51) vanish when the derivative is taken. However, since the approximation error caused by event-sampling is injected through the estimation error dynamics, $\dot{\tilde{V}}$, it becomes necessary to account for the nonzero measurement errors. Using an approach similar to what was done for *Case 1*, the coefficients are updated with $B_o = W_{Mo}^4/4 + \xi_{1M}^2/[2[K_{o1} - K_{o3}]] + \xi_{2M}^2/[2K_{o3}]$; $K_{\tilde{X}} = [K_{o1} - K_{o3}]/2$; $K_{\tilde{V}} = [K_{o1} - 2]/2$; and $K_{Wo} = -N_o/2$. With these changes in mind, the expression for $\dot{V}_{o\Xi}$ is rewritten with

$$\dot{V}_{o\Xi} \leq -K_{\tilde{X}}\|\tilde{X}\|^2 - K_{\tilde{V}}\|\tilde{V}\|^2 - K_{Wo}\|\tilde{W}_{o\Xi}\|_F^2 + B_o + \frac{1}{4}L_\sigma\|\Xi_{SX}\|^4 + \frac{1}{4}L_\sigma\|\hat{\Xi}_{SX}\|^4 + \frac{1}{4}L_\sigma\|\check{\Xi}_{SV}\|^4. \quad (9.56)$$

  In this case, the measurement errors cannot be assumed to be bounded and it becomes necessary to address their effects. This could be accomplished by designing an event-execution law that takes the form

$$\|\Xi_\chi\|^4 \leq \gamma_\chi\mu_\chi\|e_\chi\|^2, \quad (9.57)$$

  where, in general, $0 < \gamma_\chi, \mu_\chi < 1$ are design constants and $e_\chi = \chi_d - \chi$ is the tracking error corresponding to the measurement error. An execution-law bearing strong resemblance to (9.57) is what is presented in this chapter. However, the benefits of this design cannot be easily seen by considering the observer dynamics alone and (9.57) is given here only for illustration purposes. When the tracking errors are addressed in the closed-loop dynamics, we shall demonstrate how an execution law in the form of (9.57) can be used to eliminate the measurement errors from the observer subsystem.
- The results for *Case 1* and *Case 2* can be combined in order to make conclusions which apply for all time. However, since the dynamics in *Case 2* can only be fully assessed in the

closed-loop, this final combination is not be done here, but, instead, is shown for the entire UAV system. From the results that are presented, however, it can be concluded that, with an appropriately designed event-execution law, the observer with an intermittently updated NN qualifies as a candidate for an event-sampled output feedback controller.

Remark 9.6. *As we shall see in the subsequent sections, a single event-execution law is designed for the whole system. In other words, the measurement errors that originate in the observer are combined with the measurement errors in the controller and a single condition is used as the basis by which events occur. Moreover, when an event does occur, both the observer NN as well as the controller are updated with the most recent position and orientation sensor measurements and velocity observer estimates.*

Next, the event-sampled controller design is presented. First, the virtual controller is briefly addressed, then the kinematic and dynamic controllers is designed under the influence of event-sampling.

9.2.3 CONTROL OF QUADROTOR UAV

A natural progression for the derivation of the controller would be to begin with the design of the kinematic controller, to proceed with the virtual controller, and to conclude with an analysis for the dynamic controller. This progression is followed in (Dierks and Jagannathan, 2009c). However, in order to incorporate the effects of event-sampling, it is, perhaps, easier to first address the stability of the virtual controller and then consider the kinematic and dynamic controllers. The reason for this is that the assessment of the virtual controller's stability does not involve any explicit presence of event-sampling measurement errors and its analysis can be quickly summarized. An important consideration that needs to be made in the development of event-sampled controllers is in determining how and where the controller injects measurement errors into the system. In the development for the virtual controller, only the stability of the virtual control estimates is considered and the injection of any term into the system is altogether absent. Instead, it is only through the analysis for the kinematic and dynamic controllers, where there is an injection of errors caused by event-sampling. For this reason, the stability of the virtual control estimates is considered first and then the kinematic and dynamic controllers is considered under the influence of event-sampling.

9.2.3.1 Virtual Control Design

In the developments made in this subsection, the stability of the desired virtual control estimates, $\hat{\Theta}_d$ and $\hat{\omega}_d$, as well as the boundedness of the virtual control NN weight estimates, $\hat{W}_\Omega$, are considered. Since the desired virtual controls are written in terms of the UAV's measured position and orientation, there is an explicit presence of event-sampling measurement errors. However, the derivations made for the virtual controller here can only assess the stability of the estimates and not how they are injected into the system.

Begin by defining the virtual controller (Dierks and Jagannathan, 2009c)

$$
\begin{aligned}
\dot{\hat{\Theta}}_{d\Xi}(t) &= T\hat{\Omega}_{d\Xi} + K_{\Omega 1}\tilde{\Theta}_{d\Xi} \\
\dot{\hat{\Omega}}_{d\Xi}(t) &= \hat{f}_{\Omega 1\Xi} + K_{\Omega 2}T^{-1}\tilde{\Theta}_{d\Xi} \\
\hat{\omega}_{d\Xi}(t) &= \hat{\Omega}_{d\Xi} + T^{-1}K_{\Theta}e_{\Theta\Xi} + K_{\Omega 3}T^{-1}\tilde{\Theta}_{d\Xi},
\end{aligned}
\tag{9.58}
$$

where $\hat{f}_{\Omega 1\Xi}$ is the event-sampled NN estimation of the unknown function, $f_{\Omega 1\Xi}(x_\Omega) = f_{\Omega\Xi} + T^T\tilde{\Theta}_{d\Xi} - K_{\Omega 3}\dot{T}^{-1}\tilde{\Theta}_{d\Xi}$ with $f_{\Omega\Xi} = \dot{T}^{-1}\dot{\Theta}_{d\Xi} + T^{-1}\ddot{\Theta}_{d\Xi}$. Specifically, its estimation is given by $\hat{f}_{\Omega 1\Xi} = \hat{W}_{\Omega\Xi}^T\sigma\left(V_\Omega^T\hat{x}_{\Omega\Xi}\right) = \hat{W}_{\Omega\Xi}^T\hat{\sigma}_{\Omega\Xi}$, where its input is $\hat{x}_{\Omega\Xi} = \left[1, \rho_d, \dot{\rho}_d^T, \ddot{\rho}_d^T, \dddot{\rho}_d^T, \Theta_{d\Xi}^T, \hat{\Omega}_{d\Xi}, \hat{V}^T, \tilde{\Theta}_{d\Xi}\right]^T$. Here, the subscript Ξ is used to reinforce the idea that the virtual control NN weight estimates are updated only at event-sampling instants. Additionally, $e_{\Theta\Xi}$ is the UAV's event-sampled orientation tracking error, which is addressed later, and $K_{\Omega 1}$, $K_{\Omega 2}$, $K_{\Omega 3}$, and K_Θ are positive design constants.

Next, choose the NN weight update law

$$\dot{\hat{W}}_{\Omega\Xi}(t) = F_\Omega \hat{\sigma}_{\Omega\Xi} \tilde{\Theta}_{d\Xi}^T - \kappa_{\Omega 1} F_\Omega \hat{W}_{\Omega\Xi}, \tag{9.59}$$

where $F_\Omega = F_\Omega^T > 0$ and $\kappa_{\Omega 1} > 0$ are constant design parameters. Then, using (9.58) and (9.59), the virtual control estimation error dynamics can be determined and the first derivative of the Lyapunov candidate describing the virtual control system, $V_{\Omega\Xi} = \frac{1}{2}\tilde{\Theta}_{d\Xi}^T \tilde{\Theta}_{d\Xi} + \frac{1}{2}\tilde{\omega}_{d\Xi}^T \tilde{\omega}_{d\Xi} + \frac{1}{2}\mathrm{tr}\{\tilde{W}_{\Omega\Xi}^T F_\Omega^{-1} \tilde{W}_{\Omega\Xi}\}$, can be found to satisfy (Dierks and Jagannathan, 2009c)

$$\begin{aligned} \dot{V}_{\Omega\Xi} \leq & -\left[K_{\Omega 1} - K_{\Omega 3} - \frac{N_\Omega}{\kappa_{\Omega 1}}\right] \|\tilde{\Theta}_{d\Xi}\|^2 \\ & -\left[\frac{K_{\Omega 3}}{2} - \frac{N_\Omega}{\kappa_{\Omega 1}}\right] \|\tilde{\omega}_{d\Xi}\|^2 - \frac{\kappa_{\Omega 1}}{4} \|\tilde{W}_{\Omega\Xi}\|_F^2 + \eta_\Omega, \end{aligned} \tag{9.60}$$

where $\eta_\Omega = \kappa_{\Omega 1} W_{M\Omega}^2 + \xi_{\Omega M}^2 / [2K_{\Omega 3}]$ and N_Ω is the number of hidden layer neurons in the virtual control NN. By observation of (9.60), it can be seen that, with appropriate selection of design parameters, all signals in the virtual controller remain bounded (Dierks and Jagannathan, 2009c). Next, the kinematic control and dynamic control is considered under the influence of event-sampling.

9.2.3.2 Injection of Event-Sampled Desired Virtual Control

The tracking errors that correspond to the desired virtual control inputs are with respect to position and orientation. Begin by defining the position tracking error

$$e_\rho(t) = \rho_d(t) - \rho(t). \tag{9.61}$$

The dynamics of (9.61) are found to be

$$\dot{e}_\rho(t) = \dot{\rho}_d(t) - Rv(t). \tag{9.62}$$

In order to stabilize (9.62), the desired velocity is selected to be

$$v_d(t) = R^T \left[\dot{\rho}_d(t) + K_\rho e_\rho(t)\right], \tag{9.63}$$

where $K_\rho = \mathrm{diag}\{k_{\rho x}, k_{\rho y}, k_{\rho z}\}$ is a design matrix with all positive constants.

Since the desired velocity is a term that is injected into the system by the event-sampled controller, it becomes necessary to consider (9.63) in the presence of measurement errors. Observe that the measurement error that is injected into the system can be introduced into the analysis by noting that, from (9.44), the event-sampled position measurement is given by $\rho_\Xi = \rho + \Xi_\rho$, which allows (9.61) to be rewritten as

$$e_{\rho\Xi} = \rho_d - \left[\rho + \Xi_\rho\right] = e_\rho - \Xi_\rho, \tag{9.64}$$

where $\Xi_\rho = [\Xi_x, \Xi_y, \Xi_z]^T$ is the vector of measurement errors corresponding to the quadrotor's measured position. Using (9.64) in (9.63) reveals

$$\begin{aligned} v_{d\Xi} &= R^T \left[\dot{\rho}_d + K_\rho \left[e_\rho - \Xi_\rho\right]\right] \\ &= R^T \left[\dot{\rho}_d + K_\rho e_\rho\right] - R^T K_\rho \Xi_\rho. \end{aligned} \tag{9.65}$$

Next, define $e_v = v_{d\Xi} - v$ and note that, from this, $v = v_{d\Xi} - e_v$. Then, using $v_{d\Xi}$ as a virtual control input in the tracking error dynamics and substituting (9.65) into (9.62) gives

$$\dot{e}_{\rho\Xi}(t) = -K_\rho e_\rho(t) + Re_v(t) + K_\rho \Xi_\rho(t). \tag{9.66}$$

Next, the desired virtual control input corresponding to the quadrotor's orientation is considered. Begin by defining the orientation tracking error

$$e_\Theta(t) = \Theta_d(t) - \Theta(t), \tag{9.67}$$

where $\Theta_d = [\phi_d, \theta_d, \psi_d]^T$ is the desired orientation. Recall that ψ_d is an external input to be selected by the designer. Furthermore, it is shown in (Dierks and Jagannathan, 2009c) how ϕ_d and θ_d can be calculated in terms of $\dot{\rho}_d$, $\ddot{\rho}_d$, ψ_d, K_ρ, and the unknown function $f_{c1}(x_{c1})$. The NN approximation for f_{c1} is given by

$$\hat{f}_{c1} = \hat{W}_{c1}^T \sigma\left(V_{c1}^T \hat{x}_{c1}\right) = \hat{W}_{c1}^T \hat{\sigma}_{c1} = \left[\hat{f}_{c11}, \hat{f}_{c12}, \hat{f}_{c13}\right]^T,$$

where the input is $\hat{x}_{c1} = \left[1, \dot{\rho}_d^T, \ddot{\rho}_d^T, \hat{V}, \Theta^T, \tilde{X}^T\right]^T$. These estimates can then used in the derivation for the actual dynamic control.

Moving on, the dynamics of (9.67) are found to be

$$\dot{e}_\Theta(t) = \dot{\Theta}_d(t) - T\omega(t). \tag{9.68}$$

In order to stabilize (9.68), the desired angular velocity is selected to be

$$\omega_d(t) = T^{-1}\left[\dot{\Theta}_d(t) + K_\Theta e_\Theta(t)\right], \tag{9.69}$$

where $K_\Theta = \text{diag}\{k_{\Theta 1}, k_{\Theta 2}, k_{\Theta 3}\}$ is a design matrix with all positive constants. Since the desired angular velocity is a term that is injected into the system by the event-sampled controller, it becomes necessary to consider (9.69) in the presence of measurement errors. This is accomplished by observing that the event-sampled tracking error can be expressed as

$$e_{\Theta\Xi}(t) = \Theta_d(t) - [\Theta(t) + \Xi_\Theta(t)] = e_\Theta(t) - \Xi_\Theta(t), \tag{9.70}$$

where $\Xi_\Theta = \left[\Xi_\phi, \Xi_\theta, \Xi_\psi\right]^T$ is the vector of measurement errors corresponding to the quadrotor's measured orientation. Using (9.70) in (9.69) reveals

$$\begin{aligned}\omega_{d\Xi}(t) &= T^{-1}\left[\dot{\Theta}_d(t) + K_\Theta\left[e_\Theta(t) - \Xi_\Theta(t)\right]\right]\\ &= T^{-1}\left[\dot{\Theta}_d(t) + K_\Theta e_\Theta(t) - K_\Theta \Xi_\Theta(t)\right].\end{aligned} \tag{9.71}$$

Next, define $e_\omega = \omega_{d\Xi} - \omega$ and note that, from this, $\omega = \omega_{d\Xi} - e_\omega$. Then, using $\omega_{d\Xi}$ as a virtual control input in the tracking error dynamics and substituting (9.71) into (9.68) gives

$$\dot{e}_{\Theta\Xi}(t) = -K_\Theta e_\Theta(t) + Te_\omega(t) + K_\Theta \Xi_\Theta(t). \tag{9.72}$$

It is the tracking error dynamics given by (9.66) and (9.72) that are used when the closed-loop dynamics are considered.

Remark 9.7. *In contrast to the results in (Dierks and Jagannathan, 2009c), the tracking error dynamics, (9.66) and (9.72), contain additional terms, $K_\rho \Xi_\rho$ and $K_\Theta \Xi_\Theta$, respectively. These terms are the artifacts that result from event-based sampling.*

9.2.3.3 Event-Sampled Output Feedback Dynamic Control

The actual control input consists of two parts: u_1 is a scalar corresponding to the total thrust and $u_2 = [u_{21}, u_{22}, u_{23}]^T$ gives the rotational torques corresponding to roll, pitch, and yaw directions, respectively. These two parts are considered separately in the following.

9.2.3.4 Total Thrust

The time-sampled total thrust control input is given by (Dierks and Jagannathan, 2009c)

$$\begin{aligned} u_1(t) =& mk_{v3}\hat{e}_{vz} \\ &+ m\left[c_{\phi d}s_{\theta d}c_{\psi d} + s_{\phi d}s_{\psi d}\right]\left[\ddot{x}_d + k_{\rho x}\dot{x}_d - \hat{v}_{R1} + \hat{f}_{c11}\right] \\ &+ m\left[c_{\phi d}s_{\theta d}s_{\psi d} - s_{\phi d}c_{\psi d}\right]\left[\ddot{y}_d + k_{\rho y}\dot{y}_d - \hat{v}_{R2} + \hat{f}_{c12}\right] \\ &+ mc_{\phi d}c_{\theta d}\left[\ddot{z}_d + k_{\rho z}\dot{z}_d - \hat{v}_{R3} + \hat{f}_{c13} - g\right], \end{aligned} \tag{9.73}$$

where the gain, k_{v3}, is an element in the design matrix, $K_v = \text{diag}\{k_{v1}, k_{v2}, k_{v3}\}$, with all positive elements; $\hat{e}_v = \left[\hat{e}_{vx}, \hat{e}_{vy}, \hat{e}_{vz}\right]^T = v_d - \hat{v}$ with $\hat{v}$ being the translational velocity observer estimate; $\hat{v}_R = \left[\hat{v}_{R1}, \hat{v}_{R2}, \hat{v}_{R3}\right]^T = K_\rho R\hat{v}$; and $\hat{f}_{c1} = \left[\hat{f}_{c11}, \hat{f}_{c12}, \hat{f}_{c13}\right]$ is the NN estimate introduced in the previous subsection. Since the estimates from the observer are being stored in the controller and only being updated intermittently, it becomes necessary here to consider explicit measurement errors corresponding to the estimated state-vector. As a result, the terms $\hat{e}_v$ and $\hat{v}_R$ both have an explicit presence of measurement errors.

In order to incorporate the measurement errors in the analysis, it becomes necessary to expand certain computations so that the terms $\hat{e}_{vz}$, $\hat{v}_{R1}$, $\hat{v}_{R2}$, and $\hat{v}_{R3}$ can be extracted. First, in order to be able to consider $\hat{e}_{vz} = v_{dz} - \hat{v}_z$, it is necessary to consider the desired velocity (9.65) under the influence of event-sampling. By expanding the matrix multiplications, the expression for $v_{dz\Xi}$ is obtained as

$$v_{dz\Xi} = v_{dz} + \bar{R}_{3R}K_\rho \Xi_\rho, \tag{9.74}$$

where $\bar{R}_{3R}$ is the third row of R^T. Next, a similar procedure is used to find $\hat{v}_{R1}$, $\hat{v}_{R2}$, and $\hat{v}_{R3}$ under the influence of event-sampling. Using $\hat{v}_{x\Xi} = \hat{v}_x + \hat{\Xi}_{vx}$, $\hat{v}_{y\Xi} = \hat{v}_y + \hat{\Xi}_{vy}$, and $\hat{v}_{z\Xi} = \hat{v}_z + \hat{\Xi}_{vz}$, it is discovered that

$$\begin{aligned} &\hat{v}_{R1\Xi} = \hat{v}_{R1} + k_{\rho x}R_{1R}\hat{\Xi}_v, \qquad \hat{v}_{R2\Xi} = \hat{v}_{R2} + k_{\rho y}R_{2R}\hat{\Xi}_v, \\ &\hat{v}_{R3\Xi} = \hat{v}_{R3} + k_{\rho z}R_{3R}\hat{\Xi}_v, \end{aligned} \tag{9.75}$$

where R_{1R}, R_{2R}, and R_{3R} are the first, second, and third rows of R, respectively, and $\hat{\Xi}_v = \left[\hat{\Xi}_{vx}, \hat{\Xi}_{vy}, \hat{\Xi}_{vz}\right]^T$ is the vector of measurement errors corresponding to the translational velocity estimates. Finally, using (9.74) and (9.75) in (9.73) reveals

$$\begin{aligned} u_{1\Xi} = u_1^{f\Xi} + mk_{v3}\left[R_{3R}^T K_\rho\right]\Xi_\rho - \\ m\left[k_{\rho x}R_{1R} + k_{\rho y}R_{2R} + k_{\rho z}R_{3R} + \left[\begin{array}{ccc} 0 & 0 & k_{v3} \end{array}\right]\right]\hat{\Xi}_v, \end{aligned} \tag{9.76}$$

where $u_1^{f\Xi}$ is identical to u_1 (9.73), but assumes the event-sampled NN estimates, $\hat{f}_{c1\Xi}$; the implicitly affected NN estimation has no effect on further analyses. The control input, $u_{1\Xi}$, is designed in order to stabilize the translational velocity tracking error dynamics, which are given by

$$\begin{aligned} \dot{e}_{v\Xi}(t) = -S(\omega)e_v - \frac{1}{m}G(R_d) - \bar{\tau}_{d1} \\ + R_d^T\left[\ddot{\rho}_d + K_\rho\dot{\rho}_d - K_\rho R\hat{v} + f_{c1}(x_{c1})\right] - \frac{1}{m}u_{1\Xi}E_z. \end{aligned} \tag{9.77}$$

Since the event-sampled control input is the sum of the time-sampled control input and the measurement error terms, the results of substituting the expression for $u_{1\Xi}$ into the tracking error dynamics (9.77) can be used to easily find that (Dierks and Jagannathan, 2009c)

$$\begin{aligned} \dot{e}_{v\Xi}(t) = -\left[S(\omega) + K_v\right]e_v - K_v\tilde{v} + R_d^T\tilde{W}_{c1\Xi}\hat{\sigma}_{c1\Xi}^T + \xi_{c1} \\ + \left[k_{v3}\left[R_{3R}^T K_\rho\right]\Xi_\rho - \left[k_{\rho x}R_{1R} + k_{\rho y}R_{2R}\right.\right. \\ \left.\left. + k_{\rho z}R_{3R} + \left[\begin{array}{ccc} 0 & 0 & k_{v3} \end{array}\right]\right]\hat{\Xi}_v\right]E_z, \end{aligned} \tag{9.78}$$

where $\xi_{c1} = R_d^T W_{c1\Xi}^T \tilde{\sigma}_{c1\Xi}^T + R_d^T \varepsilon_{c1} - \bar{\tau}_{d1}$, $\tilde{W}_{c1\Xi} = W_{c1} - \hat{W}_{c1\Xi}$, and $\tilde{\sigma}_{c1\Xi} = \sigma_{c1\Xi} - \hat{\sigma}_{c1\Xi}$. In contrast to (Dierks and Jagannathan, 2009c), the dynamics (9.78) have the additional measurement error terms that result from event-sampling.

Later, the tracking error dynamics given by (9.78) are combined in an augmented vector along with the angular velocity tracking error dynamics, where they are both considered together. Before doing that, however, the event-sampled control inputs corresponding to the rotational torques and the angular velocity tracking errors are presented.

9.2.3.5 Rotational Torques

First, consider the angular velocity tracking error dynamics given by

$$J\dot{e}_\omega(t) = f_{c2}(x_{c2}) - u_2(t) - \tau_{d2}(t) - T^T e_\Theta(t), \tag{9.79}$$

where $f_{c2}(x_{c2})$ is an unknown function whose NN approximation is given by $\hat{f}_{c2} = \hat{W}_{c2}^T \sigma_{c2}(V_{c2}^T \hat{x}_{c2}) = \hat{W}_{c2}^T \hat{\sigma}_{c2}$ with an input $\hat{x}_{c2} = \left[1,\ \hat{\omega}^T,\ \dot{\hat{\Omega}}_d^T,\ \tilde{\Theta}_d^T,\ e_\Theta^T\right]$. Next, the rotational torque control input is given by (Dierks and Jagannathan, 2009c)

$$u_2(t) = \hat{f}_{c2} + K_\omega \hat{e}_\omega(t),$$

where $K_\omega = \text{diag}\{k_{\omega 1}, k_{\omega 2}, k_{\omega 3}\}$ is a design matrix with all positive constants, and $\hat{e}_\omega = \hat{\omega}_d - \hat{\omega}$. The event-sampled control input $u_{2\Xi}$ injects explicit measurement errors into the system through the $\hat{e}_\omega$ term. Observing that

$$\hat{\omega}_d(t) = \hat{\Omega}_d + T^{-1} K_\Theta e_\Theta(t) + K_{\Omega 3} T^{-1} \tilde{\Theta}_d(t),$$

it can be seen that, here, a measurement error corresponding to the measured orientation is injected into the system. Using (9.70) it is found that

$$\hat{\omega}_{d\Xi} = \hat{\omega}_d - T^{-1} K_\Theta \Xi_\Theta.$$

Now, noting that $\hat{\omega}_\Xi = \hat{\omega} + \hat{\Xi}_\omega$, it is revealed that the event-sampled control signal

$$u_{2\Xi}(t) = \hat{f}_{c2\Xi} + K_\omega \hat{e}_\omega(t) - K_\omega \left[T^{-1} K_\Theta \Xi_\Theta(t) - \hat{\Xi}_\omega(t)\right], \tag{9.80}$$

where $\hat{f}_{c2\Xi}$ is the event-sampled NN estimate given earlier and $\hat{\Xi}_\omega = \left[\hat{\Xi}_{\omega x}, \hat{\Xi}_{\omega y}, \hat{\Xi}_{\omega z}\right]^T$ is the vector of measurement errors corresponding to the rotational velocity estimates. Next, making use of the fact that $\hat{e}_\omega = e_\omega - \tilde{\omega}_d + \tilde{\omega}$, as well as adding and subtracting $W_{c2}^T \hat{\sigma}_{c\Xi}$, the event sampled tracking error dynamics (9.79) can be rewritten as

$$J\dot{e}_{\omega\Xi}(t) = \tilde{W}_{c2\Xi}^T \hat{\sigma}_{c2\Xi} - K_\omega e_\omega + K_\omega \tilde{\omega}_d - K_\omega \tilde{\omega} - T^T e_\Theta + \xi_{c2} - K_\omega \left[T^{-1} K_\Theta \Xi_\Theta - \hat{\Xi}_\omega\right], \tag{9.81}$$

where $\tilde{W}_{c2\Xi}^T = W_{c2}^T - \hat{W}_{c2\Xi}^T$, $\xi_{c2} = \varepsilon_{c2} + W_{c2}^T \tilde{\sigma}_{c\Xi} - \tau_{d2}$, and $\tilde{\sigma}_{c2\Xi} = \sigma_{c2} - \hat{\sigma}_{c2\Xi}$.

Next, define the augmented vector, $e_{S\Xi} = \left[e_{v\Xi}^T,\ e_{\omega\Xi}^T\right]^T$, with which the translation and angular velocities can be considered together. With this, it becomes necessary to also define $\bar{J} = [I_{3\times 3}, 0_{3\times 3}; 0_{3\times 3}, J]$, a constant matrix; $K_S = [K_v, 0_{3\times 3}; 0_{3\times 3}, K_\omega] > 0$, a positive definite design matrix; $S_S(\omega) = [S(\omega), 0_{3\times 3}; 0_{3\times 3}, 0_{3\times 3}]$, where $e_{S\Xi}^T S_S(\omega) e_{S\Xi} = 0$; $\bar{T} = [0_{3\times 6}; 0_{3\times 3}, T]$; $\bar{e}_\Theta = \left[0_{1\times 3}, e_\Theta^T\right]^T$; $\bar{\tilde{\omega}}_d = \left[0_{1\times 3}, \tilde{\omega}_d^T\right]^T$; $\xi_c = \left[\xi_{c1}^T, \xi_{c2}^T\right]^T$; and $A_d = \text{diag}\{R_d, I_{3\times 3}\}$, with $R_d = R(\Theta_d)$. Additionally, $\tilde{f}_{c\Xi} = \tilde{W}_{c\Xi}^T \hat{\sigma}_{c\Xi}$ with $\tilde{W}_{c\Xi} = \text{diag}\left\{\tilde{W}_{c1\Xi}, \tilde{W}_{c2\Xi}\right\}$ and $\hat{\sigma}_{c\Xi} = \left[\hat{\sigma}_{c1\Xi}^T, \hat{\sigma}_{c2\Xi}^T\right]^T$ and $\tilde{V}$ is the velocity tracking error vector defined in the observer development. Finally, in order to make provisions for the effects of event-sampling, define the augmented measurement error vector, $\hat{\Xi}_{SV} = \left[\hat{\Xi}_v^T, \hat{\Xi}_\omega^T\right]^T$. The augmented coefficient matrix, $K_{V\Xi}$, corresponding to Ξ_{SV} can be found in terms of the gain matrices

K_ρ and K_ω as well as the elements of R and the gain k_{v3}. With these, the tracking error dynamics described by (9.78) and (9.81) can be rewritten with the single expression

$$\bar{J}\dot{e}_{S\Xi}(t) = A_d^T \tilde{f}_{c\Xi} - [K_S + S_S(\omega)]\, e_S - K_S\tilde{V} - \bar{T}^T \bar{e}_\Theta + K_S\tilde{\bar{\omega}}_d + \xi_c + K_{V\Xi}\hat{\Xi}_{SV} + K_{X\Xi}^V \Xi_{SX}, \quad (9.82)$$

where $\Xi_{SX} = \begin{bmatrix} \Xi_\rho^T, & \Xi_\Theta^T \end{bmatrix}^T$ is the augmented measurement error vector corresponding to the position and orientation measurements and the coefficient matrix $K_{X\Xi}^V$ accounts for the Ξ_ρ and Ξ_Θ from (9.78) and (9.81); the augmented coffecient matrix $K_{X\Xi}^V$ can be found in terms of gain matrices K_ρ, K_Θ, and K_ω as well as the elements of T^{-1}.

With these results, the final two results may be presented. In Theorem 9.5, for the purposes of analysis, the time-sampled controller is considered and the explicit measurement errors that would be injected into the system by event-sampling are viewed as bounded inputs. In this way, the ISS-like behavior of the system is demonstrated. In Theorem 9.6, the assumption on the boundedness of the measurement errors is relaxed and it is shown that the measurement errors are, in fact, bounded with the implementation of an appropriately selected event-execution law.

9.2.4 QUADROTOR UAV STABILITY

Theorem 9.5. *(ISS-like Behavior of Quadrotor System): Consider the dynamics described by (9.43). Let the NN observer be defined by (9.46) and let the observer NN weights be updated at event-sampling instants with (9.50) with initial weights in a compact set; additionally, let the event-sampled virtual controller be defined by (9.58) and let the virtual control NN weights be updated at event-sampling instants with (9.59) with initial weights in a compact set. Moreover, consider the event-sampled desired virtual control inputs and actual control inputs, (9.65), (9.71), (9.76), and (9.80), respectively, that are designed to stabilize the event-sampled tracking error dynamics given by (9.66), (9.72), and (9.82). Additionally, let the NN weights corresponding to the actual control be updated at event-sampling instants with*

$$\dot{\hat{W}}_{c\Xi} = F_c \hat{\sigma}_{c\Xi} [A_d \hat{e}_S]^T - \kappa_{c1} F_c \hat{W}_{c\Xi}, \quad (9.83)$$

with initial weights in a compact set, and where $\kappa_{c1} > 0$ and $F_c = F_c^T > 0$ are constant design parameter. Finally, let the measurement errors that would be injected into the system as a result of intermittent sampling be bounded such that $\|\Xi_{SX}\| \le \Xi_{X\max}$, $\|\hat{\Xi}_{SX}\| \le \hat{\Xi}_{X\max}$, $\|\dot{\Xi}_{SX}\| \le \dot{\Xi}_{X\max}$, and $\|\hat{\Xi}_{SV}\| \le \hat{\Xi}_{V\max}$. Then, there exist positive design constants K_{o1}, K_{o2}, K_{o3}, $K_{\Omega1}$, $K_{\Omega2}$, and $K_{\Omega3}$, and positive-definite design matrices K_ρ, K_Θ, K_v, and K_ω, such that the observer estimation errors, $\tilde{X}$ and $\tilde{V}$, the NN weight estimation errors, $\tilde{W}_{o\Xi}$, the desired virtual control estimation errors, $\tilde{\Theta}_{d\Xi}$ and $\tilde{\omega}_{d\Xi}$, the virtual control NN estimation errors, $\tilde{W}_{\Omega\Xi}$, the actual control NN weight estimation errors, $\tilde{W}_{c\Xi}$, and the position, orientation, and translational and rotational velocity tracking errors, e_ρ, e_Θ, and e_S, respectively, are all locally UUB.

The key idea of the proof is to construct a Lyapunov candidate function and analyze its time-derivative. In particular, let the positive-definite Lyapunov candidate incorporating all the signals of the closed-loop system is given by

$$V_{UAV\,\Xi} = K_{S\max}^2 V_{o\Xi} + K_{S\max}^2 V_{\Omega\Xi} + V_{c\Xi},$$

where $K_{S\max}$ is the maximum singular value of K_S and

$$V_{c\Xi} = \frac{1}{2}e_\rho^T e_\rho + \frac{1}{2}e_\Theta^T e_\Theta + \frac{1}{2}e_S^T \bar{J} e_S + \frac{1}{2}\mathrm{tr}\left\{\tilde{W}_c^T F_c^{-1} \tilde{W}_c\right\}. \quad (9.84)$$

The first derivative of this Lyapunov candidate function can be shown to be negative semi-definite, and hence, it can be concluded that all signals in the closed-loop are locally UUB. Detailed proof can be seen in Szanto (2016).

Remark 9.8. *By defining the augmented vector*

$$\zeta = \left[\|\tilde{X}\|, \|\tilde{V}\|, \|\tilde{\Theta}_{d\Xi}\|, \|\tilde{\omega}_{d\Xi}\|, \|e_K\|, \dots \|e_S\|, \|\tilde{W}_{o\Xi}\|_F, \|\tilde{W}_{\Omega\Xi}\|_F, \|\tilde{W}_{c\Xi}\|_F\right]^T,$$

the final time-derivative of the Lyapunov function can be written in the form $\dot{V}(\zeta) < -\Delta(\|\zeta\|) + \Lambda(\|\eta_{UAV}\|, \|\Xi_{UAV}\|)$, *where the positive part,* Λ, *is viewed as an input to the closed-loop system and is a function of bounded measurement and NN reconstruction errors. It can, therefore, be concluded that the continuously sampled, closed-loop system has a local ISS-like Lyapunov function associated with it. Together with the assumption that the system (9.43) is locally Lipschitz, this result satisfies all conditions necessary to show that there exists positive, nonzero inter-event periods (Tabuada, 2007). This provision is necessary in order to ensure the avoidance of Zeno behavior.*

As previously mentioned, the results of Theorem 9.5 are contingent on the boundedness of the event-sampling measurement errors. However, in order to implement the event-sampled controller, these results, by themselves, are not sufficient. In addition, it is necessary to demonstrate the boundedness of the measurement errors. The following theorem addresses the boundedness of measurement errors by considering two cases: the first case analyzes the dynamics and the influences of $\dot{V}_{c\Xi}(t)$ and $\dot{V}_{o\Xi}(t)$ when the measurement errors are zero and the second case considers the system with nonzero measurement errors. It is in the analysis of the second case, an event-execution law is designed using Lyapunov stability analysis.

Theorem 9.6. *(Boundedness of Measurement Errors (Szanto, 2016)): Consider the dynamics described by (9.43). Let the NN observer be defined by (9.46) and let the observer NN weights be updated at event-sampling instants with (9.50) with initial weights in a compact set; additionally, let the event-sampled virtual controller be defined by (9.58) and let the virtual control NN weights be updated at event-sampling instants with (9.59), initialized within a compact set. Moreover, consider the event-sampled desired virtual control inputs and actual control inputs, (9.65), (9.71), (9.76), and (9.80), respectively, that are designed to stabilize the event-sampled tracking error dynamics given by (9.66), (9.72), and (9.82). Furthermore, let the NN weights corresponding to the actual control be updated at event-sampling instants with (9.83) with initial weights in a compact set. Finally, let the event-sampling measurement errors satisfy the condition* $\|\Xi_{XUAV}\| + \|\Xi_{VUAV}\| \leq \gamma_{SX}\mu_{SX}\|e_K\|^2 + \gamma_{SV}\mu_{SV}\|e_S\|^2$, *where* Ξ_{XUAV} *and* Ξ_{VUAV} *are augmented measurement error vectors corresponding to the quadrotor's measured output and its estimated velocity, respectively;* e_K *and* e_S *are the augmented tracking error vectors corresponding to the quadrotor's measured output and its estimated velocity; and* $0 < \gamma_{SX}, \gamma_{SV}, \mu_{SX}, \mu_{SV} < 1$ *are all design constants. Then, there exist positive design constants* K_{o1}, K_{o2}, K_{o3}, $K_{\Omega1}$, $K_{\Omega2}$, *and* $K_{\Omega3}$, *and positive-definite design matrices* K_ρ, K_Θ, K_v, *and* K_ω, *such that the observer estimation errors,* $\tilde{X}$ *and* $\tilde{V}$, *the NN weight estimation errors,* $\tilde{W}_{o\Xi}$, *the desired virtual control estimation errors,* $\tilde{\Theta}_{d\Xi}$ *and* $\tilde{\omega}_{d\Xi}$, *the virtual control NN estimation errors,* $\tilde{W}_{\Omega\Xi}$, *the actual control NN weight estimation errors,* $\tilde{W}_{c\Xi}$, *and the position, orientation, and translational and rotational velocity tracking errors,* e_ρ, e_Θ, *and* e_S, *respectively, are all locally UUB.*

The key idea of this proof is to use the event-triggering conditions to bound the measurement errors in the Lyapunov time-derivative expression obtained in the results of Theorem 9.5.

9.2.5 NUMERICAL EXAMPLE

The objective of this simulation example is to illustrate the effects of event-sampling. With this in mind, simulations were performed using the event-sampled controller presented in this section as well as its time-sampled counterpart presented in (Dierks and Jagannathan, 2009c). In order to evaluate the controller's performance, the averages of the control inputs, tracking errors, and observer

Table 9.5
Output feedback controller design for a quadrotor UAV

Observer dynamics	$\dot{\hat{X}}(t) = A\hat{Z} + K_{o1}\tilde{X},\ \dot{\hat{Z}}(t) = \hat{f}_{o1\Xi} + \bar{G} + K_{o2}A^{-1}\tilde{X} + M^{-1}U_{\Xi},$ $\hat{V}(t) = \hat{Z} + K_{o3}A^{-1}\tilde{X}$
Virtual controller	$\dot{\hat{\Theta}}_{d\Xi}(t) = T\hat{\Omega}_{d\Xi} + K_{\Omega 1}\tilde{\Theta}_{d\Xi},\ \dot{\hat{\Omega}}_{d\Xi}(t) = \hat{f}_{\Omega 1\Xi} + K_{\Omega 2}T^{-1}\tilde{\Theta}_{d\Xi},$ $\hat{\omega}_{d\Xi}(t) = \hat{\Omega}_{d\Xi} + T^{-1}K_{\Theta}e_{\Theta\Xi} + K_{\Omega 3}T^{-1}\tilde{\Theta}_{d\Xi}$
Desired virtual control inputs	$v_{d\Xi} = R^T\left[\dot{\rho}_d + K_\rho e_\rho\right] - R^T K_\rho \Xi_\rho$ $\omega_{d\Xi}(t) = T^{-1}\left[\dot{\Theta}_d(t) + K_{\Theta}e_{\Theta}(t) - K_{\Theta}\Xi_{\Theta}(t)\right]$
Observer NN weight update rule	$\dot{\hat{W}}_{o\Xi}(t) = F_o\hat{\sigma}_o\tilde{X}^T - \kappa_{o1}F_o\hat{W}_{o\Xi}$
Virtual controller NN weight update rule	$\dot{\hat{W}}_{\Omega\Xi}(t) = F_\Omega\hat{\sigma}_{\Omega\Xi}\tilde{\Theta}_{d\Xi}^T - \kappa_{\Omega 1}F_\Omega\hat{W}_{\Omega\Xi}$
Actual controller NN weight update rule	$\dot{\hat{W}}_{c\Xi} = F_c\hat{\sigma}_{c\Xi}\left[A_d\hat{e}_S\right]^T - \kappa_{c1}F_c\hat{W}_{c\Xi}$
Event-triggering condition	$\lVert\Xi_{XUAV}\rVert + \lVert\Xi_{VUAV}\rVert \le \gamma_{SX}\mu_{SX}\lVert e_K\rVert^2 + \gamma_{SV}\mu_{SV}\lVert e_S\rVert^2$

estimation errors for both time- and event-sampled controllers are summarized. Additionally, the effects of varrying the parameters γ_{SX} and γ_{SV} are considered.

The simulations performed in (Dierks and Jagannathan, 2009c) took into account disturbances such as unknown aerodynamic effects, blade flapping, and signal noise. Moreover, it introduced a parameter, α, which describes how the thrust is redirected as a result of, in part, wind conditions; by taking this parameter to be initially zero and then suddenly increasing it to 20^0 at $t = 20$ s, the effects of an external influence on the system, such as a gust of wind, can be illustrated. All of the considerations that were taken in (Dierks and Jagannathan, 2009c) are taken here. In general, event-triggering mechanisms for strict-feedback systems can be implemented in numerous ways. In this Chapter, the event-sampling scheme employed is one such that the measurement errors and tracking errors corresponding to the UAV's position and velocity are combined and the combinations become the basis by which an event occurs; specifically, an event takes place when there is a failure in the condition

$$\lVert\Xi_{XUAV}\rVert^2 + \lVert\Xi_{VUAV}\rVert^2 \le \gamma_{SX}\mu_{SX}\lVert e_K\rVert^2 + \gamma_{SV}\mu_{SV}\lVert e_S\rVert^2.$$

Identical simulation parameters and controller gains were used in both simulations. The gains selected in (Dierks and Jagannathan, 2009c) were used here with the following exceptions: The orientation control gains were chosen to be $K_\Theta = \text{diag}\{40,40,40\}$ and the angular velocity control gains were selected as $K_\omega = \text{diag}\{35,35,35\}$. Additionally, the desired trajectory remained identical to what was considered in (Dierks and Jagannathan, 2009c), with the only changes being $\omega_x = \omega_y = 0.06\pi$, $r_x = r_y = 0.1$, $r_z = 0.5$, and $\omega_\psi = 0.03\pi$. Finally, for the results that are illustrated in the figures, the event-execution parameters were chosen to be $\gamma_{SX} = \gamma_{SV} = 0.95$.

The event-sampled quadrotor UAV trajectory is shown in Figure 9.5. The effects of the sudden disturbance at $t = 20$ s can be clearly seen in the UAV position error. Although the effects of the

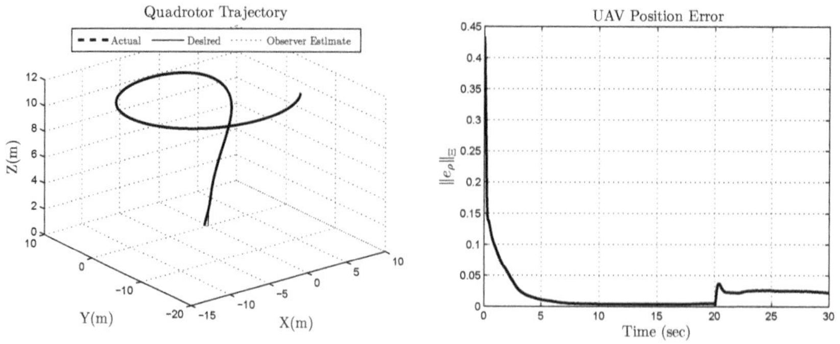

Figure 9.5 UAV Trajectory Tracking.

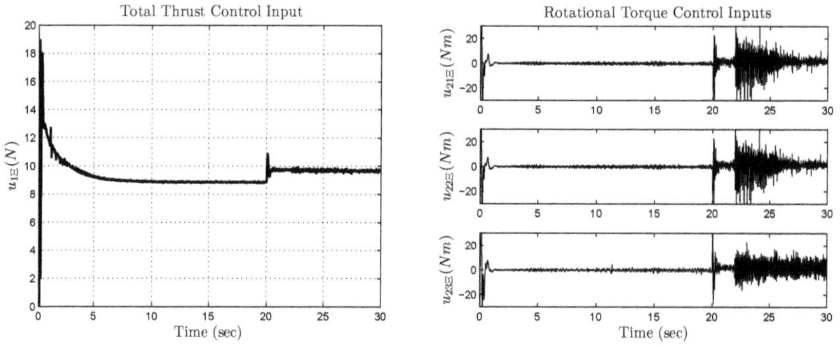

Figure 9.6 Control Inputs.

disturbances are clearly visible, the controller's ability to compensate and recover is also evident. The recovery, however, is not without expense: Figure 9.6 clearly shows an increase in the total thrust and the rotational torque control inputs when the value of α jumps from 0° to 20°.

The results shown in Figures 9.5 and 9.6 demonstrate the stability of the event-sampled controller. However, with regard to the effects of event-based sampling, these results are not tremendously revealing. In an effort to illustrate these effects, consider the results shown in Figure 9.7. The occurrence of events is shown. By normalizing the total number of available samples on the $x-$axis to one and by scaling the number of events with an equivalent factor, it can be seen that about 60% of the total samples are event-sampling instants. In other words, the remaining 40% of the samples are instants when it was unnecessary to update the controller. These results can be summarized by stating that the implementation of the event-sampled controller yielded a 40% reduction in the number of sampling instants used by the controller.

9.2.6 EFFECTS OF EVENT-SAMPLING

As a final assessment of the effectiveness of event sampling, consider the information provided in Tables 9.6 and 9.7. Firstly, the effects of changing the event-execution parameters, γ_{SX} and γ_{SV}, are explored and, secondly, the relationship between the number of events and controller performance is assessed. Whereas previous results spoke only to the stability of the controller, the information in Tables 9.6 and 9.7 will allow the performance of the event-sampled controller to be compared to that of the time-sampled controller.

Before considering the data, a few remarks are made concerning the notations in Tables 9.6 and 9.7. Firstly, the selection of $\gamma_{SX} = \gamma_{SV} = 0$ is equivalent to implementing the time-sampled

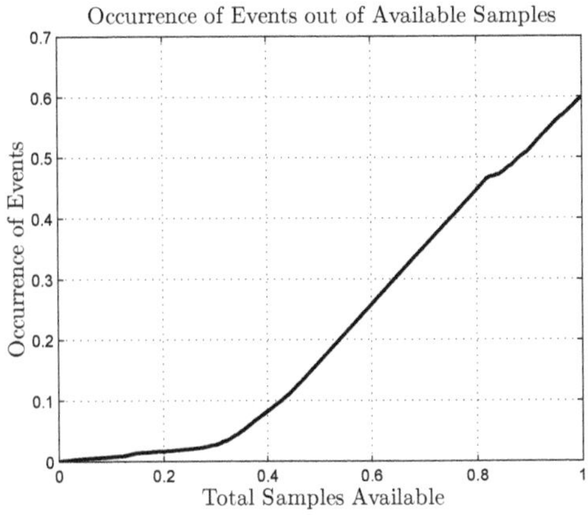

Figure 9.7 Effectiveness of Event-Sampling

Table 9.6
Effects of Event-Sampling on Mean Squared Errors and Control Effort Means

γ_{SX}, γ_{SV}	Γ	$\aleph_{e\rho}$	$\aleph_{e\Theta}$	$\aleph_{ev}$	$\aleph_{e\omega}$	$\aleph_{\tilde{\rho}}$
0	1	0.0026	0.0019	0.2608	6.094	3.29×10^{-4}
0.01	0.8050	0.0293	0.0218	2.936	95.93	2.89×10^{-4}
0.1	0.7003	0.0249	0.0236	2.448	92.69	3.06×10^{-4}
0.5	0.6254	0.0152	0.0189	1.516	48.72	3.35×10^{-4}
0.95	0.5705	0.0155	0.0252	1.630	38.97	3.08×10^{-4}

controller; hence, the first row will serve as a standard to which the event-sampled cases can be compared. Secondly, the number of events that occur out of the total available samples is given by $\Gamma = (Number\,of\,Events)\,/\,(Total\,Samples Available)$; for the time-sampled case, the value for this parameter is unity. Thirdly, as a basis for comparisons, the mean squared errors, $MSE\,(\bullet)$, are considered for the tracking and observer estimation errors corresponding to the position, orientation, and translational and angular velocities. The values summarized in Tables 9.6 and 9.7 are calculated with $\aleph_j = \sum_{i=x,y,z} MSE\,(j_i)$ for $j = e_\rho, e_\Theta, e_v, e_\omega, \tilde{\rho}, \tilde{\Theta}, \tilde{v}, \tilde{\omega}$. Finally, in order to analyze control efforts under the influence of event-sampling, the means of the control inputs, $\bar{u}$, are considered.

First, observe that the number of events increases as γ_{SX} and γ_{SV} are increased; in other words, the number of computations executed by the controller decreases with increasing γ's. This behavior is explained by noting that, with smaller γ's, the upper bounding threshold on the measurement errors is decreased; with smaller thresholds, it takes less amount of time for the measurement errors to grow, reach its threshold and trigger an event. If the threshold is made zero by selecting $\gamma_{SX} = \gamma_{SV} = 0$, an event is triggered every instant that finite measurement errors exist and, practically, the event-sampled controller exhibits time-sampled behavior.

Next, concerning tracking errors, there appear to be marginal differences in the mean squared errors corresponding the position and orientation. With respect to translational and angular velocities, it is clear that the performance of the time-sampled controller is better; this, however, is not to say that the event-sampled controller performs poorly in these areas. As a matter of fact, given the exceptional position and orientation tracking error performances, it would seem that the effects of event-sampling on the velocities are inconsequential. These conclusions can be very easily made for the observer estimation errors as well. Especially in the case of the observer estimation errors corre-

Table 9.7
Effects of Event-Sampling on Mean Squared Errors and Control Effort Means

$\aleph_{\tilde{\Theta}}$	$\aleph_{\tilde{v}}$	$\aleph_{\tilde{\omega}}$	$\bar{u}_1$	$\bar{u}_{21}$	$\bar{u}_{22}$	$\bar{u}_{23}$
0.0029	0.0033	0.3117	9.430	0.7554	1.014	1.155
0.0127	0.0040	3.787	9.430	0.7554	1.015	1.136
0.0106	0.0040	2.470	9.426	0.6790	1.005	1.089
0.0081	0.0042	1.467	9.425	0.6090	0.9772	1.002
0.0103	0.0042	1.115	9.426	0.6618	0.9345	0.9668

sponding to translational velocity, it appears that event-sampling has very little effect. Finally, it can be seen that, with event-sampling, the amount of control effort that is needed does not change substantially. It is evident that, especially with the rotational torques, greater control effort is required, but the additional amount is insignificant relative to the total.

The effects of event sampling are summarized by the information in Tables 9.6 and 9.7: The use of event-sampling gives flexibility in the amount of computations executed by the controller; moreover, while the reduction in computations does come at a cost with regards to performance, the fidelity of the controller is not significantly compromised.

9.3 DISTRIBUTED SCHEDULING PROTOCOL AND CONTROLLER DESIGN FOR CYBER PHYSICAL SYSTEMS

In CPS, multiple real-time dynamic systems are connected to their respective controllers through a shared communication network, as opposed to a dedicated line. Existing centralized or distributed scheduling schemes prove unsuitable for such CPS, as they overlook the behavior of real-time dynamic systems in the network protocol design. As highlighted in Chapters 6-8, large-scale systems adhere to asynchronous sampling conditions, yet multiple subsystems might concurrently trigger events, attempting to utilize the shared network for information transmission. In cases where the network bandwidth falls short, *packet collisions* can result in data loss. Therefore, in this part of the chapter, a distributed scheduling protocol design via cross-layer approach is presented. This protocol, as we shall see, seeks to optimize the performance of CPS by maximizing a utility function, which is generated by using the information collected from both the application and network layers. Subsequently, an adaptive model based optimal event-triggered control scheme is designed for each real-time dynamic system with unknown system dynamics in the application layer. Compared with traditional scheduling algorithms, the distributed scheduling scheme via cross-layer approach, developed by Xu (2012) and (Xu and Jagannathan, 2012), not only allocates the network resources efficiently but also improves the performance of the overall real-time dynamic system.

9.3.1 BACKGROUND

Several researchers, as noted by Tian et al. (2010), recognize the potential advantages of integrating control and networking protocol designs, offering benefits such as cost savings, enhanced adaptability, reliability, and usability. This integration has given rise to the CPS (Xia et al., 2011a,b). In CPS, where control and communication subsystems are closely intertwined, specialized control and communication schemes must be devised, taking into account their interdependence. Notably, Xia et al. (Xia et al., 2011a) proposed a cyber-physical control scheme that considers the effects of a fixed communication network to maintain the stability of the CPS's control system. Additionally, in their work (Xia et al., 2011b), the authors evaluated the performance of the widely used IEEE

802.11 protocol in the context of CPS. Nevertheless, a recurring theme in these studies is the lack of consideration for real-time interactions between control and communication subsystems. An optimal algorithm for CPS should harness these real-time interactions to enhance the performance of both subsystems. To address the intricate interplays among different layers effectively, a crucial approach is cross-layer design (Srivastava and Motani, 2005). Cross-layer design refers to an approach where communication protocols from different components of open systems interconnection (OSI) layers collaborate or interact to achieve specific optimization or performance goals. The OSI model is a conceptual framework developed by the International Organization for Standardization (ISO), aiming to provide a shared foundation for coordinating the development of standards to facilitate system interconnection. Within the OSI reference model, the communication between systems is segmented into distinct abstraction layers. It is noteworthy, however, that most cross-layer designs are predominantly implemented for data link and physical layers (Srivastava and Motani, 2005), often neglecting the application layer. In the context of CPS, it becomes imperative to jointly consider control design at the application layer and protocol design for communication at the data link layer. According to the IEEE 802.11 standard, the carrier sense multiple access (CSMA) protocol is introduced for scheduling communication links in a distributed manner (Jiang and Walrand, 2009). In this protocol, a communication link wishing to transmit does so only if it does not detect an ongoing transmission from the network. However, the prevalent use of random access schemes in most CSMA-based distributed scheduling, focusing solely on enhancing data link layer performance, can adversely impact the application layer (i.e., the control system). Consequently, these protocols are deemed suboptimal and unsuitable within the context of CPS as they have the potential to degrade CPS performance. Simultaneously, as we have seen in the earlier chapters, at the application layer, achieving optimal control design is a formidable challenge, particularly in the presence of uncertain real-time system dynamics. Traditional optimal control schemes, sampled periodically, necessitate substantial network resources.

In this section, we shall explore the application of event-triggered learning-based controllers in a cross layer design scheme in the context of CPS that includes an event-triggered controller design in the application layer and a distributed scheduling algorithm in the data-link layer. The key components of this application include:

1. distributed scheduling via cross layer approach that improves performance of CPS by minimizing the cost function from both data link and application layers
2. an adaptive model-based optimal event-triggered control scheme that is designed in a forward-in-time manner and without using the knowledge of system dynamics

Different from the discussions earlier in this chapter as well as in the earlier chapters, we shall see that the event-triggered control scheme presented in this section is based on events that are initiated not only by the control system but also via the shared network performance.

9.3.2 THE SCHEDULING AND CONTROL PROBLEMS IN CPS

Consider the case where multiple subsystems or CPS, controlled in real-time, try to communicate to their respective controllers through a shared communication network. Without loss of generality, we shall assume that these systems are homogeneous (structurally similar). On the other hand, to save the network resources, event-triggered system is used instead of a traditional time-driven sampling. Since the all the CPS are homogeneous, consider a CPS pair (cyber and physical system components) represented as

$$x_{i,k+1} = A_i x_{i,k} + B_i u_{i,k}, \tag{9.85}$$

where $x_{i,k}$ and $u_{i,k}$ are CPS system states and control inputs, respectively, and A_i, B_i denote system matrices for i^{th} CPS pair. However, the error between the system states used in the controller and actual values might increase quickly in ZOH event-triggered control scheme. For overcoming this drawback, we shall develop an adaptive model-based event-triggered system. Besides event-trigger mechanism, an adaptive model $(\hat{A}_{i,k},\hat{B}_{i,k})$ is used for the controller to estimate the system state vector when controller has not received any information from the sensor. The estimated system state vector can be represented as

$$\hat{x}_{i,k+1} = \hat{A}_{i,k}\hat{x}_{i,k} + \hat{B}_{i,k}u_{i,k}, \tag{9.86}$$

for each i. Recall that the adaptive model will be updated once when the most recent system state vector is received at the controller. Eventually, the adaptive model and estimated system states will converge close to the actual system states respectively, which in turn will improve the performance of the event-triggered control system.

9.3.3 CROSS-LAYER DESIGN FOR CPS

First, the event-triggered control design and distributed scheduling protocol are implemented at all CPS pairs, which are sharing the communication network. Each CPS pair tunes its adaptive model-based optimal event-triggered controller design by using a distributed scheduling algorithm, computes its value function based on tuned control design, and transmits the information to the data link layer. Second, data link layer can update the scheduling of the CPS pair based on network traffic payload from data link layer and the value function information received from the application layer.

9.3.3.1 Distributed Scheduling Algorithm for CPS

Without loss of generality, we shall assume that a traditional wireless ad-hoc network protocol is implemented in other layers. For optimizing the performance of multiple CPS pairs, including the performance from both application layer and data link layer, an optimal cross-layer distributed scheduling algorithm is developed by incorporating control system information from application layer. Firstly, the cost function for the CPS pair is represented as

$$J_{i,k} = x_{i,k}^T Q_i x_{i,k} + u_{i,k}^T S_i u_{i,k} + \beta_i R_{i,k}, \tag{9.87}$$

where $R_{i,k}$ is i^{th} CPS pair average traffic payload during $[0,kT_s]$ (T_s is the periodic sampling time) and β_i is the weight of average traffic payload for the ith CPS pair. A large β_i indicates that the average traffic payload will adversely influence the total cost and should be reduced by appropriate design of the scheduling protocol.

For M CPS pairs, i.e., for $i = 1,\ldots,M$ in (9.86) and (9.87), the overall cost function can be represented as

$$J_k = \sum_{i=1}^{M} J_{i,k} = \sum_{i=1}^{M} (x_{i,k}^T Q_i x_{i,k} + u_{i,k}^T S_i u_{i,k} + \beta_i R_{i,k}(\pi)), \tag{9.88}$$

with π denoting the scheduling policy. Next, the optimal design of multiple CPS pairs should minimize the cost function (9.88), i.e.,

$$J_k^* = \min_{u,\pi} \sum_{i=1}^{M} (x_{i,k}^T Q_i x_{i,k} + u_{i,k}^T S_i u_{i,k} + \beta_i R_{i,k}(\pi)), \tag{9.89}$$

where $u = (u_1^T,\ldots,u_M^T)^T$ is the control policy and π is the scheduling policy.

Obviously, each pair of CPS has two possible status (for scheduling) at any time: 1) the CPS pair is scheduled; and 2) the CPS pair is not scheduled. Note that whether or not a CPS pair is scheduled depends upon this status, which can minimize cost value. For instance,

Case 1: The ith CPS pair has been scheduled

$$J^{s,1}_{i,k} = x^T_{i,k} Q_i x_{i,k} + x^T_{i,k} \Lambda_i x_{i,k} + \beta_i R^Y_{i,k}, \tag{9.90}$$

where $\Lambda_i = \hat{K}^T_{i,k} S_i \hat{K}_{i,k}$ and $R^Y_{i,k}$ is the average traffic payload when the ith CPS pair has been scheduled.

Case 2: The ith CPS pair has not been scheduled

$$J^{s,2}_{i,k} = x^T_{i,k} Q_i x_{i,k} + \hat{x}^T_{i,k} \Lambda_i \hat{x}_{i,k} + \beta_i R^N_{i,k}, \tag{9.91}$$

where $R^N_{i,k}$ is the average traffic payload when the ith CPS pair has not been scheduled.

Then, the difference between these two cases can be considered as utility function and expressed as

$$\Delta J^s_{i,k} = \pi_{i,k} \phi(e_{i,k}) - \pi_{i,k} \beta_i D_{i,k}, \tag{9.92}$$

where $D_{i,k} = R^Y_{i,k} - R^N_{i,k} = (\frac{N_k+1}{kT_s} - \frac{N_k}{kT_s}) N_{i,bit} = \frac{1}{kT_s} N_{i,bit}$ with $N_{i,bit}$ denoting the number of bits for packetizing the sensed event at the ith CPS pair, $\pi_{i,k}$ is the schedule indicator of the ith CPS pair, $e_{i,k} = x_{i,k} - \hat{x}_{i,k}$, and $\phi(e_{i,k}) = (\hat{x}^T_{i,k} \Lambda_i \hat{x}_{i,k} - x^T_{i,k} \Lambda_i x_{i,k})$. It can be seen that when $\Delta J^s_{i,k} > 0$, scheduling the ith CPS pair can reduce the cost. Therefore, one may schedule the ith CPS pair when $\Delta J^s_{i,k} > 0$. It is important to note that there may be multiple CPS pairs eligible to transmit simultaneously, i.e., the utility functions of several CPS pairs are higher than zero, indicating that all of these CPS pairs have to be scheduled. However, according to the literature on networking (see Sarangapani and Xu (2018)), only one CPS pair can access the network. Hence, for optimizing the performance of network, the optimal scheduling policy should maximize the total utility function, that is

$$(\Delta J^s_k)^* = \max_{\pi} \sum_{i \in G_k} \Delta J^s_{i,k}, \tag{9.93}$$

where G_k is the CPS pair set with positive value of utility function at time kT_s, i.e., all the ith CPS pair with $\Delta J^s_{i,k} > 0$. The main idea behind the distributed scheduling algorithm is to separate the transmission time of different CPS pairs by using backoff interval (BI) (Mazo and Tabuada, 2011; Xu, 2012), which is designed based on a related utility function in a distributed manner. For example, to solve the optimal scheduling problem (9.93) for multiple pairs of CPS, the BI can be designed as

$$BI_{i,k} = \kappa \times (\exp^{-\Delta J_{i,k}} + n_{i,k}) \quad \text{for } l \in G_k, \tag{9.94}$$

where κ is a scaling factor and $n_{i,k}$ is a random variable sampled from a Gaussian distribution, and $L = \min_{i,j \in G_k} (\exp^{\Delta J_{i,k}} - \exp^{\Delta J_{j,k}})$ is the range of the random value $n_{i,k}$.

Result 1: (Xu and Jagannathan, 2012; Xu, 2012) Given the multiple CPS pairs and event-triggered control scheme, the distributed scheduling scheme selects the adaptive model-based event-triggered CPS pair with highest utility function value since it has the shortest backoff interval (i.e. BI) and highest priority to access the shared communication network. In addition, this algorithm can render best performance schedules for every CPS pair.

9.3.3.2 Adaptive Model-Based Event-Triggering Protocol Design

First, the adaptive state estimator design is presented. For the ith CPS pair, the event-triggered control system and adaptive state estimator with received information can be represented as

$$x_{i,k+1} = A_i x_{i,k} + B_i u_{i,k} = \theta_i^T z_{i,k} \tag{9.95}$$

$$\hat{x}_{i,k+1} = \hat{A}_{i,k}\hat{x}_{i,k} + \hat{B}_{i,k}u_{i,k} = \hat{\theta}_{i,k}^T z_{i,k}, \tag{9.96}$$

where $\theta_i = [A_i B_i]^T$ and $\hat{\theta}_{i,k} = [\hat{A}_{i,k}\hat{B}_{i,k}]^T$ denote the target and estimated system matrices for the ith CPS pair, respectively, and $z_{i,k} = [x_{i,k}^T, u_{i,k}^T]^T$, represents the augmented state and control vectors. The update law for the ith CPS pairs' estimated parameter vector $\hat{\theta}_{i,k}$ can be designed as

$$\hat{\theta}_{i,k+1} = \hat{\theta}_{i,k} + \alpha_{i,e}\gamma_{i,k} z_{i,k} e_{i,k}^T, \tag{9.97}$$

where $e_{i,k+1} = x_{i,k+1} - \hat{x}_{i,k+1}$ is the state estimation error, $\alpha_i, e < 1$ is a positive tuning parameter, and $\gamma_{i,k}$ is an indicator to the status of the event-triggering condition. Recall that the infinite-horizon value function of adaptive model-based event-triggered control system for i^{th} CPS pair can be defined as

$$V(x_{i,k}) = \sum_{l=k}^{\infty} (x_{i,l}^T Q_i x_{i,l} + u_{i,l}^T S_i u_{i,l}) = x_{i,k}^T P_i x_{i,k}. \tag{9.98}$$

Here P_i is the solution to the algebraic Riccati equation corresponding to the ith CPS pair. Then the Hamiltonian for the system is represented as

$$H(x_{i,k}, u_{i,k}) = r(x_{i,k}, u_{i,k}) + V(x_{i,k+1}) - V(x_{i,k}), \tag{9.99}$$

with $r(x_{i,k}, u_{i,k}) = x_{i,k}^T Q_i x_{i,k} + u_{i,k}^T S_i u_{i,k}$ is the one-step cost. Based on the standard optimal control theory, the optimal control input can be represented as

$$u_{i,k}^* = K_i^* x_k = -(S_i + B_{i,k}^T P_i B_{i,k})^{-1} B_{i,k}^T P_i A_{i,k} x_{i,k}, \tag{9.100}$$

where K_i^* is the optimal feedback gain.

On the other hand, we can define the optimal action-dependent value function as

$$V(x_{i,k}, u_{i,k}) = [x_{i,k}^T \quad u_{i,k}^T]\Theta_i[x_{i,k}^T \quad u_{i,k}^T]^T \tag{9.101}$$

with the matrix Θ_i given by

$$\Theta_i = \begin{bmatrix} \Theta_i^{xx} & \Theta_i^{xu} \\ \Theta_i^{ux} & \Theta_i^{uu} \end{bmatrix} = \begin{bmatrix} A_i^T P_i A_i + Q_i & A_i^T P_i B_i \\ B_i^T P_i A_i & B_i P_i B_i + S_i \end{bmatrix}. \tag{9.102}$$

According to (9.102), the optimal control gain for adaptive model-based event-triggered control system pair can be represented in terms of value function parameters, Θ_i, as $K_i^* = -(\Theta_{i,k}^{uu})^{-1}\Theta_{i,k}^{ux}$. Note that if the parameter vector Θ_i can be estimated online, then system dynamics are not needed to calculate the optimal control gain for each of the ith adaptive model-based event-triggered control system pair. Then the action-dependent value function can be represented as

$$V(\hat{x}_{i,k}, u_{i,k}) = \hat{z}_{i,k}^T \Theta_i \hat{z}_{i,k} = \rho_i^T w_{i,k}, \tag{9.103}$$

where $\hat{z}_{i,k} = [x_{i,k}^T \quad u_{i,k}^T]^T$ and $w_{i,k} = (\hat{z}_{i,k1}^2, \ldots, \hat{z}_{i,k1}\hat{z}_{i,kj}, \hat{z}_{i,k2}^2, \ldots, \hat{z}_{i,k(j-1)}\hat{z}_{i,kj}, \hat{z}_{i,kj}^2)$ is the regression vector obtained as polynomials using the Kronecker product operation, and $\rho_i = vec(\Theta_i)$, as we have defined in Chapters 3 and 6 while developing the event-based Q-learning algorithm.

The estimated Bellman equation with estimated state can be represented as $\hat{V}(\hat{x}_{i,k+1}, u_{i,k+1}) - \hat{V}(\hat{x}_{i,k}, u_{i,k}) + r(\hat{x}_{i,k} u_{i,k}) = e_{i,k}^{TD}$, where $e_{i,k}^{TD}$ is the temporal difference (TD) error. The estimated value function for the ith CPS adaptive model-based event-triggered control system pair can be expressed as $\hat{V}(\hat{x}_{i,k}, u_{i,k}) = \hat{\rho}_{i,k}^T w_{i,k}^e$. Then the dynamics of the TD error can be rewritten as

$$e_{i,k}^{TD} = r(\hat{x}_{i,k}, u_{i,k}) + \hat{\rho}_{i,k}^T \Delta W_{i,k}^e \tag{9.104}$$

with $\Delta W_{i,k-1}^e = w_{i,k}^e - w_{i,k-1}^e$. Next, an auxiliary error vector incorporating the history of cost-to-go function is defined as

$$\Pi_{i,k} = \Gamma_{i,k-1} + \hat{\rho}_{i,k}^T \Delta W_{i,k-1}^e, \tag{9.105}$$

where $\Gamma_{i,k-1} = [r(\hat{x}_{i,k-1}, u_{i,k-1}), r(\hat{x}_{i,k-2}, u_{i,k-2}), \ldots, r(\hat{x}_{i,k-1-j}, u_{i,k-1-j})]$ and the regression matrix $\Delta W_{i,k-1}^e = [\Delta W_{i,k-1}^e \cdots, \Delta W_{i,k-1-j}^e]$. Then the update law for the matrix $\hat{\Theta}_i$ corresponding to the ith CPS pair can be defined as

$$\hat{\rho}_{i,k+1} = \Delta W_{i,k}^e (\Delta W_{i,k}^{eT} \Delta W_{i,k}^e)^{-1} (\alpha_{i,\rho} \Pi_{i,k}^T - \Gamma_{i,k}^T) \tag{9.106}$$

with a tuning parameter $0 < \alpha_{i,\rho} < 1$. Eventually, recalling (9.102), the optimal control gain can be developed by using the estimated states as

$$\hat{u}_{i,k} = \hat{K}_{i,k} \hat{x}_{i,k} = -(\hat{\Theta}_{i,k}^{uu})^{-1} \hat{\Theta}_{i,k}^{ux} \hat{x}_{i,k}. \tag{9.107}$$

Result 2: (Xu and Jagannathan, 2012; Xu, 2012) Let $u_{i,0}$ be an initial admissible control policy for i^{th} pair CPS adaptive model-based event-triggered control system. Let the adaptive update law be given by (9.106). Then there exists a positive constant $0 < \alpha_{i,\rho} < 1$ such that the estimated parameter and optimal signal converges to the actual parameter and optimal signal respectively.

9.3.4 EXAMPLE

Example 9.1. *In this example, the cross-layer CPS co-design is evaluated. The CPS includes six pairs that are located within* $300m \times 300m$ *area, randomly. For maintaining the homogeneous property, all six pairs are using the similar control system. These examples are obtained from works by Mazo and Tabuada (2011) and Xu and Jagannathan (2012). The discrete-time model is given as*

$$x_{k+1} = \begin{bmatrix} 1.1138 & -0.0790 \\ 0.0592 & 0.8671 \end{bmatrix} x_k + \begin{bmatrix} 0.2033 \\ 0.1924 \end{bmatrix} u_k, \tag{9.108}$$

with sampling interval $T_s = 0.15$ *seconds, the number of bits for the six quantized sensed data for the CPS pairs are defined as* $N_{bit} = [10\ 8\ 6\ 7\ 8\ 4]$.

First, the performance of the optimal adaptive model- based event-triggered control is shown. An average value of state regulation errors for the six CPS pairs is shown in the Figure 9.8. The results indicate that optimal adaptive model-based event-triggered control design presented in this section can force the regulation errors to zero asymptotically, ensuring all CPS pairs are stable. Then the performance of adaptive model-based event-triggered CPS's event-triggering error and threshold are shown for one of the subsystems. As shown in Figure 9.9, when an event is triggered and scheduled, the estimation error will be reset to zero since actual CPS state will be received at the controller. On the other hand, if the event is not triggered and scheduled, the estimation error increases due to inaccurate adaptive model. Once the adaptive parameters are estimated accurately, the estimation error converges to zero. Next, the performance of the cross-layer distributed scheduling has been evaluated. For comparison, classical widely used embedded round robin (ERR) (Mazo and Tabuada, 2011) and Greedy scheduling (Mazo and Tabuada, 2011) are added. In Figure 9.10, the cost function of multiple pairs of CPS with three different scheduling schemes is compared. The cross-layer distributed scheduling maintains the lowest value while costs of multiple pairs of

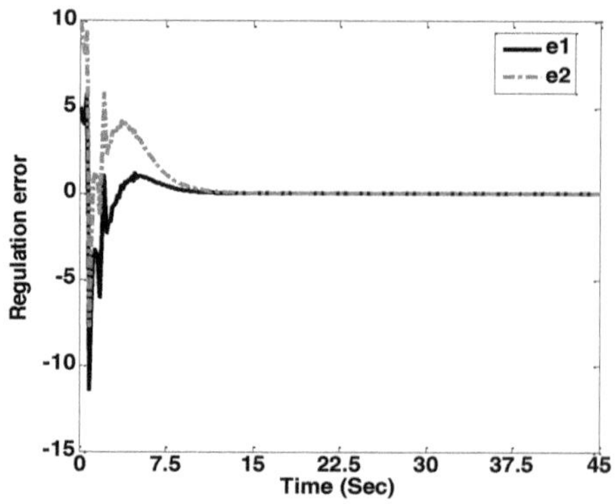

Figure 9.8 State regulation errors.

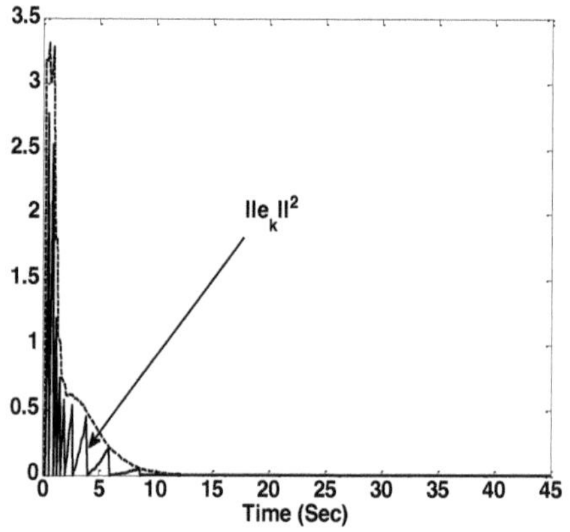

Figure 9.9 Event-triggered estimation error.

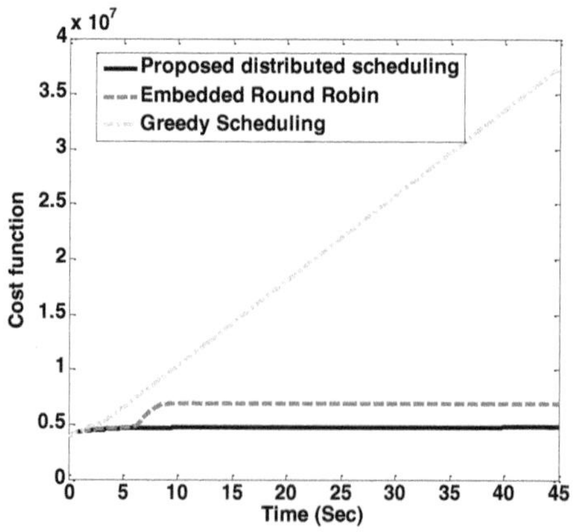

Figure 9.10 The cost function comparison (Xu, 2012).

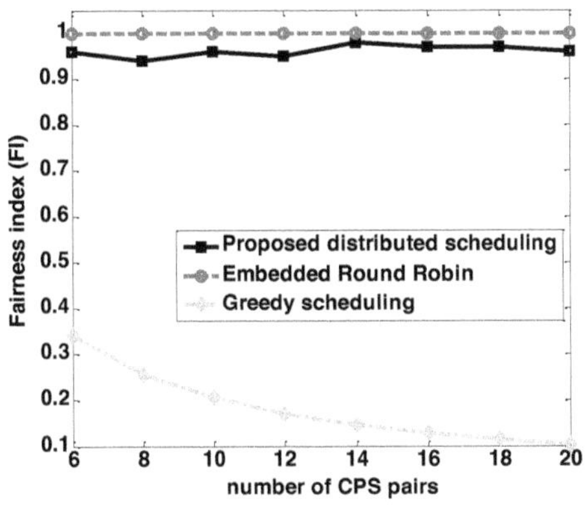

Figure 9.11 The fairness comparison (Xu, 2012).

CPS with ERR and Greedy scheduling are much higher. This suggests that the distributed scheduling scheme can improve the performance of multiple pairs of CPS. In Figure 9.11, fairness indices of the distributed scheduling protocol presented in this section and widely used ERR schemes are recorded. They seem to perform similarly and are very close to one, whereas the same metric for the Greedy scheduling is much less than one. The ERR method, though is fair, has higher cost than the distributed scheduling protocol.

9.4 SUMMARY AND CONCLUDING REMARKS

In conclusion, this chapter presented the implementation of an approximation-based control approach for a robot manipulator using only the joint position vector within an event-driven NN learning framework. Two control configurations were introduced, along with two event-triggering conditions in each configuration. The analysis revealed that the bounds on the closed-loop signals were smaller in the first configuration, where the observer was co-located with the sensor and had continuous access to the output. Event-triggering conditions were derived based on NN weights, striking a balance between computational complexity and event generation. Analytical bounds were calculated using Lyapunov stability theory, ensuring stability of the tracking error system and NN weights. Furthermore, an event-sampled output-feedback NN controller was developed for an underactuated quadrotor UAV system.The controller performed well compared to its time-sampled counterpart, offering engineering flexibility by providing a trade-off between computational efficiency and tracking/estimation performance. Depending on the specific requirements, the proposed event-sampled controller offers a viable solution. Also, in this chapter, we studied the importance of cross-layer co-design for multiple pairs of CPS. While it is important to optimize the controllers, in a shared communication network, optimizing and scheduling the transmission times will not only improve the performance of the control system but also maximize the utility of the shared communication network. Amid the escalating complexity of CPS within safety- and infrastructure-critical domains, there arises an expanding demand for co-design techniques rooted in data-driven learning. These techniques aim to synthesize optimal control and scheduling policies tailored for large-scale systems. Additionally, the heightened flexibility and interoperability of CPS expose them to increased vulnerability concerning adversarial attacks. While reaping the advantages of data-driven optimal control techniques, ensuring their safety and resilience against adversarial threats remains an ongoing challenge.

Bibliography

A. Al-Tamimi, F. L. Lewis, and M. Abu-Khalaf. Discrete-time nonlinear hjb solution using approximate dynamic programming: Convergence proof. *IEEE Trans. Syst., Man, Cybern., B*, 38(4): 943–949, Aug. 2008.

Anuradha M Annaswamy and Alexander L Fradkov. A historical perspective of adaptive control and learning. *Annual Reviews in Control*, 52:18–41, 2021.

A. Anta and P. Tabuada. To sample or not to sample: self-triggered control for nonlinear system. *IEEE Trans. on Automat. Contr.*, 55:2030–2042, 2010.

G. Antonelli. Interconnected dynamic systems: An overview on distributed control. *IEEE Control Systems*, 33(1):76–88, 2013.

K. E. Arzen. A simple event-based pid controller. In *Proceedings of the 14th World Congress of IFAC*, volume 18, pages 423–428, Beijing, China, Jul. 1999.

Karl Johan Åström and Bo Bernhardsson. Comparison of periodic and event-based sampling for first-order stochastic systems. *IFAC Proceedings Volumes*, 32(2):5006–5011, 1999.

Karl Johan Astrom and Bo M Bernhardsson. Comparison of Riemann and Lebesgue sampling for first order stochastic systems. In *Proceedings of the 41st IEEE Conference on Decision and Control, 2002.*, volume 2, pages 2011–2016. IEEE, 2002.

Karl Johan Åström and Richard M Murray. *Feedback systems: an introduction for scientists and engineers*. Princeton university press, 2021.

K.J. Aström and B. Wittenmark. *Adaptive Control*. Dover Publications, 1995.

D. D. Bainov and P. S. Simeonov. *Impulsive differential equations: periodic solutions and applications*. Longman scientific & technical, 1993.

Leemon C Baird. Reinforcement learning in continuous time: Advantage updating. In *Proceedings of 1994 IEEE International Conference on Neural Networks (ICNN'94)*, volume 4, pages 2448–2453. IEEE, 1994.

L. Bakule. Decentralized control: An overview. *Annual Reviews in Control*, 32(1):87–98, 2008.

Andrew R. Barron. Universal approximation bounds for superpositions of a sigmoidal function. *IEEE Transactions on Information Theory*, 39(3):930–945, 1993.

A. G. Barto, R. S. Sutton, and C. W. Anderson. Neuronlike adaptive elements that can solve difficult learning control problems. *IEEE Transactions on Systems, Man, and Cybernetics*, SMC-13(5): 834–846, Sept 1983. ISSN 0018-9472. doi: 10.1109/TSMC.1983.6313077.

Andrew G Barto, Warren Buckler Powell, Jennie Si, and Donald C Wunsch. *Handbook of learning and approximate dynamic programming*. Wiley-Interscience, 2004.

Tamer Basar and Pierre Bernhard. *H-infinity optimal control and related minimax design problems: a dynamic game approach*. Springer Science & Business Media, 2008.

Richard Bellman. Dynamic programming. *Science*, 153(3731):34–37, 1966.

Dimitri Bertsekas. *Dynamic programming and optimal control: Volume I*, volume 4. Athena scientific, 2012.

Dimitri P Bertsekas. Value and policy iterations in optimal control and adaptive dynamic programming. *IEEE transactions on neural networks and learning systems*, 28(3):500–509, 2015.

L Bittner. Ls pontryagin, vg boltyanskii, rv gamkrelidze, ef mishechenko, the mathematical theory of optimal processes. viii+ 360 s. new york/london 1962. john wiley & sons. preis 90/-. *Zeitschrift Angewandte Mathematik und Mechanik*, 43(10-11):514–515, 1963.

V. G. Boltyanskii, R. V. Gamkrelidze, and L. S. Pontryagin. *The Mathematical Theory of Optimal Processes*. Interscience Publishers, 1961.

Stephen P Boyd and Lieven Vandenberghe. *Convex optimization*. Cambridge university press, 2004.

Steven J Bradtke, B Erik Ydstie, and Andrew G Barto. Adaptive linear quadratic control using policy iteration. In *Proceedings of 1994 American Control Conference-ACC'94*, volume 3, pages 3475–3479. IEEE, 1994.

Roger Brockett. The early days of geometric nonlinear control. *Automatica*, 50(9):2203–2224, 2014.

Eduardo Camponogara and Marcelo Lopes de Lima. Distributed optimization for MPC of linear networks with uncertain dynamics. *Automatic Control, IEEE Transactions on*, 57(3):804–809, 2012.

CC Cheah, X Li, X Yan, and D Sun. Simple pd control scheme for robotic manipulation of biological cell. *IEEE Transactions on Automatic Control*, 60(5):1427–1432, 2015.

Chien Chern Cheah, Xiang Li, Xiao Yan, and Dong Sun. Observer-based optical manipulation of biological cells with robotic tweezers. *IEEE Transactions on Robotics*, 30(1):68–80, 2014.

Chi-Tsong Chen. *Linear system theory and design*. Saunders college publishing, 1984.

M.Z.Q. Chen, Liangyin Zhang, Housheng Su, and Chanying Li. Event-based synchronisation of linear discrete-time dynamical networks. *Control Theory Applications, IET*, 9(5):755–765, 2015. ISSN 1751-8644. doi: 10.1049/iet-cta.2014.0595.

Zheng Chen and S Jagannathan. Generalized hamilton–jacobi–bellman formulation-based neural network control of affine nonlinear discrete-time systems. *IEEE Transactions on Neural Networks*, 19(1):90–106, 2008.

Tao Cheng, Frank L Lewis, and Murad Abu-Khalaf. A neural network solution for fixed-final time optimal control of nonlinear systems. *Automatica*, 43(3):482–490, 2007.

Yi Cheng and Valery Ugrinovskii. Event-triggered leader-following tracking control for multivariable multi-agent systems. *Automatica*, 70:204–210, 2016.

Randy Cogill. Event-based control using quadratic approximate value functions. In *Proceedings of the 48h IEEE Conference on Decision and Control (CDC) held jointly with 2009 28th Chinese Control Conference*, pages 5883–5888. IEEE, 2009.

George Cybenko. Approximation by superpositions of a sigmoidal function. *Mathematics of Control, Signals and Systems*, 2(4):303–314, 1989.

Bruno da Silva and Andrew Barto. Td-deltapi: A model-free algorithm for efficient exploration. In *Proceedings of the AAAI Conference on Artificial Intelligence*, pages 886–892, 2012.

S. N. Dashkovskiy, B. Rüffer, and F. R. Wirth. Small gain theorems for large scale systems and construction of ISS Lyapunov functions. *SIAM Journal on Control and Optimization*, 48(6): 4089–4118, 2010.

José de Jesús Rubio. Sliding mode control of robotic arms with deadzone. *IET Control Theory & Applications*, 11(8):1214–1221, 2016.

José de Jesús Rubio. Discrete time control based in neural networks for pendulums. *Applied Soft Computing*, 68:821–832, 2018.

T. Dierks and S. Jagannathan. Optimal control of affine nonlinear discrete-time systems. In *Proc. Medit. Conf. Control Autom.*, pages 1390–1395, Jun. 2009a.

T. Dierks and S. Jagannathan. Optimal control of affine nonlinear continuous-time systems. In *Proc. IEEE Amer. Control Conf.*, pages 1568–1573, Jun. 2010a.

T. Dierks and S. Jagannathan. A self-tuning optimal controller for affine nonlinear continuous-time systems with unknown internal dynamics. In *2012 IEEE 51st IEEE Conference on Decision and Control (CDC)*, pages 5392–5397, Dec 2012a. doi: 10.1109/CDC.2012.6425986.

Travis Dierks and S Jagannathan. Optimal tracking control of affine nonlinear discrete-time systems with unknown internal dynamics. In *Decision and Control, 2009 held jointly with the 2009 28th Chinese Control Conference. CDC/CCC 2009. Proceedings of the 48th IEEE Conference on*, pages 6750–6755. IEEE, 2009b.

Travis Dierks and S Jagannathan. Output feedback control of a quadrotor uav using neural networks. *IEEE transactions on neural networks*, 21(1):50–66, 2009c.

Travis Dierks and S Jagannathan. Online optimal control of affine nonlinear discrete-time systems with unknown internal dynamics by using time-based policy update. *IEEE Transactions on Neural Networks and Learning Systems*, 23(7):1118–1129, 2012b.

Travis Dierks and Sarangapani Jagannathan. Optimal control of affine nonlinear continuous-time systems using an online hamilton-jacobi-isaacs formulation. In *49th IEEE Conference on Decision and Control (CDC)*, pages 3048–3053. IEEE, 2010b.

D. V. Dimarogonas and K. H. Johanson. Event-triggered control for multi-agent systems. In *Proc. IEEE Conf. Decision and Contr.*, pages 7131–7136, 2009a.

D. V. Dimarogonas and K. H. Johanson. Event-triggered cooperative control. In *Proc. Europ. Contr. Conf.*, pages 3015–3020, 2009b.

Lu Dong, Xiangnan Zhong, Changyin Sun, and Haibo He. Event-triggered adaptive dynamic programming for continuous-time systems with control constraints. *IEEE Transactions on Neural Networks and Learning Systems*, 28(8):1941–1952, 2017.

M. C. F. Donkers and W. P. M. H. Heemels. Output-based event-triggered control with guaranteed l-infinity-gain and improved and decentralized event-triggering. *IEEE Transactions on Automatic Control*, 57(6):1362–1376, Jun. 2012.

MCF Donkers and WPMH Heemels. Output-based event-triggered control with guaranteed $\mathscr{L}_\infty$-gain and improved event-triggering. In *Proceedings of 49th IEEE Conference on Decision and Control (CDC)*, pages 3246–3251, 2010.

R. Dorf, M. Farren, and C. Phillips. Adaptive sampling frequency for sampled data control systems. *IRE Transactions on Automatic Control*, 7(1):38–47, Jan. 1962.

RC Dorf and RH Bishop. Modern control systems, pearsons, 2000.

Kenji Doya. Reinforcement learning in continuous time and space. *Neural computation*, 12(1): 219–245, 2000.

Philip G Drazin and Philip Drazin Drazin. *Nonlinear systems*. Cambridge University Press, 1992.

W. B. Dunbar. Distributed receding horizon control of dynamically coupled nonlinear systems. *IEEE Transactions on Automatic Control*, 52(7):1249–1263, July 2007. ISSN 0018-9286. doi: 10.1109/tac.2007.900828.

P. Ellis. Extension of phase plane analysis to quantized systems. *IRE Transactions on Automatic Control*, 4(2):43–54, Nov. 1959.

A. Eqtami, D. V. Dimarogonas, and K. J. Kyriakopoulos. Event-triggered control for discrete-time systems. In *Proc. Amer. Contr. Conf.*, pages 4719–4724, 2010.

Mirosław Galicki. Finite-time control of robotic manipulators. *Automatica*, 51:49–54, 2015.

Huijun Gao and Tongwen Chen. Network-based h_∞ output tracking control. *IEEE Transactions on Automatic control*, 53(3):655–667, 2008.

W. Gao, Y. Jiang, Z.P. Jiang, and T. Chai. Output-feedback adaptive optimal control of interconnected systems based on robust adaptive dynamic programming. *Automatica*, 72:37–45, 2016.

E. Garcia and P. J. Antsaklis. Model-based event-triggered control with time-varying network delays. In *Proc. IEEE Conf. Decision and Contr.*, pages 1650–1655, 2011.

E. Garcia and P. J. Antsaklis. Parameter estimation in time-triggered and event-triggered model-based control of uncertain systems. *International Journal of Control*, 85(9):1327–1342, Apr. 2012.

E. Garcia and P. J. Antsaklis. Model-based event-triggered control for systems with quantization and time-varying network delays. *IEEE Transactions on Automatic Control*, 58(2):422–434, Feb 2013. ISSN 0018-9286. doi: 10.1109/tac.2012.2211411.

Shuzhi Sam Ge, Chang C Hang, Tong H Lee, and Tao Zhang. *Stable adaptive neural network control*, volume 13. Springer Science & Business Media, 2013.

Rafal Goebel, Ricardo G Sanfelice, and Andrew R Teel. Hybrid dynamical systems. *IEEE control systems magazine*, 29(2):28–93, 2009.

Tom Gommans, Duarte Antunes, Tijs Donkers, Paulo Tabuada, and Maurice Heemels. Self-triggered linear quadratic control. *Automatica*, 50(4):1279–1287, 2014.

Ian Goodfellow, Yoshua Bengio, and Aaron Courville. *Deep learning*. MIT press, 2016.

Graham C Goodwin and Kwai Sang Sin. *Adaptive filtering prediction and control*. Courier Corporation, 2014.

Michael Green and John B Moore. Persistence of excitation in linear systems. In *American Control Conference, 1985*, pages 412–417. Ieee, 1985.

M. Guinaldo, D. V. Dimarogonas, K. H. Johansson, J. Sánchez, and S. Dormido. Distributed event-based control for interconnected linear systems. In *2011 50th IEEE Conference on Decision and Control and European Control Conference*, pages 2553–2558, Dec 2011. doi: 10.1109/cdc.2011.6160580.

María Guinaldo, Daniel Lehmann, J Sanchez, Sebastián Dormido, and Karl Henrik Johansson. Distributed event-triggered control with network delays and packet losses. In *2012 IEEE 51st IEEE Conference on Decision and Control (CDC)*, pages 1–6. IEEE, 2012.

A. Gusrialdi and S. Hirche. Communication topology design for large-scale interconnected systems with time delay. In *American Control Conference (ACC), 2011*, pages 4508–4513. IEEE, 2011.

Wassim M Haddad, VijaySekhar Chellaboina, and Sergey G Nersesov. Impulsive and hybrid dynamical systems. *Princeton Series in Applied Mathematics*, 2006.

Yoram Halevi and Asok Ray. Integrated communication and control systems: Part i—analysis. *Journal of Dynamic Systems, Measurement, and Control*, 110(4):367–373, 1988.

Yujuan Han, Wenlian Lu, and Tianping Chen. Consensus analysis of networks with time-varying topology and event-triggered diffusions. *Neural Networks*, 71:196–203, 2015.

Tomohisa Hayakawa and Wassim M Haddad. Stable neural hybrid adaptive control for nonlinear uncertain impulsive dynamical systems. In *Proceedings of the 44th IEEE Conference on Decision and Control*, pages 5510–5515. IEEE, 2005.

Simon Haykin. *Neural Networks: A Comprehensive Foundation*. Macmillan College Publishing Company, 1994.

Kaiming He, Xiangyu Zhang, Shaoqing Ren, and Jian Sun. Deep residual learning for image recognition. *Proceedings of the IEEE Conference on Computer Vision and Pattern Recognition (CVPR)*, pages 770–778, 2016a.

Wei He, Yiting Dong, and Changyin Sun. Adaptive neural impedance control of a robotic manipulator with input saturation. *IEEE Transactions on Systems, Man, and Cybernetics: Systems*, 46 (3):334–344, 2016b.

Wei He, Haifeng Huang, and Shuzhi Sam Ge. Adaptive neural network control of a robotic manipulator with time-varying output constraints. *IEEE Transactions on Cybernetics*, 47(10):3136–3147, 2017.

W. P. M. H. Heemels and M. C. F. Donkers. Model-based periodic event-triggered control of linear systems. *Automatica*, 49(3):698–711, Mar. 2013.

W. P. M. H. Heemels, K. H. Johansson, and P. Tabuada. An introduction to event-triggered and self-triggered control. In *Proceedings of the 51st IEEE Conference on Decision and Control*, pages 3270–3285, Maul, Hawaii, USA, Dec. 2012.

WP Maurice H Heemels, Andrew R Teel, Nathan Van de Wouw, and Dragan Nesic. Networked control systems with communication constraints: Tradeoffs between transmission intervals, delays and performance. *IEEE Transactions on Automatic control*, 55(8):1781–1796, 2010.

WPMH Heemels, JH Sandee, and PPJ Van Den Bosch. Analysis of event-driven controllers for linear systems. *International journal of control*, 81(4):571–590, 2008.

T. Henningsson, E. Johannesson, and A. Cervin. Sporadic event-based control of first-order linear stochastic systems. *Automatica*, 44(11):2890–2895, Nov. 2008.

Geoffrey E Hinton and Ruslan R Salakhutdinov. Reducing the dimensionality of data with neural networks. *Science*, 313(5786):504–507, 2006.

Sandra Hirche, Tilemachos Matiakis, and Martin Buss. A distributed controller approach for delay-independent stability of networked control systems. *Automatica*, 45(8):1828–1836, 2009.

Kurt Hornik, Maxwell Stinchcombe, and Halbert White. Multilayer feedforward networks are universal approximators. *Neural Networks*, 2(5):359–366, 1989.

Zhong-Sheng Hou and Zhuo Wang. From model-based control to data-driven control: Survey, classification and perspective. *Information Sciences*, 235:3–35, 2013.

D. Hristu-Varsakelis and P. R. Kumar. Interrupt-based feedback control over a shared communication medium. In *Proceedings of the 41st IEEE Conference on Decision and Control*, pages 3223–3228, Las Vegas, Nevada, USA, Dec. 2002.

S. L. Hu and D. Yue. Event-triggered control design of linear networked systems with quantization. *ISA Transactions*, 51(1):153–162, Jan. 2012.

Sunan Huang, Kok Kiong Tan, and Tong Heng Lee. Decentralized control design for large-scale systems with strong interconnections using neural networks. *IEEE Transactions on Automatic Control*, 48(5):805–810, May 2003. ISSN 0018-9286. doi: 10.1109/tac.2003.811258.

Don R. Hush and Barry G. Horne. Progress in supervised neural networks. *IEEE Signal processing magazine*, 10(1):8–39, 1993.

Boris Igelnik and Yoh-Han Pao. Stochastic choice of basis functions in adaptive function approximation and the functional-link net. *IEEE Transactions on Neural Networks*, 6(6):1320–1329, 1995.

O. C. Imer and T. Basar. To measure or to control: optimal control with scheduled measurements and controls. In *Proceedings of the American Control Conference*, pages 14–16, Minneapolis, MN, USA, Jul. 2006.

P Ioannou. Decentralized adaptive control of interconnected systems. *IEEE Transactions on Automatic Control*, 31(4):291–298, 1986.

Petros Ioannou and Baris Fidan. *Adaptive control tutorial*. SIAM, 2006.

Kaabche Issam and Geng Qingbo. Research on control strategies for the stabilization of quadrotor uav. In *Fifth International Conference on Intelligent Control and Information Processing*, pages 286–292. IEEE, 2014.

S. Jagannathan. *Neural Network Control of Nonlinear Discrete-time Systems*. CRC Press, Boca Raton, FL, 2006.

Mohammad Jamshidi. *Large-scale systems: modeling, control, and fuzzy logic*. Prentice-Hall, Inc., 1996.

Libin Jiang and Jean Walrand. A distributed csma algorithm for throughput and utility maximization in wireless networks. *IEEE/ACM Transactions on Networking*, 18(3):960–972, 2009.

Y. Jiang and Z.P. Jiang. Robust adaptive dynamic programming for large-scale systems with an application to multimachine power systems. *IEEE Transactions on Circuits and Systems II: Express Briefs*, 59(10):693–697, 2012.

Yu Jiang and Zhong-Ping Jiang. Global adaptive dynamic programming for continuous-time nonlinear systems. *IEEE Transactions on Automatic Control*, 60(11):2917–2929, 2015.

Z. P. Jiang and Y. Wang. Input-to-state stability for discrete-time nonlinear system. *Automatica*, 37: 857–869, 2001.

Z.P. Jiang, A. R. Teel, and L. Praly. Small-gain theorem for ISS systems and applications. *Mathematics of Control, Signals, and Systems (MCSS)*, 7(2):95–120, 1994.

Z.P. Jiang, I.M.Y. Mareels, and Y. Wang. A Lyapunov formulation of the nonlinear small-gain theorem for interconnected ISS systems. *Automatica*, 32(8):1211–1215, 1996.

Marcus Johnson, Rushikesh Kamalapurkar, Shubhendu Bhasin, and Warren E Dixon. Approximate n-player nonzero-sum game solution for an uncertain continuous nonlinear system. *IEEE Transactions on Neural Networks and Learning Systems*, 26(8):1645–1658, 2015.

Thomas Kailath. *Linear systems*, volume 156. Prentice-Hall Englewood Cliffs, NJ, 1980.

Rudolf E. Kalman. Contributions to the theory of optimal control. *Boletin de la Sociedad Matematica Mexicana*, 1960a.

Rudolf E. Kalman. A new approach to linear filtering and prediction problems. *Journal of Basic*

Engineering, 82(1):35–45, 1960b.

Rudolf E Kalman and John E Bertram. Control system analysis and design via the "second method" of lyapunov: I—continuous-time systems. *Journal of Basic Engineering*, 1960.

Rudolf Emil Kalman. Mathematical description of linear dynamical systems. *Journal of the Society for Industrial and Applied Mathematics, Series A: Control*, 1(2):152–192, 1963.

Rushikesh Kamalapurkar, Huyen Dinh, Shubhendu Bhasin, and Warren E Dixon. Approximate optimal trajectory tracking for continuous-time nonlinear systems. *Automatica*, 51:40–48, 2015.

Iasson Karafyllis and Miroslav Krstic. Adaptive certainty-equivalence control with regulation-triggered finite-time least-squares identification. *IEEE Transactions on Automatic Control*, 63 (10):3261–3275, 2018.

Iasson Karafyllis, Maria Kontorinaki, and Miroslav Krstic. Adaptive control by regulation-triggered batch least squares. *IEEE Transactions on Automatic Control*, 65(7):2842–2855, 2019.

Mehrdad R Kermani, Rajni V Patel, and Mehrdad Moallem. Multimode control of a large-scale robotic manipulator. *IEEE Transactions on Robotics*, 23(6):1264–1270, 2007.

H. K. Khalil. *Nonlinear Systems*. Prentice Hall, Upper Saddle River, NJ, 2002.

Mohammad Javad Khojasteh, Pavankumar Tallapragada, Jorge Cortés, and Massimo Franceschetti. The value of timing information in event-triggered control. *IEEE Transactions on Automatic Control*, 65(3):925–940, 2019.

Minho Kim. A simple and fast approach to design neural network approximators using the random vector functional link network. *Proceedings of IEEE International Conference on Neural Networks*, pages 2136–2140, 1996.

Young Ho Kim and Frank L Lewis. Neural network output feedback control of robot manipulators. *IEEE Transactions on Robotics and Automation*, 15(2):301–309, 1999.

Donald E. Kirk. *Optimal Control Theory: An Introduction*. Dover Publications, 2004.

Bahare Kiumarsi, Kyriakos G Vamvoudakis, Hamidreza Modares, and Frank L Lewis. Optimal and autonomous control using reinforcement learning: A survey. *IEEE Transactions on Neural Networks and Learning Systems*, 29(6):2042–2062, 2017.

Morris Kline. *Mathematical Thought from Ancient to Modern Times*. Oxford University Press, 1990.

Bart Kosko. *Neural Networks and Fuzzy Systems: A Dynamical Systems Approach to Machine Intelligence*. Prentice Hall, 1992.

Alex Krizhevsky, Ilya Sutskever, and Geoffrey E Hinton. Imagenet large scale visual recognition challenge. In *Advances in neural information processing systems*, volume 25, 2012.

P. R. Kumar and P. Varaiya. *Stochastic Systems: Estimation, Identification, and Adaptive Control*. Prentice-Hall, 1986.

Sun Yuan Kung. *Digital Neural Networks*. Prentice Hall, 1993.

B. C. Kuo. *Analysis and Synthesis of Sampled Data Control Systems*. Prentice Hall, Englewood Cliffs, NJ, 2012.

Huibert Kwakernaak and Raphael Sivan. *Linear optimal control systems*, volume 1. Wiley-interscience New York, 1972.

GC Layek et al. *An introduction to dynamical systems and chaos*, volume 449. Springer, 2015.

Yann LeCun, Bernhard E Boser, John S Denker, Donnie Henderson, Richard E Howard, Wayne Hubbard, and Lawrence D Jackel. Backpropagation applied to handwritten zip code recognition. In *Neural Computation*, pages 541–551, 1989.

Yann LeCun, Léon Bottou, Genevieve B Orr, and Klaus-Robert Müller. Efficient backprop. In *Neural networks: Tricks of the trade*, pages 9–50. Springer, 2002.

DongBin Lee, Timothy C Burg, Bin Xian, and Darren M Dawson. Output feedback tracking control of an underactuated quad-rotor uav. In *2007 American Control Conference*, pages 1775–1780. IEEE, 2007.

J. Y. Lee, J. B. Park, and Y. H. Choi. Integral reinforcement learning for continuous-time input-affine nonlinear systems with simultaneous invariant explorations. *IEEE Transactions on Neural Networks and Learning Systems*, 26(5):916–932, May 2015. ISSN 2162-237X. doi: 10.1109/TNNLS.2014.2328590.

Tong Heng Lee and Christopher John Harris. *Adaptive neural network control of robotic manipulators*, volume 19. World Scientific, 1998.

D. Lehmann and J. Lunze. Event-based output-feedback control. In *Proceedings of the* 19th *Mediterranean Conference on Control and Automation*, pages 982–987, Corfu, Greece, Jun. 2011.

Michael Lemmon. Event-triggered feedback in control, estimation, and optimization. *Networked control systems*, pages 293–358, 2010.

Martin D. Levine. *Vision in Man and Machine*. McGraw-Hill, 1991.

F. L. Lewis, S Jagannathan, and A Yesildirak. *Neural network control of robot manipulators and non-linear systems*. CRC Press, 1998.

F. L. Lewis, D. Vrabie, and K. G. Vamvoudakis. Reinforcement learning and feedback control: Using natural decision methods to design optimal adaptive controllers. *IEEE Control Systems*, 32(6):76–105, Dec 2012a. ISSN 1066-033x. doi: 10.1109/mcs.2012.2214134.

Frank L. Lewis, Darren M. Dawson, and Chaouki T. Abdallah. Neural network control of robot manipulators and nonlinear systems. *Series in Systems and Control*, 1999.

Frank L Lewis, Draguna Vrabie, and Vassilis L Syrmos. *Optimal control*. John Wiley & Sons, 2012b.

Jr-Shin Li and Navin Khaneja. Control of inhomogeneous quantum ensembles. *Physical review A*, 73(3):030302, 2006.

Daniel Liberzon. *Calculus of Variations and Optimal Control Theory: A Concise Introduction*. Princeton University Press, 2011.

Luen-Woei Liou and Asok Ray. A stochastic regulator for integrated communication and control systems: Part i—formulation of control law. *Journal of dynamic systems, measurement, and control*, 113(4):604–611, 1991.

Richard P. Lippmann. An introduction to computing with neural nets. *IEEE ASSP Magazine*, 4(2): 4–22, 1987.

D. Liu, D. Wang, D. Zhao, Q. Wei, and N. Jin. Neural-network-based optimal control for a class of unknown discrete-time nonlinear systems using globalized dual heuristic programming. *IEEE Transactions on Automation Science and Engineering*, 9(3):628–634, July 2012. ISSN 1545-5955. doi: 10.1109/tase.2012.2198057.

Derong Liu and Qinglai Wei. Finite-approximation-error-based optimal control approach for discrete-time nonlinear systems. *IEEE Transactions on Cybernetics*, 43(2):779–789, 2013.

Derong Liu, Ding Wang, and Hongliang Li. Decentralized stabilization for a class of continuous-time nonlinear interconnected systems using online learning optimal control approach. *IEEE Transactions on Neural Networks and Learning Systems*, 25(2):418–428, 2014.

T. Liu and Z.P. Jiang. A small-gain approach to robust event-triggered control of nonlinear systems. *IEEE Transactions on Automatic Control*, 60(8):2072–2085, 2015.

Yen-Chen Liu and Nikhil Chopra. Control of robotic manipulators under input/output communication delays: Theory and experiments. *IEEE Transactions on Robotics*, 28(3):742–751, 2012.

L. Ljung. *System Identification: Theory for the User*. Prentice-Hall, 1999.

Robert E. Lucas and Nancy L. Stokey. Optimal fiscal and monetary policy in an economy without capital. *Journal of Monetary Economics*, 12(1):55–93, 1983.

G. Luders and K. Narendra. An adaptive observer and identifier for a linear system. *IEEE Trans. on Automat. Contr.*, 18:496–499, 1973.

David G Luenberger. *Dynamic Systems*. J. Wiley Sons, 1979.

Jan Lunze and Daniel Lehmann. A state-feedback approach to event-based control. *Automatica*, 46 (1):211–215, 2010.

Tarek Madani and Abdelaziz Benallegue. Sliding mode observer and backstepping control for a quadrotor unmanned aerial vehicles. In *2007 American control conference*, pages 5887–5892. IEEE, 2007.

M. Mazo and P. Tabuada. Decentralized event-triggered control over wireless sensor/actuator networks. *IEEE Transactions on Automatic Control*, 56(10):2456–2461, Oct 2011. ISSN 0018-9286. doi: 10.1109/tac.2011.2164036.

M. Mazo Jr. and M. Cao. Decentralized event-triggered control with asynchronous updates. In *Proceedings of the 50th Decision and Control and European Control Conference*, pages 2547–2552, Orlando, FL, USA, Dec. 2011.

M. Mazo Jr. and D. V. Dimarogonas. On self-triggered control for linear systems. In *Proceedings of the American Control Conference*, pages 3371–3376, Baltimore, MD, USA, Jun. 2010.

Warren S McCulloch and Walter Pitts. A logical calculus of the ideas immanent in nervous activity. *The Bulletin of Mathematical Biophysics*, 5(4):115–133, 1943.

Shahab Mehraeen and S Jagannathan. Decentralized optimal control of a class of interconnected nonlinear discrete-time systems by using online hamilton-jacobi-bellman formulation. *IEEE Transactions on Neural Networks*, 22(11):1757–1769, 2011.

Xiangyu Meng and Tongwen Chen. Event-driven communication for sampled-data control systems. In *2013 American Control Conference*, pages 3002–3007. IEEE, 2013.

Anthony N Michel. Impulsive and hybrid dynamcial systems: Stability, dissipativity and control (wm haddad et al.; 2008)[bookshelf]. *IEEE Control Systems Magazine*, 28(2):87–88, 2008.

Marvin Minsky and Seymour Papert. *Perceptrons: An Introduction to Computational Geometry.* MIT Press, 1969.

Hamidreza Modares and Frank L Lewis. Linear quadratic tracking control of partially-unknown continuous-time systems using reinforcement learning. *IEEE Transactions on Automatic control*, 59(11):3051–3056, 2014a.

Hamidreza Modares and Frank L Lewis. Optimal tracking control of nonlinear partially-unknown constrained-input systems using integral reinforcement learning. *Automatica*, 50(7):1780–1792, 2014b.

Adam Molin and Sandra Hirche. On the optimality of certainty equivalence for event-triggered control systems. *IEEE Transactions on Automatic Control*, 58(2):470–474, 2013.

Vignesh Narayanan and S Jagannathan. Distributed adaptive optimal regulation of uncertain large-scale linear networked control systems using **Q**-learning. In *Proceedings of IEEE Symposium Series on Computational Intelligence*, pages 587–592, 2015.

Vignesh Narayanan and S Jagannathan. Approximate optimal distributed control of uncertain non-linear interconnected systems with event-sampled feedback. In *Proceedings of IEEE 55th Conference on Decision and Control (CDC)*, pages 5827–5832, 2016a.

Vignesh Narayanan and S Jagannathan. Distributed adaptive optimal regulation of uncertain large-scale interconnected systems using hybrid q-learning approach. *IET Control Theory & Applications*, 10(12):1448–1457, 2016b.

Vignesh Narayanan and S Jagannathan. Event-sampled adaptive neural network control of robot manipulators. In *Neural Networks (IJCNN), 2016 International Joint Conference on*, pages 4941–4946. IEEE, 2016c.

Vignesh Narayanan and S Jagannathan. Event-triggered distributed control of nonlinear interconnected systems using online reinforcement learning with exploration. *IEEE transactions on cybernetics*, 48(9):2510–2519, 2017.

Vignesh Narayanan, S Jagannathan, and Kannan Ramkumar. Event-sampled output feedback control of robot manipulators using neural networks. *IEEE transactions on neural networks and learning systems*, 30(6):1651–1658, 2018a.

Vignesh Narayanan, Avimanyu Sahoo, and S Jagannathan. Optimal event-triggered control of non-linear systems: A min-max approach. In *2018 Annual American Control Conference (ACC)*, pages 3441–3446. IEEE, 2018b.

Vignesh Narayanan, Avimanyu Sahoo, S Jagannathan, and Koshy George. Approximate optimal distributed control of nonlinear interconnected systems using event-triggered nonzero-sum games. *IEEE Transactions on Neural Networks and Learning Systems*, 30(5):1512–1522, 2018c.

Kumpati S Narendra and Anuradha M Annaswamy. *Stable adaptive systems*. Courier Corporation, 2012.

Kumpati S Narendra and Snehasis Mukhopadhyay. To communicate or not to communicate: A decision-theoretic approach to decentralized adaptive control. In *Proceedings of American Control Conference (ACC)*, pages 6369–6376. IEEE, 2010.

Kumpati S Narendra and Kannan Parthasarathy. Identification and control of dynamical systems using neural networks. *IEEE Transactions on Neural Networks*, 1(1):4–27, 1990.

K. Ogata. *Discrete Time Control Systems*. Prentice Hall, Englewood Cliffs, NJ, 2011.

Yongping Pan, Yiqi Liu, Bin Xu, and Haoyong Yu. Hybrid feedback feedforward: An efficient design of adaptive neural network control. *Neural Networks*, 76:122–134, 2016.

Jaeson Park and I. W. Sandberg. Universal approximation using radial-basis-function networks. *Neural Computation*, 3(2):246–257, 1991.

Alexander Pekarovskiy, Thomas Nierhoff, Sandra Hirche, and Martin Buss. Dynamically consistent online adaptation of fast motions for robotic manipulators. *IEEE Transactions on Robotics*, 34 (1):166–182, 2018.

G. Pekir and A. Shiryaev. *Optimal stopping and free-boundary problems*. Lectures in Mathematica. Birkhauser Verlag Press, Basel, Switzerland, 2006.

Chen Peng, Yang Song, Xiang Peng Xie, Min Zhao, and Mei-Rui Fei. Event-triggered output tracking control for wireless networked control systems with communication delays and data dropouts. *IET Control Theory & Applications*, 10(17):2195–2203, 2016.

Pierre Peretto. *An Introduction to the Modeling of Neural Networks*. Cambridge University Press, 1992.

Thanh Ngoc Pham, Hieu Trinh, and Amanullah Maung Than Oo. Distributed control of hvdc links for primary frequency control of time-delay power systems. *IEEE Transactions on Power Systems*, 34(2):1301–1314, 2019. doi: 10.1109/TPWRS.2018.2869984.

A. M. Phillips and M. Tomizuka. Multi-rate estimation and control under time-varying data sampling with applications to information storage devices. In *Proceedings of the American Control Conference*, pages 4152–4155, Seattle, WA, USA, Jun. 1995.

L. S. Pontryagin, V. G. Boltyanskii, R. V. Gamkrelidze, and E. F. Mishchenko. *The Mathematical Theory of Optimal Processes*. Interscience Publishers, 1962.

Romain Postoyan, Adolfo Anta, Dragan Nešić, and Paulo Tabuada. A unifying lyapunov-based framework for the event-triggered control of nonlinear systems. In *2011 50th IEEE conference on decision and control and European control conference*, pages 2559–2564. IEEE, 2011.

Romain Postoyan, Marcos Cesar Bragagnolo, Ernest Galbrun, Jamal Daafouz, Dragan Nešić, and Eugênio B Castelan. Event-triggered tracking control of unicycle mobile robots. *Automatica*, 52: 302–308, 2015.

Danil V Prokhorov and Donald C Wunsch. Adaptive critic designs. *IEEE transactions on Neural Networks*, 8(5):997–1007, 1997.

Danil V Prokhorov, Roberto A Santiago, and Donald C Wunsch. Adaptive critic designs: A case study for neurocontrol. *Neural Networks*, 8(9):1367–1372, 1995.

M. Rabi and J. S. Baras. Level-triggered control of scalar linear system. In *Proceedings of the Mediterranean Conference on Control and Automation*, pages 1–6, Athens, Greece, Jul. 2007.

M. Rabi, K. H. Johansson, and M. Johansson. Optimal stopping for event-triggered sensing and actuation. In *Proceedings of the* 47th *IEEE Conference on Decision and Control*, pages 3607–3612, Cancun, Mexico, Dec. 2008.

Frank P. Ramsey. A mathematical theory of saving. *The Economic Journal*, 38(152):543–559, 1928.

Frank Rosenblatt. The perceptron: a probabilistic model for information storage and organization in the brain. *Psychological Review*, 65(6):386, 1958.

Halsey Lawrence Royden and Patrick Fitzpatrick. *Real analysis*, volume 2. Macmillan New York, 1968.

Walter Rudin. *Principles of mathematical analysis*. New York: McGraw-Hill, 1953.

David E. Rumelhart, Geoffrey E. Hinton, and Ronald J. Williams. Learning representations by back-propagating errors. *Nature*, 323(6088):533–536, 1986.

P. M. Sadegh. Functional link net: A nonlinear polynomial neural network. *Journal of Intelligent & Robotic Systems*, 7(4):403–423, 1993.

A. Sahoo, H. Xu, and S. Jagannathan. Neural network-based adaptive event-triggered control of nonlinear continuous-time systems. In *2013 IEEE International Symposium on Intelligent Control (ISIC)*, pages 35–40, Aug 2013a. doi: 10.1109/ISIC.2013.6658613.

A. Sahoo, H. Xu, and S. Jagannathan. Neural network-based event-triggered state feedback control of nonlinear continuous-time systems. *IEEE Transactions on Neural Networks and Learning Systems*, 27(3):497–509, March 2016. ISSN 2162-237X. doi: 10.1109/TNNLS.2015.2416259.

Avimanyu Sahoo. *Event sampled optimal adaptive regulation of linear and a class of nonlinear systems*. PhD thesis, Missouri University of Science and Technology, 2015.

Avimanyu Sahoo and S Jagannathan. Event-triggered optimal regulation of uncertain linear discrete-time systems by using q-learning scheme. In *53rd IEEE Conference on Decision and Control*, pages 1233–1238. IEEE, 2014.

Avimanyu Sahoo and Sarangapani Jagannathan. Stochastic optimal regulation of nonlinear networked control systems by using event-driven adaptive dynamic programming. *IEEE transactions on cybernetics*, 47(2):425–438, 2016.

Avimanyu Sahoo and Vignesh Narayanan. Optimization of sampling intervals for tracking control of nonlinear systems: A game theoretic approach. *Neural Networks*, 114:78–90, 2019.

Avimanyu Sahoo, Hao Xu, and S Jagannathan. Adaptive event-triggered control of a uncertain linear discrete time system using measured input and output data. In *2013 American Control Conference*, pages 5672–5677. IEEE, 2013b.

Avimanyu Sahoo, Hao Xu, and S Jagannathan. Neural network-based event-triggered state feedback control of nonlinear continuous-time systems. *IEEE Transactions on Neural Networks and Learning Systems*, 27(3):497–509, 2015.

Avimanyu Sahoo, Vignesh Narayanan, and S Jagannathan. Optimal sampling and regulation of uncertain interconnected linear continuous time systems. In *Proceedings of IEEE Symposium Series on Computational Intelligence (SSCI)*, pages 1–6, 2017a.

Avimanyu Sahoo, Hao Xu, and S Jagannathan. Approximate optimal control of affine nonlinear continuous-time systems using event-sampled neurodynamic programming. *IEEE Transactions on Neural Networks and Learning Systems*, 28(3):639–652, 2017b.

Avimanyu Sahoo, Vignesh Narayanan, and S Jagannathan. A min–max approach to event-and self-triggered sampling and regulation of linear systems. *IEEE Transactions on Industrial Electronics*, 66(7):5433–5440, 2018.

Robert M Sanner and Jean-Jacques E Slotine. Gaussian networks for direct adaptive control. In *1991 American control conference*, pages 2153–2159. IEEE, 1991.

Jagannathan Sarangapani and Hao Xu. *Optimal Networked Control Systems with MATLAB*. CRC Press, 2018.

Shankar Sastry and Marc Bodson. *Adaptive control: stability, convergence and robustness*. Courier Corporation, 2011.

Michael Sfakiotakis, Asimina Kazakidi, Theodoros Evdaimon, Avgousta Chatzidaki, and Dimitris P Tsakiris. Multi-arm robotic swimmer actuated by antagonistic sma springs. In *Intelligent Robots and Systems (IROS), 2015 IEEE/RSJ International Conference on*, pages 1540–1545. IEEE, 2015.

Hu Shousong and Zhu Qixin. Stochastic optimal control and analysis of stability of networked control systems with long delay. *Automatica*, 39(11):1877–1884, 2003.

Jennie Si, Andrew G Barto, Warren B Powell, and Don Wunsch. *Handbook of learning and approximate dynamic programming*, volume 2. John Wiley & Sons, 2004.

Dragoslav D Siljak. *Decentralized control of complex systems*. Courier Corporation, 2011.

Dragoslav D Siljak and AI Zecevic. Control of large-scale systems: Beyond decentralized feedback. *Annual Reviews in Control*, 29(2):169–179, 2005.

P. K. Simpson. Artificial neural systems: A new tool for spatial analysis. *Landscape and Urban Planning*, 21:37–51, 1992.

Ruizhuo Song, Frank L Lewis, and Qinglai Wei. Off-policy integral reinforcement learning method to solve nonlinear continuous-time multiplayer nonzero-sum games. *IEEE Transactions on Neural Networks and Learning Systems*, 28(3):704–713, 2017.

Yan Song and Xiaosheng Fang. Distributed model predictive control for polytopic uncertain systems with randomly occurring actuator saturation and packet loss. *IET Control Theory & Applications*, 8(5):297–310, 2014.

E. D. Sontag. Input to state stability: basic concepts and results. In *Nonlinear and Optimal Control Theory*, pages 163–220. Springer, Berlin/Heidelberg, 2008.

J. T. Spooner and K. M. Passino. Decentralized adaptive control of nonlinear systems using radial basis neural networks. *IEEE Transactions on Automatic Control*, 44(11):2050–2057, Nov 1999. ISSN 0018-9286. doi: 10.1109/9.802914.

Vineet Srivastava and Mehul Motani. Cross-layer design: a survey and the road ahead. *IEEE communications magazine*, 43(12):112–119, 2005.

Alan Wilbor Starr and Yu-Chi Ho. Nonzero-sum differential games. *Journal of Optimization Theory and Applications*, 3(3):184–206, 1969.

C. Stocker and J. Lunze. Event-based control of nonlinear systems: An input-output linearization approach. In *Proceedings of the 50th Decision and Control and European Control Conference*, pages 2541–2546, Orlando, FL, USA, Dec. 2011.

Gilbert Strang. *Introduction to linear algebra*. SIAM, 2022.

Dirk J. Struik. *A Source Book in Mathematics, 1200-1800*. Source Books in the History of the Sciences. Harvard University Press, 1986.

Christian Stöcker and Jan Lunze. Event-based control of nonlinear systems: An input-output linearization approach. In *2011 50th IEEE Conference on Decision and Control and European Control Conference*, pages 2541–2546, 2011. doi: 10.1109/CDC.2011.6160526.

Changyin Sun, Hejia Gao, Wei He, and Yao Yu. Fuzzy neural network control of a flexible robotic manipulator using assumed mode method. *IEEE Transactions on Neural Networks and Learning Systems*, 2018.

Mingxuan Sun, Shuzhi Sam Ge, and Iven MY Mareels. Adaptive repetitive learning control of robotic manipulators without the requirement for initial repositioning. *IEEE Transactions on Robotics*, 22(3):563–568, 2006.

Ilya Sutskever, Oriol Vinyals, and Quoc V. Le. Sequence to sequence learning with neural networks. *Advances in Neural Information Processing Systems*, 27:3104–3112, 2014.

Richard S Sutton and Andrew G Barto. *Reinforcement learning: An introduction*. MIT press Cambridge, 1998.

Nathan Szanto. *Event-sampled direct adaptive neural network control of uncertain strict-feedback system with application to quadrotor unmanned aerial vehicle*. Masters Theses. 7616., 2016.

Nathan Szanto, Vignesh Narayanan, and S Jagannathan. Event-sampled direct adaptive nn output- and state-feedback control of uncertain strict-feedback system. *IEEE transactions on neural networks and learning systems*, 29(5):1850–1863, 2017a.

Nathan Szanto, Vignesh Narayanan, and S Jagannathan. Event-sampled control of quadrotor unmanned aerial vehicle using neural networks. In *2017 American Control Conference (ACC)*, pages 2956–2961. IEEE, 2017b.

T. Söderström and P. Stoica. *System Identification*. Prentice-Hall, 1989.

Paulo Tabuada. Event-triggered real-time scheduling of stabilizing control tasks. *IEEE Transactions on Automatic Control*, 52(9):1680–1685, 2007.

Pavankumar Tallapragada and Nikhil Chopra. Event-triggered dynamic output feedback control for lti systems. In *2012 IEEE 51st IEEE Conference on Decision and Control (CDC)*, pages 6597–6602. IEEE, 2012.

Pavankumar Tallapragada and Nikhil Chopra. On event triggered tracking for nonlinear systems. *IEEE Transactions on Automatic Control*, 58(9):2343–2348, Sept 2013. ISSN 0018-9286. doi: 10.1109/tac.2013.2251794.

Pavankumar Tallapragada and Nikhil Chopra. Decentralized event-triggering for control of nonlinear systems. *IEEE Transactions on Automatic Control*, 59(12):3312–3324, 2014.

Pavankumar Tallapragada and Jorge Cortés. Event-triggered stabilization of linear systems under bounded bit rates. *IEEE Transactions on Automatic Control*, 61(6):1575–1589, 2015.

Guosong Tian, Yu-Chu Tian, and Colin Fidge. Performance analysis of ieee 802.11 dcf based wncs networks. In *IEEE Local Computer Network Conference*, pages 496–503. IEEE, 2010.

Kyriakos G Vamvoudakis and Frank L Lewis. Multi-player non-zero-sum games: Online adaptive learning solution of coupled hamilton–jacobi equations. *Automatica*, 47(8):1556–1569, 2011.

Kyriakos G Vamvoudakis, Hamidreza Modares, Bahare Kiumarsi, and Frank L Lewis. Game theory-based control system algorithms with real-time reinforcement learning: how to solve multiplayer games online. *IEEE Control Systems*, 37(1):33–52, 2017a.

Kyriakos G Vamvoudakis, Arman Mojoodi, and Henrique Ferraz. Event-triggered optimal tracking control of nonlinear systems. *International Journal of Robust and Nonlinear Control*, 27(4): 598–619, 2017b.

Aswin N Venkat, Ian A Hiskens, James B Rawlings, and Stephen J Wright. Distributed mpc strategies with application to power system automatic generation control. *IEEE transactions on control systems technology*, 16(6):1192–1206, Nov 2008. ISSN 1063-6536. doi: 10.1109/tcst.2008.919414.

N. Vignesh and S. Jagannathan. Distributed event-sampled approximate optimal control of interconnected affine nonlinear continuous-time systems. In *2016 American Control Conference (ACC)*, pages 3044–3049, July 2016. doi: 10.1109/acc.2016.7525383.

Antonio Visioli, Giacomo Ziliani, and Giovanni Legnani. Iterative-learning hybrid force/velocity control for contour tracking. *IEEE Transactions on Robotics*, 26(2):388–393, 2010.

Holger Voos. Nonlinear state-dependent riccati equation control of a quadrotor uav. In *2006 IEEE Conference on Computer Aided Control System Design, 2006 IEEE International Conference on Control Applications, 2006 IEEE International Symposium on Intelligent Control*, pages 2547–2552. IEEE, 2006.

D. Vrabie, O. Pastravanu, M. Abu-Khalaf, and F. L. Lewis. Adaptive optimal control for continuous-time linear systems based on policy iteration. *Automatica*, 45(2):477–484, 2009a.

Draguna Vrabie, Kyriakos Vamvoudakis, and Frank Lewis. Adaptive optimal controllers based on generalized policy iteration in a continuous-time framework. In *2009 17th Mediterranean Conference on Control and Automation*, pages 1402–1409. IEEE, 2009b.

Gregory C Walsh, Hong Ye, and Linda G Bushnell. Stability analysis of networked control systems. *Control Systems Technology, IEEE Transactions on*, 10(3):438–446, 2002.

D. Wang, D. Liu, Q. Zhang, and D. Zhao. Data-based adaptive critic designs for nonlinear robust optimal control with uncertain dynamics. *IEEE Transactions on Systems, Man, and Cybernetics: Systems*, Pp(99):1–12, 2015. ISSN 2168-2216. doi: 10.1109/tsmc.2015.2492941.

Ding Wang, Derong Liu, Hongliang Li, and Hongwen Ma. Neural-network-based robust optimal control design for a class of uncertain nonlinear systems via adaptive dynamic programming. *Information Sciences*, 282:167–179, 2014.

Ding Wang, Haibo He, and Derong Liu. Improving the critic learning for event-based nonlinear

$h_i nfty$ control design. *IEEE transactions on cybernetics*, 47(10):3417–3428, 2017.

Fei-Yue Wang, N. Jin, D. Liu, and Q. Wei. Adaptive dynamic programming for finite-horizon optimal control of discrete-time nonlinear systems with ε-error bound. *IEEE Transactions on Neural Networks*, 22(1):24–36, Jan. 2011.

S. Wang and E.J. Davison. On the stabilization of decentralized control systems. *IEEE Transactions on Automatic Control*, 18(5):473–478, 1973.

Xiaofeng Wang and Naira Hovakimyan. $\mathscr{L}_1$ adaptive control of event-triggered networked systems. In *Proceedings of the 2010 American Control Conference*, pages 2458–2463. IEEE, 2010.

Xiaofeng Wang and Michael Lemmon. On event design in event-triggered feedback systems. *Automatica*, 47(10):2319–2322, 2011a. ISSN 0005-1098.

Xiaofeng Wang and Michael D Lemmon. Event design in event-triggered feedback control systems. In *Decision and Control, 2008. CDC 2008. 47th IEEE Conference on*, pages 2105–2110. Ieee, 2008.

Xiaofeng Wang and Michael D Lemmon. Event-triggering in distributed networked systems with data dropouts and delays. In *International Workshop on Hybrid Systems: Computation and Control*, pages 366–380. Springer, 2009a.

Xiaofeng Wang and Michael D Lemmon. Self-triggered feedback control systems with finite-gain $\mathscr{L}_2$ stability. *IEEE Transactions on Automatic Control*, 54(3):452–467, 2009b.

Xiaofeng Wang and Michael D Lemmon. Event-triggering in distributed networked control systems. *IEEE Transactions on Automatic Control*, 56(3):586–601, 2011b.

Xiaoli Wang, Yiguang Hong, Jie Huang, and Zhong-Ping Jiang. A distributed control approach to a robust output regulation problem for multi-agent linear systems. *IEEE Transactions on Automatic control*, 55(12):2891–2895, 2010.

Christopher John Cornish Hellaby Watkins. *Learning from delayed rewards*. King's College, Cambridge United Kingdom, 1989.

Xinjiang Wei and Lei Guo. Composite disturbance-observer-based control and h_∞ control for complex continuous models. *International Journal of Robust and Nonlinear Control: IFAC-Affiliated Journal*, 20(1):106–118, 2010.

Robert Weinstock. *Calculus of Variations: With Applications to Physics and Engineering*. Dover Publications, 1974.

P. J. Werbos. A menu of designs for reinforcement learning over time. *J. Neural Networks Contr.*, 3:835–846, 1983.

P. J. Werbos. Optimization methods for brain-like intelligent control. In *Decision and Control, 1995., Proceedings of the 34th IEEE Conference on*, volume 1, pages 579–584 vol.1, Dec 1995. doi: 10.1109/cdc.1995.478957.

Paul Werbos. *Beyond Regression: New Tools for Prediction and Analysis in the Behavioral Sciences*. PhD thesis, Harvard University, 1974.

Paul J Werbos. Backpropagation through time: What it does and how to do it. *Proceedings of the IEEE*, 78(10):1550–1560, 1989.

Paul J Werbos. *Approximate Dynamic Programming for Real-Time Control and Neural Modeling*, pages 493–525. Van Nostrand Reinhold, 1991a.

Paul J Werbos. Adp: Goals, opportunities and principles. *IEEE Transactions on Systems, Man, and Cybernetics*, 22(3):346–357, 1992.

P.J. Werbos. An overview of neural networks for control. *IEEE Control Systems Magazine*, 11(1): 40–41, 1991b. doi: 10.1109/37.103352.

Feng Xia, Xiangjie Kong, and Zhenzhen Xu. Cyber-physical control over wireless sensor and actuator networks with packet loss. *Wireless networking based control*, pages 85–102, 2011a.

Feng Xia, Alexey Vinel, Ruixia Gao, Linqiang Wang, and Tie Qiu. Evaluating ieee 802.15. 4 for cyber-physical systems. *EURASIP Journal on Wireless Communications and Networking*, 2011: 1–14, 2011b.

B. Xu, C. Yang, and Z. Shi. Reinforcement learning output feedback nn control using deterministic learning technique. *IEEE Transactions on Neural Networks and Learning Systems*, 25(3):635–641, March 2014a. ISSN 2162-237x. doi: 10.1109/tnnls.2013.2292704.

H. Xu and S. Jagannathan. Stochastic optimal controller design for uncertain nonlinear networked control system via neuro dynamic programming. *IEEE Transactions on Neural Networks and Learning Systems*, 24(3):471–484, March 2013. ISSN 2162-237x. doi: 10.1109/tnnls.2012.2234133.

Hao Xu. *Stochastic optimal adaptive controller and communication protocol design for networked control systems*. ProQuest LLC, 2012.

Hao Xu and S Jagannathan. A cross layer approach to the novel distributed scheduling protocol and event-triggered controller design for cyber physical systems. In *37th Annual IEEE Conference on Local Computer Networks*, pages 232–235, 2012. doi: 10.1109/LCN.2012.6423616.

Hao Xu, S Jagannathan, and Frank L Lewis. Stochastic optimal control of unknown linear networked control system in the presence of random delays and packet losses. *Automatica*, 48(6): 1017–1030, 2012.

Hao Xu, S Jagannathan, and FL Lewis. Stochastic optimal design for unknown linear discrete-time system zero-sum games in input-output form under communication constraints. *Asian Journal of Control*, 16(5):1263–1276, 2014b.

X. Yang, H. He, and D. Liu. Event-triggered optimal neuro-controller design with reinforcement learning for unknown nonlinear systems. *IEEE Transactions on Systems, Man, and Cybernetics: Systems*, pages 1–13, 2017. ISSN 2168-2216. doi: 10.1109/TSMC.2017.2774602.

Xiong Yang and Haibo He. Adaptive critic learning and experience replay for decentralized event-triggered control of nonlinear interconnected systems. *IEEE Transactions on Systems, Man, and Cybernetics: Systems*, 50(11):4043–4055, 2020. doi: 10.1109/TSMC.2019.2898370.

William Henry Young. On classes of summable functions and their fourier series. *Proceedings of the Royal Society of London. Series A, Containing Papers of a Mathematical and Physical Character*, 87(594):225–229, 1912.

Yao-Chi Yu, Vignesh Narayanan, and Jr-Shin Li. Moment-based reinforcement learning for ensemble control. *IEEE Transactions on Neural Networks and Learning Systems*, 2023.

Huaguang Zhang, Qinglai Wei, and Yanhong Luo. A novel infinite-time optimal tracking control scheme for a class of discrete-time nonlinear systems via the greedy hdp iteration algorithm. *IEEE Transactions on Systems, Man, and Cybernetics, Part B (Cybernetics)*, 38(4):937–942, 2008a.

Huaguang Zhang, Qinglai Wei, and Yanhong Luo. A novel infinite-time optimal tracking control scheme for a class of discrete-time nonlinear systems via the greedy hdp iteration algorithm. *IEEE Transactions on Systems, Man, and Cybernetics, Part B (Cybernetics)*, 38(4):937–942, 2008b.

Huaguang Zhang, Yanhong Luo, and Derong Liu. Neural-network-based near-optimal control for a class of discrete-time affine nonlinear systems with control constraints. *IEEE Transactions on Neural Networks*, 20(9):1490–1503, 2009.

Huaguang Zhang, Lili Cui, Xin Zhang, and Yanhong Luo. Data-driven robust approximate optimal tracking control for unknown general nonlinear systems using adaptive dynamic programming method. *IEEE Transactions on Neural Networks*, 22(12):2226–2236, 2011a.

Huaguang Zhang, Lili Cui, Xin Zhang, and Yanhong Luo. Data-driven robust approximate optimal tracking control for unknown general nonlinear systems using adaptive dynamic programming method. *IEEE Transactions on Neural Networks*, 22(12):2226–2236, 2011b.

Wei Zhang, Michael S Branicky, and Stephen M Phillips. Stability of networked control systems. *IEEE control systems magazine*, 21(1):84–99, 2001.

Yi Zheng, Shaoyuan Li, and Hai Qiu. Networked coordination-based distributed model predictive control for large-scale system. *IEEE Transactions on Control Systems Technology*, 21(3):991–998, 2012.

X. Zhong and H. He. An event-triggered adp control approach for continuous-time system with unknown internal states. *IEEE Transactions on Cybernetics*, Pp(99):1–12, 2016. ISSN 2168-2267. doi: 10.1109/tcyb.2016.2523878.

Xiangnan Zhong, Zhen Ni, Haibo He, Xin Xu, and Dongbin Zhao. Event-triggered reinforcement learning approach for unknown nonlinear continuous-time system. In *2014 International Joint Conference on Neural Networks (IJCNN)*, pages 3677–3684. IEEE, July 2014. doi: 10.1109/ijcnn.2014.6889787.

Xiaojun Zhou, Chaojie Li, Tingwen Huang, and Mingqing Xiao. Fast gradient-based distributed optimisation approach for model predictive control and application in four-tank benchmark. *IET Control Theory & Applications*, 9(10):1579–1586, 2015.

Milton Keynes UK
Ingram Content Group UK Ltd.
UKHW020824141024
449569UK00008B/543